Modern China

GARLAND REFERENCE LIBRARY OF THE HUMANITIES
VOLUME 1519

Modern China

An Encyclopedia of History, Culture, and Nationalism

Editor
Wang Ke-wen

GARLAND PUBLISHING, INC.
A MEMBER OF THE TAYLOR & FRANCIS GROUP
New York & London
1998

Library of Congress Cataloging-in-Publication Data

Modern China : An encyclopedia of history, culture, and nationalism / editor
    Wang Ke-wen.
                p.   cm. — (Garland reference library of the humanities :
        vol. 1519)
        Includes index.
        ISBN 0-8153-0720-9 (alk. paper)
            1. Nationalism—China—History—19th century—Encyclopedias.
        2. Nationalism—China—History—20th century—Encyclopedias.   I. Ke-wen,
        Wang   II. Series.
        JC311.M54   1997
        951' .003—dc21   951'   97–19299
                                                                                                                                CIP

Cover art: Photograph of Tiananmen Square, Beijing, China by Grant Faint,
        The Image Bank, NY.

Cover design: Robert Vankeirsbilck.

Printed on acid-free, 250-year-life paper
Manufactured in the United States of America

Contents

Introduction

It has been said that every Chinese living in modern times was, or is, a nationalist. This statement at once reveals two notable characteristics of modern Chinese nationalism: its pervasive influence on the Chinese populace, and its lack of clarity as a concept when applied to the complex and changing Chinese realities. Since the emergence of foreign and domestic crises in the mid-nineteenth century, nearly all Chinese leaders have professed their desire to "save the country" *(jiuguo)*, a desire that may be generally described as nationalistic. *Jiuguo,* however, has been cited to define, and defend, such a wide range of frequently contradictory intellectual or political stances in China that its meaning has become increasingly elusive.

Both Zeng Guofan and Hong Xiuquan, fighting on opposing sides during the Taiping Rebellion, claimed confidently to be nationalistic. So did the revolutionary Sun Yatsen and his monarchist opponents, Kang Youwei and Liang Qichao; or the May Fourth youth and their conservative cultural and political rivals; or Chiang Kaishek's Guomindang[1] and Mao Zedong's Communists. A similar "patriotic" *(aiguo)* claim also predominated the self-portrayals of Yuan Shikai, Wang Jingwei, Zhang Xueliang, Deng Xiaoping, as well as those of the student demonstrators at Tiananmen Square in 1989. In their view, and in the eyes of their countrymen, nationalism is an idea so noble that its very evocation permits a positive assessment of the actions of its proponents, and so flexible that it can be tailored to justify almost any course of action.

Western scholarship on modern China reflects this omnipresence—and elusiveness—of Chinese nationalism. Paul A. Cohen, for example, traced an "economic nationalism" in the thought of Wang Tao in the 1860s[2]; Hao Chang highlighted the "spread of nationalism among the upper class" during the Reform movement of the 1890s[3]; Mary C. Wright identified nationalism as the "moving force" of the sociopolitical changes that culminated in the Revolution of 1911[4]; Arthur Waldron discerned a connection between the upsurge of "radical nationalism" and the introduction of World War I-style warfare to the second Zhili-Fengtian War of 1924[5]; John Israel analyzed "student nationalism" in the prewar period[6]; Chalmers A. Johnson attributed wartime mass support for the Communist revolution to "peasant nationalism"[7]; and William E. Griffith described nationalism as a key contributing factor to the Sino-Soviet split in the 1960s.[8] Lately, the cultural change brought about by post-Mao reforms has led some scholars to conclude that nationalism is replacing communism as the dominant ideology in contemporary China.

Historians have argued about the role that nationalist sentiment has played in various stages and aspects of modern China's development; yet they have seldom offered a clear definition as to what that sentiment was or is. To some extent, the confusion reflects the uncertainty the Chinese themselves had felt in grasping a relatively new concept. Nationalism, as a coherent ideology, did not take shape in China until the last decades of the nineteenth century. The conventional wisdom about Chinese nationalism has been that the universalist ideal of Confucianism, what Joseph R. Levenson called "culturalism," prevented the Chinese from developing a genuine nationalist consciousness before the modern era.[9] As suggested by the term *tianxia,* or "all under the heaven," the traditional Chinese elite regarded its "celestial empire" as the most advanced, in fact the only, civilization in the world. This civilization it believed to be universally appealing and applicable, thus enjoying the potential to expand beyond the borders of China. Based on such a belief, imperial Chinese considered anyone who practiced a Confucian-based Chinese way of life as "Chinese," and any government that ruled China through Chinese institutions and ideas as a "Chinese government." They made no attempt to distinguish themselves from other peoples in a political-ethnic sense. According to the culturalism theory, this absence of a "national identity" in the traditional Chinese consciousness posed an immense obstacle for the Chinese when they wished to secure their place in the modern world of nation-states.

Other scholars have challenged this view. They argue that the Han people, the traditional residents of China proper, have long been aware of the ethnic distinction between themselves and the non-Han "barbarians." Although disguised by culturalist rhetoric, the Chinese in fact had traditionally defined their empire as a Han state. In times of strength and peace, the Confucian elite often employed culturalist arguments to rationalize the outward expansions of the empire; when facing external threat, it quickly retreated to the ethnic views that the masses had always held. This pattern, proponents of the Han nationalism theory point out, was clearly demonstrated in the Han loyalist movements during the Mongol and Manchu conquests of China. Recently James Townsend, trying to bridge the two opposing views, pointed out that culturalism itself may be regarded as a form of nationalism because it attempted to define Chinese ethnicity by asserting the cultural—and even political—distinctions between the (Han) Chinese and others.[10]

The above debate, still unresolved, only highlights the extent of China's identity crisis in the modern era, when both Han nationalism and Confucian culturalism were faced with serious challenges. By the mid-nineteenth century, China had been under the "alien rule" of the Manchus for more than two hundred years. The discontent of the Han Chinese had motivated several major disturbances, notably the Taiping Rebellion of the 1850s and 1860s, but they were effectively suppressed by the Qing government. Western intrusion in the 1840s both confused and clarified the issue of Chinese nationalism. As the threat of the West, and later of Japan, became intensified, the Chinese for the first time accepted the notion of China as a member of the international community. That realization also convinced them of the need for all Chinese to unite against the foreign powers who attempted to deny China an international status equal to that of other countries.

The problem for the Chinese, however, was how to define the term "all Chinese." Most of the elite Chinese understood "Chinese" as the people being currently governed by the Qing empire. For the early reformers who came to realize the existence of a "family of nations," of which China was a member, there was no other way to define the identity and sovereignty of China but by recognizing the political legitimacy of the Qing. Yan Fu, who introduced a Social Darwinist world view to his fellow countrymen in the late nineteenth century, argued that supporting the existing Chinese state, i.e., the Qing, was necessary for the country's reform and survival.

In the meantime, the repeated failure of the Manchu court in resisting Western and Japanese assaults reinforced Han nationalism among other, mostly young, Chinese. The latter came to believe that the "non-Chinese (non-Han)" ethnic background made the Manchus unmotivated, and thereby unqualified, to protect the Chinese state. A necessary step in securing the survival of China was therefore to overthrow the Manchu rule and restore the country to the Han Chinese. Here, again, the Han nationalists, as those at the end of the Song and Ming dynasties, defined China as a Han state. And it was in this anti-Manchu discourse that they began to appreciate the Western notion of nation-state. They also adopted the Japanese terms *minzu* and *minzu zhuyi* to translate the Western concepts of "nation" and "nationalism."[11]

The anti-Manchuism of the Han revolutionaries at the turn of the century undermined the foundation of the existing Chinese state and prepared the ground for future ethnic problems in

China. It also led them to adopt an ambivalent position with regard to foreign meddling in Chinese politics. Unlike that of the Taiping rebels, the ethnic sentiment of the revolutionaries was fostered by a sense of urgency to save China from Western and Japanese aggression.[12] Yet in order to accomplish their anti-Manchu goal, the Han revolutionaries sought support and assistance from Japan and the Western powers. Foreign help was necessary, they argued with nationalistic fervor, to overthrow a pseudo-Chinese regime that failed to defend China against the foreigners. Similar arguments and actions were to reappear time and again later in the history of modern China.

The success of the anti-Manchu revolution in 1911 solved none of the problems surrounding the muddled current of Chinese nationalism. China might have been restored to the Han Chinese, but her status in the international community did not improve. The imperialist encroachment and exploitation that had plagued the Qing empire devolved upon the new Republic. Domestically, the elimination of Manchu domination liberated the Han, but also threatened to fragment the Chinese state. In order to ensure the survival of China in its present size and shape, the revolutionaries quietly abandoned their demand for the "expulsion" of the Manchus. They soon redefined the Chinese nation, or *Zhonghua minzu*, to include the Manchus as well as other ethnic groups formerly governed by the Qing. In 1912, Sun Yatsen proclaimed the forging of the five ethnic groups (i.e., Han, Manchus, Mongols, Tibetans, and Muslims) into one nation. Probably intentionally, the term which Sun and the new Republic used to describe a commonwealth of the five ethnic groups, *gonghe,* was also used to identify the new republican polity.

Although never explicitly stated, the five-ethnic-group commonwealth *(wuzu gonghe)* rested upon Han culture, and since 1912 the Chinese state has actively promoted the acculturation of other ethnic groups into the Han mainstream. This, however, has proved to be a difficult process. As the subsequent Mongolian and Tibetan independence movements indicated, *Zhonghua minzu* remains more of a myth than a reality. Even in the post-imperial era, China is not a genuine nation-state.[13] This fact has seriously weakened the country's ability to defend her territorial integrity against twentieth-century imperialist inroads. Russian interference in Mongolia and Xinjiang, Japanese aggression in Manchuria and Mongolia, and British involvement in Tibet were but the most notable examples of the exploitation of modern China's identity crisis by the outside world.

On the other hand, the Chinese nationalists, mostly Han, have chosen to ignore the nationality issue and concentrate on saving a China that is defined by the state, that inherited the population and territory of the former Qing empire. To borrow a conceptual framework suggested by Anthony D. Smith, the Chinese have discarded "ethnic nationalism," which advocates the political independence or statehood of an existing ethnic group, in favor of "state nationalism," a scheme whereby a unified nation is created on the basis of an existing state.[14]

The rise of "state nationalism" in China was justified by mounting external threats to the Chinese state in the twentieth century. Ironically, it was also assisted by a few seemingly anti-nationalist forces. One such force was regionalism or provincialism, a latent trend in Chinese economic and political life that usually surfaced during periods of dynastic decline. Regionalist tendencies reemerged in the wake of the Taiping Rebellion and paralleled the fall of the Qing empire, culminating in the warlordism of the 1910s and 1920s. They could be detected in almost every major political event from the late nineteenth to the mid-twentieth centuries: the Self-Strengthening movement of the 1870s to the 1890s, the Rights-Recovery movement of the 1900s to the 1910s, the Revolution of 1911, the Federalist movement of the 1920s, and the Communist base areas of the 1930s and 1940s.

Although ostensibly divisive, these regionalist movements often justified their actions by resorting to nationalistic arguments. The region or province, they contended, could serve as a foundation of national regeneration at a time when the state (represented by the central government) failed to safeguard national interests. Notably absent in the rhetoric and action of these movements was the promotion of regional culture or ethnicity as a permanent focus of identity and loyalty. Instead, its adherents espoused such notions as the "model province" in their effort to strengthen regional autonomy, which was perceived as a temporary alternative and an eventual stepping-stone to nationalism. This half-hearted regionalism was naturally vulnerable. When arguments arose, with increasing persuasiveness after the 1930s, that a unified and centralized state was within reach and could better protect China, regionalist movements capitulated. Centralization and unity were obviously more in tune with the statist approach to nationalism.

Not all forms of regional or provincial sentiments, however, have been overcome by nationalist appeals in China. As some of the following entries suggest, loyalty to one's native place, be it a province or a city, or to one's family ties has constituted a major distraction that has interfered with the full experience of modern Chinese national consciousness. Those loyalties have generally failed to sustain a political alternative to state nationalism, but they have been sufficiently potent to prevent the latter from monopolizing the self-identity of the Chinese.

Another force that characterized, and contributed to, the growth of modern Chinese nationalism was "New Culture" iconoclasm. Originating in the early Republic and flourishing during the May Fourth era, the "New Culture" advocates strove to save China by denouncing, or renouncing, the country's cultural heritage. They saw in the latter an obstacle to the country's embracing of the "new" (Western) civilization, which they deemed as essential to the survival of China in the modern world. Their position was no less contradictory than that of the anti-Manchu revolutionaries during the late Qing era. By attacking elite Chinese tradition, the "New Culture" advocates in a sense rejected the Chinese cultural identity and repudiated what had made the Chinese "Chinese." Unlike nationalists in most other modern societies, who often exalted their national traditions as a source of inspiration and a focus of allegiance, the Chinese iconoclasts expressed their nationalism by promoting foreign cultures. This irony they themselves refused to recognize. In their minds, China was defined simply as the existing Chinese state, regardless of its cultural content. In fact, they believed, rejecting the "cultural China" was necessary for the preservation of a "political China." Cultural iconoclasm reinforced the legitimacy of "state nationalism."

An equally prominent group of Chinese intellectuals defended China's cultural heritage in the May Fourth era, but it was the anti-traditionalist iconoclasts who shaped the minds of the young Chinese during the following decades. This iconoclastic nationalism reinforced the westernization trend in almost all aspects of twentieth-century Chinese life. In literature and the arts, as well as in government institutions and customs, adoption of foreign modes became fashionable and progressive—and nationalistic. The inherent tension between Chinese identity and the Western model was never resolved.

The rejection of Chinese tradition paved the way for the acceptance by the Chinese youth of various foreign ideas, including socialism and communism. Again, it was mainly nationalism that drove twentieth-century Chinese to the supposedly "internationalist" political creeds. To some Chinese Marxists, the appeal of Lenin's anti-imperialist call far outweighed the problems posed by Marx's criticism of "narrow nationalism." They found little contradiction in defending the need for a Communist revolution in China in nationalist terms. The domestic oppressors of the Chinese masses—warlords, landlords, and capitalists—were lackeys of foreign imperialists, they argued. The internal struggle to liberate the Chinese masses, therefore, would also liberate the country as a whole from imperialist oppression. In this sense, the Chinese revolutionary movement was simultaneously nationalist and internationalist.

Anti-imperialism became indispensible in the ideological formulation of the Chinese revolution. At first directed against the Western powers but later shifted increasingly toward Japan, anti-imperialist sentiment further persuaded the Chinese to ignore internal ethnic or class differences and focus their attention on the external threat. Pressing imperialist encroachment helped to sustain and strengthen the appeal of national unity as an urgent goal. After the May Fourth era, as Chinese politics was transformed by the introduction of the mass movement, anti-imperialism competed with class interests in mobilizing the populace for mass action.[15] To a large degree, anti-imperialist mass movements paved the way for first the Guomindang, and then the Chinese Communists, to seize national power during the first half of this century.

The connection between nationalism and the Communist revolution in the 1930s and 1940s has been the subject of heated debate among Western scholars. Chalmers Johnson's contention that anti-Japanese nationalism had motivated Chinese peasants to support the Chinese Communist movement has been refuted by later, more detailed studies of wartime rural China.[16] Yet none of the new studies denies the fact that wartime nationalism created circumstances in China that were instrumental in the survival and growth of the Communists. Nor have these studies altered the picture of wartime urban China, where the anti-imperialist tradition of the May Fourth and May Thirtieth movements persuaded more and more city residents to side with the anti-Japanese Communists.

Anti-imperialism continued to be a central theme in Chinese politics even after the Communist victory and the founding of the People's Republic on the mainland. It helped the "New China" to define its global role, although in the process the nationalist and internationalist dimensions of the concept sometimes blurred.[17] The participation of China in the Korean War of the 1950s, her border conflicts with India and the Soviet Union in the 1960s, and her war with Vietnam in the 1970s were all justified, to various degrees, by anti-imperialist rhetoric. These external crises usually resulted in enhanced domestic popular support for the Chinese state. The unfinished civil war between the Communists and the Guomindang, which has left the country divided, also necessitated the promotion of anti-imperialist sentiments by both sides of the conflict. For decades, the People's Republic attributed the survival of the Guomindang in Taiwan to American imperialist intervention, whereas the Guomindang accused mainland Communists of being a tool of Soviet imperialism. Both contentions have lost their currency since the early 1970s, but nationalism still provides the ground for Beijing and Taibei to justify their separate existence and, at the same time, to share the goal of eventual reunification.[18]

The trends and tendencies that have shaped the development of modern Chinese nationalism in the past are still present at the end of the twentieth century. Some of them have assumed new forms, with new momenta. The issue of China's ethnic composition remains unresolved. Outer Mongolia became an independent state in 1946, a fact which the Guomindang regime in Taiwan refuses to recognize even today. Tibet, having been put under effective Chinese control by the People's Republic in 1950, is actively seeking independence under a leadership in exile.

Tibetan nationalism poses a direct challenge to the Chinese ideal of *Zhonghua minzu*. To the Chinese nationalists, compromising this ideal is unthinkable; it would deny the Chinese state the right to govern not only the Tibetans but other ethnic minorities in the country, thereby reducing China to a Han state. By openly supporting the Tibetan independence movement, the Western countries shared the movement's position of rejecting the notion of a multi-ethnic "Chinese nation." Many Chinese, fresh with their memory of repeated Western attempts to "divide and rule" China during the past 150 years, cannot help but see the Tibetan problem as a symptom of continuing imperialist encroachment on China. Ethnic nationalism thus clashed with anti-imperialism. Both sides, it seems, are not prepared to back down.

Slightly different sentiments and views may be found in the issue of Hong Kong. No nationalistic Chinese would have opposed the British colony's return to China in 1997, which symbolized the demise, in one form at least, of Western imperialism in China. Yet distinct historical experiences since the 1840s, and different political-economic systems since 1949, have created an alien identity in the Hong Kong community that has seriously weakened its subscription to Chinese state nationalism. To an extent, the community's interests have converged with those of Great Britain, which desired to prolong her control of this last bastion of her old colonial empire. While the People's Republic eagerly tried to attract the loyalty of Hong Kong residents by appealing to their anti-imperialist sentiments, it had to concede that some of those "compatriots" have sided with the "imperialists."

Hong Kong residents defended their ambivalent attitude toward the People's Republic by stressing the benefits that an autonomous Hong Kong would have brought to the future development of China, economically and politically. Here the half-hearted regionalist argument reappeared: the maintenance of a form of regional autonomy is not anti-nationalistic, but a desirable and necessary stage in nation-building. The argument applied not only to Hong Kong, but to Taiwan and other areas in China as well. In the era of post-Mao economic reforms, the rapidly developed coastal provinces often employ, though implicitly, such a regionalist rationale in resisting central control and asserting local initiatives.

The case of Taiwan stands somewhere between those of Tibet and Hong Kong. Like Hong Kong, the island has formed an identity that is distinct from China's on the basis of its unique historical experience and separate political-economic systems. Yet unlike Hong Kong, and like Tibet, that distinct identity has led some Taiwanese (of Han origin) to reject Chinese nationalism and advocate Taiwanese independence. "Formosan nationalism," as some scholars have called it, seems to support David M. Potter's observation that nationalism often finds its root not in common culture, but in common interests.[19] The issue will continue to jeopardize China's national integration and international status.

Nevertheless, culture remains an important dimension of contemporary Chinese nationalism. Nearly eighty years after the May Fourth movement, the legacy of "New Culture" iconoclasm is still alive. Under the current policy of "reform and open-up" *(gaige kaifang),* new influences from the outside world have refreshed the Chinese mind and provoked another round of critical evaluation by the Chinese of their own tradition. Although this time the tradition that is under scrutiny and attack is the "new tradition" of Maoist Communism, it is not uncommon to find the "old tradition," including both the Confucian elite culture and the peasant folk culture, once again becoming targets. Some Chinese in fact argued that the country's feudal tradition should be partially blamed for the triumph and duration of the Maoist rule. In other words, the "new tradition" was established on the basis of the "old tradition." Such an assertion has led many contemporary Chinese intellectuals to condemn China's cultural heritage, much like their May Fourth predecessors had done in the latter's search for causes of the failure of the Chinese Republic. The tone of their self-criticism is harsh, but their goal is to rejuvenate the country, which is unmistakenly nationalistic.

Meanwhile, Beijing and Taibei continue to invoke their common cultural heritage, which usually implies Han ethnicity and the Confucian-based tradition, as the basis of their claim of influence, if not sovereignty, over overseas Chinese. Both governments interpret the support for the Chinese state by overseas Chinese as a patriotic gesture. The Guomindang even allows overseas Chinese to be represented in its regime in Taiwan. Culturalism, apparently, has not completely disappeared.

A century and a half after China's entrance into the modern world, the Chinese still struggle to define their "nation," or, more precisely, to make their "nation" and "state" congruent. In terms of culture or ethnicity, a Chinese nation remains in flux. The Chinese state, moreover, is divided and uncertain about its proper shape and size. Despite all this, and probably because of all this, nationalism continues to be one of the most influential sentiments and highest principles among the Chinese. In a recent study of nationalism in modern China, aptly titled *Awakening and Confusion,* the Chinese author describes his subject as such a powerful "intellectual current of the time" *(shidai sichao)* that it commands almost a religious devotion of the Chinese people.[20]

It is with a recognition of this extraordinary appeal, and ambiguity, that the following entries have been selected and presented. These entries, illustrating various facets of modern China's cultural and historical experiences, share the common theme of the search for a national identity and the construction of a national community by the Chinese. At the same time, they reveal the extent of conflict and tension that have characterized the Chinese efforts. It is a story that is still far from being concluded. To comprehend this story is essential to our understanding of the past, present, and future of China.

Notes

1. The conventional English translation of the Guomindang as the "Nationalists," and its seizure of national power as the "Nationalist Revolution," has been a misnomer. The name literally means "National People's Party," which has no relevance to the term or concept of nationalism. To avoid confusion, the present volume refers to the Party as the Guomindang (GMD).
2. Paul A. Cohen, *Between Tradition and Modernity: Wang T'ao and Reform in Late Ch'ing China* (Cambridge, MA: Harvard University Press, 1974), 198–207.
3. Hao Chang, "Intellectual Change and the Reform Movement, 1890–8," in *The Cambridge History of Modern China*, vol. 11, eds. John K. Fairbank and Kwang-ching Liu (Cambridge, England: Cambridge University Press, 1980), 333.
4. Mary C. Wright, "Introduction: The Rising Tide of Change," in *China in Revolution: The First Phase, 1900–1913,* ed. Mary C. Wright (New Haven, CT: Yale University Press, 1968), 3–23.
5. Arthur Waldron, *From War to Nationalism: China's Turning Point, 1924–1925* (Cambridge, England: Cambridge University Press, 1995).
6. John Israel, *Student Nationalism in China, 1927–1937* (Stanford, CA: Stanford University Press, 1966).
7. Chalmers A. Johnson, *Peasant Nationalism and Communist Power: The Emergence of Revolutionary China, 1937–1945* (Stanford, CA: Stanford University Press, 1966).
8. William E. Griffith, *The Sino-Soviet Rift* (Cambridge, MA: The MIT Press, 1964), 230.
9. Joseph R. Levenson, *Confucian China and Its Modern Fate: A Trilogy,* vol. 1 (Berkeley: University of California Press, 1968), 95–108.
10. James Townsend, "Chinese Nationalism," in *The Australian Journal of Chinese Affairs* 27 (January 1992): 108–109.
11. For a discussion of the use of the terms *minzu* and *minzu zhuyi,* see Frank Dikötter, *The Discourse of Race in Modern China* (Stanford, CA: Stanford University Press, 1992), 108–110.
12. Dikötter observes an upsurge of "race nationalism," including the notion of the "yellow race" versus the "white race," among both the revolutionaries and the reformers at the turn of the century. Ibid., 107–115, 123–125.
13. John Fitzgerald offers a similar observation when he describes modern China as a "nationless state." John Fitzgerald, "The Nationless State: The Search for a Nation in Modern Chinese Nationalism," *The Australian Journal of Chinese Affairs* 33 (January 1995): 75–104.
14. Anthony D. Smith, *Theories of Nationalism* (New York, NY: Harper & Row, 1971), 176. The terms are suggested in James Townsend, op. cit., 104.
15. For a discussion of the complex relations among class, nation, and the state in the ideological formulation of the Chinese revolution in the 1920s, see John Fitzgerald, op. cit., 90–97.
16. See, for example, Donald G. Gillin, "'Peasant Nationalism' in the History of Chinese Communism," *Journal of Asian Studies* 23, no. 2 (February 1964): 269–289; Chen Yung-fa, *Making Revolution* (Berkeley: University of California Press, 1986).
17. The People's Republic prefers the term "patriotism" *(aiguozhuyi)* to "nationalism" *(minzu zhuyi)* so as to conform to its internationalist official ideology.
18. In 1995, Taiwan's efforts to seek *de facto,* if not *de jure,* independence, and the perceived American support for those efforts, has led the People's Republic to revive its attack on U.S. "imperialistic intervention in Chinese affairs."
19. David M. Potter, "The Historian's Use of Nationalism and Vice Versa," *American Historical Review* 67 (1962): 924–950.
20. Tang Wenquan, *Juexing yu miwu* (awakening and confusion) (Shanghai: Renmin chubanshe, 1993), 10–11.

Entries by Subject

Soong Qingling
Soong, T.V.
Stilwell, Joseph W.
Sun Chuanfang
Sun Yatsen
Ting, V. K.
Tan Kah Kee
Tan Sitong
Tang Shaoyi
Tao Xingzhi
Wang Jingwei
Wang Ming
Wang Tao
Wei Yuan
Wenxiang
Woren
Wu Peifu
Wu Tingfang
Wu Zhihui
Xu Shichang
Xu Jiyu
Yan Fu
Yan Xishan
Yang Du
Yang Shangkun
Ye Mingchen
Yen, James
Yuan Shikai
Yung Wing
Zeng Guofan
Zhan Tianyou
Zhang Binglin
Zhang Jian
Zhang Xueliang
Zhang Xun
Zhang Zhidong
Zhang Zuolin
Zhao Ziyang
Zheng Guanying
Zhou Enlai
Zhu De
Zou Rong
Zuo Zongtang

Political Organizations
Anfu Club
Anhui Clique
Beiyang Army
Blue Shirts
C. C. Clique
China Arise Society (Huaxinghui)
Chinese Communist Party
Chinese Revolutionary Party
Chinese Youth Party
Comintern

Democratic League
Democratic Parties
Democratic Progressive Party
Emperor Protection Society
 (Baohuanghui)
Fengtian Clique
Gang of Four
Guangxi Clique
Guomindang, 1912–1914
Guomindang, 1919–
Internationalists
Left Guomindang
National Salvation Association
National Socialist Party of China
Progressive Party (Jinbudang)
Restoration Society (Guangfuhui)
Revive China Society (Xingzhonghui)
Revolutionary Alliance (Tongmenghui)
Society for the Study of European
 Affairs
Third Party
Zhili Clique

Popular Uprisings
Anti-American, Anti-Government
 Demonstrations
Boxer Uprising
Canton-Hong Kong Strike
December Ninth Movement
Democracy Wall
February Twenty-Eighth Incident
Hankou-Jiujiang Incident
Hong Kong Riots of 1967
March Eighth Incident
May Fourth Movement
May Thirtieth Movement
Muslim Uprisings
Nian Rebellion
Railway Protection Movement
Sanyuanli Incident
Taiping Rebellion
Taiwan Minzhuguo
Tiananmen Incident of 1976
Tiananmen Incident of 1989
Wuchang Uprising
Zilijun Uprising

Publications
China's Destiny
China White Paper
Dagongbao
Independent Review
Minbao
New Democracy
New People Miscellany (Xinmincongbao)

Chronology

1898	Zhang Zhidong advocated *ti-yong* theory; Hundred Days Reform failed; Empress Dowager Cixi resumed power; Boxer Uprising began in north China; lease of new territories.
1899	Kang Youwei organized Baohuanghui in Canada; United States announced Open Door policy with China.
1900	Qing court declared war against foreign powers; regional officials proclaimed southeast autonomy; Russians occupied Manchuria; Yen Fu published translation of Thomas Huxley's *Evolution and Ethics*.
1901	Boxer Protocol.
1902	Liang Qichao's *Xinmin congbao* began publication in Japan.
1903	Chinese students in Japan organized Anti-Russian Volunteer Army; *Subao* case tried in Shanghai.
1904	Outbreak of Russo-Japanese War; organization of Guangfuhui and Huaxinghui in Japan; British invasion of Tibet.
1905	Anti-American boycott; civil service examinations abolished; Tongmenghui formed in Japan; *Minbao* began publication; suicide of Chen Tianhua.
1906	Qing court announced preparations for constitutionalism; Constitutional movement began.
1907	Execution of Qiu Jin.
1908	Emperor Guangxu and Empress Dowager Cixi died.
1909	Zhan Tianyou completed Beijing-Kalgan Railway; provincial assemblies established.
1910	National assembly established.
1911	Railway Protection movement in Sichuan; Wuchang Uprising; independence of the provinces.
1912	Founding of the Republic of China; Qing dynasty ended; Yuan Shikai assumed Presidency; Guomindang established.
1913	Formation of Jinbudang; assassination of Song Jiaoren; Yuan Shikai obtained Reorganization Loan; Second Revolution failed.
1914	Outbreak of World War I; Sun Yatsen organized Chinese Revolutionary Party in Japan; British-Tibetan agreement.
1915	Japan presented Twenty-One Demands; Yuan Shikai launched monarchical attempt; *New Youth* began publication.
1916	National Protection movement; Yuan Shikai died; Cai Yuanpei became chancellor of Beijing University.
1917	Attempt to reestablish the Qing court by Zhang Xun; Sun Yatsen established first Canton regime; Hu Shih proposed literary reform.
1918	World War I ended; Duan Qirui negotiated Nishihara loans; Lu Xun published *A Madman's Diary*.
1919	Treaty of Versailles; May Fourth movement; Sun Yatsen reorganized Chinese Revolutionary Party into Chinese Nationalist Party (Guomindang).
1920	Zhili-Anhui War; Federalist movement began in Hunan.
1921	Chinese Communist Party (CCP) established; Washington Conference.
1922	First Zhili-Fengtian War; Chen Jiongming expelled Sun Yatsen from Canton; James Yen experimented with mass education programs in Hunan.
1923	Sun-Jaffe Manifesto; formation of first Guomindang–Chinese Communist Party (GMD–CCP) United Front; Sun Yatsen returned to Canton; Canton Customs Crisis.
1924	Second Zhili-Fengtian War; Merchant Corps Incident in Canton; Mongolian People's Republic established in Outer Mongolia.
1925	Sun Yatsen died; May Thirtieth Incident in Shanghai; Shakee Massacre in Canton; Canton–Hong Kong Strike.
1926	March Eighteenth Massacre in Beijing; Northern Expedition began.
1927	Hankou-Jiujiang Incident; Nanjing Incident; Nanjing-Wuhan split; dissolution of the first GMD–CCP United Front.
1928	Jinan Incident; Northern Expedition completed; Guomindang commenced political tutelage.

1929	Chinese Eastern Railway Incident; Disbandment Conference failed; Guomindang government obtained tariff autonomy; Chinese Communist Party established Jiangxi Soviet.
1930	War of the Central Plains; Chiang Kaishek began Bandit-Suppression campaigns against Chinese Communist Party; League of Chinese Left-Wing Writers formed.
1931	Nanjing-Canton split; Manchurian Incident; Ma Zhanshan organized the Northeast Anti-Japanese Volunteer Army.
1932	January Twenty-Eighth Incident; National Emergency Conference at Loyang; Japan organized Manchukuo.
1933	Tanggu Truce; Feng Yuxiang organized Chahar People's Anti-Japanese Allied Army; Fujian Rebellion.
1934	Chinese Communist Party began Long March; Guomindang launched New Life Movement.
1935	Chinese Communist Party relocated in Yan'an; Japan instigated north China autonomy; December Ninth Movement.
1936	Guangdong-Guangxi Rebellion; Xian Incident; Japanese-sponsored independence of Inner Mongolia.
1937	Outbreak of second Sino-Japanese War; Nanjing Massacre; formation of the second GMD-CCP United Front.
1938	Battle of Taierzhuang; People's Political Council established in Wuhan.
1939	Guomindang government moved to Chongqing.
1940	Wang Jingwei regime established in occupied China; publication of Mao Zedong's *New Democracy*; Battle of Hundred Regiments.
1941	New Fourth Army Incident; outbreak of World War II.
1942	Chinese Communist Party launched Rectification campaign in Yan'an; Burma campaigns.
1943	Abolition of unequal treaties; Cairo Conference; Chiang Kaishek's *China's Destiny* published.
1944	Joseph Stilwell recalled; formation of Democratic League; establishment of the East Turkestan Republic in Xinjiang.
1945	Yalta Conference; World War II ended; Taiwan returned to China; Sino-Soviet Treaty of Friendship and Alliance.
1946	Political Consultative Conference convened in Chongqing; outbreak of GMD-CCP civil war.
1947	February Twenty-Eighth Incident in Taiwan; Anti-American, Anti-government demonstrations; Marshall mission failed.
1949	United States published *China White Paper*; Chinese Communist Party defeat of Guomindang on the mainland; founding of the People's Republic of China (PRC); Mao Zedong declared "Leaning to One Side."
1950	Outbreak of Korean War; United States protection of GMD government in Taiwan; Sino-Soviet Treaty of Friendship, Alliance and Mutual Assistance; People's Republic of China troops entered Tibet; land reform; promulgation of marriage law.
1952	Establishment of Autonomous Regions of National Minorities; Sino(ROC)-Japanese Peace Treaty.
1953	Collectivization of agriculture; First Five-Year Plan.
1954	First Quemoy-Matsu Crisis; Sino(ROC)-American Mutual Defense Treaty.
1955	Bandung Conference.
1956	Hundred Flowers and Anti-Rightist campaigns.
1958	Great Leap Forward began; second Quemoy-Matsu Crisis.
1959	Tibetan Uprising began.
1960	Sino-Soviet split.
1962	Sino-Indian border conflict; ROC military harassments of mainland coast.
1964	First successful test of atomic bomb by PRC.
1966	Cultural Revolution began; purge of Liu Shaoqi.
1967	Hong Kong riot; first successful test of H-bomb by PRC.
1969	Zhenbao Island Incident.

1971	Diaoyutai demonstrations by Chinese students in the United States; People's Republic of China replaced Republic of China to represent China in the United Nations; Lin Biao died in plane crash.
1972	United States president Richard Nixon and Japanese prime minister Tanaka Kakuei visited China; Japan shifted diplomatic recognition from Republic of China to People's Republic of China.
1975	Chiang Kaishek died in Taiwan, succeeded by son Jingguo.
1976	Tiananmen Incident; Mao Zedong died; arrest of Gang of Four.
1978	United States shifted diplomatic recognition from Republic of China to People's Republic of China; Sino-Japanese Treaty of Peace and Friendship; Democracy Wall movement.
1979	Sino-Vietnamese War.
1980	Deng Xiaoping launched "reform and open-up" policy.
1982	Sino-British Agreement on Hong Kong.
1986	Democratic Progressive Party established in Taiwan; China criticized "bourgeois liberalization."
1988	Li Denghui succeeded Jiang Jingguo as Republic of China President in Taiwan; relaxation of mainland-Taiwan relations.
1989	Soviet president Mikhail Gorbachev visited China; Tiananmen demonstrations and massacre.
1996	PRC staged missile exercises near Taiwan; Li Denghui elected Republic of China president in Taiwan's first direct presidential election.
1997	Deng Xiaoping died; Hong Kong returned to China.

Contributors

David L. Anderson
Department of History
University of Indianapolis

Lynda S. Bell
Department of History
University of California, Riverside

Gerald W. Berkley
Department of History
University of Guam

Henry Y.S. Chan
Department of History
Moorhead State University

Ming K. Chan
Department of History
University of Hong Kong

Wellington K.K. Chan
Department of History
Occidental College

David Wen-wei Chang
Department of Political Science
University of Wisconsin, Oshkosh

Iris Chang
Center for Chinese Studies
University of California, Berkeley

Li-fen Chen
Division of Humanities
The Hong Kong University of Science and
    Technology

Yung-fa Chen
Institute of Modern History
Academia Sinica (Taiwan)

Gregory K.K. Chiang
Department of Chinese
Middlebury College

Hungdah Chiu
School of Law
University of Maryland

Min-chih Chou
East Asia Library/Department of Asian
    Languages and Literature
University of Washington

Hong-yuan Chu
Institute of Modern History
Academia Sinica (Taiwan)

Paul Clark
East-West Center, Honolulu

Edwin Clausen
Department of History
Pacific Lutheran University

Nicholas R. Clifford
Department of History
Middlebury College

Parks M. Coble
Department of History
University of Nebraska, Lincoln

Craig Dietrich
Department of History
University of Southern Maine

William J. Duiker
Department of History
The Pennsylvania State University

Lu Fang-shang
Institute of Modern History
Academia Sinica (Taiwan)

Lee Feigon
Department of History and East Asian Culture
Colby College

Robert D. Fiaola
Department of History
Concordia College

Lanny B. Fields
Department of History
California State University, San Bernadino

Douglas Fix
Department of History
Reed College

Poshek Fu
Department of History
University of Illinois, Urbana-Champaign

He Gaochao
Division of Social Science
Hong Kong University of Science and
    Technology

Michael Gasster
Department of History
Rutgers University

Bryna Goodman
Department of History
University of Oregon

Tze-ki Hon
Department of History
State University of New York, Geneseo

Chün-tu Hsüeh
Huang Hsing Foundation (USA)

James L. Huffman
Department of History
Wittenberg University

Dan N. Jacobs
Department of Political Science
Miami University

Roger B. Jeans
Department of History
Washington and Lee University

Luo Jiu-jung
Institute of Modern History
Academia Sinica (Taiwan)

William A. Joseph
Department of Political Science
Wellesley College

Ellen R. Judd
Department of Anthropology
University of Manitoba

Thomas L. Kennedy
Department of History
Washington State University

Jeffrey Kinkley
Department of History
St. John's University

Chiu-chun Lee
Department of History
Chinese Culture University (Taiwan)

Marilyn Levine
Division of Social Sciences
Lewis-Clark State College

Charlton M. Lewis
Department of History
Brooklyn College, CUNY

Peter M. Lichtenstein
Department of Economics
Boise State University

Edward A. McCord
Department of History
George Washington University

Andrea McElderry
Department of History
University of Louisville

Harvey Nelson
Department of International Studies
University of South Florida

J. Kenneth Olenik
Department of History
Montclair State College

David Pong
Department of History
University of Delaware

Jonathan Porter
Department of History
University of New Mexico

Murray A. Rubinstein
Department of History
Baruch College, CUNY

John Schrecker
Department of History
Brandeis University

Peter J. Seybolt
Department of History
University of Vermont

James D. Seymour
East Asian Institute
Columbia University

Lawrence N. Shyu
Department of History
University of New Brunswick

Louis T. Sigel
Department of History
Eastern Kentucky University

Martin Singer
Department of History
Concordia University

Lawrence Sullivan
Department of Political Science
Adelphi University

Lung-kee Sun
Department of History
University of Memphis

Chia-lin Pao Tao
Department of East Asian Studies
University of Arizona

Anthony Y. Teng
Department of History
Rhode Island College

Ranbir Vohra
Department of Political Science
Trinity College

Fan-shen Wang
Institute of History and Philology
Academia Sinica (Taiwan)

Wang Ke-wen
Department of History
St. Michael's College

Tien-wei Wu
Department of History
Southern Illinois University

Raymond F. Wylie
Department of International Relations
Lehigh University

Joseph K.S. Yick
Department of History
Southwest Texas State University

Ka-che Yip
Department of History
University of Maryland, Baltimore County

Xu Youwei
Department of History
China Textile University (China)

Peter G. Zarrow
Department of History
University of New South Wales

Shi-ping Zheng
Department of Political Science
University of Vermont

Zhou Qiuguang
Department of History
Hunan Normal University (China)

John Zou
Institute of East Asian Studies
University of California, Berkeley

Political map of contemporary China

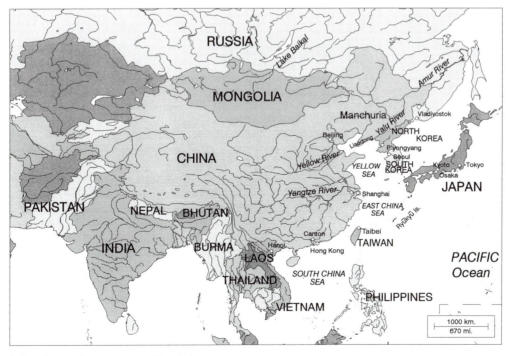

Political map of contemporary East Asia

Modern China

A

Amur River Massacres

In 1900, imperial Russia dispatched 200,000 troops into China as part of an international expedition to suppress the Boxer Uprising and to rescue the foreign embassies in Beijing. In July, the Russian army imposed a blockade along the Amur River, which served as the Sino-Russian border at the time. Most of the northern bank of the river, an area densely populated with Chinese residents, had been ceded to Russia in the Treaty of Aigun in 1858, but part of the area was still under Chinese jurisdiction. In an attempt to reduce Chinese influence in that area, the Russians massacred more than seven thousand Chinese residents along the northern bank (as in Hailanpao) and burned their houses. The Chinese authorities in Heilongjiang Province, south of the river, could offer little protection to those Chinese. After the incident, Russia annexed the entire northern bank.

The Russian army proceeded to occupy Manchuria during the expedition and refused to withdraw after the suppression of the Boxers. It was not until her defeat by Japan in the Russo-Japanese War (1904–05) that Russia evacuated southern Manchuria. She finally gave up northern Manchuria after World War I (1914–18).

Wang Ke-wen

References

Quested, R. K. I. *"Matey" Imperialists? The Tsarist Russians in Manchuria, 1895–1917.* Hong Kong: Oxford University Press, 1982.

Anarchist Movement

Although anarchism is internationalist in ideology and cosmopolitan by nature, Chinese anarchists demonstrated nationalist impulses as well as attacked what they regarded as narrow nationalism. The anarchist movement flourished in a radical atmosphere from about 1905 to the late 1920s, and its influences persisted considerably longer. During this period of intense and widespread nationalism, anarchists argued that their revolution would lead to the demise of the state, national borders, and perhaps even national identity and to the rise of a worldwide egalitarian, cooperative social system. Nonetheless, they were anti-imperialists, who supported movements to gain freedom from foreign domination and, before 1911, promoted the anti-Manchu republican revolution. Criticized by self-avowed nationalists and national revolutionaries, anarchists argued that the true interests of the Chinese people lay in an international system of strictly voluntary organizations; some argued that indeed the good aspects of Chinese culture would flourish if the internal repression and external exploitation inherent in a state system were absent.

Most Chinese anarchists, although consistently deprecating chauvinism, encouraged nationalist movements as positive steps taken by oppressed peoples toward the achievement of a real revolution. Liu Shipei in 1907 in some respects anticipated Lenin's theses on imperialism. Liu foresaw that populist national liberation struggles would weaken the ruling classes of the colonial powers and help to precipitate revolutions in Europe and America. However, along with Zhang Binglin at the time, Liu favored a pan-Asianist, anti-imperialist movement—one that would forge links with Western radicals and lead a world revolution. In Liu's analysis, imperialism was rooted in capitalism and in old notions of in-group exclusivity and racism. Nationalist movements were therefore an important step, but only a first step, in creating a truly new order.

Before 1911, anarchists were firmly in the anti-Manchu camp. Although some emphasized the dangers of a nationalist revolution, which would re-create the faults of the Manchu regime under Han Chinese leadership, most joined the umbrella revolutionary organization, the Tongmenghui. Wu Zhihui and several other anarchists strenuously argued that the Manchus' grasp on power was especially pernicious and that revolution appropriately started with their destruction.

After the Revolution of 1911, some of the first-generation anarchists turned to cultural and, above all, educational reform in an effort to raise the Chinese people's "level of civilization." This eventually brought them into the Guomindang of Sun Yatsen and Chiang Kaishek. If "labor-learning" became a motif in Chinese radicalism generally, their anarchism, though continuing to be cited as a final goal, became attenuated. Liu Sifu (Shifu) assumed leadership of the movement after the founding of the Republic, giving it a strong moral thrust. He sharply distinguished his anarcho-communism from other forms of socialism. A number of his followers went on to leading positions in academia and the labor movement.

The May Fourth movement of 1919 represented an outburst of nationalist feeling, but it was also an era of social radicalism, and anarchism therefore played an ideological role through the 1920s. Nationalists tended to merge society into the state in an effort to strengthen China; these tendencies were prevalent in the Guomindang and the Chinese Communist Party. Anarchists would, in contrast, merge the state into society and replace governmental functions with voluntary organizations. Yet even with an overlay of internationalism, anarchism was not directly opposed to many nationalist goals. Above all, anarchists offered a critique of capitalism that explained the sources of imperialism. Although many anarchists regarded class analysis a useful tool and promoted working class movements, some assailed communists for using class struggle to divide the people. Eventually, Chinese Marxists combined social revolution and nationalism with effective organization in a way that anarchist revolutionaries found impossible to achieve.

The appeal of anarchism as an ideology was undoubtedly weakened by its criticisms of nationalism. Chinese anarchism was a modern incarnation of humanist and universalist elements of the traditional Chinese world view. The anarchists' main focus remained a social and cultural revolution, and Chinese radicalism as a whole was most receptive to anarchist influences in these realms rather than on the political stage. However, anarchists inevitably wove strands of nationalist feelings into their doctrines. They argued that only an international, anti-authoritarian revolution would enable the Chinese to flourish, along with the world's other peoples. In their view, a revolution that strengthened the state would fail to produce a society with greater freedom, but would inevitably create a new hegemonic system.

References

Dirlik, Arif. *Anarchism in the Chinese Revolution.* Berkeley: University of California Press, 1991.
———. *The Origins of Chinese Communism.* Oxford: Oxford University Press, 1989.
Zarrow, Peter. *Anarchism and Chinese Political Culture.* New York, NY: Columbia University Press, 1990.

Peter G. Zarrow

Anfu Club

A political faction that dominated the Chinese parliament in the late 1910s, the Anfu Club supported Duan Qirui's government and was generally regarded as the civilian branch of Duan's Anhui Clique.

Following the aborted attempt by Zhang Xun to restore the Qing dynasty in July 1917, the Beijing government fell under the control of Premier Duan Qirui. Duan proposed the election of a new parliament as the basis of what he called the "re-established Republic." In March 1918, Duan's principal followers, Wang Yitang and Xu Shuzheng, organized the Anfu Club, named after their meeting place in Beijing's Anfu Alley, to ensure the election of pro-Duan politicians into the new Parliament.

The Anfu Club was remarkably successful in its operations. When the new parliament opened in August, the club controlled 70 percent of the seats. From late 1918 to late 1920, the Anfu politicians effectively controlled the parliament, which soon came to be known as the "Anfu Parliament." Under the leadership of Wang Yitang, they proposed and decided on legislations as a group, and then, with their majority, they imposed their will on the parliament. The club supported Duan's pro-Japanese policies and strengthened Duan's legitimacy as the national leader. By then, however, the Chinese Republic had become engulfed by warlordism, and the central political institutions as a whole hardly exerted any real influence over the political situation in the country.

In July 1920, Duan's Anhui Clique was defeated by its rival, the Zhili Clique, in the Zhili-Anhui War, resulting in the collapse of Duan's government. In August, the Zhili Clique entered Beijing and dissolved the "Anfu Parliament." The Anfu Club thereafter disappeared from the Chinese political scene. Some of its members later served as Japanese puppets during the Sino-Japanese War of 1937–45.

Wang Ke-wen

References

Nathan, Andrew J. *Peking Politics, 1918–1923: Factionalism and the Failure of Constitutionalism.* Berkeley: University of California Press, 1976.

Anhui Clique

See DUAN QIRUI

Anti-American, Anti-Government Demonstrations

The anti-American, anti-government demonstrations were an anti-civil war movement that lasted from October 1945 to April 1949 and was mainly a Communist-instigated movement to undermine Guomindang (GMD) authority. The demonstrations condemned the "brutality" of the United States in China and its support for the GMD, and accused the GMD of initiating the civil war and mistreating and suppressing the Chinese people. Thus the Communists and their urban allies succeé`ed in accelerating the collapse of the GMD.

After the war with Japan was over, the GMD government pursued an unskillful program of reorientation and examinations in the recovered territories, which alienated the "puppet" teachers and students and gave the Chinese Communist Party (CCP) an opportunity to denounce the "reactionary" nature of the government. The first Communist student demonstra-

tion was the peaceful Anti-Examination movement (October 1945–June 1946) that started in Beijing-Tianjin, followed by the bloody December First movement (1945) in Kunming. The emergence of slogans such as calls "to end one-party [GMD] dictatorship" and "to withdraw the American troops in China," and the inability of the government to control these demonstrations, were early signs of GMD weakness.

The period between June 1946 and July 1947 marked the high tide of the anti-American, anti-government demonstrations. The CCP exploited the alleged rape of a Beijing University coed (Shen Chong) by two American marines on December 24, 1945, by organizing a student-led Protest the Brutality of the American Military Personnel in China movement (December 1946–January 1947). The GMD could not control the students, and its opposition to the students' demands for withdrawal of all American influence compromised its stated commitment to Chinese nationalism. The Anti-Brutality movement thereby enabled the CCP to grasp the banner of Chinese nationalism and to lead the students. Partly influenced by the Shen Chong affair, The United States ordered most of the American troops to leave China by the end of 1947. The objectives of the Communist-instigated American Troops Quit China movement (1947) was therefore satisfied.

The pro-government demonstrations, especially the Anti-Soviet, Anti-Communist movement (February 1946), subdued the Communist-instigated "student tides" only temporarily, but did not succeed in seriously discrediting the CCP and the Soviet Union. In May 1947, a new wave of student demonstrations protested China's economic plight. By publicizing the issues of hunger, the government's huge military budget, and GMD repression, the Communists convinced some Chinese of the reactionary nature of the GMD government. The Anti-Hunger, Anti-Civil War movement (May 1947) proved so effective in undermining the GMD's prestige that Zhou Enlai and Mao Zedong glorified it as the "Second Battle Front," in contrast with the military "First Battle Front" in the countryside.

In July 1947, the GMD issued an order to suppress the Communists, but it could not restrain student power nor stop the demonstrations. The GMD could not break the Communist hold on the various student self-governing organizations or destroy the Communist-controlled All-China Student Association. In May and June 1948, the Communists launched a protest against American support of Japan—the last openly anti-American, anti-government demonstration. This time, the slogans included "Long live the independence of the Chinese nation" and "Stop the second Marco Polo Incident [of July 7, 1937]." The Communists claimed that the demonstrations exposed the treachery of American imperialism and the traitorous actions of the GMD.

In August 1948 the GMD was resolved to crush the Communist student movement once and for all. But the August Nineteenth Great Arrest (1948) of students and other social elements failed; this incident marked the beginning of the end of the GMD's political control in urban China. The last anti-government protest before the Communist conquest of Nanjing (April 24, 1949) was the six-thousand-strong student demonstration in the GMD capital on April 1, 1949, which demanded the GMD's acceptance of the Communist peace offer and an end to American meddling.

Until at least 1947, most students and other social elements supported neither the GMD nor the CCP overtly. This situation then changed. Student-based demonstrations ultimately discredited the GMD, but not the CCP. The anti-American, anti-government demonstrations decisively benefited the Communists during the civil war.

Joseph K. S. Yick

References

Pepper, Suzanne. *Civil War in China: The Political Struggle, 1945–1949*. Berkeley: University of California Press, 1978.

Wasserstrom, Jeffrey W. *Student Protests in Twentieth-Century China: The View from Shanghai*. Stanford, CA: Stanford University Press, 1991.

Anti-American Boycott

The boycott of 1905 in protest against American immigration policy was one of the first attempts in modern China at using economic means to achieve nationalistic political ends.

In 1904, the U.S. Congress passed a bill that permanently excluded Chinese immigration from American territories. The news enraged many Chinese, who saw the law as a form of racial discrimination. The Qing government immediately began negotiations with

the United States in hopes of changing this new legislation. To demonstrate their dissatisfaction with the American policy, and to strengthen the Qing government's position in the negotiations, Chinese merchants in Shanghai, Nanjing, Canton, and other major cities organized a boycott of American goods and services in 1905. In their proclamations, the merchants pointed out that cheap American products had earned huge profits for American businesses but had driven Chinese laborers out of work. As a result, many Chinese went to the United States to work on its railways and in its factories. Instead of showing their gratitude for the contributions that the Chinese had made to their economic well-being, the Americans were now depriving the Chinese workers of their opportunity to make a living.

The boycott movement was careful not to alienate the entire American population. It described its move as a "civilized action" and blamed the recent legislation on narrow-minded American workers. It pleaded for sympathy from "the enlightened people in America" as well as from "other civilized countries." When five American missionaries were killed near Canton during the boycott, the boycott leaders immediately disassociated themselves from the incident. The Qing government viewed the merchants' action with a degree of approval, realizing for the first time the value of a mass movement as a diplomatic weapon. It did not officially support the boycott, however, because of the understandable fear that the movement might lead to an uncontrollable outburst of anti-foreign chaos.

In response to the boycott, the American minister in Beijing issued protests and an American fleet arrived in Shanghai, threatening military actions. But no armed conflict occurred. Toward the end of 1905, as the United States promised to treat non-laboring Chinese visitors in America fairly, Qing officials urged the merchants to end the boycott. The boycott had lost momentum by then, and it gradually stopped, having lasted for about half a year.

The economic impact of the boycott on American trade was limited. It did not produce the desired result in terms of the immigration issue, although it accidentally helped the local gentry and government in Hubei and Hunan to cancel a railway concession held by the American China Development Company. Nevertheless, the movement was an unprecedented expression of modern nationalism among China's emerging elite—the urban bourgeoisie. In contrast to the anti-foreign violence of the Boxer Uprising of 1900, the anti-American boycott of 1905 was characterized by reasoned arguments and calculated measures, indicating the growth of national consciousness and a more restrained way of exercising public pressure. The experience prepared the Chinese elite for the Rights-Recovery movement and the Railway Protection movement in the following years.

Wang Ke-wen

References

Cohen, Warren I. *America's Response to China*. Revised edition. New York, NY: Columbia University Press, 1990.

Field, Margaret. "The Chinese Boycott of 1905." *Harvard Papers on China* 2 (1957): 63–98.

Iriye, Akira. *Across the Pacific: An Inner History of American-East Asian Relations*. Revised edition. Chicago, IL: Imprint Publications, 1992.

Anti-Christian Movement

Anti-Christian movements in twentieth-century China differed markedly from nineteenth century anti-Christian activities, when Confucian scholars rejected Christianity as being subversive of the traditional order, and the people expressed their frustration and hostilities toward the intrusion of Western missionaries in riots or attacks. By the 1910s, most new-style intellectuals had been converted to a faith in science. They believed that China's modernization and survival demanded the adoption of Western science and learning. To them, Christianity—and indeed all religions—was a reactionary force that should be discarded. Moreover, amid the growing anti-imperialist sentiments that castigated the Western powers for their political and economic exploitation of China, many also denounced Christian missionaries as the vanguards of Western imperialism.

In early 1922, against this background of rising nationalism and intellectual ferment, anti-Christian student organizations in Shanghai, Beijing, and other cities, as well as many new intellectual leaders, opposed the April meeting of the World Student Christian Federation at Qinghua University. The protest, confined largely to the printed media, focused primarily on the "unscientific" and "outdated" nature of Christianity. The rising tide of anti-imperialist sentiment after 1923, however, caused the anti-Christians, mostly students now supported by the Guomindang and Communists, to attack the missionary establishment—with its churches, schools, and hospitals—as the harbingers of cultural imperialism. In 1924, the Beijing government launched a movement to impose state control over mission schools. The anti-imperialist stance of the anti-Christian movement was accentuated after the May Thirtieth Movement of 1925, which strengthened the people's hostility against Christian institutions, now regarded as an integral part of Western imperialism, threatening China's survival as a nation.

Disturbances against churches, mission schools, and hospitals occurred throughout the country and continued into 1926 and 1927 during the Northern Expedition. The attacks culminated in the Nanjing Incident of March 1927, when anti-foreign and anti-missionary activities erupted after troops seized the city. The anti-Christian movement forced many missionaries to reexamine their objectives and methods in China and encouraged many Chinese Christians to work for the indigenization of the church. After 1927, the Nanjing regime curbed student activism and attempted to seek Western help in China's reconstruction. This led to the decline of organized anti-Christian activities, although the Chinese Communists continued their anti-religious, including anti-Christian, campaign in areas under their control.

With the Communist victory in 1949, the new government reorganized the churches according to the "three-self" model: self-support, self-propagation, and self-government, which in practice meant the complete severance of all ties with Western Christian bodies which the government denounced as imperialists—and placed control of all religious activities in the hands of the Religious Affairs Bureau of the United Front Department. To some extent, the Communist government tolerated religious activities until the outbreak of the Cultural Revolution, when Christians and believers of other faiths were persecuted by the Red Guards, who set out to destroy old ideas and customs in their attempt to build a new revolutionary China. By the late 1970s, the government had adopted a new policy of reconstruction and modernization, accompanied by a more pragmatic approach toward the church: it reopened some churches and officially reaffirmed a policy of toleration.

The government, however, has continued to reject religion as a legitimate belief system.

Ka-che Yip

References

MacInnis, Donald. *Religious Policy and Practice in Communist China—A Documentary History.* New York, NY: Macmillan, 1972.

Yip, Ka-che. *Religion, Nationalism and Chinese Students: The Anti-Christian Movement of 1922–1927.* Bellingham: Western Washington University, 1980.

Anti-Footbinding Movement

Footbinding was a practice among Chinese women that began around the Five Dynasties (907–960) or Song dynasty (960–1279). First started in the upper classes, it had become a widespread custom by the Ming (1368–1644) and Qing (1644–1912) periods. Girls between five and eight years of age would have their feet tightly bound with cloths, gradually crushing the bones, until the feet were deformed and kept at a small size. The bound feet of a woman were considered to be beautiful by Chinese men, and families normally enforced the practice with their daughters in order to make them presentable for marriage. The custom physically crippled China's female population and prevented women from having extensive social contact, thus keeping them dependent on the males. However, some ethnic minorities, such as the Manchus and the Hakka, did not adopt this Han practice.

As early as the eighteenth century, a few Chinese scholars had begun to criticize the custom, but not until the end of the nineteenth century were serious efforts made, mostly by the gentry class, to advocate its abolition. The first anti-footbinding society was founded by Kang Youwei in Canton in 1892; its membership eventually exceeded 10,000. Similar societies soon appeared in other cities, including one established by some Western women residents in Shanghai in 1895. These organizations promoted the cause through propaganda, and their members often vowed not to allow their sons to marry girls with bound feet. During the Hundred Days Reform of 1898, Kang Youwei included the prohibition of footbinding as one of his reform proposals. His disciple and colleague, Liang Qichao, as well as the female revolutionary Qiu Jin, was also outspoken against footbinding. In 1902 even the Qing government urged the people to terminate this "evil practice."

After the Revolution of 1911, the new Republic abolished footbinding, together with the Manchu hair-style ("pig-tails") for men. But popular resistance, often by women themselves, caused the practice to linger on for many more years in the rural areas. In the May Fourth era, leading advocates of westernization again identified footbinding as a major symbol of China's backwardness. Hu Shih ridiculed footbinding and opium-smoking as the country's "national essence." As did Kang Youwei in the 1890s, the reform-minded intellectuals of the 1910s and 1920s perceived the elimination of such embarrassing customs as necessary for the modernization of China. Their concern for the well-being of Chinese women was based on, and conditioned by, nationalism. Crippling Chinese women, for example, was said to have affected the physical health of Chinese children and hindered the country's economic productivity. Ultimately, the attack on footbinding was accompanied by attempts to raise women's status in society and represented a major step toward the liberation of modern Chinese women.

Wang Ke-wen

References

Bastid-Bruguiere, Marianne. "Currents of Social Change." *Cambridge History of China,* ed. John K. Fairbank and Kwang-ching Liu, vol. 11, 535–602. Cambridge, England: Cambridge University Press, 1980.

Croll, Elizabeth. *Feminism and Socialism in China.* New York, NY: Schocken Books, 1980.

Anti-Imperialism

This elusive phenomenon may include aspects of patriotism, nationalism, or xenophobia. Although elements of anti-imperialism may be found in earlier times, the concept is perhaps most usefully restricted to the emergence, at the end of the nineteenth century, of Chinese resistance to the continued expansion of the power and privileges that foreigners enjoyed under unequal treaties. The opposition to Russian incursions into Manchuria in 1903–04, and the anti-American boycott in 1905, are early examples of the phenomenon, as is the Rights-Recovery movement, including the attempt to gain control over foreign railway concessions, that flowered in the closing years of the Qing.

Although overt anti-imperialism was largely absent from the Revolution of 1911, the circumstances surrounding Japan's Twenty-One Demands of 1915 heightened fears in China of continued foreign depredations. Yet anti-imperialism did not reach its full development until the early years of the Republic, particularly after the May Fourth movement of 1919. By the 1920s, variants of Lenin's doctrine of imperialism as the highest stage of capitalism had taken hold among advanced thinkers of both the Guomindang and the Chinese Communist Party. This gave a modern theoretical base to what had heretofore been an ill-defined movement and allowed anti-imperialism to form one of the foundations of the first United Front (1923–27).

By now, anti-imperialism had come to mean opposition not only to political and economic concessions, but to foreign cultural manifestations as well. This was evident in the anti-Christian movement of the 1920s. Resentment against foreign privilege, particularly in the cities, was considerably heightened by the outbreak of the May Thirtieth movement of 1925, and the Northern Expedition that followed. In particular, the protagonists of those movements sought to build an advanced nationalism by linking foreign privilege and foreign oppression to the depredations of warlordism and civil war, and after 1928, the new Guomindang government at Nanjing began to negotiate a recovery of the rights lost under the unequal treaties.

While Great Britain had been the main focus of anti-imperialism in the 1920s, Japan became the target of the 1930s. Following the loss of Manchuria to Japan in 1931, the Communists exploited Nanjing's apparent passivity in the face of Japanese aggrandizement, using the National Salvation movements to build up their support, particularly among students and urban intellectuals, in the period before the emergence of the second United Front (1937–45).

With the defeat of Japan in 1945, and the withdrawal of other chief targets of anti-imperialism, the Communists sought to portray Chiang Kaishek as Washington's puppet, not only during the civil war (1945–49) and the Korean War (1950–53) but during the years of confrontation in the Taiwan Straits in 1954–55 and 1958. From the mid-1960s well into the 1970s, however, the Soviet Union replaced the United States as the arch-enemy. The Chinese Communists described Moscow as practicing "socialist imperialism" under the rule of the "new czars" striving for world hegemony. Only in the last decade, as China has emerged as a less strident voice in world affairs, has Beijing somewhat muted its anti-imperialist rhetoric.

Some critics maintain that anti-imperialism often did no more than substitute an attack on foreigners for a genuine analysis of China's domestic ills. Although such a description might fit Chiang Kaishek's *China's Destiny* (1943), most anti-imperialism cannot be so easily categorized. Late Qing republican revolutionaries blamed the weakness of a foreign (Manchu) dynasty for China's inability to resist Japanese and Western aggrandizement, and the May Fourth movement perceived the whole Confucian tradition as one of the causes for China's backwardness. Prior to 1949, at least, the Communists tended to see imperialism and "feudalism" as two wings of an unholy alliance designed to keep China poor and in a position to be exploited (as Mao Zedong, for example, wrote in his 1939 work, "The Chinese Revolution and the Chinese Communist Party"). In any event, the anti-imperialist movement was responsible for certain gains in modern China: the weakening of foreign privilege and of its base in the unequal treaties in the 1920s and 1930s, and the development of a broad sense of national identity and mass nationalism, particularly in the war against Japan.

Nicholas R. Clifford

Anti-Japanese Base Areas
See BORDER REGIONS

Anti-Japanese Boycott
In the first half of the twentieth century, popular nationalism became a potent force in Chinese politics, particularly in urban areas. Students, professionals, and businessmen fought to "save China" at a time of weakness and foreign invasion. One important component of this nationalist force was the anti-Japanese boycott, which figured prominently in such events as the May Fourth movement and the May Thirtieth movement. The boycotts were particularly significant because they attracted the support not only of radical groups, such as the students, but usually had the backing of more conservative elements, such as chambers of commerce and

business guilds. Chinese capitalists often faced stiff competition from foreign businesses, and boycotts were a way of opening the door for Chinese manufacturing and commerce.

Although the anti-American boycott of 1905 is generally considered the first such significant action in China, Japan was the most frequent target of boycotts. The *Tatsu Maru* Incident of February 1908, in which the Qing government apologized for alleged slights to the Japanese flag, occasioned the first serious boycott aimed at Japan. A more successful boycott, which reduced Japanese exports to China for several months, occurred in 1915 in response to Japan's Twenty-One Demands.

The May Fourth movement of 1919, in response to Japanese actions in Shandong province, led to a renewal of the boycott. Student groups throughout China organized the boycott, the effects of which were felt until 1921. As was often the case with boycotts, however, the goal of the organizers was not simply to damage Japanese economic interests but also to pressure the Chinese government to resist Japanese encroachments. The Beiyang government in Beijing became as much the students' target as the Japanese. The cycle of boycotts continued throughout the 1920s. Although Great Britain became the primary target in the anti-foreign boycott at the time of the May Thirtieth movement of 1925, the original target had been Japan, which was responsible for the killing of Chinese workers striking at a Japanese mill in Shanghai. Anti-Japanese actions resumed in 1928 and 1929 following the Jinan Incident.

The intense boycott movements of the 1920s played into the hands of the Guomindang (GMD) government in Canton. Allied with the new Chinese Communist Party, the Guomindang tapped into the large pool of activists that grew out of the May Fourth–May Thirtieth tradition. After Chiang Kaishek's break with the Communists in April 1927, however, the GMD found the boycott movement a mixed blessing. As head of a new, and relatively weak, government in Nanjing, Chiang sought to avoid antagonizing his powerful neighbor by settling the Jinan Incident on terms favorable to Japan. The boycott activity, moreover, was a mass movement of the type that Chiang came increasingly to distrust.

The contradictions between Chiang's goals and those of boycott organizers became clear in the 1930s. The summer of 1931 saw the beginnings of what would become the most intense and successful of all the anti-Japanese boycotts. Beginning with the Wanbaoshan Incident of July 1931, the movement peaked with the Manchurian Incident in September and the fighting between China and Japan at Shanghai in early 1932. After the fighting at Shanghai ended and the League of Nations was unable to force a Japanese withdrawal from the northeast, Chiang decided upon a policy of appeasing Japan and pursuing the civil war against the Communists. Under such conditions, the GMD government found itself, in the mid-1930s, in the awkward position of trying to terminate the anti-Japanese boycott movement. Japanese sales in China had fallen by as much as 75 percent in the year following the Manchurian Incident, and Tokyo made suspension of the boycott a condition for coexistence with Chiang.

Beginning in May 1932, therefore, the Nanjing government actively suppressed anti-Japanese boycott activity. Throughout the remaining years of the Nanjing Decade, when calls for boycotting Japanese products followed in the wake of new Japanese pressures, such as the war at the Great Wall in 1933 and the Amo Statement of 1934, Chiang was placed in the awkward position of opposing the boycott, while simultaneously depicting himself as the leader of Chinese nationalism. Groups sympathetic to the Chinese Communist Party (CCP) used this issue to embarrass Chiang.

The anti-Japanese boycott movement failed to stop Japanese imperialism in China. Although Japan's exports to China often decreased for months at a time because of the boycotts, Japanese business eventually recovered. More importantly, Japanese extremists used the anti-boycott movement to justify a more aggressive policy toward China. Only through armed conquest of China, they argued, could Chinese resistance to "economic cooperation" with Japan be ended. In retrospect, the most important legacy of the boycott movement was not its effectiveness in halting Japanese imperialism but its politicization of China's urban populace. Boycotts allowed ordinary people to participate in "saving the nation" and contributed to the growth of nationalism in China. In the 1920s, this sentiment fueled the Guomindang's "National Revolution"; in the 1930s, it aided the Communists.

Parks M. Coble

References

Coble, Parks M. *Facing Japan: Chinese Politics and Japanese Imperialism, 1931–1937*. Cambridge, MA: Harvard University Press, 1991.

Jordan, Donald. *Chinese Boycotts versus Japanese Bombs: The Failure of China's "Revolutionary Diplomacy," 1931–1932*. Ann Arbor: University of Michigan Press, 1931.

Remer, C. F. *A Study of Chinese Boycotts with Special Reference to Their Economic Effectiveness*. Taibei: Cheng-wen Publishing Co., 1966.

Anti-Manchuism

Opposition to the Manchus by Han Chinese took several different forms and changed over time. It also coexisted with extensive Chinese-Manchu interaction, including cooperation and varying degrees of cultural assimilation. Thus "anti-Manchuism" is a rather elusive concept in itself, and its connection with nationalism is even more problematic.

The Manchus are a Tungusic people native to northeast Asia, particularly identified with the three provinces comprising China's northeast, the area once known as Manchuria. They were part of a culturally diverse confederation of peoples known as Jurchens, whose ancestors had moved south, occupied north China, and created the Jin dynasty (1115–1234). In 1616, the Jurchen Khan in Manchuria declared the establishment of the Later Jin. Twenty years later they took the name Manchu and renamed their kingdom Qing. By 1644, Qing forces had taken Beijing; they then proceeded to consolidate their rule over China during the next forty years. The dynasty fell in 1912.

Chinese opposition to the Manchus can be traced to the earliest years of extensive contacts between the two peoples. Organized resistance to the Manchus was evident, for example, when the Jurchens took control of Liaodong between 1618 and 1621, and it continued sporadically for years thereafter. The opposition ranged from random or isolated actions such as poisoning the food and water of the invaders to organized rebellions against their rule (*e.g.,* in 1623 and 1625). A group of prominent seventeenth-century intellectuals, most notably Gu Yanwu and Wang Fuzhi, transformed hostility toward the Manchus into a doctrine that may be termed anti-Manchuism.

Zahng Binglin. (Courtesy of Nationalist Party Archives.)

Wang was especially remarkable for the sustained vigor of his struggle against the Manchus and for his systematic attempt to express his anti-Manchuism in a broad historical and philosophical context. Wang mobilized a force to resist Qing troops in 1648; after being defeated, he joined remnant Ming forces and fought on until 1650. For the remainder of his life he pursued his studies and refused to have any dealings with the Manchus. His research led him to the conclusion that the fundamental principles of heaven, earth, and man required "an absolute distinction between societies." Although he acknowledged that similarities existed among human beings, for example in the bone structure and sense organs of Chinese and Manchus, he nevertheless insisted that Chinese "must be distinguished absolutely from the barbarians." Worthy rulers and great states had a solemn duty to protect their own kind and their own groups, especially against foreign invasion and conquest, and this was best assured by ethnic separatism.

Ideas such as Wang's could not circulate

freely in the Qing period, and Wang's writings remained largely unknown until late in the dynasty's existence. But anti-Manchu ideas took root in secret societies, some of which professed loyalty to the Ming and claimed to have been inspired by Gu, Wang, and other early Qing opponents of the Manchus. Such links cannot be fully confirmed by historical evidence, but secret societies such as the Triads did continue throughout the Qing dynasty to stand for its overthrow and for the restoration of the Ming. What is difficult to determine is the extent to which their political anti-Qing sentiments were linked to an ethnic anti-Manchuism of the Wang Fuzhi variety or to anything that today might be regarded as nationalism.

Similar analytical problems exist with respect to the anti-Manchuism of the Taiping Rebellion (1850–64) and the republican revolutionary movement (1895–1912). As with the secret societies, many scholars stress the political anti-Qing ideas of both, implying that the Taipings and republican revolutionaries would have opposed the dynasty just as strongly had it been Chinese. But others insist that the ethnic anti-Manchuism was also important to one or another or both of them. This makes the task of relating anti-Manchuism to modern Chinese nationalism a highly complex enterprise; the issues are blurred, and their resolution is not easily subject to empirical analysis.

Undisputedly, Wang Fuzhi's ideas had great influence on major late-Qing thinkers and movements. Among the Taipings, at least one leader, Hong Rengan, was familiar with the ideas of Wang and Gu Yanwu, and he made an appeal (rare for the Taipings) to the Chinese elite that was based on ethnic nationalist grounds reminiscent of those ideas. But Taiping anti-Manchuism was also shaped by the general (*i.e.*, not specifically anti-Manchu) anti-Qing sentiments concerning foreign conquest and oppression. Still more to the point, Taiping anti-Manchuism was most distinctive in its religious content. The Taiping leader Hong Xiuquan proclaimed that the Manchus were more than barbarian usurpers, they were devils who had stolen China from God; it was God, indeed, who had decreed that Hong should destroy them.

The republican revolutionaries used lavish anti-Manchu rhetoric, and on numerous occasions their revolutionary propaganda employed crude racist language. Thus, for example, they described the Manchus as "an inferior minor-ity" and an "evil race" whose wickedness was not limited to their political policies but was "rooted in the nature of the race and can neither be eliminated nor reformed." Such propaganda has come to be regarded partly as a tactic to overcome division in the revolutionary movement and to arouse mass support, and partly as a scapegoating device to lay the blame for China's weakness and defeats on the Manchu rulers.

Some revolutionaries, notably Zhang Binglin, the most prominent scholar in the anti-Qing camp, had a broader foundation for their anti-Manchuism. Widely read in history and philosophy, Zhang was a particular admirer of the Ming loyalists and had adopted as a *hao* (literary name) Taiyan, a reference to Huang Zongxi and Gu Yanwu. Zhang specifically traced his anti-Manchuism to Huang, Gu, Wang Fuzhi, and other Ming loyalists. His critique of the Manchus and the Qing regime drew on an exceptionally wide range of ideas, and his writings include some blatant anti-Manchu racism. On balance, however, most analysts of Zhang's many-sided, labyrinthine, and at times quirky thought conclude that his anti-Manchuism was fundamentally an expression of his nationalism, that his nationalism reflected above all his anti-imperialism, and that his anti-Manchuism was a statement about Chinese cultural and political identity more than racism. In this context it is significant that Zhang later omitted his crudest anti-Manchu writings from his collected works and that he wrote no more such text after the Qing fell. Similarly, it is noteworthy that the fall of the Qing was not accompanied by widespread anti-Manchu actions on the part of the Han Chinese population, although some ethnic clashes did occur, and that the Manchu imperial house was treated leniently, even generously, in comparison with those of other fallen empires in the modern world.

Han Chinese anti-Manchuism seems to have been primarily a political phenomenon associated chiefly with resentments concerning conquest by and subordination to foreigners, intensified by the problems China faced in the nineteenth and early twentieth centuries and the strong currents of modern nationalism that stirred China in the same period. Further study of it is being carried on in the wider context of Chinese ethnocentrism and Han perceptions of non-Han peoples, and these studies may be expected to produce substantial gains in our still limited understanding of anti-Manchuism.

Michael Gasster

References

Dikötter, Frank. *The Discourse of Race in Modern China.* Stanford, CA: Stanford University Press, 1992.

Gasster, Michael. *Chinese Intellectuals and the Revolution of 1911: The Birth of Modern Chinese Radicalism.* Seattle: University of Washington Press, 1969.

Laitinen, Kauko. *Chinese Nationalism in the Late Qing Dynasty: Zhang Binglin as an Anti-Manchu Propagandist.* London, England: Curzon Press, 1990.

Anti-Revisionism

Anti-revisionism is an ideological theme that preoccupied Mao Zedong for two decades beginning in the mid-1950s. It is a main component of Mao's theory of "continuing the revolution under the dictatorship of the proletariat." Mao's concern about the danger of "revisionism" to Communism ultimately led him to initiate the Cultural Revolution in 1966 to combat "revisionists" at home and abroad.

Mao reportedly first mentioned the term "revisionism" in May 1957, in a speech that prompted the Anti-Rightist movement. Although at the time the political campaign was directed more at Chinese intellectuals and non-Communists who had criticized the Communist Party, Mao became increasingly concerned about events in the Soviet Union, precipitated by Khrushchev's secret speech against Stalin in 1956. Mao apparently concluded that a similar fate might befall him should he fail to prevent the emergence of "revisionism."

Mao first identified "revisionists" in the international Communist movement. In a speech in March 1960, he condemned the Yugoslavs as "revisionists" and the Soviets as "semi-revisionists." Soon Mao deleted the prefix "semi-" in referring to the Soviet "revisionists." At a party cadre meeting in January 1962, Mao announced that "the Party and state leadership of the Soviet Union have now been usurped by the revisionists." The attack was seen by many as part of Mao's attempt to assert

A

Mao Zedong greeting Soviet leader Nikita Khrushchev in Beijing, 1959. (Xinhua News Agency.)

China's independence from Soviet influence and control.

Having issued several warnings about "revisionism" in the international Communist movement, Mao then focused his attention on the domestic front. In 1963, he instructed the Party to organize the Socialist Education movement in the countryside. Mao also criticized Chinese literature, art, film, and drama for harboring "feudalistic and bourgeois tendencies." On April 10, 1964, Mao asked a foreign Communist Party delegation to "help the Chinese Marxists fight against the Chinese revisionists." At a work conference in the same year, Mao challenged his colleagues: "If revisionism appears in the Central Committee, what are you going to do? It is possible that it will appear, and this is a great danger." Clearly, by then Mao had reached the conclusion that "opposing and preventing revisionism" was the most urgent task facing the Chinese Communists.

Finally, in 1966, Mao decided to launch the Cultural Revolution to wipe out the Chinese "revisionists." The Party's official notice of May 16, written under Mao's instructions, called on the entire party to expose, attack, and purge those "counter-revolutionary revisionists who were trying to usurp the political power." During this mass campaign, Mao's chief lieutenants and many Party officials were accused of becoming "China's Khrushchev" and "revisionists trying to restore capitalism." In condemning the "revisionists," the Chinese people also underwent a mind-twisting process of thought reform, called "fighting self and opposing revisionism."

Mao's obsession with the anti-"revisionist" struggle continued until his death in 1976. Since then the term "revisionism" has almost disappeared from Party newspapers and official publications, perhaps because "revisionism" reminds the surviving leaders, including Deng Xiaoping, of the attacks and persecutions they suffered during the Cultural Revolution.

Shi-ping Zheng

References

Schram, Stuart R. "Mao Tse-tung's Thought from 1949–1976." *The Cambridge History of China,* ed. Roderick MacFarquhar and John K. Fairbank, vol. 15, 1–104. Cambridge, England: Cambridge University Press, 1991.
Starr, John Bryan. *Continuing the Revolution: The Political Thought of Mao.* Princeton, NJ: Princeton University Press, 1979.

Anti-Rightist Campaign
See HUNDRED FLOWERS CAMPAIGN

Anti-Russia Volunteer Army
This short-lived militia, which lasted from April 29 to May 7, 1903, was organized by the Chinese radicals in Japan as a protest against Russian aggression in Manchuria. After 1900 the number of Chinese students in Japan increased by leaps and bounds. Exposed to ideas of nationalism and Social Darwinism, some of them became politically conscious and critical of the weak Manchu (Qing) government. Further news of foreign encroachments on Chinese rights stimulated the young radicals into action.

In the spring of 1903, Chinese students in Tokyo had demonstrated against French imperialist activities in southern China. A larger student movement developed when, on April 28, 1903, a Japanese newspaper unveiled Russia's seven demands issued to the Manchu government as a precondition for the withdrawal of Russian troops in Manchuria, which had been stationed there since the Boxer Uprising of 1900. The next day, the aroused Chinese students, led by Niu Yongjian, Tang Erhe, and Ye Lan, met at Kinki Hall in Kanda and decided to form a force, known as the Anti-Russia Volunteer Army *(JuE yiyongjun)*, to fight the aggressors. By April 30 about 130 students had joined the student corps, another 50 agreed to work at the headquarters in Tokyo, and 12 women students signed up for nursing duties.

On May 2, the Anti-Russia Volunteer Army changed its name to Student Army *(Xueshengjun)* and elected Lan Tianwei as its chief commanding officer. It dispatched telegrams to student activist groups in China. In response, members of the Education Association and the Patriotic School formed the Shanghai Anti-Russia Volunteer Army. At the same time, the Student Army sent two representatives to China to offer the government its services. Suspecting the army of subversive intentions, Qing officials persuaded the Japanese government to ban Chinese student activities.

On May 7, the Student Army was disbanded. In its place the militants formed the Military Affairs Discussion Society, which was soon dissolved by the Tokyo authorities. They then established the Association for National Military Education *(Junguomin jiaoyuhui)* on May 11. Ostensibly a patriotic society, it was secretly anti-dynastic. When rumors reached the association that the two representatives of the former Student Army had been executed by the Manchu government in Tianjin, the radicals organized a secret assassination corps and pledged to overthrow the Qing dynasty through propaganda, assassinations, and uprisings. They returned to China and founded two separate revolutionary societies: the Huaxinghui (China Arise Society) and the Guangfuhui (Restoration Society). The formation of the Anti-Russia Volunteer Army and its subsequent evolution signified the transformation of the nationalist student movement from anti-imperialism to anti-Manchuism at the turn of the century.

Henry Y. S. Chan

References

Harrell, Paula. *Sowing the Seeds of Change: Chinese Students, Japanese Teachers, 1895–1905.* Stanford, CA: Stanford University Press, 1992.

Schiffrin, Harold. *Sun Yat-sen and the Origins of the Chinese Revolution.* Berkeley: University of California Press, 1970.

Arrow War

During the fifteen years following the Treaty of Nanjing, which ended the Opium War of 1839–1842, tension continued in Sino-Western relations. The Western powers were frustrated by the lack of Chinese cooperation in implementing the treaty, as officials in Canton still refused to allow Westerners to enter the city. The Chinese, on the other hand, were constantly annoyed by new Western demands. Defeat in the Opium War apparently did not change the self-image of China as the "celestial empire," nor her attitude toward the "barbarians." The West, especially the British, was eager to "teach China another lesson" in order to force her to accept Western rules in the conduct of international relations.

Treaty revision offered the West a convenient excuse to take a bellicose action. The Treaty of Nanjing, as well as the treaties that China had subsequently concluded with the United States and France, had stipulated that it was to be revised in twelve years. In 1854, the Treaty of Nanjing was slated for revision. The British, joined by the Americans and the French, took this opportunity to demand an expansion of trade opportunities. The Chinese government ignored their demands.

Two incidents in 1856 reinforced Western determination to go to war. In February, Chinese officials in Guangxi arrested and executed a French Catholic missionary. In October, a Chinese ship, the *Arrow,* registered in Hong Kong and flying the British flag, was searched by Chinese officials in Canton on suspicion of piracy. The latter was known as the *Arrow* Incident. The British gunboats stationed outside of Canton immediately retaliated by bombarding the city. In 1857, a joint British-French expeditionary force seized Canton. Failing to obtain a satisfactory response from Beijing, the expeditionary force, now accompanied by American and Russian "observers," sailed to north China and landed at Dagu, with Tianjin and Beijing well within reach.

In panic, the Qing court hastily signed the Treaty of Tianjin with the British in June 1858. The British acquired the right to post a resident minister in Beijing; British ships gained permission to sail up the Yangtze River; and British subjects could travel in all parts of the Chinese interior. In addition, ten new treaty ports were opened; the Chinese government was to protect Christian missionaries and converts; and war indemnities were paid to the British. The opium trade, the cause of the first war in 1839, was finally legalized.

Wang Ke-wen

References

Hurd, Douglas. *The Arrow War: An Anglo-Chinese Confusion, 1856–1860.* New York, NY: Macmillan, 1967.

Wakeman, Frederick, Jr. *Strangers At the Gate: Social Disorder in South China, 1839–1861.* Berkeley: University of California Press, 1966.

Wong, J. Y. "The Arrow Incident: A Reappraisal." *Modern Asian Studies* 9, no. 3 (1975): 303–20.

Assassinationism *(Ansha zhuyi)*

Ansha zhuyi, a neologism which first appeared in Chinese revolutionary literature around 1902, was derived from the Japanese term *ansatsu shugi,* referring to populist terrorism in nineteenth-century Russia. The violent tactic gained wide acceptance among Chinese radicals, and this resulted in waves of revolutionary assassinations in the last decade of the Qing dynasty.

The use of violence to achieve political

objectives was not foreign to the Chinese. For generations Chinese authors had glorified the tradition of romantic heroism, as manifested in the courageous missions of the historical *cike* (assassins). Members of secret societies applied the tactic against their enemies. In the Huizhou Uprising of 1900, some Japanese *shishi* (men of purpose) volunteered to assassinate senior Qing officials in central China. For various reasons, Sun Yatsen cancelled the operation. But Shi Jianru resorted to it in a vain attempt to save the revolutionaries from defeat.

Through Japanese translations, the Chinese radicals found their situation identical with that of the Russian populists. The Manchu government's suspicious attitude toward the students' Anti-Russia movement in 1903 incited the militants to action. Thus Gong Baoquan formed an assassination corps in Tokyo and founded the Guangfuhui (Restoration Society) in Shanghai, which advocated the use of violence against the Qing dynasty. Cai Yuanpei, Liu Shipei and Yang Shouren publicized the populist method in *Zhejiangzhao (Tides of Zhejiang), Jingzhong ribao (The Alarm Bell)*, and *Subao (Jiangsu Gazette)*. Lin Xie praised the tradition of the historical assassins in his writings for *Zhongguo baihuabao (Chinese Vernacular Journal)*. Under their influence, three assassinations occurred in 1904. The next year, Wu Yue's attempt on five Qing officials at the Beijing railway station shook the capital. His posthumous writings, which later appeared in *Minbao (The People's Report)*, epitomized the morality of a modern Chinese assassin. Citing Russian nihilist experiences, Wu dashingly announced the beginning of the age of assassination in China. He eulogized the romantic tradition of the *xia* (knights-errant) and justified the act of self-sacrifice in Confucian and Buddhist terms.

The incidents between 1904 and 1905 were propaganda by deed in the sense that the lone assassins sacrificed themselves for the propagation of the revolutionary message. In subsequent years, most of the operations were team efforts, with the tactical objective of weakening the local government through the elimination of senior officials, thus paving the way for uprisings. Revolutionary writers launched another propaganda wave in *Minbao, Xinshiji (New Century)*, and *Tianyi (Heavenly Justice)* to promote the use of assassinations when the revolutionary morale was in the doldrums as a result of repeated failures in 1906 and 1907. A

new round of assassinations began in 1909, consisting of both solo missions and group operations. In 1910, Wang Jingwei and his team ventured north against the Prince Regent. Even Sun Yatsen and Huang Xing briefly advocated this violent tactic after the debacle of the Canton Uprising of April 1911.

In the end it was uprisings that brought down the Manchu regime. Some of the radicals gradually turned their interest from Russian populism to anarchism. Assassinationism had, however, indirectly contributed to the intensification of violence in politics. Later, the warlords adopted similar tactics against the revolutionaries, and the Guomindang government against dissidents. This in part accounted for the high intensity of violence in republican China.

Henry Y. S. Chan

References
Krebs, Edward. "Assassination in the Republican Revolutionary Movement." *Ch'ingshi wen-ti* (December 1981): 45–81.
Price, Don. *Russia and the Roots of the Chinese Revolution.* Cambridge, MA: Harvard University Press, 1974.

Atomic Bomb

China was the fifth country in the world to develop nuclear weapons, after the United States, Soviet Union, Great Britain, and France. The history of the evolution of the Chinese atomic bomb may be broken roughly into several stages: the establishment of the infrastructure (1955–58), the period of Soviet assistance (1958–60), the "stage of standing firm" (1960–62), when the program hit the nadir of its difficulties, and the "stage of flowering" (1962–64), after which nuclear development proceeded at a rapid rate.

Hostilities with the United States had forced China to venture into the nuclear age. On two occasions the United States had threatened to use nuclear weapons against the People's Republic: in 1953, when the Eisenhower administration contemplated the use of the atomic bomb to end the war in Korea, and then in 1954, when Secretary of State John Foster Dulles hinted at massive retaliation against China in response to events in Indochina. These two crises drove the Politburo of the Chinese Communist Party to consider building China's own nuclear arsenal. Funding for science and technology programs increased dramatically between 1955 and 1956, and the Chinese leadership appointed a committee comprising Chen Yun, Nie Rongzhen, and Bo Yibo to coordinate the organization of the nuclear weapons program. Several government agencies established between 1955 and 1958 mobilized the scientific community.

In 1955, the Soviet Union promised to assist China in building a nuclear arsenal. In January of that year, the USSR offered China research facilities, uranium, technical experts, missiles, and a prototype atomic bomb. In return, China pledged to provide the USSR with raw materials. With Soviet assistance, the Chinese began to build a gaseous diffusion plant at Lanzhou, in Gansu province.

The Chinese experienced great difficulties in the early stages of their atomic bomb program. The country embarked on a prospecting campaign for uranium in the provinces of Liaoning, Guangdong, and Hunan, where miners fell victim to disease, radiation poisoning, and cave-ins. This effort coincided with the Anti-Rightist of 1957 and the Great Leap Forward of 1958 to 60, during which time many of the top intellectuals in China were purged.

The worst period came in 1960, when Mao and Khrushchev clashed and ended friendly relations between Beijing and Moscow. The Soviets reneged on their promises to deliver a prototype bomb and withdrew all of their technical advisors from China. They left the Lanzhou gaseous diffusion plant unfinished and took with them most of the crucial blueprints and plans. To add to China's difficulties, the country was stricken with a devastating famine.

Fortunately, the Chinese government had an elite group of native scientists who had received their training abroad. Prominent among them were Qian Sanqiang (nuclear physics under Irene Joliet-Curie in Paris), Peng Huanwu (quantum physics with Max Born at Edinburgh University), Wang Ganchang (nuclear physics, University of Berlin), Guo Yonghuai (aerodynamics, California Institute of Technology), Qian Weichang (jet propulsion laboratory of Caltech), and Qian Xuesen (aerodynamics, Caltech). These scientists proved critical to the development of the Chinese nuclear bomb and missile program. In the 1960s, a number of important nuclear facilities emerged: three major nuclear bases and a research center in Hengyang, Jiuquan, Lanzhou, and Qinghai, respectively. At the Ninth Academy in Qinghai,

China's first successful test of atomic bomb in 1964. (Xinhua News Agency.)

the "Los Alamos" of China, the country's best engineers finally designed the first Chinese atomic bomb.

On October 16, 1964, China detonated its first atomic bomb in the Xinjiang desert. The bomb had an enriched core of uranium-235 with a 20-kiloton yield. Two years later, on October 27, 1966, China recklessly (albeit successfully) tested a nuclear missile simultaneously with a nuclear warhead—the first and only country in the world to do so.

The scientists then devoted their energies to the building of a hydrogen bomb. On May 9, 1966, the Chinese tested a 200- to 300-kiloton-yield uranium device with lithium-6, followed by another test of a 300- to 500-kiloton-yield uranium-lithium device on December 28, 1966. Half a year later, on June 17, 1967, the Chinese successfully exploded a 3-megaton, multistage H-bomb. The speed with which the Chinese developed their H-bomb after the detonation of their first atomic bomb was remarkable, considering that it had taken the USSR four years and France eight years to make the transition between fission and fusion devices. It had taken China only thirty-two months.

Experts believe that China's greatest leap in nuclear technology occurred over a single decade, from the mid-1960s to the mid-1970s. This development coincided with the chaotic years of the Cultural Revolution, but scientists working on the nuclear bomb and missile programs received special protection. The program spread to more than forty sites, including five major weapons factories, two nuclear research institutes, six nuclear reactors, and a Lop Nor test site in Xinjiang. In November 1976, China detonated a 4-megaton-yield thermonuclear warhead during a ballistic missile training exercise—capping ten years of research and development, most of it performed in relative isolation.

Within the space of thirty years, China had transformed itself from a backward military power to one capable of delivering nuclear warheads intercontinentally. By the 1980s, China had accumulated an impressive nuclear arsenal and had become the world's fourth-largest arms supplier. If "wealth and power" for their country has been the goal of all nationalistic Chinese since the late nineteenth century, then the development of nuclear weapons by the People's Republic has at least partially realized that goal.

Iris Chang

References

Hahn, Bradley. "China's Nuclear History." *The China Business Review* vol. 12, no. 2 (July-August 1985): 28–31.

Lewis, John, and Xue Litai. *China Builds the Bomb*. Stanford, CA: Stanford University Press, 1988.

Pollack, John. "China as a Nuclear Power." *Asia's Nuclear Future*, ed. William Overholt, 35–65. Boulder, CO: Westview Press, 1979.

August Thirteenth Incident

It is now a "historical fact" that China's war of resistance against Japan began on July 7, 1937. But to most Chinese observers at the time, the July seventh Marco Polo Bridge Incident was perhaps another humiliating incident like the Mukden Incident of 1931, which resulted in the Japanese occupation of Manchuria. In their minds, the war started with the outbreak of hostilities in Shanghai on August 13, 1937.

On the morning of August 13, Japanese marines crossed the Shanghai-Wusong Railway to attack the Chinese army stationed around the North Station in Zhabei, and the fighting quickly spread to other parts of the city—except the foreign settlements. The attack was probably aimed as a preemptive strike against the increasing movement of Chinese troops into greater Shanghai since July 7. Shanghai, republican China's largest metropolis, had been the major source of revenue for the Guomindang government. To protect his power base as well as to plead for international intervention against Japanese aggression, Chiang Kaishek committed not only half a million soldiers but also his best-trained elite corps to defend the city. The Chinese army fought heroically, courageously holding on to its defensive line in the face of Japanese naval and aerial predominance. When they lost a strategic position during the day, they took it back in hand-to-hand combat at night, while the Japanese bombing was less effective.

The most dramatic act of Chinese heroism in the August Thirteenth Incident was the resistance of the "Lone Battalion" *(gujun)*. In late October, the Japanese broke through the Chinese line at Dachang, a strategic town eight miles north of Zhabei. The 524th Regiment of the 88th Army was ordered to serve as a rear guard for the Zhabei troops in retreat. This seemed to be a doomed cause. Under Colonel Xie Jinyuan, the 800-strong regiment fortified itself in a warehouse bordering the Suzhou Creek and held out for four days against constant Japanese bombardments and heavy machine-gun fire. The regiment finally withdrew on October 31 only under Chiang Kaishek's order. This remarkable resistance made the "Lone Battalion" into a symbol of the defense of Shanghai.

On November 12, a fortnight after the retreat of the "Lone Battalion," Shanghai fell and remained under Japanese occupation throughout the eight years of war. The Battle of Shanghai nevertheless destroyed the Japanese illusion of gaining an easy victory in China. Instead of conquering China in a matter of months with only a quarter million troops, as Japan had boasted it could do, Japan was forced to commit over 300,000 soldiers to break the Chinese resistance in Shanghai alone. Soon it had to reconsider its overall strategy in the Sino-Japanese War.

Poshek Fu

References

Ch'i, Hsi-sheng. *Nationalist China at War: Military Defeats and Political Collapse, 1937–1945.* Ann Arbor: University of Michigan Press, 1982.

Wilson, Dick. *When Tigers Fight: The Story of the Sino-Japanese War, 1937–45.* New York, NY: The Viking Press, 1982.

Autonomous Regions of National Minorities

Before its ascent to national power, the Chinese Communist Party had been sympathetic toward the struggle for autonomy, even independence, by China's national minorities. In the 1930s, the Jiangxi Soviet formally supported the self-determination of national minorities and the formation of a multinational Chinese federation modeled on the Soviet Union. During the Sino-Japanese War of 1937 to 1945, the Party modified its position and advocated instead the minorities' self-government within the Chinese state. This latter principle was translated into policy after the Communist victory in 1949. Since then the People's Republic of China (PRC) has constructed an administrative framework for the autonomy of the country's minority peoples and regions, while actively promoting their integration into the Han-dominated Chinese state through internal immigration and education.

In 1952, the PRC promulgated the General Program for the Implementation of Regional Autonomy and established the Autonomous Regions *(zizhiqu)* for national minorities. Five such regions were formed in the following years: Inner Mongolia, Xinjiang-Uighur, Hui, Zhuang, and Tibet. Less important national minorities were recognized through smaller administrative units—the Autonomous Prefecture *(zhou)*, County *(xian)*, and Village *(xiang)*. This administrative arrangement was subsequently adopted by the PRC Constitutions of 1954, 1975, and 1978.

The government recognized fifty-four national minorities *(shaoshu minzu)* in 1957; one more was added in 1979. A 1990 census indi-

Market scene in the Xinjiang-Uighurs Autonomous Region. (Xinhua News Agency.)

cated that these minorities constituted about 8 percent of China's population but inhabited more than half of the country's territory. In the autonomous areas the minorities enjoy full PRC citizenship as well as government protection of their languages and customs. In general, central policies and programs have been implemented more flexibly, and at a slower pace, in these areas than elsewhere in China. Most of the local cadres in these areas, moreover, have been chosen from the relevant minorities. The government established Nationalities Institutes *(minzu xueyuan)*, totaling twelve in the 1990s, to train minority cadres for these responsibilities.

Despite these efforts, however, attempts at central control have provoked occasional unrest in the Autonomous Regions, such as the Muslim revolts in Xinjiang in the 1980s and the Tibetan problem since the late 1950s. Another source of the minorities' discontent has been the government's aggressive policy of Han migration into their areas. With the possible exceptions of Tibet and Xinjiang, Han people now form the majority of the population in the Autonomous Regions. This has eroded the minorities' traditional culture and lifestyle.

Full autonomy of the minorities often exists in name rather than in reality under the PRC, but the system of Autonomous Regions does represent an official recognition of the multiethnic composition of the Chinese state and, to a degree, a respect for the cultural heritages of the non-Han peoples.

Wang Ke-wen

References

Dreyer, June Teufel. *China's Forty Millions: Minority Nationalities and National Integration in the People's Republic of China.* Cambridge, MA: Harvard University Press, 1976.

Heberer, Thomas. *China and Its National Minorities: Autonomy or Assimilation?* Armonk, NY: M. E. Sharpe, 1989.

Mackerras, Colin. *China's Minorities: Integration and Modernization in the Twentieth Century.* Hong Kong: Oxford University Press, 1994.

B

Bandit-Suppression Campaigns

Following the collapse of the first United Front in 1927, the Chinese Communist Party (CCP) launched a series of unsuccessful armed uprisings against the Guomindang (GMD), and by 1928 had established Red Army bases in the Middle Yangtze region. As soon as the GMD consolidated its position as the national government, and Chiang Kaishek stabilized his leadership in the GMD, the GMD turned its attention to the residual Communist forces.

From late 1930 to early 1934, the GMD government launched five offensives against the central CCP base in the Jiangxi-Fujian border area. Officially designated as "Bandit-Suppression Campaigns," these offensives were initially carried out by local Hunan troops who came increasingly under the command of Chiang's Whampoa forces. The latter, however, still relied on the militarists in Guangdong and Hunan for assistance. The first four campaigns (December 1930–January 1931, April–May 1931, July–September 1931, and January–April 1933) all ended in failure. The government troops suffered heavy casualties in the face of Mao Zedong's guerrilla warfare.

In September 1933, Chiang moved his military headquarters to Nanchang and started the fifth campaign. This time, assisted by German advisers (notably Hans von Seeckt) and modern weaponry, Chiang adopted the blockhouse-blockade strategy in surrounding and diminishing the Communist base. Meanwhile, he used the traditional system of mutual responsibility, *baojia*, to tighten government control over the Communist-infested rural areas. He described this as a "seventy-percent political and thirty-percent military" plan. Despite the interruption of the Fujian Rebellion in November 1933, the fifth campaign finally succeeded in breaking into the central CCP base in early 1934. With most of its forces wiped out by Chiang's troops, the CCP abandoned its Jiangxi Soviet base and began the Long March to southwest and northwest China.

The significance of the Bandit-Suppression Campaigns in relation to Chinese nationalism lay in the fact that they embodied Chiang's policy of "domestic pacification before external resistance" *(annei rangwai)* in the prewar years. In the face of increasing Japanese encroachments in Manchuria and north China, Chiang still believed that the residual Communist influence in rural China posed a greater threat to his government and the country than the Japanese. During the period of the five campaigns he repeatedly made territorial concessions to Japan in the north, hoping to delay a confrontation with that foreign aggressor until the CCP was eliminated. This policy contradicted the wish of the majority of nationalistic Chinese in the 1930s. Many of them saw the Bandit-Suppression Campaigns as a futile and unnecessary civil war, which wasted the country's resources that should have been utilized to fight Japan. In the end, the campaigns accomplished their military goals but cost Chiang and the GMD dearly in terms of popularity and legitimacy.

Wang Ke-wen

References

Liu, F. F. *A Military History of Modern China, 1924–1949.* Princeton, NJ: Princeton University Press, 1956.
Wei, William. *Counter-revolution in China: The Nationalists in Jiangxi during the*

Soviet Period. Ann Arbor: University of Michigan Press, 1985.

Bandung Conference

The first international consultation among the newly independent countries of the Third World was the Bandung Conference. Held in Bandung, Indonesia, from April 18 to 25, 1955, the conference signified the beginning of the non-aligned movement.

Among the representatives from twenty-nine Asian and African countries the most notable were China's Premier Zhou Enlai, India's Nehru, Egypt's Nasser, Indonesia's Sukarno, and Burma's U Nu. China's participation in the Bandung Conference represented a major foreign policy effort to reach out to the non-Communist Asian and African countries. During the conference, Premier Zhou successfully established close relations with many Afro-Asian leaders who came to recognize and welcome China's new role in international affairs.

China's foreign policy adjustments followed the death of Stalin in 1953 and the end of the Korean War in the same year. While the People's Republic had been "leaning to one side" (the Soviet side) before, it now began to seek sympathy and support among the countries of "Third Forces," those who were neither active partners of the American policy of containment against China, nor close allies of the Soviet Union.

China first approached India, the largest Asian country that had declined to join the American efforts of containment against China. In June 1954, Chinese Premier Zhou and Indian Prime Minister Nehru met in New Delhi. The two leaders agreed upon the Five Principles of Peaceful Coexistence as a basis for conducting relations between the two countries. These five principles included: (1) mutual respect for sovereignty and territorial integrity; (2) mutual non-aggression; (3) mutual non-interference in internal affairs; (4) equality and mutual benefit; and (5) peaceful coexistence.

On the basis of the Five Principles, China also improved its relations with another large neighboring country in Asia, Burma. At the Bandung Conference, Chinese diplomats not only successfully renewed acquaintance with their Asian counterparts but established contact with the government leaders of African states for the first time. After India and Burma, China won another notable friend, Egypt, in 1955.

Zhou Enlai's extended talks with Egyptian President Nasser at Bandung laid down a solid foundation for closer relations between the two countries in later years. Gestures of good will also characterized Zhou's meetings with the government leaders of Indonesia, the Philippines, Thailand, and Pakistan, which led to certain mutual understandings on nationality, security, and border issues.

The participating countries at the Bandung Conference accepted China's Five Principles. The conference came to symbolize a strong desire by the Third World countries to seek an active role in international affairs in a world dominated by the United States and the Soviet Union. It established a basis for the Asian and African countries, who shared similar social and economic problems and a common experience in colonialism, to work as an independent bloc.

The Bandung Conference proved to be a huge diplomatic success for the People's Republic, which in turn was credited to a large extent to the outstanding performance by Premier Zhou. Since the conference, China has insisted that the Five Principles of Peaceful Coexistence be extended to her relations with the socialist states and later with all countries. Although China's foreign policy behaviors do not always match these lofty principles, the Five Principles have been frequently cited in China's foreign policy statements as the basis for conducting international relations.

Shi-ping Zheng

References
Garver, John W. *Foreign Relations of the People's Republic of China.* Englewood Cliffs, NJ: Prentice-Hall, 1993.

Kim, Samuel S. *The Third World in Chinese World Policy.* Princeton, NJ: Princeton University Press, 1989.

Barbarian Affairs *(Yangwu/Yiwu)*

"Barbarians" *(yi or yidi)* was the term the Chinese traditionally used to refer to countries or societies outside of the reach of Chinese cultural and political influence. In early modern times it was applied to the Westerners who made their way to China, beginning with the Age of Discovery. In the nineteenth century, *"yiwu"* (barbarian affairs) became an official term for China's foreign relations with the Western countries. After the *Arrow* War (the Second Opium War) in 1858–60, the word *"yi"* disappeared from official Chinese usage at the request of the West. Since most of the Westerners arrived in China via sea routes, they were then called *"yangren"* (people from the ocean), and relations with the West became *"yangwu"* (ocean affairs).

Meanwhile, as the Chinese leaders gradually came to appreciate the power of Western technology and institutions, they also included the introduction and promotion of those aspects of Western civilization in the meaning of *"yangwu."* The "Self-Strengthening Movement" in the latter half of the nineteenth century was sometimes referred to as the "Yangwu Movement," and supporters of that movement emerged as the "Yangwu Faction." One of the first steps that movement took, however, suggested a change in traditional language and concept. In 1861, the Qing government established the Zongli Yamen to serve as China's first Foreign Ministry. The full name of this office was "General Office for Managing the Affairs of the Various Countries" *(Zongli geguo shiwu yamen),* in which the term *"yangwu"* or *"yiwu"* was no longer present. Such a change marked a significant development in modern Chinese national consciousness. It symbolized the abandonment of the traditional self-image of "celestial empire" and "all under the heaven" *(tianxia),* and its replacement by a non-judgemental recognition of the international community.

Wang Ke-wen

Battle of Hundred Regiments

For three years after the outbreak of the Sino-Japanese War in 1937, forces commanded by the Chinese Communist Party (CCP) avoided major confrontations with the invading Japanese. They were generally outnumbered and out-equipped by the enemy, and they received little assistance from the Guomindang government.

In 1940 this strategy changed. From August 20 to December 5, the CCP's Eighth Route Army launched a series of sustained offensives against the enemy in an effort to break the Japanese blockade on the Communist bases in north China. More than one hundred regiments of the army, with about 400,000 men, were mobilized for the offensives, giving them the name the Battle of Hundred Regiments.

The battle, which raged along the railways in Hebei and Shanxi, included three stages:

From August 20 to early September, the CCP forces aimed to destroy Japanese communication lines; from early September to early October, they attacked Japanese strongholds along these lines; and from early October to December 5, they repelled Japanese retaliatory "mopping-up" campaigns.

In themselves the offensives were successful. About 25,000 Japanese troops were reportedly killed and serious destructions or disruptions crippled railways, roads, bridges, and the important Jingjing coal mines. The CCP forces themselves suffered 17,000 casualties. In the long run, however, the battle provoked ferocious pacification efforts by the Japanese, including the "three-all" policy (kill all, burn all, loot all) that lasted for nearly three years.

Years later, the CCP commander of the battle, Peng Dehuai, came under criticism for having planned and ordered the offensives without full consultation with Mao Zedong and the Yan'an leadership. It may well have been the case. Nevertheless, the official CCP history still praised the battle, which is said to have prevented the Guomindang from capitulating to the Japanese. The battle also proved the Communists' contribution to the anti-Japanese war effort and effectively supported their claim that they too were nationalists.

Wang Ke-wen

References

Eastman, Lloyd E., et al. *The Nationalist Era in China, 1927–1949.* Cambridge, England: Cambridge University Press, 1991.

Wilson, Dick. *When Tigers Fight: The Story of the Sino-Japanese War, 1937–1945.* New York, NY: The Viking Press, 1982.

Battle of Taierzhuang

The Battle of Taierzhuang was one of the largest military victories won by the Chinese during the second Sino-Japanese War (1937–45).

In early 1938, invading Japanese forces advanced toward the city of Xuzhou after taking Nanjing, the Chinese capital. Their aim was to control the vital Tianjin-Pukou Railway in east China. In late March the Japanese Tenth Division, led by General Isogai Rensuke, encountered the Chinese forces defending Xuzhou at the strategic town of Taierzhuang in southern Shandong. The Chinese forces, totaling 800,000 men, greatly outnumbered their adversaries but were less well equipped than the mechanized Japanese army. The defense was under the command of General Li Zongren, but the actual fighting was conducted by Sun Lianzhong's divisions. After weeks of fierce fighting in and around Taierzhuang, the Japanese troops were defeated on April 7th. Nearly 20,000 Japanese were killed and a large number of weapons were captured by Sun's troops. Among Chinese casualties was a division commander, Wang Mingzhang. The battle marked the first major Chinese victory since the outbreak of the Sino-Japanese War in mid-1937. It was an important boost to Chinese morale in the face of a long and hard war of resistance.

Wang Ke-wen

References

Ch'i, Hsi-sheng. *Nationalist China at War: Military Defeats and Political Collapse, 1937–1945.* Ann Arbor: University of Michigan Press, 1982.

Wilson, Dick. *When Tigers Fight: The Story of the Sino-Japanese War, 1937–1945.* New York, NY: The Viking Press, 1982.

Beijing Convention

The Treaty of Tianjin, signed after the *Arrow War* of 1857–58, not only failed to settle the old conflicts between China and the West, but itself became a source of new problems. The Chinese government, in fact, regretted the conclusion of the treaty almost immediately after the Anglo-French joint expeditionary force left north China.

In 1859, representatives of Great Britain and France sailed to the Dagu forts, outside of Tianjin, as part of their journey to Beijing for the ratification of the Treaty of Tianjin. To their surprise, Chinese forces at Dagu attacked and repelled their ships, resulting in heavy British and French losses. The incident shocked and angered the governments as well as the populace of the two European countries. In 1860, a new Anglo-French joint expedition was sent to China and it easily took Dagu and Tianjin. The Qing government was indecisive as to whether to seek peace or to go to war. In a sense, the Westerners were taking advantage of an unusually weak moment of the Qing government, as it was confronted with the formidable Taiping Rebellion in central and south China. In September, foreign troops advanced toward Beijing and Emperor Xianfeng

and his court fled to Inner Mongolia, leaving Prince Gong in the capital to surrender to the expedition. Before the surrender was effected, however, the British and French forces looted and burned down the Summer Palace.

A new treaty, or more precisely, the terms of China's surrender, was known as the Beijing Convention. It basically confirmed the Treaty of Tianjin, but doubled the indemnities China had to pay (from 4 million to 8 million taels of silver) and added Tianjin to the list of new treaty ports. Moreover, Kowloon (the peninsula opposite Hong Kong island) was ceded to Great Britain in perpetuity.

The two Anglo-French joint expeditions of 1857–58 and 1860 have also been referred to as the "Second Opium War." In many ways they exerted a greater shock to educated Chinese than did the initial Opium War of 1839–1842. While the latter was but a local incident in south China, the former resulted in the occupation of the Chinese capital and the destruction of the imperial residence. Few Chinese could doubt the seriousness of the challenge posed by the West to their country, and the superior military strength the West possessed, after this humiliating event.

Wang Ke-wen

References

Beeching, Jack. *The Opium Wars in China, 1834–1860.* London, England: Hutchison, 1975.

Graham, Gerald. *The China Station: War and Diplomacy, 1830–1860.* New York, NY: Oxford University Press, 1978.

Beijing Opera

Beijing Opera is the dominant form of traditional Chinese drama, a combination of singing, dancing, and acrobatic performance, in the nineteenth and twentieth centuries. Beijing Opera *(Jingju),* however, belies its name in two ways. Historically speaking, it did not originate in Beijing. Geographically, an account of its success always must be a tale of two cities, of two forms of life, of Beijing and Shanghai.

The eighteenth-century predecessor of Beijing Opera was certainly more southern in character. The four Anhui troupes, which later comprised the core of the new opera, were brought to the capital by the Qing emperor Qianlong (1736–95) from his Jiangnan tours. For much of the nineteenth century, this Anhui-

Beijing opera performance, with famous actor Mei Lanfang. (Xinhua News Agency.)

style performance coexisted with other regional varieties at the lower end of the operatic culture in Beijing. The leading opera at the time was *Kunju,* or Kunshan Opera, which, though diminishing in popular appeal, still commanded prestige as the paragon of Jiangnan (Lower Yangtze) sophistication. Yet already, actors serving in the Anhui troupes demonstrated remarkable plasticity in assimilating features from other popular genres, especially those of Hubei and Hebei origins. From Cheng Changgeng to Tan Xinpei, the later decades of the century saw incessant effort to transform the Anhui-originated style into a hybrid performance as *the* popular opera in the capital city.

In the meantime, the post-Taiping prosperity of Shanghai created unprecedented demands for popular entertainment and a fertile ground of competition for regional troupes across the country. It was in this context that the popular opera of Beijing, then termed *luantan,* or "random plucking," as in opposition to the rigorous *Kunju,* entered Shanghai as "Beijing" Opera. Long a part of teahouse activities and family celebrations at the court or noble residences at the capital, Beijing Opera now became a properly theatrical phenomenon in a commercial city where numerous stages were constructed to accommodate large audiences hungry for auditory and visual pleasures. Practices in make-up,

costumes, and stage settings were subjected to comprehensive reconsideration in relation to film, modern drama, and other productions of public entertainment. With its trademark adaptability, Beijing Opera thus married Beijing manpower and Shanghai technology in a bid for transregional significance beyond the walls of the old capital.

The founding of the Republic in 1912 had both positive and negative impacts on Beijing Opera's quest for national prominence. The banning of male prostitution was detrimental, because the female roles were often played by young men trained at their masters' "private residences," which also catered to sensual pleasures. The May Fourth intellectuals' call for replacing corrupt forms of pleasure with the modern, European-style drama *(huaju)* further jeopardized its legitimate cultural position. But for the fallen gentry-literati, who used to pursue Beijing Opera as a mere pleasurable frivolity, it now became a major forum to address their past glory. Attempts were made to elevate Beijing Opera from the dilapidated infrastructure to the position of a specimen of traditional Chinese culture at peril in modern times. The performing tours by Mei Lanfang in Japan, the United States, and the Soviet Union in the 1920s were so orchestrated that they generated a spectacle of "Chinese classicism" powerful enough to win applause from the general public as well as drama critics in the outside world.

By the end of the 1920s, Beijing Opera had firmly established itself as the "national drama" *(guoju)* of China. In 1931 Mei Lanfang, probably the most popular Beijing Opera actor in modern China, founded the National Drama Study Association *(guoju xuehui)* for the promotion of the opera. He praised the opera as not only the drama in national tradition, but "the drama that best represents the nation." Such a claim has been avidly supported by all Chinese governments ever since. The stakes it held for China's national identity was such that, under Japanese occupation during the war, Mei's retirement and Zhou Xingfang's staging of patriotic events became pregnant with political meanings. The Communists' unparalleled interest in popular culture granted Beijing Opera, in the 1950s and early 1960s, its long-sought official endorsement as the shining example of China's classical performing tradition. During the Cultural Revolution (1966–76), it also served as a basis for the production of the eight "model plays" *(yangbanxi)*, thus becoming a mouthpiece for political propaganda. Since the 1980s, however, Beijing Opera's claim on nationwide attention has been weakening in mainland China. Even the massive celebration of Mei Lanfang's and Zhou Xingfang's birthday centennial in 1994 seems to have achieved little in engendering new popular interest.

John Zou

References

Mackerras, Colin P. *The Chinese Theatre in Modern Times: From 1840 to the Present.* Amherst: University of Massachusetts Press, 1975.

———. *The Rise of the Peking Opera, 1770–1870: Social Aspects of the Theatre in Modern China.* Oxford: Clarendon Press, 1972.

Beijing University

Beijing University, the first Western-style educational institution in China, was founded in 1898 as part of the modernization effort connected with the Hundred Days Reform. It served at first primarily to educate future members of the governmental bureaucracy. Even after the abolition of the civil service examination system in 1905, for many years it tended to be a training ground in Confucian principles for bureaucrats.

But the role of the university changed in the first decade of the republican era. In December 1916, the well-known Chinese educator Cai Yuanpei became chancellor and immediately set out to transform the institution into a vehicle for the introduction of Western ideas and values into China. As a means of promoting this effort, he appointed a number of well-known supporters of westernization, such as Chen Duxiu, Hu Shih and Li Dazhao, to leading positions at the university.

Cai's main purpose as chancellor of Beijing University was to bring about vital reforms in China's educational, political, and social institutions. But the so-called "New Culture" movement which emerged as a consequence of that effort coincided with a period of rising national consciousness in China, provoked in part by a generation of humiliations imposed by the Western powers. More recently, patriotic sentiment was aroused by the Twenty-One Demands presented by Japan to the government of Yuan Shikai in Beijing.

In 1919, students and faculty from the university played a leading part in the demonstration in Beijing against Japan's acquisition of the German concession areas in Shandong province, which historically became known as the May Fourth movement. Many students were jailed for disrupting the peace, but the news of their actions reached far beyond the city walls of Beijing and aroused patriotic sentiment among people of various classes throughout China. The May Fourth movement was critical in promoting the rise of Chinese nationalism.

In the years that followed, students and faculty at Beijing University continued to play a leading role in the effort to build a new China. Two prominent faculty members, Chen Duxiu and Li Dazhao, became founding members of the Chinese Communist Party. Members of the institution participated actively in the tumultuous riots in 1935 demanding that the government of Chiang Kaishek adopt a tougher stand against Japanese aggression in north China. During the civil war of 1945 to 1949, Beijing University became a nerve center of political activities against the Guomindang regime and American intervention in China. The tradition of political activism continued into the Communist period, when students at the institution became leading participants in the Great Proletarian Culture Revolution (1966–76).

William J. Duiker

References

Israel, John. *Student Nationalism in China, 1927–1937.* Stanford, CA: Stanford University Press, 1966.

Tse-tsung, Chow. *The May Fourth Movement: Intellectual Revolution in Modern China.* Cambridge, MA: Harvard University Press, 1960.

Beiyang Army

The Beiyang Army was a Western-style military force organized primarily under the influence of Yuan Shikai at the end of the Qing dynasty. The army played a dominant role in Chinese politics from the late Qing through the first half of the republican period.

The original foundation of the Beiyang Army was the Newly Created Army *(Xinjian lujun),* one of China's first Western-style military forces established by Yuan Shikai in 1895. After succeeding to Li Hongzhang's positions as Zhili governor-general and commissioner of the northern ports *(beiyang dachen)* in 1901, Yuan expanded this force to create the Beiyang Army. By 1906, the army contained six divisions, making it China's largest military force.

The formation of the Beiyang Army occurred within the context of growing nationalist concerns about the possible disintegration of

the Chinese state in the face of imperialist pressure. The creation of the Beiyang Army, along with other Western-style "New Armies" in the provinces, was part of a broad official reform movement that sought to strengthen the foundations of the Chinese state, and the Qing dynasty, by institutional changes based on Western models. The Beiyang Army, however, failed to live up to either its nationalist or dynastic mission. The Revolution of 1911 intervened before the Beiyang Army was called upon to test its mettle against China's foreign foes. In the Revolution of 1911 itself, the Beiyang Army first supported the Qing against revolutionary forces, then heeded Yuan Shikai's call for the abdication of the Manchu emperor. Thus, the Beiyang Army alienated Han nationalist supporters of the revolution even while betraying the dynasty it was created to defend.

After the Revolution of 1911, Yuan Shikai, as president of the Republic, further expanded the Beiyang Army and used it to support his effort to reestablish centralized bureaucratic control over the entire country. During this period, the term "Beiyang Army" was used to identify all the northern military forces that allied themselves with Yuan Shikai, even if they were only weakly associated with the original six Beiyang divisions. While it might be possible to attribute nationalist mo-

B

The Beiyang warlords in 1917. (Courtesy of Nationalist Party Archives.)

tivations to Beiyang Army support for Yuan's program of national unification, its nationalist credentials were later tainted by serving as Yuan's personal tools in his attempt to make himself emperor.

After Yuan Shikai's death in 1916, Beiyang Army units remained the most important military forces in north and central China, and the national government at Beijing remained under the domination of Beiyang Army commanders for the next decade. The Beijing government was therefore generally referred to as the Beiyang government. Nonetheless, the Beiyang Army was no longer a united military or political force. Even before Yuan's death, the army had begun to factionalize and individual commanders had begun to assert a large degree of political autonomy. After Yuan's death, these commanders competed among themselves, as well as with non-Beiyang rivals, in a series of civil wars to strengthen their own personal military and political powers. In the eyes of Chinese nationalists, then, Beiyang commanders had become warlords, whose personal political ambitions stood in the way of national unity. Not surprisingly, the overthrow of Beiyang warlords became a main objective of the Northern Expedition launched by the Guomindang in 1926. The success of this military campaign, and the establishment of a new central government at Nanjing in 1927, finally terminated the political dominance of the Beiyang Army.

Edward A. McCord

References

MacKinnon, Stephen R. "The Peiyang Army, Yuan Shih-k'ai, and the Origins of Modern Chinese Warlordism." *Journal of Asian Studies* 32, no. 2 (May 1973): 405–23.

———. *Power and Politics in Late Imperial China: Yuan Shi-kai in Beijing and Tianjin, 1901–1908.* Berkeley: University of California Press, 1980.

Beiyang Government (1916–27)

See BEIYANG ARMY

Black Flag Army

The Black Flag Army was an anti-government army organized by Liu Yongfu in Guangxi following the failure of the Taiping Rebellion (1851–64). Liu, a native of Guangdong, grew

Liu Yongfu. (Courtesy of Nationalist Party Archives.)

up in Guangxi and joined the Taiping rebels in 1857. Months after the fall of the Heavenly Kingdom, Liu brought his men, totaling fewer than three hundred, into the mountainous area along the Sino-Vietnamese border. They adopted the black-colored symbol of a local temple as their flag and came to be known as the Black Flag Army. In 1867, the army moved into northern Vietnam (Annam) and grew rapidly in size. Liu received an official appointment from the king of Annam after his army defeated the local rebels.

As France increased her encroachment upon Vietnam in the 1870s, the Vietnamese government enlisted the help of the Black Flag Army to resist French invasion. While the Chinese (Qing) government was still unwilling to intervene openly, Liu's troops had engaged the French forces in the Hanoi area as early as in 1873. In 1883 the Chinese government finally decided to assist her tributary state, and with encouragement from the Qing, Liu secured several victories over the French forces in northern Vietnam.

When the Sino-French War (1884–85) broke out, the Black Flag Army was incorporated into the Qing military establishment and participated in the war. After the war the army returned to China and was reduced to about one thousand men. During the first Sino-Japanese War (1894–95) Liu led the army to Taiwan, where it fought against the invading Japanese forces. In 1895, the Qing ceded Taiwan to Japan. Liu played a major role in the attempt to create an independent republic on the island (Taiwan Minzhuguo) to resist Japanese control. The Black Flag Army was destroyed during Japan's subsequent military conquest of Taiwan.

Wang Ke-wen

References

Eastman, Lloyd E. *Throne and Mandarins: China's Search for a Policy during the Sino-French Controversy, 1880–1885.* Cambridge, MA: Harvard University Press, 1967.

McAleavy, Henry. *Black Flags in Vietnam: The Story of a Chinese Intervention.* New York, NY: Macmillan, 1968.

Blue Shirts (Lixingshe)

A secret political organization in the Guomindang (GMD) during the 1930s was popularly known as the Blue Shirts. This group's real name was the "Three Peoples' Principles Earnest Action Society *(Sanminzhuyi lixingshe,* or *Lixingshe).*

In reaction to the chaotic political situation in China and in the Guomindang during the early 1930s, a group of young graduates of the Whampoa Military Academy, mostly former members of the anti-Communist Sun Wenist Society *(Sun Wen zhuyi xuehui),* decided to organize a new intra-party group to "save the country and the Party." This new organization, "unified in will, strict in discipline, clear in responsibilities and swift in action," was to strive for the unification of China under the GMD and the revitalization of the GMD under the leadership of Chiang Kaishek. Its initial organizers included Teng Jie, Gan Guoxun, He Zhonghan and Deng Wenyi. Deng, an aide-de-camp to Chiang Kaishek at the time, submitted their proposal to Chiang and obtained the latter's approval and support. In March 1932, the society was secretly founded in Nanjing with Chiang as its supreme leader.

With headquarters at Nanjing, the society established provincial branches, county branches, and district cells throughout the country. Both the headquarters and the provincial branches were governed by a directory council and a supervisory council. Surrounding the *Lixingshe* were two concentric circles of "front" organizations. The inner circle consisted of the clandestine Revolutionary Soldiers Association *(Geming junren tongzhihui)* and the Revolutionary Youth Association *(Geming qingnian tongzhihui),* established for the purpose of recruiting members from the military and the schools, respectively. The outer circle was a mass organization called the China Revival Society *(Zhonghua fuxingshe,* or *Fuxingshe).* There were additional related groups and training institutes. Total membership of the *Lixingshe* did not exceed three hundred throughout its tenure, but the *Fuxingshe* at its peak had as many as 500,000 members. The society published a number of newspapers and journals, including *China Daily* (Zhongguo ribao) and *Future (Qiantu).*

The society had a three-fold goal: to support Chiang Kaishek as the national and GMD leader, to oppose Japanese aggression, and to suppress the Communists. It actively led or participated in a series of GMD endeavors in the 1930s, collectively known as the National Revival movement, including the New Life movement, the National Economic Reconstruction movement and the National Military Training movement. It also diligently executed Chiang's policy of "domestic pacification before external resistance." The "Special Service Section" of the society, headed by Dai Li, was responsible for the assassination of anti-Chiang democrats such as Shi Liangcai and Yang Xingfo in Shanghai. In ideological and organizational orientations the society was clearly influenced by European fascism. It advocated charismatic one-man rule, party dictatorship and a form of national socialism.

Among the salient characteristics of the *Lixingshe* was its anti-Japanese nationalism. Even before the Sino-Japanese War broke out in 1937, the nationalist activity of the society, such as the promotion of anti-Japanese feelings and the assassination of Chinese collaborators, had drawn serious attention from Japan. This was evidenced by the He-Umezu Agreement of 1935, in which the Japanese army in North China demanded that the Chinese authorities suppress "organizations such as the Blue Shirts and the *Fuxingshe* which are jeopardizing Sino-Japanese relations." During the first year of the war, the society helped conduct intelligence work, assist anti-Japanese organizations and carry out armed resistance in the occupied territories.

In May 1938, the society was formally dissolved in Wuhan. Under Chiang's instruction, its members joined the newly formed "Three People's Principles Youth Corps," a semi-factional organization in the GMD. Dai Li's "Special Service Section" was reorganized into the Military Committee's Bureau of Investigation and Statistics *(Juntong),* still under his control, which was active in wartime Chinese intelligence.

Xu Youwei

References

Chang, Maria Hsia. *The Chinese Blue Shirt Society.* Berkeley: University of California Press, 1985.

Eastman, Lloyd E. *The Abortive Revolution.* Cambridge, MA: Harvard University Press, 1974.

Border Regions

Throughout the Sino-Japanese War of 1937 to 1945, the Chinese Communist Party (CCP) formed border-region *(bianqu)* governments in north and central China. The border region governments were so named because of their geographical location. They always claimed to rule a region that squatted over the borders of more than two provinces. The CCP chose, in general, to develop such a region into a "base area" *(genjudi)* because here enemy control was the weakest. In the Northwest, the CCP had developed a base area in ShaanGanNing (Shaanxi-Gansu-Ningxia) before the war. After the outbreak of the war, the Communist forces crossed the Yellow River and went into action behind Japanese lines. Using ShaanGanNing as a model, they gradually developed similar base areas in JinSui (Shanxi-Suiyuan), JinChaJi (Shanxi-Chahar-Hebei), JinJiLuYu (Shanxi-Hebei-Shandong-Henan), EYuWan (Hubei-Henan-Anhui), and SuWan (Jiangsu-Anhui), forming border-region governments in those areas.

After its relocation in ShaanGanNing in 1935, the CCP center built an independent government there, but the formation of the second United Front required it to forsake separatism and to nominally accept the sovereignty of the Guomindang (GMD) government. Before the Xian Incident of December 1936, the CCP had only seven counties within that border region untouched by fighting with the GMD army. The incident enabled it to reverse its fortune and expand its territory. In late 1944, the ShaanGanNing border-region government claimed to have rule over a territory of 256,300 square miles and a population of 1.5 million (it actually included some areas under the GMD's *de facto* rule before 1940). This border region, where the Communist Party center was located, supposedly served as an example for other base areas, although the actual geographical and socio-economic conditions in other areas often made variations in the CCP practice inevitable.

To prepare for the coming reconciliation with the GMD government, the CCP held popular elections in February 1937 at the administrative levels from village to county. Since the Party had initiated an effective program of land redistribution prior to the elections, the Party's candidates easily won a majority of votes on the basis of peasant support. The landlords, allowed to participate in the elections, could win only a few seats because of their numerical insignificance. This democratization then enabled the Party to resist, on the grounds of popular will, any GMD demands that it deemed contrary to its political interests.

In September 1937, two months into the war, the Communists formally announced the formation of the ShaanGanNing border region government with Lin Boqu as chairman. Nominally subordinate to the GMD government, the border region in fact subjected itself only to the control of the CCP and implemented only the CCP policies. It was a state within a state, seeking to expand its power and to compete with the GMD by championing the anti-Japanese cause.

The CCP considered its border region government a united front organization, representing the interests of all anti-Japanese classes, including landlords and capitalists. But neither did the earlier reform measures allow nor did the wartime political environment encourage them to conspicuously include representatives from the landlord classes. After a honeymoon period of two years, the GMD and the CCP began in 1939 to part ways and to compete with each other for the control of the areas behind Japanese lines. The situation prompted the GMD to impose political and economic blockades on the ShaanGanNing border region. To defuse landlords' hostility and mistrust, the CCP repeatedly held border-region-wide elections, emphasizing its intention to strengthen the united front. The Party not only managed to include many more old elites in the border-region assembly but also enlisted some of them into the administration. It described its approach as the "three-third system," with one-third of the assembly seats going to Party members, one-third to "leftists" (CCP sympathizers), and one-third to political neutralists. It also used the inclusion of non-CCP members to highlight the GMD monopoly of power at various levels of government in other parts of China. Despite its democratic appearance, ShaanGanNing was ruled by the CCP from behind the scenes.

Situated on a rugged terrain of a loess plateau, ShaanGanNing was one of the most impoverished and backward areas in China. The formation of the anti-Japanese United Front enabled the Party center to dispatch about 40,000 soldiers and relieve itself of much financial burden. The funds provided by the GMD government accounted for more than half of the border region's budget and reached an all-time high of nearly 90 percent in 1939. Using the appropriated funds frugally and efficiently, the Party exempted merchants from commodity taxes and freed the majority of impoverished peasants from any tax burdens. The area, which had suffered from a protracted civil war, experienced a quick economic recovery.

When Chiang Kaishek ordered the blockade of ShaanGanNing in 1939, he continued to appropriate funds for the border region government and the Communist forces. The GMD government's appropriation still accounted for about 50 percent of the border region's revenue in 1940. In the intensified frictions and conflicts between the two parties, the CCP annexed the rich Suide area from the GMD. But when Chiang finally terminated all appropriations and imposed a more stringent blockade on the eve of the New Fourth Army Incident of 1941, it resulted in a three-year economic crisis for the CCP. To make the situation worse, the Japanese army escalated its counterinsurgency behind the lines and prevented other base areas from financially helping ShaanGanNing. To overcome this crisis, the Party resorted to a dramatic increase of its financial extraction. Merchants and peasants complained about the tax burden, and some peasants fled to evade the heavy taxation.

In a rural setting, the CCP had to boost agricultural production. Through the so-called Yan'an Way, the Party claimed to have eventually overcome the financial crisis by 1944. In addition to a policy of crack forces and simplified administration, the Party sought to make its bureaucracy more responsive to peasant needs and aspirations by rusticating the intellectual cadres and integrating them through ideological remodeling, or rectification (zhengfeng), campaigns. The Party mobilized cadres and soldiers for agricultural production and carried out such reform campaigns as reducing rents and interest rates. Having thus won support from the peasants, the Party stepped up its efforts to organize rural cooperatives and mutual aid teams, emphasizing the principle of voluntary participation and reinforcing the traditional custom of mutual help. Allegedly the Yan'an Way emphasized the "Mass Line" (mass mobilization) and depended upon peasants' wisdom and initiative. It not only salvaged the almost bankrupted border-region government but also transformed the outlook of the backward and impoverished villages.

The Party's efforts brought about dramatic changes in the border region during the war, yet there was also a dark side to this picture. To supplement its income, for example, the CCP secretly grew and marketed opium in large scale. The income from opium accounted for more than one-third of the Party's financial income from 1942 to 1945. The new rural policy also encouraged agricultural intensification, which inflicted environmental damages in the area. Yet the myth of the "Yan'an Way" was created and has been celebrated ever since. Later, whenever the Party initiated a mass campaign in rural areas, it would invariably conjure up the "Yan'an Way" as an ideal. But the accumulated result of the Yenan experience was disappointing. The ShaanGanNing region remains one of the poorest areas in China today. After Mao Zedong's death in 1976, the People's Republic pledged not to launch mass campaigns again. Emulating the "Yan'an Way" gradually became an outdated Party practice, and by Deng Xiaoping's era it had become an anachronism recalled only by a few nostalgic cadres.

Yung-fa Chen

References

Schran, Peter. *Guerrilla Economy: The Development of the Shensi-Kansu-Ninghsia Border Region, 1937–1945.* Albany:

B

State University of New York Press, 1976.

Selden, Mark. *The Yenan Way in Revolutionary China*. Cambridge, MA: Harvard University Press, 1971.

Van Slyke, Lyman P. "The Chinese Communist Movement during the Sino-Japanese War." *The Cambridge History of China,* ed. John K. Fairbank and Albert Feuerwerker, vol. 13, 609–722. Cambridge, England: Cambridge University Press, 1986.

Borodin, Mikhail (1884–1951)

Mikhail Borodin was Moscow's most prominent prefect in China during the Chinese revolution of 1923–27. Borodin (née Gruzenberg) was born into a Jewish family in Yanovichi, Russia, in 1884. He participated in the 1905 revolution, thereby becoming a member of the Bolshevik establishment. The Czarist crackdown in 1906 forced him to flee abroad. By 1908 he was in Chicago, where he attended nearby Valparaiso University and opened a school for new arrivals from Russia, which became a center for the city's Russian-Jewish-Socialist community. When the 1917 revolutions broke out, he succumbed to revolutionary fervor and returned to Moscow the following year.

During 1918–21 Borodin served as a Bolshevik agent in Scandinavia, western Europe, and America and operated behind the scenes of the first and second Comintern congresses. While working in England in 1921, he was arrested by Scotland Yard, imprisoned for six months, and deported to Russia. These experiences won him the reputation in Comintern circles of being a skilled agent, able to serve the revolutionary cause in the hostile imperialist world.

In early 1923, Moscow, in accord with the Sun-Jaffe Manifesto, established relations with Sun Yatsen's recently reinstalled government in Canton. The Kremlin sought an experienced agent to send to Sun. That individual would have to know how to organize, as well as speak English, as Sun did. Borodin qualified; he was assigned as Moscow's representative to the Guomindang (GMD) and reached Canton in October 1923.

Almost from the moment of his arrival in south China, Borodin encountered opposition from the right wing of the GMD and from the Chinese Communist Party (CCP). The latter could not comprehend why Moscow was dealing with the bourgeois Sun, who sometimes doubted his own wisdom of having admitted a Russian commissar to his inner circle. But five weeks later, as Sun's regime was once again about to be driven from the South, Borodin and the cadre of military officers dispatched from Moscow stiffened the forces defending Sun and drove the enemy back. The overjoyed Sun became convinced that at last he had found the "Lafayette" he had long been seeking to help him reunify China.

After November 1923, Sun and Borodin maintained a close working relationship. Borodin persuaded Sun to hold a GMD Congress, which he manipulated, and with Sun's approval he reorganized the GMD along Russian Communist Party lines. He persistently sought to strengthen the GMD, much to the consternation of the Chinese Communists. He organized a non-warlord army for Sun's long-dreamed-of Northern Expedition and established the Whampoa Military Academy for the training of its officer corps. By mid-1924, as the Canton regime began to gain authority and stability, Borodin had developed a reputation in non-Communist leftist circles as a miracle-worker. He and Sun did not agree on everything—especially not on economic reforms—yet both recognized their need for one another.

Although pleased with the progress being made in building an effective political and military force in the South, Sun wanted to reunify China more swiftly. In November 1924, Sun held a reunification conference with the northern warlords. When Sun died in Beijing in March 1925, the Soviets feared for their future in Canton without his protecting presence. Borodin was ordered to uphold Moscow's interests in the anticipated power struggle. This he did throughout 1925. Borodin threaded his way among the various power claimants while seeking to strengthen Moscow's grasp. He used the new-type Soviet-trained military and propaganda forces to extend GMD control in Guangdong province.

As the GMD forces consolidated their power throughout Guangdong, Borodin increased his political control, but so did those who opposed the GMD-Soviet alliance. The question for Borodin was, should the revolution be "deepened," *i.e.,* made more pervasive in the province, or be "broadened," *i.e.,* spread throughout the country. In February 1926, Borodin consulted with a secret Kremlin commission in Beijing on the next move in China. His advice to "broaden" the revolution met with Moscow's approval. But before he could return south to implement the decision, the future of the Chinese revolution was taken out of Russian hands.

Chiang Kaishek, who succeeded to Sun, had become increasingly suspicious because Moscow favored his rivals. During Borodin's absence, Chiang became convinced that he was being "frozen out"; on March 20, 1926, he seized control of the Canton regime and placed its Russian advisors under house arrest. In Moscow, the central concern of the moment for Stalin was to win his power struggle with Trotsky. Stalin feared the consequences of the Soviet being ousted from the Chinese revolution, plus the likely embarrassing revelation that he had ordered Borodin to support the bourgeois GMD at the expense of the CCP. Such an intelligence would provide the Trotskyite opposition with damaging material. He therefore ordered Borodin to get back into the revolution at any cost in Canton.

In Canton, Borodin accepted Chiang Kaishek's terms for a renewed Soviet association: Soviet support for the Northern Expedition to unite China; the return of Soviet General Blyukher (known in China as Galen), with whom Chiang had been associated in Guangdong and whom he trusted; further diminution of the role of the CCP; and the termination of any leftist criticism of Chiang. Borodin hoped that once the revolution had spread to the North, the Soviets and their Chinese supporters would be able to escape from Chiang's grasp.

The Northern Expedition, which began in July 1926, enjoyed an immediate and dramatic success. By October, all of China south of the Yangtze River was under GMD control. Even before, the situation in Canton started to turn bleak for Borodin and his leftist allies. In November, Borodin moved the revolutionary capital northward from Canton to Wuhan, which had a large industrial proletariat and therefore was judged to have more revolutionary potential than Canton. He tried to convince Chiang to join him in Wuhan, but Chiang refused, well aware of the radical reputation of the Wuhan workers. Chiang established his capital in the more congenial Nanchang and prepared to move on Shanghai, where he had friends and strong foreign support.

From December 1926 through April 1927, Wuhan was a revolutionary hotbed, with workers launching increasingly radical demonstra-

tions. The split between Borodin and Chiang deepened. The Wuhan regime had little armed strength on which it could depend. Although the city's proletariat was radical, it could not be organized in time to defend the revolution against Chiang—and Borodin knew it. His presentiment proved accurate shortly after Shanghai fell to Chiang in April 1927. The latter turned on the Communists, first locally and then throughout the territories which he controlled, and had them executed by the thousands. The Wuhan regime soon followed Chiang's footsteps in terminating its alliance with the Soviets and the CCP. With the game over, Borodin left China in July.

Although he continued to enjoy Stalin's protection, Borodin never again received an assignment that matched the authority he had held before. The failure in China further diminished Stalin's interest in fostering revolution abroad, and Borodin was shifted from international activities to positions in the Soviet industrial bureaucracy. He was eventually appointed editor of the *Moscow News,* an English-language paper founded by Anna Louise Strong for foreigners living in the Soviet capital. Borodin held that post until 1949, when, in the midst of one of Stalin's anti-nationalist paroxysms, he was arrested for his close association with Strong, whom Moscow regarded as being a Maoist sympathizer, and because he was of Jewish origin. Borodin was sent to the camps in Siberia, where he died in 1951. The Soviet Union restored his reputation in 1964.

Dan N. Jacobs

References

Holubnychy, Lydia. *Michael Borodin and the Chinese Revolution, 1923–1925.* Ann Arbor, MI: University Microfilms International, 1979.

Jacobs, Dan N. *Borodin: Stalin's Man in China.* Cambridge, MA: Harvard University Press, 1981.

Wilbur, C. Martin, and Julie Lien-ying How, eds. *Missionaries of Revolution: Soviet Advisers and Nationalist China, 1920–1927.* Cambridge, MA: Harvard University Press, 1989.

Bourgeois Liberalization

The economic reforms and renewed contacts with the capitalist West following Deng Xiaoping's consolidation of power in 1978 brought about an unprecedented relaxation in the cultural and political atmosphere in Communist China. Western lifestyle became accepted in large cities, and calls for western-style democracy by some intellectuals found enthusiastic audience among the educated youth. The Chinese Communist Party (CCP), under the direction of Deng's right-hand man, Hu Yaobang, seemed to adopt a tolerant attitude toward these developments in the early 1980s. Conservatives in the Party were alarmed.

The term "bourgeois liberalization" was introduced by Deng himself in 1980 in reference to foreign ideas and practices which deviated from his Four Cardinal Principles, *i.e.*, socialist line, proletarian dictatorship, CCP leadership, and Marxism-Leninism-Mao Zedong thought. Criticism of "bourgeois liberalization" was then frequently found in the official media throughout the 1980s. In 1983–84 the criticism briefly merged with an Anti-Spiritual Pollution campaign, in which the Party attacked Western influences deemed threatening to its political leadership and ideological control.

In December 1986, student demonstrations demanding political reforms occurred in major cities. The CCP conservatives, led by Peng Zhen and Deng Liqun, escalated their attacks on "bourgeois liberalization," which they believed had caused the demonstrations. They orchestrated the dismissal of Hu Yaobang as Party general secretary and the expulsion from the Party liberal-minded intellectuals Fang Lizhi, Liu Binyan and Wang Ruowang. The witch-hunt was soon curbed by Deng Xiaoping, but since then the Chinese government has used, from time to time, the same rhetoric against "excessive Western influence."

To a degree the CCP's ideological offensive against "bourgeois liberalization" resembles the late Qing formula of "Chinese substance *(ti)* and Western functions *(yong)*." Although the "substance" the Chinese leaders defended in the 1980s was itself a foreign import (Marxism), they displayed and evoked sentiments reminiscent of those in the 1890s in their denunciation of the polluting effects of Western ideas on the existing social-political order in China. In the 1990s, as economic success enhanced China's self-confidence, and mutual suspicion clouded China's relations with the West, the Chinese government's criticism of "bourgeois liberalization" connotes an increasingly nationalistic implication.

Wang Ke-wen

References
Nathan, Andrew J. *Chinese Democracy.* Berkeley: University of California Press, 1985.
Sullivan, Lawrence R. "Assault on the Reforms: Conservative Criticism of Political and Economic Liberalization in China, 1985–86." *China Quarterly* 114 (June 1988): 198–222.

Boxer Protocol
See BOXER UPRISING

Boxer Uprising

On June 21, 1900, the Manchu court, under the leadership of Empress Dowager Cixi, declared war on all the foreign powers which had representatives in Beijing. This act had been set in motion by the rise of a nationalistic group, which claimed both spirit-possession and physical invulnerability. Some ten days before the declaration of war, this assemblage, which came to be known in the West as the Boxers, had swarmed into the capital and burned churches and foreign residences, killed Chinese Christian converts, and exhumed graves of foreign missionaries. They then began what was to be a fifty-five-day siege of foreign legations in Beijing.

The end of this uprising was swift and tragic. By mid-August 1900, the armies of seven foreign powers (Germany's forces arrived later) had entered the capital and begun wreaking a terrible revenge. In addition to killing many of the rebels, scores of innocent Chinese, who were either mistaken for Boxers or who just happened to be in the wrong place at the wrong time, were slaughtered. The foreign troops also engaged in a concomitant orgy of looting, rape, and arson. These punitive acts, and the subsequent Boxer Protocol, provided additional fuel for the nationalistic spirit that was flickering in China.

Geographically, the Boxers originated in the northwestern part of Shandong province—an area characterized by flat land, cereal agriculture, dense population, and impoverished villages. The region was also prone to human and natural disasters. The people of northwest Shandong had a long tradition of heterodox religious sects, martial arts, and dramatic local opera. The heterodox practices included charms, spells, invulnerability, and spirit-pos-

Foreign troops approaching Beijing to suppress the Boxer Uprising, 1900. (Courtesy of Nationalist Party Archives.)

session. Martial practices emphasized boxing and swordsmanship. Most of the village operas drew on deities from novels such as the *Romance of the Three Kingdoms, Journey to the West,* and *The Enfeoffment of the Gods.* With these three activities conjoined, the Boxers had their primary inspiration.

The Boxers targeted not the Qing dynasty but rather the growing foreign threat and Christian aggressiveness, in particular German Catholic missionaries. Many of these individuals had been especially offensive in their intervention in secular disputes. There was also a link between German missionary activity and German imperialism in Shandong. In 1897, Germany used the pretext of an attack on missionaries to occupy the Shandong port city of Qingdao. The German commercial and military presence which followed tended to further embolden the missionaries, who then became even more enmeshed in China's domestic politics.

Partially in response to the German incursion, and partially in reaction to the ruinous socioeconomic conditions in the region, especially the massive floods of 1898, the Society of Righteous and Harmonious Fists *(Yihetuan)* or Boxers rose in northwest Shandong in the spring of 1898. Exactly who was responsible for starting the first Boxer group is unknown, but once begun the movement rapidly spread. Recruitment was relatively simple. Young men from one village would hear of the practice nearby and go to observe. They witnessed a simple ceremony which induced a trance, causing the youthful initiates to believe that they were possessed by a folk deity. The "Spirit Boxer" ritual then led to a conviction of invulnerability. Organizationally, the Boxers were essentially egalitarian. Each village's boxing group would have a leader, known as "Senior Brother-Disciple." Ordinary members knew each other as "Brother-Disciples." However, because the spirit ritual was so easily learned, and all who learned it became equally divinely possessed, all were, in fact, on the same exalted level.

In the summer of 1899, the Boxers began to engage in acts of violence against Catholic missionaries in Shandong. Local government officials tended to look the other way, in effect indicating that they considered such actions to be an effort by ordinary villagers seeking their own way of countering Christian abuses of power. Soon the Boxers came to realize that they also enjoyed support from individuals high in the Qing court, including the empress dowager. In response to this patronage, Boxers began streaming into the national capital by the thousands in early June of 1900. The tragedy which followed has already been noted.

The Boxer Protocol, which officially marked the end of the uprising, was signed by officials of the Chinese government and representatives of eleven foreign powers on September 7, 1901. Included in the document were provisions for the punishment of those considered most grievously responsible for the rebellion; some sixty-seven million pounds in indemnity; the stationing of foreign troops in China; and the suspension of civil service examinations in forty-five cities for a period of five years. These latter items, *i.e.*, military occupation and interruption of the examination system, played an extremely significant role in the development of Chinese nationalism in the twentieth century. The first served as a constant reminder of China's humiliation, and the second caused China's elite to look elsewhere for ways to assist their country in its time of need.

Gerald W. Berkley

References

Buck, David D., ed. *Recent Studies of the Boxer Movement*. Special issue of *Chinese Studies in History*, 1987.

Esherick, Joseph W. *The Origins of the Boxer Uprising*. Berkeley: University of California Press (1987).

Purcell, Victor C. *The Boxer Uprising*. Cambridge, England: Cambridge University Press, 1963.

Burlingame Mission

In 1867, on the advice of Robert Hart, Inspector General of China's maritime customs, the Qing government decided to send a diplomatic mission abroad and cultivate friendly relations with the West. The Zongli Yamen, however, found it more suitable to trust this task to a foreigner than to any Chinese official. It appointed the United States minister in Beijing, Anson Burlingame, who was about to retire, as China's ambassador-extraordinary to all the major Western countries. A British and a French diplomat in China, as well as some Chinese officials, also joined the mission as Burlingame's assistants.

The mission left China in May 1868 and visited Washington, London, Paris, Stockholm, Copenhagen, The Hague, Berlin, St. Petersburg, Brussels, and Rome during the following two years. In February 1870, while visiting St. Petersburg, Burlingame died of illness. The mission continued to visit two more countries under the Manchu official Zhigang, then hastily ended its journey.

Burlingame did improve China's international image and status during the trip. He delivered goodwill speeches that depicted China as open and eager to learn from the West, a portrayal that attracted the Western public but shocked the Chinese government. While in the United States, he negotiated, without consultation with Beijing, supplementary articles that revised the Sino-American Treaty of Tianjin (1858) and protected China's sovereignty. In England, Burlingame persuaded the British government to adopt a lenient attitude toward China, and thus helped to conclude the Alcock Convention (1869), which was somewhat favorable to China. At Burlingame's request, most of these Western countries paid lip service to China's territorial integrity and independence, but no tangible long-term benefit was conceded to China.

Although it was common to employ the service of foreigners in many of China's westernizing projects at the time, the Burlingame mission indicates a degree of reluctance and ignorance on the part of the Qing government to its entrance into the international arena. "Barbarian affairs" *(yiwu)*, it seems, were still believed to be best left in the hands of the "barbarians" themselves. Not until the late 1870s did China begin to appoint her own officials to reside in the West as ministers.

Wang Ke-wen

References

Biggerstaff, Knight. "The Official Chinese Attitude Toward the Burlingame Mission." *American Historical Review* (July 1936), 682–702.

Hsu, Immanual C. Y. *China's Entrance into the Family of Nations: The Diplomatic Phase, 1858–1880*. Cambridge, MA: Harvard University Press, 1968.

Williams, F. W. *Anson Burlingame and the First Chinese Mission to Foreign Powers*. New York, NY: Scribner's, 1912.

Burma Campaigns

The anti-Japanese battles fought by Chinese troops in Burma during 1942 to 1944 were collectively known as the Burma campaigns. Following the outbreak of the Pacific War in 1941, the Japanese quickly conquered the British and French colonies or spheres of influence in Southeast Asia. In January 1942, the Japanese army advanced from Thailand into the British colony of Burma. In order to prevent the

Japanese from cutting the Burma Road, China's main line of communication to the outside world during the war, the Chinese Expeditionary Army *(yuanzhengjun)* entered Burma from western Yunnan. The army, about 100,000 men in strength, was under the nominal command of Luo Zhuoying and Du Yuming, but its actual commander was the American advisor to Chiang Kaishek, Joseph W. Stilwell. In March, as the British forces in Burma were about to collapse under Japanese attacks, the Expeditionary Army came to their rescue in the Thai-Burmese border area.

Fierce battles took place in Toungoo and Yenangyaung, yet eventually the Japanese took both positions. After being rescued by the Chinese, the British forces fled into India, thereby exposing the rear of the Chinese Expeditionary Army to Japanese assault. In May the Japanese severed the Chinese line of provision and crossed the Chinese-Burmese border into China. In June, the besieged Expeditionary Army broke into two groups; one returned to western Yunnan while the other retreated into India. The long and chaotic retreat through the Burmese jungles resulted in heavy casualties in both groups. By the time they returned to safety, only 40,000 men were left in the army.

At the insistence of Stilwell, the Chinese government soon began the planning of a counter-attack to recover northern Burma with American assistance. A joint Sino-America force (called the Chinese-Army-in-India) was organized on the basis of the Expeditionary Army in India, with Stilwell as commander and Zheng Dongguo as his deputy. The Expeditionary Army in western Yunnan was expanded and placed under the command of Chen Cheng. In October 1943, as the Allies were winning in the Pacific, the Chinese-Army-in-India crossed the high mountains along the Burmese-Indian border and attacked the Japanese troops in northern Burma.

The force achieved a series of major victories in late 1943 and early 1944 with American air support. In March the Chinese forces in western Yunnan also crossed the Nu River and launched a successful offensive from the other side, thereby scissoring the Japanese. Jungle battles, described by George Marshall as "the most difficult campaign of World War Two," raged in the region for another year. The Battle of Myitkyina in May–August 1944 was especially praised by the Allies as a demonstration of the superb leadership of Stilwell and the bravery of the Chinese army.

In January 1945, the two groups of the former Expeditionary Army finally met at Maymyo. Two months later the Burma campaign ended. More than fifty cities and towns in northern Burma were recovered from the Japanese and the critical overland route to India was reopened. The Japanese suffered a loss of 30,000 men. This was the only occasion in World War II that Chinese forces fought beyond the Chinese border for the Allies. The impressive results enhanced China's international prestige.

Wang Ke-wen

References

Fischer, Edward. *The Chancy War: Winning in China, Burma and India in World War Two*. New York, NY: Orion Books, 1991.

Romanus, Charles, and Riley Sunderland. *Time Runs Out in CBI*. Washington, DC: Department of the Army, 1959.

Wilson, Dick. *When Tigers Fight: The Story of the Sino-Japanese War, 1937–1945*. New York, NY: The Viking Press, 1982.

C

Cai E (1882–1916)
See NATIONAL PROTECTION MOVEMENT

Cai Yuanpei (1868–1940)
Revolutionary, educator, and leading intellectual in modern China, Cai Yuanpei was born in Shaoxing, a thriving market town in Zhejiang province. After earning the *jinshi* degree in 1890, he accepted employment as a compiler with the Hanlin Academy in Beijing, but resigned from office in 1898 after the defeat of Kang Youwei's Hundred Days Reform. Shortly after, he settled in Shanghai.

Cai's decision to abandon a bureaucratic career was motivated in considerable measure by strong patriotic feelings. Like many members of his generation, he was concerned about the humiliation of China at the hands of foreign powers, and had decided that radical change was the only way to prevent a total collapse. After his arrival in Shanghai he became involved in educational activities and joined with others in establishing a Patriotic Academy *(Aiguo Xueshe)* in the international settlement in Shanghai. He also joined the anti-Manchu revolutionary group Guangfuhui (Restoration Society) and after the establishment of Sun Yatsen's Tongmenghui (Revolutionary Alliance) in Tokyo in 1905, he directed the organization's branch in Shanghai.

But Cai was already more than just an ardent nationalist. As a youth he had been strongly impressed by the humanitarian aspects of the Confucian vision and as he entered his mature years harbored a passionate commitment to the concept of *datong,* or universal peace. Such feelings were strengthened after he left China to study in Europe in 1906. While studying philosophy and the social sciences in Germany, he became acquainted with the ideas of the Russian anarchist Peter Kropotkin and a vocal supporter of the latter's belief that harmony and mutual aid, not national competition and conflict, were the fundamental law of human nature.

Cai Yuanpei retained this commitment to the concept of global unity to the end of his life. On returning to China in early 1912 to accept the position of minister of education in the new Republic of China, he presented an educational program based on five principles, one of which was the concept of world-outlook education. But Cai's effort to build a new educational system based on internationalism rather than nationalism ran counter to the growing emphasis on national revival and was rejected by his colleagues.

Before the end of the year Cai had resigned his position in protest against the policy of President Yuan Shikai and returned to Europe to resume his studies. In 1917 he returned to China to become chancellor of Beijing University. During the next several years he transformed the institution into the vibrant heart of intellectual activity in republican China. While much of the concern of faculty and students was focused on the reform of Chinese political and social institutions, national issues also received close attention, and the university played a major role in the May Fourth movement in 1919.

During the 1920s, Cai continued to play an active part in educational activities, and in 1922 the Beijing government adopted a new program that embodied his views on the importance of an international dimension to the school curriculum. But such ideas were opposed by key members of Sun Yatsen's Guomindang, and

Cai Yuanpei. (Courtesy of Nationalist Party Archives.)

after the establishment of the Nanjing regime in 1928, a new educational program was adopted that reflected nationalist leanings rather than cosmopolitanism.

Cai shared many of the national concerns of his countrymen. In his later years he was vocally critical of Japanese aggression in north China and wrote articles on the enduring value of traditional Chinese culture. He also grew critical of the Nanjing regime. In 1932 Cai, together with Sun Yatsen's widow Soong Qingling, founded the Chinese League for the Protection of Human Rights in Shanghai. Until his death in 1940, he argued passionately that for humankind to endure, narrow nationalism had to be replaced by a broader universal vision of the human experience.

William J. Duiker

References

Duiker, William J. *Ts'ai Yuan-p'ei: Educator of Modern China*. University Park: Pennsylvania State University Press, 1978.

Cairo Conference

The Cairo Conference and the Teheran Conference, which followed immediately, were convened during World War II to help Joseph Stalin, Winston Churchill, and Franklin Roosevelt decide when a second European front should be opened and when the Soviet Union would enter the war in the Pacific. In the six-day meeting (November 22–27, 1943), at which China was represented by Chiang Kaishek, discussions also centered on whether the United States could use recaptured Pacific islands as staging locations to bomb Japan. This latter action could have reduced China's military importance in the war.

The Cairo Declaration, issued on December 1, 1943, after the approval of the Soviet Union, demanded for the first time the unconditional surrender of Japan. It also specified that all Chinese territories lost to Japan would be returned to China and that Japanese possessions outside of the archipelago, including Sakhalin and the Kurile Islands, would be returned to the Soviet Union. Some Japanese mandatories in the Pacific would be taken by the United States.

In a Christmas message Roosevelt told Americans that as a result of the conference, "we and the Republic of China are closer together than ever before in deep friendship and in unity of purpose." Despite his effusive words, the Cairo Conference and a number of unofficial meetings held during those six days reflected Sino-American disagreement and revealed a United States president who was less than enamored with Chiang Kaishek.

The Cairo Conference witnessed significant disagreement over the shape of postwar East Asia. Chiang Kaishek was concerned that if China's military significance in the war against Japan was diminished, the country's ability to determine its own destiny would be reduced. Churchill seemed to lend some credibility to Chiang's concerns as he advocated the primacy of the European theater and a reduced stature for Chiang: "The talks of the British and American staffs were sadly distracted by the Chinese story. . . ."

Rancor also existed between the Americans and British, with reference to Burma. General Joseph Stilwell, who ironically had been asked along by Chiang Kaishek, recounted that British field marshal Sir Alan Brooke "got nasty and [Admiral] King got good and sore. King almost climbed over the table at Brooke. God he was mad. I wished he had socked him." The British also worried that if Chiang and Roosevelt became too cozy, the American president might urge the British to grant independence to their Asian colonies, especially Hong Kong.

It appeared clear in 1945 that Japan would not participate in rebuilding postwar Asia. At the same time, Roosevelt was also discontented with Chiang Kaishek. Perhaps the clearest indication of this was the president's remark to Stilwell that the United States would support whoever was "next in line," if Chiang were to be overthrown. This comment reflected a deeper attitude that was antithetical to increasingly virulent Asian nationalism. Before Stilwell met with Roosevelt in Cairo, he saw Harry Hopkins, an aide who accompanied Roosevelt to Cairo. Hopkins told the surprised American general that he expected Chiang soon to be doing the bidding of the United States and that the United States intended to determine on its own how territory would be distributed in the postwar period. In fact, he pointedly suggested, the United States would demand bases in "Formosa, the Philippines, and anywhere we damned please." The ramifications of this attitude are numerous, but the results of American arrogance confronting Asian nationalism can be witnessed in the tension with the People's Republic of China prior to the normalization of relations in 1979.

Edwin Clausen

References

Clemens, Diane S. *Yalta.* New York, NY: Oxford University Press, 1970.

Neumann, William L. *After Victory: Churchill, Roosevelt, and Stalin and the Making of the Peace.* New York, NY: Harper & Row, 1967.

Schaller, Michael. *The U.S. Crusade in China, 1938–1945.* New York, NY: Columbia University Press, 1979.

Canton Customs Crisis

In October 1923, Sun Yatsen's "National Government" in Canton notified the foreign diplomatic body in Beijing of its intention to collect the "customs surplus" (annual customs revenue after deductions of payments for foreign loans and indemnities) from the foreign-controlled Maritime Customs Service at Canton. Sun's previous Canton regime had received a share of this fund during 1919–1920; he now demanded a resumption of that practice. The request was in part prompted by his regime's financial difficulties, and in part motivated by his desire to demonstrate the regime's independence from the Beijing government, to which the "customs surplus" was normally delivered.

The notification came at a time when Sun had just begun to reorganize his Guomindang under Soviet guidance and when the Canton regime was under attack by Chen Jiongming's forces. The foreign powers were neither impressed by Sun's recent pro-Soviet stance nor optimistic about his regime's chance to survive. On December 14, the diplomatic body formally informed the Canton regime that it would not permit the regime to collect the local "customs surplus" and would use force to prevent such an attempt. Sun, however, regarded the issue as not only critical to the financial stability of his revolutionary base but symbolic to the political legitimacy of the Canton regime. On December 19, he ordered the the Canton Maritime Customs Service to turn its revenue over to his government. He also asked the inspector-general, Sir Francis Aglen, to pay all arrears of the "customs surplus" due the government since 1920, and threatened to reorganize the service if his orders were not obeyed. Meanwhile anti-imperialist protests raged in the local Chinese press.

In retaliation, sixteen foreign warships—including six American and five British—gathered at the port of Canton in a show of force. The inspector-general refused to obey Sun's orders, but Sun did not make further moves. Both the United States and Great Britain, who were concerned about the Hong Kong-Canton trade, did not want to resort to war. On January 4, 1924, the American minister to China, Jacob Gould Shurman, arrived in Canton to mediate the dispute. The warships soon began to depart, and the crisis passed. In April 1924, the foreign diplomatic body in Beijing agreed to turn over a portion of the "customs surplus" in Canton to Sun's regime. The crisis enhanced Sun's anti-imperialist views as well as the solidarity of his new revolutionary camp. It reinforced his resolution to form a united front with the Soviet Union and the Chinese Communists.

Wang Ke-wen

References

Wilbur, C. Martin. *Sun Yat-sen: Frustrated Patriot.* New York, NY: Columbia University Press, 1976.

Canton Regimes (1917–26)
See CONSTITUTION PROTECTION MOVEMENT

Canton System

The system of Sino-Western trade prior to the 1842 Treaty of Nanjing is known as the Canton system. The system was first established in 1760 by the Qing Dynasty, in which only the southern port of Canton (Guangzhou) was open to Western trade and contact. Foreign merchants were allowed to stay in an area ouside the city walls of Canton, where their "factories" (warehouses) were located, and they were not allowed to bring their wives and families.

In conducting their trade in Canton, foreigners had to deal only with a group of government-authorized Chinese merchants called Cohong, who monopolized the Chinese side of Sino-Western trade and provided living accommodations for the foreigners. No direct communication between foreign merchants and the Chinese officials, or between the Western and Chinese governments, was permitted under this system.

Western toleration of this restrictive trade diminished as the West, led by Great Britain after the eighteenth century, became increasingly confident of its industrial and military strength. Lord Macartney's mission to Beijing in 1793 was but the most prominent example of British efforts to persuade the Qing government to change the Canton system. The failure of those efforts was an important contributing factor to the Opium War of 1840–1842. The Treaty of Nanjing signed after the war finally abolished the system and replaced it with a new set of arrangements defined by the unequal treaties.

Wang Ke-wen

References

Fairbank, John K. *Trade and Diplomacy on the China Coast.* Cambridge, MA: Harvard University Press, 1953.

Greenberg, Michael. *British Trade and the Opening of China, 1800–42.* Cambridge, England: Cambridge University Press, 1951.

Canton–Hong Kong Strike

The 1925 British massacre of Chinese demonstrators in Shanghai, known as the May Thirtieth Incident, provoked a nationwide anti-British protest which involved some 130 reported strikes throughout China. The most significant, longest lasting, and indeed, the climax of this anti-imperialistic movement was the Canton–Hong Kong General Strike-Boycott from June 1925 to October 1926. From beginning to end, it was a political mobilization sponsored by the Guomindang–Chinese Communist Party (GMD–CCP) United Front in Canton, using grassroots economic warfare against British imperialism.

The Shakee Massacre of June 23, 1925, in which British troops, firing from their concession on Shameen Island across the river from Canton city, killed 52 and wounded 117 Chinese demonstrators on the city side of the river, escalated the protest in support of the May Thirtieth strikers into an all-out struggle against the British in the Canton delta. At its peak, the strike-boycott, drawing some 250,000 Hong Kong strikers and their families back to the Canton delta, paralyzed the colony's economy and came close to liquidating British interests in south China. Hong Kong's total trade fell by 50 percent, shipping tonnage diminished by almost 40 percent, stock market share values dropped by 40 percent, property prices and rents decreased by 60 percent, and two runs were made on two local banks.

However, statistics on Hong Kong's economic calamity could not convey the full dimension of the physical destitution, personal sacrifices, nationalistic satisfaction, and political consequences of the strike-boycott, which directly involved the GMD regime in Canton and its coalition partner, the CCP. Under the CCP's All China Federation of Trade Unions, the Canton–Hong Kong Strike Committee assumed charge of the whole movement with its own three-thousand-strong armed pickets and a budget of some five million dollars. The committee's armed capacity to exercise quasi-police function earned it the label of "a state within a state" or "a Red labor regime" in Canton.

With the presence of 250,000 strikers in the Canton delta, the strike-boycott greatly aided the CCP and the GMD's left wing; it also alarmed the GMD's right wing. The very effectiveness of this Communist-led mass mobilization intensified internal discord within the GMD. Yet the nationalist appeal of the movement remained so strong that even the ascending GMD Right under Chiang Kaishek could not terminate it immediately after his March

1926 coup d'état against the Left. Only half a year later, as the Northern Expedition reached central China, the Canton regime unilaterally ended the General Strike-Boycott on the Chinese National Day, October 10, 1926, while maintaining the boycott against British goods.

The strike-boycott was primarily a patriotic movement using economic means for political ends. Its continuation was subjected to the political consideration of its sponsors, which by late 1926 considered it a drain on its financial resources and even a diplomatic obstacle *vis-à-vis* the West. Despite the fact that the GMD-CCP United Front ended the movement without fulfilling the Hong Kong strikers' demands against British colonialism, the British government in December 1926 announced a new friendly policy toward the rising force of Chinese nationalism, as represented by a victorious GMD in its Northern Expedition. In this sense, the Canton–Hong Kong Strike generated great momentum and provided a solid mass support for the Guangdong home base of the United Front and forced a realignment in Sino-British-Hong Kong relations.

Ming K. Chan

References

Chan, Ming K. "Hong Kong in Sino-British Conflict: Mass Mobilization and the Crisis of Legitimacy, 1912–26." *Precarious Balance: Hong Kong Between China and Britain, 1842–1992*, ed. Ming K. Chan. Armonk, NY: M. E. Sharpe, 1994.

Chesneaux, Jean. *The Chinese Labor Movement, 1919–1927*. Stanford, CA: Stanford University Press, 1968.

Cao Kun (1862–1938)

Militarist and leader of the Zhili Clique, Cao Kun may be best known as the only president in the republican era who bribed his way into that office. He thus came to epitomize the corrupt politics that many nationalists in modern China vowed to eliminate.

Born in Tianjin, Cao was said to have been a cloth peddler before joining the Huan Army in 1881. He rose to senior ranks in the Beiyang Army under Yuan Shikai after the first Sino-Japanese War (1894–95) and was given the responsibility of guarding the imperial capital when the Revolution of 1911 broke out. In 1912 his troops mutinied in Beijing and Tianjin, probably at the order of Yuan, which gave Yuan

the excuse to organize his new republican government in the North. Cao supported Yuan's aborted monarchical attempt in 1915, but two years later opposed Zhang Xun's effort to restore the Qing emperor. Following the death of Feng Guozhang in 1919, Cao succeeded Feng as leader of the Zhili Clique. The next year he defeated Duan Qirui in the Zhili-Anhui War and then Zhang Zuolin in the first Zhili-Fengtian War of 1922. In 1923, Cao, who now controlled Beijing, forced President Li Yuanhong to step down and paid each member of the parliament five thousand dollars to vote for him as the new President.

Cao's presidency was shortlived. In 1924 his general Feng Yuxiang defected to the Fengtian side in the second Zhili-Fengtian War and captured Beijing. Cao was placed under house arrest and soon forced to resign. Released in 1926, Cao sought protection from his former Zhili colleague Wu Peifu, but never returned to public office. He spent his last years in the Concessions in Tianjin and reportedly refused to become a Japanese puppet after the Manchurian Incident in 1931. He died during the second Sino-Japanese War.

Wang Ke-wen

References

Nathan, Andrew J. *Peking Politics, 1918–1923: Factionalism and the Failure of Constitutionalism*. Berkeley: University of California Press, 1976.

C. C. Clique

"C. C." was apparently an informal, though popular, reference to the faction, led by Chen Guofu and Chen Lifu, that dominated the Guomindang (GMD) party apparatus throughout its rule on the mainland. It stood for either the Chen brothers or "Central Club," *i.e.*, the central headquarters of the GMD. Guofu and Lifu were nephews of an early assistant to Sun Yatsen and patron of Chiang Kaishek, Chen Qimei (Yingshi), who was killed by Yuan Shikai in 1916. Since the days of the Canton regime in the early 1920s, the Chen brothers had performed critical services to Chiang by seizing control of the Party for him. Rumors of the existence of the C. C. Clique first appeared in 1927, after Chiang had purged the Communists and other leftists from the GMD and entrusted the party machine to the Chen brothers.

By 1930, the power of Guofu and Lifu in

the GMD headquarters at Nanjing was unchallenged; through efforts from the top, they also extended their influence to the Party branches in the provinces. After supervising the Party's Organization Department for many years, Guofu was appointed as governor of Jiangsu in 1933 and later held other positions, but his influence in the Party never decreased. Lifu was the Party's secretary-general from 1929 to 1932 and head of the Organization Department from 1933 to 1936. After 1928, he was also in charge of the Party's security agency, the Investigation Section, later the Bureau of Investigation and Statistics, or *Zhongtong*. The bureau competed with Dai Li's military secret police, *Juntong*, in suppressing Communists and dissidents on behalf of Chiang's regime.

During the early 1930s, the C. C. Clique formalized its existence by establishing the Association of Loyal Comrades of the Guomindang *(Zhongshi tongzhihui)* in the capital. The association resembled the Blue Shirts in organization, with a second-tier group called the Blue-Sky White-Sun Society *(Qingtian bairituan)* and many other front organizations. In 1938 Chiang Kaishek ordered the clique to dissolve and merge with the Blue Shirts into the Three Peoples' Principles Youth Corps, yet the clique continued to exist. One of its remaining institutional bases was the Central Political Academy administered by Guofu. Partly because of Lifu's personal background (he received a Master's degree at the University of Pittsburgh), the clique was especially influential in China's academia and schools. During the Sino-Japanese War of 1937–45 Lifu was appointed minister of education; the faction's influence in cultural and education institutions was further strengthened. In these areas, the C. C. Clique came into bitter conflict with Chiang Kaishek's son, Jingguo, in the 1940s. Following the GMD's retreat to Taiwan in 1949, Guofu (who died in 1951) and Lifu retired from politics, and the faction soon disappeared.

Whereas Guofu may be regarded as the real founder of "C. C.," Lifu defined the ideological position for the faction. Under Lifu's guidance, the C. C. Clique advocated a restoration of China's cultural tradition. National regeneration, Lifu stressed, had to be based on national self-confidence, which could be found only by embracing the country's glorious heritage. To a degree, Lifu was expanding on an ideological line first introduced by Dai Jitao,

linking Sun Yatsen's doctrines to Confucianism. An important articulation of the clique's ideological view was the "Declaration of Cultural Construction on a Chinese Basis" of January 1935, issued by ten university professors and published in the "C. C." organ *Wenhua jianshe (Cultural Construction)*. The document was said to have been drafted by Lifu. Lamenting the decline of Chinese culture under the assault of Western influences, the declaration called for the development of "Chinese characteristics" in China's politics, society and thought. It proposed a selective syncretism of Chinese and Western cultures with an emphasis on the fundamentality of Chineseness. This cultural conservatism represented a strand of ultranationalist, traditionalist thinking in the GMD.

Wang Ke-wen

References

Chang, Sidney H., and Ramon H. Myers, eds. *The Storm Clouds Clear Over China: The Memoir of Ch'en Li-fu*. Stanford, CA: Hoover Institution Press, 1994.

Eastman, Lloyd E. "The Kuomintang in the 1930s." *The Limits of Change: Essays on Cultural Alternatives in Republican China*, ed. Charlotte Furth, 191–210. Cambridge, MA: Harvard University Press, 1976.

Chahar People's Anti-Japanese Allied Army

In May 1933, Feng Yuxiang organized his former followers in the Northwest Army and established the Chahar People's Anti-Japanese Allied Army in Kalgan, with himself as commander. Other important officers in the army included Fang Zhenwu and Ji Hongchang; part of the army was composed of remnants of the Northeast Anti-Japanese Volunteer Army from Manchuria. Indirectly assisted by the Chinese Communists, Feng and his followers denounced the recent Sino-Japanese Tanggu Truce as traitorous and vowed to fight independently against the invading Japanese.

In July, the army won a number of victories against the Japanese forces in northern Chahar. Regarding Feng's action as a threat to Sino-Japanese rapprochement and to its authority, the Guomindang government in Nanjing immediately exerted political and military pressure against the army. In August Feng was forced to dissolve the army and retire. Fang and

Ji, however, continued their fight under the new title of Anti-Japanese and Traitor-Pacification Army. They were eventually defeated under a joint attack by the Japanese and Nanjing's forces in October.

Under the banner of anti-Japanese nationalism, the Chahar army exploited prevailing Chinese popular sentiments and briefly revived Feng Yuxiang's military and political career. It was yet another example of how nationalist causes and regionalist ambitions could enter an ironic marriage of convenience in prewar China.

Wang Ke-wen

References

Conle, Parks M. *Facing Japan*. Cambridge, MA: Harvard University Press, 1991.

Sheridan, James E. *Chinese Warlord: The Career of Feng Yu-hsiang*. Stanford, CA: Stanford University Press, 1966.

Chang, Carsun (Zhang Junmai, 1887–1969)

Nationalism was a constant force in the life of Carsun Chang. As a youth, he joined a student volunteer corps whose mission was to expel the Russians from Manchuria. While teaching in Hunan province shortly afterwards, he lectured his students on the aggression of the foreign powers. As a student in Japan prior to the Revolution of 1911, he expressed anxiety concerning Japanese expansionism in Asia. Following the revolution, he clashed with Yuan Shikai over the issue of Mongolian independence, fearing that Manchuria and Tibet would also be lost. While hopeful, following World War I, that the League of Nations could protect China, he argued that until China put its house in order, foreign powers would continue to take advantage of it. Hence, he asserted that imperialism was not the sole reason why China had failed as a nation, and he opposed ultranationalism and its "empty shouting" of "down with imperialism."

Nationalism was a key element in the platform of Chang's National Socialist Party of China *(Zhongguo guojia shehuidang)*, founded in 1932 in response to the Japanese threat. The party "took the nation as the starting point" and believed that nationalism was the "modern foundation for the establishment of the state." Its first congress (1934) emphasized nationalism and called for national unity against foreign aggression, while at its second congress (1936) it demanded immediate resistance to Japan.

During the 1930s, Chang's preoccupation with the nation was revealed in his frequent writings on such topics as "national democracy," "national socialism," "national revival," and China's "national characteristics." He searched for provincial reconstruction movements that could serve as models for reforming the Chinese nation, while complaining of the weakness of the Chinese people's national consciousness.

Chang's party took issue with the Chinese Communists, arguing that "nationalistic sentiments are stronger than class feelings." Chinese capitalists and workers were united against the Japanese invasion, Chang declared after the outbreak of the Sino-Japanese War, while the USSR's success was due to the "nationalistic character" of its socialist reconstruction.

Chang was a member of that wing of the republican political world loosely referred to as the "third force," third parties and minority parties and groups. His own "third-force" position may be seen in his opposition, from the early 1920s, to both the Chinese Communist Party and the Guomindang. Following the Communist victory in China in 1949, he served as representative in the United States of an organization termed the "Third Force." Officially called the Fighting League for Chinese Freedom and Democracy, it lasted only a few years (1952–54). Its nationalism took the form of opposing the Soviet Union, while accepting American aid and attempting to form an alliance with anti-Communist Vietnam and South Korea. Chang died in San Francisco in 1969.

Roger B. Jeans

References

Chang, Carsun. *Third Force in China*. New York, NY: Bookman, 1952.

Jeans, Roger B. "The Trials of a Third-Force Intellectual: Zhang Junmai (Carsun Chang) During the Early Nanjing Decade, 1927–1931." *Roads Not Taken*, ed. Roger B. Jeans, 37–60. Boulder, CO: Westview Press, 1992.

Tan, Chester. *Chinese Political Thought in the Twentieth Century*. New York, NY: Anchor Books, 1971.

Chefoo Convention

See MARGARY AFFAIR

Chen Duxiu (1879–1942)

Chen Duxiu was the founder and first general secretary of the Chinese Communist Party (CCP). One of the leading political and intellectual figures of China before he became a Communist, Chen launched the "New Culture" movement with his publication of the highly influential *New Youth* magazine in 1915. Among his many other contributions to the political and cultural development of the modern Chinese nation was his establishment of the use of punctuation in modern written Chinese.

In the pre-1911 period, Chen published the *Anhui Vernacular Journal,* said to be the first vernacular newspaper in China and one that galvanized support for the activities of the young anti-Qing revolutionaries in Anhui. Its appeals to past nationalist heroes, its use of the vernacular, and its attempts to introduce ideas of science and democracy in Anhui presaged many of the themes later to be repeated in *New Youth.* Chen also helped to organize a number of other anti-Qing revolutionary and nationalist associations, including the National Essence Society, a group of neo-conservatives seeking to restore the traditions and ideals of the Chinese past. His concern for preserving a strong and prosperous Chinese society ultimately led Chen away from this group and toward the study of Western ideas. He established *New Youth* in 1915 to awaken the young people of China to these concerns, which he believed vital for the preservation of the Chinese people.

In 1917, Chen became the dean of the College of Arts and Letters of Beijing University. His *New Youth* magazine now commanded a national following, and Chen gained a wide platform for his attacks on Confucian tradition and family values, his advocacy of the use of the vernacular in Chinese writing, and his interest in science and democracy.

In late 1920, Chen abandoned his advocacy of Western democracy and began the organization of a Leninist-style party in China. In 1921, the Party elected him its first general secretary. Initially, Chen believed that China under the leadership of his new Communist Party would be able to avoid the horrors of capitalist development that had occurred in the West and develop as a strong independent state under a Socialist government. But after repeated setbacks and much pressure from the Soviet Comintern, Chen accepted the idea that a bourgeois revolution would have to occur in China before Socialism could be achieved and that to accomplish this, the CCP would have to ally itself, at least temporarily, with Sun Yatsen's Guomindang (GMD).

Although Chen expressed constant doubts about the wisdom of continuing the alliance with the GMD and several times advocated dissolving the compact, he shouldered the responsibility for implementing the United Front. At the same time, he developed the Party into a strong independent organization. After Chiang Kaishek's forces turned on the Communists in April 1927, a younger generation of Party members purged Chen from the Party leadership. Under Stalin's prodding, the Party labeled Chen an opportunist and blamed him for the failure of the United Front.

In 1929, after Chen continued to criticize the CCP's policies, the Party expelled him. He joined a Trotskyist leftist opposition group, but was jailed by the Guomindang in 1932, which effectively ended his political career. Released in 1937, he died in obscurity in Sichuan during the Sino-Japanese War.

Lee Feigon

References

Feigon, Lee. *Chen Duxiu: Founder of the Chinese Communist Party.* Princeton, NJ: Princeton University Press, 1983.

Chen Gongbo (1892–1946)

Chen Gongbo was a founding member of the Chinese Communist Party, a left-wing leader and theorist of the Guomindang, and a principal leader of the pro-Japanese Wang Jingwei regime during the second Sino-Japanese War.

Born in Ruyuan, Guangdong, Chen as a youth followed his father in participating in local anti-Manchu activities. After the Revolution of 1911, he pursued higher education at the prestigious Beijing University. Although not actively involved in the May Fourth Movement of 1919, he was influenced by the new ideological currents and, shortly after graduation, became an active member in the early Communist organizations in Canton. In 1921 he attended the First National Congress of the Chinese Communist Party in Shanghai. However, he soon withdrew from the Party and left for the United States to study.

Upon receiving a master's degree in economics at Columbia University, Chen returned to China in 1925. At the invitation of Liao Zhongkai, he joined the Guomindang in Canton and was appointed to a number of important Party and government positions. When Liao was assassinated in August 1926, Chen succeeded him as head of the GMD's Peasant Department. In the post-Sun Yatsen power struggle within the Party Chen became a follower of Wang Jingwei. He played a major role in Wang's Wuhan regime in 1927, and from 1928 to 1930 organized Wang's supporters in opposition to the Nanjing government under Chiang Kaishek. Their criticism of Chiang's conservative leadership won them the appelation of the "Left GMD." The "Left GMD" instigated a series of political and military attacks on Nanjing, culminating in the "Enlarged Session" opposition at Beiping in 1930. All of them, however, were unsuccessful.

In 1932, Chen followed Wang Jingwei into a coalition with Chiang and served as minister of industry in the Nanjing government. He held that position until 1935, when Wang was wounded by an assailant and forced to resign as premier. When the Sino-Japanese War broke out in 1937, Chen briefly toured Europe as a special envoy of the government in quest of international assistance to China's war effort. In 1938, while heading the GMD's provincial branch in Sichuan, he reluctantly joined Wang's "peace movement" and flew to Hanoi. Yet he refused to accompany Wang to Shanghai to negotiate a separate peace with Japan. After staying in Hong Kong for more than a year, Chen was finally persuaded by his loyalty and affection to Wang to become a member of Wang's collaborationist regime in Nanjing in early 1940. For the next five years, Chen served first as head of the regime's legislative Yuan and then, after Wang's death in 1944, as chairman of the regime. When Japan surrendered in 1945, he sought temporary refuge in Japan but was soon brought back to China for trial. He was convicted of high treason and executed in 1946.

Wang Ke-wen

References

Wilbur, C. Martin. "The Variegated Career of Ch'en Kung-po." *Revolutionary Leaders of Modern China*, ed. Chün-tu Hsueh, 455–470. New York, NY: Oxford University Press, 1971.

So, Wai-chor. *The Kuomintang Left in the National Revolution, 1924–1931.* Hong Kong: Oxford University Press, 1991.

Chen Jiongming (1878–1933)

C

Chen Jiongming, a militarist and ruler of Guangdong in the early 1920s, was best known for his 1922 *coup d'état* that toppled Sun Yatsen's second Canton regime.

Chen was a native of Guangdong. Well educated, he established himself early in life. He became a member of the newly formed provincial assembly in 1908 but soon turned to revolution and joined Sun Yatsen's Tongmenghui. Subsequently he participated in several uprisings organized by Sun. During the Revolution of 1911 Chen led the People's Army *(minjun)* in the East River area of Guangdong and then succeeded Hu Hanmin as Guangdong's military governor. In 1913 he supported Sun's second revolution. When it failed, he fled to Southeast Asia, where he joined the Society for the Study of European Affairs *(Oushi yanjiuhui)*. The society, organized by Huang Xing and Li Genyuan, was not in accord with Sun's Chinese Revolutionary Party in Japan. In 1916, Chen returned to China and participated in the National Protection movement *(Huguo yundong)* that toppled Yuan Shikai.

When Sun established the first Canton regime in 1917 to challenge the Beijing government, he gave Chen a small army and a base in western Fujian. This army was the only force that Sun could depend upon, as the troops in Guangdong were under the control of local warlords who merely used Sun. In 1918, Sun was ousted from Canton. Two years later Chen, whose army had grown much in size, was ordered by Sun to launch an attack from Fujian on the Guangdong warlords. Chen's forces won a quick victory and Sun established the second Canton regime in 1920. To reward Chen, Sun appointed him as governor of Guangdong and commander of the Guangdong army. In reality, Chen became Sun's partner and military support in the regime.

As *de facto* ruler of Guangdong, Chen devoted much of his attention to the reconstruction of the province while trying to maintain peace between the province and the northern warlords. He favored the Federalist movement *(liansheng zizhi)* at the time, believing that a form of provincial autonomy was a necessary step toward the rebuilding of the Republic. In this sense his provincialism was motivated, ironically, by nationalism. Chen's vision and policy obviously conflicted with those of Sun Yatsen, who was eager to defeat the Beijing government and reunify the country under his leadership. In 1921 Sun was elected "Extraordinary President" by the second Canton regime; he further appointed Chen as minister of interior and minister of the army.

This, however, did not help to bridge the differences between the two men. Despite Chen's disapproval, Sun soon launched his Northern Expedition against Beijing. The expedition drained the military and financial resources which Chen needed for his provincial reconstruction, and he was reluctant to assist Sun's campaigns. In April 1922, Sun removed Chen from most of his posts and returned from the front to Canton to review the situation there. Chen left the city to avoid Sun. In June, Chen's troops in the city revolted and attacked Sun's office and residence. Sun narrowly escaped to a gunboat outside of the port of Canton. Two months later he went to Shanghai; the second Canton regime collapsed.

During the following year, Chen maintained peace and order in Guangdong and presided over the drafting of a provincial constitution. But Sun Yatsen, aided by a new alliance with Russia, directed a counterattack on Chen. Troops loyal to Sun again attacked from Fujian and took over Canton, where Sun established the third Canton regime in 1923. Chen retreated to the East River area. In late 1925, shortly after Sun's death, the forces of the Canton regime thoroughly defeated Chen, who fled to Hong Kong. In his final years, Chen wrote on his views of national reconstruction and organized a small political party, but he was no longer relevant to Chinese politics.

Wang Ke-wen

References

Hsieh, Winston. "The Ideas and Ideals of a Warlord: Ch'en Chiung-ming (1878–1933)." *Harvard Papers on China,* no. 16 (December 1962): 198–251.

Wilbur, C. Martin. *Sun Yat-sen: Frustrated Patriot.* New York, NY: Columbia University Press, 1976.

Chen Tianhua (1875–1905)

Chen Tianhua was an anti-Manchu revolutionary and propagandist during the late Qing. Born in Hunan to a poor family, Chen did not begin his education until he was fifteen. He enrolled into the new-style Qiushi Academy in his hometown Xinhua in the late 1890s, the heyday of the Reform movement in Hunan, and was apparently influenced by the reformist current of the time.

After receiving the *shengyuan* degree in 1902, Chen was sponsored by the academy to study in Japan, starting in 1903. As a student in Tokyo, he soon became involved in the political activities among overseas Chinese and turned from reform to revolution. In April that year Chinese students in Japan rose to protest against the refusal of Russia to withdraw her troops sent to Manchuria during the Boxer Uprising of 1900. Chen became a leading propagandist of this movement. In addition to sending letters of protest, written in his blood, to China, Chen penned numerous articles for student publications. He also joined the Anti-Russian Volunteer Army *(JuE yiyongjun)* organized by the students, who wished to expel the Russians from Manchuria by force. The organization quickly evolved into the anti-Manchu Association for the National Military Education *(Junguomin jiaoyuhui).* A few months later, Chen returned to China as a representative of the association to promote revolution.

In early 1904 Chen, together with his fellow Hunanese Huang Hsing and Song Jiaoren, founded the underground revolutionary society Huaxinghui (China Arise Society) in Changsha. He worked with other members of the society to incite armed uprisings among the Qing troops and secret societies. When those efforts failed, he again escaped to Japan. In 1905 Chen became a founding member of the Tongmenghui (Revolutionary Alliance) and helped to draft its constitution. He also wrote for the alliance organ *Minbao* on anti-Manchuism and republicanism. In November 1905 the Japanese government, pressured by the Qing, cracked down on the revolutionary activities of the Chinese students. In protest, Chen committed suicide by drowning himself in the sea on December 8.

Chen was a radical anti-Manchu nationalist. Like many Chinese youth in Japan at the turn of the century, he was convinced that China was about to be destroyed by the foreign powers and was bitter about the Manchu government's inability to defend Chinese rights and independence. In his enormously popular pamphlets written in colloquial style, *Menghuitou* (Turning Around) and *Jingshizhong* (Bell of Warning), Chen attacked both the "foreign devils" and the weak-kneed Manchus. He called for a violent overthrow of the Qing dynasty and the militarization of the Chinese population to resist foreign encroachment. Although his career and life were short, Chen's nationalist thought reflected the general sentiment of his time and remained influential after his death.

Wang Ke-wen

References

Gasster, Michael. *Chinese Intellectuals and the Revolution of 1911: The Birth of Modern Chinese Radicalism.* Seattle: University of Washington Press, 1969.

Young, Ernest P. "Problems of a Late Ch'ing Revolutionary: Ch'en T'ien-hua." *Revolutionary Leaders of Modern China,* ed. Chun-tu Hsueh, 210–247. New York, NY: Oxford University Press, 1971.

Chen Yun (1905–95)

Chen Yun, leader of the Chinese Communist Party (CCP) and the People's Republic of China (PRC), was an economic planner and theorist.

Chen was born in Jiangsu province; his original name was Liao Chenyun. Orphaned as a child, he went to work in a Shanghai factory after finishing elementary school. In the mid-1920s, Chen joined the CCP and became a labor union organizer. In 1927 he participated in the Shanghai uprisings led by Zhou Enlai that secured the city for the Guomindang-CCP Northern Expedition against the warlords. Following the collapse of the first United Front later that year, Chen led a failed uprising in his hometown, then fled to the Jiangxi Soviet established by Mao Zedong. There he rose quickly in Party rank and by 1931 had entered the CCP's Politburo. Although not an "internationalist" himself, Chen maintained close ties with Wang Ming, who controlled the Party leadership at the time. Chen survived the Long March (1934–1935) and then accompanied Wang to represent the CCP at the Comintern in Moscow in 1935 through 1937.

During the second Sino-Japanese War Chen worked in the CCP base in Yan'an and was head of the Party's Organization Department during the Rectification campaign in 1942 through 1944. His major responsibility after 1940, however, was economic planning. He led the battle against the Guomindang's economic blockade of Yan'an and soon became an expert in guerrilla economy and finance.

After the founding of the People's Republic, Chen emerged as one of the seven members of the Standing Committee of the Politburo, which was the center of power in the PRC. In 1956 he became vice-chairman of the CCP. His most important appointment, however, was chairman of the State Finance and Economic Committee, which supervised the development and restructuring of the Chinese economy on a socialist model. Chen's early tasks included rebuilding China's industry and infrastructure that had been ruined by the war and eliminating the rampant inflation that had paralyzed the country before 1949. In the mid-1950s, Chen supported the Russian-style Five Year Plan but also advocated "self-reliance," *i.e.,* economic independence from the Soviet Union. A pragmatic economic planner, he opposed Mao's Great Leap Forward, which led to his fall from power in 1958. After that, he kept a low profile and was not abused during the Cultural Revolution (1966–76).

Shortly after Mao's death and the purge of the Gang of Four, Chen resurfaced as a major policymaker in the PRC. He chaired, for example, the CCP's Central Commission for Inspecting Discipline in the 1980s. Chen had favored expanding the market and a degree of decentralization in the 1950s, but his views now were more cautious than those of the reformers in the post-Mao era. Under the leadership of Deng Xiaoping, Chen has been generally viewed as a "conservative," meaning that he preferred a gradual approach to economic reform and the retention of some basic characteristics of the socialist system in China. This position alienated him from reformers, such as Hu Yaobang and Zhao Ziyang, and persuaded him to support the suppression of the Tiananmen Incident in 1989. When Chen died in 1995, the official elegy praised him as "one of the founders of China's socialist economic reconstruction."

Wang Ke-wen

References

Bachman, David M. *Chen Yun and the Chinese Political System.* Berkeley: University of California Press, 1985.

Lardy, Nicholas R., and Kenneth Lieberthal, eds. *Chen Yun's Strategy for China's Development: A Non-Maoist Alternative.* Armonk, NY: M. E. Sharpe, 1983.

Chennault, Claire L. (1890–1958)

Claire L. Chennault retired from the United States Air Force in 1936, only to become a private adviser to Chiang Kaishek after 1937. He became an ardent admirer of the Generalissimo and his wife, and Chiang sought to use this admiration to facilitate his plans for fighting the war against Japan.

To this end, Chennault, together with T. V. Soong, approached the United States Secretary of the Treasury Henry Morgenthau, Jr., in 1940 about the establishment of a "Special Air Unit" in China that would bomb the Japanese islands. As the secretary seemed ready to pave the way, the plans were scrapped because of the intervention of Secretary of War Henry Stimson and Army Chief of Staff General George Marshall. President Franklin Roosevelt then proposed a compromise, resulting in a secret Executive Order permitting American military pilots to sign up with a private company once they resigned their commissions. They would be part of the "American Volunteer Group" and were to fly planes provided to China under a lend-lease program. The group formed the core of the "Flying Tigers."

The Flying Tigers had approximately 100 pilots and were stationed at Kunming, China, and in Burma, until the Japanese occupied that country. When the United States entered World War II, Chennault returned to active duty and became the head of the China Air Task Force. This eventually evolved into the Fourteenth Air Force, with Chennault as its commander.

Chennault was a leading proponent of fighting the Japanese by air, and in this capacity he received the ardent support of Chiang Kaishek, who preferred to keep his best troops to blockade the Communists in the Northwest. General Joseph Stilwell, Chennault's immediate superior in China, preferred to prosecute the war on the ground and often blamed China's problems on Chiang Kaishek. The different beliefs on how best to fight the war and over the efficacy of Chiang often embroiled the two men in the internal affairs of China.

Chennault became a spokesperson for Chiang and the Guomindang; he attempted to influence more than the course of the war against the Japanese. This became especially true after the end of the war, when, in 1946, he returned to China to found the Civil Air Transport (CAT), ostensibly an air cargo carrier. He moved from the mainland when Chiang's government went to Taiwan after its defeat in the civil war of 1945–49.

Following the resurrection of the Flying Tigers in the form of the Civil Air Transport, American war planes and CAT pilots flew missions for the Guomindang (GMD) armies for the duration of the civil war. This intervention in the internal conflict continued after the formation of the People's Republic of China (PRC) in 1949, when in the mid-1950s CAT became Air America. As the CIA's airline, it helped to sponsor border armies dedicated to the overthrow of the government of the PRC, and it facilitated the opium trade out of the Golden Triangle as part of its involvement in the Vietnam War. Certain grades of this opium, especially the infamous Tiger and Globe and the Double U-O Globe brands, often ended up on American streets or for use by American soldiers in Vietnam and Thailand.

No one could have foreseen that one legacy of the Flying Tigers would be Air America. One reason for the formation of the Flying Tigers was to strengthen the bond between the United States and the GMD. Chiang and his party could not muster the support garnered by the Chinese Communist Party (CCP), in part because of the nationalism the CCP represented by fighting the Japanese in the countryside. Lacking popular support, certainly among the rural population in China, Chiang and his government relied on outside support, primarily from the United States. The inability of the United States to modify its own agenda in the face of Asian nationalism and self-determination brought it full force into the maelstrom first of Chinese nationalism, and eventually that of Vietnam. Claire Chennault and the Flying Tigers symbolized this inability and the failure of American foreign policy in the region in general.

Edwin Clausen

References

McCoy, Alfred. *The Politics of Heroin in Southeast Asia.* New York, NY: Harper & Row, 1972.

Schaller, Michael. *The United States and China in the Twentieth Century.* New York, NY: Oxford University Press, 1979.

Scott, Robert L. *Flying Tiger: Chennault of China.* New York, NY: Doubleday, 1959.

Chiang Kaishek (Jiang Jieshi, 1887–1975)

Leader of China during the interwar years and World War II, Chiang Kaishek spent the last twenty-six years of his life in de facto exile on the island of Taiwan.

Born to a merchant family in Fenghua, Zhejiang province, Chiang lost his father at the age of nine and was raised by his mother. After attending schools in his home province, he unsuccessfully attempted to pursue his studies in Japan. He returned to China and enrolled in the Baoding Military Academy in 1907. The next year he was sent to Japan again to attend a military school in Tokyo. While there, Chiang became an anti-Manchu revolutionary and joined Sun Yatsen's Tongmenghui. When the Revolution of 1911 erupted, he rushed home and participated in the uprisings in Zhejiang. Chiang soon became a protégé of Chen Qimei, one of Sun's chief assistants in the revolutionary movement. In 1912 he carried out the assassination of Tao Chengzhang, Chen's rival in post-revolutionary Shanghai.

Following the failure of the second revolution against Yuan Shikai and the murder of Chen by Yuan's men, Chiang's political career reached a low point. From 1916 to 1918, with the help of his wealthy fellow-provincials Zhang Jingjiang and Dai Jitao, also followers of Sun Yatsen, Chiang sustained himself by investing in Shanghai's stock market. Meanwhile he offered occasional services to Sun in the latter's repeated attempts to establish an anti-Beijing regime in Canton. When Sun was ousted from Canton by Chen Jiongming in 1922, Chiang immediately went south and fought alongside Sun on board a gunboat. His loyalty was said to have impressed Sun tremendously, and the relationship between the two men was strengthened.

In 1923, Sun established a United Front with Moscow and the Chinese Communist Party (CCP). He sent Chiang to the Soviet Union to study its political and military affairs. Although Chiang was not favorably impressed by what he saw there, this experience enabled him in the following year to become commandant of the new military academy at Whampoa, which was planned and funded with Russian assistance. Heading the Whampoa Academy proved to be a critical political resource in Chiang's later career.

When Sun died in 1925, the hitherto politically insignificant Chiang found his first opportunity to advance himself in the Guomindang (GMD). During the post-Sun succession struggle Chiang's military strength became an enormous asset to him, as he moved quickly up the ladder of power. By late 1925 he was ruling Canton with Wang Jingwei. In March 1926, he ousted Wang in a *coup d'état* known as the Zhongshan Gunboat Incident. The coup was in part aimed at Moscow and the CCP, because Chiang sensed that they supported Wang instead of himself. Yet he also recognized the need for Soviet help to execute his plan of national unification, so he quickly reached a rapprochement with the Left once his power in Canton was consolidated.

In 1926, Chiang launched his Northern Expedition from Canton to reunify the country. Initial success in the campaigns enhanced Chiang's prestige, but also deepened the tension between Chiang and his intra-party rivals, and between the GMD and the CCP. Later that year, anti-Chiang members in the GMD, under the leadership of the Soviet adviser Mikhail Borodin, collaborated with the CCP to move the GMD government from Canton to Wuhan and thereby to reduce Chiang's power. Chiang realized that the United Front had outlived its usefulness to him. In March 1927, his troops took over the Lower Yangtze cities of Nanjing and Shanghai. The alarmed Western powers now promised him assistance that would more than substitute for Soviet aid, on condition that he break up with the Left. In April, Chiang ordered a purge of Communists and leftists from the GMD, having them killed by the thousands, and then founded his own government in Nanjing. Three months later the Wuhan government, out of its own concerns, followed suit. By early 1928 Chiang was again leader of a reunited GMD. In that capacity he completed the final stage of the Northern Expedition, often by concluding deals with regional warlords, and brought China under the GMD banner.

During the "Nanjing Decade" (1927–37), Chiang was the *de facto* ruler of China. His government in Nanjing, however, was threatened by increasing encroachment on Chinese territories by Japan and residual opposition from the regional warlords and the CCP. Chiang's overall strategy was to practice "domestic pacification before external resistance." He made a series of territorial and other concessions to Japan, especially after the Manchurian Incident in 1931, while concentrating on defeating his domestic rivals. Chiang's rapid and ruthless rise to power had produced numerous enemies within the GMD, and throughout the decade they collaborated with the regional warlords to challenge Nanjing. The Beiping regime of 1930, the Canton regime of 1931, the Fujian Rebellion of 1933 and the Guangdong-

Guangxi Incident of 1936 were but the most notable examples of such challenge. Chiang suppressed all of them, using a combination of force and bribery. Meanwhile, from 1930 to 1934, Chiang launched five Bandit-Suppression Campaigns against the Communist base in Jiangxi, eventually forcing the CCP to escape to the Northwest.

The Nanjing government maintained close ties with the Western powers. By marrying the American-educated Soong Meiling (sister of Madame Sun Yatsen) and by converting to Christianity, Chiang himself won Western friendship and support. In the 1930s he became especially interested in Nazi Germany, whose ideological influence and military assistance were evident in his campaigns against the CCP and his New Life movement of 1934. In part with Western help, the Nanjing government developed the infrastructure of China's society and economy. Most of it, however, was limited to the coastal cities, where the GMD control was relatively stable. As a national leader, Chiang showed little understanding or concern for China's rural problems and apparently believed that the Communist influence in the countryside could be eliminated by force alone.

Yet in the short run, the source of the government's unpopularity lay in its weak-kneed policy toward Japan. Most nationalistic Chinese saw Chiang's "pacification first, resistance later" strategy as selfish and unpatriotic. In December 1936, while inspecting troops in Xian, Chiang was placed under house arrest by one of his generals, the former Manchurian warlord Zhang Xueliang. The Xian Incident ended peacefully in two weeks, after Chiang accepted Zhang's demands to stop the anti-Communist campaigns and begin the preparation for a war against Japan.

That war eventually broke out in July 1937. While Chiang suffered disastrous military defeats in the first year of the war, losing almost the entire coastal areas to the invading Japanese, his prestige as the leader of national resistance and salvation rose steadily. A second United Front with the Communists was formed, in which the CCP agreed to support the GMD but was allowed to keep its army. From 1938 to 1941, Chiang's wartime government in Chongqing fought a hard war in the unoccupied territories with little foreign help and scarce resources. The Japanese attack at Pearl Harbor in 1941 came as a timely relief for Chiang. After that, the Chongqing government relied heavily on United States aid for the continuation of the war. Adopting the strategy of "trading space for time," Chiang was able to tie down a large portion of the Japanese forces in China while engaging in as few costly battles with the enemy as possible.

As the GMD-CCP relations worsened after 1941, Chiang devoted at least as much attention to the Communists as that given to the Japanese. He ordered a blockade of the Communist base in Yan'an and kept his best troops and weapons, provided by the United States, for a possible military showdown with the CCP. This policy was a major cause of his clash with the American adviser General Joseph Stilwell in 1944. Nevertheless, Chiang was supported by the United States as China's heroic leader throughout the war. In 1943 he was invited to attend the Cairo Conference with Franklin Roosevelt and Winston Churchill, and China rose to the status of one of the "Big Four."

Upon the Japanese surrender in 1945, Chiang and his government returned triumphantly to Nanjing. The long war, however, had left his Party and army demoralized and corrupt; the rampant inflation in the formerly unoccupied territories now spread to the entire country, and most of north China had fallen into the hands of the CCP. Following one year of unsuccessful negotiations, the civil war between the GMD and the CCP erupted in 1946. In 1948, Chiang was elected as the "Constitutional President" of China, but resigned in less than one year as his government was losing the civil war. In 1949 the GMD government was driven out of the mainland by the CCP. Chiang and remnants of his following found refuge in Taiwan.

The outbreak of the Korean War once again saved Chiang from total defeat. In 1950, the United States, which had given up on Chiang one year earlier, decided to provide military and financial aid to Taiwan as part of a general policy of "containment" against international communism. For the next two decades, American protection and assistance proved to be the most important factor in the survival of Chiang and his government in Taiwan.

On the island, Chiang resumed the presidency, and was "reelected" four times until his death. His government continued to claim sovereignty over the mainland and, with American support, was recognized as the "sole legitimate government of China" by most countries and international organizations before the mid-

1970s. The GMD government was never democratic while it ruled the mainland. Heeding the lesson of 1949 and cognizant of the shrinkage of its territory to a small island, the GMD government tightened its control over the population. Chiang's most trusted assistant was his eldest son, Jingguo, whose secret police ruthlessly suppressed anyone suspected of sympathizing with either the People's Republic on the mainland or the emerging Taiwanese independence movement.

Political stability, American aid, and appropriate development policies produced rapid economic growth in Taiwan during the 1960s and 1970s. In the late 1960s, Chiang initiated the Chinese Cultural Revival movement, an updated version of his New Life movement three decades earlier, in part as an ideological counterattack against Mao Zedong's Cultural Revolution. Yet the international support that Taiwan enjoyed gradually faded. New strategic considerations led the United States to improve relations with the People's Republic in the early 1970s. As a result, Taiwan lost her seat in the United Nations in 1971 and the diplomatic recognitions of many countries, including Japan, thereafter. This was a severe blow to Chiang, whose health was in decline, and he died in 1975. With the demise of Chiang, his dream of "recovering the mainland" also vanished. His leadership on the island was passed to Jingguo.

Few would question the fact that Chiang was a nationalist. He clearly desired and strove for a strong and unified China. In the war years, especially, leadership in the resistance against Japanese aggression made Chiang a symbol of Chinese nationalism in the eyes of millions of Chinese and their Western allies. Yet Chiang's vision of, and approaches to, national reconstruction were limited. A professional soldier, he little appreciated the role of the masses in the political process and often resorted to military or militaristic means to solve the country's problems. At times, he regarded personal power as more important than the interests of his Party, or the latter's benefit as tantamount to the well-being of the entire country. After 1949, his government survived in Taiwan under American protection, not unlike Sun Yatsen's Soviet-backed Canton regime in the early 1920s. Until his death, Chiang maintained that there is only one China, but his opposition to the People's Republic in effect caused a prolonged division of the country.

Wang Ke-wen

References

Eastman, Lloyd E. *The Abortive Revolution: China under Nationalist Rule, 1927–1937*. Cambridge, MA: Harvard University Press, 1972.

———. *Seeds of Destruction: Nationalist China in War and Revolution, 1937–1949*. Stanford, CA: Stanford University Press, 1984.

Loh, Pichon. *The Early Chiang Kai-shek: A Study of His Personality and Politics, 1887–1924*. New York, NY: Columbia University Press, 1971.

China Arise Society (Huaxinghui)

The Huaxinghui was one of the revolutionary societies organized by the student activists at the heels of the Anti-Russia movement in 1903. When the Anti-Russia Volunteer Army was forced to disband in Japan, the radicals turned against the incompetent Qing government and vowed to continue the struggle in China. In late 1903, Huang Hsing, Song Jiaoren, and other returned students met in Changsha, Hunan, to form a revolutionary society under the cover of a mining company called the Huaxing Corporation. On February 15, 1904, the Huaxinghui was formally established, with the election of Huang Hsing as its president.

While there is no record of the society's socioeconomic program, its strongly nationalistic political goal was to overthrow the Qing dynasty. Unlike the Xingzhonghui (Revive China Society), the Huaxinghui did not seek help from foreigners or overseas Chinese. It was an elite organization whose members were mostly Hunanese returned students, many of whom had received some form of military training in Japan. Huang Hsing, in fact, patterned his forces after the Japanese army.

In revolutionary strategy, Huang Hsing advocated regional uprisings. His plan was to start a revolt in Changsha, which would be followed by simultaneous uprisings in the neighboring provinces, so that the revolutionaries would occupy central China to challenge the imperial court in the North. Agents of the society established bases in Hubei, Jiangxi, Zhejiang, Jiangsu, and Sichuan. An affiliated society, the Tongchouhui (Common Enemy Society), was formed to enlist the support of secret societies, especially the Gelaohui (Elder Brothers Society).

The Changsha revolt, arranged for November 16, 1904, on the occasion of Empress Dowager Cixi's birthday celebrations, never took place. One of the members of the society had inadvertently leaked the plot to the local authorities. As the government was searching for the conspirators, Huang Hsing fled to Shanghai where he planned another uprising. The conspiracy ended with his arrest, following an assassination incident in the international settlement. He was released after the police found that he was not implicated in the case. Together with other members of the Huaxinghui, he went to Japan in late 1904.

In Tokyo, Song Jiaoren and Chen Tianhua inaugurated a nationalist journal called the *Twentieth-Century China*. In 1905, when Sun Yatsen arrived in Japan with the idea of forming a united revolutionary organization, Miyazaki Torazo introduced him to the leaders of the Huaxinghui. They supported Sun's plan and joined the new society, the Tongmenghui (Revolutionary Alliance), *en masse*. The Huaxinghui thus ceased to exist after 1905. Its former leaders, especially Huang Hsing, Song Jiaoren, and Chen Tianhua, contributed enormously to the development of the Tongmenghui and the revolutionary movement. The *Twentieth-Century China* was renamed *Minbao (The People's Report)* to become the Tongmenghui's propaganda organ.

Henry Y. S. Chan

References

Hsueh, Chun-tu. *Huang Hsing and the Chinese Revolution*. Stanford, CA: Stanford University Press, 1961.

Liew, K. S. *Struggle for Democracy: Sung Chiao-jen and the 1911 Chinese Revolution*. Berkeley: University of California Press, 1971.

China Merchants' Steam Navigation Company

The China Merchants' Steam Navigation Company, established in 1872, was China's first steamship line. Zhili governor-general and commissioner of Northern Ports Li Hongzhang received imperial sanction to establish the company as an outlet for ships constructed at the Jiangnan Arsenal and the Fuzhou Dockyard, both of which Li urged to convert from military to commercial construction. Li saw the China Merchants' Company as a means to break the monopoly by foreign shipping companies of China's coastal trade. But a commercial challenge to established foreign lines, such as Russell and Company, Butterfield and Swire, and Jardine Matheson, was beyond the capacity of China's emergent capitalists. This led Li to propose government-merchant cooperation in a loose organizational structure, which had been previously employed by state monopolies, known as *Guandu Shangban* (government supervised merchant enterprises). Private investors provided the funding, and the government extended official sponsorship, supervision, and loans.

From 1873 to 1885, management was entrusted to two merchant investors, Tong Kingsing (Tang Tingshu) and Xu Run. In 1885, management fell into the hands of Sheng Xuanhuai, an official with strong merchant connections, who held control until 1902. In 1909, official supervision passed from the commissioner of Northern Ports to the ministry of Posts and Communications. Following the establishment of the Republic in 1912, the China Merchants' Steam Navigation Company operated essentially as a private concern subject to intermittent government intervention. Then, from 1927 to 1933, it was reorganized and taken over by the Guomindang government. During World War II, company headquarters relocated from Shanghai to Hong Kong and ultimately to China's wartime capital in Chongqing. Postwar assets included 460 vessels exceeding 330,000 tons. Although the new Communist government took over the China Merchants' Steam Navigation Company in 1949, it was reestablished as a wholly government-owned and operated company by the Guomindang government in Taiwan.

The China Merchants' Steam Navigation Company was an early manifestation of economic nationalism. It represented a broadening of the scope of self-strengthening from the purely government-owned national defense industries of the 1860s to privately-owned enterprises designed to break the stranglehold of foreign powers on the Chinese economy. To aid the China Merchants' Company in its struggle against foreign competition, the Qing government granted a monopoly on the transport of tribute rice from the Yangtze delta to Tianjin. In 1877, when vessels constructed in domestic yards proved unsuited for commercial use, the company acquired the fleet of the American-owned Shanghai Steam Navigation Company to accommodate its expanding activities. The draining of profits by management and stockholders, however, limited the growth of the company's fleet and inhibited the expansion of operations. Moreover, competition from foreign companies intensified, and their share of China's domestic shipping increased sharply into the early twentieth century.

Thomas L. Kennedy

References

Feuerwerker, Albert. *China's Early Industrialization: Sheng Hsuan-huai (1844–1916) and Mandarin Enterprise.* Cambridge, MA: Harvard University Press, 1958.

China White Paper

By the end of 1949, the political waters in the United States were tempestuous and the impending victory of the Chinese Communist Party in the Chinese civil war exacerbated the situation. Opponents of the Truman administration, mostly Republican, attacked the government for what they considered to be a lackluster performance in support of the Guomindang and Chiang Kaishek. Further, an anti-Communist mood that set the stage for the McCarthy hysteria swirled across the country, as Whittaker Chambers accused Alger Hiss, Judith Coplon was accused of conspiracy, and eleven Communist Party members faced a Smith Act trial in New York City.

This acrimonious setting characterized the temperament of the time and was the context which spawned the "China White Paper." In part to counter Republican charges of a "failure in China" and to distance itself from claims of being soft on Communism in Asia and at home, the U.S. State Department, following directions from President Harry Truman and Secretary of State Dean Acheson, compiled a voluminous report justifying American policies in China, with special emphasis on the 1944 to 1949 period. The two-volume report, issued in August 1949, is mostly a compilation of documents or excerpts from documents, all taken from the files of the State Department. The report is introduced by a "Letter of Transmittal," written by Secretary of State Acheson.

At its core, the report placed the blame for the victory of the Chinese Communists squarely on the shoulders of Chiang Kaishek and the Guomindang, citing rampant incompetence, corruption, and borderline totalitarianism. The conclusion was that the United States could do nothing for a government that alienated its people, despite the fact that it had tried to give it all the support it could. The only alternative was full-scale military intervention, something the report deemed unthinkable. The authors of the report concluded that such an invasion would have created massive Chinese resistance, engendered the disapproval of most Americans, and would have constituted a reversal of traditional American policy.

In his letter of transmittal, Acheson seemed to affirm the futility of American intervention, while at the same time trying to appease right-wing critics. The Secretary of State wrote that "[t]he unfortunate but inescapable fact is that the ominous result of the civil war in China was beyond the control of the government of the United States. . . . It was a product of internal Chinese forces, forces which this country tried to influence but could not." Almost in the same breath, Acheson went on to characterize the Communists in terms most nefarious, depicting them as destroyers of Chinese culture, civilization, and of a supposed special friendship that had existed between China and the United States. He concluded that the Communists were pawns of a foreign country (Soviet Union), and without being explicit, he dismissed Chinese nationalism and the fact that for over one hundred years China had been struggling to regain its sovereignty. The importance of Chinese nationalism was quickly lost in the political scramble to appear in step with the emerging anti-Communism.

Reacting to what he perceived to be a misrepresentation of history and reality by the United States, Mao Zedong wrote five articles (the last five articles in Volume IV in his *Selected Works*) repudiating Acheson's conclusions. Mao contended that the United States refused to recognize the right of nations to self-determination and depicted the primary thrust of imperialism as the attempt to destroy socialism. The "White Paper," and especially Acheson's introduction, rubbed Chinese nationalism and China's historical sensitivity to imperialism the wrong way.

Mao's repudiation of the "White Paper" came only after repeated attempts to keep Communist China's options open. Mao and other Chinese leaders, including Zhou Enlai, attempted to keep communications open with Americans and to explore alternatives to "leaning to one side." George Kennan, author of the 1947 "Mr. X" article, counseled American flexibility in the face of Chinese explorations. But

Acheson seemed intractable, even before the "White Paper" was issued. He had ordered American diplomats in China not to respond to any Chinese overtures. In fact, two weeks before the publication of the "White Paper," Acheson had appointed a special State Department committee to review contingencies for stopping "the extension of communist domination on the continent of Asia or in the Southeast Asia area." He instructed the committee through one of its members to be sure that "we are neglecting no opportunities that would be within our capabilities to achieve the purpose of halting the spread of totalitarian communism in Asia."

With the Republican right, led by such notables as Walter Judd and Senators William Knowland and H. Styles Bridges, leading the charge and McCarthyism just around the corner, any rational assessment of nationalism and revolution in Asia fell by the wayside. The words of Walter Lippmann, who questioned how the United States could have given so much support to the Guomindang in the first place, fell on deaf ears. The political environment in the United States precluded any attempts to understand the strength of nationalism in Asia; hostility toward China after 1949 eventually translated into war in Korea and in Vietnam. Asian nationalism fell prey to American ideological rigidity and United States designs for a post-World War II "new world order."

Edwin Clausen

References

Department of State. *The China White Paper.* Originally issued as *United States Relations with China with Special Reference to the Period 1944–1949,* 2 vols. Stanford, CA: Stanford University Press, 1967.

Dulles, Foster Rhea. *American Policy Toward Communist China: The Historical Record, 1949–1969.* New York, NY: Crowell, 1972.

Schaller, Michael. *The United States and China in the Twentieth Century.* New York, NY: Oxford University Press, 1979.

China's Destiny

China's Destiny (Zhongguo zhi minyun) is a long treatise published in 1943 that represents the clearest and most systematic articulation of the nationalist ideas of Chiang Kaishek. The treatise was published, in book form, under Chiang's name, but it is widely believed to have been penned by his secretary Tao Xisheng with careful guidance from Chiang himself. It soon became required reading for Guomindang members, government employees, and students. A revised edition, with minor changes, appeared in 1944.

Divided into eight chapters, the treatise is in part an interpretive narration of the recent history of China and in part a platform for her "revolutionary reconstruction." It displays strong Han nationalism in its description of the cultural and historical roots of the "Chinese nation" *(Zhonghua minzu)* and even stronger anti-imperialism in its criticism of the unequal treaties that had been imposed on China by the West since the Opium War (1840–42). It also laments the westernization trends that resulted from the May Fourth movement of 1919. The movement, it argues, helped to spread communism and liberalism in China, both of which disrupted the Chinese social order and undermined her national spirit. Echoing his ideological mentor Dai Jitao, Chiang supports the revival of traditional (Confucian) values as the foundation of the Chinese state. The treatise concludes by suggesting that only Sun Yatsen's Three Peoples' Principles, representing the best of old and new in China, could guide the country to her proper destiny.

The purpose of publishing the treatise was apparently to celebrate the abolition of the unequal treaties in 1942 and to deliver a warning to the Chinese Communists, whose relations with Chiang's government were deteriorating. As a Chinese leader who had been relying heavily on Western support since the late 1920s, and even more so since the outbreak of the war, however, Chiang demonstrated a degree of anti-Western sentiment that was surprising to many. Yet it may have been an unusually candid expression of his true feelings and beliefs with regard to China's place in the world. Together with *China's Destiny*, Chiang published another treatise titled *Chinese Economic Theory*, but the latter was soon withdrawn from circulation because of its questionable arguments.

Wang Ke-wen

References

Chiang Kai-shek. *China's Destiny & Chinese Economic Theory.* Notes and commentary, Philip Jaffe. New York, NY: Roy Publishers, 1947.

Chinese Communist Party (Zhongguo Gongchandang)

The party that led the Communist revolution during the 1920s to the 1940s and the ruling party of the Chinese mainland since 1949 is known as the Chinese Communist Party (CCP).

The Chinese Communist Party was founded by a group of intellectuals in 1921, in the midst of the radicalism of the post–May Fourth era, with the assistance of the Comintern. Its founding leaders were Chen Duxiu and Li Dazhao, professor and library curator, respectively, of the prestigious Beijing University. Shortly after its organization, the CCP received instructions from the Comintern to form a United Front with a much more experienced and well-known political group, the Guomindang (GMD) under Sun Yatsen, by joining the GMD as individuals. With some reluctance the CCP obeyed.

The years of the first United Front (1923–27) proved to be enormously beneficial to the young CCP. Sharing the GMD's base in Guangdong, the Communists experimented with their theories of mass mobilization while learning political skills from its senior partner in the alliance. Under the guidance of the Soviet advisers to the GMD, especially Mikhail Borodin, the CCP expanded rapidly within the GMD.

From 1924 to 1926, the CCP membership grew from a few hundred to nearly 20,000.

The development alarmed the GMD and, soon after Sun Yatsen's death in 1925, tension between the two parties turned into open conflict, which was galvanized by a post-Sun succession struggle in the GMD. In 1927, during the Northern Expedition, the United Front collapsed. Chiang Kaishek, the new leader of the GMD, surprised the CCP by launching a bloody purge of his Communist allies in Shanghai, having thousands killed. Before the year's end the CCP was forced underground and its membership diminished from over 60,000 to fewer than 10,000.

The first general secretary of the Party, Chen Duxiu, was blamed and punished by Moscow for this debacle, although much of it was in fact caused by the miscalculation of Stalin. In the late 1920s the CCP was in disarray. Its confused leadership, first under Qu Qiubai and then under Li Lisan, attempted a series of abortive urban uprisings while a few others developed armed bases in China's countryside. Among the latter, the base at Jinggang Mountains, Jiangxi, established by Mao Zedong and Zhu De, was the most successful. Mao's strategy of combining guerrilla warfare

C

Communist leaders in the early 1960s: (left to right) Zhu De, Zhou Enlai, Mao Zedong, Liu Shaoqi. (Xinhua News Agency.)

with land revolution attracted poor peasants to form the new basis of the Communist revolution in China and soon proved to be the only way for the CCP to fight a protracted civil war against the ruling GMD. As a result, Mao's influence in the Party increased; in 1931 he was elected chairman of the Chinese Soviet Republic in Jiangxi.

In the early 1930s, the pro-Moscow leadership of the CCP challenged Mao's power as well as his rural strategy. The "internationalists," led by Wang Ming, who controlled the Party center and regarded Mao's peasant revolution as unorthodox and opportunistic, briefly eclipsed Mao's leadership in Jiangxi during 1933 to 1935. Meanwhile, the Jiangxi Soviet was the target of five Bandit-Suppression Campaigns waged by Chiang Kaishek between 1930 and 1934. Mao's peasant guerrillas successfully repelled the first four attacks, but in 1934 were defeated by the fifth offensive. Abandoning its Jiangxi base, the CCP embarked on the Long March across half of China. At Zunyi in 1935, in the middle of the march, Mao blamed the recent failure on the "internationalists" and seized the Party leadership. Henceforth, for the next forty years, he remained the supreme leader of the CCP. In late 1935, after marching six thousand miles and losing 90 percent of the original force, the CCP relocated itself in the northwestern province of Shaanxi. The pursuing GMD army soon besieged this new CCP base.

The mounting crisis in Sino-Japanese relations saved the CCP from total extermination by the GMD government. As the government's policy of "domestic pacification before external resistance" caused widespread dissatisfaction among the nationalistic Chinese, the CCP shrewdly exploited the anti-Japanese feelings in the country and demanded national solidarity against Japanese aggression. The call, which also complied with the new Moscow strategy, gained sympathy and support from many educated urban Chinese. After the Xian Incident of 1936, Chiang Kaishek finally agreed to stop his anti-CCP campaigns and prepare for war against Japan. When the Sino-Japanese War broke out in 1937, the CCP formed another United Front with the GMD government and participated in the war effort.

During the war, the Communists concentrated their main attention on expanding their own territorial base and military strength. Moderating the land revolution of the Jiangxi period, the Party now formulated a program that included tax and rent reductions, democratic reforms, and mass mobilization (the "mass line") to attract sustained peasant approval. With this support, it established a number of border-region governments in the vast areas nominally under Japanese occupation.

Again, the expansion of the CCP alarmed the GMD. In 1940 the GMD-CCP rivalry culminated in the New Fourth Army Incident in southern Anhui, and after that the wartime United Front existed only in name. The GMD forces imposed a blockade on the CCP base in Yan'an and prevented the CCP from sharing any of the American aid that began to arrive after the outbreak of World War II. Nevertheless, as the GMD government became increasingly corrupt and demoralized during the last years of the war, the vigorous CCP came to represent the hope of a new China in the eyes of many. Party membership rose from 40,000 in 1937 to 1.2 million in 1945. In the meantime, the CCP took measures to strengthen ideological unity as well as the leadership of Mao Zedong in the Party. The Rectification campaign of 1942 to 1945 enforced Party discipline with terror tactics throughout the Communist areas, which tranformed the newly recruited urban intellectuals into loyal Party members. "Mao Zedong thought" was formally accepted as the new orthodoxy of Party ideology.

By the end of the war, the CCP controlled most of the rural areas in north and central China, and commanded an armed force of nearly one million. Most scholars have now rejected the thesis that attributes the Communist victory in China to "peasant nationalism." Separately, however, "peasant" and "nationalism" were indeed the keys to the wartime success of the CCP, which in turn was crucial to its triumph in 1949.

On October 1, 1949, the CCP founded the People's Republic at Beijing after easily defeating the GMD in the civil war of 1945–1949. In its own words, the Party was now "entering the cities," commencing the new task of national administration and socialist reconstruction. In the early 1950s, the Party built an extensive network of branches (bureaus and committees) throughout the country, from the Party center down to the grass-roots level, for the effective mobilization and control of the population. Party membership, meanwhile, increased from 4.5 million in 1950 to 6.2 million in 1953 and cadres with professional training quickly replaced the uneducated guerrilla soldiers.

As the Party's power became consolidated and its popularity peaked, in part as a result of land reform and the Korean War, Mao's leadership in the Party also became dictatorial. In the second half of the 1950s, Mao imposed his will on the Party and launched the Hundred Flowers campaign, the Anti-Rightist Campaign and the Great Leap Forward, resulting in the alienation of intellectuals and peasants from the Party. The summary purge of Peng Dehuai, who criticized Mao's campaigns at the Lushan Conference of 1959, further established the chairman's absolute authority.

Mao and the Chinese Communist movement had maintained only tenuous ties with Moscow from the mid-1930s to its victory in 1949. During the first decade of its existence, facing hostility from the West, the People's Republic reluctantly "leaned to one side," *i.e.,* to the Soviet Union, in the international community. This position severely compromised the nationalist appeal that had brought the CCP to power. As soon as Mao's government was able to stand on its own, therefore, the CCP broke with Moscow. After 1960, until the Sino-American rapprochement in the early 1970s, the CCP was isolated from almost all of the world's major powers. In the meantime, the People's Republic claimed leadership among the Third World countries. Mao's rural strategy served as a model for leftist revolutionary movements throughout Southeast Asia, Latin America, and Africa.

After the disaster of the Great Leap Forward Mao temporarily yielded power to the more realistic Liu Shaoqi and Deng Xiaoping, who soon resurrected the gradualist approach to economic development of the early 1950s. But Mao still held the CCP chairmanship and soon became the object of an intensive personal cult. By the mid-1960s, Mao had concluded that the bureaucratized Party, now with 17 million members, had ceased to be an effective instrument in continuing his revolution in China. In 1966 he started the Great Proletarian Cultural Revolution, calling on the youthful Red Guards to attack the "capitalist roaders," namely, Liu, Deng and their followers, in the Party. Within months, not only a majority of the old Party leadership was destroyed but the entire Party machine was paralyzed by the violent purges from outside—ordered by its own chairman. Soon the CCP branches at all levels were replaced by "Revolutionary Committees," which were dominated by

Maoist radicals. A group of loyal supporters of Mao, including Mao's wife Jiang Qing, took over the Party center.

In 1969, Mao designated Lin Biao, whose People's Liberation Army had helped Mao to restore order in the country after the initial chaos of the Cultural Revolution, as vice-chairman of the Party and his "revolutionary successor." Yet a power struggle soon surfaced between Lin and Jiang, leading to the sudden death and denunciation of Lin in 1971. Following the crisis, Mao felt it necessary to rebuild the old Party structure and reestablish some of the purged leaders, such as Deng Xiaoping. In the first half of the 1970s, as senility prevented Mao from supervising daily administration, another intra-Party rivalry between the "moderates" under Deng Xiaoping and the "radicals" under Jiang Qing erupted.

The moderates eventually triumphed after Mao's death in 1976. With the backing of the military, Deng and his followers purged Jiang's faction, now labeled the "Gang of Four," and seized the Party leadership. Following a brief interregnum under Hua Guofeng's chairmanship, Deng assumed full control over the Party in 1979. He dissolved the Red Guards and abolished the "Revolutionary Committees." In the early 1980s, Deng launched his "Party consolidation" *(zhengdang)* to cleanse the CCP, whose membership totaled 48 million by the end of the decade, of the radical influence of the Cultural Revolution. A reregistration of Party membership took place, more younger cadres were brought into the Party leadership, and the post of general secretary was restored to replace the chairmanship instituted for Mao in 1945. The CCP also abandoned the Maoist campaigns and focused instead on the orderly implementation of the "four modernizations" and market-oriented economic reforms.

Economic growth, decentralization of power, and the "open-up" policy in the 1980s, however, led to a liberalization of the society and the undermining of the CCP's monopoly over resources. Concern over the pace of reform and the issue of Party control once more divided the Party into conservatives and reformers. To balance himself between the two camps, and thereby maintain his supreme leadership, Deng Xiaoping was forced to purge his own followers: Hu Yaobang in 1987 and Zhao Ziyang in 1989. The new prosperity also created opportunities for Party corruption. Between 1987 and 1989 over 100,000 CCP members suffered punishments for having violated discipline. The Tiananmen Incident of 1989 further eroded the legitimacy of the Party as China's ruler. Into the 1990s, the CCP faced a worsening "crisis of faith" among its own members and a "crisis of confidence" among the Chinese people. Deng's death in 1997 also resulted in a new crisis in Party leadership.

Wang Ke-wen

References

Ch'i, Hsi-sheng. *Politics of Disillusionment: The Chinese Communist Party under Deng Xiaoping, 1978–1989*. New York, NY: M. E. Sharpe, 1992.

Dittmer, Lowell. *China's Continuing Revolution: The Post-Liberation Epoch, 1949–1981*. Berkeley: University of California Press, 1987.

Harrison, James P. *The Long March to Power: A History of the Chinese Communist Party, 1921–1972*. New York, NY: Macmillan, 1972.

Chinese Eastern Railway Incident

The Chinese Eastern Railway, which extended the Trans-Siberian Railway across northern Manchuria to Vladivostok, had been ceded to Russian control since its construction during the late Qing. In 1924, a Sino-Soviet agreement established joint management of the railway by the two countries, but the local authorities in Manchuria often complained about Soviet propaganda and trade-union activities along the railway. As China was nominally unified under the anti-Communist government of the Guomindang (GMD) in 1928, the national and regional (Manchurian) leaders decided to regain control of the railway from the Soviet Union.

In May 1929, Zhang Xueliang, the *de facto* ruler of Manchuria, ordered the search of the Soviet Consulate in Harbin and the arrest of thirty-nine consulate employees on charges of suspected subversive activities. He also closed down the trade union of the Chinese Eastern Railway. The Soviet Union immediately issued a protest and demanded the release of its personnel. The GMD government in Nanjing supported Zhang's action. Chiang Kaishek, the government leader, visited north China personally and reinforced the defense along the Sino-Soviet border. In early July, Zhang's Northeastern (Manchurian) Army seized control of the railway and expelled all of its high-ranking Russian employees. His regional government then officially declared the recovery of Chinese ownership of the railway and abolished the Russian-owned agencies in Manchuria, including the bureaus of telegraph service, commercial shipping, gas supply, and commerce.

On July 14, Moscow warned the Chinese government to redress its actions with an ultimatum, and three days later it broke off diplomatic relations with China. On July 20, Soviet troops crossed the Sino-Soviet border in northern Manchuria and attacked Chinese positions along three routes. The Northeastern Army soon collapsed and retreated. Military setbacks forced the GMD government to seek international help. Through the mediation of Great Britain, France, and the United States, Chinese and Soviet representatives entered negotiations. The GMD government still tried to retain some of the rights it had recovered by force, but Moscow was uncompromising and continued its military actions.

In November Chiang Kaishek faced another warlord rebellion in China, whereupon the Manchurian authorities assumed the responsibility of negotiations. On December 22, the two parties signed an agreement at the border town of Khabarovsk. Under the agreement, peace was restored and the Soviet troops withdrew to their positions before the conflict. The difficult issue of the Chinese Eastern Railway was left to a formal Sino-Soviet conference, to be convened at a later date. The GMD government, however, declared the agreement null and void because it had been concluded without Nanjing's approval. After a lengthy stalemate, negotiations between Nanjing and Moscow resumed in October 1930, yet it did not reach any conclusion before the Japanese conquest of Manchuria in September 1931.

Several factors contributed to the outbreak of the Chinese Eastern Railway Incident. The GMD government in Nanjing was in a frenzied anti-Communist mood after the collapse of the first GMD-CCP United Front in 1927. Chiang Kaishek welcomed any excuse to sever ties with his former Soviet ally. Moreover, the new government was experimenting with the so-called "revolutionary diplomacy" at the time, which advocated a forceful approach to the recovery of China's sovereign rights that had been lost to the various foreign powers in the unequal treaties. Zhang Xueliang, who had just succeeded his father Zhang Zuolin as ruler of Manchuria in 1928, capitalized on these developments to create the crisis. Less experienced than the old Zhang in dealing with Soviet influence in his region, the "Young Marshal" hoped to establish himself as an anti-imperialist and anti-Communist leader with a militant action against the Russians.

Both Zhang and Nanjing overestimated their own strength. The quick defeat of the Northeastern Army demonstrated the weakness of China's national defenses. In order to regain China's national independence, the GMD government had to strengthen its military forces, which indeed became one of its main efforts in the following years. The Sino-Soviet negotiation in 1929 also convinced Nanjing that the international community felt little sympathy for its "revolutionary diplomacy." It soon shelved the policy. The incident, however, had certain positive side-effects for China. By assisting Zhang Xueliang's initial actions, and by rejecting the agreement which he later concluded, the GMD government succeeded in extending a degree of its influence into Manchuria, a region over which it had no control previously.

Wang Ke-wen

References

Iriye, Akira. *After Imperialism: The Search for a New Order in the Far East, 1921–1931.* Cambridge, MA: Harvard University Press, 1965.

Tang, Peter S. H. *Russian and Soviet Policy in Manchuria and Outer Mongolia, 1911–1931.* Durham, NC: Duke University Press, 1959.

Chinese Maritime Customs

The Chinese Maritime Customs Service was probably the most influential of the Sino-foreign hybrids that grew up under the treaty system during the century after the Opium War. Growing out of the unresolved problems following the Treaty of Nanjing (1842), and the problems besetting the Yangtze valley during the Taiping Rebellion (1851–64), its origin can be seen in the foreign inspectorate of Customs established by the consuls in Shanghai in 1853. After the Treaty of Tianjin (1858), Horatio Nelson Lay was appointed chief commissioner of customs and began to spread the Shanghai model to the other open ports. Promoted to inspector-general in 1861, he was dismissed two years later, and his deputy, Robert Hart, took his place, moving the customs administration from Shanghai to Beijing in 1865.

Under Hart, the customs expanded beyond mere revenue collection, taking under its jurisdiction questions of pilotage, aids to navigation, as well as river conservancy measures. In 1896, the government created a national post office under the inspector-general's supervision, a measure that Hart and such reformist officials as Li Hongzhang had been urging for years.

Insisting that he served China, and not the foreign powers, Hart built the customs into a service that provided Beijing with a reliable revenue, and that was also a force for the maintenance of imperial authority at a time when centrifugal tendencies were loosening Beijing's hold on the provinces. He also sought to maintain the integrity of the customs against the challenges presented by the increasing demands by foreigners for economic and territorial concessions and the growth of spheres of influence. Moreover, by the early twentieth century, the customs revenues became pledged in their entirety to repay the foreign loans and indemnities to which China now became subject.

It fell to Hart's successor, Sir Francis Aglen (1908–27) to try to hold the administration together during the Revolution of 1911, and the period of disunion that followed. It was a trying time, when various local authorities sought to gain access to the customs revenues, and when China took its first steps toward tariff autonomy, although the Special Conference on the Chinese Tariff (1925–26) failed to make much progress. In 1927, after Aglen fell out with the Guomindang authorities, Sir Frederick Maze became inspector-general, and it was he who dealt with the questions posed by the restoration of tariff autonomy, and by the Japanese invasion of 1937. He was forced then to make a controversial agreement in 1938 to place the revenues collected in occupied ports in Japanese banks. After the outbreak of the Pacific War in 1941, Japan seized control of the coastal customs, and Maze moved his office to southwestern China, where the Guomindang still ruled. In 1943, the American Lester Little succeeded Maze as the last of the foreign inspector-generals. He gave up his post at the end of the war.

The Chinese Maritime Customs, although in a sense dominated by the British, has nonetheless been called the first international civil service. While nationalists might see it as a symbol of foreign control over Chinese revenues, it was, in the minds of its directors at any rate, an agency devoted to the orderly maintenance of Chinese trade, and therefore an agency working ultimately for China's good and advancement.

Nicholas R. Clifford

References

Wright, Stanley F. *China's Struggle for Tariff Autonomy.* Shanghai: Inspectorate General of Customs, 1938.

———. *Hart and the Chinese Customs.* Belfast: Wm. Mullan, 1950.

Chinese Nationalist Party

See GUOMINDANG, 1919–

Chinese Representation Question in the United Nations

The Republic of China (ROC) was an original member of the United Nations and a permanent member of the Security Council. On October 1, 1949, the victorious Chinese Communist forces proclaimed in Beijing the establishment of the People's Republic of China (PRC). On November 18, 1949, the PRC requested that the United Nations immediately deprive the ROC delegation of "all rights to further represent the Chinese people in the United Nations" and demanded that its own delegation be seated in the United Nations. Thus began a twenty-two-year struggle between two rival Chinese governments over the Chinese representation question in the United Nations. On December 8, 1949, the ROC government moved to Taibei, Taiwan, and has been there ever since.

Until 1961, the General Assembly of the United Nations decided not to place the Chinese representation question on the agenda of the General Assembly for debate, thereby permitting the ROC delegation to retain its seat in the General Assembly. Between 1961 and 1970, the General Assembly formally included this question on its agenda, but annually decided that this item was an "important question" under Article 18 of the United Nations Charter, thereby making any Assembly decision on it subject to a two-thirds vote. In view of this arrangement, the Albanian proposal of "Restoration of All the Rights of the People's Republic of China and the Expulsion of the Representatives of Chiang Kaishek" was annually defeated.

In August 1971, the United States and several other states proposed a "dual representation" approach to the Chinese representation question, which would seat the PRC in the Security Council, but both the PRC and the ROC would serve in all other United Nations organs. However, on October 25, 1971, the General Assembly, by a vote of 55 in favor to 58 against (with 15 abstentions), rejected a United States-sponsored draft resolution that requested the General Assembly to declare any proposal, which would result in depriving the ROC of representation in the United Nations, to be an important question under Article 18 of the Charter requiring a two-thirds majority vote.

Then, the General Assembly by a vote of 76 in favor to 35 against (with 17 abstentions), adopted an Albanian-sponsored proposal, as resolution 2758 (XXVI), of restoring all rights to the PRC and of recognizing the representatives of the PRC government as the only legitimate representation of China to the United Nations. The resolution also called for the United Nations to expel forthwith the representatives of "Chiang Kaishek" [i.e., the ROC] from the United Nations and all the related UN organizations.

The representatives of the ROC responded by withdrawing from the United Nations before the General Assembly voted on this resolution. From then on, the PRC took over the Chinese seats in the United Nations and all related UN organizations. Since 1993, the ROC has started a campaign to restore its participation in the United Nations, but is encountering strong opposition from the PRC.

Hungdah Chiu

References

Chiu, Hungdah. "Communist China's Attitude Toward the United Nations: A Legal Analysis." *American Journal of International Law* 62, no. 1 (January 1968): 33–37.

"China." *UN Monthly Chronicle* 8, no. 10 (November 1971): 34–61.

"The Membership of the Republic of China in the United Nations." *Chinese Yearbook of International Law and Affairs* 11 (1991–92): 271–6.

Chinese Revolutionary Party

In August 1913, following the failure of the Second Revolution against Yuan Shikai, Sun Yatsen led members of the parliamentary

Guomindang into another exile in Japan. Sun decided to regroup his followers, continue the anti-Yuan effort, and plan for a third revolution. He reorganized the parliamentary Guomindang into the Chinese Revolutionary Party (Zhonghua gemingdang) and began to recruit new members in September. On June 22, 1914, the Chinese Revolutionary Party held its first congress in Tokyo. Representatives from eighteen provinces in China elected Sun as the Party's "leader" (zongli); Sun assumed office on July 8.

The Party headquarters at Tokyo included five departments: General Management, Party Affairs, Military Affairs, Political Affairs, and Foreign Affairs. Party branches were established in various provinces and major cities in China, with additional Revolutionary Army Commands formed in important regions or provinces to direct anti-Yuan uprisings. The Party also had branches and fund-raising agencies outside of China. The domestic Party branches were to launch military revolts, while those overseas were to support the revolts with financial contributions. Between 1914 and 1915 the Party recruited about three thousand members.

The Chinese Revolutionary Party arose as a reaction against the parliamentary Guomindang of the early Republic. In contrast to the loosely organized Guomindang, the new Party drastically tightened its organization and discipline. This was evidenced especially by the nearly dictatorial power enjoyed by the Party leader. The Party not only gave the leader (Sun) full authority to organize members and appoint officers at all levels, but also required every member to pledge a loyalty oath to the Leader, which had to be certified with a seal and fingerprints. Moreover, the Party constitution established three types of Party members, according to their date of entry, and gave these "original," "assisting," and "ordinary" members differing privileges. All of these arrangements were based on Sun's idea of "Party rule." The Chinese Revolutionary Party was to forfeit parliamentary politics and become a secret organization, working to establish one-party dictatorship in China. Many former members of the old Guomindang, including Huang Hsing, Li Liejun, Bo Wenwei, and Zhu Zhixin, either refused to join the new Party or decided to organize separate groups on their own. The revolutionaries thus split.

Japan's presentation of the Twenty-One Demands to Yuan Shikai's government in January 1915 mobilized the nationalist sentiment of the Chinese and created a general feeling of the need for national solidarity. Many former Guomindang members, such as those who had organized the Society for the Study of European Affairs (Oushi yanjiuhui), publicly called for the cessation of internal strife and national unity in the face of external threat. Although Sun Yatsen maintained his own Japanese connections, he ordered the Chinese Revolutionary Party to issue announcements disclosing the secret dealings that Yuan had with the Japanese. On May 9, Yuan accepted most of the Twenty-One Demands, which disillusioned the Chinese public. Those who had initially disagreed with Sun's anti-Yuan strategies gradually changed their minds. At the same time, Sun relaxed the rules of the Chinese Revolutionary Party to allow those who held contentious views to become members. As a result the Party's anti-Yuan military operations in Shanghai, Shandong, and Guangdong gained strength after 1915.

In 1916, Yuan's attempt to make himself an emperor provoked the revolt of the National Protection Army in Yunnan. The Chinese Revolutionary Party immediately joined the revolt. Following Yuan's death, the Party moved its headquarters from Tokyo to Shanghai and soon engaged in the Constitution Protection movement (Hufa yundong) to oppose the Beiyang government in Beijing. In October 1919, Sun reorganized the Party into the Chinese Nationalist Party (Guomindang).

Lu Fang-shang

References

Friedman, Edward. *Backward toward Revolution: The Chinese Revolutionary Party, 1914–1916.* Berkeley: University of California Press, 1974.

Yu, George T. *Party Politics in Republican China: The Kuomintang, 1912–1924.* Berkeley: University of California Press, 1966.

Chinese Youth Party

The Chinese Youth Party (Zhongguo qingniandang) was a partial successor to the Young China Association of the May Fourth period. The association split along ideological lines in the early 1920s as a result of the radicalization of the Chinese intelligentsia. In 1921, the Chinese Communist Party (CCP) was formed with the assistance of the leftist members of the association. To counter the CCP influence, a group of anti-Communist members of the association, then studying in France under the work-study program *(qingong jianxue)*, organized the Chinese Nationalist Youth Corps *(Zhongguo guojiazhuyi qingniantuan)* in 1923. In 1929 the organization was renamed the Chinese Youth Party. Its leader was Zeng Qi; important members included He Luzhi, Li Huang, Zuo Shunsheng, Chen Qitian, and Yu Jiaju.

The Chinese Youth Party advocated the doctrine of *guojia zhuyi*, which may be translated as "nationalism," as a repudiation of the Communist proposal of "internationalism." It did not use the common Chinese translation of "nationalism," *minzu zhuyi*, probably because the latter term had been used by Sun Yatsen's Guomindang (GMD). Perceiving itself to be the carrier of the May Fourth nationalist tradition, the Party summarized its political objectives by reiterating a popular May Fourth movement slogan, *neichu guozei waikang qiangquan* (eliminate domestic traitors and resist foreign oppressors). It vowed to strive for a unified and independent China, and attacked the CCP as an instrument of Russian imperialism. The Party also supported a democratic political system and a middle-of-the-road economic system that was neither capitalist nor socialist.

A weekly, *The Awaking Lion (Xingshi),* founded in Shanghai in 1924, served as the Party's organ. Throughout most of the 1920s, the Party engaged in a hard political battle, in China as well as in Europe, against the emerging GMD-CCP United Front. It sided with the Beiyang warlords during the GMD's Northern Expedition, and continued to oppose the GMD even after the latter had broken with the CCP and nominally unified the country. From 1927 to 1934, the Party criticized the GMD's one-party dictatorship and was therefore suppressed by the Nanjing government. In the wake of the Manchurian Incident in 1931, the Party made an unsuccessful attempt to organize an anti-Japanese army in north China.

The Chinese Youth Party finally reached a rapprochement with the ruling GMD in the mid-1930s. When the Sino-Japanese War broke out in 1937, the Party supported the anti-Japanese United Front led by the GMD. In 1938 it participated in the GMD government's People's Political Council, whose members also included Chinese Communists. Meanwhile, Zeng Qi stayed in the occupied territories and was reportedly in contact with Wang Jingwei's pro-Japanese regime. In 1941,

following the *de facto* GMD-CCP schism, the Party joined with a few other minor parties to form the Democratic League, designed as an independent force between the two major parties. Zuo Shunsheng was elected as the league's secretary-general.

During the initial postwar years, the Party was an active member of the Chinese People's Political Consultative Conference, which tried to mediate between the GMD and the CCP and establish a multiparty government for China. When that plan failed and the civil war ensued, the Party, still bitterly anti-Communist, declared its loyalty to the GMD and participated in the GMD's "constitutional government" in 1947. It ceased to resist the trend of polarization in Chinese politics.

In 1949, the Chinese Youth Party followed the GMD to Taiwan. On the island it served as a window-dressing for the constitutional structure of the GMD rule, receiving regular subsidies from the government. A few of its members, however, did have occasional involvement in opposition politics. The Party has been weak and divided during the past four decades.

Wang Ke-wen

References

Chan, Lau Kit-ching. *The Chinese Youth Party, 1923–1945.* Hong Kong: University of Hong Kong Press, 1972.

Fung, Edmund S. K. "The Alternative of Loyal Opposition: The Chinese Youth Party and Chinese Democracy, 1937–1949." *Modern China* 17, no. 2 (April 1991): 260–89.

Levine, Marilyn A. *The Found Generation: Chinese Communists in Europe during the Twenties.* Seattle: University of Washington Press, 1993.

Christian Missionaries

The role Western missionaries played in the evolution of Chinese nationalism is a complex one. In essence, two major themes may be discerned. The first is the way the missionaries—as modernizers—helped to introduce the Chinese to Western political ideas. The second is the way the Chinese elites and masses reacted to the missionaries as agents of Western cultural and economic imperialism.

From the time of their first entry into China in the late sixteenth century, missionaries, Catholic and later Protestant, attempted to establish institutions and introduce ideas that were designed to transform China into a replica of a Western—and by inference—a modern nation. Such Jesuit Catholic exemplars as Matteo Ricci, Adam Schall, and Theophile Verbiest were proponents of Western learning. They spent their careers attempting to introduce the Ming and then the Qing courts to Western concepts of such pure sciences as physics, astronomy, of the more practical arts of military science, and of Western political/moral philosophy and Christian theology. Robert Morrison, the Protestant pioneer, saw himself as a westernizer as well as a Christianizer. He and his British and American compatriots established schools, opened infirmaries and hospitals, and set up printing companies. Each of these institutions provided venues for the introduction of Western cultural, religious, scientific, and political ideas into China.

The missionary role in China, Catholic as well as Protestant, expanded dramatically in the years after the Opium wars. From 1860 until 1898, the missionaries established networks of schools from primary to college level, set up sophisticated hospitals that also served as training centers for the Chinese, and expanded the scope of their publication efforts. After the xenophobic Boxer Uprising (1899–1901) had run its course, the missionaries were again able to expand their efforts. During these years a secular gospel was taught along with the Gospel of the Living Christ.

The writings of such key figures as the late imperial reformers Wang Tao and Liang Qichao, republican thinkers and church activists Ding Guangxun and Y. T. Wu, suggest that the missionaries were successful in their efforts to inform key intellectuals about Western political ideas. Within the larger body of late nineteenth-century European and American political thought were essays and books on issues of state-to-state relations, and on a conception of the nation-state and of nationalism. These ideas were conveyed to the Chinese in lectures given in mission schools and in articles and books that appeared in the mission press. They helped the Chinese define their own concepts even as they clarified their own reactions to Western imperialism.

This role of missionary as teacher of political/nationalist ideas can be seen as the positive side of the missionary impact. But the missionary as preacher of an alien faith system also evoked a different form of nationalistic response, one that was antagonistic and often violent. The scholarly gentry of the late Qing saw the missionaries challenging their intellectual/ moral domination of the masses and reacted by stirring the common people to action. The many volumes of the *Missionary Cases (Jiaowudang)* that make up part of the Zongli Yamen archives demonstrate the depth and breadth of this gentry-led Chinese antagonism. The Tianjin Incident of 1870 is one dramatic example of the way this gentry-related antagonism could turn violent.

The Boxer Uprising which targeted Western missionaries, both Catholic and Protestant, demonstrates another aspect of the anti-missionary feeling. It was a popular, religiously sectarian response to what was seen as missionary and Chinese Christian arrogance and usurpation of authority. Even after the rebellion was formally quelled, popular disturbances, although of lesser intensity, continued during the "golden age" of 1860–98.

The early 1920s witnessed yet another form of Chinese response to the missionary enterprise. This Anti-Christian, Anti-Religions movement and the later Education Rights movement can be seen as examples of a modern nationalistic response to Western religious imperialism, one that was organized and led by key figures within the May Fourth community. The Guomindang and Chinese Communist Party (CCP) cadres soon adopted these ideas and disseminated them: when the Northern Expedition took place in 1926 and 1927, the missionaries found themselves targets of the onrushing military and mass-movement tide. Chiang Kaishek made skillful use of the rising anti-missionary sentiment to gain control of the Western-run/mission-run school and university systems. The CCP would complete his work in the late 1940s.

Murray A. Rubinstein

References

Lattourette, Kenneth Scott. *A History of Christian Missions in China.* New York, NY: Macmillan, 1929.

Neils, Patricia, ed. *United States Attitudes and Policies Toward China: The Impact of the Missionaries.* Armonk, NY: M. E. Sharpe, 1990.

Rubinstein, Murray A. "Religion, Revolution, and Anti-Foreignism." *American ASIAN Review* 4, no. 4 (Winter, 1986): 1–28.

C

Cinema

Although films were shown in Shanghai in 1896, shortly after they first appeared in Europe and the United States, cinema was regarded as a foreign art form through much of its history in China. This foreignness has inhibited the use of film to express nationalist purposes. In two decades, however—the 1940s and 1980s—film was the major means for popular expression of views of the country shaped by the traumas of war with Japan and the Cultural Revolution.

The first Chinese-made films were silent versions of scenes from Beijing Opera made in the 1910s. Since then, this most national of art forms has been often adapted to the film screen. When a film industry emerged in the 1920s, it was centered in Shanghai and competed in a marketplace dominated by imported films, chiefly from Hollywood. This foreign domination of the Chinese film market has persisted to the present. Competition with Hollywood films generally encouraged imitation of American themes and styles, although reformist filmmakers extended their range to include stories involving working-class protagonists. Filmmakers were also not immune to rising anti-Japanese, nationalist sentiments; several films, including Sun Yu's *The Highway* (*Dalu*, 1934), carried disguised messages directed against an unidentified enemy.

During the Sino-Japanese War (1937–45), filmmaking continued in Japanese-occupied Manchuria and Shanghai, as well as less vigorously in Guomindang-held areas. The war exposed film artists to a full range of Chinese society and experiences. This helps to explain the extraordinary qualities of films such as *The Spring River Flows East* (*Yijiang chunshui xiang dong liu*; directed by Cai Chusheng and Zheng Junli, 2 parts, 1947 and 1948) in capturing the national spirit of the age.

After 1949, the film studios were nationalized. A new, foreign esthetic was introduced in the form of "socialist realism" from Stalin's Soviet Union. The Chinese Communist leaders regarded film as a major means to create and disseminate a mass, national culture. Accordingly, they paid close attention to filmmakers and their films, particularly during campaigns such as the Anti-Rightist campaign and the Great Leap Forward (1958). By this time, the adoption of a new slogan, combining "revolutionary realism and revolutionary romanticism," reflected a further effort to find a Chinese film esthetic. Musical adaptations, such as

Third Sister Liu (*Liu Sanjie*; dir. Su Li, 1960), represented this new effort.

The film industry ceased production in 1966, with the start of the Cultural Revolution. Work resumed in 1971, with adaptations of the revolutionary "model plays" (modernized operas and ballets), perpetuating in film what the cultural authorities deemed the most Chinese of performing arts. The Cultural Revolution saw a heightened emphasis on the propaganda potential of film, as new feature films emerged from the reopened studios after 1973.

The Cultural Revolution indirectly inspired a new generation of film artists, whose experimental films in the 1980s came closer to a national film esthetic than any previous generation's work. The Chinese "New Wave" in the 1980s, launched internationally by *The Yellow Earth* (*Huang tudi*; directed by Chen Kaige, 1984), was the product of the so-called fifth generation. Most of these young artists had been "sent down" to the countryside in the late 1960s. Like their film predecessors in the war with Japan, these youths were exposed to a full range of society. When men and women such as Chen Kaige, Tian Zhuangzhuang, Zhang Yimou and Hu Mei graduated from the Beijing Film Academy in 1982, they had the technical skills to express their ideas about being Chinese. They created films such as the Tibetan saga *The Horse Thief* (*Daoma zei*; directed by Tian Zhuangzhuang, 1986), the rollicking and optimistic *Red Sorghum* (*Hong gaoliang*; directed by Zhang Yimou, 1987), and the distinctly feminist *Army Nurse* (*Nu'er lou*; directed by Hu Mei and Li Xiaojun, 1985). Although these "art house" style films could not compete with foreign films and the more pedestrian Chinese productions, they received increasing recognition at international film festivals. In the 1990s, Zhang Yimou and others continue to make films from a deeply national perspective, paradoxically with the assistance of foreign investments.

Hong Kong filmmaking since the 1940s has been invigorated by an influx of mainland artists. Artistic innovation, often drawing upon popular national traditions of martial artists and knights errant, has been a hallmark of Hong Kong cinema. In the early 1980s, a new generation of filmmakers, like their later counterparts on the mainland, breathed new life and social concern into Hong Kong films. In Taiwan, also, as the ex-Shanghai artists ran out of ideas and local audiences grew restless, a new wave of younger artists emerged. Hou Xiaoxian and Yang Dechang (Edward Yang) rank as world-class film directors, although their work is deeply rooted in Chinese historical experience and culture.

Paul Clark

References

Berry, Chris, ed. *Perspectives on Chinese Cinema*. London, England: British Film Institute, 1991.
Clark, Paul. *Chinese Cinema: Culture and Politics since 1949*. Cambridge, England: Cambridge University Press, 1988.

Civil Service Examinations

The civil service examinations were a system of examinations for the recruitment of government officials in imperial China. First introduced in the Sui (581–617) and Tang (617–907) dynasties, the system was significantly refined during the Song (960–1279). From Song until the end of Qing (1644–1911) the examinations not only served as almost the exclusive means for Chinese men to enter the prestigious officialdom but shaped the values and structure of the society.

In its final form, the system consisted of three or four levels of written tests: local *(shengyuan)*, provincial *(juren)* and metropolitan/palace *(jinshi)* examinations. They tested the candidates on their knowledge of Confucian classics, current affairs and government, and on their writing skill. It was highly competitive and generally fair, and it more or less opened the bureaucracy to talents. In the later centuries, however, the system became increasingly dogmatic and restrictive. The content of the examinations prevented Chinese intellectuals from pursuing other useful studies, especially the natural sciences, and the "eight-legged" *(baguwen)* essay style required by the examinations undermined the candidates' intellectual creativity.

Criticisms of the examination system could be found before modern times, but they received serious attention only after the intrusion of the West in the mid-nineteenth century. Reform-minded Chinese, such as Wang Tao and Zheng Guanying, attacked the system for its exclusion of Western learning, which China's self-strengthening required. During the Hundred Days Reform of 1898, Kang Youwei also included examination reforms as a major component of his platform. However, that platform was not implemented because the reform movement soon failed.

In the early 1900s, the Empress Dowager Cixi, facing domestic and foreign pressure for fundamental changes, took an action even more drastic than Kang's proposal. In 1901, she abolished the "eight-legged" essay style, and in 1905, she abolished the examination system altogether. The action liberated the minds of educated Chinese which, in a sense, had been imprisoned by this institution for nearly one thousand years. Yet it also produced far-reaching repercussions in the society in the decades that followed.

Among the most significant consequences of the abolition of the examination system was the disappearance of the gentry class. The gentry *(shenshi)*, whose status had been defined solely by success in the examinations, had served for centuries as the social and political elite in Chinese society. With the collapse of its institutional basis in 1905, the gentry ceased to be an active class. Its various social and political roles were gradually assumed by landlords, bureaucrats, merchants, or local bullies in the twentieth century. To a degree, this change weakened the moral fiber that had helped to maintain China's traditional social order.

The Qing government, moreover, did not replace the examinations with an effective system of modern schools. A seven-tier school system, which would require twenty-five years to complete, was promulgated but did not go into effect. No clear pattern of advancement, therefore, was available to those who were ambitious or interested in pursuing a government career. As a result, thousands of young men (and some women) sought higher education in foreign countries as a substitute for the old examination degrees. Most of these youths went to Japan and, after seeing the progress that country had made during the past half-century, they soon lost faith in the Qing. The anxiety about their own futures, combined with the shocking foreign experiences, created a profound sense of crisis that in the end marginalized and radicalized a generation of Chinese youth. The abolition of the examination system paved the way for the Qing dynasty's own downfall.

Wang Ke-wen

References

Franke, Wolfgang. *Reform and Abolition of the Traditional Chinese Examination System*. Cambridge, MA: Harvard University Press, 1960.

Miyazaki, Ichisada. *China's Examination Hell: The Civil Service Examinations in Imperial China.* Trans. Conrad Schirokauer. New Haven, CT: Yale University Press, 1976.

Civil War, 1945–49

The civil war of 1945 to 1949 was the military showdown between the ruling Guomindang (GMD) and the Chinese Communist Party (CCP) which resulted in a Communist victory and the founding of the People's Republic of China.

The civil war began when, in the immediate wake of the Sino-Japanese War (1937–45), the CCP and the GMD, in their rush to capture the formerly Japanese-occupied and "puppet"-controlled areas, clashed with one another. Until October 1, 1949, when the People's Republic of China was established, the GMD-CCP conflict was marked by massive internal violence and foreign involvement: the Soviet Union invaded northeast China (or Manchuria), America intervened in north China, and the Japanese assisted both the GMD and the CCP.

When the war with Japan was over, the CCP appeared to be nationalistic and stressed the theme of "peace, democracy, and unity" during its negotiations with the GMD from August 1945 to June 1946. Simultaneously, however, the Communists were busily capturing territories. In the GMD-controlled urban areas, the CCP mobilized students and other social groups to denounce American support for the GMD while keeping quiet about the military aid it had received from the Soviet Union. The Soviet troops, in fact, looted the cities and industrial plants in Manchuria and turned over to the CCP large quantities of Japanese weapons before permitting the GMD to enter the region in May 1946.

With American assistance and Japanese cooperation, the GMD recovered most of the major cities in formerly occupied China. But the corruption and unreasonable policy of the GMD takeover alienated the populace and prompted some Chinese in those cities to wonder whether life might have been better under Japanese rule. While the United States Marines publicly helped the GMD to secure the big cities in north China, the American mediation effort under General George C. Marshall (from December 1945 to January 1947) to create a

coalition government in China failed because of the deep-seated mistrust between the two Chinese parties. Yet the mediation blocked a GMD chance, when it still enjoyed military superiority, to defeat the CCP by force.

In urban China, the GMD failed to employ its mass movement—particularly the Anti-Soviet, Anti-Communist movement (February 1946)—to condemn the pro-Soviet CCP effectively and to eradicate its student-centered subversive activity. On the other hand, by 1948, the CCP had succeeded in manipulating the national sentiment to discredit the GMD and the United States through the use of two political movements: Protest the Brutality of the American Military Personnel in China movement (December 1946–January 1947) and Anti-Hunger, Anti-Civil War movement (May 1947). By the summer of 1948, the CCP's People's Liberation Army had begun to turn the tide of the war against the GMD, which became further weakened by the Communist-controlled student movement in the cities. Meanwhile, even huge amounts of American financial aid could not halt the galloping inflation under the GMD government, which demolished the last remnant of the urban support it enjoyed.

The GMD and the CCP utilized Japanese and "puppet" (Chinese collaborator) troops during the civil war. The Japanese holdovers on the GMD side, especially those who enrolled in Yan Xishan's army in Shanxi, were an embarrassment to the GMD government and detracted from the image of victory that the government hoped would secure the loyalty of the people. The Communists, quietly but more successfully, also recruited Japanese and "puppet" troops to fight the GMD. Their strength was enhanced by these troops, especially in the Northeast.

The defeat of the GMD in the decisive battles of Liaoxi-Shenyang, Haui-Hai, and Beijing-Tianjin (October 1948–January 1949) sealed its doom in north China. In January 1949 Chiang Kaishek stepped down as president of the GMD government. His successor, Li Zongren, attempted to negotiate a peace settlement with the CCP in order to keep south China in GMD hands. But the triumphant CCP would not be stopped by negotiations now. In April, the People's Liberation Army crossed the Yangtze River and swept southward; the demoralized GMD forces surrendered to the CCP *en masse*. Li's government first moved to Canton and then to Chongqing. By the end of 1949, the entire mainland of China had been taken by the

CCP. Chiang, who had tried to control the situation from behind the scenes, relocated the GMD to the island of Taiwan.

The civil war was a life-or-death struggle between two bitter enemies that culminated their conflict since the mid-1920s. Under the slogans of "Down with Chiang Kaishek and liberate the people of the whole country" and "Suppress the rebellion [of the Red Bandits] and reconstruct the nation," the CCP and the GMD made use of nationalist appeals in attacking each other. However, they both introduced foreign elements in an internal war that disregarded the war weariness of the Chinese at the end of World War II and the common plea for peace, cooperation, and reform in the country. Chinese nationalism, therefore, was twisted by the two political parties to justify the pursuit of a non-nationalistic war, which caused tremendous losses to the people.

Joseph K. S. Yick

References

Hsu, Immanuel C. Y. *The Rise of Modern China.* 4th ed. New York, NY: Oxford University Press, 1990.

Spence, Jonathan D. *The Search for Modern China.* New York, NY: Norton, 1990.

Yick, Joseph K. S. "Civil War, 1945–49." *Historical Dictionary of Revolutionary China, 1839–1976.* New York, NY: Greenwood, 1992.

Cohong

Cohong was an essential component of the Canton system of Sino-Western trade before the Opium War of 1839 to 1842. Organized by the *hong* (a corruption of *yanghang,* meaning "foreign-trade companies") merchants, this guild monopolized Chinese trade with the West in the port of Canton.

Cohong was first established in 1720. It was then disbanded twice and eventually resurrected in 1782. Officially totaling thirteen, the actual membership number fluctuated during the Qing dynasty. The *hongs* were authorized by the Chinese government as the sole agents of the limited foreign trade in Canton. They not only handled the business transactions but also provided necessary accommodations and management for the Western merchants staying in Canton. To the government, they served as guarantors of good conduct and tax payment by the "barbarians." All communications between these foreigners and the Chinese government had to be transacted through the *hongs.*

The guild embodied the restrictive and discriminatory nature of the Canton trade and was the focus of resentment and criticism among Westerners seeking commercial interests in China. Following China's defeat in the Opium War, Cohong was abolished by the Sino-British Treaty of Nanjing in 1842. Yet the need of the foreign merchants for Chinese partners to arrange the Chinese side of their business remained. The functions of Cohong fell to private agents, the *compradors,* many of whom originally had been associated with the *hongs.*

Wang Ke-wen

References

Greenberg, Michael. *British Trade and the Opening of China, 1800–42.* Cambridge, England: Cambridge University Press, 1951.

Collectivization of Agriculture

In December 1953, the Chinese Communist Party formally inaugurated a fifteen-year program for the collectivization of agriculture. The plan, which had the approval of Mao Zedong, was to be carried out gradually in three stages, beginning with "mutual aid teams," followed by lower-level (semi-socialist) Agricultural Producers' Cooperatives (APC), and concluding in higher-level (socialist) cooperatives. In a "mutual aid team" four to eight peasant households shared their tools, livestock, and labor, while retaining individual ownership of land and personal property; in a lower-level APC, land, tools, and livestock were jointly owned and managed by twenty to fifty households, and the output was shared according to each peasant's contribution of labor and land; in the higher-level APC, comprising 100 to 300 households, land contribution would no longer count toward output-sharing.

By the end of 1954, 58.4 percent of the peasant households had established "mutual aid teams" and 2 percent, lower-level APCs. In mid-1955, Mao suddenly decided to hasten the process of collectivization because he believed that any delay would increase the capitalist tendencies reemerging in the countryside, as evidenced by some of the land-owning peasants getting richer than the others. His other reason was that collectivization would result in a rapid increase in agricultural production.

As far as collectivization went, Mao's campaign achieved phenomenal success. By 1957, 93.3 percent of the peasant households were in higher-level APCs, and another 3.7 percent in lower-level APCs. However, agricultural production as a whole rose only marginally and still lagged far behind the rapidly increasing industrial demands for agricultural products. At the same time, a growing population was generating unemployment and the APCs had increased the quantity of surplus labor. While orthodox economists debated various methods to solve the problem of economic growth, Mao, having regained absolute control of the Party, forced his solution on China by inaugurating the Great Leap Forward program in 1958.

The vast-scale projects of the Great Leap Forward demanded such heavy inputs of labor that the minute APCs became an obstacle to unified action. This resulted in the emergence of much larger units—the "people's communes" (average size: 4,600 households), which managed their own industry, agriculture, trade, education, health, social welfare, and military affairs. In Mao's view, the communes advanced the cause of socialism by communalizing the personal and working lives of the peasants. The failure of the Great Leap Forward and peasant discontent with the communes, however, caused some of the collectivization policies to be rescinded and the peasants to be allowed to retain private ownership of their houses and other personal properties.

After the death of Mao Zedong in 1976, Deng Xiaoping, in a radical reversal of Maoist economic policies, disbanded the entire collectivization process. By 1982, the communes and the collectives had disappeared; land was redivided into parcels and leased to individual peasant households, which were entitled to produce what they wished as long as they met their tax obligations.

Ranbir Vohra

References

Riskin, Carl. *China's Political Economy: The Quest for Development Since 1949.* Oxford, England: Oxford University Press, 1987.

College of Foreign Languages (Tongwenguan)

In 1862, at the recommendation of Prince Gong, the Qing government ordered the establishment of Tongwenguan (College of Foreign Languages) in Beijing for the training of Chinese interpreters and potential diplomats. It was the first government school for Western studies under the Qing. Administered by the newly founded Zongli Yamen, the college initially recruited only teenage Manchu boys to study English, French, and Russian, as well as Chinese. It later recruited Manchu and Chinese youth under the age of twenty-five. In 1867, the college expanded its curriculum to include mathematics, astronomy, physics, chemistry, biology, and Western histories and laws. Courses in German and Japanese were added in the following years. At first, the duration of the program was three years, but it was extended to five and eight years in 1876.

Most of the instructors at the college were foreigners. W. A. P. Martin, the American missionary, served as dean of the college from 1869 to 1895. The British inspector-general of the Chinese Maritime Customs, Robert Hart, exercised considerable power over the budget and personnel of the college during his tenure. Similar schools, also called Tongwenguan, flourished in Shanghai and Canton following the establishment of the Beijing school.

Tongwenguan represented one of late-Qing China's major attempts to understand and communicate with the West, and it was an important part of the self-strengthening movement of the 1860s to the 1880s. As such, it was also at the center of political controversy. The expansion of its curriculum in 1867, for example, came only after a fierce debate between reformers and conservatives, who accused the school's mission as being one to "barbarianize" Chinese youth. Although the reformers, led by Prince Gong, eventually obtained imperial approval not only to expand the college's curriculum but also to recruit degree-holders as its students, in the end few members of the official-gentry elite enrolled themselves in the college. In 1902, Tongwenguan was merged with other institutions to form the predecessor of Beijing University.

Wang Ke-wen

References

Biggerstaff, Knight. *The Earliest Modern Government Schools in China.* Ithaca, NY: Cornell University Press, 1961.
Cohen, Paul A., and John C. Schrecker, eds. *Reforms in Nineteenth-Century China.* Cambridge, MA: Harvard University Press, 1976.

Comintern

The Comintern, also known as the Communist International, the Third International, the CI, KI, and, simply, "the International," existed from 1919 to 1943 as the arm of the Soviet Communist Party to spread the revolution in the world. In China, the Comintern played significant roles in both the Nationalist revolution of the 1920s and the Communist revolution in the 1930s.

The First, or Marxist, International was founded in 1864 and collapsed in the 1870s, destroyed by factional dispute. The Second, or Socialist, International (which still exists) foundered on the shoals of nationalism during World War I. Among Bolsheviks, discussions about founding a new international began early in the war, but nothing concrete emerged until 1919, more than a year after the October revolution.

Why Lenin waited so long to establish his own formal international apparatus has never been satisfactorily explained. The standard Bolshevik rationale has been that the times were not opportune before 1919. But, since Lenin believed that the only way the Russian revolution could survive was if it quickly spread to the capitalist West, his procrastination is difficult to understand. Reasons offered include his preoccupation with Russian problems; his relative disinterest in any revolution except the one in Russia; and his belief that the revolution in the West would ignite spontaneously.

In early 1919, perhaps prodded by the summoning of a revivification congress by the Second International, Lenin ordered the founding congress of the Comintern, which met in Moscow from March 2 through 6, 1919. Because Soviet Russia was isolated from the world, few of the leftists who might have been attracted to the congress heard about it, and only a few delegates from abroad arrived specifically for the meetings. But an official count listed 52 delegates from 21 countries. The stated objective of the new international as adopted by the congress was to support the proliferation of revolution. However, all talk of cooperation with other left-leaning groups was rejected and denounced as opportunism.

At the end of the congress, the Comintern dispatched agents abroad to organize movements allied to Moscow. During the following year parties adhering to the Comintern, most of them little more than shadow organizations, appeared in dozens of countries. In the course of that year, leftist revolutions failed in Hungary, Bavaria, and Slovakia. Those fiascoes, plus the difficulties the revolution was experiencing in Russia, led Lenin to conclude that, for now, revolutionary opportunity had passed and it was time to retreat, both at home and abroad. Now was the time to prepare for the long haul, he argued. Those who insisted on pushing revolution further were to be regarded as adventurists, who were frightening international capitalism into taking up arms against working-class interests and thereby endangering the successes that had already been accomplished in Soviet Russia.

By the time the Second Comintern Congress convened in July 1920, Lenin had decided that the purpose of the Comintern should no longer be to foster revolution, but to establish Moscow's control of the Comintern apparatus and to weed from the latter's ranks those who could not be depended upon to take Kremlin orders. Many of those at the second congress, in contrast to the first congress, were representatives of real, if weak parties, and had traveled to Russia specifically for the meetings. Contrary to Lenin's ideas, however, they were not interested in reining in the revolution. Excited by the news of the Red Army's triumphant race across Poland, the delegates balked at accepting Lenin's proposal of retreat and the congress was temporarily adjourned. Only after the Red Army had been stopped, and under Russian pressure, did the congress reconvene and accept Lenin's analysis. Contrary to those of the first congress, the resolutions of the second congress included ordering Communists to collaborate with non-Communists in trade-unions, youth, and national liberation organizations, with the intention of gradually taking them over.

Following the second congress, and throughout the remainder of Comintern history, the Comintern unrelentingly glorified the idea of world revolution. Nevertheless, its propaganda, policies, and activities were invariably an extension of Soviet interests, which the Soviet leadership often deemed to conflict with immediate revolutionary exploits. The Comintern became a chief vehicle whereby Moscow's adherents and agents abroad received funds and instructions, and through which the Kremlin's participation in revolutionary and national-revolutionary movements was directed and masked. The fiction was being maintained that the Comintern was completely independent of the Soviet government, neither having anything to do with the other.

C

Actually, the more important the movement and situation, the more directly Stalin and the Politburo became involved, as in China and Germany in the 1920s.

In 1921, Comintern agents helped established the Chinese Communist Party (CCP). Two years later the Comintern reached an agreement with Sun Yatsen's Guomindang (GMD), offering the latter aid in exchange for the formation of a united front between the GMD and the CCP. From 1923 to 1927, Comintern agents, notably Mikhail Borodin, were instrumental in the development of the United Front and the Nationalist Revolution. After the collapse of the United Front, the Kremlin focused its attention on the endangered CCP. A group of Comintern-trained Chinese Communists, known as the "Internationalists," dominated the CCP leadership during 1931 to 1935.

The "Internationalists" were among the better-known East Asian Communists who were members of the Comintern apparatus during the 1920s and 1930s; others included Ho Chi Minh, Sen Katayama and Musso. While some members of the Comintern apparatus and congresses opposed the primacy that Russian interests enjoyed in the international arena, their numbers diminished. By the end of the 1920s, Comintern ranks had been cleared of all those who failed to enthusiastically accept Moscow's control.

The rise of Mao Zedong to supremacy in the CCP during the late 1930s, however, weakened the Comintern influence in the Chinese Communist movement. Mao, who had no personal ties to the Comintern, asserted a degree of independence for the CCP from Moscow's control. This emphasis on a nationalist dimension of the Chinese revolution was to have important ramifications in Sino-Soviet relations after 1949.

In 1943, during World War II, Stalin became convinced that the West was delaying the launch of a second front in Europe because it did not want to help a country that for a quarter century had called for its destruction. He decided to show his good will by eliminating the Comintern. The official date of its demise was May 1943. Stalin's ability to terminate an international organization with such ease indicates the degree to which the Comintern had become his personal instrument.

After World War II, Moscow established a smaller successor organization, the Communist Information Bureau or Cominform, whose membership was limited to Communist Parties in power plus the large French and Italian Parties. The Cominform fell victim to the centrifugal forces that developed in the international movement following Stalin's death in 1953 and was dissolved in April 1956. On several subsequent occasions, Khrushchev and Brezhnev tried to create new international organizations, but other Communist countries, fearful of renewed attempts by Moscow to dominate the movement, frustrated their efforts.

Dan N. Jacobs

References

Degras, Jane, ed. *The Communist International: Documents.* 3 Vols. London, England: Oxford University Press, 1956, 1960, 1965.

Hulse, James W. *The Forming of the Communist International.* Stanford, CA: Stanford University Press, 1964.

Nollau, Gunther. *International Communism and World Revolution: History and Methods.* New York, NY: Praeger, 1961.

Comprador

From the eighteenth to the mid-nineteenth century, the *comprador* played a critical role as the intermediary between foreign and Chinese merchants in the treaty ports of China. Often misunderstood, *compradors* have been vilified by both conservative Chinese nationalists and by Chinese Marxist-Leninists as turncoats and "slaves of Western imperialists" who helped foreign merchants gain greater access to China's domestic market. Such a view has been based on the theories, including those by V. I. Lenin, J. A. Hobson, and J. Myrdal, which postulate that Western economic expansion of trade with China and other less-developed countries have been conducted at the latter's expense, weakening them and making them poorer. On the other hand, several other studies, including those of Carl Riskin and Chi-ming Hou, have argued that, on balance, Western trade has contributed positively to China's economic development. They suggested that the trade has provided China with new infusions of capital, new types of markets in goods and services, the transfer of managerial and technological knowledge, as well as the training of a modern professional personnel. Chinese *compradors* were heavily engaged in all of these activities, thus facilitating the modernization of the Chinese economy.

The Chinese term for *comprador, maiban,* was first used for a group of official purveyors of the Ming Dynasty (1368–1664). Sometime during the eighteenth century, as *maiban* became licensed purveyors employed by Chinese *hong* merchants, who alone could trade with Europeans, the term *comprador* (meaning "purchaser" in Portuguese) was adopted. Then, starting in the 1830s, independent foreign merchants began to hire them as their resident assistants, treasurers, and guarantors of their Chinese staff. These responsibilities quickly expanded to include guaranteeing all business transactions between their foreign employers and other Chinese merchants.

Even as purveyors and treasurers, the early *compradors* were already known to conduct some trading on their own accounts. After the Opium War (1840–42) and the abolition of the *hong* system, the latter activities had increased so much that they became the *compradors'* dominant concerns. Foreign merchants did not mind this because they never penetrated into China's interior market; instead they needed *compradors* who were already reputable and well connected merchants in their own right, and whose networking could bring them more business. Those who responded were often exceptional entrepreneurs ready to innovate and to adapt to cultural differences. Thus, in the tea trade, for example, several *compradors* would go "upcountry" to buy tea directly from the growers, assuring foreign traders both source and price stability. For native banks, they also introduced the "chop" loan, a short-term credit instrument linking Chinese and Western financial institutions to better serve an expanding credit market. Then, as other Chinese merchants were still hesitant about investing in modern industry, *compradors* poured in with capital and management skill. By the 1870s, several left their foreign employment to take charge of joint government-private ventures. Among the first group were Takee (Yang Fang) and Ahyue (Lin Xianyang), *compradors* respectively for Jardine and Matherson and Russell's during the 1850s. The second, even more prominent, group included Tong King-sing (Tang Tingshu), Xu Run, and Zheng Guanying, who left major foreign companies in order to partially own and manage the China Merchants' Steam Navigation Company, the Kaiping Mines, and the Shanghai Cotton Cloth Mills, among others.

The *compradors'* powerful influence, great wealth, and independent business, while maintaining employment and partnership with Western merchants, continued during the republican era. In the 1920s, many prominent *compradors,* such as the Shanghai banker Yu Qiaqing, became important allies of the Guomindang. Yet as bridges to the West, their economic contribution and cultural identity were often marginalized. After 1949, with China under Communist control, they were condemned wholesale. Only since the 1980s, under Deng Xiaoping's new "open-up" policy of economic reforms, have mainland scholars begun to reassess their roles in a favorable light. Meanwhile, at the popular level, new Chinese entrepreneurs taking up business relationships with Western enterprise are half-jokingly called "red *compradors.*"

Wellington K. K. Chan

References

H. Hao, Yen-p'ing. *The Comprador in Nineteenth Century China: Bridge Between East and West.* Cambridge, MA: Harvard University Press, 1970.

Concessions and Settlements

The terms "concessions" and "settlements" refer to different types of foreign jurisdictions in the treaty ports of China. Although legally they differed, the words were conventionally used with little distinction. A concession was a piece of land, granted or leased directly by the Chinese government to a foreign power in return for payment of a nominal ground rent; a settlement was a place set aside where foreigners might live and conduct business, dealing directly with the Chinese owners of the land in making their arrangements.

The first foreign settlements were established soon after the opening of the original five treaty ports by the Treaty of Nanjing (1842). By the early twentieth century, some forty-nine ports had been opened. Foreign settlements or concessions could be found in thirteen of them, although some had more than one (for instance, there were eight concessions in Tianjin, five at Hankou, and two each at Canton and at Shanghai). Two cities (Shanghai and Xiamen) had international settlements, in which the representatives of various foreign countries cooperated; in most other cases, concessions were granted to individual powers.

The settlements were usually located at the edges of cities, and occasionally on islands in the harbor (Gulangyu at Xiamen; Shamian in Canton). At first, the reservation of particular tracts of land for foreign residence and trade was simply a convenience for both sides in a country where foreigners were otherwise debarred from residing or owning property. Gradually, however, the settlements assumed a political and jurisdictional life of their own. Profiting from the provision of extraterritoriality, the larger settlements established municipal administrations, governed along Western lines, with the power of taxation to maintain the sorts of municipal services that the foreigners wanted: gas, sewage, electricity, education, and policing. As increasing numbers of Chinese moved into the foreign settlements, questions of legal jurisdiction arose, which were never satisfactorily resolved. In Shanghai, where an international settlement and a French concession existed, the foreign areas came to dominate the economic and commercial life of the city, and to contain roughly half of its population; by the 1930s, over one and a half million Chinese lived under foreign governance in that city alone, while the foreign residents numbered only about 50,000.

The large numbers of foreigners, the presence of foreign legal and administrative practices, of Western educational institutions, newspapers, and journals gradually gave rise to a "treaty port culture," which affected both foreigners and Chinese. By the late nineteenth century, with the development of a sense of China's nationhood, the arrangements that had made foreign settlements possible came to be seen not as a convenience, but as an infringement on China's sovereignty. Particularly in the wake of the May Fourth movement (1919), there were an increasing number of calls for the return of the foreign settlements. These demands gathered strength after the May Thirtieth movement (1925) and the successful completion of the Northern Expedition (1926–28). Some concessions were returned to China (the former holdings of Russia and the Central Powers after Versailles, the British concessions at Hankou and Jiujiang in 1927, for instance), but most waited upon the negotiations, undertaken in the early 1930s, for an end to the extraterritoriality on which they rested. It was World War II that brought the concessions to an end. In 1943, Great Britain and the United States abandoned their extraterritorial rights in China. France followed suit in 1946. With those treaty provisions gone, there was no longer any basis for the earlier system.

Nicholas R. Clifford

References

Fairbank, John K. *Trade and Diplomacy on the China Coast*. Cambridge, MA: Harvard University Press, 1953.

Willoughby, Westel W. *Foreign Rights and Interests in China*. Revised and enlarged edition. Taibei: Cheng-wen Publishing Co., 1966.

Constitution Protection Movement

The Constitution Protection movement, (hufa yundong) in support of the provisional constitution *(yuefa)* of 1912, allowed Sun Yatsen to establish a rival government in Canton during 1917 to 1923.

After the death of Yuan Shikai in June 1916, Li Yuanhong succeeded Yuan as president of the Republic, but Premier Duan Qirui held the actual power in the government. Duan, who headed the emerging Anhui Clique of the Beiyang warlords, opposed the provisional constitution that Sun Yatsen had promulgated before yielding the presidency to Yuan in 1912. Sun was furious. He regarded the provisional constitution as the fundamental law of the country. Although it differed from his ideal blueprint for nation-building, *Design for Revolution (Geming fanglue)*, Sun believed that it could provide a basic constitutional structure for the Republic before the drafting of a formal constitution. In July 1917, in the wake of the abortive attempt by Zhang Xun to restore the Qing monarchy, Duan refused to reestablish the parliament that was organized on the basis of the Provisional Constitution. Sun immediately called for a nationwide opposition to Duan's government in defense of the old constitutional order. This was the beginning of the Constitution Protection movement.

Under Sun Yatsen, the Constitution Protection movement underwent three stages. The first stage began with Sun's departure from Shanghai in July 1917. He led most of the members of parliament, as well as the Chinese navy, and arrived in Canton to establish a military government there. Assuming the title of "Generalissimo" *(dayuanshuai)*, he claimed his Canton regime to be the legitimate government of China, but in effect it controlled only a few provinces in the South and Southwest. It nevertheless challenged the authority of the government in Beijing, and China became formally divided into two rival states. The first stage ended in May 1918, when the Guangxi militarists, upon whom Sun was relying, reorganized the leadership of the military government into a council system, with Sun as one of the seven chief executives *(zongcai)* in the council. Deprived of power, Sun was forced to leave Canton for Shanghai.

In late 1920, under Sun's instruction, the Guangdong forces commanded by Chen Jiongming defeated the Guangxi militarists and recovered Canton. Chen invited Sun back to Canton and established the second Canton regime, signaling the commencement of the second stage of his Constitution Protection movement. The Sun-Chen cooperation lasted less than two years. In May 1921 the old parliament in Canton elected Sun as "Extraordinary President" of the Republic. One year later, however, Chen Jiongming staged a *coup d'état* and expelled Sun from Canton. The second stage thus ended.

The third and final stage of the movement extended from late 1922 to late 1923. In the winter of 1922, the Guangxi and Yunnan forces who supported Sun attacked Chen Jiongming and again recovered Canton. On February 4, 1923, Sun resumed the post of "Generalissimo" in Canton and revived the Constitution Protection effort. At this time, the situation in the North also changed. After winning the first Zhili-Fengtian War of 1922, the Zhili Clique declared its support for the old constitutional order. It restored Li Yuanhong as president of the Beijing government and reestablished the old parliament. Most members of the old parliament therefore left Canton and returned to Beijing, thereby undermining the legitimacy of Sun's third Canton regime.

The Zhili Clique under Cao Kun and Wu Peifu, however, was merely using the provisional constitution as an instrument to expel the previous government in Beijing and to destroy Sun's opposition in the South. As soon as these objectives were accomplished, it took over the government for itself. In June 1923, Cao Kun forced Li Yuanhong out of office and then bribed the parliament into electing him as the new president. Meanwhile, Wu Peifu prepared to reunify the country by force. Facing increasing threats from the North and disgusted by the corruption of the old parliament, Sun decided to terminate the futile Constitution Protection movement and start a new revolution. Still preserving his regime in Canton, he soon formed an alliance with the Soviet Union and reorganized his party, the Guomindang, for the task of the National Revolution.

Lu Fang-shang

References
Wilbur, C. Martin. *Sun Yat-sen: Frustrated Patriot*. New York, NY: Columbia University Press, 1976.
Yu, George T. *Party Politics in Republican China: The Kuomintang, 1912–1924*. Berkeley: University of California Press, 1966.

Constitutional Movement

The Constitutional movement, which advocated the establishment of constitutional monarchy in China, was a failed alternative to republican revolution during the last years of the Qing dynasty.

Since the late nineteenth century reformist thinkers, such as Wang Tao and Zheng Guanying, had been suggesting that China adopt the Western system of constitutional monarchy. The system subsequently became the goal of the Hundred Day Reform of 1898 and, after this movement's failure, the rallying point of its exiled participants as they organized an opposition movement overseas. In the early 1900s, Liang Qichao, leader of that opposition movement, engaged in a fierce debate with the followers of Sun Yatsen in Japan on the merits and feasibility of constitutional reform versus revolution in China. Meanwhile, high officials in China such as Zhang Zhidong and Liu Kunyi also urged the Qing court to adopt a constitution. Faced with domestic and foreign pressures for reform in the wake of the Boxer Uprising (1899–1901), Empress Dowager Cixi at last began to consider such proposals favorably. She apparently believed that a constitutional reform would restore confidence among the country's educated elite in the government and to help stem the rising tide of revolution.

The Qing government planned a gradual transformation into the constitutional system. In December 1905, it dispatched five high officials on a tour to Japan and Europe to investigate the practice of constitutional governments. Upon their return in July 1906, the government announced its intention to adopt a constitution, without indicating any time-table for such an effort. The announcement nevertheless encouraged reform-minded gentry, who soon began to petition for the speedy adoption of a constitution. Later that year, gentry leaders Zheng Xiaoxu, Zhang Jian, and Tang Shouqian organized the Association for the Preparation of Constitutional Government *(Yubei lixian gonghui)* in Shanghai. Similar organizations sprang up in various provinces.

During the next four years the gentry advocates for constitutional government, now known as the constitutionalists *(lixianpai),* persistently pushed for thorough and rapid reform. They gathered signatures, issued declarations, sent delegations to Beijing, and created a powerful petition movement with the skillful use of public meetings, modern newspapers, and pressure politics. In 1908 the overseas constitutionalists, led by Liang Qichao, also transferred their organization to China and participated in the movement.

As a step toward the constitutional system, the Qing had ordered the founding of government-appointed national and provincial assemblies in 1907. When the provincial assemblies *(ziyiju)* and the national assembly *(zizhengyuan)* were finally established in 1909 and 1910, respectively, these advisory bodies immediately fell under the control of the constitutionalists and became the latter's instruments. The petitions succeeded in forcing the Qing court to announce, in 1908, a plan of adopting a constitution and electing a parliament within nine years. A new wave of protests by the constitutionalists against this lengthy period thereupon followed. This time, they were joined by governors and generals in the provinces. In 1910 the government took punitive actions against some of the petition leaders while reluctantly abridging the preparation period to three years.

Although forced to compromise on the time-table for reform, the Qing court was determined to control the degree of reform. In the "Imperial Outline of Constitution" issued in 1908 it clearly adopted the Meiji Constitution of Japan as its model and tried to concentrate power in the hands of the constitutional monarch. In 1911, the court established an experimental cabinet, with nine out of its thirteen members Manchu, and seven of those Manchu selected from the imperial family. Prince Qing was prime minister.

The cabinet was disillusioning to many constitutionalists. Frustrated by the slow pace and the limited scope of the reform, they began to question the sincerity of the Qing court in establishing a genuine constitutional government. As a result, their protests became increasingly radical in content as well as in rhetoric. At the same time, the movement had politicized these gentry activists and increased their confidence in employing new forms of organization and activity to exert political influence.

In mid-1911, radical gentry activists in Sichuan, Hunan, Hubei, and Guangdong played a leading role in the Railway Protection movement. When that incident triggered the Wuchang Uprising in October, the constitutionalists in south and central China quickly abandoned their hope for constitutional reform and defected to revolution. Experienced and well-connected in politics, they easily mobilized the provincial assemblies and pressured the provincial governments to declare their independence from the Qing. The constitutionalists' support for the revolutionaries was indeed the key to the success of the Revolution of 1911. This also explains why after the revolution the former constitutionalists were far more influential in the provinces than the revolutionaries.

The Constitutional movement of 1906 to 1911 represented a moderate approach to China's political modernization. Whether it was based on a sophisticated understanding of the functions of the constitution or not, the support for a constitutional system had become consensual among all Chinese political activists by the beginning of the twentieth century. The major difference between the constitutionalists and the revolutionaries was their attitude toward the Qing. Almost all of the constitutionalists were Han Chinese, and as such they naturally sympathized with the anti-Manchu sentiments of the revolutionaries. Yet as members of the established gentry elite they preferred a gradual reform within the framework of the dynasty to its violent overthrow, which they feared would lead to political and social upheavals, as well as foreign intervention. In addition, foreign models such as Meiji Japan indicated to them the effectiveness of a constitutional monarchy in bringing about national unity and strength. They therefore chose to tolerate and cooperate with the Manchu ruler. The fact that they defected to the revolution in 1911 illustrates that their loyalty to the Qing was by no means absolute or irrational. In this sense, the constitutionalists, while supporting a traditional monarchy, may have been more inclined toward modern Chinese nationalism, which envisioned a multiethnic Chinese state, than were the anti-Manchu revolutionaries.

Wang Ke-wen

References
Chang, P'eng-yuan. "The Constitutionalists." *China in Revolution: The First Phase,*

1900–1913, ed. Mary C. Wright, 143–183. New Haven, CT: Yale University Press, 1968.

Esherick, Joseph. *Reform and Revolution in China: The 1911 Revolution in Hunan and Hubei.* Berkeley: University of California Press, 1976.

Schoppa, R. Keith. *Chinese Elites and Political Change: Zhejiang Province in the Early Twentieth Century.* Cambridge, MA: Harvard University Press, 1981.

Constitutional Orthodoxy *(Fatong)*

By the last years of the Qing dynasty there had emerged among the Chinese elite a consensus about constitutionalism. Republican revolutionaries and supporters of the Qing monarchy alike saw constitutionalism, a Western concept, as essential to China's new political order. Once the dynasty was replaced by a republic, however, constitutions proved to be far more difficult to implement than to draft.

Several attempts were made to formulate a constitution during the republican era. Shortly after the Revolution of 1911 the provisional government under Sun Yatsen drafted and promulgated a provisional constitution *(yuefa)* to define the general political structure of the new Republic. The new president, Yuan Shikai, soon abrogated the document. A preliminary draft constitution produced by the first parliament of the Republic in 1913 suffered a similar fate. In 1914, Yuan promulgated a new provisional constitution, but it perished with his government in 1916. From 1917 to 1923, Sun Yatsen led a Constitution Protection movement in Canton, vowing to defend the original provisional constitution against it being trampled by the Beiyang warlords. Meanwhile the Beiyang warlords, who controlled the central government in Beijing, tried to draft their own constitution. In 1923, the Beijing government under Cao Kun's Zhili Clique drafted and promulgated a constitution. Since Cao was notorious for his election to the presidency through bribery, and since his government collapsed after the second Zhili-Fengtian War in 1924, the Zhili Clique's constitution received little serious attention from either the people or the succeeding governments in China.

Upon its nominal reunification of the country in 1928, the Guomindang (GMD) government announced the commencement of a period of Political Tutelage *(xunzheng),* under

which party dictatorship by the GMD was the norm. An intra-party debate, however, soon arose concerning the necessity of providing a "Provisional Constitution for Political Tutelage." In 1930, the Beiping opposition, organized by anti-Chiang Kaishek militarists and Party leaders, drafted such a document as evidence of its intention to replace Chiang's dictatorship with democracy. Chiang consulted this document when he, having defeated the Beiping opposition by force, ordered the drafting of his own provisional constitution for political tutelage in 1931. On this issue Chiang clashed with Hu Hanmin, who saw no need for such a document, and their dispute caused the Nanjing-Canton split later that year. Chiang's provisional constitution merely translated the reality of GMD rule into a legal document, offering no real protection of people's rights or freedoms.

As the era of political tutelage approached the end of its six-year limit that was set by the GMD itself, Chiang's government began the drafting of a formal constitution in preparation for the transition to the period of constitutional democracy *(xianzheng)*. After three years' effort, a draft constitution was promulgated in 1936 yet was never implemented. One of the reasons for this failure was the Japanese invasion in 1937, which prevented the government from convening a national assembly to ratify the constitution, although the GMD's sincerity in actually putting the constitution into effect, thus terminating its own dictatorship, was also in question.

After the end of the Sino-Japanese War in 1945, the GMD government began to draft a new constitution. By then, the civil war between the GMD and the Chinese Communist Party (CCP) had erupted and the CCP was opposed to any drafting without its participation. The GMD, however, decided to use the constitution to show its own support for democracy and soon completed the draft with the help of a few minor parties. A GMD-controlled national assembly ratified and promulgated the constitution in 1947.

Less than two years after the promulgation of the 1947 constitution, the GMD government was driven out of the mainland by the CCP. On its island refuge of Taiwan, the GMD continued to call itself the "constitutional government" of China, although its constitution was effectively nullified by a martial law that returned all power to the Party. The People's Republic founded by the CCP on the mainland promulgated its own constitution in 1954. That socialist democratic constitution was subsequently revised many times, often to adjust it to changing political situations, and was as irrelevant to the state and society of China as its counterpart in Taiwan. Since the late 1980s both the mainland and Taiwan have been experimenting with a new stage of constitutionalism. The post-Mao reforms in the mainland have created a need for some form of constitutional order to regulate the much liberalized domestic activity and to consolidate popular support, while the end of the Chiang family's rule in Taiwan has provided an opportunity for its government and people to revive and revise the constitution into a realistic guide to the island's politics.

Although as the fundamental law of the country the constitution has had little impact on the lives of the Chinese in the twentieth century, as a political symbol it often has been the subject of controversy and allegiance. The Beiyang warlords and Sun Yatsen in the 1910s and 1920s, and the GMD from the 1940s to the present, have used the defense of a constitution as the rationale for their engagement in power struggles. The term *fatong* (constitutional orthodoxy) emerged during the early Republic to describe the political legitimacy endowed by a certain constitution. It apparently derived from a traditional Confucian term, *daotong* (orthodoxy of the Way), which may be loosely translated as moral tradition. In an age when the value of a constitution was universally accepted, the term suggested that a constitution, however created, could automatically give one authority, much as the Confucian teachings did in the past. Such efforts to mystify the constitution in the end vulgarized it, making the realization of constitutional democracy in China even more difficult.

Wang Ke-wen

References

Ch'en, Jerome. "Historical Background." *Modern China's Search for a Political Form,* ed. Jack Gray, 1–40. London, England: Oxford University Press, 1969.

Constitutions
See CONSTITUTIONAL ORTHODOXY *(Fatong)*

Critiques of Ancient History (Gushibian)
See GU JIEGANG

Culturalism
See HAN NATIONALISM

D

Dagongbao (L'Impartial)

Founded in Tianjin in 1902, *Dagongbao* was generally regarded as the most influential privately-owned newspaper in Republican China.

The newspaper was not successful in the beginning. Its original owner, the reform-minded Manchu Catholic Ying Hua, sold the newspaper to an Anhui Clique politician in 1916. For the next decade or so it became the mouthpiece of the pro-Japanese Anfu Club, and in 1925 it was forced to suspend publication following the downfall of that faction.

One year later, the newspaper resumed publication under the guidance of a new group of owners—the triumvirate of Wu Dingchang, Hu Zhengzhi, and Zhang Jiluan. It underwent a dramatic transformation in organization and outlook. Wu, an experienced politician and banker, provided the newspaper with the necessary political and financial support. Hu had been general manager and editor-in-chief of the newspaper between 1916 and 1925; he now concentrated on management. And the writings of Zhang, a well-known journalist, soon attracted nationwide attention. Jointly the "Big Three" designed the motto of the new *Dagongbao*: "non-partisan, never sold-out to political or commercial pressures, no advancement of private interests, and not blind to the truth." By the 1930s, it had become one of the most prestigious and best-selling daily newspapers in the country.

In 1935 the Nanjing government recruited Wu, who came to be associated with the Political Study Clique in the ruling Guomindang (GMD). Thereafter the newspaper, while generally liberal, sometimes reflected the views of certain groups in the government and became increasingly more moderate in its criticism of the GMD. It was a strong supporter, for example, of Chiang Kaishek's policy of "domestic pacification before external resistance" with regard to the Chinese Communists and the invading Japanese. In 1936, it began the publication of a Shanghai edition.

After the outbreak of the Sino-Japanese War, *Dagongbao* moved with the government first to Hankou and then to Chongqing. It subsequently published separate editions in Guilin and Hong Kong. The wartime editorials by Zhang Jiluan, before his death in 1941, often spoke for the nationalist Chinese in support of the war effort. However, *Dagongbao* also was seen as being close to the political and business establishment. Following the Japanese surrender the newspaper returned to Tianjin and Shanghai, and the Hong Kong edition was restored in 1948. Its staff was divided in supporting the GMD and the Chinese Communist Party (CCP) during the civil war of 1945–1949. Wang Yunsheng, who succeeded Zhang Jiluan as editor-in-chief, sympathized with the CCP, whereas Hu Zhengzhi and Wu Dingchang still sided with the GMD. Yet overall the newspaper took a pro-government stand.

Wu resigned as head of *Dagongbao* in 1948 and Hu died in 1949. In 1953, under the People's Republic, the Tianjin and Shanghai editions combined in Tianjin, then moved to Beijing in 1956. Shortly after the beginning of the Cultural Revolution in 1966, the newspaper ended its publication on the mainland. The pro-CCP Hong Kong edition has continued its publication to this date.

Wang Ke-wen

References
Pepper, Suzanne. *Civil War in China: The*

Political Struggle, 1945–1949. Berkeley: University of California Press, 1978.

Ting, Lee-hsia Hsu. *Government Control of the Press in Modern China, 1900–1948.* Cambridge, MA: Harvard University Press, 1975.

Dai Jitao (1891–1949)

Guomindang leader and theorist, Dai Jitao's interpretation of the Three Peoples' Principles was the ideological foundation of Chiang Kaishek's Nanjing government.

A native of Zhejiang but born in Sichuan, Dai Jitao (Chuanxian) became an anti-Manchu revolutionary during his studies in Japan in 1905–1909. In 1910 he edited and wrote for revolutionary newspapers in Shanghai under the penname "Tianchou." Wanted by the Qing government, he fled to Southeast Asia and joined Sun Yatsen's Tongmenghui (Revolutionary Alliance) shortly before the Revolution of 1911. In the early years of the Republic, Dai founded his own newspaper, *Minquanbao (People's Rights),* and was briefly involved in the organization of the Liberal Party *(Ziyoudang).* In 1913, he participated in the anti-Yuan Shikai "Second Revolution" and, upon its failure, fled to Japan with Sun Yatsen. From then on Dai became a close assistant to Sun. During 1917 to 1923, while Sun made several attempts to establish a regime at Canton and rejuvenate his party, renamed the Guomindang (GMD) in 1919, Dai served as Sun's secretary and played an important role in Party propaganda. In the wake of the May Fourth movement, Dai edited *Xingqi pinglun (Weekly Review),* a GMD organ in Shanghai, and introduced Marxist theories into China. He was said to have helped with the organization of the Chinese Communist Party (CCP) but refused to join the CCP when it was founded in 1921, because of his personal ties to Sun.

In 1924, Sun reorganized the GMD in Canton, under the guidance of the Soviet Union, and Dai was appointed into the new Party leadership. Although once displaying an academic interest in Marxism, Dai now turned uneasy with the GMD-CCP United Front and suspicious of the CCP's intention in the alliance. After Sun's death in March 1925, Dai stayed in Shanghai. He wrote two controversial pamphlets, *The Philosophical Foundation of Sun-Wenism* and *The National Revolution and the Chinese Guomindang,* which questioned the wisdom, as well as the feasibility, of the current cooperation between the GMD and the CCP, and proposed to replace the Marxist doctrine of class struggle with a "class harmony" based on the Confucian concept of humanity *(ren'ai).*

Dai also claimed that Sun's political ideas had inherited China's moral tradition *(daotong),* which could be traced to the ancient sage-kings and to Confucius. This attempt to Confucianize Sun's Three Peoples' Principles, in sharp contrast to the internationalist revolutionary line which the United Front maintained at the time, quickly attracted widespread attention. Dai's prestige in the GMD and his skillful exploitation of the influential Confucian tradition provided a timely ideological basis for the conservative elements in the Party who opposed the United Front. The leftists branded Dai's theory "Dai-Jitaoism" and accused him of distorting the teaching of Sun. When some of the anti-United Front leaders in the GMD organized the Western Hills meeting near Beijing in November 1925, they were apparently inspired by Dai's works, although Dai himself eventually disassociated himself from the faction.

Dai's theory also influenced his one-time protégé, Chiang Kaishek. When Chiang launched his "party purification" and terminated the United Front in April 1926, he adopted Dai's interpretation of the Three Peoples' Principles as the ideological rationale for his political action. Class harmony under a traditionalist and nationalist framework, and the emphasis on a Confucianist moral approach to China's "revolutionary reconstruction," characterized the ideological orientation of Chiang's Nanjing government in the 1920s and 1930s. Dai supervised Chiang's ideological press organ *Xinshengming* (New Life Monthly), in 1926 to 1930, and under Chiang, Dai became the mentor of other leading theorists, such as Zhou Fohai. During the Nanjing Decade (1927–37) Dai headed the Party's Propaganda Department, the government's Examination Yuan and many other high positions, but he was never politically powerful. His support for Chiang, nevertheless, lent a degree of legitimacy to Nanjing as the successor to Sun's mantle. Dai became a devout Buddhist in his later years. He committed suicide on the eve of the collapse of the GMD on the mainland in 1949.

In the GMD's transition "from revolution to restoration," to borrow the expression of Mary C. Wright, Dai Jitao's role was indispensable. His reinterpretation of Sun Yatsen's ideas countered the iconoclast currents of the May

Fourth era and reaffirmed the fundamentality of Confucian tradition in the Chinese revolution. Frustrated by China's political weakness, Dai found comfort and hope in the Chinese cultural past and saw it as the potential rallying point for the national revolution (guomin geming). Such an appeal to the national heritage not only helped Chiang Kaishek to establish an anti-Communist regime in China under the GMD banner in the 1920s, but paved the way for the incorporation of Fascism into the ideological program of the regime in the 1930s.

Wang Ke-wen

References

Mast, Herman III. "Tai Chi-t'ao, Sunism and Marxism During the May Fourth Movement in Shanghai." *Modern Asian Studies* 5, no. 3 (July 1971): 227–49.

——— and William Saywell. "The Culturalism of Political Despair: Tai Chi-t'ao and Chiang Kai-shek." *Asia Quarterly* no. 3 (1972): 227–44.

———. "Revolution Out of Tradition: The Political Ideology of Tai Chi-t'ao." *Journal of Asian Studies* 34, no. 1 (November 1974): 73–98.

Dai Li (1897–1946)

Dai Li was head of the secret police and military intelligence in Guomindang China. Born to a middle-income family in Jiangshan, Zhejiang province, Dai lost his father as a child. He enrolled in a middle school in Hangzhou in 1914, but soon dropped out and began a ten-year period of roving and wandering. During this period, he became acquainted with Chiang Kaishek and Dai Jitao in Shanghai, which changed his life. In 1926, Dai went to Canton to study at the Whampoa Military Academy and joined the Guomindang (GMD). As a student at Whampoa, he took the initiative to gather information on his classmates for Chiang, the commandant. His service apparently impressed Chiang, because during the Northern Expedition of 1925 to 1927 he was ordered to spy for the National Revolutionary Army in the warlord territories. In 1932, Dai participated in the organization of the Blue Shirts (or *Lixingshe*), a pro-Chiang faction within the GMD, and became head of its "Special Service Section." He was in charge of the faction's clandestine information-gathering activity in government agencies, as well as private

organizations, throughout the country. Due to this experience Chiang appointed him in 1934 as chief of the second section of the first formal secret police organization under the GMD government, the Military Commission's Bureau of Investigation and Statistics (*Juntong*).

In the prewar years, Dai aggressively executed Chiang's policy of "domestic pacification before external resistance." He ordered the assassination of Chiang's political enemies, such as Shi Liangcai and Yang Xinfo, and helped to sabotage the Fujian Rebellion of 1933 and the Guangdong-Guangxi Incident of 1936. At the same time, his men were responsible for killing several notable figures whom the government suspected of collaborating with the Japanese. Japan therefore viewed Dai as a major anti-Japanese leader in the GMD. During the Xian Incident of 1936, Dai went to Xian in an attempt to rescue Chiang, which furthered Chiang's trust and appreciation of his service.

Shortly after the outbreak of the Sino-Japanese War in 1937 Dai organized wartime intelligence in Shanghai and established the National Salvation Army (*Zhongyi jiuguojun*), an anti-Japanese guerrilla force in eastern China directly controlled by the Bureau of Investigation and Statistics. When Wang Jingwei went to Hanoi to lead the peace movement in 1938, Dai's men arranged an aborted attempt on Wang's life. Thereafter Dai's agents executed other "traitors" in the Japanese-occupied territories.

In 1938, Chiang established another Bureau of Investigation and Statistics under the GMD's Central Committee and transferred members of the C. C. Clique from the Military Committee's Bureau to the new organization. Dai was then promoted to head the Military Committee's Bureau. In 1943 Dai also became director of the Sino-American Institute for Special Techniques in Chongqing, which enlisted American assistance in the training of Chinese secret agents and police. On the whole, the operations of the Military Committee's Bureau constituted an important part of China's war effort.

As the second United Front between the GMD and the Chinese Communist Party deteriorated in the final years of the war, Dai's tasks included the imprisonment and killing of Communists and anti-GMD elements as well as spying on the Japanese invasion. From 1943 to 1945, he was also in charge of suppressing the smuggling of goods into and out of areas under the GMD government's control. This in fact allowed him to participate in that smuggling operation and obtain enormous profit for himself and the bureau. Following the Japanese surrender in 1945, Dai's men were among the first to appear in the formerly occupied territories to confiscate properties that belonged to "traitors" (collaborators). This offered them yet another opportunity to engage in corruption. Seven months later, Dai was killed in a plane crash.

Known as "China's Himmler," Dai often symbolized the "white terror" under the GMD. He was ruthless in consolidating the power of the Party, and the power of Chiang Kaishek, in China. On the other hand, the anti-Japanese activities he conducted for the Blue Shirts and for the Military Committee's Bureau were undeniably driven by nationalist impulses. To him, protecting Chiang's leadership was as critical to the survival of China as undermining the Japanese invasion. That end justified all means.

Xu Youwei

References

Eastman, Lloyd E. *The Abortive Revolution: China Under Nationalist Rule, 1927–1937.* Cambridge, MA: Harvard University Press, 1974.

Schaller, Michael. *The U.S. Crusade in China, 1937–1945.* New York, NY: Columbia University Press, 1979.

Dalai Lama

See TIBETAN INDEPENDENCE MOVEMENT

Datong

Datong, which literally means "great unity," is a concept that represents one of the most enduring images of the good society in Chinese tradition. *Datong* developed out of an eclectic background during the Warring States era (403–221 B.C.) and became an important part of Confucian thought from the Han dynasty (202 B.C.–A.D. 220) onwards. The term refers primarily to the social order and suggests a society that would relate like a great family, provide human equality, and integrate the best in human experience. *Datong* also developed connotations of an international order of universal peace and harmony. This was because of its familial overtones as well as its association with the universal political claims of the Zhou dynasty (1027?–221 B.C.). In its international

sense, the term was commonly linked to the idea of *taiping*, "universal peace."

In the early twentieth century *datong* was often equated with Western socialism. Like socialism, the concept of *datong* might, because of its universalistic aspect, seem theoretically antithetical to nationalism. This was sometimes the case, most importantly in the thought of Wang Yangming, who is said to have received one of his profound insights into human equality and harmony while living in exile among tribesmen in the South. However, as with socialism, *datong* has been in fact often tied to nationalism. Indeed, the very thinkers and movements identified with the concept frequently also promoted nationalism. A major reason for this connection is because *datong* as a social ideal and nationalism as a political creed were both features of the general pattern of Chinese oppositional thought.

Gu Yanwu, the early Qing scholar whose Han nationalist thought deeply affected the anti-Manchu revolutionaries of the late Qing, was also an important advocate of *datong* ideals. The same was true of the Taiping rebels, who had powerful nationalist elements in their ideology, but advocated *datong* as a social ideal (a link reflected in the name of their movement).

The two most important *datong* thinkers of the late nineteenth and early twentieth centuries were Kang Youwei and Sun Yatsen. Both advocated the egalitarian, socialist ideals of *datong* and desired a universal world order that would abolish nation-states. Kang spelled out these desiderata in his *Datongshu* (On the Datong). Similarly, the dual ideals of social equality and international brotherhood are enshrined in the second line of the national anthem of the Republic of China, with its hope that mankind will "enter the *datong.*" At the same time, however, Kang and Sun were fervent nationalists who opposed imperialism and struggled for the national independence of China. In their views, an independent China would serve as a basis, indeed a stepping-stone, for the universal order of *datong.* The compatibility of socialism and cosmopolitanism with nationalism is, of course, also evident in the ideology of Chinese Communism.

John Schrecker

References

John Schrecker. *The Chinese Revolution in Historical Perspective.* New York, NY: Praeger, 1991.

Dazhai and Daqing

In 1964, Chinese Communist Party (CCP) chairman Mao Zedong forwarded the slogan "In agriculture, learn from Dazhai! In industry, learn from Daqing!" as a call to the people to take these two production units as the models for China's economic development. Dazhai, a small village in Shanxi province, and Daqing, a large oil field in Heilongjiang, were regarded as the embodiments of Mao's emphasis on human will as the decisive factor in development, and his dictum to put "politics in command" of production.

Dazhai and Daqing became important symbols of Mao's Cultural Revolution quest to keep the People's Republic of China (PRC) on the socialist road. The two models also served as concrete examples of Mao's attempt to forge a distinctive Chinese path to modernization that could serve as an inspiration to other developing countries. They can therefore be regarded as part of the effort to bolster the PRC's international prestige and Chinese nationalism in the late Maoist era.

The Dazhai model consisted of a number of specific features to be emulated by other rural communities. Dazhai was touted for its emphasis on self-reliance and mass mobilization, rather than on state financial support or technological inputs, as the foundations of its success in raising production and overcoming natural impediments to development. The Dazhai "work-point system," in which peasant incomes were determined by a process of self-assessment and public evaluation that measured both work performance and political attitude, was hailed as a revolutionary breakthrough toward a more egalitarian method of distribution in the agricultural sector. Dazhai also used a more radical system of financial reconciliation ("brigade-level accounting") than that practiced by nearly all other rural communes at the time. Dazhai's stringent policies restricting private plots, household side-line production, and free markets were deemed exemplary measures for "cutting off the tail of capitalism" in the Chinese countryside.

During its heyday as a national model, Dazhai was led by Chen Yonggui, a peasant who had become village Party secretary in the early 1950s. In the 1960s and 1970s, Chen rose to important county, provincial, and ultimately national positions, including vice-premier and CCP Politburo member. Following the death of Mao Zedong in 1976, Dazhai initially achieved even more prominence as a model of agricultural development because of its close association with interim leader Hua Guofeng.

But the ascendancy of Deng Xiaoping and the implementation of market-oriented economic reforms led to a thorough repudiation of the Dazhai model in the early 1980s. Dazhai was criticized for promoting extreme leftism in its highly egalitarian distribution policies, for magnifying the role of class struggle in the countryside, and for falsifying grain production figures. Its much-vaunted self-reliance was also said to have been a sham when it was revealed that Dazhai had actually been receiving large state subsidies and other forms of aid for years. By late 1980, Chen Yonggui had lost all his official positions; he died in March 1986.

The Daqing oil field was first opened for production in 1959, and the heroic saga of its discovery and early development became an important part of the Daqing model. By the mid-1960s, Daqing was supplying over half of China's total national production of crude oil. Its major economic significance was the role it played in breaking China's dependence on imported oil.

The ideological significance of Daqing was based on its system of revolutionary enterprise management, its political rectitude, and its unique pattern of industrial development. The oil field was administered according to the principle of "democracy in politics, production, and economics," which stressed cadre participation in labor and worker participation in management. Daqing also stressed moral rather than material incentives and placed great emphasis on the study of "Mao Zedong thought" as spurs to worker productivity.

Daqing received praise for its integration of town and countryside within a single production unit, a key component of the Maoist model of development. Rather than building a gigantic Soviet-style "oil city" near the production site, Daqing consisted of dozens of scattered "residential points" of 100,400 families clustered around small towns. These communities engaged in agricultural production which made Daqing self-sufficient in food and were the locales of educational, health, and other service facilities utilized by the oil workers and their dependents.

Although Daqing's luster as a model faded in the post-Mao era, it has never been subjected to the kind of blistering criticism that was leveled at Dazhai. Indeed, in 1989, the thirtieth anniversary of the opening of the oil field was celebrated with some fanfare in the PRC. Daqing continues to be one of the major sources of China's domestic oil production.

William A. Joseph

References

Chan, Leslie W. *The Taching (Daqing) Oil Field: A Maoist Model for Economic Development.* Canberra: Australian National University Press, 1974.

Tsou, Tang, Marc Blecher, and Mitch Meisner. "National Agricultural Policy: The Dazhai Model and Local Change in the Post-Mao Era." *The Transition to Socialism in China,* ed. Mark Selden and Victor Lippit. Armonk, NY: M. E. Sharpe, 1982.

Debate of Maritime Defense versus Frontier Defense

In the early 1870s, as Muslim rebellions and the Ili Crisis emerged in China's northwestern frontier and the Ryukyu-Formosa Incident threatened her southeast coast, a policy debate arose within the Qing government concerning the relative urgency of the empire's maritime and inland defenses.

At the time, the Qing court was considering the request by Zuo Zongtang, governor-general of Shaanxi and Gansu, to organize a costly expedition against the Russian-supported Muslim rebellion in Xinjiang. Leaders of the Self-Strengthening movement, such as Prince Gong, Wenxiang, and Li Hongzhang, objected to Zuo's plan. They perceived the menace of Japan, shown in her recent expansion to Ryukyu and Formosa (Taiwan), as deserving greater attention than Russia. Li and other coastal officials proposed instead the creation of a modern army along the coast to strengthen China's maritime defense.

Advocates of maritime defense argued that Xinjiang was far from the capital, surrounded by strong neighbors (*e.g.,* Russia and Great Britain), and consisted of barren land and therefore did not warrant the effort and precious financial resources of the government to recover and defend. They further suggested that to adopt a conciliatory posture in the inland frontier, *i.e.,* to suspend the Xinjiang expedition, could preserve the dynasty's strength for aggressive actions at a more appropriate time in the future.

Zuo Zongtang had his supporters at the court. To counter Li's arguments, they indicated that Xinjiang, although located in the north-

west, shielded Mongolia and thus indirectly the capital. Moreover, it was an area conquered by the dynastic forefathers and should never be given up. They did not question the importance of naval development, but pointed out that coastal defense had already been funded regularly and sufficiently, now inland defense should receive its share. Zuo's faction emphasized that the Russian advance in Xinjiang posed far more an immediate threat to national security than did any possible attack from the sea. In fact, they predicted, if the Muslim rebellion in Xinjiang was not suppressed, a continuing Russian aggression in the northwest would motivate other Western powers to invade along the coast. The Russian problem was therefore "a sickness of the heart," whereas the Western and Japanese problem "a sickness of the limbs."

The Qing court eventually agreed with Zuo, though it continued to support the projects of naval development. In 1875, the court appointed Zuo as commissioner of the Xinjiang campaign. Two years later, Zuo successfully suppressed the Muslim rebellion and pacified the region. The Russian occupation of Ili, however, was not resolved until 1881.

The controversy regarding maritime and frontier strategies revealed the unprecedented challenges China faced during the second half of the nineteenth century. Since the Opium War of 1839–42, Western military threat from the sea had exposed the weakness of China's coastal defense, yet Russian and British encroachments in Inner Asia also reminded the Chinese of the necessity of maintaining a strong inland defense. In the wake of the two Opium wars and the Taiping and Nian rebellions, this dilemma was exacerbated by the increasing financial burdens of the Qing. The two camps in the debate expressed opposing views of the country's priorities, but both represented the national concern of protecting China's territorial integrity and international status in modern times.

Wang Ke-wen

References

Hsu, Immanuel C. Y. "The Great Policy Debate in China, 1874: Maritime Defense vs. Frontier Defense." *Harvard Journal of Asiatic Studies* no. 25 (1965): 212–28.

Debate of Revolution *versus* Constitutionalism

See MINBAO; XINMIN CONGBAO

Debate on Chinese Social History

In the May Fourth movement era, the Marxian view of Chinese society largely ignored the issue of class struggle. With the formation of the Guomindang-Chinese Communist Party (GMD-CCP) United Front in 1923 and the May Thirtieth movement in 1925, the class issue became important to political activists and radical intellectuals alike. From 1925 to 1927, as a rift appeared in the GMD-CCP coalition, "class analysis" of Chinese society emerged as a central ideological concern for those caught in the crisis. In Moscow, Trotsky called for an immediate break between the CCP and the GMD in order to stage a socialist revolution in China. He criticized Stalin's thesis that China was still a feudal society. In China, following the collapse of the United Front in 1927, various factions in both parties began to present their divergent Marxian views to justify their political programs. Wang Jingwei's Left GMD was the first to do so. What ensued was a debate among Chinese Marxists on the nature and history of Chinese society; the debate reached its climax during 1931 to 1933 in the pages of Shanghai's *Reading Magazine (Dushu zazhi)*.

The Left GMD theorist, Tao Xisheng, first enunciated the thesis of the Chinese society as one of "commercial capitalism." He averred that feudalism had been dissolved by the formation of commercial capitalism two millennia ago, resulting in commercialized landownership and bureaucratic hegemony. Foreign imperialism in the modern era actually reinforced indigenous usurious capitalism. Such a view reflected the position of the Left GMD, which supported a political revolution against imperialism, bureaucrats, and warlords.

The Chinese Stalinists in the CCP reversed Tao's thesis, arguing that Chinese society was still feudal, and only its superstructure differed from Western feudalism. They focused exclusively on the "mode of exploitation" which, they argued, was largely "extra-economical" (or feudal) in China. The Stalinists therefore advocated a program of anti-feudal, anti-imperialist revolution led by the proletariat.

The Chinese Trotskyites believed that "remanent feudal factors" in China were rendered insignificant by imperialism, or global capitalism. Land in China had been a commodity even before imperialist intrusion, and now the country had become part of the world market. The Trotskyites split into diverse views. Ren Shu, for example, discerned advanced capitalism in China. For Liu Renjing, Chinese capitalism still relied on feudal exploitation. Yan Lingfeng suggested that imperialism was steadily eroding the feudal vestiges.

After 1931, the debate also branched into historical studies. On the nature of imperial China, five major schools took shape: (1) the ex-Communist Zhu Qihua's "feudal" thesis; (2) Tao Xisheng's "early capitalism under feudalistic hegemony" thesis; (3) the Trotskyite Li Ji's "pre-capitalism" thesis; (4) the "society under absolute monarchy" thesis argued by the *Reading Magazine* faction, notably Wang Lixi and Hu Qiuyuan; and (5) the heretical "Asiatic mode of production" thesis, aired by L. Madgyar, E. Varga, and K. Wittfogel within the Comintern.

Among the above models, the "Asiatic" position enjoyed no support in China; the most popular was the "post-feudal" theses. The latter and its variants, such as "pre-capitalism" and "absolutism," relied on Marx's definition of "commercial capital" as corrosive to the natural economy. The "feudal" thesis, on the other hand, denied "commercial capital" the capability to form a new mode of production. Both the "post-feudal" and "feudal" positions attributed long-term socio-economic stagnancy to China's undeveloped international commerce.

The debate also dwelled on the presence or absence of slavery in Chinese history, an issue raised by Guo Moruo's study of ancient China. Guo attempted to combine Engels' and L. Morgan's theories, thereby causing some interpretive confusions, but his schema reaffirmed in Chinese history a linear succession of modes of production, which was basically a Stalinist view.

The fact that so many top scholars and writers participated in this debate attested to the popularity of Marxism within the Chinese intelligentsia at the time. The Left GMD and the Chinese Trotskyites introduced some of the original theories in the debate. The ruling GMD faction, under Chiang Kaishek, rejected Marxian views completely, whereas the CCP mainstream rigidly defended the Stalinist dogma. The debate did not end in a clear victory in the 1930s, but the Stalinists ultimately "won" the dispute with their political victory in 1949.

Lung-kee Sun

References
Dirlik, Arif. *Revolution and History: The Origins of Marxist Historiography in China, 1919–1937.* Berkeley: University of California Press, 1978.

Debate on Democracy and Dictatorship

As the six-year political tutelage of the Guomindang (GMD) was nearing its end in 1935, a debate emerged among the Chinese intellectuals on the merits of democracy versus dictatorship in China. The debate took place in the country's leading journals and newspapers, such as *Duli pinglun (Independent Review)*, *Dagongbao (L'Impartial)*, *Dongfang zazhi (The Eastern Magazine)* and *Guowen zhoubao (National News Weekly)*, from 1933 through 1936.

In 1934, the GMD government, following the timetable it had announced earlier, began to prepare for the conclusion of its Party rule and the transition to constitutional democracy. Many intellectuals, both within and outside the government, voiced objections. Frustrated by the failure of the democratic experiment in the early Republic, and inspired by the anti-democratic trends in the West after World War I, they believed that China should adopt "enlightened despotism," or simply despotism, not liberal democracy. These intellectuals argued that China, as a nation, was not prepared for democracy. The Chinese people, they suggested, lacked either the education or the cultural background to foster the sense of nationhood and citizenship that was required for democratic institutions to succeed. Moreover, democracy could not provide the kind of efficient and farsighted leadership that China badly needed. As Mussolini's Italy, Hitler's Germany, and Stalin's Russia demonstrated to them in the early 1930s, a capable dictatorship could rescue a country from chaos and defeat and deliver it to unity and strength. Advocates for dictatorship in the debate included T. F. Tsiang (Jiang Tingfu), V. K. Ting (Ding Wenjiang), Wu Jingchao, Chen Zhimai, and Qian Duansheng, all of them Western-trained scholars.

Defenders of democracy were also educated in the West, such as Hu Shih, Zhang Foquan, and Peng Xuepei. Their arguments, however, focused less on the strength of democracy than on the weaknesses of the GMD's Party rule. Since the dictatorship of the GMD had proved to be disastrous, they contended, it must be replaced by a new system. While not necessarily in disagreement with their opponents on China's need for effective government and strong central authority, they argued that democracy is more stable and dependable than dictatorship. Hu Shih described democracy as a form of "kindergarten government," in contrast to the outstanding ability and knowledge that would be required for the leader of a dictatorship, and therefore suited the environment of contemporary China.

To an extent the intellectual mood, as illustrated in this debate, was capitalized by the ruling GMD to prolong its grasp of power. In 1932 Chiang Kaishek secretly approved of the organization of the Blue Shirts *(Lixingshe)*, an intra-party faction that promoted fascist ideas and activity in the country. If he was reluctant to conclude the "Political Tutelage" on time, the pro-dictatorship arguments offered by the scholars gave him the timely intellectual support for seeking an alternative to democracy. Although not entirely the result of the debate, the "Political Tutelage" did not end in 1935 as planned but lasted for another twelve years.

T. F. Tsiang soon joined the Nanjing government, yet few other participants in the debate supported Chiang Kaishek or the GMD. It does not seem that their position in the debate was motivated by selfish political interests. Rather, the main theme of the debate was the concern for national well-being. The pro-dictatorship side was willing to sacrifice individual liberty for the sake of national stability and power, while the pro-democracy side often pointed out the usefulness of representative government in enhancing national solidarity. After decades of domestic disturbance and foreign encroachment, the educated Chinese were in a state of despair, longing for any means that could restore the country to a position of strength and respectability. The debate in the early 1930s clearly reflected this feeling.

Wang Ke-wen

References

Eastman, Lloyd E. *The Abortive Revolution: China under Nationalist Rule, 1927–1937*. Cambridge, MA: Harvard University Press, 1974.

Debate on Science and Philosophy of Life

The debate on science and philosophy of life in 1923 was a controversy that divided Chinese intellectuals concerning the importance of science in modern life. Informed by the European debates on freedom versus necessity, mind versus matter, and ethics versus science, the Chinese intellectuals argued whether or not science could offer a view of life to humankind. Although it employed much philosophical jargon, the debate in fact addressed the relative merit of Chinese and Western cultures. For some Chinese intellectuals, the Chinese culture would bring a human face to the increasingly technological world shaped by Western culture.

The idea of "strengthening China by learning from the West" dominated the Chinese intellectual scene from the Opium War (1840–42) to the First World War (1914–18). For more than half a century, the West seemed to have offered the Chinese solutions to their quest for modernity; and Western superiority was understood to be rooted in science. But the massive devastation in Europe during the First World War altered the Chinese view of the West. The Chinese saw Western science bringing forth deadly destruction rather than offering more material benefits to humankind. Instead of enhancing world peace, the Western political system produced greed and animosity. Suddenly, some Chinese intellectuals discovered that their own culture might have something of value to offer to the world.

This Chinese re-visioning of the West received its most artful expression in the writings of Liang Qichao. Upon his return from a trip to Europe in 1919, he published his famous *Reflections on a European Journey (Ouyou xinyinglu)*, lamenting the malaise he saw in Europe and consoling his countrymen for having a humanistic tradition that could not be found in Europe. Liang Qichao's view was extended by Liang Shuming. In his *Eastern and Western Cultures and Their Philosophies (Dongxi wenhua jiqi zhexue)*, written in 1921, Liang Shuming argued that Western material culture represented only the first stage of human development, and it would soon be replaced by the Chinese culture of moderation and the Indian culture of asceticism.

But the two Liangs' view did not attract much attention until a European-trained philosopher, Carsun Chang (Zhang Junmai), rearticulated their view in the form of the incompatibility between science and the philosophy of life. In a 1923 speech to students at Qinghua University in Beijing, Chang spoke about the limitations of science in enriching human spiritual life. According to Chang, science concerned itself with objectivity, logical explanation and analytical method. It differed diametrically from human spiritual life, which was subjective, intuitive, and synthetic. Due to their opposite natures, Chang concluded, no matter how developed science might be, it could never solve problems involving the philosophy

of life. To solve philosophical problems, Chang advised his audience to consult the Chinese humanistic tradition, especially neo-Confucianism of the Song and Ming dynasties.

Shortly after Carsun Chang's speech was published, the Glasgow-trained geologist, V. K. Ting (Ding Wenjiang), expressed his disapproval. Ting called Chang "a metaphysical ghost" who deceived himself by indulging in speculative inquiry. Advocating "the omnipotence of science," Ting argued that science could provide solutions to all facets of human life, spiritual and material alike. Armed with its rational mode of thinking and its empirical emphasis, science was the only reliable means for humankind to know the world and to change it. For Ting, science was more than a technique; it was a rational world view that characterized modernity. First practiced by Westerners, science was a universal human knowledge, accessible to all peoples regardless of race, culture, and language. For Ting, to be modern, one had to be first and foremost scientific. From Ting's perspective, Carsun Chang's fault was twofold: (1) he stressed the particularity of Chinese humanistic tradition as something distinguishing the Chinese from other peoples; and (2) he denied science as the common factor in the modern world.

The Ting-Chang debate quickly mushroomed into an impassioned polemic. Within a year, the polemic involved a large number of scholars and resulted in numerous publications regarding whether the Western example had to be accepted as the universal model for modernization, or whether there could be a specific Chinese road to modernity.

Tze-ki Hon

References

Kwok, D. W. Y. *Scientism in Chinese Thought 1900–1950*. New Haven, CT: Yale University Press, 1965.

Debates on Chinese and Western Cultures
The Western intrusion inevitably gave birth to an intellectual puzzle in modern China: the confrontation between the two cultures. China's worsening position in this encounter generated self-doubt within the intelligentsia. In the 1890s, Yan Fu compared the Chinese ethos unfavorably with the Western one. During the Hundred Days Reform of 1898, Hunanese reformists Fan Zhui and Yi Nai advocated full-scale Westernization

as a way of securing China's survival in the world (it was the earliest instance of wholesale westernization). Zhang Zhidong, a high Qing official, opposed the reformists' Westernism with his famous *ti-yong* theory, which restricted Western influences to "functions" *(yong)* serving the Chinese "substance" *(ti)*.

The May Fourth movement era witnessed a major confrontation between westernizers and defenders of Eastern culture. Beginning in 1915, a series of skirmishes occurred between the two camps. Conservatives such as Du Yaquan, Zhang Shizhao, and Zhu Diaosun countered the Westernism of Chen Duxiu, Wu Zhihui and Zhang Dongsun with their prediction of the spiritual leadership of the East in the future global cultural synthesis. To them, the destruction of Europe during World War I suggested that the Western culture was spiritually bankrupt and therefore unworthy of Chinese adoption. The debate continued into the 1920s, against the backdrop of Rabindranath Tagore's visit in China, the publications of Liang Qichao's European travelogues, and Liang Shuming's book on Eastern and Western cultures. It overlapped with another debate, on "science versus the philosophy of life."

In 1923, Hu Shih made a scathing critique of Liang Shuming's mystic portrayal of Eastern culture. In 1926, he further attacked the spiritual claim of the Eastern culture camp by stating that the East was inferior to the West materially and spiritually. In 1929, in an English article for the *Chinese Christian Year-Book,* Hu introduced the slogan "wholesale westernization" *(quanpan xihua)* as a national goal. He recast it into "wholehearted globalization" *(quanpan shijiehua)* in 1935, when another cultural debate was occasioned by the ten professors' "Declaration of Cultural Construction on a Chinese Basis." The slogan "wholesale westernization" was then picked up by Chen Xujing, who became its most fervid champion. The Nanjing regime under Chiang Kaishek, on the other hand, promoted the revival of traditional morals with its New Life movement.

The question resurfaced in Taiwan in the 1960s. The "wholesale westernizer" Li Ao laid claim to Hu Shih's mantle. Li used cultural iconoclasm to discredit the gerontocratic Guomindang (GMD) rule on the island. He was not rebutted by traditionalists, but by ex-radicals such as Hu Qiuyuan. The debate soon degenerated into an exchange of insults and mutual incrimination of Communist affiliations. Meanwhile, the liberal dissident Yin Haiguang reexamined the cultural issue with American social sciences theories. He substituted "wholesale westernization" with the new concept of modernization based on science, democracy, and moral reconstruction. In 1967, the GMD regime offered its own response to the culture debate by launching the Chinese Cultural Revival movement *(Zhonghua wenhua fuxing yundong)*. It reaffirmed Chinese tradition and saw its modern embodiment in Sun Yatsen's Three Peoples' Principles. The regime soon silenced Yin Haiguang by depriving him of his professorship at the National Taiwan University. In 1971, Li Ao also landed in jail for sedition.

The crisis of Marxism in post-Mao China led to the resurrection of Westernism on the mainland. Its exponents, Fang Lizhi, Wang Ruowang and Liu Binyan, were criticized in the 1987 official campaign against the "spiritual pollution," which was said to have been caused by bourgeois liberalization. They were specifically accused of advocating "wholesale westernization" and expelled from the Chinese Communist Party (CCP). The television series "River Elegy" *("Heshang")*, produced by a group of young intellectuals in the late 1980s, also met official censure for its glorification of the "maritime culture" *(i.e.,* the West) at the expense of the "Yellow River culture" *(i.e.,* China). Under the CCP, socialism was the official Chinese "substance" which the (capitalist) Western "functions" can only supplement but not replace. The culture debate continues.

Lung-kee Sun

Debates on the National Form of Literature

The Literary Revolution of the May Fourth era gave birth to a vernacular-based "new literature" which challenged the classical literature. The vernacular champions at the same time discovered an indigenous folk literature, different from both the classical Chinese *(wenyan)* and the westernized new style of writing. They found folk literature less artificial, and thus more representative of the people, than the commercialized popular literature—the "mandarin duck and butterfly" genre, for example. In the late 1920s, left-wing writers, regarding literature as an important instrument in advancing their political cause, launched an abortive attempt to create "revolutionary literature" as a genre. The failure of the latter also led Communist ideologues, notably Qu Qiubai, to ponder in the 1930s on the westernized literature's shortcomings and the advantages of literary "massification" *(dazhonghua), i.e.,* adopting literary forms familiar to ordinary Chinese.

The need was greatly accentuated by the Japanese invasion, when Chinese intellectuals tried to use literature to enhance nationalist sentiments. After the Manchurian Incident of 1931, Gu Jiegang, a stalwart of the folk literature movement, launched a propaganda journal, *Popular Readings (Tongsu duwu),* which employed the old story hawkers' techniques. When the Sino-Japanese War broke out in 1937, he used folksongs for anti-Japanese propaganda in *The Common People (Laobaixing).* This led to a discussion in central and southern China on the use of popular "old forms" in wartime literature. Among the discussants were the famous writers Lao She and Mao Dun, but the latter wrote from Hong Kong that "old forms," while necessary for communication, needed renovation as well.

The All-China Association of Literary Circles for the Resistance to Japan, founded in Hankou in May 1938, raised the slogan of "essays going to the village, essays joining the military rank." The use of "old forms" thus became critical in this task. Initially, the Chinese Communists, due to their anti-feudal biases, had reservations about this approach. The Wuhan Chinese Communist Party (CCP) organ, under the control of Wang Ming, criticized the Popular Readings Publishing Society, a pioneer of using "old forms," for its regressive tendencies.

Meanwhile, the CCP headquarters at Yan'an was launching its own campaign of sinification. Mao Zedong, in *The Chinese Communist Party's Position in the National War* (1938)—a critique of Wang Ming's dogmatism—introduced the Soviet term, "national form" *(minzu xingshi).* He argued that Chinese Marxism should have "Chinese style and Chinese manner delightful to the eyes and ears of the common people of China." The essay shaped the ongoing discussion on the use of "old forms" in literature.

Following Mao's essay, Yan'an launched an intensive discussion on the "national form" in culture, involving Zhou Yang, Ai Siqi, He Qifang, and others and the discussion spread to the Shanxi-Chahar-Hebei base area. The Communists emphasized the dialectical unity of old and new cultural forms but insisted that the content must be contemporary. Mao again spoke authoritatively in 1940 which defined "today's new culture" as "new democratic contents couched in national form," thus giving his approval to the use of indigenous "old forms."

A similar debate was also raging in the wartime capital of the Guomindang (GMD) government, Chongqing. In 1940, Gu Jiegang's associate in the Popular Readings Publishing Society, Xiang Linbing (Zhao Jibin), presented the thesis that only the folk form can be the central fountainhead of Chinese literature's national form. His denigration of westernized May Fourth literature provoked rebuttals from Ge Yihong and Hu Feng, who saw little redeeming value in "old forms." Hu especially exalted the cosmopolitanism of the new literature of the May Fourth movement. Both camps found supporters in Guilin, Kunming, Chengdu, Shanghai, and Hong Kong.

Two forums on literature's "national form" were held in Chongqing, in April and June 1940. Involved in this debate were such notable intellectuals as Ai Qing, Chen Jiying, Guo Moruo, Hu Sheng, and Pan Zinian. In early 1941, another forum on "national form" in drama was held in Chongqing. As the wartime GMD-CCP United Front was ending, the GMD newspapers charged that the notion of "national form" was in fact a disguise of "alien contents" in Chinese forms. Meanwhile, forums continued to be held in Yan'an and other CCP base areas. A 1941 forum in southeast Shanxi stated that the central fountainhead of literature's "national form" was "the battle of real life." Another forum on "national form" of poetry occurred in Pingshan, Hebei, involving the poet Tian Jian. The debate subsided after 1941, yet the issue of "national form" remained.

The event was the largest-scale of its kind in the republican era, and it portended the CCP-orchestrated nationwide intellectual debates under the People's Republic. The wartime condition imposed a near consensus among Chinese intellectuals regarding the function of literature as a tool to promote nationalism. Yet the exaltation of literature in "Chinese style and Chinese manner, delightful to the eyes and ears of the common people of China," persisted into the Communist era.

Lung-kee Sun

December Ninth Movement

The December Ninth movement was one of the largest anti-Japanese student protests in the Republican era.

Anti-imperialist sentiment had long been a primary moving force behind the student movement in modern China. After the Manchurian Incident of 1931, most nationalistic Chinese regarded Japan as the country's number one imperialist enemy. During the early 1930s, the Japanese expanded their territorial control in north China and the Guomindang (GMD) government in Nanjing, following a policy of "domestic pacification before external resistance," made repeated concessions to the Japanese. On December 7, 1935, Nanjing approved the establishment of the Hebei-Chahar Political Affairs Committee *(JiCha zhengwu weiyuanhui)* in Beiping, a semi-autonomous and seemingly pro-Japanese organization, as *de facto* administration in north China. This was a major step in Japan's effort to promote north China autonomy, as a preparatory stage of her annexation of the northern provinces.

Students in Beijing (Beiping) had been in the vanguard of the national student movement since the May Fourth demonstration in 1919. Now at the forefront of the Japanese encroachment, they immediately organized themselves for a massive protest. On December 9, thousands of university and middle-school students staged a demonstration in the city. The demonstrators held a mass meeting in front of the office of General He Yingqin, the leading GMD official in north China, and voiced their protest against the "North China Autonomy" conspiracy. They also demanded the disclosure of Sino-Japanese negotiations, an end to China's civil wars, and the protection of freedom of association and speech by the government. Following the meeting the students paraded through the streets, shouting slogans that were both anti-Japanese and critical of the Nanjing government. They soon clashed with the police and fighting ensued. More than one hundred demonstrators were injured in the struggle, and more than thirty of them arrested. The incident enraged the students, who launched a strike the next day. Another massive demonstration was held on December 16. Again the demonstrators ran into conflict with the police, resulting in more injuries and arrests. By then, the actions of the Beiping students had received nationwide sympathy and support. Students in other cities joined the protest. Faced with this outpouring of youthful anger, the Hebei-Chahar Political Affairs Committee postponed its date of establishment.

The Communist underground in Beiping assisted the December Ninth movement in both its organization and propaganda. The Chinese Communist Party (CCP), which had just completed its Long March to the Northwest, found the north China incident a convenient diversion of the GMD's attention and an opportunity to show its solidarity with the patriotic students. It succeeded in achieving these aims. A group of student leaders, including Huang Hua, Jiang Nanxiang and Yao Yilin, soon joined the CCP in Yan'an. Decades later, Huang became foreign minister of the People's Republic, Jiang education minister, and Yao vice-premier. Some other participants of the movement emerged as prominent officials in the GMD regime in Taiwan after 1949. Although these student activists parted ways in their later careers, in December 1936 they were united by a common sense of national crisis and fervent nationalism. Their radical anti-Japanese sentiment typified the militant anti-imperialism of the student movement in the 1920s and 1930s, and to a degree reflected the mood of the country on the eve of the second Sino-Japanese War (1937–45). Incidents such as the December Ninth demonstration also revealed the unpopularity of Nanjing's policy of "domestic pacification before external resistance" and forced the GMD to confront Japan in a forceful way in July 1937.

Wang Ke-wen

References

Israel, John. *Student Nationalism in China, 1927–1937.* Stanford, CA: Stanford University Press, 1966.

———, and Donald W. Klein. *Rebels and Bureaucrats: China's December 9ers.* Berkeley: University of California Press, 1976.

Lutz, Jessie G. "December 9, 1935: Student Nationalism and the China Christian Colleges." *Journal of Asian Studies* (August 1967): 627–48.

Democracy Wall

Because of its proximity to Tiananmen Square, a stretch of brick wall near Xidan Street in downtown Beijing became a focal point and a symbol of the democracy movement in 1978–79. Subsequently, the brick wall became known as "Democracy Wall."

The "Democracy Wall" was born in March 1978, less than two years after Mao Zedong died, when posters appeared on the wall celebrating the mass demonstration at Tiananmen Square in 1976 and criticizing the leftist leaders who were still in power. The posters attracted large crowds of educated youth, students, academics, and city residents, who came to the wall to discuss and debate issues ranging from the official verdict on the Tiananmen Incident of 1976, Maoist policies, personal persecution and injustice, democratic reform, and human rights. As more and more people gathered in front of the wall every day, public forums, rallies and even demonstrations were held, at which copies of unofficial journals and pamphlets circulated.

Following instructions from the Beijing municipal committee of the Chinese Communist Party (CCP), plainclothes police were taking notes, secretly making identifications, harassing participants, and threatening the organizers. The central authorities, however, appeared quite tolerant of the "Democracy Wall" activities. For several months, no major repression occurred against the participants. Deng Xiaoping probably calculated that popular dissent symbolized by the "Democracy Wall" could strengthen his position in the upcoming battle with the Maoist leaders at the central work conference in November and the third plenum of the CCP's Eleventh Central Committee in December 1978. In two separate meetings with visiting Japanese Socialist party leader, and American syndicated columnist Robert Novak in November 1978, Deng Xiaoping suggested that the Chinese people had their constitutional right to write big-character posters. Putting up posters was a normal phenomenon, and it was a sign of China's stability.

Deng, however, quickly changed his mind. After China suffered defeats in the Sino-Vietnamese War of February–March 1979, with heavy Chinese casualties, Deng came under much pressure from conservative leaders. In the meantime, Wei Jingsheng, an electricity worker and a former army soldier, placed on "Democracy Wall" a new poster in criticism of Deng, entitled "Do we want democracy or new dictatorship?" Wei suggested that Deng Xiaoping's four modernizations (industry, agriculture, national defense, and science and technology) were not enough because China needed a "fifth modernization"—democracy. Frustrated and irritated, Deng decided to abandon his social allies to calm the conservative opposition in the Party leadership.

In a major policy speech made on March 30, Deng labeled the "Democracy Wall" activists as "counter-revolutionaries and bad elements" who "were associated with political forces in Taiwan and abroad." Deng further set limits on China's modernization programs by putting forward "Four Cardinal Principles" (the socialist system, the dictatorship of the proletariat, the Party leadership, and Marxism-Leninism-Mao Zedong thought).

The police crackdown soon came. Putting up posters on "Democracy Wall" was banned, gatherings were prevented, and leaders of the democracy movement were arrested. Among them was Wei Jingsheng, who was sentenced in October 1979 to 15 years in jail for the alleged crime of having revealed state secrets to foreign journalists. Wei remained in prison for the next 14 years; he was released in September 1993, a few days before Beijing's failed bid to host the Olympic Games in the year 2000.

Shi-ping Zheng

References

Goodman, David S. G. *Beijing Street Voices: the Poetry and Politics of China's Democracy Movement.* London, England: M. Boyars, 1981.

MacFarquhar, Roderick. "The Succession to Mao and the End of Maoism." *The Cambridge History of China,* vol. 15, ed. Roderick MacFarquhar and John K. Fairbank, 305–401. Cambridge, England: Cambridge University Press, 1991.

Democratic League

The largest of many groups which sought to offer alternatives to the Guomindang and the Chinese Communists, the Chinese Democratic League (DL) *(Zhongguo minzhu tongmeng)* was formed through the gradual amalgamation, beginning in 1939, of six minor intellectual associations: the National Salvation Association, Vocational Educational Group, Chinese Youth Party, Third Party, Rural Reconstruction Association, and Democratic Socialist Party. During the ensuing years, various appellations were used for the organization, with the name Democratic League being adopted in 1944, when Zhang Lan was elected its chairman (until 1955). It had a seat (along with the Guomindang and the Chinese Communist Party) in the People's Political Council.

In addition to being a third force, the league sought to be a bridge between the two militarized parties, so that collectively the three parties could better resist Japan and promote China's development. As relations between the Chinese Communist Party (CCP) and the Guomindang (GMD) deteriorated, the league attempted to be a mediating force. However, the league gradually lost its impartiality as its leaders became disenchanted with the GMD and sympathetic with the CCP, in whose government they sometimes accepted positions. Chiang Kaishek became increasingly hostile toward the organization. After the war, it became dangerous for DL leaders to operate openly in GMD-controlled parts of the country (one DL figure was murdered after holding a press conference), and soon the DL used British Hong Kong as its main base. Eventually, the GMD government insisted that the league be dissolved, which officially occurred in 1947.

After 1949, entities such as the league (whose members were now known collectively as "democratic parties and groups") were reorganized by, and brought under the control of, the Communist government. Several parties left the DL to assume separate existences under the Communists or under the GMD regime in Taiwan. The league was allowed to continue to recruit members, but it operated under severe restrictions. Its size was to be determined by the CCP, and it could only recruit members in certain cities and from among educational and cultural circles, primarily educators and technicians. Although DL personages could occasionally run for public office, the elections were always managed by the Communists, and once in office, league officials had little or no influence.

The league had 30,000 members in 1956, and during the 1957 "Hundred Flowers" thaw grew perhaps several-fold. Some DL leaders hoped that the organization could become a force in Chinese politics, but the Anti-Rightist campaign put an end to that aspiration. Thereafter, the league was in eclipse until the late 1970s, when it was revived and permitted to expand its activities. In the early 1990s, its membership exceeded 100,000. The organization publishes the monthly magazine *Qunyan* *(Voice of the Masses)*, which has been liberal by Chinese standards in the late 1980s.

James D. Seymour

References

Seymour, James D. *China's Satellite Parties.* Armonk, NY: M. E. Sharpe, 1987.

Democratic Parties

Before 1949, there emerged in China various political organizations which sought to serve as middle-class alternatives to the Communists and the Guomindang. After the Communists gained control of the country, these parties were reorganized and turned into satellites of the Chinese Communist Party (CCP) under a "united front" that was intended to serve as the institutional embodiment of Chinese nationalism. Each party represented a particular constituency, but in general they comprised urban intellectuals.

These organizations were now called "democratic parties and groups" (DPGs)—the term "democratic" intended to demonstrate the tolerance of China's leaders toward the bourgeoisie. But often these groups were controlled by people who were Communists with dual party membership. The minor "parties" (the term is something of a misnomer) were regarded not only as having some propaganda value, but also as serving as potential links with overseas Chinese, and—most important—as being in a position to contribute to China's economic development. They were not supposed to take any political initiatives. They generally maintained a major presence in the Chinese People's Political Consultative Conference and its local urban counterparts, which are powerless bodies.

With the exception of two brief periods, the parties gave at least the outward appearance of being loyal followers of the Communists. The first exceptional period was the 1956 to 1957 "Hundred Flowers" thaw, when encouraged by Mao Zedong, DPG members and others criticized the CCP. Many of the participants began serving long prison sentences during the Anti-Rightist campaign. The parties remained moribund until the late 1970s, when they were revived in an effort to broaden the political base of China's leaders.

In the late 1980s, at the height of the Zhao Ziyang reforms, the parties once again became self-assertive. Beginning in the mid-1980s, some sentiment arose in China for a genuine multiparty system. In response to the demand in liberal circles for such a chance, the moderates in the CCP took a number of steps, including the reco-optation of the democratic parties. At the beginning of 1989, just a few months before the Tiananmen Incident that rocked China and brought down his administration, Zhao Ziyang declared that building the multiparty system was the year's principal task. Around 1989, some of the parties made a bid for expanded autonomy and clout, and many of their members approved of the student demonstrations at Tiananmen and elsewhere in China. But the DPGs soon became pawns in the struggle between the reformers and conservatives in the CCP.

In approximate descending order of size, the parties are: the Democratic League (comprised of intellectuals), National Construction Association (business circles), Association for Promoting Democracy (school teachers), Peasants and Workers Party (health professionals), Jiusan Society (higher intellectuals), Revolutionary Guomindang (people with GMD background or ties), Taiwan Autonomy League (Taiwanese), and the Chinese Zhigongdang (triads and returned "overseas Chinese"). Combined the parties had 337,000 members in 1990.

As political organizations, the DPGs are not held in high esteem by the public. Whatever respect they have earned is owed largely to the various public services they perform in education, economic consultation work, and other non-political venues.

James D. Seymour

References

Seymour, James D. *China's Satellite Parties.* Armonk, NY: M. E. Sharpe, 1987.

Democratic Progressive Party (Minzhu Jinbudang)

The first genuine opposition party under the Guomindang rule in Taiwan since 1949 is known as the Democratic Progressive Party (DPP).

Founded on September 28, 1986, the Democratic Progressive Party was the product of the Taiwanese opposition movement that emerged in the early 1970s. Although there had been an abortive attempt at forming an opposition party, under the leadership of Lei Zhen, in 1960, it was not until the regular holding of supplementary elections to the island's national representative bodies (Legislative Yuan and National Assembly) after 1972 that a significant native political opposition began to take shape. As the Republic of China suffered economic crises and increasing diplomatic isolation in the 1970s, the Guomindang (GMD) government under Jiang Jingguo, who was about to succeed his father Chiang Kaishek, responded by tolerating greater political participation on the island. Elections under the GMD government

were not entirely open and fair, but the non-GMD candidates gradually developed an electoral base by the end of the decade, with about 25 percent of the popular vote.

In the election of 1978, the opposition candidates for the first time organized a non-GMD campaign corps. The momentum for an opposition coalition continued to grow despite the 1979 GMD crackdown, known as the Gaoxiong Incident. After securing another electoral victory in 1983, with more than 30 percent of the popular vote, the non-GMD politicians established the Non-GMD Public Policy Association. Although not a political party in name, as the island was still under martial law that prohibited such formation, the association functioned more or less like a political party, with local branches and *ad hoc* campaign offices. This trend toward formal organization reached its peak in 1986, when, on the eve of another election, the opposition candidates suddenly announced the formation of the DPP in Taibei.

Surprisingly, the GMD government did not retaliate against the opposition with another crackdown. Jiang Jingguo, who was seriously ill at the time, chose to be tolerant. In July 1987, he lifted the thirty-year-old martial law, formally sanctioning the organization of new political parties in Taiwan. Since then a number of other opposition parties have been established, but the DPP remains the largest and most important one, gaining 25 to 30 percent of the popular vote in every election.

The DPP, and for that matter the opposition movement since the 1970s, has always implicitly favored Taiwanese independence. Led almost exclusively by native Taiwanese politicians, the party constantly challenges the GMD's claim to represent all of China and demands a new political identity for the island in the international community. After Jiang Jingguo's death in January 1988, a rapprochement developed between Taiwan and the mainland, and the DPP has been outspoken in cautioning against that development. Meanwhile, as political liberalization in Taiwan continued, many members of the overseas Taiwanese independence movement returned home and joined the DPP, which further strengthened the voice for independence in the party. With this call for independence, the DPP has antagonized the People's Republic on the mainland. In 1996, the radical pro-independence members of the DPP broke with the Party and organized the Nation-Building Party (Jianguodang).

Wang Ke-wen

References

Tien, Hung-mao. *The Great Transformation: Political and Social Change in the Republic of China.* Stanford, CA: Hoover Institution Press, 1989.

Tsang, Steve, ed. *In the Shadow of China: Political Developments in Taiwan since 1949.* Hong Kong: Hong Kong University Press, 1993.

Deng Xiaoping (1904–1997)

Deng Xiaoping was the paramount leader of the Chinese Communist Party (CCP) and the People's Republic of China in the post-Mao era.

Deng was a native of Sichuan province. In 1920, at the age of 16, he was selected through a competitive examination to study in France. He became a Communist while studying there and was Zhou Enlai's trusted right-hand man in the European branch of the CCP in the early 1920s. Deng returned to China in 1926 after a brief study sojourn in the Soviet Union. He was soon assigned by the Party as a Communist organizer-infiltrator in the Guomindang military, when the GMD and the CCP were in their first United Front against warlords. When the split occurred in 1927, Deng and his military unit, then stationed in Guangxi province, revolted. Following the failure of that revolt, he joined Mao Zedong's Communist forces in Jiangxi province.

In the Jiangxi Soviet, Deng suffered his first political setback in 1931 when he supported Mao's guerrilla war strategy against the pro-Moscow "Internationalists" in the Party. It nevertheless indicated his early loyalty to Mao. He then participated in the Long March of 1934 to 1935 and moved with the CCP to the Northwest. Deng did not achieve distinction in the Party until after World War II, when he proved to be an able battlefield strategist and efficient coordinator-planner during the GMD-CCP civil war of 1945 to 1949.

After the founding of the People's Republic, Deng was the all-powerful ruler of southwestern China, in charge of political, military, and party policies in that region. In 1955, he arrived in Beijing to become the CCP's general secretary (under Mao's chairmanship), finance minister in Premier Zhou Enlai's cabinet, and one of several vice-premiers. He remained the administrative head of the Party and a key policymaker in the government for one full decade, until his removal from office at the start of the Cultural Revolution in 1966. By then, Deng had become well-known and broadly connected in the Party, the military, and the government. From 1966 to the early 1970s, Deng was Mao's purge victim in a labor reform camp in Jiangxi. He had ample time to reflect on how to find new approaches to move the country into a peaceful revolution that would terminate the chaos created by Mao and his radical followers.

After his second return to power in 1973, Deng tried to rescue the country from the ruins of the Cultural Revolution. As Zhou Enlai's "acting premier," when Zhou was sick in his hospital bed, Deng came under the radicals' attack. In the wake of the Tiananmen Incident of 1976, he was again purged. In 1977, after the death of Zhou and Mao, Deng returned to power for the third time. He soon defeated Premier Hua Guofeng, Mao's chosen successor, in a power struggle, and became the top leader among equals in the so-called post-Mao collective leadership. He remained in that position until his death, implementing internal reforms and opening China to the outside world.

Deng's peaceful revolution is forging ahead without the benefit of a new ideology to replace Marxism or the Mao Zedong thought—seen by some as a crisis of ideological void. Officially, his reforms remain embedded within the ideology of Marxism; they neither adhere to, nor formally condemn, its fundamental tenets. Yet it is undeniable that his reforms are likely to build, eventually, a non-communist and non-capitalist system in China. Deng pragmatically called this novel modernization "Socialism with Chinese characteristics." The successes in economic achievement since the late 1970s have separated Deng's China from the discredited Communist countries in Eastern Europe and in the former Soviet Union. Tremendous economic changes continue to take place in China during the 1990s, as the government created millions of urban jobs and massive numbers of farmers left agriculture for the private or market economy. Foreign investments have come from western Europe, Japan, and North America. Special economic zones have been established along the China coast to facilitate joint economic ventures between China and foreign companies.

Deng's promise was to quadruple, by the year 2000, the living standard of China from that of 1980 by achieving success in four areas—industry, science, agriculture, and defense. He also

Deng Xiaoping and British Prime Minister Margaret Thatcher after the signing of Sino-British Agreement on Hong Kong, 1984. (Xinhua News Agency.)

advocated Party reform in favor of younger and better educated cadres, forcing partial early retirement among senior members. To set an example, Deng himself gradually resigned from his position as vice-premier, chief of staff of the People's Liberation Army, and the chairmanship of the CCP's Military Commission. However, economic success bred demands for greater political reform, and in this respect Deng was slow to act. Beginning in the mid-1980s, there were several large-scale street demonstrations and intellectual criticisms against political authoritarianism and official corruption. The most serious expression of such discontent was the Tiananmen Incident of 1989, which Deng brutally suppressed.

Stubborn and self-centered, Deng possessed an iron will and the courage to speak his mind, and he did so until his third downfall in 1976. Upon his final rehabilitation in 1977, he pledged at the conclusion of the eleventh Party Congress to "work more and speak less." He

has, since then, indeed articulated very little on either Marxist ideology or intra-party struggle. Deng's one-line guide of conduct to the post-Mao CCP has been "practice is the sole test for truth." He also refused to use Mao's methods against political opponents within the Party. Nevertheless, Deng was not prepared to change the Communist rule. He advocated the so-called Four Cardinal Principles—CCP leadership, democratic centralism, socialist path, and Marxist-Leninist-Mao Zedong thought—as the foundations, and limits, of his reforms. Yet when confronted with the drastic changes in China's economy, politics and social conditions, Deng seemed to ignore these slogans; but this talented and pragmatic leader successfully reversed Mao's fanatical policies and provided the country with a relatively long period of stability and prosperity. Deng died on February 19, 1997. According to *Yale Daily News* (February 20, 1997), "The first test of Deng's legacy will be whether his handpicked successor, Communist Party General Secretary Jiang Zemin, and the other younger technocrats he installed in the 1990s, will weather political maneuvering that is expected to intensify in the coming months."

David Wen-wei Chang

References

Chang, David Wen-wei. *China Under Deng Xiaoping: Political and Economic Reform.* New York, NY: St. Martins, 1991.

Evans, Richard. *Deng Xiaoping: And the Making of Modern China.* New York, NY: The Viking Press, 1994.

Shambaugh, David, ed. *Deng Xiaoping in the Scale of History.* Oxford, England: Oxford University Press, 1994.

Deng Yanda (1895–1931)

Founder and leader of the Third Party movement between 1927 and 1931, Deng Yanda occupies a unique position in the history of Republican China. A native of Guangdong, Deng was an instructor at the Whampoa Military Academy before rising to political prominence during the Northern Expedition (1926–28). He played a major role in the Wuhan regime of 1927 and, following the collapse of that regime, became a leading opponent to Chiang Kaishek and the Nanjing government. Deng was arrested and executed by Chiang in 1931.

Deng provided the Third Party (formally called the Chinese Revolutionary Party or the Provisional Action Committee of the Guomindang) with its core principles and ideology, a blend of Sun Yatsen's Three Peoples' Principles, rationalism, and historical materialism. While Deng utilized Marxian analytical categories, he retained a Kantian skepticism regarding the transformation of reason into religion. Undercurrents of skepticism and confidence in a critical spirit colored his understanding of the modern concept of nationalism.

Deng's ideas on nationalism was part of his general world view. He accepted historical materialism as the foundation for his analysis of China, but he softened materialism with a persistent skepticism about the limitations of human reason. He regarded economic analysis as essential, but rejected any attempt to universalize the data of limited experience or dogmatic sectarianism. He utilized the Marxist imperialism paradigm to explain China's position in the world but he rejected the Third or Second International programs for China. Deng considered both Socialist Internationals agents for specific national interests.

While Deng defined China in the context of universally unfolding economic forces, he insisted on the unique, Chinese quality of conditions and events. As he wrote on many occasions, China's revolution was not the French Revolution nor was it the Bolshevik Revolution. Rather, China needed a national revolution of the common people *(minzu de pingmin geming)*. His choice of the term *minzu* for the concept of nation was drawn from Sun Yatsen's principles. Like his mentor, Deng assumed that China possessed a unique racial-ethnic quality and a history and economy which reflected this uniqueness. The special ethnic quality of Deng's nationalism surfaces in his retention of Sun's concept of ethnic pluralism. China's revolution was not only for Chinese but also for the autonomy and independence of other ethnic groups (Mongols and Manchus, for example), with which China shared historical and geographical associations.

In its practical application, Deng's nationalism retained Sun's program. He declared a willingness to establish relations with all countries that would treat China as an equal. His opposition to imperialism was tempered by the sobering assumption that capitalism and its international manifestation would persist for a long time. Deng's pragmatic approach to international relations was further reinforced by doubts regarding socialist internationalism. His immediate objectives were to rewrite the "unequal treaties" and establish international relations on a basis of equality. He further saw the need for international assistance in China's modernization and expressed a willingness to use foreign capital and expertise, provided they came in a non-exploitative package.

Deng understood the practice of revolution, including its anti-imperialist, nationalist component, as inseparable from the organization, politicization, and mobilization of a multiclass social configuration which he called the common people *(pingmin)*. The *pingmin* included peasants, workers, and the urban petit-bourgeoisie, or all those who "work to eat and are the victims of imperialist or feudal exploitation." The enemies of revolution included the Nanjing government under Chiang Kaishek and the Chinese Communist Party, which was being manipulated by the Third International. Deng reasoned that only the common people, who were victims of exploitation and oppression, would be capable of breaking the bonds of imperialism and feudalism. Using the concept of the *pingmin,* he was able to bridge the conceptual gulf between class struggle and his conviction that China needed a national revolution built on unique historical and cultural experience.

Finally, Deng was rather unique during the 1920s and 1930s for his sensitivity to the cultural dimension of revolution and national identity. Rejecting Comintern internationalism and what he called a reactionary Confucian-Christian amalgamation forming in Nanjing, Deng was confident that a new common people's culture which would bear distinctive Chinese characteristics would emerge from the process of revolutionary change. His common people's revolution would not preclude the need or desirability for unique national cultures. Quite the contrary, revolution would allow China to produce new and better expressions of cultural forms relevant to the masses of the common people. He saw opportunities for unique Chinese contributions to the new evolving world order.

J. Kenneth Olenik

References

Olenik, J. Kenneth. "Teng Yen-ta and the Theory of Mass Revolution in Kuomintang Ideology." *Asian Thought & Society* 3, no. 8 (September 1978): 178–92; 3, no. 9 (October 1978): 297–307.

Diaoyutai Controversy

The Diaoyutai Islets, or Senkaku Gunto in Japanese, consist of five uninhabited islets and three rocks in the East China Sea northeast of Taiwan. Diaoyutai, the largest of the group, is about 1.667 square miles in size, Huangwei about 0.416 square miles, and the remaining three islets each are smaller than Huangwei. They are all situated at the edge of the East China Sea continental shelf as it extends from the Chinese mainland and Taiwan, and are geographically separated from the continental shelf of Japan and the Ryukyu Islands by the Okinawa Trough, which is more than 3000 feet deep. The islets have had little economic value except as a base for fishing.

In 1968, a study by the United Nations Economic Commission for Asia and the Far East revealed that the sea-bed of the East China Sea could be one of the richest oil-deposit areas in the world. Suddenly ownership of the islets became important because the country that owned them could lay claim to the adjacent territorial sea and continental shelf. This is especially important for Japan, because the islets would serve as the only basis for her claim to a share of the East China Sea continental shelf. When the United States announced that it planned to return the Ryukyu Islands (Okinawa) to Japan in 1972 and that Senkaku (Diaoyutai), which had been administered as part of the Ryukyus, would also revert to Japan, the dispute involving the People's Republic of China (PRC), the Republic of China (ROC) and Japan over the sovereignty of the islets arose.

The Japanese position is that after 1885, Japan conducted several surveys of the Senkaku Islands and found no trace of Chinese control. Therefore, Japan asserts, a valid cabinet decision on January 14, 1895, incorporated these islands into the Japanese territory of Nansei Shoto within the Ryukyu Island group. Consequently, it argues that these islands were not included in the island territories of Taiwan and the Pescadores, which were ceded to Japan after the first Sino-Japanese War of 1894 to 1895 but returned to China in 1945. When Japan renounced Taiwan and the Pescadores in the 1951 San Francisco Peace Treaty, she did not renounce the Senkaku Islands, which instead were placed by that treaty under United States administration, together with other islands in the Ryukyu Island group. Under the United States-Japan Agreement Concerning the Ryukyu Islands (signed on June 17, 1971 and in force on May 15, 1972), administration over the Senkaku Islands was to be returned to Japan. Japan further points out that since the entry into force of the 1951 San Francisco Peace Treaty, the PRC and the ROC have raised no objection to the fact that the Senkaku Islands were included in the area placed under United States administration.

The PRC and the ROC maintain that the Diaoyutai Islets were Chinese territory for centuries. According to both Chinese governments, the Diaoyutai Islets were first discovered by the Chinese and were recorded as early as 1532 in the *Shiliuqiulu* (Record of the Ryukyu Mission) compiled by the Chinese official Chen Gan. The islets were also included within China's sea defense line in the 1561 *Chouhai tubian (Compilation of Maps on Managing the Sea),* edited by the Chinese official Hu Zhongxian. Moreover, in the 1862 *Huangchao zhongwai yitong yutu (Unified Maps for the Imperial Dynasty),* the

Diaoyutai Islets were marked as Chinese territory. Finally, the Chinese point out that a map in a well-known 1785 Japanese publication, entitled *Sanguo tonglan tushuo (Illustrated Map and Explanations of Communications Among Three Countries [China, Japan, and Korea])*, clearly makes the Diaoyutai Islets part of China's Fujian province.

With respect to the Japanese incorporation of the Diaoyutai Islets in 1895, the Chinese view is that the Japanese victory over China in 1895 rendered China unable to resist the Japanese annexation. The 1895 Treaty of Shimonoseki ceded to Japan "Taiwan, together with all islands appertaining to Taiwan," which included the Diaoyutai Islets. When the Japanese renounced their claim to Taiwan and the appertaining islands after World War II, in the 1951 San Francisco Peace Treaty and the 1952 Japan–ROC Peace Treaty, they lost the Diaoyutai to China.

The dispute first surfaced in mid-1970 between the ROC and Japan. Later that year, when the ROC and Japan were considering shelving the dispute to engage in a joint exploration for oil, the PRC entered the dispute. The ROC also pressed the United States not to return the Senkaku Islands to Japan in 1972, but the United States refused to accede to the ROC's wishes. Instead, the United States pledged to remain neutral in the dispute and stated that the return of administrative rights over Senkaku to Japan would not affect the sovereign claim of any state to the islands. In December 1971, the ROC government included the Diaoyutai Islets in the administrative district of Yilan county of Taiwan province. In September 1972, Japan severed diplomatic relations with the ROC and established diplomatic relations with the PRC. Since then, the ROC has not been in a legal position to negotiate the matter with Japan, although she has on several occasions issued statements reaffirming her claim to the islets.

At the time of the establishment of diplomatic relations between the PRC and Japan in 1972, both countries had reportedly agreed to table the issue. When Japan signed a Treaty of Peace and Friendship with the PRC in 1978, the PRC allegedly told Japan that the issue should be left for the next generation to settle.

The Diaoyutai controversy created one of the largest and most significant overseas Chinese student movements in the post-World War II era. Motivated by strong patriotic feelings, and inspired to an extent by the anti-Vietnam War movement in America, Chinese students in the United States, all of them from Taiwan, organized massive and prolonged demonstrations in America to protest the transfer of the Diaoyutai Islets to Japan. The Defend Diaoyutai movement began with the first demonstrations held in seven American cities in January 1971 and culminated in a major demonstration, with nearly four thousand participants, in Washington, D.C., in April 1971. The students issued their protest, attacking the transfer, to the governments of Japan and the United States. They demanded tougher measures of their own government in Taiwan. The impact of the movement was felt in Europe, Japan, and in Taiwan, where college students briefly organized their own protest under the close surveillance of the ROC government.

Frustrated by the ROC's weakness and dependence on the United States, and impressed by the PRC's propaganda about its ongoing Cultural Revolution, the protesting students in America gradually developed a pro-PRC stance. In mid-1971, the movement began to transform itself into a unification movement, which advocated the reunification of China under the seemingly strong PRC government. With the formal transfer of the islands by the United States to Japan in May 1972, the Diaoyutai demonstrations ended but the unification movement lingered on. The fervor eventually subsided when the PRC also displayed moderation in its communication with Japan on this issue in late 1972.

The students who participated in the Defend Diaoyutai movement saw themselves as successors to the student demonstrators of the May Fourth movement. Indeed, they shared similar nationalistic concerns with the May Fourth generation as they directed their attack on both the imperialists (especially Japan) and an incompetent Chinese government. There are, however, important differences between these students and the May Fourth youth. The foreign environment in which these students lived created in them an acute sense of alienation and a romantic desire for a strong China. They were also presented with an alternative "motherland," *i.e.*, the PRC, that appeared to satisfy their emotional needs, if not their political demands. In the end most of them, comprising the elite of Taiwan's educated youth, shifted their allegiance from the ROC to the PRC. Although the Diaoyutai demonstrations, like those in the May Fourth movement, failed to accomplish their immediate goal, they politicized a whole generation of overseas Chinese students and enhanced their patriotism.

Hungdah Chiu
Wang Ke-wen

References

Chao, K. T. "East China Sea: Boundary Problems Relating to the T'iaoyu Tai Islands." *Chinese Yearbook of International Law and Affairs* 2 (1982): 45–80.

Chen, Tao. "The Sino-Japanese Dispute Over the Tiao-yu-tai (Senkaku) Islands and the Law of Territorial Acquisition." *Virginia Journal of International Law* (1974): 221–66.

Li, Victor H. "China and Off-Shore Oil: The Tiao-yu Tai Dispute." *Stanford Journal of International Law* (1975): 143–62.

Disbandment Conference

The completion of the Northern Expedition in 1928 brought nominal unification of China under the Guomindang (GMD). The new national government at Nanjing, however, was by no means in effective control of the provinces beyond the Lower Yangtze region. The power of the regional militarists was one of the major threats to the Nanjing Government and its leader, Chiang Kaishek. Some of these militarists, such as the Guangxi Clique and Feng Yuxiang, had joined the GMD before the Northern Expedition, whereas others, notably Yan Xishan, had defected to the GMD camp during the expedition. Eager to bring the country under the GMD flag, Chiang had initially tolerated their regional autonomy in exchange for their cooperation in the campaign against other warlords. As a result, the domains of the leading militarists had been further expanded. By the end of 1928, in addition to Zhang Xueliang's continuing rule of Manchuria, Feng Yuxiang had dominated the Northwest and Shandong, Yan Xishan had controlled Shanxi and most of north China, and the Guangxi Clique under Li Zongren had stretched its influence from its home base of Guangxi to Guangdong and the Middle Yangtze. The military strength of the three army groups commanded by Feng, Yan, and Li far exceeded that of the First Army Group under Chiang Kaishek himself.

Therefore, among Chiang's first priorities after the Northern Expedition was to reduce

D

Guomindang military leaders upon the completion of the Northern Expedition: (left to right) Chiang Kaishek, Feng Yuxiang, Li Zongren, Yan Xishan. (Courtesy of Nationalist Party Archives.)

the power enjoyed by these regional rulers. On January 1, 1929, Chiang invited them to participate in the National Army Disbandment Conference *(bianqian huiyi)* at Nanjing. The purpose of the conference was to drastically reduce the size of the country's military establishment, which totaled 2.3 million men at the time, for the new era of peace. At the same time, it is clear that Chiang wanted to use army reduction as a pretext to weaken his regional rivals. Chiang's rivals were well aware of his intentions and they decided to oppose it. None of the proposals discussed during the one-month conference had a chance to be implemented. Instead, the militarists soon returned to their provinces and prepared for a military confrontation with Chiang.

In March the Guangxi Clique, whose relations with Chiang had deteriorated most rapidly since 1928, rose first in rebellion. One of its rationales was that Chiang's army reduction plan favored his own First Army Group at the expense of others. Feng Yuxiang followed the Guangxi Clique's example in May. These revolts initiated a period of continuous civil wars in China, culminating in the "War of the Central Plains" (*Zhongyuan dazhan*) in 1930. In this last conflict, Feng, Li Zongren, and Yan Xishan joined hands and fought against Chiang in one of the largest civil wars in the republican era. They were supported by Chiang's intra-party rivals, especially the Left Guomindang under Wang Jingwei, in organizing a short-lived regime, the Enlarged Session of the GMD Central Committees, in Beiping. The Left Guomindang also persuaded a few other militarists, including Zhang Fakuei and Tang Shangzhi, to participate in the rebellion. Chiang suppressed all of these revolts in 1929 and 1930, some by force and others through bribery; yet he never fully solved the problem of regional militarism throughout the Nanjing Decade (1927–37).

The Disbandment Conference thus precipitated a confrontation between Chiang Kaishek's Nanjing government and the regional militarists who had assisted in the Northern Expedition. The root of this confrontation lay in Chiang's expedient strategy of incorporating these militarists into the GMD regime before 1928. Although the militarists' revolts constituted only one of several crises that Nanjing faced at the time, they diminished its legitimacy and undermined its effectiveness as the new national government of China.

Wang Ke-wen

References

Bedeski, Robert E. *State-Building in Modern China: The Kuomintang in the Prewar Period.* Berkeley: Center for Chinese Studies Publications, University of California, 1981.

Leang-li, Tang. *The Inner History of the Chinese Revolution.* Reprint edition. Westport, CT: Hyperion Press, 1977.

Domestic Pacification before External Resistance (*Annei Rangwai*)

See BANDIT-SUPPRESSION CAMPAIGNS; NANJING DECADE

Duan Qirui (1865–1936)

Leader of the Beiyang government and founder of the Anhui Clique, Duan was generally regarded as a warlord, but his supporters praised him as the man who "reestablished the Republic."

Born in Hefei, Anhui, Duan had graduated from the Tianjin Military Academy and studied military science in Germany before joining the Beiyang Army established by Yuan Shikai. He rose quickly in the ranks and by the time of the outbreak of the Revolution of 1911 had become the commander of the Second Army. While leading the battle against the revolutionaries in Hubei, he acted under Yuan's order to pressure the Qing court to abdicate. For this he was rewarded with the position of Minister of Army in the new republican government, with Yuan as president. He actively assisted Yuan in suppressing the Second Revolution of 1913, but distanced himself from Yuan's monarchist plan in 1915. After the downfall of Yuan, Duan became premier of the new government in Beijing and soon clashed with President Li Yuanhong. In mid-1917 he was dismissed from the post by Li, but Li himself was subsequently ousted by Zhang Xun in Zhang's attempt to restore the Qing court. Duan, with forces loyal to him, launched an expedition against Zhang from Tianjin. Zhang was defeated in a few days, and Duan resumed the premiership, claiming that he had "re-established" the Republic.

During the following years, Duan tried to unify the country by force, for which he negotiated a series of loans from Japan and organized an army under the pretext of preparing China for participation in World War I. Military support for Duan came from the Anhui Clique, a group of fellow Anhui militarists, while political backing issued from the Anfu Club, a civilian arm of the Anhui Clique that dominated the new Parliament of 1918. He resigned from the post of premier in 1918, but still controlled the Beijing government as commissioner of Border-Defense and commissioner of War Participation, until the defeat of his Anhui Clique in the Zhili-Anhui War of 1920.

Ostensibly in semi-retirement in Tianjin, Duan quietly worked for a "triangle pact" among the Anhui Clique, the Fengtian (Manchurian) warlord Zhang Zuolin, and Sun Yatsen's Guomindang in Canton. Their common enemy was the Zhili Clique that was in power in Beijing at the time. In 1924, the Zhili Clique was finally toppled in the Second Zhili-Fengtian War, and Duan was invited to head the new Beijing government under the title of provisional executive. As such, he aborted the plan for a peaceful unification of the country by breaking off with Sun Yatsen, and ordered the March Eighteenth Massacre against the Beijing students in 1926. One month later he was ousted by Feng Yuxiang.

From 1926 to 1936, under the rule of the Guomindang, Duan lived first in Tianjin and then in Shanghai, and ceased to be active in politics. In 1931, after the Manchurian Incident, the government invited him to attend the National Emergency Conference *(guonan huiyi)* in Loyang, and in 1935 appointed him a member of the National Government Committee. He declined both offers. He is also said to have rejected, in his last years, a proposal by Japan to become its puppet in north China.

Duan was a nationalist who believed that China's stability and prosperity could be achieved only by being unified under his own leadership. In this respect, his view echoed that of Chiang Kaishek, who once had been his student at the Baoding Military Academy. Chiang also shared with Duan the insistence that force had to be used to achieve the unification of China. Both men ultimately failed in that effort.

Wang Ke-wen

References

Chi, Hsi-sheng. *Warlord Politics in China, 1916–1928*. Stanford, CA: Stanford University Press, 1976.

Nathan, Andrew J. *Peking Politics, 1918–1923: Factionalism and the Failure of Constitutionalism*. Berkeley: University of California Press, 1976.

D

E

East Turkestan Republic

The East Turkestan Republic was a pro-Soviet state established by Turkish Muslims in Xinjiang province from 1944 through 1949.

The predominant population of the Ili region in northwestern Xinjiang were Kazaks and Uighurs. During the late Qing, the area had witnessed the Muslim rebellion led by Yakub Beg and the establishment, in 1865, of an independent kingdom in Kashgar. Yakub Beg's kingdom had received Russian and British support.

In November 1944, another large-scale anti-Chinese revolt broke out in northwestern Xinjiang, which was adjacent to Soviet Central Asia. In January 1945, the Muslim rebels, most of them Uighurs, established the East Turkestan Republic in the Ili region and declared its secession from China. The republic tried to protect the local Turkish culture from Han influence and to develop close economic ties with the Soviet Union. Backed by Moscow, it was mostly a Soviet design to weaken the rule of the Chinese Guomindang (GMD) government on China's western frontier, but also suggested a degree of Uighur nationalism.

The GMD government, then at war with Japan, sought a peaceful solution to the crisis. After long negotiations, the government signed an agreement with the Ili regime in 1946. The agreement led to the organization of a coalition provincial government in Xinjiang in Urumchi, with the participation of the Ili leaders. This coalition government, however, was short-lived. In mid-1947, prominent Ili leaders, such as Akhmedjan and Saifudin, resigned from the government and again demanded full autonomy of the Ili region. In August 1948, they organized the Democratic League for the Protection of Peace in Xinjiang as the new title for the Ili regime. Although the regime still attacked the past and present Chinese rule of Xinjiang, it began to side with the Chinese Communist Party (CCP) in the ongoing Chinese civil war.

When the CCP emerged triumphant in the civil war in late 1949, the provincial government of Xinjiang surrendered to the CCP. The Ili regime, now openly supportive of the CCP, also allowed its armed forces to be incorporated by the newly arrived People's Liberation Army. Saifudin, himself a member of the Russian Communist Party, soon led a delegation to attend the founding of the People's Republic of China (PRC) in Beijing. Shortly after, the CCP announced that another Ili delegation, which included Akhmedjan and other more outspoken advocates of Uighur nationalism, had perished in a plane crash in Manchuria. Saifudin thus became the only surviving leader of the Ili regime, and he pledged loyalty to the PRC. He later joined the CCP and became head of the Xinjiang-Uighur Autonomous Region under the PRC.

Wang Ke-wen

References

Gladney, Dru C. *Muslim Chinese: Ethnic Nationalism in the People's Republic.* Cambridge, MA: Harvard University Press, 1991.

Moseley, G. *A Sino-Soviet Cultural Frontier: The Ili Kazakh Autonomous Zhou.* Cambridge, MA: Harvard University Press, 1966.

Eighth Route Army

The Eighth Route Army was the main armed

force of the Chinese Communist Party (CCP) during the Sino-Japanese War of 1937 to 1945. The CCP's Red Army in the Northwest was reorganized into the Eighth Route Army of the Guomindang (GMD) government's National Revolutionary Army following the formation of the second GMD-CCP United Front in the early months of the war. Zhu De became its commander and Peng Dehuai the deputy commander. Nominally under the unified command of the GMD, the Eighth Route Army was in fact an independent force still under the CCP's total control.

In September 1937, the Eighth Route Army was renamed the Eighteenth Army Group and ordered to participate in the battles in north China. However, the Eighth Route Army *(balujun)* remained the most commonly used reference to the CCP forces throughout the war and even became synonymous with the CCP itself. It was this army that launched the Battle of Hundred Regiments against the invading Japanese in late 1940. Meanwhile, the army's guerrilla warfare behind the enemy lines was extremely successful not only in establishing for the CCP numerous base areas or border-region governments in the occupied territories, but in creating a popular image of the CCP as a patriotic force fighting for the country's survival. Such an image, together with the army's effective propaganda and intelligence tactics, helped to recruit a large number of Chinese peasants into its ranks. By the end of the war, the Eighth Route Army, or the Eighteenth Army Group, had increased to about one million men.

Yet during the last years of the war, as the United Front deteriorated, the main responsibility of the northern Shaanxi units of the Eighth Route Army was in fact the defense of the CCP base in Yan'an against the GMD blockade. It played an important role, for example, in the Great Production Campaign *(dashengchan yundong)* that built up the economic base of the ShaanGanNing (Shaanxi-Gansu-Ningxia) border region. After the war and during the GMD–CCP civil war, the CCP forces were renamed the People's Liberation Army.

Wang Ke-wen

References

Griffith, Samuel B., II. *The Chinese People's Liberation Army.* New York, NY: McGraw-Hill, Inc. 1967.

Elder Brother Society (Gelaohui)

The Elder Brother Society (Gelaohui) probably emerged along with the Heaven and Earth Society (Tiandihui) and the White Lotus Sect (Bailianjiao) in the late seventeenth century, when Ming loyalists went underground to form or join secret organizations in order to continue their nationalistic struggle against the Qing conquest of China. Geographically, the Elder Brother Society originated in western China— either in Sichuan or Guizhou—then expanded into the Yangtze valley. The main vehicle of this expansion may have been Zeng Guofan's Hunan Army during the Taiping Rebellion (1850–64). According to one estimate, some 30 percent to 40 percent of new peasant recruits in Zeng's army were Gelaohui members.

When the Hunan Army disbanded, after the suppression of the Taipings, many of these former soldiers found quiet life in their villages boring and ventured into the cities along the Yangtze. They recruited merchants and artisans into the society, and well-to-do persons also joined the Gelaohui to protect their possessions against other outlaws. As a result of these successful recruitment efforts, the Gelaohui became the predominant secret society in central China during the last fifty years of the Qing dynasty.

Organizationally, the Gelaohui appears to have had a loose network without a central headquarters or leader. Individual units or cells, scattered throughout central China, wove themselves into the fabric of Chinese society. A chief dragon head *(zheng longtou)* led each lodge *(tang)*, with numerous officers serving under his authority. Each society applicant had to have a Gelaohui sponsor and to undergo an initiation ceremony, which consisted of taking a blood oath of loyalty. Once recruited, members identified themselves through an elaborate system of hand and body gestures.

The Gelaohui were nationalistic, but as many other secret societies, they were too dispersed, too loosely organized, and too enmeshed in the existing political system to be the leading force in the drive to oust the Qing. This is not to say, however, that their activities are not noteworthy. In 1870 and 1871, the society engaged in uprisings in several districts in Hunan. The primary motivating factor appears to have been social and economic malaise. In 1891, the society fomented nationalistic riots in the lower and middle Yangtze. This activity was designed to embarrass the Manchu government by antagonizing the foreign powers. In the summer of 1900, dissident literati recruited a large Gelaohui army in Hunan and Hubei, known as the *Zilijun* (Independent Army), in an abortive revolt against the Qing.

During the final years of the Qing, the Gelaohui often joined hands with the anti-Manchu revolutionaries. In 1904 Huang Hsing prepared for his Huaxinghui (China Arise Society) revolt by mobilizing a Gelaohui force for his insurrection at Changsha. Although detected and suppressed, this endeavor enhanced anti-government sentiment in the society. The sentiment manifested itself again in December 1906 in the Ping-Liu-Li Uprising, a massive revolt along the Hunan-Jiangxi border. Tactics utilized by the Gelaohui in this adventure included guerrilla techniques, such as ensuring rapid mobility by carrying only minimal supplies and using crack marksmen to guard their rear during a retreat. The revolt was finally suppressed by government armies dispatched from four provinces; defeat cost the Gelaohui much of their political vitality in central China.

In view of this fact, it is not surprising that the Gelaohui did not play a leading role in the Revolution of 1911, despite some assertions to the contrary. To be sure, the society was active in aiding the Tongmenghui (Revolutionary Alliance) to occupy several towns and cities in Sichuan. The Gelaohui also provided similar services in Canton and Xian, but to credit the society with any sort of leadership in the founding of the Republic is excessive. During the Second Revolution of 1913, when the Guomindang (GMD) tried to rise against Yuan Shikai, the Gelaohui reportedly also provided troops with which to attack Yuan's government from central China.

In addition to providing assistance to the Guomindang, the Gelaohui developed links with the Chinese Communist Party (CCP) in the 1920s and 1930s. Several well-known Communist personalities, including Zhu De, Wu Yuzhang, Liu Zhidan, and He Long, were highly placed in the society. Zhu had joined the Gelaohui in Sichuan in 1911 and had risen to become a dignitary in the society. He credited the society with the idea of the cell system of organization that the GMD and the CCP utilized. Wu, who also joined the society in Sichuan, was at some point elected a "Great Elder." Liu was one of the founders of the Soviet in North China prior to the Long March, and he was an exemplary member of the Gelaohui. He Long, whose father had been a renowned leader in the society,

supposedly inherited his prestige. His rank and fame in the Gelaohui were such that, according to one source, he was able to enlist an entire lodge into the People's Liberation Army.

Mao Zedong, while apparently not a member of the Gelaohui, thought very highly of its revolutionary virtues. In 1936, he wrote an appeal to the society in an attempt to forge a connection between the anti-Manchu nationalism of the Gelaohui and the anti-Japanese nationalism of the Chinese Communists. Mao's missive concluded with a spirited call: "Let the Gelaohui and the whole of the Chinese people unite to strike at Japan and to restore China!" After the Communist victory of 1949, however, the Elder Brother Society disappeared from the Chinese social and political scene.

Gerald W. Berkley

References

Lewis, Charlton M. "Some Notes on the Gelaohui in Late Qing China." *Popular Movements and Secret Societies in China 1840–1950,* ed. Jean Chesneaux, 97–112. Stanford, CA: Stanford University Press, 1972.

Puyraimond, Guy. "The Ko-lao Hui and the Anti-Foreign Incidents of 1891." Ibid., 113–24.

Emperor Guangxu (1871–1908)

The ninth emperor of the Qing dynasty, Guangxu's personal name was Zaitian, and he was the second son of Prince Yihuan. He was chosen in 1875, at the age of four, to succeed Emperor Tongzhi (who died without an heir) by his aunt, Empress Dowager Cixi, because Zaitian was the prince closest to Cixi by blood. This would guarantee Cixi's firm control over the infant emperor. On January 15, 1875, Cixi officially assumed the position as co-regent (with Empress Dowager Xiaozhen, the natural mother of Zaitian) of the throne until Guangxu was of age. The act violated the dynastic laws of succession; yet it was carried out without objection.

Emperor Guangxu was therefore raised under the total domination of Cixi, who maintained full influence over him. When Guangxu came of age in 1887, Cixi, through political manipulation, continued to control the court and the government even though she had been "retired" to her summer palace near Beijing. Reportedly, all important state papers and key

Empress Dowager Cixi. (Courtesy of Nationalist Party Archives.)

1898, Guangxu became more eager to pursue the new reforms. After January 29, 1898, Kang was granted a special right to have direct access to Emperor Guangxu. From February to May of 1898, Kang drafted his reform proposal, which included (1) a national polity under Emperor Guangxu's leadership modeled after Peter the Great of Russia and Emperor Meiji of Japan; (2) reorganization of the national government based on the new ideas under the leadership of the new reform-minded intellectuals; and (3) provincial governments to be given authority to initiate changes according to national needs.

On June 11, 1898, Emperor Guangxu agreed to institute the reform proposal and issued an imperial decree for the general government reform (known as the Hundred Days Reform) which lasted until September 20, when Empress Dowager Cixi unleashed her power and put an immediate stop to it. Guangxu was placed under house arrest and Kang Youwei fled to Japan. Cixi thereupon resumed her control of the government. Guangxu once again became nothing more than a puppet emperor under the shadow of his aunt until his death on November 14, 1908. Guangxu was succeeded by his nephew, Emperor Xuantong (or Puyi) in December 1908.

Anthony Y. Teng

References

Fairbank, John K., ed. *The Cambridge History of China*, vols. 10 and 11. Cambridge, England: Cambridge University Press, 1978, 1983.

Hsu, Immanuel C. Y. *The Rise of Modern China*, 4th ed. New York, NY: Oxford University Press, 1990.

Hummel, Arthur W. *Eminent Chinese of the Ch'ing Period*, vol. 1. Washington, DC: United States Government Printing Office, 1943.

government appointments still went to Cixi for final approvals.

Although Guangxu was a weak emperor, he was inquisitive and possessed a keen, open mind about national and international affairs. He was interested in new ideas introduced to China at this time by Westerners, and particularly concerned about the national identity and survival of China in the face of the menace from the West.

The defeat and humiliation suffered by China during and after the Sino-Japanese War of 1894 to 1895 shocked Guangxu in such a way that he became immensely worried about China's survival and wanted to seek his own way to avert its demise. A young and dynamic scholar, Kang Youwei, who had similar concerns about China as Guangxu did, attracted the emperor's attention. Kang Youwei had repeatedly sent memorials to Guangxu expressing his ideas for urgent reform of the Chinese government. When Guangxu's imperial tutor Weng Tonghe supported Kang's advocacies in early

Emperor Protection Society (Baohuanghui)

Also named Zhongguo weixinhui (Chinese Reform Association) or Baojiu daQing Guangxu huangdi hui (Society to Save the Guangxu Emperor of the Great Qing Dynasty), Baohuanghui was founded by Kang Youwei on July 20, 1899, in Victoria, British Columbia, with the support of Chinese-Canadian leaders such as Li Fuji (Lee Fook Kee) and Ye En (Yip On). Formed in the wake of the abortive Hundred Days Reform outside China, the organization emphasized in its charter the goals of restoration of the emperor, promotion of commerce, national revival through institutional reforms, and salvation of the Yellow race. The last point was further elaborated in the bylaws of the San Francisco branch, which stated that the purpose of the society was to elevate the Chinese to a level equal to that of any other civilized race. It was the sentiment of nationalism and the concern for Chinese rights in foreign countries which drew both rich and poor overseas Chinese to Baohuanghui. In a few years, eleven regional headquarters and 103 chapters were operating in the Americas, and in East and Southeast Asia.

For the dissemination of reformist ideas, newspapers such as *Qingyibao* (Pure Discussions) were published, and Chinese schools were established in Macao, Hong Kong, Yokohama, Tokyo, Honolulu, Singapore, Rangoon, San Francisco and Victoria. To obtain more funds for the society, the Baohuanghui ventured into businesses and successfully developed a chain of corporations, which engaged in publishing, servicing and banking activities.

Twice the society conspired against Empress Dowager Cixi; both attempts ended in failure. During the Boxer Uprising of 1900, the Baohuanghui mobilized its resources to support the loyalist Zilijun (Independence Army) revolt staged by Tang Caichang in central China. It was soon suppressed by Zhang Zhidong, governor-general of Hunan and Hubei. Kang Youwei afterward sent one of his aides to assassinate the Empress Dowager Cixi in Beijing, but the plot was aborted when it was discovered by the metropolitan police in 1906.

By 1906, however, the revolutionaries had become the major rival of the Baohuanghui. Much earlier, some Japanese *shishi* (men of purpose) had tried in vain to mediate between Sun Yatsen and the reformers for cooperation against the Manchu government. Down to 1904, the Baohuanghui still held the upper hand in competition with the revolutionary Xingzhonghui (Revive China Society) for funds and membership. The situation changed with the formation of the Tongmenghui (Revolutionary Alliance) in 1905 and with the polemic that took place between the revolutionary *Minbao* (The People's Report) and the reformist *Xinmin congbao* (The New People Miscellany) the next year. When the Qing government announced its constitutional program, the reformers responded by changing the name of their society to Diguo xianzhenghui (Imperial Constitutional Association) in 1907. The society then gradually lost its membership to its rival, Tongmenghui. Its decline was further accelerated by the collapse of its commercial empire after the death of Emperor Guangxu in 1908.

The Baohuanghui clearly represented the thinking of a major group of late Qing political activists, who believed that preserving the Manchu government was critical to the survival of the Chinese state, or even the Chinese race. The foundation of their reform proposal, which lay in the person of the young Emperor Guangxu, proved to be too narrow and transient, but later many Baohuanghui leaders lent their support to the Constitutional Movement of 1909–11.

Henry Y.S. Chan

References

Chan, Henry Y. S. "The Reformer as Conspirator: K'ang Yu-wei versus the Empress Dowager, 1904–1906." *Chinese Studies in History,* vol. 25, no. 4 (1992), 38–50.

Larson, Jane Leung. "New Source Materials on Kang Youwei and the Baohuanghui." *Chinese America: History and Perspectives* (1993), 151–198.

Ma, L. Eve Armentrout. *Revolutionaries, Monarchists, and Chinatowns.* Honolulu: The University Press of Hawaii, 1990.

Emperor Tongzhi (1856–75)

See TONGZHI RESTORATION

Emperor Xianfeng (1831–61)

The Qing monarch who ruled China from 1851 to 1861. Emperor Xianfeng's reign, marked by domestic rebellions and foreign invasions, was one of the darkest periods in the history of the Dynasty.

Succeeding the throne at the age of twenty, Xianfeng (personal name Yiju) faced the aftermath of the Opium War (1840–42), an unprecedented experience in Chinese history. He was more hostile toward the "barbarians" than his father, Emperor Daoguang, had been, and apparently regretted some of the compromises in the postwar treaties. This hard-line policy partly contributed to the Sino-Western disputes on treaty revisions during his reign, which eventually led to the *Arrow* War, or the second Opium War, in 1858 to 1860. In 1860, the British-French joint expeditionary forces invaded and occupied Beijing, whereupon Xianfeng's court hastily fled to the Inner Mongolian province of Jehol. This was the first time in Qing history that the capital had fallen into the hands of the "barbarians." Xianfeng soon died of illness in Jehol; he never saw the Forbidden City again.

The attack from the West, however, was not the most serious threat that Xianfeng's government encountered. The same year his father died, the Taiping Rebellion (1850–64) broke out in the South. By 1852, the rebels had entered the Yangtze valley, and the following year they established their own government at Nanjing. From then on, until Xianfeng's death, the rebels fought a prolonged civil war with the Qing government. Not only did the Qing lose control over most of central and south China, but its legitimacy as the ruler of China was at stake. When Xianfeng died in his Jehol exile, the Taipings had just defeated the main forces of the Qing in the Lower Yangtze, and the dynasty seemed on the verge of collapse.

Xianfeng's only son and heir apparent was given birth by his concubine, Cixi (Yehonala). After his death, Cixi and the empress Cian were both made empresses dowager. Cixi then collaborated with Xianfeng's younger brother, Prince Gong, in staging a *coup d'état* and taking control of the court. She became *de facto* ruler of the Chinese empire for the next half-century.

Wang Ke-wen

Emperor Xuantong
See Puyi, Henry

Empress Dowager Cixi (1835–1908)

China's *de facto* ruler during the second half of the nineteenth century and one of the most powerful women in Chinese history, Empress Dowager Cixi was born Yehonala, daughter of Huizheng of the Manchu Bordered Blue Banner. She was chosen in 1851 to enter the imperial court as a concubine to Emperor Xianfeng. Cixi was not the Emperor's senior consort at this time, yet using her beauty, intelligence, and ability to manipulate power, she drew herself closer to Xianfeng. She eventually became his favorite concubine and gave birth, in 1856, to Xianfeng's only son, Zaichun.

Thereafter Cixi became a very influential member of the court.

Following the death of Emperor Xianfeng in 1861, Cixi's son was enthroned as Emperor Tongzhi at the age of five. Empresses Cixi and Cian (Emperor Xianfeng's senior consort) were appointed to be the young emperor's co-regents. Naturally, Cixi was the more powerful regent; and for the first time in her life she was able to experience the sweet taste of power. However, Cixi knew that if she wanted more control of the court, she had to cooperate closely with her brother-in-law Prince Gong, who was popular, influential, and powerful in Beijing.

The political alliance between Cixi and Prince Gong climaxed in the coup d'état of 1861, in which Cixi helped Prince Gong oust his ultra-conservative enemies, such as Suxun, Prince Yi, and Prince Zheng. The power balance between Cixi and Prince Gong in the 1860s and 1870s seemed to have brought new strength to China, known as the Tongzhi Restoration, with Prince Gong as the leader in the Qing court to support the Self-Strengthening programs for the industrialization and modernization of China. It, however, meant that China would have to open its door more widely to the West. Empress Dowager Cixi, with the support of the conservative official Woren, opposed these changes. A power struggle thus developed between Cixi and Prince Gong.

Emperor Tongzhi came of age in 1872; Cixi remained in power and became even more ambitious in the years after 1873. When Emperor Tongzhi died in 1875, Cixi was able to place her four-year-old nephew, Zaitian, on the throne as Emperor Guangxu. This arrangement would obviously guarantee Cixi's continued control over the emperor and the court.

Empress Dowager Cixi's domination of the government after 1875 weakened China considerably. Internally, her corruption, which included the embezzlement of public funds, virtually paralyzed many modernization programs initiated by Prince Gong and such Han Chinese leaders as Zeng Guofan. In 1884, Prince Gong was finally dismissed by Cixi. In 1898, even Emperor Guangxu rebelled against Cixi and recruited the young and reform-minded scholar Kang Youwei to launch the Hundred Days Reform (June 11 to September 20, 1898). The reform failed and Cixi resumed her regency by the end of 1898. Externally, Cixi's conservatism worried foreign powers in China. As foreign encroachments on China reached new heights in the Sino-French War of 1884 to 1885, the Sino-Japanese War of 1894 to 1895, and the territory-lease treaties with France, Germany, Russia, and Great Britain in 1898 and 1899, Cixi became extremely anti-foreign. Her frustration over the government's inability to resist foreign intrusion led her to support the Boxer Uprising of 1900, which in the end not only humiliated China but also bankrupted Chinese finances. This alienated the Han Chinese leaders and stimulated such political activists as Sun Yatsen to engage in anti-Manchu revolutionary movements.

After the Boxer Uprising, Cixi finally gave approval to a series of belated reforms in education, the military, and the restructuring of the government. But her health deteriorated considerably, and she died on November 15, 1908, one day after the death of Emperor Guangxu. Many Chinese, especially Han nationalists, have argued that Cixi's main concern was the survival of the Manchu court in China, not the survival of China as a nation facing the menace of the West. A more sympathetic view, however, portrays her as a shrewd leader who, limited by personal background and knowledge, failed to comprehend and solve the unprecedented problems confronting both China and the Manchu court.

Anthony Y. Teng

References

Haldane, Charlotte. *The Last Great Empress of China*. Indianapolis, IN: Bobbs-Merrill, 1967.

Hussey, Harry. *Venerable Ancestor: The Life and Times of Tz'u Hsi, Empress of China*. Westport, CT: Greenwood Press, 1970.

Seagrave, Sterling. *Dragon Lady: The Life and Legend of the Last Empress of China*. New York, NY: Alfred A. Knopf, 1992.

Ever-Victorious Army

The Ever-Victorious Army was a Western mercenary force that assisted the Qing government to fight the Taiping Rebellion during the early 1860s.

As the Taiping rebels approached the Shanghai area in 1860, the business community in the city saw the need to organize its own defense against the Taipings because the Qing army seemed unable to stop the rebels' advances. The plan soon received approval and assistance from local Chinese officials. In 1861 a foreign rifle squadron *(yangqiangdui)* was formed under the command of an American mercenary, Frederick T. Ward. Most of its soldiers were foreign deserters or discharged seamen. The initial performance of this force was unimpressive. It suffered a series of defeats in the Songjiang-Qingpu line, yet it was allowed to continue its service. By this time, the Western powers, having secured significant benefits from the Qing government in the Treaty of Tianjin and the Beijing Convention, had abandoned their neutrality in the Taiping Rebellion and actively assisted the Qing to suppress the Taipings. Ward's army became a symbol and a major instrument in that assistance.

In September 1861, after scoring its first victory, Ward expanded his troops by recruiting four thousand to five thousand local Chinese into its ranks. These men were trained by about one hundred Western officers, with Western weapons and in Western uniforms. A few hundred Filipinos also joined the army. The Qing court formally named it the Ever-Victorious Army *(Changshengjun)* in March 1862. During the following months, the army launched several successful offensives on the Taipings with the support of the British authorities in the area. In September, Ward was killed in a battle and his deputy, Henry A. Burgevine, succeeded him. In March 1863, the British officer Charles G. Gordon ("Chinese Gordon") was appointed as the new commander. From late 1863 to early 1864, the army fought in coordination with the Huai Army under Li Hongzhang in the southern Jiangsu area, and made an important contribution to the recovery of Taicang, Suzhou, and Changzhou. Gordon was rewarded with prestigious official titles by the Qing. Upon the defeat of the Taipings in May 1864, the Ever-Victorious Army disbanded.

The employment of the Ever-Victorious Army by the Qing government was a partial implementation of the policy of "borrowing the barbarian troops for the suppression of the rebels" proposed by Prince Gong and leaders of the gentry armies. The very existence of the army suggests the degree of Western intrusion into China's domestic affairs in the mid-nineteenth century. At the same time, however, the organization, equipment, and weaponry of the army provided its Chinese allies such as Zeng Guofan and Li Hongzhang with first-hand knowledge of the superior performance of Western military forces. Shortly after the suppression of the rebellion, these gentry-officials started the Self-Strengthening movement with a main focus on introducing Western military technology to China. The Ever-Victorious Army, together with other foreign rifle squadrons such as the French Ever-Triumphant Army *(Changjiejun)*, played a critical role in stimulating that movement.

Wang Ke-wen

References

Smith, Richard J. *Mercenaries and Mandarins: The Ever-Victorious Army in Nineteenth Century China.* New York, NY: KTO Press, 1978.

Spence, Jonathan D. *To Change China: Western Advisers in China, 1620–1960.* New York, NY: Little, Brown, 1969.

Extraterritoriality

The Chinese government's exclusion of foreign merchants at trading ports from its jurisdiction could be traced to as early as Song dynasty (960–1279). In 1835, the Qing government signed an agreement with the khanate of Kokand (in today's Xinjiang), granting its representatives the power to govern and tax the Central Asian merchants at the trading posts on China's western border. This was the first, although little noted, precedent of the Chinese recognition of extraterritoriality.

After China's defeat in the Opium War (1839–42), the Sino-British Treaty of Nanjing granted the same extraterritoriality rights to Great Britain. According to the treaty, British subjects in China were exempt from Chinese laws. In the case of British subjects involved in disputes with Chinese citizens, the British would be tried by the British Consul, under British laws, while the Chinese would be judged according to the laws of China. The provision, applied to both civil and criminal cases, gave British subjects in China a legal privilege that even the highest Chinese official did not enjoy.

Extraterritoriality was then extended to other Western powers and to Japan in subsequent treaties concluded between China and those countries. It provided the legal basis for the establishment of foreign concessions and settlements in China's treaty ports. In Shanghai, for example, a Sino-foreign mixed court was established to try cases in its foreign settlement. The

The signing of Sino-American new treaties to end the unequal treaties, 1943. (Courtesy of Nationalist Party Archives.)

significance of extraterritoriality as a violation of China's sovereignty, however, was not appreciated by the Qing government initially. It did not challenge the traditional Chinese notion of *tianxia* and universal kingship. But as the Chinese were gradually exposed to the new knowledge of international relations and international law, and as disputes between the Chinese and foreigners in China became frequent, the Chinese began to recognize extraterritoriality as an insult to Chinese independence. This foreign privilege thus symbolized the "unequal treaties" and the inferior status that China bore in the world community. It was a major cause of frustration and grievance for all nationalist Chinese.

As early as in the 1880s, reformist officials and intellectuals, such as Zeng Jize and Wang Tao, had called for the abolition of extraterritoriality. One of the main goals of the legal reform during the last years of the Qing dynasty was to attack the rationale of extraterritoriality, namely, the "backwardness and barbarity" of China's legal codes. During the late 1920s, the newly established Guomindang (GMD) government negotiated aggressively with the foreign powers for the abolition of this privilege, with little success. Not until the outbreak of World War II did the Western countries finally agree to return full sovereignty to China, their wartime ally. Extraterritoriality was abolished in 1943, when the GMD government signed new and equal treaties with the Allied Powers.

Wang Ke-wen

References

Fairbank, John King. *Trade and Diplomacy on the China Coast: The Opening of the Treaty Ports, 1842–1854.* Cambridge, MA: Harvard University Press, 1953.

Fishel, Wesley R. *The End of Extraterritoriality in China.* Berkeley: University of California Press, 1952.

Fletcher, Joseph. "The Heyday of the Ch'ing Order in Mongolia, Sinkiang and Tibet." *Cambridge History of China,* ed. John K. Fairbank, vol. 10, 351–408. Cambridge, England: Cambridge University Press, 1978.

E

F

Fascism

Originating in Europe as a reaction against the rise of communism in the early twentieth century, fascism is generally understood as a totalitarian ideology which attempts to protect the capitalist order by organizing a multiclass, corporative state under a charismatic leader. It became one of the most influential political movements in republican China.

Following its triumph in Italy in the 1920s, fascism was introduced to China as a fashionable political trend in Europe. The life story of Benito Mussolini, his domestic and foreign policies, and the political and social conditions of Italy attracted the attention of many Chinese, especially the Chinese media. Among the latter *Dongfang zazhi (The Eastern Magazine), Guowen zhoubao (National News Weekly)* and the newspaper *Shenbao* probably published the largest number of reports, comments, and translations on this subject. In addition, some Italian and Japanese fascists visited China and promoted the ideology. The initial Chinese reaction to fascism was mixed—most people regarded it as no more than an interesting foreign idea. Its impact on China's domestic development was at first limited.

The political situation in the late 1920s and early 1930s made it possible for fascism to reappear on the Chinese scene with a new momentum. In 1928 the Guomindang (GMD) government under Chiang Kaishek announced the beginning of political tutelage in China. The country was thus put under an anti-Communist party dictatorship that resembled the fascist rule in Italy. On May 5, 1931, Chiang declared in his opening speech at the National People's Conference that only the "fascist political theory" could guarantee "the most effective rule" in a country. His words ushered in a national frenzy for the propagation of fascist theory and practice.

In propaganda, a circle of GMD theorists around Chiang now proposed that "only fascism can save China." Borrowing the *ti-yong* theory of the late Qing, they suggested that, for the Party, the Three Peoples' Principles constituted *ti* (substance) while fascism could serve as *yong* (function). A number of propagandist organizations affiliated with the GMD, such as the Chinese Cultural Association *(Zhongguo wenhua xuehui)* and Chinese Cultural Construction Association *(Zhongguo wenhua jianshe xuehui)*, were active in formulating a theoretical framework for the integration of fascism with the GMD ideology. In line with the fascist exaltation of national heritage, they also sought to promote China's cultural tradition as a way of restoring national pride and self-confidence.

In organization, the most representative example of Chinese fascist groups was the Blue Shirts (or *Lixingshe*) established in early 1932. A pro-Chiang faction in the GMD, the society was the moving force behind the National Revival movements *(Minzu fuxing yundong)* initiated by Chiang in the 1930s, which included the New Life movement, the National Military Training movement and the National Economic Reconstruction movement, all with strong fascist overtones. The society often praised and quoted Mussolini and Hitler in its publications.

The rise of the fascist movement in China was closely related to the Sino-German and Sino-Italian diplomatic ties. Before the outbreak of the Sino-Japanese War (1937–45), Guomindang China was friendly with both Nazi Germany and Fascist Italy. German military advisers, in particular, played a major role in Chiang's anti-Communist Bandit-Suppression Campaigns during 1930 to 1934. The formation of the German-Italian-Japanese Axis in the mid-1930s inevitably undermined this friendship and the popularity of fascism in China. During and after the war, while open promotion of the ideology gradually disappeared in China, the reality of a fascist-type rule under the GMD remained.

Like all other ideologies or movements imported from the West in twentieth-century China, the Chinese version of fascism displayed some prominent distinctions from its Italian and German models. In the 1930s, fascism was understood by most of its Chinese advocates as a form of national solidarity, achieved under the guidance of a powerful party and a charismatic leader, which was seen as necessary in bringing about domestic order and in protecting the country from foreign oppression. The slogan "one nation, one ideology, one leader," a popular way of explaining the ideology in China, was enormously appealing to those Chinese who were frustrated by the endless civil wars and alarmed by the increasing threat from Japan. To them the fast recovery of Italy and Germany after World War I proved the effectiveness of this new method of state-building and national strengthening. In this sense the popularity of fascism in China was a clear expression of Chinese nationalism.

Xu Youwei

References
Chang, Maria Hsia. *The Chinese Blue Shirt Society: Fascism and Developmental Nationalism.* Berkeley, CA: Center for Chinese Studies Publications, University of California, 1985.

Eastman, Lloyd E. *The Abortive Revolution: China under Nationalist Rule, 1927–1937.* Cambridge, MA: Harvard University Press, 1974.

February Twenty-Eighth Incident
Analyzed variously as urban riot, political rebellion, or popular uprising, this 1947 conflict between Taiwanese civilians and the Guomindang-appointed Chen Yi administration is probably the single most important event in Taiwan's post-World War II history. The incident's tragic unfolding and brutal suppression created distrust between native Taiwanese and Chinese mainlanders and influenced the overall development of Taiwanese nationalism.

The confrontation began on February 27, 1947, when Monopoly Bureau agents harassed a woman selling contraband cigarettes in north Taibei, touching off angry protests. However, the incident is remembered for the mass demonstrations in central Taibei the following morning, which ended in violent attacks on mainlanders after military guards fired on protesters from the governor-general's headquarters. Within days, the upheaval had spread throughout the island. In Taibei and other urban centers, Taiwanese elites initiated negotiations with the authorities to seek a reasonable and thorough resolution of the incident, though more radical demands surfaced in central Taiwan. Students and youth were mobilized to maintain civil order, to take over official offices and protect arms depots.

Chen Yi's initial response was conciliatory, but with the help of subordinates he encouraged dissension within the settlement committees while gathering intelligence for later prosecution of participants. He also requested military reinforcements from Chiang Kaishek, should a political resolution of the crisis fail. When settlement committee demands escalated beyond the resolution of the immediate conflict to include the implementation of Taiwanese self-rule, and with military reinforcements awaiting deployment nearby, Chen Yi ordered the immediate suppression of the rebellion. Military suppression was swift and brutal; only in central Taiwan, where radical activists had more support, was any serious resistance encountered. Reliable estimates of deaths caused by the incident and the subsequent suppression range from five-thousand to twenty-thousand, many of whom were innocent victims of the violence.

Historians cite numerous long-term causes for the incident: severe postwar economic and social dislocation, exacerbated by Chen Yi's inappropriate, ineffective, and discriminatory statist policies; inept, inefficient, and corrupt Guomindang rule; deployment of poorly trained and ill-disciplined military forces; fundamentally different Taiwanese and Chinese perspectives regarding immediate needs and future plans for Taiwan; and the basic lack of mutual understanding between both groups. Further consideration must be given to disparate Taiwanese experiences with Japanese colonial rule, which influenced postwar attitudes and expectations.

Without doubt, this incident has had a tremendous impact on Taiwan's postwar development. The confrontation precipitated a fundamental and broad-based reassessment of both Guomindang and Japanese rule on Taiwan. Proponents of Taiwanese independence often trace the genesis of their movement to the 1947 incident. Students of Taiwan's postwar development have highlighted the substantial loss of native elites during the suppression, which facilitated rapid Guomindang implementation of land reform and other policies. Finally, the long-term, fundamental distrust between Taiwanese and mainlanders owes its existence to the incident and its suppression.

Douglas Fix

References

Kerr, George. *Formosa Betrayed.* Boston, MA: Houghton Mifflin, 1965.

Lai, Tse-han et al. *A Tragic Beginning: The Taiwan Uprising of February 28, 1947.* Stanford, CA: Stanford University Press, 1991.

Federalist Movement *(Liansheng Zizhi)*

The Federalist movement, which flourished briefly in the early 1920s, called for the reorganization of the Chinese state into a federation of self-governing provinces. Although originally promoted by well-meaning nationalists as a means to stop political conflict and civil war, in practice the movement was used by warlords to justify the preservation of autonomous regional power bases.

In the late-nineteenth and early-twentieth centuries, a number of Chinese intellectuals, including both revolutionaries and reformers, developed an admiration for the Western federalist system of government and proposed this as most suited to China's vast territory and the diversity of conditions among its provinces. With the north-south division of the country during the Revolution of 1911, federalist proposals were temporarily shelved in the interest of national unification. After the establishment of Yuan Shikai's dictatorship, public interest in federalism reemerged as a means of opposing Yuan's rule. After Yuan's death, discussion of the idea again temporarily subsided.

Federalism gained its greatest popularity in the context of the incessant military conflicts between, and among, northern and southern warlords that arose following the emergence of the Constitution Protection movement in 1917. Seeing no hope for national unification under either northern or southern forces, Xiong Xiling, a former early republican premier, issued a telegram in January 1918 advocating federalism as a means of eliminating civil war and restoring peace. After the northern warlord Zhang Jingyao was expelled from Hunan in July 1920, Tan Yankai, Hunan's military governor, became the first provincial leader to accept Xiong's proposal. Seeking to keep his province out of future north-south military conflicts, Tan called for local self-rule in his province (*Xiangren zhiXiang* or "the rule of Hunan by Hunanese") and a federation of self-governing provinces *(liansheng zizhi).* Xiong Xiling and Liang Qichao then provided Hunan with a plan for the implementation of provincial self-government which they hoped would lead to political reforms and the expansion of democracy. Taking the federalist system of the United States as their model, they urged each province to draft a constitution initiating provincial autonomy. Next, a conference of these self-governing provinces would be called to establish a federal government.

A Federalist movement emerged as Hunan's proposal for provincial self-government received enthusiastic support from warlords in south and southwestern China. The federalist slogan was also raised by progressive forces in a number of provinces seeking to end the rule of outside warlords. For example, in 1924, a self-governing federation of Jiangsu, Zhejiang, and Anhui provinces was advocated as a means of opposing the northern warlord Sun Chuanfang. Nonetheless, nationalist criticism of the Federalist movement increased as the idea of provincial self-government was manipulated by warlords to defend their regional power bases. The Federalist movement came to an end when the Northern Expedition initiated by the Guomindang in 1926 provided new hope for national unification.

Zhou Qiuguang

References

Chesneaux, Jean. "The Federalist Movement in China, 1920–3." *Modern China's Search for a Political Form,* ed. Jack Gray, 96–137. London, England: Oxford University Press, 1969.

Schoppa, Keith R. "Province and Nation: The Chekiang Provincial Autonomy Movement, 1917–1927." *Journal of Asian Studies* 36, no. 4 (August 1977), 661–674.

Feng Guifen (1809–74)

Feng Guifen was one of the earliest reformist thinkers of the late Qing. Born to a wealthy family in Suzhou, Jiangsu, he was a student of Lin Zexu. He received a *Jinshi* degree in 1832 and was subsequently appointed a Hanlin scholar. When the Taiping Rebellion broke out in the 1850s, Feng organized anti-Taiping militia in his home town. Following the fall of Suzhou to the rebels in 1860, he sought refuge in Shanghai and again participated in organizing the defense of the city with the help of the Western troops in the area. The effectiveness of Western weapons shocked and impressed Feng. In 1861 he wrote *Jiaobinlu kangyi (Straightforward Words from the Lodge of Early Zhou Studies)*, which established him as one of the earliest reformist thinkers in nineteenth-century China. The book argued for a rational foreign policy and the introduction of Western science and technology. "When methods are faulty," it declared, "we should reject them even though they are of ancient origins; when methods are good, we should benefit from them even though they are those of the barbarians." China, therefore, need not be restricted by her own traditional ways but should seek whatever means that could strengthen her in the face of the new threat from the West. Such a view was indeed revolutionary in his time.

Like Wei Yuan and Wang Tao, Feng was deeply influenced by the Statecraft School *(Jingshi xuepai)* of the late Qing. His writings discussed not only the necessity and urgency of learning from the West but a wide range of reforms in taxation, economy, and the examination system. He suggested a form of public opinion survey as the basis of government policies, which may be described as proto-democratic. The proposals Feng made were said to have had a profound impact on Li Hongzhang, whom he briefly assisted in 1862. Moreover, his idea of preserving "China's ethical and social tradition as her basis, while supplementing it with the methods of achieving wealth and power from the Western nations," provided the philosophical foundation for the Self-Strengthening movement of the 1870s and 1880s.

Wang Ke-wen

References

Cohen, Paul A., and John E. Schrecker, eds. *Reform in Nineteenth Century China.* Cambridge, MA: Harvard University Press, 1976.

Wright, Mary C. *The Last Stand of Chinese Conservatism: The T'ung-chih Restoration, 1862–1874.* Stanford, CA: Stanford University Press, 1966.

Feng Guozhang (1859–1919)

The death of Yuan Shikai in 1916 led to a split of his Beiyang Army into several rivaling warlord factions. Among them the Zhili Clique under Feng Guozhang was the most powerful at the time.

A native of Zhili, Hebei, Feng had studied military affairs in Japan before becoming chief assistant to Yuan Shikai in the organization of the Beiyang Army. Later he was given the assignment of founding the prestigious and influential Baoding Military Academy. Together with Duan Qirui and Wang Shizhen, they were known as the three prominent leaders of the Beiyang Army, second only to Yuan himself. When the Revolution of 1911 broke out, Feng, then commander of the Qing government's First Army, was ordered to attack the revolutionaries in Wuhan. He duly followed Yuan's instructions in the political maneuvering of the subsequent months that in the end brought Yuan the presidency of the new Republic.

Under Yuan's presidency, Feng served as governor of Zhili and then of Jiangsu, and played an important role in the suppression of the Second Revolution of 1913. When Yuan tried to make himself emperor in 1915, Feng led his Beiyang colleagues in voicing their disapproval, which dealt a severe blow to Yuan's effort. After Yuan's failure and subsequent death, Li Yuanhong succeeded Yuan as president and Feng was elected vice-president. By then, the Zhili Clique had been formed with Feng as its leader. In 1917, Feng became president after Li had fled Beijing in Zhang Xun's attempt to restore the Qing court. As president, Feng was crippled by Duan Qirui's Anhui Clique that controlled the Parliament. He was forced out of office by the Parliament in 1918 and died the next year. The leadership of his Zhili Clique passed to Cao Kun and Wu Peifu.

Wang Ke-wen

References

Ch'i, Hsin-sheng. *Warlord Politics in China, 1916–1928.* Stanford, CA: Stanford University Press, 1976.

Nathan, Andrew J. *Peking Politics, 1918–1923: Factionalism and the Failure of*

Constitutionalism. Berkeley: University of California Press, 1976.

Feng Yuxiang (1882–1948)

Widely recognized as one of the most colorful and controversial military figures during China's warlord period (1916–28), Feng Yuxiang steered his career precariously through the swift currents of change in modern Chinese history. Born in 1882 into a poverty-stricken soldier's family, Feng received hardly any formal education and was enlisted at the tender age of eleven through his father's connection. Feng could truly claim to be a child of the army. Through rigorous physical training, perseverance, a thirst for knowledge, and self-discipline, he grew up to be a man of splendid physique, well versed in the written language, and quite knowledgeable of world affairs, which was unusual for a professional soldier who had risen through the ranks in China's turbulent age.

Growing up from a humble childhood experience in the age of imperialism in China, Feng developed a life-long sympathy with the lot of common folks and a loathing for corruption and extravagance, as well as an intense patriotism and the desire for progress. Feng's nationalist credentials and republican sympathy were shown early in his involvement in the unsuccessful Luanzhou Uprising in November 1911, his active role in defeating Zhang Xun's Qing restoration plot in July 1917, and his action to expel Puyi and his anachronistic imperial court from the Forbidden City in Beijing in October 1924. Feng's early conversion to Christianity—he became known as "the Christian General"—can be seen in the same vein, because he discerned in Christianity moral values for the betterment of the individual and the attainment of social order and progress. By his disposition and the evolution of his thinking, Feng was, among all warlord generals, the most likely one to be drawn into China's nationalist revolution in the 1920s.

As a military man, Feng fully understood the importance of his army. He paid meticulous care to the upkeep, training, and welfare of his troops, and sought at every available opportunity to strengthen and expand the army under his command. Feng's military career prospered; he became a brigade commander in 1914 when he was only thirty-two. He was a strict disciplinarian with his soldiers and demanded unquestioning obedience from his officers. He set himself as an example in leading a simple, unpretentious, and even frugal life. Feng's army earned its fame as one of the few tough fighting units among the warlord armies, and one of the best disciplined forces during the whole republican period.

From 1914 to 1926, Feng was fully involved in the frequent rivalry, intrigues, and battles associated with the warlord era. He was first identified with the Zhili Clique; then, after his coup of October 1924, he broke with the clique and renamed his army the *Guominjun* (National People's Army). However, his army came to be popularly known as the Northwest Army both because of its region of control and with reference to its principal rival, the Manchurian, or Northeast Army.

The year 1926 marked a turning point in Feng's career. Facing the combined attack of the Fengtian Clique and the reorganized forces under the Zhili leader Wu Peifu, Feng's army retreated to Inner Mongolia and suffered serious setbacks. Feng journeyed to the Soviet Union trying to obtain aid. During his trip he joined the Guomindang (GMD) and accepted the policy of the United Front between the GMD and the Chinese Communist Party (CCP). After his return to China in September, with Soviet advisers and limited Soviet supplies, Feng regrouped his scattered forces and formally accepted the title of Commander of the Second Army Group of the National Revolutionary Forces. Feng's army played an active role in the second stage of the GMD's Northern Expedition, which succeeded in reunifying China and ending the warlord period. However, the United Front could no longer be maintained, and the GMD purged the Communists in 1927. Feng decided to side with the GMD's top military leader, Chiang Kaishek, and ended his ties with the Soviet Union.

Emerging as one of the most powerful military leaders after the Northern Expedition, Feng soon found himself on the opposite side from Chiang Kaishek on various issues. The rift eventually led to civil wars in 1929 to 1930, which involved virtually all other important military leaders in the country. Feng's army suffered defeat and defection. The mighty Northwest Army disintegrated, and many of its units were absorbed by Chiang's Central Army. Feng was forced into retirement and never resumed military command. Deprived of military power but still enjoying a fine reputation, Feng soon became an outspoken arch-nationalist in China's struggle against Japanese aggression. In 1933, he led the abortive attempt to organize an anti-

Japanese army in Chahar. From 1935 to 1945, Feng, from his largely honorary position as vice-chairman of the Military Commission, carried out his anti-Japanese activities with dedication and enthusiasm.

During the latter years of the Sino-Japanese War, Feng became increasingly critical of the wartime government under Chiang Kaishek and was politically leaning toward the CCP and the liberal Democratic League. After the end of the war, Feng visited the United States on a mission to study water conservancy projects. The rapidly changing situation in China's civil war made him break openly with Chiang Kaishek and the GMD government. On July 31, 1948, Feng and his family boarded the Russian ship *Pobeda* on their way back to China via the Soviet Union. A fire reportedly broke out on September 1 when the ship was approaching Odessa. Feng and his youngest daughter were among the victims of this accident. His widow later confirmed that Feng died of a heart attack caused by asphyxiation.

Lawrence N. Shyu

References

Sheridan, James E. *Chinese Warlord: The Career of Feng Yu-hsiang.* Stanford, CA: Stanford University Press, 1966.

Fengtian Clique
See ZHANG ZUOLIN

Five Principles of Peaceful Coexistence
See BANDUNG CONFERENCE

Five-Year Plans

In the People's Republic of China, five-year plans are produced by the State Planning Commission in conjunction with planning personnel in provincial and local enterprises and governments. There are also annual plans, ten-year, and longer-range plans. China's Soviet-inspired central plans are based on the belief that, by controlling the output of products, prices, and allocation among sectors and regions, the state can foster rapid economic growth while also promoting egalitarianism and other social goods, such as education and health.

Nationalism shapes this system in two respects. First, economic growth affects China's standing in the world, and five-year plans are the road to growth. Secondly, nationalism implies uniting the constituent parts of China, specifying how the government will integrate sectoral, regional, class, or other particular interests and also privileging national investment over personal consumption.

Since the economy was socialized under collective agriculture and state enterprises in the mid-1950s, there have been eight five-year plans: First, 1953–57; Second, 1958–62; Third, 1963–67; Fourth, 1971–75; Fifth, 1976–80; Sixth, 1981–85; Seventh, 1986–90; and Eighth, 1991–95. But these plans did not determine economic life as much as this list suggests. Four were defunct: the second was overtaken by the Great Leap Forward (1958–60), while the third, fourth, and fifth were negated by the Great Proletarian Cultural Revolution (1966–69) and its aftermath.

Nor were the other five-year plans (the first, sixth, seventh, and eighth) determinant. In the case of the first plan, statistical services and other administrative capabilities were just being developed as the five-year period concluded. The bureaus were then partly dismantled during the Great Leap Forward and the Great Proletarian Cultural Revolution.

In the 1980s and 1990s, planning capabilities were reestablished, but the seventh (1986–90) and eighth (1991–95) five-year plans were compromised by economic overheating and the 1989 Tiananmen demonstrations. Plans were often late in being finalized: the sixth (1981–85) was not approved until late 1982, and the eighth (1991–95) was still being debated in March 1991. On the other hand, work on the Seventh (1986–90) did begin as early as 1982. In any case, in so huge a country, the state's ability to oversee production and exchange of all intermediate and final products is limited.

In the 1980s, reliance on central planning diminished, as belief in markets increased. Also, the center's levers of control weakened further with administrative decentralization and the rapid growth of out-of-plan enterprises and foreign participation in the economy. Still, China continues to produce these plans and to measure success against the stated goals. The goals continue to emphasize the most rapid possible development of China's economy and internal coordination, stability, and balance the two aspects of nationalism suggested above.

Craig Dietrich

References

Hamrin, Carol Lee. *China and the Challenge of the Future: Changing Political Patterns.* Boulder, CO: Westview Press, 1990.

Howe, Christopher, and Kenneth R. Walker. *The Foundations of the Chinese Planned Economy: A Documentary Survey, 1953–1965.* London and Basingstoke, England: Macmillan, 1989.

Lieberthal, Kenneth, and Michel Oksenberg. *Policy Making in China: Leaders, Structures, Processes.* Princeton, NJ: Princeton University Press, 1988.

Flying Tigers

See CHENNAULT, CLAIRE L.

Four Modernizations

The "four modernizations" has been the stated goal of Chinese economic policymaking in the post-Mao era. First articulated by Zhou Enlai in the mid-1970s, the "four modernizations" ordered the priorities of Chinese economic development in the following order of importance: agriculture, industry, national defense, and science and technology.

The "four modernizations" represents a shift in emphasis from "putting politics in command" to "putting economics in command"; from stressing political goals to stressing economic goals; from transforming the social relations of production to transforming the forces of production; from employing idealism and utopianism to employing pragmatism ("seek truth from facts") in designing socioeconomic policy. In other words, the "four modernizations" program represents the rejection of Cultural Revolution ideology and of radical left excesses. Virtually all political factions in post-Mao China accepted the broad goals of the four modernizations. How these modernizations would be accomplished, however, remained extremely controversial.

Immediately after the deaths of Zhou Enlai and Mao Zedong, a period of constant evaluation, reevaluation, investigation, experimentation, debate, and criticism commenced. It seemed that everything was under scrutiny. Radical Maoist idealism had indeed been replaced by economic pragmatism, but a sharp division existed between those proposing the pursuit of a Maoist-inspired modernization strategy that relied on collectivist principles and policies and an alternative strategy based on individual initiative, economic rationality, market forces, and an open door to the West.

The former camp, led by Hua Guofeng, promoted the "Learn from Dazhai" campaign. The campaign wanted to duplicate the impressive accomplishments of the Dazhai commune to achieve the "four modernizations." For Hua, the Dazhai commune provided evidence that the communal organization of China's agricultural sector and the policy of self-reliance could succeed in modernizing China. It would also eliminate the differences between the urban and rural economies (and hence, between workers and peasants), a goal which Mao himself had set. With the modernization of agriculture, the modernization of industry, national defense, and science and technology would follow. In 1978, Hua outlined an ambitious ten-year plan to achieve the "four modernizations" along these lines.

Hua's opponent, Deng Xiaoping, had an alternative plan for achieving the "four modernizations." His plan was to rehabilitate those people purged by radical leftists and Maoists, to implement a program based on opening the door to the West, to introduce foreign technologies and investment, and to train Chinese students overseas. Deng's goal was to make China into a "powerful modern socialist state by the year 2000" and to realize sufficient economic growth so that China's annual per capita GNP would reach $1,000 by the year 2000.

The third plenum of Eleventh Central Committee of the Chinese Communist Party in December 1978 ratified the Dengist modernization strategy and rejected the economic plan of Hua Guofeng. A remarkable decade of economic transformation followed. The agricultural sector was decollectivized and the communal system dismantled. The household "responsibility system" was introduced in its place, which ultimately led to the reform of the entire Chinese economy.

Peter M. Lichtenstein

References

Ch'i, Hsi-sheng. *Politics of Disillusionment: The Communist Party under Deng Xiaoping, 1978–1989.* Armonk, NY: M. E. Sharpe, 1991.

Perry, Elizabeth J., and Christine Wong, eds. *The Political Economy of Reform in Post-Mao China.* Cambridge, MA: Harvard University Press, 1985.

Fujian Rebellion

After the January Twenty-eighth Incident in 1932, the Nineteenth Route Army, which had fought heroically against the Japanese in Shanghai, was transferred to Fujian to participate in Chiang Kaishek's anti-Communist campaign. The next year the Japanese invaded along the Great Wall, and the Nineteenth Route Army requested to be sent to the North to reinforce the Chinese resistance there. The Nanjing government refused.

In Fujian, leaders of the army, notably Chen Minshu, Jiang Guangnai and Cai Tingkai, were influenced by leftist political groups such as the Third Party, formerly under Deng Yanda. They soon decided to rebel against Nanjing in the name of anti-Japanese nationalism. In October 1933, the army reached a secret "anti-Japan, anti-Chiang" agreement with the Chinese Communist Party (CCP) in Jiangxi, and in November it established the People's Revolutionary Government at Fuzhou, the provincial capital, to challenge the Nanjing government. Li Jishen, a former commander of Chen, Jiang and Cai, became head of the Fuzhou regime, which renamed the Chinese Republic from *Zhonghua minguo* to *Zhonghua gongheguo*. A Producer People's Party *(Shengchan renmin-dang),* with Chen Minshu as its general-secretary, was organized to lead the Fuzhou regime. The Party's platform, which included such items as abolishing the unequal treaties and implementing land reform, was anti-imperialist and moderately socialist. The immediate demand of the regime was to end Chiang Kaishek's policy of "domestic pacification (against the CCP) before external resistance (against Japan)."

The rebellion disrupted the fifth "Bandit-Suppression Campaign" launched by Chiang Kaishek in September 1933. The CCP's Jiangxi Soviet, however, failed to form an active alliance with the rebels in their opposition to Nanjing. The anti-Chiang militarists in neighboring Guangdong, dismayed by the rebels' radicalism, also refused to offer assistance. In January 1934, Chiang ordered his troops to attack Fuzhou. The Nineteenth Route Army proved to be militarily ineffective this time, and the Fuzhou regime quickly collapsed. Part of the army was later absorbed by the Guang-dong militarists.

Wang Ke-wen

References

Dorrill, William F. "The Fukien Rebellion and the CCP: A Case of Maoist Revisionism." *China Quarterly* no. 37 (Jan.–Mar. 1969): 31–53.

Eastman, Lloyd E. *The Abortive Revolution: China under Nationalist Rule, 1927–1937.* Cambridge, MA: Harvard University Press, 1974.

Hsi, Angela N. S. "Socialist Reform and the Fukien Rebellion, 1932–34." *Journal of Asian History* 11, no. 1 (1977), 1–25.

Fuzhou Naval Dockyard

See SHEN BAOZHEN

G

Gang of Four

The Gang of Four, a radical faction within the Chinese Communist Party (CCP), dominated the Party and the government during the Cultural Revolution of 1966 to 1976.

The leader of the gang was Jiang Qing, Mao Zedong's wife. The other three members of the gang were Zhang Chunqiao, Yao Wenyuan, and Wang Hongwen. Zhang, a writer and propagandist, had headed the Propaganda Department of the CCP branch in Shanghai before the Cultural Revolution. Yao's specialty resembled Zhang's; he had worked for the Party newspapers in Shanghai. The two men attracted Jiang Qing's attention and patronage during the early 1960s, when they supported her reform of Chinese drama.

In 1965, Yao's harsh attack on Wu Han's play, *Hairui's Dismissal from Office*, spearheaded a cultural campaign carefully planned by Mao and Jiang, which led to the Great Proletarian Cultural Revolution. In 1966, Zhang and Yao followed Jiang into the powerful Politburo. Zhang also shared with Jiang the deputy directorship of the Central Cultural Revolutionary Small Group, of which Yao was a member.

Wang Hongwen was a worker in a Shanghai cotton mill when the Cultural Revolution started. His radical and active leadership in the worker rebellion in Shanghai during the early months of the campaign, however, soon made him a favorite of Jiang Qing and Zhang Chunqiao. In February 1967, Wang and Zhang successfully seized power in Shanghai from the old Party establishment. To reward Wang's contribution, Jiang elevated him to chair the presidium of the CCP's Ninth Congress in 1969. Wang thus became the "model revolutionary worker" that provided Jiang's group with a proletarian touch.

All of these four radicals rose to political prominence with the help of the violent Cultural Revolution, and they pressed for the continuation and expansion of the campaign in order to further eliminate the old Party and government leadership. Their power reached its peak after the death of Lin Biao in 1971. In 1973 Wang Hongwen became vice-chairman of the CCP, in 1975 Zhang Chunqiao was appointed vice-premier of the PRC, and throughout the early 1970s Yao Wenyuan directed the Party's propaganda machine. Yet the power base of the radicals appeared to be limited—they were in total control of the media and some mass organizations, but had little influence in the military and the government. Their ruthlessness and arrogance also produced enemies. In May 1975, Mao Zedong reportedly admonished Jiang and her followers "not to function as a gang of four." This was the origin of the term, although it was not made public until their downfall in 1976.

During the final days of Mao, Jiang's faction engaged in a bitter power struggle with the moderates under Premier Zhou Enlai and Deng Xiaoping, another vice-premier. The faction apparently wanted Jiang to succeed Mao's Party leadership and Zhang the leadership in the government. When Zhou Enlai died in January 1976, however, they failed to seize his vacated position but instead allowed a neutral figure, Hua Guofeng, to become premier. Hua soon proved to be an obstacle to the faction as he began to establish his own power base. On September 9 Mao died. In the following weeks, the moderates and the radicals hastily prepared for a showdown. Deng Xiaoping, who had been purged in the wake of the Tiananmen Incident in April that year, secretly returned from the

South to Beijing. His allies in the military, represented by Ye Jianying, approached Hua Guofeng for cooperation. The commander of the security force in Beijing, Wang Tongxing, also lent his support to the moderates.

In the early morning of October 6, Hua invited Jiang, Zhang, Yao, and Wang to the government compound in Beijing for a Politburo meeting. When the latter three arrived they were summarily arrested by Wang Tongxing's men; Jiang was arrested at her house. The coup d'état was so swiftly carried out that the radicals were unable to offer any resistance. No disturbance took place either in the capital or in the radicals' base, Shanghai. The next day the CCP announced the purge of Jiang and her followers, calling them the "Gang of Four." They were described as a "counterrevolutionary clique" that had used the Cultural Revolution to advance their own power and sabotage the Party. Hua, Ye, and Deng emerged from the coup as the new leadership of the CCP and the PRC, and the radical policies of the Cultural Revolution were gradually overturned.

From November to December 1980, the Gang of Four, together with Mao's theorist Chen Boda and a few former followers of Lin Biao, were placed on public trial. The gang members were accused of having unjustly persecuted, hurt, or murdered hundreds of thousands of people, resulting in the death of nearly 35,000, during 1966 to 1976. Almost all the disasters created by the Cultural Revolution were blamed on them. In January 1981, Jiang and Zhang were sentenced to death (with a two-year suspended execution), Wang was given life imprisonment and Yao twenty years imprisonment. Wang later died of illness in jail; Jiang committed suicide in 1991.

Unquestionably, the Gang of Four was at least tacitly supported by Mao in its various activities. Jiang Qing's most important qualification in exercising power was that she was Mao's wife. To an extent the gang served as an instrument for Mao to realize his radical vision of "permanent revolution" as a form of national development, yet in the process the gang also used Mao to enhance its own position and influence. Together, the "gang of five" created a decade of destruction and terror in China.

Wang Ke-wen

References

Bonavia, David. *Verdict in Peking: The Trial of the Gang of Four.* New York, NY: Putnam, 1984.

Chi, Hsin. *The Rise and Fall of the "Gang of Four."* New York, NY: Books New China, 1977.

Gao Gang (1902–54)

Gao Gang was the first major Communist leader purged under the People's Republic. Born in Hengshan, Shaanxi, Gao joined the Chinese Communist Party (CCP) in 1926 and soon organized Party units in the local armies that were affiliated with the Guomindang (GMD). During the early 1930s he served as political commissar in a number of Red Army units in the Northwest. Such a position made him an important ally when Mao Zedong and his exhausted survivors of the Long March reached the area in 1935. As the local boss, Gao was appointed chief political commissar and vice-chairman of the CCP's Northwest Revolutionary Military Committee.

Gao's power and status remained high throughout the Sino-Japanese War (1937–45). He served in various prominent positions in the ShaanGanNing border region, including as secretary of the Party's Northwest Bureau. When the civil war between the Guomindang and the CCP commenced in 1946, Gao was transferred to the Northeast (Manchuria). By the end of that war he was concurrently secretary of the Northeast Bureau, chairman of the Northeast People's Government, and commander-in-chief and political commissar of the Northeast Military Zone. With Party, government, and military leadership all concentrated in his hands, he was described as the "Czar of Manchuria."

After the founding of the People's Republic, Mao rewarded Gao with the prestigious vice-chairmanship of the Central People's Government while allowing him to maintain his control over the Northeast. But suspicion soon arose within the top leadership of the CCP regarding Gao's attitude toward the Soviet Union, whose influence in the Northeast was particularly strong. Gao had visited the Soviet Union and concluded economic agreements there even before the People's Republic was established, and in the early 1950s he was the foremost advocate of Soviet-style industrial development in China. It has been alleged that Gao tried to create an "independent kingdom" for himself in the Northeast by maneuvering between Beijing and the adjacent Soviet Union.

In 1953, shortly after being transferred to

Beijing to chair the new State Planning Commission, Gao was accused of "engaging in activities aimed at splitting up the Party and usurping state leadership." His co-conspirator was said to be Rao Shushi, one-time head of the CCP's Organization Department. In 1954, following a CCP central plenum that condemned his alleged crimes, Gao killed himself. To the end he denied the accusations lodged against him by his comrades, and his suicide was considered as a form of protest. He was posthumously expelled from the Party the next year.

The purge of Gao Gang, known as the Gao-Rao Affair, marked the first major intra-party strife of the CCP in the history of the People's Republic. It is especially noteworthy because it involved not only a case of region versus center, but of foreign influence in domestic politics. As a revolutionary movement the CCP had claimed opposition to imperialism, yet tolerated, however uneasily, Soviet guidance before 1949. It was therefore particularly sensitive to the issue of Soviet interference or dominance once it came to power. The removal of Gao temporarily improved Sino-Soviet relations and made China more of an equal partner in that relationship, but it also foreshadowed the eventual split between the two Communist giants.

Wang Ke-wen

References

Meisner, Maurice. *Mao's China: A History of the People's Republic.* New York, NY: The Free Press, 1977.

Teiwes, Frederick C. *Politics at Mao's Court.* Armonk, NY: M. E. Sharpe, 1990.

Gentry

The study of the Chinese gentry—its role and influence in traditional Chinese society, its response to change in the late nineteenth century, and its survival into the twentieth-century context of nationalism and revolution—and attempts to define the term have engendered a considerable body of literature. Because of the gentry's central position in society as mediators between the state and the lower classes, and because of the evolution of the class, definition of the gentry and its role in the nationalist movement has remained problematic.

The use of the term "gentry" has been borrowed from its English cognate as a convenient approximation, relying on the inexact analogy between the English landed-gentry's domination of rural society and the social leadership of the Chinese local and regional elite. The term is generally used as a translation for the Chinese *shenshi* or *shenjin*. *Shen,* literally a sash or girdle worn by officials, connotes official status in the traditional Chinese bureaucracy; *jin,* meaning collar, has a similar significance. *Shih* means scholar. Accordingly, a number of alternative terms have found common application in addition to merely "gentry": "scholar-gentry," "scholar-officials" and "official-gentry."

Some writers have avoided the ambiguities inherent in these terms by using the word "elite" instead, often distinguishing among local, regional, and national elites. In this usage, the gentry is usually identified with the local and/or provincial elites. But as elite may include certain intellectual or economic groups which are not usually considered to belong to the gentry, most writers have preferred to use "gentry" for want of a more acceptable term.

Until major changes in the traditional order emerged in the mid-nineteenth century, the gentry may be distinguished as a distinct social class comprising the social and political leadership, below the level of the dynastic aristocracy, at the local and regional levels. Membership in the gentry was based solely on official appointment in the bureaucracy or qualification for such an appointment. Acquisition of one of the higher academic degrees in the civil service examination system normally qualified a person for official appointment, but did not ensure it. Holders of the metropolitan *jinshi* degree, the provincial *juren* degree, and sometimes the sub-provincial *gongsheng* degree, were likely to receive official appointments and therefore be regarded as members of the gentry class. There is some disagreement, however, on whether holders of the lowest level regular degree, the *shengyuan,* and the purchased *jiansheng* degree should be considered to belong to the gentry, as they were not qualified for office holding.

Following these criteria, then, the gentry comprised active officials serving in the capital and in districts away from their home; retired officials, dismissed officials, and officials temporarily on leave for mourning and residing in their home districts; higher degree holders, usually residing in their home districts, who were potential officials; and lower degree holders. It is sometimes useful to distinguish between the "upper gentry," consisting of officials and those qualified to be officials, and "lower gentry,"

G

consisting of mainly *shengyuan* and *jiansheng* who were scholars but not officials, often employed as teachers in village schools or as family tutors. In the nineteenth century, there were roughly one-and-a-half million gentry in these two categories.

The most important criterion defining gentry membership was, therefore, access to officialdom, either by being an official, having the potential to become one by holding an appropriate degree, or having regular social and political access to other officials by virtue of social status. Landlords were not members of the gentry, but wealth in land or other forms could provide the leisure which made possible the education necessary to earn a degree in the civil service examinations, thus acquiring gentry status.

The mid-nineteenth century marked the beginning of a transitional period in the history of the gentry as a class. Responding to the crises of domestic social upheaval culminating in the Taiping Rebellion, as well as the military and economic incursions of Western imperialism, the late traditional social-political order began to disintegrate and become more fluid. The late nineteenth century witnessed an expansion in the purchase of offices and academic titles, at first for the government to raise revenues to combat the Taipings, but later by merchants and new entrepreneurs eager to improve their social standing. Increasingly, wealth—both from commerce and land—provided direct access to gentry status. At the same time, members of the gentry were moving into newly emerging and increasingly prestigious careers as military officers, educated professionals, and entrepreneurs.

Until about 1900, the traditional educational achievement of status through the examination system remained the principal route to social and political leadership. Yet throughout this transitional period the gentry was being enlarged and replaced by a more diverse class or classes. This new bourgeoisie consisted of intellectuals educated abroad, military officers of the new self-strengthening armies, and professionals associated with new commercial and industrial enterprises. Imbued with the lingering prestige of traditional models, gentry culture, if not actual gentry status, persisted into the early twentieth century, but its content and the profile of its membership changed. The abolition of the civil service examination system in 1905 belatedly sounded the death knell of formal traditional gentry status.

The gentry did not respond to or partici-pate in the emerging nationalism in any creative and lasting sense. Rather, it was its successors, the new social and economic elites, who did. Undoubtedly, the traditional Confucian view of *tianxia*, a comprehensive supranational ethical order with a common ideology and culture, largely preempted a sense of modern nationalism among the gentry. In the threatening crisis of the Taiping Rebellion, Zeng Guofan appealed to the gentry to rise to the defense of tradition against a threat perceived as alien. Although the implication was the preservation of the dynasty as well, that conclusion was ambiguous even then. The issue arose again in the 1890s after the Sino-Japanese War, with appeals to unite against the foreign threat to China's integrity and survival. By then, however, the dynasty had lost most of its credibility, and the new appeals were laced with nationalist goals and programs and the agenda of representative government. Thereafter, patriotism in defense of the country no longer meant defense of the dynasty. But it was, after all, the dynastic system that had established and preserved the traditional route to elite status through the examination system.

Beginning as early as 1904 in some areas, and especially after 1909, local and provincial representative assemblies, established as part of the reform program, became a new vehicle for local political leadership. At first members of the traditional gentry dominated the assemblies; however, they increasingly admitted people with other than traditional academic qualifications, and by the second decade of the century, the balance had radically changed and the gentry monopoly was broken. Unlike the traditional gentry, the new social elites were deeply infected with nationalism. The representative assemblies readily abandoned the dynasty and embraced the Republic in 1911. These same groups also welcomed the Guomindang victory under Chiang Kaishek in the next decade. By then, the transition to a new social and political elite was complete.

The traditional gentry endured as long as late traditional or even to some extent early modern society (depending on one's interpretive preferences) endured. But it was too much wedded to that evolving historical pattern to survive the more revolutionary transition to the modern world. Thus, for the modern world of China, roughly from the late nineteenth to the early twentieth centuries, it is more appropriate to speak of "new elites" or "transitional elites" of various kinds—intellectual, political, social, and economic—than to insist on the "gentry" designation. The traditional elite evoked by the latter could no longer provide a basis for the reintegration of a new Chinese nation, and consequently it disappeared in the space of a few decades.

Jonathan Porter

References
Ch'ü, T'ung-tsu. *Local Government in China under the Ch'ing.* Cambridge, MA: Harvard University Press, 1962.

Eastman, Lloyd E. *Family, Fields, and Ancestors: Constancy and Change in China's Social and Economic History, 1550–1949.* New York, NY: Oxford University Press, 1988.

Ho, Ping-ti. *The Ladder of Success in Imperial China: Aspects of Social Mobility, 1368–1911.* New York, NY: Columbia University Press, 1962.

Government-Supervised, Merchant-Operated Enterprises

See GUANDU SHANGBAN

Great Leap Forward

The Great Leap Forward (GLF), which was initiated in 1958, then relaxed and revived in 1959 and 1960, was a Maoist attempt to achieve an economic breakthrough for China. The main focus was agriculture, with the establishment of rural people's communes, but it also included industry, especially steel production, and it radicalized every aspect of life.

Mao Zedong's controversial "high tide" development strategy, which emerged during the First Five-Year Plan (1953–57), entailed mobilizing through collectives, setting audacious goals, and using small-scale rural technology, while maintaining investments in heavy industry. In 1957, Mao convinced key Party leaders to support this approach to rapid economic development.

GLF schemes, such as the tens of millions of "backyard steel furnaces," were often poorly conceived, implemented with excessive zeal and insufficient skill. The consequences were disastrous. The years 1959 through 1961, when the campaign was officially terminated, witnessed a massive economic decline, including famines that claimed millions of lives.

Although GLF symbols emphasized social-

ism and class struggle, the movement did manifest a dedication to nationalism. All Chinese leaders regarded rapid modernization as an imperative for the survival of their backward country. Tellingly, the GLF was launched with a call to "catch up with Great Britain" in steel and other industrial production within fifteen years.

Additionally, Chinese nationalism focused on the United States and the Soviet Union. Anti-American sentiments had prevailed since the Korean War (1950–53) and deepened because of American support for the Guomindang (GMD) regime on Taiwan. In August 1958, as the GLF was launched, the Chinese began to bombard the GMD-held island of Quemoy (Jinmen), just off Fujian province. This injected a war fever into the GLF.

Still more dramatic was the reaction of Chinese nationalism to the internationalism of the USSR. By the mid-1950s, Chinese leaders realized that their development must be less imitative of Russia. But the GLF did not originate as a challenge to Moscow. Indeed, Mao was inspired by Nikita Khrushchev's efforts at economic acceleration and by Soviet achievements in satellites and missiles in launching the GLF. However, once launched, the GLF triggered deep Sino-Soviet stresses.

Khrushchev was working to reduce the Soviet Union's confrontation with the United States and to slow the arms race, but Mao believed that the Communist bloc should press its advantages. This set the stage for deepening differences. The Soviets disparaged the GLF and the communes. They disapproved of the Quemoy bombardment and gave lukewarm support. They took a neutral stance on the Sino-Indian border conflict (1959–62). And they refused to proceed with an agreement to provide China with nuclear technology. In late 1959, Khrushchev faced a frigid reception when he visited Beijing (directly from his meetings with American president Dwight D. Eisenhower). In the summer of 1960, he withdrew all Soviet technicians from China, initiating a long-term split between the two countries.

The withdrawal of Soviet assistance was often cited by the Chinese government as a major cause of the economic disaster in the early 1960s, which in fact resulted largely from the GLF. In the wake of this Maoist experiment, the country was paralyzed by hunger, unemployment and lawlessness. It is estimated that abnormal mortalities totaled around sixteen million from 1958 to 1962. Food shortages forced China

"Backyard furnaces" in the Great Leap Forward, 1958. (Xinhua News Agency.)

to import wheat from Canada and Australia. Both heavy and consumer industries experienced steep decline. China was falling further behind the industrialized countries of the West.

Facing the apparent failure of the GLF, Mao Zedong stepped down as chairman of the People's Republic, although he refused to take full responsibility for the campaign or admit its complete failure. His successor, Liu Shaoqi, soon took meaures to return China to a moderate and realistic path to economic growth.

Craig Dietrich

References

MacFarquhar, Roderick. *The Origins of the Cultural Revolution, 2: The Great Leap Forward 1958–1960.* New York, NY: Columbia University Press, 1983.

Great Proletarian Cultural Revolution

The Great Proletarian Cultural Revolution (GPCR) was initiated in 1966 by Mao Zedong, in association with his wife, Jiang Qing, Defense Minister Lin Biao, and other leading radicals, in order to attack and eliminate revisionists within the Chinese Communist Party (CCP). It effectively ended in 1969 (although some analysts treat the GPCR as continuing until Mao's death in 1976). Tens if not hundreds of thousands of intellectuals and Party members—including then head of state Liu Shaoqi—were purged and persecuted, and unknown thousands killed. In all, perhaps one hundred million people were affected.

By the mid-1960s, Mao had grown increasingly dissatisfied with the moderate policies of the current leadership, *i.e.,* Liu Shaoqi and Deng Xiaoping, and had concluded that only by bringing in forces from outside the Party apparatus could he regain control over the Party line. In the summer of 1966, students in every city responded to Mao's call to attack revisionist authorities. Motivated by idealism as well as personal dissatisfaction, they formed organizations, as did workers. Soon there were competing revolutionary coalitions everywhere containing Red Guards, Revolutionary Rebels, Red Laborers, Scarlet Guards, and numerous others, all claiming to represent Chairman Mao. They hauled officials and intellectuals before mass "struggle" meetings and otherwise persecuted them. They ransacked intellectuals' homes. They also factionalized and fought each other, quite beyond the control of Beijing. By 1967 and 1968, violent confrontations were widespread. The People's Liberation Army was called to restore order in 1968 and early 1969.

The GPCR had positive nationalistic dimensions. Chinese proudly hailed Mao Zedong as the greatest Marxist-Leninist of the age. To counter the Soviet threat and the American war in Vietnam (1965–73), Lin Biao developed a guerrilla defense strategy that supposedly freed China from dependency on other countries. To the Third World, Lin preached revolutionary nationalism, offering the Chinese revolution as a model for enveloping and defeating imperialism.

It was characteristic of the GPCR that most expressions of nationalism went to excess. China temporarily ceased functioning internationally as a normal state. In 1967, all ambassadors but one were recalled. Hostility toward the USSR led to border incidents and military confrontations in 1969. Propaganda assaults spared few countries. A mob burned the British Embassy's chancery in 1967. Chinese who

Red Guards in the Great Proletarian Cultural Revolution, 1966. (Xinhua News Agency.)

had diligently served the country were punished for past connections with foreigners. Foreign culture was totally repudiated.

The GPCR's glorification of class struggle also weakened that aspect of nationalism which unifies a country's particular interests. A line had to be drawn between the bad and the good, even within families. Opportunism and fear corroded humane values. Patron-client cronyism increased, as people scurried for refuge or advancement.

Mao, Jiang, and their followers also attacked the past. The campaign against "the four olds" in 1966 targeted China's cultural legacy. Traditional arts were tabooed. Religion came under attack, a critical issue for many minority groups. In Tibet, especially, the GPCR led to massive destruction of temples and monasteries, which retarded the difficult task of integrating Tibet into the Chinese nation.

On balance, like most other aspects of the Great Proletarian Cultural Revolution, nationalism presented itself pathologically. By the early 1970s, more normal forms were reappearing, as in the case of the rapprochement with the United States (1972). After Mao's death in 1976, the new Chinese Communist leadership denounced the GPCR as a "leftist error" made by the chairman and the Gang of Four.

Craig Dietrich

References

Thurston, Anne F. *Enemies of the People: The Ordeal of the Intellectuals in China's Great Cultural Revolution.* Cambridge, MA: Harvard University Press, 1988.

White, Lynn T., III. *Policies of Chaos: The Organizational Causes of Violence in China's Cultural Revolution.* Princeton, NJ: Princeton University Press, 1989.

Green Gang (Qingbang)

The Green Gang was a secret society originated as a self-protective organization of sailors, dock coolies and transportation workers on the Grand Canal in the early Qing. Following strict rules and complex rituals (vaguely related to a Buddhist sect), gang members were identified by artificial "generations" and grouped into regional "boats." Initially it was a public association recognized by the government, but as the government gradually felt threatened by its mass mobilizing ability, the gang went underground in the early eighteenth century. By then, the gang had spread to the Yangtze River valley and recruited people in other professions, as well as the unemployed, into its ranks. After the decline of the grain tribute system (*caoyun*) along the Grand Canal in the mid-nineteenth century, the gang transformed itself into a mafia-type underworld in eastern and central China's cities and towns.

In the meantime, the base of the gang in the Lower Yangtze became the core of Western penetration in China. With the establishment of foreign concessions and settlements in the treaty ports, the gang found new opportunities to survive and thrive in the abnormal environment of Sino-Western condominium. It was especially powerful in Shanghai, where the gang controlled the police of the city's international settlement and French concession. The power of the gang first impressed the foreign powers when one of its leaders, Huang Jinrong, successfully negotiated the release of Western hostages during the Lincheng Incident in 1923. After that, the gang's influence was further tolerated in the treaty ports, with its hands in gambling, prostitution, and other illegal activities.

The Green Gang was not political in its origin, although some of its members did participate in anti-Manchu activities during the Qing. In the twentieth century, however, it assumed a unique political role. Since the gang provided a source of organized manpower and a clandestine network, and since foreign concessions and settlements often served as havens for political dissidents, revolutionaries from the late Qing to the 1930s all sought assistance or protection from the gang. In 1927, Chiang Kaishek, who allegedly had associated himself with the gang in his early years, employed the gang in his bloody "Party Purification" against the CCP in Shanghai. In reward for the gang's contribution to that effort, the gang leaders Huang Jinrong, Du Yuesheng and Zhang Xiaolin were appointed to high military ranks under the Guomindang (GMD) government. In addition, the gang was allowed to dominate the "yellow unions" in Shanghai and other major cities as an instrument of the GMD in suppressing the CCP-led labor movement. During the Sino-Japanese War of 1937 to 1945, Du Yuesheng worked closely with Dai Li in organizing the government's anti-Japanese underground in Shanghai. Elsewhere and other members of the gang, however, sometimes collaborated with the Japanese. The CCP's New Fourth Army also maintained contacts with the gang in its effort to expand into the Lower Yangtze.

Shortly after the CCP came to power in 1949, the gang was crushed by the new regime. Some of its residual elements remained active in Taiwan and Hong Kong during the 1950s and 1960s, but the gang ceased to exist in China under the CCP.

Wang Ke-wen

References

Martin, Brian G. *The Shanghai Green Gang: Politics and Organized Crime, 1919–1937.* Berkeley: University of California Press, 1996.

Wang, Y. C. "Tu Yueh-sheng (1888–1951): A Tentative Political Biography." *Journal of Asian Studies* 26 (May 1967), 433–55.

Gu Jiegang (1893–1980)

A leading historian and populist in modern China, Gu Jiegang majored in philosophy at Beijing University and, as a member of the New Tide Society, published several articles in the society's *New Tide* journal. Shortly after graduating, Gu launched the Critiques of Ancient History *(Gushibian)* movement that sharply criticized unrealistic yet commonly held notions about China's antiquity. In the 1920s, Gu incited controversy by claiming that because the sage king Great Yü's name contained the "insect" glyph, he was really a mythic and not a historical figure. Between 1926 and 1941, he published seven thick volumes on Chinese ancient history, and they included hundreds of articles by various authors. The premier volume included an intellectual biography of Gu's early life and was later translated into English by Arthur W. Hummel as *The Autobiography of a Chinese Historian* (1931).

Through the Ancient History Debate movement, large numbers of works bearing false authorship and outright forgeries were detected. From this body of research, Gu postulated that the later the ancient legends were added, the earlier the period to which they were attributed. By removing the so-called legendary periods, the traditionally held span of recorded history was shortened from five to three thousand years. This raised the ire of those who upheld a strong nationalist agenda, and Gu came under severe criticism by his contemporaries for his comments.

In spite of these attacks, Gu Jiegang proved his patriotism in 1925 when, in the aftermath of the bloody May Thirtieth Incident, he edited "Saving Our Country," a literary supplement in the newspaper *Qingbao*. In the same vein, he also composed the nationalistic farmers' folk song entitled "Song of Deep Sorrows."

There was an important shift in Gu's work after the Manchurian Incident in 1931. Alarmed by the threat of a subjugated China, Gu strongly urged historians to make their work more relevant to political realities. In his own writings, he devoted considerable energies to the study of geographical history because of its importance to political affairs. In 1935 he became head of the Yugong Society for Chinese geographical history. Gu argued in the society's manifesto that, because of imperialist encroachments along China's borders, it was necessary to investigate the history of the borderlands.

Besides these efforts, the national crisis also pushed Gu to produce more popular writings in a vernacular style in order to awaken the patriotic feelings of the common people. After the loss of Jehol to the Japanese army in 1933, Gu believed it was his responsibility to fan the flames of nationalism in the hearts and minds of the masses into resistance against Japanese aggression. He wrote poster slogans, pamphlets, narrative ballads to be accompanied by beating drums, and even serialized cartoons. The success of his efforts was demonstrated by the wide popularity his works enjoyed among the public.

Afterward, Gu also received support from the political leader of north China, Song Zheyuan, to publish additional popular writings. At its peak, under Gu, the Popular Reading Publishing Society issued eight weekly pamphlets, and hired a blind singer to perform his folk songs. Gu's patriotic actions incurred Japanese surveillance even before the military engagement at the Marco Polo Bridge in 1937. Upon the outbreak of war, he was outlawed by the Japanese army and fled to northwest China. In Gansu he fought on by establishing the People's Society and continued distributing patriotic literature to the public. In these years, he published over six hundred items, which amounted to some fifty million copies.

In 1938, Gu arrived in Kunming, where he edited the "Borderland Literary Supplement" for newspapers. In this period he also published his "China as a Unified Whole" article to repudiate Japanese assertions that historically China had legitimate claims over only the eighteen core provinces, but had no authority over the outlying border regions. With other scholars, he organized the Society for the Study of China's Border Regions.

A contradiction between historical objectivity and nationalistic fervor soon surfaced in Gu's arguments. In "China as a Unified Whole," Gu asserted that certain minority groups in southeastern China were originally ethnically different from the Han Chinese and that they had only been gradually assimilated. This line of thinking bolstered the struggles of separatist groups in the southwest who received support from Japan. The Japanese asserted that the peoples of Yunnan and Guangxi provinces were mostly of Thai ancestry and that they should be realigned with Thailand to form a Grand Thai alliance.

In the years of civil war between the Guomindang and the Chinese Communists (1945–49), Gu was engaged in a publishing company and taught part-time. After 1952 he resumed teaching as a full-time professor at Fudan University and, in 1954, was appointed to a research position in the Chinese Science Academy's Institute of History. He held this last post until his death in 1980. In his later life, Gu led the project to punctuate the *Twenty-Four Dynastic Histories (Ershisi hi)* and the *Draft History of the Qing Dynasty (Qingshigao)*. As a mark of his scholarly productivity, it has been estimated that Gu wrote over seven hundred titles, including numerous papers and books, during his lifetime.

Fan-shen Wang

References

Hummel, Arthur W. *The Autobiography of a Chinese Historian*. Leyden: E. J. Brill, 1931.

Schneider, Laurence A. *Ku Chieh-kang and China's New History*. Berkeley: University of California Press, 1971.

Guandu Shangban

Guandu shangban, alternatively rendered in English as "government-supervised, merchant-operated enterprises" or "officially supervised merchant undertakings," refers to the form of organization employed by certain Chinese business firms established in the 1870s, 1880s, and 1890s. Beginning in the 1870s, Zhili governor-general Li Hongzhang, a leader of the Self-Strengthening movement, mobilized merchant capital under government protection to establish profit-oriented basic industries in support of national defense production. Li subsequently broadened this effort, establishing light industries designed to improve China's commercial

G

position. Based loosely on the government-supervised merchant-operated Salt Monopoly, these new industries solicited merchant capital usually from the treaty ports, but were headed by an official or a prominent private individual through whom government extended protection. Government protection or monopoly rights, granted to the new industries to help them become competitive with foreign firms, may be understood as an expression of incipient economic nationalism.

The most well-known government-supervised merchant firms were the China Merchants' Steam Navigation Company (1872), the Kaiping Coal Mines (1877), the Shanghai Cotton Cloth Mill (1878), the Imperial Telegraph Administration (1881), the Moho Gold Mines (1887), the Hanyang Ironworks (1890), the Daye Iron Mines (1890), the Pingxiang Coal Mines (1890) and the Imperial Bank of China (1896). Li Hongzhang was the principal sponsor of the early government-supervised merchant industries. By the late 1880s, governor-general of Hunan and Hubei Zhang Zhidong and others were active in establishing such firms.

Although the founders of government-supervised merchant industries hoped to ward off foreign domination of China's basic industries and realize profits through reliance on domestic rather than foreign capital, the industries developed problems that undermined these goals. Their profit-oriented operations under grants of government protection, or *de facto* monopolies, discouraged the establishment of competing private firms. Private shareholders generally invested their profits in land or in traditional economic enterprises, thereby eschewing reinvestment and updating obsolete equipment. Official managers tolerated bureaucratic abuses such as nepotism, cronyism, and corruption; they hired foreign personnel to staff key positions and accepted foreign loans, resulting in foreign dependence and opening the way for foreign control.

By the late 1880s, the failure of the government-supervised merchant industries to strengthen China's economy led Zhang Zhidong to establish *Guanshang heban* (joint government-merchant) industries: the Hubei Cotton Cloth Mill (1889) and the Hubei Cotton Spinning Mill (1894). Though these firms were intended to give merchants a greater voice in management and access to government capital, the shortcomings of official management continued to plague them. The bureaucratic control and low rate of reinvestment that undermined the government-supervised merchant-operated firms and the joint government-merchant firms, by 1900, led to the initiation of privately financed and managed *(shangban)* business firms, in a further manifestation of economic nationalism.

Wellington K. K. Chan

References

Chan, Wellington K. K. *Merchants, Mandarins and Modern Enterprise in Late Ch'ing China.* Cambridge, MA: Harvard University Press, 1977.

Feverwerker, Albert. *China's Early Industrialization: Shen Hsuan-huai (1844–1916) and Mandarin Enterprise.* Cambridge, MA: Harvard University Press, 1958.

Guangdong-Guangxi Incident

In June 1936, the militarists controlling the southern provinces of Guangdong and Guangxi declared their intention to march their forces to north China in an attempt to resist Japanese aggression. This move, while ostensibly patriotic, was in fact a challenge to the authority of the Nanjing government on the issue of national defense.

Since the end of the Guomindang's Fourth Party Congress in 1931, Guangdong and Guangxi had been independent of Nanjing's control. The congress marked the permanent break between Chiang Kaishek and Hu Hanmin, who subsequently found support among the military rulers in Guangdong and Guangxi and established the Southwestern Political Affairs Committee in Canton. Supposedly a branch of the national government in Nanjing, the committee in effect had been used by those military rulers, including Chen Jitang, Li Zongren, and Bai Chongxi, to continue the practice of regional warlordism, and Hu had been their political patron. In May 1936, Hu died in Canton. With the realization that Nanjing would not tolerate their independent status once their protector was gone, the Guangdong-Guangxi militarists decided to make the first move.

In preempting Nanjing's strike on them, the southern provinces seized the issue of resistance against Japan. The continuous encroachment on Chinese land and sovereignty by Japan since the Manchurian Incident of 1931 had provoked feelings of anti-Japanese nationalism throughout China, and the compromising policy adopted by Nanjing in dealing with Japan had been severely criticized by many, including Hu Hanmin. A few weeks after Hu's death, the Southwestern Political Affairs Committee issued a circular telegram denouncing the recent reinforcement of Japanese troops in north China, and on June 1 the committee formally requested the Nanjing government to allow the movement of its troops to north China for a war against Japan. The Guangdong-Guangxi army soon entered Hunan.

Nanjing reacted promptly. While commending their patriotism, Chiang quickly sent his troops to defend Hunan and to ensure the loyalty of the Hunan militarist He Jian. As the anti-Communist campaign in the Northwest still occupied Chiang's main attention and the Japanese were increasing their pressure on the North, Chiang had determined from the outset to settle the matter through political maneuvering. In late June, the southern provinces organized their Military Committee and Anti-Japanese National Salvation Army, both headed by Chen Jitang, and ordered a massive invasion of Hunan and Jiangxi. Yet there were no armed clashes.

In early July, under Chiang's persuasion and possibly through bribery, the air force and a number of leading generals in Guangdong defected to Nanjing's side. The military front of the southern provinces thereupon collapsed. In mid-July Chen Jitang announced his resignation and went to Hong Kong. The Guangxi leaders Li Zongren and Bai Chongxi remained obstinate; in August they established their own "national government" in Nanjing and tried to recapture Guangdong. After weeks of negotiation and bargaining, and with the mediation of another Guangxi leader, Huang Shaoxiong, a compromise was finally reached. In September, Li and Bai accepted new appointments by Nanjing and the crisis ended peacefully.

The incident was one of several cases in the 1930s in which regional militarists used anti-Japanese issues as a pretext to resist Nanjing's centralizing efforts. Nationalism, ironically, became a "front" for regionalism. Nanjing's successful solution of these challenges effectively enhanced the unification of the country.

Wang Ke-wen

References

Eastman, Lloyd E. *The Abortive Revolution: China under Nationalist Rule, 1927–1937.* Cambridge, MA: Harvard University Press, 1974.

Lary, Diana. *Region and Nation: The Kwangsi Clique in Chinese Politics, 1925–1937.* London, England: Cambridge University Press, 1974.

G

Guangxi Clique
See LI ZONGREN

Gung Ho Movement
Gung Ho, a movement to establish rural industrial cooperatives in China's hinterland during the second Sino-Japanese War (1937–45), was first proposed by Rewy Alley, a New Zealand official in the administration of the international settlement in Shanghai, shortly after the outbreak of the war. In August 1938 Alley obtained the support of the Guomindang (GMD) government for his idea and founded the Chinese Industrial Cooperatives Association at Hankou, with H. H. Kung as its president. The association then sponsored and guided the organization of cooperatives for the manufacture of industrial goods in the unoccupied territories. It hoped that this effort would help to spread industrial technologies, as well as expand the market for manufactured goods, to China's rural hinterland. The project was assisted by a group of leftist Western intellectuals in China, such as Edgar Snow and Helen Foster Snow (Nym Wales), and by Madame Sun Yatsen, who headed its Hong Kong Promotion Committee.

From 1939 until the end of the war, a large number of industrial cooperatives *(Gongye hezuoshe),* known as "Gonghe," or "Gung Ho" among the Westerners in China, appeared in towns and villages throughout the Northwest and the Southwest. Operated largely on a self-sufficient basis with some outside support in skills and equipments, these cooperatives produced various kinds of manufactured goods, including food, clothing, paper, and tools, for military and civilian use. It did increase rural employment and industrial production to some extent, but on the whole its impact on China's wartime economy was minimal. The massive zeal for the movement in rural China, motivated undoubtedly by wartime nationalism, nevertheless impressed many Western observers in China, and "Gung Ho" soon became an American slang for momentary, and somewhat naive, enthusiasm.

Wang Ke-wen

References

Peck, Graham. *Two Kinds of Time.* Boston, MA: Houghton Mifflin, 1967.

Guo Songtao (1818–91)

Guo Songtao was a late Qing diplomat and reformer and the first permanent Chinese diplomatic envoy to the West.

A native of Hunan, Guo received his *jinshi* degree at the age of twenty-nine and subsequently served under Zeng Guofan during the suppression of the Taiping Rebellion. In 1863, he was appointed as governor of Guangdong and, in the 1870s, transferred to the newly established Zongli Yamen in Beijing. In the wake of the Margary affair of 1875 and 1876, the Qing government dispatched an apology mission to Great Britain and then turned it into a resident delegation to that country. Because of his proven ability in handling "barbarian affairs" *(yiwu),* Guo was selected to lead the mission and become China's first resident minister abroad. He served in that post until 1878, when he was transferred to France. While in Europe, Guo was deeply impressed, and alarmed, by the power of the West. He not only found it necessary to adopt some of the Western customs in performing his duties, but advised his government to emulate Western technologies and institutions for the strengthening of China. At the same time, Guo was frustrated by the fact that the Western countries treated China as an inferior because of her weakness.

In 1877, Guo edited his diaries of the past two years, which had recorded his observations and thoughts on the Western world, and published them under the title *Shixi jicheng (The First Chinese Embassy to the West).* The book became an important source of information for contemporary Chinese intellectuals, who were eager to learn about the West, and lauded a pioneering discussion on China's need of Western-style reforms. Guo's views drew harsh criticisms from conservatives within and outside of the government. He was forced to retire from office upon returning to China in 1879 and spent his later years lecturing at an academy in his home town.

Guo was representative of a small but significant group of reform-minded officials, including Xue Fucheng, Ma Jianzhong and Zeng Jize, who served as China's first generation of diplomats in the West. Their experience in the Western countries compelled them to propose, through writing and through advising high officials such as Li Hongzhang, technological and institutional reforms in Qing China. Although unpopular at the time, their ideas helped to shape a realistic perception among the Chinese of their own place in the world and of the nature of the Western challenge.

Wang Ke-wen

References

Frodsham, J. D. *The First Chinese Embassy to the West: The Journals of Kuo Sung-tao, Liu Hsi-hung, and Chang Te-yi.* Oxford, England: Clarendon Press, 1974.

Hamilton, David. "Kuo Sung-t'ao: A Maverick Confucian." *Harvard Papers on China* 15 (1961): 1–29.

Hao, Yen-p'ing, and Erh-ming Wang. "Changing Chinese Views of Western Relations, 1840–95." *The Cambridge History of China,* ed. John K. Fairbank and Kwang-ching Liu, vol. 11, 142–201. Cambridge, England: Cambridge University Press, 1980.

Guomindang, 1912–14

Guomindang, or Nationalist Party, was the name adopted for the political party formed by Song Jiaoren in the wake of the Revolution of 1911 to contest the national legislative elections held in the winter of 1912 to 1913, the only national elections ever held in republican China.

After Sun Yatsen resigned as provisional president of the newly proclaimed Republic of China in favor of Yuan Shikai in early 1912, the main responsibility for safeguarding the revolutionary goal of establishing a republican form of government passed to Song Jiaoren. Song led the opposition to Yuan's attempts to concentrate power in his own hands with the backing of his Beiyang Clique. As head of the Political Affairs Department of the Tongmenghui (Revolutionary Alliance), Song worked to consolidate a revolutionary majority in the provisional legislature, and he promoted the idea of government by ministers who enjoyed the support of a legislative majority. In Song's view, only a legitimate popularly-based government could bring about the national solidarity required by China and gain recognition of China's sovereign rights from the foreign powers.

In August 1912, Song Jiaoren merged the majority of the Tongmenghui with members of four smaller parties: the *Tongyi gonghedang*

(United Republican Party), the *Guomin gongjinhui* (National Mutual Advancement Society), the *Guomin gongdang* (National Public Party), and the *Gonghe shijinhui* (Society for the Practical Advancement of a Republic). Consolidation gave this parliamentary party a majority in the provisional legislature, and it adopted the name "Guomindang." The chief concern of the newly formed party was to win a majority of the seats in the House of Representatives and the Senate in the forthcoming election for the first National Parliament, in the belief that electoral success at the polls would secure the Guomindang political power to realize the goal of a constitutional republic.

Song actively directed the election campaign throughout the country and personally took charge of the effort in his home province of Hunan. He led the Guomindang to a resounding victory at the polls with strong attacks on the incompetence of the authorities in Beijing. Because Song made clear his intention to use his parliamentary majority to insist on a responsible cabinet, Yuan Shikai reacted with brute force to this challenge by arranging the assassination of Song Jiaoren in the Shanghai railway station on March 20, 1913, as Song was returning to Beijing to mobilize his parliamentarians for the legislative session.

Yuan was subsequently able to bribe and intimidate the Parliament into compliance before defeating the military forces backing the Guomindang. He thereupon dissolved the parliamentary party and expelled its members in late 1913. He finally suspended the national legislature altogether in early 1914. Later that year, Sun Yatsen founded the Chinese Revolutionary Party to replace the Guomindang. The new party was a secret organization dedicated to the seizure of power by force and ultimately became the Leninist Guomindang of the 1920s.

The Guomindang of 1912 to 1914 represented an attempt by the republican revolutionaries to establish a parliamentary system in China. Its failure led to frustration and disillusionment in Sun Yatsen and his followers, who subsequently sought to reconstruct China's political order through non-democratic means.

Louis T. Sigel

References

Hsueh, Chun-tu. *Huang Hsing and the Chinese Revolution.* Stanford, CA: Stanford University Press, 1961.

Li, Chien-nung. *The Political History of China, 1840–1928.* Stanford, CA: Stanford University Press, 1967.

Liew, K. S. *Struggle for Democracy: Sung Chiao-jen and the 1911 Chinese Revolution.* Berkeley: University of California Press, 1971.

Guomindang, 1919–

The Chinese Nationalist Party, the Guomindang (GMD), was ruling party of China from 1928 to 1949 and remains the ruling party in Taiwan (1949 to the present).

In 1919, Sun Yatsen renamed his Chinese Revolutionary Party *(Zhonghua gemingdang)* the Chinese Nationalist Party *(Zhongguo guomindang),* partly as an attempt to relate it to the old Guomindang of 1912 to 1914. The history of the new Guomindang, however, did not begin until its reorganization in 1923 and 1924. In this reorganization, guided by the recent alliance between Sun and the Soviet Union, members of the Chinese Communist Party (CCP) were allowed to join the GMD, forming the first United Front. The GMD also adopted the structure of a Leninist party, with party congresses and committees at all levels. The only organizational difference between the GMD and the Russian Communist Party was that Sun's supreme leadership was institutionalized in the position of *zongli,* whose power was superior even to that of the Central Executive Committee or its Standing Committee (Politburo).

Following the reorganization, the GMD grew rapidly in size and strength in its Guangdong base from 1924 to 1927. Under the radical influence of the United Front, the Party defined its mission as the anti-imperialist, anti-militarist national revolution *(guomin geming)* and actively sought support from the masses in accomplishing that mission. In addition, the Party built a loyal army indoctrinated in its ideology. All of these efforts were carried out with Soviet aid and advice.

After Sun's death in 1925, a series of power struggles occurred within the GMD for the succession to Sun's leadership. By 1926, Chiang Kaishek, commander of the new Party army, had assumed control and launched the Northern Expedition from Guangdong to reunify the country by force. Halfway through the campaign, in 1927, Chiang purged the Communists from the Party in a bloody "Party Purification." The purge briefly caused a split in the Party, but by the end of that year the United Front was terminated and the GMD regrouped under Chiang's leadership. Chiang rejected Soviet influence and turned to the Western powers for backing and assistance. The Party's anti-imperialism became toned down.

From 1928 to 1937, the GMD ruled a nominally unified China. With its capital at Nanjing, Chiang's government was in full control only in the Lower Yangtze region. The Party declared the implementation of political tutelage *(xunzheng), i.e.,* Party rule, in accordance with the scheme of national reconstruction devised by Sun Yatsen. In effect, however, the GMD had come under the domination of the military, with Chiang holding dictatorial power. During the Nanjing Decade the GMD concentrated its attention on suppressing domestic rivals, especially the CCP, while making repeated compromises with the Japanese in northeast and north China. This policy of "domestic pacification before external resistance" provoked widespread criticism from nationalist Chinese and undermined the GMD's legitimacy as national leader. Moreover, the Party seemed to have all but abandoned its earlier revolutionary commitment and sided increasingly with the status quo. Its failure to realize any fundamental socioeconomic reform fueled the appeal of the CCP opposition.

The prestige and popularity of the GMD rose again with the outbreak of the Sino-Japanese War in 1937. Forming a new United Front with the CCP, the Party led the country in a protracted war of resistance against Japan. In 1938, Chiang Kaishek was elected the Party's *Zongcai,* a supreme position resembling Sun Yatsen's *Zongli.* With its prewar territorial and financial base in the coastal provinces occupied by Japan, the Party was forced to retreat to the Southwest hinterland. In 1939, the peace movement led by Wang Jingwei, vice-head of the GMD, briefly threatened Party unity, but the majority of the Party chose to stay with Chiang in the anti-Japanese front. After 1941, the war became linked to World War II and Chiang's government at Chongqing became an ally of the major Western powers. With American aid and support, the Chongqing government not only survived but eventually triumphed in the war. China was recognized as one of the "Big Four" in 1945.

The glory of victory, however, was short-lived. Four years after the Japanese surrender, the GMD was defeated by the CCP in the civil war and driven out of the Chinese mainland. Corruption, political repression, mismanage-ment of the economy, as well as military incompetence were among the principal factors that contributed to the rapid collapse of the GMD government. Yet with renewed American support following the Korean War (1950–53), the Party consolidated its footing on the island of Taiwan. It has controlled the island to this date. Under the leadership of Chiang Kaishek, and later his son Jingguo, the GMD government in Taiwan continued to call itself the Republic of China and claimed to be the sole legitimate government of all China. Before 1971, it retained China's seat in the United Nations.

Internally, the GMD ruled the island with an iron hand despite its 1947 announcement of entering into a constitutional democracy. Political opposition and dissidents were brutally suppressed, and the Party clung to its unrealistic goal of recovering the mainland. At the same time, intelligent import-export strategy, favorable international environment, and a successful land reform (which the Party had not implemented on the mainland) led to dramatic economic growth in Taiwan. The "economic miracle" has helped the island regime survive the increasing diplomatic isolation since the 1970s.

By the early 1990s, the rule of the Chiang family in Taiwan had ended. The GMD has become significantly indigenized. Li Denghui, a native Taiwanese, is Chairman and the vast majority of the Party membership consists of native Taiwanese. The GMD government also modified its militant anti-Communist stance and reached a rapprochement with the CCP government on the mainland. "Recovering the mainland" has been gradually replaced by the new policy of "non-hostile coexistence" with the People's Republic. The Party has become drastically different from its former self of the previous seventy years.

Wang Ke-wen

References

Ch'ien, Tuan-sheng. *The Government and Politics of China.* Cambridge, MA: Harvard University Press, 1950.

Eastman, Lloyd E., et al. *The Nationalist Era in China, 1927–1949.* Cambridge, England: Cambridge University Press, 1991.

Tien, Hung-mao. *The Great Transformation: Political and Social Change in the Republic of China.* Stanford, CA: Hoover Institution Press, 1989.

H

Hakka

A unique cultural-ethnic minority in China, the Hakka (or *Kejia*, meaning "guest families") were originally Han residents of north and central China. Around the tenth century, they migrated *en masse* to south and southeast China to escape nomadic invasions and political chaos in the north. Scattered in the coastal areas, including Jiangxi, Fujian, Guangdong, Guangxi, Hainan, and Taiwan, these "guest families" have since retained much of their northern customs and dialects and refused to be assimilated by the southern people. They insulated themselves from the surrounding population and maintained a kind of clannish existence. As time passed their northern lifestyle gradually disappeared even in the north, yet was still preserved in the southern Hakka communities.

As late-comers in the south, the Hakka often faced difficult economic conditions and local hostilities. Such an environment trained them to be a tough and independent people, engaging in frequent ethnic conflict with the native southerners. The strong character of the Hakka, as well as their poverty, have made them potential rebels or revolutionaries in Chinese history. In the mid-nineteenth century, Hakka communities in Guangdong and Guangxi formed the initial and core following of the Taiping Rebellion. In the 1920s to the 1940s, Hakkas again figured prominently as Party activists or guerrilla fighters in the Communist revolution. Many political leaders in modern China were said to be Hakka, among them Sun Yatsen, Zhu De, Deng Xiaoping, and the Soong family.

Although the Hakka, who presently constitute about 3 percent of the Chinese population, have shared with other Han Chinese the mainstream culture and nationalist (*e.g.,* anti-Manchu and anti-imperialist) sentiments, they have kept a self-identity that distinguishes them from other peoples in China. The existence of such minority groups illustrates the complexity of ethnic composition in China and the problems involved in her national integration in modern times.

Wang Ke-wen

References

Constable, Nicole. *Christian Souls and Chinese Spirits: A Hakka Community in Hong Kong.* Berkeley: University of California Press, 1994.

Erbaugh, Mary S. "The Secret History of the Hakkas: The Chinese Revolution as a Hakka Enterprise." *China Quarterly* no. 132 (December 1992): 937–68.

Leong, S. T. "The Hakka Chinese of Lingnan: Ethnicity and Social Change in Modern Times." *Ideology and Reality: Social and Political Change in Modern China, 1860–1949,* ed. David Pong and Edmund S. K. Fung, 287–326. Lanham, MD: University Press of America, 1985.

Han Nationalism

Traditionally, the Han people (*i.e.,* the Chinese living in China proper) have held two contrasting attitudes toward other nations and peoples. One stressed the importance of the degree to which a person accepted and practiced Chinese culture, regardless of his or her birth place or ethnic background. This approach is commonly called "culturalism." The other approach stressed the importance of whether or not a person was born within China as a Han. In foreign policy, this latter view asserted that a unified and effective Chinese nation, one emblematic of the aroused and cohesive actions of the Han people, could and should resist all foreign threats. Foreigners should be kept out when they were beyond the wall and driven out when they were within; dynasties of conquest were never proper. This approach can be said to represent the essence of "Han nationalism."

Scholars have been disinclined to use the word nationalism when discussing Chinese history prior to the advent of the West. In American historiography, the Chinese nationalist tradition has generally been called "xenophobia," "ethnocentrism," or "patriotism." However, nationalism is arguably the more appropriate term because it is relatively value-free, historically reasonable, and helps to relate Chinese history of the nineteenth and twentieth centuries to the past.

In the late imperial era, the period from the late Tang (618–907) onward, the official and orthodox position tended to favor culturalism, whereas the opposition was generally associated with Han nationalism. This is evident at least as far back as Han Yu's critique of Buddhism in the ninth century. In the Song (960–1127), Han nationalism continued to be central to the Fang La Rebellion, whose leader sharply attacked the accommodating policy of the government toward the northern peoples. Similarly, in the southern Song (1127–1279), Han nationalism was associated with Yue Fei, who died a martyr's death for demanding a more vigorous policy against the nomadic Jin. The link between nationalism and political opposition was bolstered by the experience of the Mongol conquest and the fact that the Yuan (1264–1328) ranked the Han of south China below all other groups in its society.

The vast rebellion under Zhu Yuanzhang which overthrew the Yuan and established the Ming (1368–1644) was extremely nationalistic and firmly established the relationship among social unrest, resistance to foreigners, and political unity. In the seventeenth century, in the years immediately following the victory of the Manchus, Han nationalism once again flourished in the opposition. Indeed, it became a hallmark of early Qing (1644–1912) thinkers such as Gu Yanwu and Wang Fuzhi. One of their major criticisms of Wang Yangming and the intellectual movement of the late Ming was that they had weakened China in the face of the northern threat.

Manchu policy, in tandem with the general decline of elite opposition during the first hundred years of the Qing, combined to reduce Han nationalism among the upper classes. As in politics in general, this change tended to distinguish the establishment from the rest of society. Important popular groups, such as the secret societies, continued to have powerful nationalistic and anti-Manchu elements in their ideology. Han nationalism was sufficiently influential with the reading public of the eighteenth century for the Qing government to undertake a literary purge to remove unflattering comments on nomads and tribesmen from Chinese texts.

Han nationalism reemerged as a powerful force in the anti-Qing revolts of the nineteenth century, such as the Taiping Rebellion. With the coming of the Western threat it was also directed toward the West and was a key factor in the Qingyi movement of the 1880s and the Reform movement of 1898. By the turn of the twentieth century, nationalism had become the dominant Chinese attitude toward foreigners.

Nevertheless, the term "nationalism" has been avoided in discussing Chinese history prior to the impact of the West because the existence of "culturalism" as the official ideal has tended to overshadow the nationalist aspect of Chinese attitudes. In addition, it has been often asserted that nationalism is bound up with a feeling of insecurity and inferiority toward foreigners that the Han did not have. However, although nationalism may be grounded in insecurity, belief in one's own cultural superiority is also compatible with the generally understood meaning of the term. Even those who do not use the term "nationalism" agree that Chinese ethnocentrism did arise as a response to the foreign pressures and occupations of the era from the Song onward, when the Han lost much of their martial vigor and were either conquered or militarily on the defensive. This situation would suggest that insecurity was indeed involved in the development of nationalism in China.

Other historical reasons also contributed to the overlooking of nationalist sentiments in Western discussions about China. First of all, the Qing, the dynasty in power when Western imperialism came on the scene, was a foreign (non-Han) one. It therefore emphasized the culturalist point of view and denigrated and repressed nationalist feelings. This situation has made a full appreciation of the latter approach more difficult. Secondly, the rise of nationalism in the West is associated with the era following the French Revolution of 1789, and it is often asserted that "traditional" societies cannot have it. This belief, accurate or not, ignores the long and continuous existence of the Chinese state and the many modern features of its sociopolitical system in the post-Tang era. Thirdly, virtually all scholars agree that China experienced a vast upsurge of nationalism by the end of the nineteenth century. Like many phenomena of that revolutionary era, the prominence of nationalism, indeed its very existence, has been attributed to the coming of the West. However, as the earlier history shows, it was precisely in times when the opposition was on the rise and when foreign pressures were felt in China that an efflorescence of nationalism was to be expected.

John Schrecker

References

Schrecker, John. *The Chinese Revolution in Historical Perspective.* New York, NY: Praeger, 1991.

Shih, Vincent Y. C. *The Taiping Ideology.* Seattle: University of Washington Press, 1967.

Hanjian

By definition *hanjian* is a betrayer of the Han people and their interests. The word "Han" has two connotations: ethnic and political. In the first sense, it refers to the Han people as an ethnic group, one distinct from the Manchus and the Mongols, for example. In the second sense, Han is the synonym of "Chinese," and is therefore a political definition. In the late Qing dynasty, the rise of Chinese nationalism under Western encroachments gave a new meaning to this term: Han came to refer to China as a nation distinct from others; all Chinese were considered Han regardless of their ethnic origins. Hence, despite the existence of Han-Manchu ethnic tensions during the late Qing, Lin Zexu, the Manchu official who was himself a Han, denounced an opium dealer as a *hanjian* for having betrayed the interests of the Chinese people. There was no mentioning whether the person in question was a Han or a Manchu. To Lin, a *hanjian* was someone who rendered assistance to the Western powers, in this case, Great Britain, to undermine China's national interests.

It was in this last sense that tens of thousands of *hanjian* stood trial after the Japanese surrender in 1945. According to one estimate by the Ministry of Judicial Administration, as of June 1947, 26,970 Chinese had been prosecuted as *hanjian* for colluding with the Japanese during the Sino-Japanese War, and as such, for violating the interests of China and its people.

The postwar *hanjian* trials conducted by the Guomindang (GMD) and the Chinese Communist Party (CCP) indicated that, apart from moral condemnation, China's political power balance in the aftermath of the war had a major impact on the ways in which trials were conducted. With the war's end, the GMD government, faced with mounting pressure from the Chinese Communists, enlisted help from former collaborators and Japanese troops to reestablish its control over the occupied territories. While this move to some degree helped to forestall the expansion of the Communists in southeast China, it contradicted the other role expected of the government, *i.e.*, to be the standard-bearer of the nation's collective moral consciousness and sense of social justice. Moreover, as the GMD government in Chongqing was the legitimate wartime government of China, the *hanjian* were tried for their double betrayal of China's national interests and of the GMD government.

In a similar vein, the CCP's treatment of the *hanjian* was closely linked to concerns of expanding and consolidating its bases in postwar China. For the Communists, the trials of the collaborators served the dual purpose of challenging the GMD government's claim to political legitimacy and of mobilizing the masses. While they pursued the former goal with a certain degree of tenacity, the latter task engaged their relentless efforts. In the CCP's definition of the *hanjian,* collaboration with the Japanese was accounted for by factors such as class origins. It was asserted that people from certain class backgrounds, such as landlords and the gentry, were more prone to collaborate with the Japanese than others. Finally, there was an economic dimension to the trials of the *hanjian* in that, to some extent, the expropriation of *hanjian* properties helped to facilitate wealth redistribution in Communist-controlled areas.

Luo Jiu-jung

References

Eastman, Lloyd E. "Facets of an Ambivalent

Relationship: Smuggling, Puppets and Atrocities during the War, 1937–1945." *The Chinese and the Japanese: Essays in Political and Cultural Interactions,* ed. Akira Iriye, 275–303. Princeton, NJ: Princeton University Press, 1980.

Hankou-Jiujiang Incident

Building on the momentum of the Guomindang-Chinese Communist Party (GMD-CCP) United Front's Northern Expedition, organized labor under leftist leadership in January 1927 literally liberated the British concessions in Hankou and Jiujiang along the Yangtze River in central China in the Hankou-Jiujiang Incident. This was the first time since the Treaty of Nanjing (1842), which ushered in the era of unequal treaties and treaty ports, that a Western power was forced to return concession territories to China under the pressure of a nationalistic outburst at the Chinese grassroots.

The roots for the retrocession of these two British concessions can be traced to June 1925, when local workers and students in Hankou and Jiujiang staged massive demonstrations to support the May Thirtieth movement protesters in Shanghai. In both cities, patriotic demonstrators clashed with British and Japanese steamship companies and the British concession police. In Hankou, British troops firing machine guns killed nine and seriously wounded more than ten Chinese protesters. On June 11, 1925, however, the armed repression of the anti-imperialistic strike-boycott by the local Chinese warlords made any concrete anti-British struggle impossible. In Jiujiang, sympathy protests of the Hankou demonstrators did not escalate into any prolonged struggle because of its suppression by the local military and police, as well as by the naval pressure exerted by British and Japanese warships sailing up the Yangtze River. This was in marked contrast to the full-scale mobilization in Canton, where the patriotic grassroots were fully supported by a revolutionary, anti-imperialist GMD regime.

In the autumn of 1926, after the Middle Yangtze valley had been liberated by the Northern Expedition forces, the labor movement mushroomed immediately. By the end of that year over two hundred labor unions with a total membership of nearly one-third of a million had been established in Wuhan. Jiangxi province witnessed the same type of unionization. This resulted in an epidemic of widespread in-

dustrial disputes. Being supported by the new government, the workers gained substantial economic improvements.

This aroused morale of central China's organized labor soon confronted British imperialism. In late December 1926, a quarter million people attended an anti-British rally in Hankou, demanding the retrocession of the British concession. When the new year celebration in January 1927 turned into mass rallies against British imperialism, the British fortified their Hankou concession with more troops and police. In an altercation on January 3, 1927, one Chinese unionist was killed by a British soldier, who also wounded several dozen Chinese in the concession. The next morning, labor union pickets and a massive turnout of city inhabitants rushed into the British concession. The British concession authorities had no choice but to evacuate their forces, inhabitants and British business concerns onto British ships in the Yangtze. By January 5, the British had relinquished the concession, and the Chinese government, under the GMD-CCP United Front, formally took over the administration.

A similar pattern occurred in Jiujiang. Upon hearing about the Hankou Incident, British nationals evacuated to British vessels in the Yangtze. On January 6, a British marine killed a Chinese union picket. This provoked a massive public protest, with several tens of thousands of Chinese rushing in to occupy the British concession. Failing to control the situation, the British requested local Chinese soldiers to move in to maintain law and order; the Chinese forces came, but on the condition that the British evacuate totally. By January 7, the Chinese government had also taken over the British concession in Jiujiang. On February 19 and 20, 1925, the British government entered into an agreement with China formally relinquishing the two concessions.

The Hankou-Jiujiang Incident was a rare case of successful collaboration between party-state and labor in a struggle against foreign imperialism, and was hailed as a victory of the "revolutionary diplomacy" with which the GMD-CCP United Front was experimenting at the time. The patriotic fervor and mobilizational momentum of the concessions' recovery also propelled organized labor to the forefront of the Chinese Revolution, as witnessed by the armed workers' liberation of Shanghai in March 1927, ahead of the Northern Expedition forces.

Ming K. Chan

References

Fung, Edmund S. K. *The Diplomacy of Imperial Retreat: Britain's South China Policy, 1924–1931.* Hong Kong: Oxford University Press, 1991.

Lee, En-han. "Chinese Restoration of British Hankow and Kiukiang Concessions in 1927." University of Western Australia, Centre for East Asian Studies, *Occasional Paper* no. 6 (August 1980).

He-Umezu Agreement

During the first half of the 1930s, following the Manchurian Incident, Japan persistently extended her *de facto* control of Chinese territory from the northeast to north China. In May 1935, two pro-Japanese journalists were assassinated in Tianjin. The Japanese Guandong Army immediately brought in reinforcements from Manchuria under the pretext that the Chinese government had assisted an element of the Northeast Anti-Japanese Volunteer Army to enter the demilitarized zone of eastern Hebei, which violated the Tanggu Agreement of 1933. It pressured the local Chinese authorities for a new settlement. In June, He Yingqin, the acting head of the Beiping branch of the Guomindang's Military Committee, concluded an agreement with Umezu Yoshijiro, commander of the Tianjin garrison of the Guandong Army. The Chinese promised to remove all Guomindang organizations and all "Central forces" (*i.e.,* troops directly controlled by the Nanjing government) from Hebei and to dissolve anti-Japanese organizations, such as the Blue Shirts, in China. They also had to replace the governor of Hebei and the mayor of Tianjin, who were deemed anti-Japanese, and to transfer the Hebei provincial government from Beiping to Baoding. All of these terms were subsequently carried out by the Chinese government. In addition, Nanjing issued a goodwill mandate *(dunmu bangjiao ling),* banning all anti-Japanese activity in the country.

The He-Umezu Agreement, as it was later called, took the form of the Chinese accepting an ultimatum from the Japanese. Acting under specific instructions from Chiang Kaishek, He Yingqin accepted the Japanese demands orally but refused to sign a written document (which reportedly included even harsher terms). He Yingqin did, however, send a note to Umezu on June 6 indicating the Chinese acceptance of those demands. Chiang at the time and Guomindang officials, including He himself, since then have insisted that the note did not amount to a formal agreement.

Nevertheless, the agreement (or oral understanding) in effect surrendered Chinese sovereignty in Hebei and recognized Japanese control over that province. The surprising ease with which the Chinese government accepted the Japanese demands encouraged the hard-liners within the Japanese military and sorely frustrated the nationalistic Chinese populace. Many Chinese were convinced, after this agreement, that the Guomindang was either unwilling or incapable of defending the country against Japanese imperialism.

Wang Ke-wen

References

Coble, Parks M. *Facing Japan.* Cambridge, MA: Harvard University Press, 1991.

Crowley, James B. *Japan's Quest for Autonomy.* Princeton, NJ: Princeton University Press, 1966.

Ho Kai (He Qi, 1859–1914)

A late Qing reformer and early prominent Chinese resident of Hong Kong, Ho Kai was a native of Guangdong province and the son of a Christian preacher who made a fortune in the construction business in Hong Kong. As a teenager, Ho went to study in England, where he received degrees in both law and medicine and married a wealthy English woman. Returning to Hong Kong in 1882, Ho practiced law and founded the Alice Memorial Hospital. He also established the College of Medicine for Chinese in Hong Kong, where Sun Yatsen received his medical training. In 1890, Ho became a member of the colony's Legislative Council. An advocate of westernized institutional reforms, Ho co-authored with former classmate Hu Liyuan *A True Interpretation of New Policies (xinzheng zhenquan),* which proposed the establishment of a parliament and the use of popular elections in China. The work was widely read in the treaty ports in the late 1890s and influenced the political views of the young Sun Yatsen. Ho was active in actual politics as well. In 1895 he assisted Sun's first armed revolt attempt in Canton. During the Boxer Uprising in 1900, he tried unsuccessfully to unite Sun with Li Hongzhang, then governor-general of Guangdong and Guangxi, to stage a secession of the two provinces. Later Ho lived to witness Sun becoming the provisional president of the Chinese Republic.

Ho's reformist ideas have been described by some as an expression of "*comprador* nationalism." Living in a British colony, Ho was anxious to see a strong and modern China in which he could take pride. At the same time, Western education and foreign residency reduced Ho's dependence on the Chinese cultural and political traditions. He was therefore bold and explicit in his call for learning from the West, especially in the area of political institutions.

Wang Ke-wen

References

Chang, Hao. "Intellectual Change and the Reform Movement, 1890–8." *Cambridge History of China,* ed. John K. Fairbank and Kwang-ching Liu, vol. 11, 274–338. Cambridge, England: Cambridge University Press, 1980.

Tsai, Jung-fang. "The Predicament of the Compradore Ideologists He Qi and Hu Liyuan." *Modern China* 7, no. 2 (April 1981): 191–225.

Hong Kong Riots of 1967

The largest mass disturbances in the British colony's modern history were the Hong Kong riots of 1967. Since its cession to Great Britain by the Treaty of Nanjing in 1842, Hong Kong has been under British colonial rule, but has maintained close cultural and economic ties to China. The colony also has served as a safe haven for political refugees and dissidents from its turbulent motherland. At times, Chinese political movements directly contributed to mass actions in the colony. The Seamen's Strike in 1922 and the Canton-Hong Kong Strike of 1925 to 1926 were notable examples.

After the founding of the People's Republic of China (PRC) in 1949, relations between the colony and China became strained despite a quick diplomatic recognition of the Beijing government by Great Britain. Small-scale disturbances occurred in the colony in the 1950s, which were either caused or exploited by the continuous political struggle between the Chinese Communists and the Guomindang in Taiwan. In 1966, a demonstration-riot targeted on the Star Ferry Company in Kowloon was said to have been instigated by the Chinese Communists.

In January 1967, the Hong Kong Seamen's Union organized a demonstration in protest against the shooting and injury of a Chinese sailor by his European captain of the Dutch Royal Interocean Lines. During the following months, conflicts broke out between workers and managements at a number of local factories: the Nam Fung Textile Mill in Tsuen Wan, the Green Island Cement Company in Hung Hom, and the Hong Kong Artificial Flower Works in San Po Kong. Drivers of several taxi companies also went on strike. In May, police were called in to suppress a demonstration staged by thousands of San Po Kong workers. In the summer, terrorist bombings occurred at various public places in the colony: government offices, streetcar and railway stations, ferries and buses, and street corners. In August, an anti-Communist radio announcer was assassinated. The public panicked; businesses slumped.

The riots were closely linked to politics in the PRC. Mao Zedong's Cultural Revolution began in mid-1966. Leftists in Hong Kong soon decided to mobilize an anti-British struggle to prove their loyalty to the new radical leadership in Beijing. In a revolutionary frenzy, the radicals seizing control of the Chinese government also hoped to liberate the British colony by way of a mass movement. In support of the revolutionary struggle in Hong Kong, the PRC stopped its supply of food and water to the colony; Red Guards demonstrated in front of the British Embassy in Beijing. External incitations, however, could not succeed without internal grievances. Working conditions in Hong Kong were miserable enough to persuade the workers to respond to the Communists' ideological and organizational guidance.

By late 1967, Beijing had moderated its attitude toward the Hong Kong issue. The PRC still wanted peaceful relations with Great Britain and other Western powers. In September, China resumed its supply of food and water. But the riot in Hong Kong did not end until February 1968, when factional struggle in the neighboring Guangdong subsided and Beijing consolidated its control over that province.

According to official records, fifty-one people were killed, and nearly one hundred wounded, in the 1967 to 1968 riots. More than five thousand people were arrested, and many others secretly deported by the British authorities. Toward the end of the riots, the residents of Hong Kong, alienated by the leftists' terrorist tactics, displayed their support for social and political order, and thus for the status quo of British rule. In the meantime, the riot forced the

British authorities to pay attention to public welfare and implement labor-protection laws. The bloody confrontation and the ensuing compromise led to the development of a new political consciousness, and self-identity, by the Hong Kong community. The colony began to distinguish its existence from both its British colonial master and from its Chinese motherland.

Wang Ke-wen

References

Jarvie, I. C., and Joseph Agassi, eds. *Hong Kong: A Society in Transition.* London, England: Frederick Praeger, 1969.

Young, John D. "The Building Years: Maintaining a China-Hong Kong-Britain Equilibrium, 1950–71." *Precarious Balance: Hong Kong Between China and Britain, 1842–1992,* ed. Ming K. Chan, 131–147. Armonk, NY: M. E. Sharpe, 1994.

Hong Rengan (1822–64)

Hong Rengan, whose leadership and westernizing reforms briefly revived the Heavenly Kingdom in its final years, was the younger cousin of the founder of the Taiping movement (1851–64), Hong Xiuquan.

Like Xiuquan, Rengan was also a failed scholar under China's examination system and therefore may have shared Xiuquan's frustration and anti-Manchu feelings. When Xiuquan and his friends established the Society of God-Worshippers in 1843, Rengan was one of its first converts. In 1847, he accompanied Xiuquan to Canton to study Christianity with the American missionary Issachar J. Roberts. Partly due to his temper and personality, however, Rengan later distanced himself from Xiuquan as the latter's religious activity became increasingly radicalized and politicized. He did not participate in the Taiping Rebellion when it broke out in 1851. After a few abortive attempts to join it later, he went to Hong Kong in 1852 to further his study of Christianity with Western missionaries. While in the British colony, Rengan acquired a great deal of knowledge about the West and of Western learning, such as the sciences.

In 1859 Rengan finally reached Nanjing, the capital of Xuiquan's Heavenly Kingdom, and rejoined his elder cousin. His arrival was timely for the Taiping movement, because it had been crippled by a series of internal conflicts. In 1856, Xiuquan's leading assistants in the rebellion, the "East King" Yang Xiuqing, the "North King" Wei Changhui and the "Assistant King" Shi Dakai, waged a bloody internecine strife among themselves and with the "Heavenly King," Xiuquan. As a result Yang and Wei were killed and Shi left Nanjing. Meanwhile, Xiuquan became increasingly detached from the reality of government and sought refuge in his religion. The Heavenly Kingdom was in a serious leadership crisis when Rengan appeared. With the complete trust of Xiuquan, he assumed control of the Nanjing regime and was soon appointed the "Shield King" and prime minister.

Rengan's ideas of reforming and strengthening the Taiping movement were embodied in a proposal which he submitted to Xiuquan shortly after he arrived in Nanjing, entitled *New Treatise for Aid in Government (Zizheng xinbian).* In addition to administrative reforms, the proposal called for the introduction of Western technologies and institutions, including railways, steamships, postal services, modern banks, mining, and industries. It also recommended the improvement of relations with the Western powers. These suggestions reflected Rengan's appreciation of the industrial civilization of the West, clearly a result of his sojourn in Hong Kong. At the same time, Rengan tried to win the support of China's educated elite by emphasizing anti-Manchu nationalism in the Taiping propaganda.

Few of Rengan's new ideas were put into practice by the Nanjing regime. Nevertheless, with the military assistance of other new leaders, especially the "Loyal King" Li Xiucheng, Rengan did succeed for a while in stabilizing the movement. After the loss of the strategic city of Anqing in 1861, however, Xiuquan lost faith in Rengan and removed him from power. On the eve of the collapse of the Heavenly Kingdom, and before his own suicide, Xiuquan again appointed Rengan as regent to his son, Hong Fu. Following the fall of Nanjing in 1864, Rengan fled from the city. He was eventually captured and executed in Jaingxi.

His reformist ideas placed Hong Rengan among the earliest advocates of Western-style modernization in nineteenth-century China. In the wake of the defeat of the Taipings, the gentry-officials who helped the Qing in the conflict launched the "Self-Strengthening movement," implementing many of the reforms suggested in Rengan's *New Treatise for Aid in Government.* Rengan was therefore a step ahead of the movement. His vision of a new China appeared to be more pragmatic and modern than that of Xiuquan's *Land System of the Heavenly Dynasty (Tianchao tianmu zhidu)*.

Wang Ke-wen

References

So, Kwan-wai, and Eugene P. Boardman. "Hung Jen-kan, Taiping Prime Minister, 1859–1864." *Harvard Journal of Asiatic Studies,* vol. 20, no. 1–2 (June 1957): 262–81.

Teng, S. Y. "Hung Jen-kan, Prime Minister of the Taiping Kingdom and His Modernization Plans." *United College Journal,* no. 8 (1970–71): 87–95.

Yuan-chung, Teng. "The Failure of Hung Jen-kan's Foreign Policy." *Journal of Asian Studies* 28 (November 1968): 125–38.

Hong Xiuquan (1814–64)

Hong Xiuquan was the leader of the Taiping Rebellion and the "Heavenly King" of the Heavenly Kingdom of Great Peace.

The son of a Hakka family in Guangdong province, Hong received classical education as a youth and tried several times to pass the civil service examination in pursuit of a government career. After the third failure, he fell seriously ill, actually a mental breakdown, and claimed to have dreamed of God in his delirium. After recovery, he took the examination the fourth time and again failed. Hong then connected his dream with the Christian tracts he had chanced upon earlier and concluded that his dream was in fact a revelation from God. He started to preach his own version of Christianity and found a few followers among his close relatives.

In 1847, Hong went to Canton to study the Bible with the American missionary Issachar J. Roberts. Upon his return home, he found out that one of his original followers, Feng Yunshan, had established the Society of God-Worshippers *(Baishangdihui)* in Guangxi with more than two thousand members. Hong was regarded as their supreme leader. During the following years, as local disturbances and ethnic conflict grew, the society attracted more followers and became a focal point of Hakka solidarity in Guangdong and Guangxi. Hong's religious teaching meanwhile became increasingly political; he now claimed that he was the second son of God, and younger brother of Jesus Christ, with a divine mission to expel the Manchu "demons" from China and establish the "heavenly kingdom" on earth. A group of new leaders also emerged from the society, including Yang Xiuqing, Xiao Chaoguei, and Shi Dakai.

In 1851, Hong led the society in an open rebellion in Jintian village, Guangxi province. The Society declared the founding of the Heavenly Kingdom of Great Peace *(Taiping tianguo),* with Hong as the "Heavenly King." Hong then appointed Feng, Yang, Xiao and Shi as secondary "Kings." The Taiping rebels launched a successful northward campaign, defeating the forces of the Qing government along the way. As they swept into the Yangtze valley, the number of the rebels grew from ten thousand to over one million. In 1853, they captured Nanjing as the capital of the Heavenly Kingdom. From Nanjing, Hong dispatched forces on a northern expedition to attack Beijing, which failed, but by 1856 the Taipings had consolidated their control over the entire Yangtze region.

In the meantime, the Taiping regime was paralyzed by internal power struggles. In a series of bloody purges and massacres in 1856, Yang Xiuqing and Wei Changhui, together with thousands of their followers, were killed, and Shi Dakai took his forces and left Nanjing. Partly disillusioned by this development and partly suffering from deteriorating mental problems, Hong paid less and less attention to administration and devoted himself completely to his religion. The actual policymaking was taken over by his brothers and, from 1859 to 1963, by his cousin Hong Rengan. Although the rebels again secured a few military victories in 1860, the political fortune of the Heavenly Kingdom was in rapid decline. The gentry-led Hunan and Huai armies, fighting for the Qing government and assisted by the Western powers, slowly recovered territories from the Taipings and besieged Nanjing. In June 1864, realizing that his cause was lost, Hong took his own life in Nanjing. One month later, the city fell. None of his followers surrendered; they either died in battle or committed suicide.

Wang Ke-wen

References

Jen, Yuwen. *The Taiping Revolutionary Movement.* New Haven, CT: Yale University Press, 1973.

Michael, Franz. *The Taiping Rebellion: History and Documents,* 3 vols. Seattle: University of Washington Press, 1966–71.

Yap, P. M. "The Mental Illness of Hung

Hsiu-ch'uan, Leader of the Taiping Rebellion." *The Far Eastern Quarterly* 13, no. 3 (May 1954): 287–304.

Hongxian Monarchy
See NATIONAL PROTECTION MOVEMENT; YUAN SHIKAI

Hu Hanmin (1879–1936)

Hu Hanmin was an anti-Manchu revolutionary, and a Guomindang leader and theoretician. A native of Guangdong, Hu had attained the *juren* degree in the examination system before going to Japan to study in 1902. In Japan, Hu was soon attracted to the revolutionary movement of Sun Yatsen and joined the Tongmenghui in 1905. As the editor of *Min-bao,* the Tongmenghui organ, Hu forcefully defended the anti-Manchu cause against attacks from the constitutionalists under Liang Qichao, and expanded on Sun's doctrines of the Three Peoples' Principles. From 1907 to 1910, Hu accompanied Sun to Southeast Asia to raise funds and organize revolts. Later, Sun appointed him as head of the south China branch of the Tong-menghui.

During the Revolution of 1911 Hu helped the revolutionaries to capture Canton and became the governer of Guangdong, one of the few provinces controlled by the Tongmenghui. When Sun Yatsen was elected provisional president of the new Republic, Hu was his secretary-general. In 1913, Hu participated in the Second Revolution led by Sun against Yuan Shikai. In the wake of its failure, he followed Sun to Japan and subsequently was in the top leadership of Sun's Chinese Revolutionary Party. From 1917 to 1923, when Sun made repeated attempts to establish an anti-Beijing regime in Canton, Hu remained Sun's most trusted lieutenant and occupied various important positions in the Canton regimes.

In 1919, Hu helped to found the journal *Jianshe (Reconstruction)* in Shanghai to serve as a mouthpiece of Sun's group in the post-May Fourth era. His writings for *Jianshe* included the earliest discussions of Marxism in China. Hu's intellectual curiosity, however, was not matched by political radicalism. When Sun entered a United Front with the Soviet Union and the Chinese Communist Party (CCP) in 1923, Hu was skeptical. He was elected into the Central Executive Committee of the reorganized Guomindang, but was soon identified as a leader of the Party's conservative (*i.e.,* anti-United Front) wing. Upon Sun's death in 1925 Hu ranked among the top contenders for the succession to Sun's leadership. A few months after the demise of Sun, however, he was defeated in the power struggle by a coalition of the radicals and the military leaders in Canton. In August 1925 Liao Zhongkai, the leader of that coalition, was assassinated. Hu was suspected of having been involved in the assassination and dispatched to the Soviet Union as a form of punishment.

When Hu returned to Canton nearly one year later, he found himself still *non grata* by Chiang Kaishek, the new leader of the Guomindang. He stayed in Shanghai in the following months as Chiang launched the Northern Expedition. Hu's political fortune changed dramatically in early 1927 when the Nanjing-Wuhan split occurred. In April, following the purge of the Communists, Chiang established his anti-United Front government in Nanjing and was in need of a prestigious Party veteran to support his cause; he chose Hu to head the new government. When Chiang resigned under the pressure of the Wuhan government in August, Hu also stepped down. He left the country for Europe in January 1928 and did not return until September.

From 1928 until his death in 1936, Hu, together with Chiang and Wang Jingwei, were the three most powerful leaders of Guomindang China. During 1928 to 1931 Hu served as head of the Legislative Yuan in the Nanjing government under Chiang. In May 1931 Hu clashed with Chiang on the issue of the constitution and presidency, and was placed under house arrest by Chiang. The incident led to the establishment, by Hu's supporters, of the Canton government in opposition to Nanjing. Hu was released following the Manchurian Incident in September, and the Canton government dissolved itself. Hu, however, never cooperated with Chiang again. After 1932, Chiang and Wang controlled the Nanjing government, while Hu led a *de facto* regional autonomy of Guangdong and Guangxi with the support of provincial militarists.

In his last years, Hu criticized Nanjing for its failure to suppress the CCP and to resist Japan. He tried to rally national support by adopting an "anti-Chiang, anti-Japan" stance, with little success. Nevertheless, his interpretations of Sun Yatsen's political doctrines remained authoritative within the Guomindang.

Wang Ke-wen

References

Barret, David P. "The Role of Hu Hanmin in the 'First United Front': 1922–27." *China Quarterly* no. 89 (January–March 1982): 34–64.

Kennedy, Melville T. "Hu Han-min: His Career and Thought," in *Revolutionary Leaders of Modern China,* ed. Chun-tu Hsueh, 271–294. New York, NY: Oxford University Press, 1971.

Hu Shih (Hu Shi, 1891–1962)

One of the most influential intellectuals in China in the first half of this century, Hu Shih was the leading spokesman of the literature revolution and an advocate for a scholarly study of fiction and plays. He played a pioneering role in promoting a modern methodology and outlook in historical and philosophical research, and was regarded as the political conscience of China at a time of oppression and frequent violation of civil liberties by the Guomindang. Above all, Hu was one of the most important individuals under whose leadership a critical reevaluation of Chinese cultural values was vigorously undertaken.

Hu Shih was born in Jixi, Anhui province. Educated in Shanghai, and later at Cornell University (1910–15) and Columbia University (1915–17), Hu spent most of his academic life at Beijing University as a professor (1917–27, 1930–38) and as its president (1945–48). He was China's ambassador to the United States (1938–42) and served as president of Academia Sinica (1958–62) in Taiwan for the last four years of his life.

One of Hu's overriding concerns was to transform China into a modern country. In this sense, he, like many other Chinese at the time, was a nationalist. But his nationalism was strongly colored by a cosmopolitan outlook and a spirit of constant self-reflection. He was active in the Cosmopolitan movement while a student in the United States, and held offices in the Cosmopolitan Club at Cornell University and nationally. He defended China's interests on many occasions in those years, but he was always mindful of a higher principle than national interests. "Above all nations is humanity," he wrote in 1914. In condemning the high-handed treatment of China by foreign powers, Hu would point out that China herself was not beyond reproach and that the fundamental strategy for China to free herself was to achieve modernization. Throughout his life, even while he defended China's interests in the international community, he was reluctant to label foreign governments as imperialistic.

Hu Shih's more concerted efforts were in the cultural and intellectual realm. He hoped that China would improve her condition through a painstaking self-reflection of her cultural and intellectual heritage and a conscious borrowing of Western values. In this regard, although his ultimate goal had a nationalistic element, he was far less nationalistic than most of his compatriots. Hu envisioned a future China whose place in the world would not depend on how strong she might become, although he certainly wanted his beloved motherland to be able to defend her dignity, but rather on how significant a contribution she might make toward improving culture and living conditions in the world. Unlike many other Chinese nationalists who were often hostile toward Western ideas, Hu was always receptive to them. While many of the conservative nationalists excessively protected the Chinese tradition, Hu was highly critical of it. In fact, his detractors complained, with some justification, that he was too well-disposed toward the West while being too negative regarding Chinese tradition.

The influence of Hu Shih's ideas, including his understanding of nationalism, is still being felt today. In republican China, before and after 1949, Hu was severely criticized by his detractors; in the People's Republic of China (PRC), he was violently assailed until recent years. The very criticisms and attacks, in fact, attested to the power of his ideas. In the PRC, Hu's reputation has been rehabilitated. Scholars there and in Taiwan who study him no longer carry the emotional burdens of yesteryears. Hu's place in modern Chinese history is now universally affirmed.

Min-chih Chou

References

Chou, Min-chih. *Hu Shih and Intellectual Choice in Modern China.* Ann Arbor: University of Michigan Press, 1992.

Grieder, Jerome B. *Hu Shih and the Chinese Renaissance: Liberalism in the Chinese Revolution, 1917–1937.* Cambridge, MA: Harvard University Press, 1970.

Hu Yaobang (1915–1989)

Hu Yaobang was the general secretary of the Chinese Communist Party (CCP) from 1981 to 1987 and a leader of post-Mao reforms.

Hu, a native of Hunan, was a teenager when he joined the Communist revolution as a bugle boy. A survivor of the Long March (1934–35), Hu was a compassionate person who championed a cause with enthusiasm and deep personal conviction. Through decades of self-education and learning on the job, Hu became a genuine Party theorist with liberal thinking and coherent analysis. Before the founding of the People's Republic, he spent much of his years as an educator in Party schools.

Dedication and hard work eventually helped Hu to rise to top leadership in the Communist Youth League, a subordinate but large-scale mass organization of carefully recruited young people under the CCP. Hu thus developed strong leadership experience in a fairly autonomous domain. Before the Cultural Revolution he worked at the provincial level in northern Sichuan and was also acting provincial Party secretary in Shaanxi. While leading the Youth League, he acquired good working relations with Deng Xiaoping, who was the CCP general secretary until 1966. During the Cultural Revolution both Deng and Hu were purged. When Deng was reinstated in 1977 for the last time, Hu was among the first to be rehabilitated by Deng and assumed directorship of the Party's Organization Department. He also headed the propaganda unit of the Party. In these capacities Hu was responsible for assigning many rehabilitated CCP leaders to important posts in the late 1970s.

When these rehabilitated leaders, most of whom supported Deng, gathered sufficient strength in leadership positions, they began to challenge Hua Guofeng, who was Party chairman and premier simultaneously. Hua had inherited and defended Mao's legacy in order to justify his own leadership, and was under severe criticism by Deng's supporters for failure to effect change and reform. Hu Yaobang provided key assistance to Deng in post-Mao Party politics, pressuring Hua to relinquish his Party leadership. Eventually, in 1980, Deng ousted Hua and appointed Hu as Party chairman. Soon that position was abolished in favor of the former secretariat, and Hu was made the general secretary of the CCP in 1981.

As head of the Party, Hu helped to create and expand the concept of "practice as the sole

Hu Yaobang in 1981. (Xinhua News Agency.)

test for truth." He remained, until his ousting in January 1987, the Party's top theorist on ideological interpretation. He communicated openly and freely and enjoyed a huge following among intellectuals and university students. In addition to carrying out Deng's economic reforms, Hu was also eager to reform the political system along with developing a new ideological cohesion for Chinese socialism. He favored the transfer of political power and leadership to a younger generation. In 1981, he proposed a peaceful reunification with the Guomindang regime in Taiwan.

Hu's dedication to rapid reform, however, antagonized the conservative Party leaders. When student demonstrations, in demand of participation in free campus elections and policy matters, occurred in many major cities (especially Shanghai and Nanjing) in late 1986, pressure mounted against Hu for his failure to restrain the students. He was forced by the conservatives to resign his post as general secretary, but allowed to retain his seat in the powerful Politburo.

Hu was close to Deng politically and was his bridge partner. His downfall inevitably harmed Deng's image as the paramount reform leader. Deng had no choice but to transfer his other trusted right-hand man, Premier Zhao

Ziyang, to be the new CCP general secretary. The premiership was thus left open for competition among the conservative Party leaders, who recommended Li Peng as China's new premier. Hu's death in April 1989 touched off a massive and continuous student unrest in Beijing. Without Hu, the students were further alienated from the government, and the moderate voice in the government was further weakened. The demonstrations eventually ended in the massacre at Tiananmen Square on June 4th.

David Wen-wei Chang

References

Burns, John P., and Stanley Rosen, eds. *Policy Conflicts in Post-Mao China.* Armonk, NY: M. E. Sharpe, 1986.

Yang, Zhongmei. *Hu Yaobang: A Chinese Biography.* Armonk, NY: M. E. Sharpe, 1988.

Hua Guofeng (b. 1921)

Hua Guofeng was Mao Zedong's immediate successor in 1976, and leader of the People's Republic and the Chinese Communist Party (CCP) during 1976 to 1981.

Born in Shanxi in 1921, Hua came from a poor peasant family and joined the Communist forces shortly after the latter completed their Long March and entered the northwestern provinces. When the People's Republic was founded in 1949, Hua was sent to Hunan to be a county Party secretary. For the next 14 years, Hua rose steadily in the Party apparatus in Hunan, supervising especially the Party work in Mao Zedong's home town Xiangtan, and was known for his contribution to the agricultural collectivization campaign. During the Cultural Revolution (1966–76) Hua's career was not hurt but helped. After organizing the Revolutionary Committee in Hunan, he was given the task to read the investigative report of Liu Shaoqi at the CCP's Central Plenum in 1968. In 1971 he was transferred to Beijing to head a special task force investigating the Lin Biao affair. He joined the Politburo in 1973 and became minister of Public Security two years later.

Hua proved that he was a capable Party bureaucrat, with a specialty in investigative works, but that hardly qualified him to be the number one successor to Mao. It was therefore a surprise to many when Mao nominated him as the new premier following the death of Zhou Enlai in April 1976. He was also made vice-chairman of the CCP's Central Committee. It was generally believed that Hua was the compromise candidate of two rival factions, the radicals under Jiang Qing and the moderates under Deng Xiaoping, in their bitter struggle for the post-Mao leadership. To certify his succession, which took place in September 1976, the CCP revealed a note Mao had given to Hua shortly before his death. It reads: "I am at ease when you are in charge."

Yet weeks after the leader's death, Hua collaborated with the moderates and the military and arrested the "Gang of Four." The move set the stage for the overturn of the radicalism of the Cultural Revolution and the initial political and economic restructuring of China. During the following four years, Hua was concurrently premier of China, chairman of the CCP's Central Committee, and chairman of the Central Military Council. He guided a limited post-Mao reform, but eventually clashed with Deng Xiaoping in a conflict of power and ideology. In 1980, Hua was removed from the premiership, and the following year he stepped down as chairman of the two top committees. He lost power completely in 1982, when he was deprived of his membership in the Politburo, and since then has remained in semi-retirement. He was the "man of transition." His leadership during the late 1970s was convenient, but critical, to the rise of Deng and the reformers in post-Mao China.

Wang Ke-wen

References

Bartke, Wolfgang, and Peter Schier. *China's New Party Leadership.* Armonk, NY: M. E. Sharpe, 1985.

Burns, John P. *Policy Conflicts in Post-Mao China.* Armonk, NY: M. E. Sharpe, 1986.

Huai Army

One of the largest and most powerful regional armies organized for the suppression of the Taiping Rebellion (1851–64), the Huai Army *(Huaijun)* was second only to the Hunan Army *(Xiangjun)* in terms of historical significance.

Shortly after the outbreak of the Taiping Rebellion, Li Hongzhang, then a Hanlin scholar, returned to his native province of Anhui and organized local militia *(tuanlian)* to fight against the rebels. Later Li joined the personal staff *(mufu)* of Zeng Guofan. In 1861, Zeng sent Li to southern Anhui for the purpose of establishing a new anti-Taiping force on the basis of local defense units. Imitating the organization and training programs of Zeng's Hunan Army, Li forged the initial 6,500 recruits into a regional army that was cemented by personal connections and loyalty to himself. Known as the Huai Army ("Huai" refers to the Huai River area of Jiangsu, Anhui, and Henan), the troops were soon transported by British steamships to Shanghai and became the major force fighting for the Qing government in the Jiangsu-Zhejiang area. It not only received assistance from the Western countries in terms of weaponry and personnel, but also fought alongside Western forces, such as the Ever-Victorious Army. The experience of Li and his officers during this period had a tremendous impact on their later attitude toward the West and their efforts to launch the Self-Strengthening movement.

By 1863, the Huai Army had grown to 40,000 men with at least 10,000 rifles and several modern cannons. In addition to Li himself, major leaders of the army included Liu Mingchuan, Zhang Shusheng, Guo Songlin, and Pan Dingxin.

Following the defeat of the Taipings, the Huai Army, now numbering 60,000, was ordered to suppress the Nian Rebellion (1855–68) in north China. During the 1870s to the 1890s, as Li rose to become the most important official in late Qing China, the Huai Army continued to be his basic military support. Although Li organized the Beiyang navy after 1875, on land he still relied upon the Huai Army; he used units of the army in the Sino-French War of 1883 to 1885 and the Sino-Japanese War of 1894 to 1895. After the disastrous defeat of Li's forces in the latter conflict, the Huai Army gradually dissolved.

Because of its association with the Beiyang forces, which many regarded as the origins of Chinese warlordism, the Huai Army is sometimes linked to the Beiyang warlords in the early Republic. While this point is debatable, there is no question that personalized armed forces such as the Hunan and Huai armies pioneered the development of warlord armies in modern China. On the other hand, from among the staff of the Huai Army there emerged a number of prominent figures in the late Qing reform: Feng Guifen, Guo Songtao, and Ding Jihchang.

Wang Ke-wen

References

Liu, Kwang-ching. "The Ch'ing Restoration." *The Cambridge History of China*, ed. John K. Fairbank, vol. 10, 409–90. Cambridge, England: Cambridge University Press, 1978,.

Spector, Stanley. *Li Hung-chang and the Huai Army.* Seattle: University of Washington Press, 1964.

Huang Fu (1880–1936)

See NORTH CHINA AUTONOMY; TANGGU TRUCE

Huang Hsing (Huang Xing, 1874–1916)

Military leader of the Revolution of 1911 which overthrew the Manchu dynasty and co-founder of the Republic of China, Huang Hsing was born in Shanhua (now Changsha), Hunan, on October 25, 1874. According to a family genealogy discovered in the 1980s, his ancestors migrated to Hunan from Jiangsi province at the beginning of the Ming dynasty. They were the descendants of Huang Tingjian, a noted poet and calligrapher of the northern Song dynasty. Huang Hsing's father was a school teacher. Huang Hsing himself received a traditional Chinese education and held a *shengyuan* degree.

In 1902, after graduating with distinction from the Academy of Hunan and Hubei at Wuchang, Huang was one of the students whom the government sent to study in Japan, where he pursued normal-school education. In Japan, he became involved in the anti-Manchu activities among Chinese students. Huang returned to Changsha to teach in the summer of 1903. In November of that year he founded the Huaxinghui (China Arise Society), and made plans for simultaneous uprisings in five cities in Hunan the following year. The government discovered the plot, and in November 1904 Huang was forced to flee, first to Shanghai and then to Japan. In August 1905, he joined hands with Sun Yatsen and others to establish the Tongmenghui (Revolutionary Alliance) in Tokyo. What had been provincial in the two men's revolutionary leadership now became national.

While Sun Yatsen was abroad most of the time, Huang Hsing directed a number of military campaigns against the Manchu government. The most important one was the Canton Uprising of March 1911. After the Wuchang Uprising in October, Huang rushed to the scene to assume command. When the provisional government of the Republic of China was established in Nanjing in January 1912, he served as Minister of War and apparently exercised even greater power and influence than Sun Yatsen in domestic politics.

Huang, along with Sun Yatsen and other revolutionary leaders and republican politicians, was exiled to Japan after the failure of the Second Revolution against Yuan Shikai. In order to recapture his leadership, Sun Yatsen organized the Chinese Revolutionary Party in Tokyo in June 1914. Most of his leading comrades, however, refused to join the party because Sun requested all party members to take an oath of personal loyalty to him. Huang went to the United States but returned to Shanghai in July 1916 and patched up his differences with Sun Yatsen, who had quietly dropped his previous demand for personal obedience from his comrades.

On October 31 of the same year, Huang died at the age of 42 of an old stomach ailment. His untimely death closed one chapter of Chinese republican revolutionary history. Unlike many other revolutionary leaders, Huang Hsing never fought for personal power. He was a born leader with a vigorous and magnetic personality. Typical of the literati of traditional China, he was gifted in the literary writing of *ci* and poetry, as well as in calligraphy. He accepted Western political philosophy, but highly valued the traditional culture of China. His ideas of nationalism and patriotism, which were the driving forces of his dedication to the revolution, came from the readings of noted Chinese scholars who stressed the differences between the Manchus and the Han Chinese. He was influenced by the history of the Taiping Rebellion and by the repeated humiliations imposed upon China by foreign powers. Although the revolution succeeded in overthrowing the Manchu dynasty and the Chinese monarchical system, it failed to create a strong, democratic and prosperous modern China.

Chün-tu Hsüeh

References

Hsüeh, Chün-tu, ed. *The Chinese Revolution of 1911: New Perspectives.* Hong Kong: Joint Publishing Co., 1986.

———. *Huang Hsing and the Chinese Revolution.* Stanford, CA: Stanford University Press, 1968.

———. "The Life and Political Thought of Huang Hsing: Co-founder of the Republic of China." *The Australian Journal of Politics and History* (April 1967): 21–33.

Hunan Army

In the wake of the Taiping rebels' northward drive through Hunan into the Yangtze valley in 1852, local gentry leaders had formed small militia units *(tuanlian)* to suppress local insurgents and bandits. These units had already enjoyed some success when Zeng Guofan, who had temporarily retired to his home in Hunan in 1852, was commissioned by the Qing court to manage militia organization in the province. Zeng assembled forces already in existence, including units led by Jiang Zhongyaun, Wang Zhen, Luo Zenan, and Hu Linyi, and regular provincial forces under the Manchu officer Taqibu. This consolidated force became the Hunan Army *(Xiangjun)*.

The Hunan Army was modeled on the military organization used by the Ming commander Qi Jiguang (1528–88) to combat Japanese pirate invasions along the coast in the mid-sixteenth century. Battalions *(ying)* of approximately six hundred men each were built up of smaller, individually trained units recruited from the sedentary rural peasant class rather than from the unreliable urban and rural transient population. Unlike soldiers in the regular armies, members of the Hunan Army were paid regularly and relatively well and were loyal to their superior officers. The principal commanders below Zeng were related through traditional patronage, kinship, and personal friendship associations, and the commander of each unit, from battalion down, recruited his immediate subordinate officers of the next lower unit, so that the entire army was pervaded by bonds of loyalty and personal obligation. To disassociate the army from the alienation caused by the depredations of the regular Qing forces and to combat the ideological appeal of the Taipings, breaches of discipline were severely punished, and soldiers were regularly lectured on Confucian morality, a harbinger of the political indoctrination of the Guomindang armies in the 1920s and the Communist armies in the 1930s and 1940s.

The first major campaigns against the Taiping forces remaining in Hunan began in early 1854, but success was mixed, with some initial defeats. A naval force was created when it became apparent that the army would require mobility on the waterways along the Yangtze River to prevent the Taipings from infiltrating back into pacified areas. By 1855, Hunan was largely secure, and the army advanced into Hubei and Jiangxi, as Zeng pushed slowly down river. Jiujiang was finally taken in 1858 after a determined campaign, and Anqing, which became a base for operations against Nanjing, was captured in 1861. Although it advanced beyond the provincial boundaries of Hunan, the army continued to draw new recruits from militia units in Hunan. During the course of the campaign, Zeng's lieutenant Zuo Zongtang recruited a separate branch of the Hunan Army to campaign in Zhejiang. Li Hongzhang's Huai Army, recruited in Anhui and patterned on the Hunan Army, was sent to Jiangsu in 1862. The Hunan Army was disbanded after the final defeat of the Taipings at Nanjing in 1864.

The development of the Hunan Army marked a significant stage in the acceleration of regional militarization extending from the nineteenth into the early twentieth century. In particular, the participation of the local gentry in military organization and leadership engendered a new level of involvement in local affairs and new career opportunities much less under the control and purview of the central government than heretofore. The increasing local autonomy thus fostered by the activities of the Hunan Army contributed to the political disintegration of modern China. At the same time, however, it created the foundation for local representative assemblies during the reform movement in the 1890s, which became a major vehicle for the expression of Chinese nationalism.

Jonathan Porter

References

Kuhn, Philip A. *Rebellion and Its Enemies in Late Imperial China: Militarization and the Social Structure, 1796–1864.* Cambridge, MA: Harvard University Press, 1970.

Porter, Jonathan. *Tseng Kuo-fan's Private Bureaucracy.* Berkeley: University of California Press, 1972.

Hundred Days Reform

From June 11 to September 20, 1898, Emperor Guangxu of the Qing dynasty issued a series of reform edicts known as the Hundred Days Reform. Influenced by the ideas of Kang Youwei, the edicts marked China's first attempt to organize national reform from the top down.

Japan's victory in the first Sino-Japanese War (1894–95) stimulated reformist zeal around the country. Study societies, newspapers, and modern schools spread through the provinces. Germany's occupation of Jiaozhou in November 1897, and the leases extorted by Russia, Great Britain, and France in March and April 1898, fed an atmosphere of crisis at the capital. Kang Youwei, a prominent young scholar and junior official, urged reform in a January 1898 interview with the Zongli Yamen and in several memorials to the throne. These efforts antagonized conservatives but encouraged the young emperor. Aided by his former tutor, Weng Tonghe, he issued an edict on June 11 announcing a program of institutional change, and on June 16 he granted Kang Youwei a lengthy audience.

That summer, influenced by Kang's ideas, the emperor issued some 130 reform decrees. Many reflected Kang's interest in education: a system of modern schools, an imperial university, an official newspaper, and revision of the civil service exams. Others enjoined industrial, commercial, and agricultural development and railway construction. The most controversial concerned government administration, including abolition of sinecures and numerous provincial offices, notably the governorships of Hubei, Guangdong, and Yunnan provinces. With their vested interests threatened, high officials waited to see what the empress dowager would do.

The Empress Dowager Cixi's power was well-known. She had placed the emperor on the throne as a child, and he owed his position entirely to her. So did officials on the Grand Council and the Six Boards. On June 15, 1898, she acted to protect her power by removing Weng Tonghe from his government posts and appointing her favorite, Ronglu, as governor-general of Zhili province in command of all troops in north China.

By early September, the reforms were becoming ominously political. The emperor dismissed senior officials in the Board of Ceremony and installed four young reformers, Yang Rui, Lin Xu, Liu Guangdi, and Tan Sitong, as secretaries in the Grand Council. Influenced by her favorites, the empress dowager began to plan a coup d'état to remove the emperor from power. As rumors spread, the reformers tried to enlist Ronglu's subordinate Yuan Shikai in a counter-coup to kill Ronglu and the empress dowager. Yuan, who controlled seven thousand modern-style troops near

Tianjin, informed Ronglu. The next day, September 21, the empress dowager imprisoned the emperor and resumed direct rule. Kang Youwei and Liang Qichao escaped to Japan, while six others, including Tan Sitong and Kang's brother, were summarily beheaded.

Suppression of the Hundred Days Reform thwarted the development of a national response to China's crisis, reaffirmed the power of reactionaries at court, and cleared the way for the Boxer Uprising of 1900. Only in 1901, with her policies in ruin, did the empress dowager begin a new reform program to reorganize the Confucian state.

Charlton M. Lewis

References

Kwong, Luke S. K. *A Mosaic of the Hundred Days: Personalities, Politics and Ideas of 1898.* Cambridge, MA: Harvard University Press, 1984.

Hundred Flowers Campaign

By 1956, leaders of the Chinese Communist Party (CCP), including Mao Zedong, had come to the conclusion that the future development of the country required the active participation of the alienated intellectuals, who had become estranged because of the many harsh ideological campaigns carried out against them by the Party. The CCP leaders believed that the intellectuals could be won over if they were granted better working conditions and a degree of intellectual freedom. In May 1956, Mao launched an innovative movement embodied in the slogan, "let a hundred flowers bloom, let a hundred schools contend." The Hundred Flowers campaign was unique because it not only encouraged "independent thinking and free discussion" (blooming and contending) among the intellectuals, but also invited them to criticize the Party bureaucracy for the mistakes it had made in dealing with the problems of the intellectuals.

The campaign was, however, slow in taking off because there was resistance from Party cadres who worried that outside criticism would lower Party prestige and weaken inner-Party unity; the intellectuals, too, fearing Party reprisal, were reluctant to express their opinions. In early 1957, Mao enunciated a new thesis concerning the settling of "non-antagonistic contradictions" between the leaders and the followers through discussion, criticism, debate and education, and he urged the Party not to be afraid of hearing criticism if it sincerely wanted to improve its work-style.

By May 1957, the fears of the non-Party intellectuals having been allayed, the Hundred Flowers campaign unfolded in earnest. The flood of criticism that followed—from members of democratic parties, writers, journalists, teachers in lower schools, colleges, and universities, other professionals, and students—revealed the intensity of the intellectuals' disenchantment with the regime. Not only individual cadres, but the whole Communist system came under attack. Some of the critics went so far as to challenge the right of the CCP to rule the country.

Shocked by the volume and bitterness of the attacks on the Party, a totally disillusioned Mao terminated the campaign in June 1957, within five weeks of its inauguration, and launched an Anti-Rightist campaign that shifted the target of criticism from the Party to the intellectuals, who were now stigmatized as bourgeois rightists and as "the enemies of the Party." Out of the nearly 550,000 intellectuals who were denounced, thousands were executed and hundreds of thousands exiled to the countryside to "rectify their thinking through labor." Not until 1979, three years after Mao's death, did Deng Xiaoping finally rehabilitate these blacklisted intellectuals and restore them to an honorable status in society.

The Party revived the Hundred Flowers policy in 1986, on the occasion of the thirtieth anniversary of Mao's campaign, as part of its limited political reform. This new exercise, too, brought few gains to the Chinese intelligentsia.

Ranbir Vohra

References

Goldman, Merle. *China's Intellectuals: Advise and Dissent.* Cambridge, MA: Harvard University Press, 1981.

I

Ili Crisis (1871–81)

The strategically important Ili valley straddled a major communication route between Russian and Chinese Turkestan. It also possessed fertile land and abundant minerals. In 1863, a Muslim force, probably inspired by the successful efforts of their coreligionists in Shanxi and Gansu, attacked the Qing garrisons. Unrest in Ili continued until 1871. Then, in response to a serious effort by Ya'qub Beg, a Muslim officer and statesman, to control Chinese Turkestan, including the Ili valley, the Russians sent a force to Ili and occupied it. They acted to prevent unrest from spreading into their territories and to seize strategic territories. Although the Russians professed to be aiding the Qing government by the occupation, the czarist government believed the valley to be lost forever by the Chinese. The Russians signed a trade treaty with Ya'qub Beg and thereby officially recognized him.

It took the Qing government until 1877, after a long, bitter campaign, to recapture the lost territories. The Manchus reasserted sovereign claim to the valuable Ili valley. Zuo Zongtang, commander of the Qing reconquest, urged the court to adopt a strong position in the matter. He soon moved his headquarters into northern Chinese Turkestan to demonstrate his and the government's resolve.

Between 1877 and 1881, two treaties were signed by Russia and China. The first was negotiated by the inept Manchu statesman, Chonghou, who failed to understand and defend his country's national interests. His Treaty of Lividia ceded 70 percent of the valley to the Russians, including strategic places. Other concessions included an indemnity of five million rubles. The stunned Manchu court, along with many patriotic Chinese, greeted this settlement with alarm. Elite pressure forced the government to adopt a hard line with the Russians. Chonghou was arrested and sentenced to death, whereupon the Chinese and the Russians traded bellicose threats and engaged in hostile actions.

A second treaty was negotiated after careful preparation by Zeng Jize, son of the eminent statesman Zeng Guofan. Tough bargaining led to a temporary stalemate. Eventually, Czar Alexander II yielded nearly all of the valley, including the strategic places, to China. A larger payment (diplomatically called military compensation) of nine million rubles helped to assuage the Russian concessions. The new settlement anchored Chinese Turkestan to the Qing empire. Provincial status came three years after the signing of the Treaty of St. Petersburg (1881). The favorable diplomatic results encouraged the more bellicose elements in Chinese elite circles. Zuo Zongtang's strong actions buttressed the tenacity of the imperial court and helped to realize provincial status for Chinese Turkestan (Xinjiang) in 1884. Sino-Russian tensions, however, remained a source of concern to the Qing.

Lanny B. Fields

References

Fields, Lanny B. *Tso Tsung-t'ang and the Muslims: Statecraft in Northwest China, 1868–1880.* Kingston, Ontario: The Limestone Press, 1978.

Hsu, Immanuel C. Y. *The Ili Crisis: A Study of Sino-Russian Diplomacy, 1871–1881.* Oxford, England: Clarendon, 1965.

Independent Review

Independent Review (Duli pinglun), a weekly publication, was started on May 22, 1932, and

Hu Shih. (Courtesy of Nationalist Party Archives.)

China's integrity, but also attacked many of the policies of China's ruling party, the Guomindang. It expressed well-informed opinions on Sino-Japanese relations and on many of the social and political issues in China. It is impossible to determine how much influence the *Review* exerted on Japanese policymakers. It is probably fair to say that the *Review* acted as a small counter force to the rule of the oppressive Guomindang. Because of the wide-ranging issues it discussed, *Independent Review* should be considered an important source for the study of China's social and political history in the 1930s.

Independent Review stopped publication in July 1937. Beiping, and North China in general, were no longer secure, as Japan had started a large-scale invasion of China in that month. Moreover, some of the founding members of the *Review* had dispersed. V. K. Ting had died; T. F. Tsiang was appointed ambassador to the Soviet Union in 1936; and one year later, Hu Shih became ambassador to the United States.

Min-chih Chou

ceased operation on July 25, 1937, after 244 issues having been published.

The *Review* was founded by a small group of university professors in Beiping (Beijing). At the time, China was in great difficulty as a result of misgovernment and Japanese aggression. The direct impetus for the founding of the *Review*, however, was the Manchurian Incident of September 18, 1931, which commenced a concerted effort by Japan to conquer China. The major purpose of the publication, as its founding members proposed, was to reflect upon the relations between China and Japan during a domestic and international crisis. In that sense, *Independent Review* reflected the nationalistic sentiments of its founders when China's survival was being threatened.

Most of the founding members of the *Review* were prominent academic leaders. Hu Shih, its driving force, was one of the founders and served much of the time as its editor-in-chief. Hu alone contributed nearly 10 percent of all the writings published in the *Review*. Other contributors included V. K. Ting (Ding Wenjiang), T. F. Tsiang (Jiang Tingfu), and Weng Wenhao.

The nationalism reflected in the *Review* was not a virulent type. Rather, it was mild, studied and balanced. The *Review* not only criticized Japan's China policy and its blatant disregard of

Inspectorate General of Customs
See CHINESE MARITIME CUSTOMS

Internationalists
The "internationalists" were a faction within the Chinese Communist Party (CCP) in the 1930s that supported, and was controlled by, the Communist International. The faction, also known as the "twenty-eight Bolsheviks," was organized by a group of former students at the Sun Yatsen University in Moscow. While at the university, these students, led by Wang Ming (Chen Shaoyu), had organized themselves in support of the university president, Pavel Mif, in the power struggle within the Russian Communist Party. In return, Mif rewarded the students with his backing in their careers in the CCP. In 1929 through 1931, these "internationalists," including Wang Ming, Bo Gu (Qin Bangxian), Lo Fu (Zhang Wentian), Wang Jiaxiang and Yang Shangkun, returned to China one by one. Meanwhile, Moscow appointed Mif as the Comintern representative in the CCP.

With Mif's encouragement and assistance, the returned students soon ousted Li Lisan and seized control of the Party leadership. Wang Ming became *de facto* head of the Party, whereas other members of the faction held high positions in the Politburo and Central Secretariat (Bo Gu was general secretary in 1934–35). From 1931 to 1935, they dominated the CCP's policymaking and overshadowed Mao Zedong, chairman of the Jiangxi Soviet. In 1934 the CCP lost its base in Jiangxi, for which CCP historians later blamed the "internationalists," and embarked on the Long March. After the Zunyi Conference in January 1935, Mao gradually forced the "internationalists" out of power. A few of them, especially Wang Ming, continued to compete with Mao for the Party leadership; others defected to Mao's camp. During the Sino-Japanese War of 1937 to 1945, Wang briefly supervised the Party's United Front with the Guomindang (GMD), still upholding the Comintern instructions. As a group, the "internationalists" ceased to be influential in CCP politics.

The "internationalists" represented the most pro-Soviet elements in the Chinese Communist movement. Trained in Moscow, they loyally followed the Comintern line and believed that the Chinese Revolution should not only be guided by the Soviet Union but modeled on the urban-based proletarian revolt of the Bolshevik Revolution. Their view overlooked the reality of Chinese society, and their rapid rise to power in the CCP caused widespread dissatisfaction among other Party members. The downfall of the "internationalists" was critical to the indigenization of the Communist movement in China and the triumph of Mao's rural strategy.

Wang Ke-wen

References

Braun, Otto. *A Comintern Agent in China, 1932–1939.* Stanford, CA: Stanford University Press, 1982.

North, Robert C. *Moscow and the Chinese Communists.* Stanford, CA: Stanford University Press, 1953.

Rue, John E. *Mao Tse-tung in Opposition, 1927–1935.* Stanford, CA: Stanford University Press, 1966.

J

January Twenty-Eighth Incident

The January Twenty-Eighth Incident is also known as the Shanghai Incident. In early 1932, shortly after the Manchurian Incident, the Japanese decided to create a new conflict in the Lower Yangtze area, China's financial and economic center, in an attempt to divert Chinese and international attention from Manchuria. In late January, the Japanese provoked a series of disputes and fightings between the Chinese and Japanese residents in Shanghai. The Japanese consulate then issued a protest against these incidents to the Shanghai municipal government, and threatened military solutions. On January 24, the Shanghai residence of the Japanese minister to China was burned down. Japan blamed the Chinese for this attack, although it may have been the work of Japanese agents, and immediately reinforced its troops in Shanghai. On January 26, the Japanese consulate again issued an ultimatum with a number of demands to the Chinese government. The Guomindang (GMD) government in Nanjing, then in a transition of leadership, adopted a conciliatory policy toward Japan. It issued an official apology and dissolved the local anti-Japanese organizations, but the Japanese were determined to use force. On the morning of January 28, Japanese troops marched out from the Japanese concession in Shanghai and attacked the Chinese forces in the city.

At the time, the city was defended by the Chinese Nineteenth Route Army. Under the command of Jiang Guangnai and Cai Tingkai, the army offered stiff resistance against the invading Japanese. Nanjing later dispatched the modernized Fifth Army to assist in the resistance effort. After one month of fierce fighting, however, the Chinese forces had to retreat. The GMD government, fearing the advance of the Japanese troops to Nanjing, moved its seat from Nanjing to Luoyang in central China. Meanwhile, the Japanese action worried the Western powers, which had vested financial and economic interest in Shanghai, and they decided to intervene. In early May, under Western pressure, the Japanese signed a truce agreement with the Chinese government. According to this agreement, the Japanese forces would withdraw into the concession, and the Chinese would not station troops in the strategic area between Shanghai and Suzhou.

The Shanghai Incident was a dubious diplomatic victory for the GMD government. When the Japanese attack occurred, the government of Sun Fo (Sun Ke), which had come to office in December 1931 as a solution to the Nanjing-Canton split, had just resigned. The crisis in Shanghai facilitated the formation of a new government under Chiang Kaishek and Wang Jingwei, and the development of the policy of "resisting while negotiating" toward Japan. This policy proved to be more effective than the "non-resistance" policy previously adopted by Nanjing in handling the Manchurian Incident. It succeeded in localizing and eventually containing the conflict with the help of the Western powers. In the long-run, however, this strategy of flexibility failed to dissuade Japan from her continuing aggression against China, and nationalist Chinese soon came to see it as a form of appeasement.

Wang Ke-wen

References

Coble, Parks M., Jr. *Facing Japan.* Cambridge, MA: Harvard University Press, 1991.

Jordan, Donald A. *Chinese Boycott vs. Japanese Bombs: The Failure of China's "Revolutionary Diplomacy," 1931–32.* Ann Arbor: University of Michigan Press, 1991.

Jiang Baili (1882–1938)

Jiang Baili was the foremost military strategist and theorist in republican China. A native of Zhejiang, Jiang (Fangzhen), was deeply affected by China's defeat in the first Sino-Japanese War (1894–95) when only thirteen. His interest in military affairs was said to have originated at this time. From 1901 to 1905, Jiang studied military science in Japan, where he became one of the best Chinese students the Japanese military schools had ever had. Then, from 1908 to 1910, he again pursued military studies in Germany. Upon returning to China, he served in the staff of the governor-general of Manchuria and became interested in the defense of the region against Russian and Japanese ambitions.

Following the founding of the Republic, Jiang, at twenty-nine, was appointed by President Yuan Shikai as commandant of the Baoding Military Academy. The academy was the most prominent higher military education institution in modern China, and through his position Jiang established teacher-student ties with many future military leaders in the republican era. In 1913, after failing to obtain necessary funds for the academy from the government, Jiang attempted to commit suicide in front of a student gathering, an act that moved the students deeply. He was merely wounded, but soon left the academy.

In the following years, Jiang was closely associated with Liang Qichao's Research Clique *(yanjiuxi)*. He accompanied Liang on a tour to Europe and edited the journal *Gaizao (Reformation)* in Shanghai. In the early 1920s, he supported the Federalist movement *(liansheng zizhi)* and helped to draft the provincial constitutions of Hunan and Zhejiang. While critical of warlordism in his writings, Jiang maintained connections with many regional militarists, some of whom had been his students at Baoding. He served successively as chief-of-staff to Sun Chuanfang and Wu Peifu in 1923 to 1925. On the eve of the Northern Expedition, Jiang assisted the Hunanese militarist Tang Shengzhi and followed Tang in defecting to the Guomindang (GMD).

However, Jiang was not on good terms with the GMD government after its nominal unification of China. In 1930 he participated in Tang Shengzhi's failed revolt against Nanjing, for which he was put under arrest for one year. Finding politics dangerous and frustrating, Jiang turned his attention to research and writing. From 1931 to 1937 he drafted several proposals for strengthening China's defense in the event of war, which apparently impressed Chiang Kaishek. In 1935, Chiang reinstated his reputation, appointed him senior military adviser to the government, and subsequently sent him to Europe to study the European countries' wartime mobilization laws. Shortly after the outbreak of the second Sino-Japanese War, Jiang was again on a mission to Europe, seeking international support for China's war effort. In 1938 he became acting president of the Army Staff College in Hankou, but soon died of an illness.

China in the republican era was plagued by wars and militarism. It seems ironic, therefore, that as the top military theorist in the country, Jiang Baili found little use of his knowledge and talents during his lifetime. He once proposed to eliminate China's warlordism by drastically reducing the number of troops and the military budget, and by establishing a national conscription/militia system. He believed that the latter system would not only undermine the warlord armies but also strengthen China's defense by integrating the civilian and military sectors of the society. Jiang's best-known work, *Guofanglun (On National Defense)*, published in 1937, argues the importance of building an economic basis for national defense. He introduced the concept of total war and suggested that, in order to win in such a war, the "living conditions" of the populace must be in line with the "battle conditions." To an extent, Jiang was influenced by the militarist values and concepts of Germany and Italy; his ideas in turn exerted an impact on Chiang Kaishek and China's overall strategy in the second Sino-Japanese War.

Wang Ke-wen

References

Boorman, Howard L., and Richard C. Howard, eds. *Biographical Dictionary of Republican China*, vol. 1. New York, NY: Columbia University Press, 1967.

Jiang Jingguo (1910–88)

Jiang Jingguo's place in modern Chinese history is determined by two salient facts. First, he was the son of Chiang Kaishek, which enabled him to inherit his father's power and position; and secondly, he built his career and assumed party-government leadership in Taiwan, the island base of a refugee regime in a divided China.

Jingguo was the eldest son of Chiang Kaishek and his first wife, Mao Fumei, whom Chiang later divorced. At the age of fifteen, he was sent by Chiang, then a rising military leader under the Guomindang-Chinese Communist Party (GMD-CCP) United Front in Canton, to study in the Soviet Union. In Moscow, Jingguo soon joined the Chinese Communist Party, and when Chiang purged the Communists from the GMD on April 12, 1927, Jingguo publicly denounced his father. For the next ten years he was opposed to, and separated from, his father. He graduated from Sun Yatsen University and a military school, worked in factories, and married a Russian woman. Not until 1937, when relations improved between the Soviet Union and China, and between the ruling GMD and the CCP, was Jingguo allowed to return to China.

Serving under his father—now the generalissimmo—Jingguo initially displayed populist tendencies that may have resulted from his Russian sojourn. In 1938, while in charge of the administration and reconstruction of southern Jiangxi, he mobilized a degree of popular support for the GMD in an area that had been ruled by the CCP for years. During the latter part of the Sino-Japanese War (1937–45), Jingguo established a power base in the Three Peoples' Principles Youth Corps and began his climb up the ladder of power in the GMD. In 1945, he returned to Moscow and assisted T. V. Soong in the negotiation of the Sino-Soviet Treaty of Friendship and Alliance, which ceded Outer Mongolia to Soviet domination. His relations with the powerful families of T. V. Soong and H. H. Kung, however, were not good. In the chaotic years of the civil war (1945–49) he persecuted members of the two families in a doomed battle against corruption in Shanghai.

Despite his growing political importance, Jingguo probably would not have succeeded his father's party and government leadership had the GMD not been defeated in the civil war. The loss of the mainland in 1949, ironically, helped to destroy all the major factions under Chiang Kaishek that might have been Jingguo's rivals for the succession to Chiang. In the days of defeat and retreat to Taiwan, Jingguo forged close ties with his father. He was still not without

Chiang Kaishek and son Jingguo in 1945. (Courtesy of Nationalist Party Archives.)

competitors, however. In the 1950s, Jingguo ousted Wu Guozhen and Sun Liren, two American-trained officials whom Chiang had promoted in order to attract United States support for Taiwan, and in the 1960s he engaged in a power struggle with Chiang's vice-president, Chen Cheng, who died in 1965.

To groom Jingguo as his heir apparent, Chiang entrusted to Jingguo the work of the youth, of the veterans, and of political indoctrination in the military. In 1965, he became Minister of Defense. Yet the cornerstone of Jingguo's power was his control of the secret police. More than anyone else in the GMD regime, Jingguo was responsible for the reign of terror in Taiwan during the 1950s and 1960s. The secret police helped him to eliminate dissidents as well as his own political enemies. By the time he assumed the headship of the Administrative Yuan (premier) in 1972, under an ailing Chiang, his position in Taiwan was unchallenged.

From 1972 onward, Jingguo's public image underwent a dramatic transformation. As *de facto* ruler of the island during 1972 to 1978 and as president of the Republic of China after 1978, he revived some of his earlier populist touch and presented himself as a progressive leader. Apparently more realistic than his father in assessing the prospect of the GMD's recovery of the mainland, he recruited a large number of Taiwanese into the regime, concentrated the regime's resources on basic constructions on the island, and adopted a pragmatic approach to the regime's foreign relations. These policies prepared Taiwan for the international isolation it has suffered since the early 1970s and laid the foundation of the island's "economic miracle" in the following decades. During his last days, Jingguo tolerated the emergence of a political opposition in Taiwan and permitted, for the first time since 1949, limited communications between the people in Taiwan and their relatives on the mainland. One of his last, and boldest, major decisions was the choice of Li Denghui, a Taiwanese agricultural economist, as his successor.

Jiang Jingguo symbolized, even more than his father had, the "Taiwan experience" that has become a challenge and an alternative to Communist China since 1949. The political stability and economic growth over which he presided in Taiwan offered a sharp contrast to the constant upheavals in the People's Republic, and in recent years the island's accomplishments have received increasing international recognition. Nevertheless, Jingguo was a regional leader in a nation divided. His approach to nation-building was not unlike that of some of the provincial militarists in the 1920s and 1930s—they all invoked nationalist appeals for the reconstruction and development of a region. Although he never gave up the principle of national reunification, in effect his rule indigenized, and thus regionalized, the GMD regime in Taiwan.

Wang Ke-wen

References

Durdin, Tillman. "Chiang Ching-kuo and Taiwan: A Profile." *ORBIS* (Winter 1975): 1023–1042.

Tien, Hung-mao. *The Great Transition: Political and Social Change in the Republic of China*. Stanford, CA: Hoover Institution Press, 1989.

Vorontsov, V. "The Dictator's Heir." *Far Eastern Affairs,* Institute of the Far East, USSR Academy of Sciences, vol. 1, 1989.

Jiang Qing (1913–91)

Jiang Qing was the wife of Mao Zedong, the leader of the so-called Gang of Four, and one of the most powerful persons in the People's Republic during the late 1960s and early 1970s.

Born Li Yunhe (or Li Jin) to a family of modest means in Shandong, Jiang Qing was orphaned as a child and raised by her grandfather. She received limited education before entering a drama school in her home province. In 1933, she joined the Chinese Communist Party (CCP) through the introduction of a man with whom she lived at the time, and who later deserted her. Jiang then moved to Shanghai, married and divorced a writer, and acted in films and plays under the name Lan Ping. Although unsuccessful as an actress, she was active in leftist circles and was once arrested by the Guomindang (GMD) government. When the Sino-Japanese War broke out in 1937, Jiang, like many other leftist artists, left Shanghai for the CCP base in Yan'an. There Jiang met Mao Zedong, who was divorcing his third wife, and quickly attracted Mao's attention. It was Mao who gave her the name Jiang Qing (Blue River) during this time. In 1939, the two married and Jiang soon gave birth to a girl.

Because of Jiang's shady personal background, the CCP leadership allegedly approved of the marriage on the condition that she would refrain from politics for twenty years. Throughout the Sino-Japanese War and the GMD-CCP civil war, therefore, Jiang merely served as Mao's personal secretary and worked for the Party's Propaganda Department, involving herself in the reform of traditional Chinese drama. In fact, during the first decade and a half after the founding of the People's Republic, she remained politically inactive and obscure.

In the early 1960s, Jiang began to establish her influence in China's cultural arena when she again pushed aggressively for the revolutionization of the Beijing Opera. Her effort was supported by a group of Party intellectuals in Shanghai, especially Zhang Chunqiao and Yao Wenyuan, who subsequently became her close followers. These Party intellectuals were also responsible for the campaign against the play

Hairui's Dismissal from Office in 1965, which ignited the flame of the Cultural Revolution.

At the beginning of the Cultural Revolution Jiang, who was then in charge of the CCP's cultural policy, was appointed deputy director of the Central Cultural Revolutionary Small Group in Beijing. In that position and as the chairman's wife, she exercised enormous power during the next ten years, purging and persecuting numerous Party leaders, intellectuals, and personal enemies. Many of the victims either knew about her early life in Shanghai or had objected to her marriage to Mao in Yan'an. She also controlled the country's cultural life. For a time, the eight "model plays" *(yangbanxi)* she had helped to produce, as examples of the revolutionary Beijing Opera, were the only officially approved entertainment for the Chinese people.

The chaos of the Cultural Revolution paved the way for Jiang's rapid ascent to Party leadership. In 1969, she was elected into the Politburo, together with her protégés Zhang Chunqiao and Yao Wenyuan. She chose a young worker from Shanghai, Wang Hongwen, to assume top positions in the Party. Jiang and her followers formed a radical faction within the CCP that advocated the continuation and expansion of the violent attacks on the establishment in the Cultural Revolution. Initially she worked closely with the Defense Minister and Mao's revolutionary successor, Lin Biao, but their relationship deteriorated as Lin and his People's Liberation Army gained increasing power after 1969. In 1971, Lin was purged and killed in a mysterious accident. From then on, Jiang and the radicals, with the backing of the ailing Mao, dominated the Party and the government.

Jiang, however, was not without rivals under Mao. The moderates led by Zhou Enlai and Deng Xiaoping opposed the excesses of the Cultural Revolution, and they enjoyed broad support among the senior cadres. In September 1976, Mao died and was succeeded by Hua Guofeng, a compromise candidate between the radicals and the moderates. Four weeks later, Hua collaborated with the moderates and ordered the arrest of Jiang and her associates, now known as the Gang of Four. The new leadership denounced the gang as a counterrevolutionary clique that had attempted to use the Cultural Revolution to destroy the CCP. In 1980 and 1981, the gang members were tried publicly and charged with the unjust persecution of hundreds of thousands during the Cultural Revo-

lution. Jiang refused to admit any wrong-doing. She was nevertheless sentenced to death, which was then commuted to life imprisonment. In May 1991, depressed and in poor health, Jiang hanged herself in her jail cell.

Wang Ke-wen

References

Terrill, Ross. *The Whiteboned Demon: A Biography of Madame Mao Zedong*. New York, NY: Morrow, 1984.
Witke, Roxane. *Comrade Chiang Ch'ing*. Boston, MA: Little, Brown, 1977.

Jiang Zemin (b. 1926)

State chairman of the People's Republic since 1993, Jiang Zemin represents the post-Tiananmen leadership of the Chinese Communist Party (CCP).

Born in Yangzhou, Jiangsu, Jiang joined the Chinese Communist Party while studying at the Jiaotong (Communications) University in Shanghai, shortly before the Communist victory in 1949. Following a brief training program in Moscow in the mid-1950s, he spent most of his career before the Cultural Revolution in areas related to engineering and China's technological development. He was apparently not seriously affected by the turmoil of the Cultural Revolution, and in the 1970s became director of the Foreign Affairs Bureau under the First Ministry of Machine Building Industry. After Deng Xiaoping returned to power in 1979, his political fortune rose steadily. In the 1980s, Jiang served as vice-minister and then minister of the Ministry of Electronics Industry before being appointed to the powerful post of mayor of Shanghai. He entered the Politburo in 1987.

During the nationwide mass protest and riots in May–June 1989, Jiang's mild but firm handling of the demonstrations in Shanghai, which did not result in terrible bloodshed as had the Tiananmen Incident in Beijing, reportedly impressed Deng Xiaoping. His technological background, moreover, made him an acceptable candidate to both the conservative and the reform factions. Following the purge of Zhao Ziyang in the wake of the incident, Jiang was selected to succeeded Zhao as secretary-general of the CCP's Central Committee. He soon became chairman of the Party's Military Commission, and in 1993 succeeded Yang Shangkun as chairman of the state (president). Although concurrently top leader of the Party, the military and the government, Jiang was overshadowed by the "supreme leader" Deng, before Deng's death in 1997, and enjoying little power-base of his own.

Nevertheless, as head of state, Jiang has been the principal spokesman, if not decision-maker, of the People's Republic of China's (PRC) policy with regard to the 1997 return of Hong Kong and the possible reunification with Taiwan. National unity has always been an aspiration of all patriotic Chinese. Inheriting a party-state which is rapidly losing its socialist character, Jiang's leadership seems to shift increasingly to Chinese nationalism as a source of appeal and legitimacy.

Wang Ke-wen

References

Bartke, Wolfgang. *Who's Who in the People's Republic of China.* Armonk, NY: M. E. Sharpe, 1991.

Jiangnan Arsenal

One of the first major endeavors of the Self-Strengthening movement in the latter half of the nineteenth century, the Jiangnan Arsenal was established by Zeng Guofan and Li Hongzhang in 1865 on the basis of several American and Chinese-owned factories in the Shanghai area. Together with similar establishments in Anqing, Nanjing (Jinling), and Tianjin, and the dockyard in Fuzhou, these projects constituted an attempt by the Qing government, or rather by its farsighted regional officials, to modernize China's military technology.

Zeng and his colleagues were deeply impressed, and alarmed, by the Western military strength they witnessed as they fought alongside Western troops during the suppression of the Taiping Rebellion. It was therefore natural for them to begin their modernizing effort in the wake of the Rebellion with projects that focused on fortified ships and powerful guns (*chuanjian paoli*). To an extent, the Jiangnan Arsenal was motivated by the burgeoning nationalism in the late Qing period.

The establishment of the arsenal was assisted by the Yale graduate Yung Wing, then a protégé of Zeng, who purchased machines from the United States for the arsenal. Ding Richang was appointed as the arsenal's first commissioner, with an American as chief supervisor and many other Westerners as engineers. The arsenal included three branches that manufactured machinery, guns, and ships. About two thousands workers were employed in the arsenal, making it one of the largest military industrial units in the world at the time. A translation bureau and a technical school were added in 1868 for the introduction of Western sciences.

That same year the arsenal produced its first steam-powered gunboat, the 185-foot-long *Yiji,* and another four followed in the next five years. In 1905 the shipyard was separated from the arsenal and managed independently. After the Revolution of 1911, the arsenal continued to operate under the new name of Shanghai Arsenal. It ceased operation following the January Twenty-Eighth Incident in 1932 and was demolished by the invading Japanese forces after their occupation of Shanghai in 1937. The shipyard, however, remained in operation throughout the war and after the Communist victory in 1949.

Wang Ke-wen

References

Kennedy, Thomas L. *The Arms of Kiangnan: Modernization in the Chinese Ordnance Industry.* Boulder, CO: Westview Press, 1978.

Ocko, Jonathan K. *Bureaucratic Reform in Provincial China: Ting Jih-ch'ang in Restoration Kiangsu, 1867–1870.* Cambridge, MA: Harvard University Press, 1983.

Wright, Mary C. *The Last Stand of Chinese Conservatism: The T'ung-chih Restoration, 1862–1874.* Stanford, CA: Stanford University Press, 1957.

Jiangxi Soviet

Reeling from the effects of Chiang Kaishek's new policy of anti-Communist suppression, which began in April 1927, leaders of the Chinese Communist Party (CCP) faced one of two alternatives—remain involved in underground political activities in urban areas or move to the countryside. Many who became the most important CCP political and military leaders in subsequent periods—Mao Zedong, Peng Dehuai, and Zhu De, among others—adopted the latter option. At first, the retreat to the countryside was regarded as a temporary expedient. But by 1928, after a series of failed attempts to seize power in urban locations, a new strategy took shape. Rural "base areas" were organized, the earliest centered on a remote location in the Jinggang Mountains, or Jinggangshan, straddling the borders of Hunan and Jiangxi provinces. At Jinggangshan, the first efforts of the CCP to organize the Red Army and carry out land reform took shape. In subsequent months, Mao and Zhu De abandoned the Jinggangshan base, and the newly formed Red Army moved its central focus of operation to a wider area in southeastern Jiangxi, bordering Fujian province. This new Central Soviet Base Area, or Jiangxi Soviet, became the central location of CCP efforts during the period from 1931 to 1934.

"Base area strategy," as the new rural-oriented policies came to be termed, involved a recognition by Mao and others that China's revolution for national salvation would have to begin from a set of rather unorthodox premises, at least according to prevailing views of the Moscow-based Communist International and a group of CCP leaders who had studied in Moscow, known as the "twenty-eight Bolsheviks." Disputes within upper-party leadership became endemic about who should be organized, the peasantry or the proletariat. Eventually, the decision was made to concentrate on the poor peasantry in a comprehensive program for political reorganization and land reform. To accomplish its new goals, the CCP also had to determine how best to link up with ongoing shifts in local power structures to build a successful revolutionary movement.

The complexities of recruiting new leadership at the local level suggest that the goals of national salvation, strong among the upper echelon of the CCP, may have been temporarily eclipsed in rural settings. In Jinggangshan, local bandit organizations had powerful leadership hierarchies, with the Hakka minority of the region playing an important part in such groups. There were also modern schools, where young intellectuals had been recruited earlier into Guomindang (GMD) or CCP membership. After a period in which the CCP recruited widely from evolving hierarchies of local leadership, it soon realized that the interests of diverse groupings in local society and their "natural" leaders—be they Hakka bandits, sons of local landlords, or rich peasants—might not be reconciled easily with the Party's larger nationalist goals. Party ranks therefore became purged as early as 1930, to eliminate uncooperative local leaders. The need to build a local leadership willing to focus on land reform and on a national war against imperialist aggression

would remain a constant struggle in subsequent periods of CCP organizing ventures.

Lynda S. Bell

References

Averill, Stephen C. "Revolution and Society in South China: Jinggangshan and the Jiangxi Revolutionary Movement." Paper for the Annual Meeting of the American Historical Association, San Francisco, CA, December 27–30, 1989.

Huang, Philip C. C., Lynda Schaefer Bell, and Kathy LeMons Walker. *Chinese Communists and Rural Society, 1927–1934.* Berkeley: University of California Press, 1978.

Kim, Ilpyong J. *The Politics of Chinese Communism: Kiangsi under Soviet Rule.* Berkeley: University of California Press, 1974.

Jinan Incident

In April 1928, the Guomindang's (GMD) Northern Expeditionary forces advanced into Shandong. The Japanese government, in order to safeguard Japan's special interest in that province, responded to the situation by reinforcing its troops stationed in Jinan, the provincial capital. The pretext of this action was to protect the lives of the Japanese in the city, but Japan was also trying to discourage the expansion of the GMD's rule, which she perceived as representing British-American interests, to north China. On May 1, the Northern Expeditionary forces entered Jinan and clashed with Japanese troops. On May 3, the GMD's special negotiator in Shandong, Cai Gongshi, was sent to negotiate the matter with the Japanese. Cai, together with sixteen of his assistants, were brutally tortured and murdered by the Japanese soldiers in Jinan.

The Jinan Incident, also known as the May Third Massacre, enraged the Chinese population and posed a dilemma to the GMD and its leader, Chiang Kaishek. The GMD had declared anti-imperialism as a principal goal of its "National Revolution," yet to confront the Japanese imperialist at this time would disrupt and derail the attack on the warlords, which was another important mission of the Party. Chiang, as commander-in-chief of the Northern Expeditionary forces, decided that completing the war against the warlords was the Party's most urgent task. He withdrew his troops from the city and made a detour in their northward march. The Japanese troops in Jinan, apparently dismayed by Chiang's reaction, launched a massive attack on the Chinese forces during the following days and occupied the city. Not until March 1929 did Japan, under the pressure of the Western powers, return Jinan to the new Chinese government under the GMD.

The tolerant attitude of Chiang and the GMD toward the incident caused popular anger and criticism in China. To many, including radical members within the GMD, this evidenced Chiang's abandonment of the anti-imperialist dimension of the "National Revolution." It was at least a mockery of the "revolutionary diplomacy" that the Party had been espousing since 1925. Avoidance of conflict with the Japanese did allow Chiang to concentrate on the final phase of the Northern Expedition and unify China by the end of 1928. The incident, however, together with the assassination of the Manchurian warlord Zhang Zuolin by the Japanese a month later, served as a reminder to Chiang and all Chinese that the immediate external threat to their country came from Japan.

Wang Ke-wen

References

Bamba, Nobuya. *Japanese Diplomacy in a Dilemma: New Light on Japan's China Policy, 1924–1929.* Kyoto: Minerva Press, 1972.

Iriye, Akira. *After Imperialism: The Search for a New Order in the Far East, 1921–1931.* Cambridge, MA: Harvard University Press, 1965.

Jordan, Donald A. *The Northern Expedition: China's National Revolution of 1926–1928.* Honolulu: The University Press of Hawaii, 1976.

Jinggang Mountains
See JIANGXI SOVIET

K

Kang Youwei (1858–1927)

Educator, philosopher, and political activist in late Qing China, Kang Youwei was best known for his advocacy of institutional reform, which culminated in the Hundred Days Reform of 1898. In his syncretic analyses of the Confucian philosophical heritage and in his patriotic political activism, Kang may be regarded as the founder of modern Chinese nationalism.

Kang was born into a scholarly family near Canton, where a prominent teacher stimulated his passion for classical studies. By the age of eighteen he believed that he could "be a sage," and "remake the world." Two years later, after an emotional crisis, he abandoned his orthodox studies, but continued to read avidly in Western materials and in the so-called New Text School of Confucianism. With eclectic scholarship, he began to create a rationale for institutional reform *(bianfa)*. His study in 1891 of the "false classics," allegedly forged during the reign of the ancient usurper Wang Mang, cast doubt on orthodox doctrines, and his *Tuogu gaizhikao (Confucius as a Reformer)* in 1897 argued that Confucius was not merely a transmitter of tradition, as conventionally held, but the creator of a new "teaching" (analogous to Christianity in the West) that encompassed all enduring truths. By drawing on an ancient notion of a succession of "three ages" from disorder toward a utopian Great Unity *(datong)*, Kang affirmed the idea of progress in China's past. Within this controversial framework he found the precedents necessary to build a modern society.

Following Japan's victory in the Sino-Japanese War of 1894 and 1895, a wave of patriotic indignation swept the country. In Beijing, Kang led 1,300 degree candidates in a petition to the emperor protesting the terms of the Treaty of

Kang Youwei. (Courtesy of Nationalist Party Archives.)

Shimonoseki (1895) and urging reform. In August he established the Society for the Study of National Strengthening *(Qiangxuehui)* and a newspaper edited by his student, Liang Qichao. Soon similar institutions spread through China's provinces as reformers urged discussion of nationalistic goals. Kang's career climaxed in 1898, as the foreign scramble for concessions precipitated a national crisis. Through the spring he pressed the throne for reform. The young Emperor Guangxu, captivated by Kang's eloquence, issued a series of reform edicts (June 11) and five days later received him for an audience. Under Kang's guidance, the decrees continued (for one hundred days) until the Empress Dowager Cixi's *coup d'état* on September 21 ended the reform movement. Kang and Liang fled to Japan and six reformers, including Tang Sitong and Kang's brother, were executed.

In exile for the next sixteen years, Kang worked to protect the emperor and promote constitutional monarchy. These efforts brought him into a losing rivalry with Sun Yatsen's Revolutionary Alliance *(Tongmenghui)*, which advocated the overthrow of the Manchus. By 1912 Kang's monarchist views had become anachronistic. Thereafter he devoted himself to promoting Confucianism as a national ethos and to the revival of the Qing dynasty. His support for the warlord Zhang Xun's two-week effort to restore the last emperor to the throne (1917) came as China was entering the May Fourth era of anti-Confucian nationalism. Kang spent his last years teaching at a private academy in Shanghai.

Charlton M. Lewis

References

Hsiao, Kung-chuan. *A Modern China and a New World: K'ang Yu-wei, Reformer and Utopian, 1858–1927.* Seattle: University of Washington Press, 1975.

Lo, Jung-pang, ed. and trans. *K'ang Yu-wei: A Biography and a Symposium.* Tucson: University of Arizona Press, 1967.

Kangda

The abbreviation of Chinese People's Anti-Japanese Military and Political University *(Zhongguo renmin kangri junzheng daxue)*, Kangda was founded by the Chinese Communist Party (CCP) in Yan'an in January 1937. Its predecessor was the Chinese People's Anti-Japanese Red Army University established a half year earlier in Wayaobao of northern Shanxi. The university, formally under the jurisdiction of the CCP's Military Affairs Committee, was planned as a training institution for Party cadres in an effort to rebuild the CCP in the wake of the disastrous losses it had suffered during the Long March.

Following the outbreak of the Sino-Japanese War in mid-1937, the university established twelve branches in the CCP base areas in north and central China and became an important instrument in the Party's wartime expansion. The main campus in Yan'an (later moved to the Taihang Mountains area) was especially useful in re-educating the many urban youths attracted there by the socialist *and* nationalist appeal of the

Kangda students in military training. (Xinhua News Agency.)

Communist movement during the War. Lin Biao (1906–71), Wang Jiaxiang (1906–74), and Xu Xiangqian (1902–93) successively served as its president. From 1936 to 1945, a total of eight classes graduated from the university, producing more than 100,000 graduates. Many of them later rose to important positions under the People's Republic. The school was renamed Chinese People's Liberation Army Military and Political University at the end of the war.

Wang Ke-wen

References

Harrison, James P. *The Long March to Power: A History of the Chinese Communist Party, 1921–72.* New York, NY: Praeger, 1972.

Koo, Wellington (Gu Weijun, 1888–1985)

Gu Weijun was a leading diplomat in twentieth-century China. Born to a wealthy family in Shanghai, Gu received a Western-style education in the city as a youth. Upon graduating from St. John's Academy in 1908, he traveled to the United States for advanced studies. In 1912, the year the Republic was founded, Gu received a Ph.D. in political science at Columbia University and returned to China.

Through the introduction of Tang Shaoyi, who later became his father-in-law, Gu worked briefly as the English secretary for President Yuan Shikai before he was transferred to the Foreign Ministry. In 1915, at age twenty-seven, he was appointed China's minister to the United States, Mexico, and Cuba. The young diplomat proved to be capable and popular, and apparently symbolized the new Republic in the eyes of the West. In 1919, Gu headed the Chinese delegation at the Paris Peace Conference which concluded World War I. However, since the Western powers at the conference agreed to Japan's succession to the German interests in Shandong, the delegation in the end refused to sign the Versailles Peace Treaty. After the conference, Gu stayed in Europe and assisted the formation of the League of Nations in 1920. That same year he became the Chinese minister to Great Britain. In 1921, Gu again represented China at the Washington Conference, where he defended China's sovereignty and territorial integrity, a novel concept to the Powers at the time, and obtained the partial return to China of the Japanese rights in Shandong.

From 1922 to 1927, Gu served in the cabinet of the Beijing government as foreign minister, finance minister and, from 1926 to 1927, as premier. Among the important diplomatic cases during this period were the Lincheng Incident of 1923 and the establishment of diplomatic relations with the Soviet Union in 1924. Gu's political prominence coincided with the warlord era, when the national government at Beijing was nothing more than an instrument of the militarist who happened to control the capital at the time. Despite domestic chaos and instability, Gu struggled to protect China's international status and image to the best of his ability.

Gu's close ties to the Beiyang warlords naturally made him an enemy of the Guomindang (GMD) government which reunified the country in 1928. After a brief period of exile overseas, he reached a rapprochement with the GMD through the mediation of the Manchurian leader Zheng Xueliang. In the wake of the Manchurian Incident of 1931, Chiang Kaishek appointed Gu foreign minister of the Nanjing government. Shortly afterward, he represented China at the League of Nations meetings on the issue of Manchuria, where his eloquent condemnation of the Japanese aggression moved the participants. Nevertheless, the final report of the Lytton Commission, organized by the league to investigate the incident, failed to satisfy China's wishes. When the second Sino-Japanese War broke out in 1937, Gu was the Chinese ambassador to France. He again represented China in seeking international mediation in the conflict at the Brussels Conference, but without success. Following the eruption of World War II in Europe and the fall of France, he was transferred to the post of Chinese ambassador to Great Britain. In that position he participated in the negotiation in 1941 to abolish British extraterritoriality in China.

In 1945, Gu was China's chief delegate to the organizational meeting of the United Nations in San Francisco, where he signed the charter of the United Nations on behalf of China. The next year he was appointed China's ambassador to the United States. As the GMD government was defeated in the civil war of 1946 to 1949, Gu was faced with the difficult task of pleading for support and assistance from an unsympathetic American government. He continued to serve as ambassador after the retreat of the GMD government to Taiwan and, in 1954, helped to negotiate the Mutual Defense Treaty between the United States and the Re-

K

public of China (Taiwan). Gu finally resigned the ambassadorship in 1956 and became a member of the International Court of Justice in the Hague. After retiring from that post in 1967, Gu moved to New York City and lived there until his death at the age of ninety-seven.

Gu's diplomatic career extended through the entire republican era. He worked to defend China's interests for a succession of Chinese governments from the Beiyang warlords to the GMD, providing a degree of continuity in China's international presence. Under some extraordinary circumstances he managed to secure a respectable place for his country in the world through peaceful and piecemeal efforts. In addition, he made significant contributions to the organization of both the League of Nations and the United Nations.

Wang Ke-wen

References

Chu, Pao-chin. *V. K. Wellington Koo: A Case Study of China's Diplomat and Diplomacy of Nationalism, 1912–1966.* Hong Kong: The Chinese University Press, 1981.

Tung, William. *V. K. Wellington Koo and China's Wartime Diplomacy.* New York, NY: St. John's University Press, 1977.

Korean War

See RESIST AMERICA AND ASSIST KOREA CAMPAIGN

Kung, H. H. (Kong Xiangxi, 1880–1967)

Financier and principal administrator in Guomindang China, H. H. Kung was born into a Shanxi family prominent in banking and business. He attended Western missionary schools in China, including the North China Union College, and then traveled to the United States where he graduated from Oberlin College in 1906 and received an MA in economics from Yale University in 1907. A devout Christian, Kung promoted Sino-American educational cooperation, particularly the Oberlin-in-China program.

It was in the political arena, however, where Kung would make his career. An active supporter of Sun Yatsen's revolutionary movement, Kung became tied to Sun through marriage in 1914, when Kung married Soong Ailing and Sun married her sister Soong Qingling. Kung served Sun in a variety of capacities, most notably in negotiating with northern militarists

on behalf of his Canton regime. Kung helped to arrange Sun's final journey to the north and was at Sun's deathbed in Beijing. Later, Kung assisted Chiang Kaishek with his negotiations with the northerners, garnering the support of Feng Yuxiang for Chiang's fledgling Nanjing regime. Kung also smoothed the way for Chiang's marriage to his wife's younger sister, Soong Meiling, thereby becoming connected to Chiang as well as Sun by marriage.

During the initial phase of the Nanjing Decade, Kung served as Minister of Commerce and Industry, promoting schemes to develop China's economy. In October 1933, Kung took over the position of Minister of Finance from his brother-in-law, T. V. Soong, a position he would hold for over one decade. Under his leadership, several critical financial steps were taken, including government seizure of the control of China's major banks in the spring of 1935 and the inauguration of a paper currency *(fabi)* reform in November 1935. The latter was a particularly significant step, as it took China off the silver standard and ended a deflationary economic crisis caused by a worldwide rise in silver prices. The move was costly, however; it earned the enmity of Japanese militarists, who saw *fabi* as challenging Japanese economic domination of China, and this fueled their desire to invade. It also opened the door to unrestricted issuance of currency, creating the conditions for China's disastrous wartime inflation.

Aside from his domestic duties, Kung became well known in the West because of his important foreign visits. In April 1932 he traveled to Europe to seek loans for China, and in 1937 he made two extended trips abroad in which he met with Roosevelt, Hitler, Mussolini, and other world leaders.

Although Kung can be credited with many achievements in buttressing the GMD government in China, his reputation today remains clouded. Kung has been blamed for the disastrous inflation which badly eroded morale in wartime China. In May 1945, he resigned his government posts, in part accepting blame for the situation. Communist writers have also criticized Kung as a "bureaucratic capitalist." Kung did, in fact, accumulate sizable wealth through his private economic activities, many undertaken in conjunction with his official roles in government banks and agencies. His wife, Soong Ailing, also developed a reputation as a speculator, using inside information, it was said, on the Shanghai currency, commodity, and stock exchanges. Whatever the truth of these allegations, Kung left for the United States in 1948. Although he made visits to Taiwan, he never joined his brother-in-law's government there.

Parks M. Coble

References

Coble, Parks M. *The Shanghai Capitalists and the Nationalist Government, 1927–1937,* 2d ed. Cambridge, MA: Harvard University Press, 1986.

K

L

Labor Movement

The modern Chinese labor movement has been closely linked with nationalistic factors in its three major layers of development, namely, ideology, organization, and mobilization. Although attempts at economic improvement motivated many Chinese labor collective undertakings from unionization to strike, bread and butter issues often could not be separated from the problem of imperialism in China.

Modern industries were first introduced into China through the treaty ports created by nineteenth-century "unequal treaties." In the modern Chinese industrial sector (which concentrated mainly in the foreign-dominated concessions and settlements), an ordinary industrial dispute between labor and capital could be easily turned into a Sino-foreign confrontation with obvious nationalistic overtones. Indeed, in late Qing and republican China, Chinese workers often became the country's frontline defense *vis-á-vis* imperialist encroachment.

Because of their strategic service functions and vital economic contribution, Chinese labor collective actions such as strike and boycott became a highly effective sanction against foreign interests. This had been demonstrated time and again in many large-scale, multiclass patriotic mobilizations, such as the 1905 to 1906 anti-American boycott, the 1919 May Fourth nationwide strikes, the 1925 May Thirtieth movement in Shanghai, the 1925 to 1926 Canton-Hong Kong general strike-boycott, and the spring 1927 retrocession of British concessions in Hankou-Jiujiang.

The labor movement was also a major asset for the political partisans of the Guomindang (GMD) and the Chinese Communist Party (CCP) which competed to maintain direct influence among organized labor. Each claimed the patriotic contributions of Chinese workers and their organizations as a vital part of their own revolutionary heritage. Sun Yatsen recruited the seamen and mechanics for his revolutionary activities from late nineteenth-century anti-Manchu attempts to the National Revolution of the 1920s. The GMD-CCP First United Front facilitated the dramatic rise of the radical labor movement in south China from 1925 to 1927. In turn, the growing influence of leftist labor also contributed to the United Front's premature breakdown in 1927 by posing a potent threat to domestic social control and to the economic interests of the GMD Right and its bourgeois allies, as well as to their rapport with the foreign powers.

The main arena of the modern Chinese labor movement seemed to be confined to a few major urban centers, but the real impact of labor collective action extended far beyond its narrow geographic base or relatively small numbers (in terms of total population). Labor events in Canton and Hong Kong, such as the 1922 seamen's strike, or in Shanghai, such as the 1925 May Thirtieth movement, at first might appear to have been isolated local labor incidents. However, they precipitated, indeed unleashed, the tidal force of massive waves of strikes and other organized labor actions that engulfed the whole Chinese society, with far-reaching domestic and even international consequences.

In fact, such labor events were not only significant to the workers themselves but had direct and crucial political, social, and economic repercussions in the shaping of the course of the modern Chinese revolution. For instance, the 1927 breakdown of the United

Front doomed the CCP's initial urban-labor strategy of revolutionary mobilization. Hence, its retreat to the countryside and its post-1927 rural-peasant-oriented strategy became natural and even inevitable. Later, in the civil war of 1946 to 1949, the CCP remounted an active urban-labor strategy in its campaign to return to the cities. During the 1927 to 1949 period, the GMD regime, fearing a reactivated radical labor movement, mainly adopted a demobilizational, even repressive control of organized labor and unionization. Yet it was not able to prevent the outbreak of strikes and other forms of collective labor action because of economic pressure, especially during the 1930s Depression and the post-World War II era of hyper-inflation.

In retrospect, the forces of nationalism, economism, and traditional/particularistic values (*i.e.,* guild mentality, local ties, and personal network) propelled the modern Chinese labor movement; its participants had a relatively weak sense of class consciousness and ideological maturity toward the classic Marxist-Leninist notion of proletarianization.

Ming K. Chan

References

Chan, Ming K. *The Historiography of the Chinese Labor Movement, 1894–1949.* Stanford, CA: Stanford University Press, 1981.

Chesneaux, Jean. *The Chinese Labor Movement, 1919–1927.* Stanford, CA: Stanford University Press, 1968.

Land Reform

For centuries the unequal distribution of land, and the resulting poverty of the majority of the rural population, had been a major source of social and political instability in China. Various peasant rebellions in country's history had identified the solution of the land problem as their primary goal, the most notable example of such rebellions in modern times being the Taiping Rebellion of 1850 to 1864. In 1905, Sun Yatsen's Tongmenghui included equalization of land rights in its four-points platform, but the Revolution of 1911 failed to address this issue.

In the 1920s, both the Guomindang (GMD) and Chinese Communist Party (CCP) called for land reform in their revolutionary programs. The GMD promised and briefly attempted to reduce land rents, but dropped the issue shortly after its capture of national power, fearing that the reform would threaten its rural political base. The CCP proposed a more radical solution to the problem, but alternated between violent land confiscation and moderate rent reduction programs in the areas under its control before 1949. Nevertheless, the CCP's promise to solve the land problem attracted for the Party continuous support from China's poor peasants.

As soon as the People's Republic was founded, the Communist government launched a nationwide land reform to eliminate landlordism and to realize a system of "land to the tillers." Guided by the Agrarian Reform Law of 1950, land was confiscated from landlords and rich peasants, and redistributed, on an equal basis, to poor peasants and hired hands. Middle peasants were largely left alone.

The reform was carried out in several stages: mobilizing the rural masses through the organization of peasant associations; identifying the rural classes (landlords, rich peasants, middle peasants, poor peasants/tenants, and hired hands); confiscating land and holding "accusation meetings"; redistributing land. During the three-year-long reform (1950–53), almost half of the country's agricultural land changed hands, and about 300 million peasants received land from the new government. But it was a bloody campaign backed by the coercive power of the state. An estimated five million people, labeled landlords or rich peasants, died by execution or in mob violence.

During the same period, a peaceful land reform was implemented in Taiwan, where the GMD had retreated after its defeat on the mainland in 1949. Pressured and assisted by the United States, the GMD launched, from 1949 to 1953, a land reform similar to the one that was being carried out in Japan under the American occupation. The reform began with a rent reduction to 37.5 percent of the main crop, followed by a sale of public land, and completed with the purchase of land from landlords by the government and the sale of such to landless peasants. As a result, about 90 percent of the agricultural land was tilled by its owners.

Thus by the early 1950s, China's age-old malaise of landlordism was finally cured, both on the mainland and in Taiwan. Together with it the power of the gentry elite, whose title had been eliminated in 1905 but whose economic base remained intact throughout the republican era, was also destroyed. It was a revolutionary change that forever reshaped the economic and political structure in the Chinese countryside.

Wang Ke-wen

References

Wong, John L. *Land Reform in the People's Republic of China: Institutional Transformation in Agriculture.* New York, NY: Praeger, 1973.

Yang, Martin M. C. *Socioeconomic Results of Land Reform in Taiwan.* Honolulu: The University Press of Hawaii, 1970.

Language Reform

Chinese language reform has been an ongoing process since the latter half of the nineteenth century. The reform included four major components: the phoneticization of Chinese, the simplification of characters, the promotion of a common spoken language, and the popularization of the vernacular.

Chinese orthography is unique in that it transcends time, dialectic differences, and even national boundaries. For thousands of years, Chinese characters survived phonological, lexical, and syntactic changes, and remained an effective communication tool for millions of Chinese who speak mutually unintelligible tongues, as well as for educated Japanese and Koreans.

Yet, interestingly enough, the reform of the Chinese written language has remained a continuing concern in modern China. The main efforts of the language reform are two-fold: to phoneticize the Chinese language and to simplify Chinese characters. Initially, these efforts were intimately linked to the social and technological changes that occurred in the late nineteenth century. After her humiliating defeat in the Opium War (1840–42), China began a period of zealous reform. In this period of national crisis, ardent nationalism went hand in hand with a sense of urgent need to emulate the West. Leading intellectuals advocated the phoneticization and simplification of the Chinese language in order to propagate literacy, the first step toward constructing a modern, scientific, and democratic China capable of resisting Western imperialism.

This period witnessed the first efforts to phoneticize Chinese, such as the Wade-Giles system of romanization and Lu Ganzhang's "new phonetic script." By the time the Republic was established in 1912, there were over twenty plans for reforming written Chinese, based variously on the use of basic strokes of the Chinese character, an English-like shorthand, or the Latin alphabet as vehicles of simplification. Various forms of phonetic substitution of written characters, such as the National Romanization *(Gwoyeu Romatzyh)* and the New Latinized Script *(Latinxua Sinwenz)*, were experimented with, but without much success. Paralleling the phoneticization effort was the attempt to simplify the characters by reducing the number of strokes. Qian Xuantong, for example, presented such a plan in 1922. Yet it was not until the establishment of the Written Language Reform Committee by the government of the People's Republic in 1954 that systematic planning and implementation of the simplification of written Chinese became a serious national effort. In 1964, a "General Table of Simplified Characters" was published, containing 2,238 simplified characters derived from 2,264 traditional characters. Today most of these characters are in general use in all People's Republic of China (PRC) publications.

Another facet of the language reform is the effort to promote a common spoken language. In the 1920s, the National Phonetic Alphabets for Mandarin Pronunciation were designed; it was a system of phonetic transcription in the primary schools to teach the national language *(guoyu)*. This system is still in use in Taiwan. In the PRC, the State Council issued a directive on the popularization of the common language *(putonghua)* in 1956. In 1958, the National People's Congress adopted the Chinese Language Phonetic Spelling Plan and promulgated what is now known as the *pinyin* system. It has been used in primary schools nationally as an aid for learning to speak *putonghua,* and as a basis for the creation of written languages for the national minorities.

The early part of the twentieth century witnessed another important shift in the use of the Chinese language. This was the vernacular *(baihua,* or "plain talk") instead of classical Chinese *(wenyan,* or "literary language") as the vehicle for writing. Advocates of *baihua,* such as Hu Shih and Chen Duxiu, suggested in the May Fourth era the creation of a national literature based entirely on the vernacular. Although the path from *wenyan* to *baihua* was a tortuous one, today most written Chinese texts resemble vernacular Chinese much more than they do classical Chinese.

Gregory K. K. Chiang

L

References

Seybolt, Peter, and Gregory Chiang. *Language Reform in China: Documents and Commentary.* White Plains, NY: M. E. Sharpe, 1979.

League of Chinese Left-Wing Writers

The 1920s witnessed the formation and collapse of the first United Front between the Guomindang (GMD) and the Chinese Communist Party (CCP). When the break came during the Northern Expedition of 1926 to 1928, many leftist intellectuals, siding with the CCP, launched a "cultural" offensive against the GMD by attacking the Nanjing government in their literary works.

In 1929, the CCP consolidated its control over the radical forces in Shanghai's literary circles. It decided to unify its followers and allies by forming the League of Chinese Left-Wing Writers. Instrumental to the league's birth was the Cultural Work Committee, headed by Pan Hannian, in the Party's Propaganda Department. At that time, CCP cells existed in various Shanghai colleges and high-schools, providing institutional support to the leftist intellectuals. The league's founding congress was held at the Communist-controlled China Art University on March 2, 1930. The founding members included Lu Xun, Mao Dun and members of the leftist literary groups, such as the Creation Society *(Chuangzaoshe)* and the Sun Society *(Taiyangshe).*

Another key component of the league, Tian Han's South Country Society *(Nanguoshe),* was also heavily represented in the League of Chinese Left-Wing Performance Troupes (later based on playwrights), a sister organization. Soon similar leagues of social scientists and fine artists were founded, many of which had overlapping memberships. In the same year, the CCP established a superordinate Chinese Left-Wing Cultural Federation, but the League of Chinese Left-Wing Writers remained the flagship of the Communist "cultural offensive." In 1931, ex-CCP general secretary Qu Qiubai assumed leadership of the league.

From 1930 to 1934, the league supported discussions on the "massification of literature," promoted resistance to Japanese aggression, and denounced the GMD government's revival of Confucian classics. In 1930, the GMD countered the development of leftist cultural organizations with its Nationalist Literature movement, which was immediately criticized by the league. In 1932, the league also battled the so-called third category of people, *i.e.,* liberal Marxists who resisted the politicization of literature. The league spawned various literary subgroups and a host of journals.

In 1931, the GMD stepped up its literary censorship and repression and executed five Communist writers of the league, later canonized by the CCP as the "five martyrs." Under the ultra-leftist leadership of Li Lisan and Wang Ming, the CCP ordered its writers to participate directly in political work and to stage open demonstrations, making them easy targets for the police. In 1933, the CCP headquarters were forced to leave Shanghai, and it became increasingly difficult to publish leftist journals. Individual league members turned to publishing their works, under pen names, in neutral newspapers and journals. In 1935, the GMD destroyed the CCP branches in Jiangsu and Shanghai, as well as its Cultural Work Committee. As a result, the Shanghai Communist underground lost contact with the Party center, then located in northern Shaanxi.

In December 1935, the league leadership received a directive from Moscow, which conveyed the idea of Wang Ming and Kang Sheng to disband the league in order to organize a broader cultural united front. The league was thus dissolved in the spring of 1936. The dissolution caused an open split between Lu Xun and Zhou Yang, the league leader. Nevertheless, during its six-year existence, the league was an important cultural arm of the CCP and laid the foundation of the Communist literary tradition in China.

Lung-kee Sun

References

Hsia, Tsi-an. *The Gate of Darkness: Studies on the Leftist Literary Movement in China.* Seattle: University of Washington Press, 1968.

Pickowicz, Paul G. *Marxist Literary Thought: The Influence of Ch'u Ch'iu-pai.* Berkeley: University of California Press, 1981.

"Leaning to One Side"

In 1949, as the People's Republic of China (PRC) was being founded, Mao Zedong declared that "the Chinese people must lean either to the side of imperialism or to the side of socialism. There can be no exception. There can be no sitting on the fence; there is no third path." The "New China," therefore, was to be on the side of socialism—and on the side of the Soviet Union. This policy of "leaning to one side" became the cornerstone of the PRC's foreign policy for the next decade and firmly placed the PRC in the Soviet bloc in the emerging Cold War.

Although not having been strongly supported by Moscow during the revolutionary years of the 1930s and 1940s, the Chinese Communist Party (CCP) nevertheless saw itself as belonging to the socialist world led by the Soviet Union. Moreover, the American assistance to the Guomindang during the civil war of 1945 to 1949 decisively alienated the CCP from the imperialist U.S., which left few foreign policy alternatives for the PRC in 1949.

In December 1949, two months after the founding of the People's Republic, Mao visited Moscow—his first and only trip abroad. There, with the assistance of Zhou Enlai, then premier and foreign minister, Mao negotiated with Stalin the basic terms of a close alliance between China and the Soviet Union. At the end of Mao's visit, on February 14, 1950, a Sino-Soviet Treaty of Friendship, Alliance, and Mutual Assistance was signed. The treaty restricted the two countries from taking hostile actions against each other, established a military alliance against possible attack by Japan "and her allies," and promised mutual economic aid. Accompanying the treaty were agreements that promised the return of Port Arthur, Dairen, and the Changchun Railway (Chinese Eastern Railway) to Chinese control, Soviet loans of $300 million to China over a five-year period, and Soviet technical assistance in China's industrialization and military modernization.

In the years that followed, numerous Soviet scientists, technicians and military advisers, totaling more than 40,000, were sent to China. They provided critical help in the early reconstruction of the PRC. By 1954, Moscow had agreed to help build 156 production projects in China, an integral part of the PRC's First Five-Year Plan (1953–57). In 1955, the Soviet Union began assisting China's nuclear development.

In exchange, China followed Soviet guidance closely on the international front. Soviet influence in all aspects of Chinese administration, society, and economy was evident. Textbooks in Chinese schools were translated from Russian; some 37,000 Chinese students went to study in the Soviet Union; and Russian arts and literature became popular among the Chinese.

Soviet assistance, material and otherwise, was much needed by the infant People's Republic, but the policy of "leaning to one side" inevitably tarnished the Chinese Communists' paradoxical claim to nationalism. China had finally "stood up," it seemed, but not yet on her own. The leaders of the PRC in the early 1950s apparently tolerated the humiliating image of a "Soviet satellite," and an image they finally shed with the Sino-Soviet split at the end of that decade.

Wang Ke-wen

References

Chai, Winberg. *The Foreign Relations of the People's Republic of China.* New York, NY: Praeger, 1972.

Nakajima, Mineo. "Foreign Relations: From the Korean War to the Bandung Line." *The Cambridge History of China,* ed. Roderick MacFarquhar and John K. Fairbank, vol. 14. Cambridge, England: Cambridge University Press, 1987: 259–89.

Left Guomindang

Origins of the Left Guomindang could be traced to the years of the First United Front between the Guomindang (GMD) and the Chinese Communist Party (CCP). As early as in 1925, shortly after the death of Sun Yatsen, the CCP had used the term to identify those GMD leaders who supported the GMD-CCP cooperation. Liao Zhongkai was the representative figure classified in this category. As relations between the two parties worsened and became tangled with the post-Sun succession struggle within the GMD, many GMD leaders came to be labeled as the "Left GMD" at one time or another. Stalin, whose orders determined the actions taken by the CCP and the Soviet advisers in China, for a while had high hopes for the elusive left-wing of the GMD to be the true partner of the CCP in the Chinese revolution.

The collapse of the United Front in 1927 was a severe blow to Stalin and the CCP, and a watershed in the history of the Left GMD. Following the demise of the leftist Wuhan regime, a group of GMD leaders questioned the new conservative line adopted by the Party's post-1927 leadership. They were again identified as the Left GMD. Some of them, such as Deng Yanda and Sun Yatsen's widow Soong Qingling,

L

still supported the United Front and went on a self-imposed exile in Europe. Deng later returned to China and organized the Third Party, which had little impact on Chinese politics in the late 1920s. Others, led by Wang Jingwei, succeeded in forming a powerful intra-party opposition to the conservative GMD leadership under Chiang Kaishek.

Wang and his followers had represented the GMD leadership during the United Front but had lost control over the Party in the political maneuvers that followed the demise of the United Front. In their attempt to recapture the Party, and to an extent speaking out of conviction, Wang's group openly criticized the corrupt and reactionary trends within the Party after the purge of 1927 and proposed to revive the radical line adopted under the United Front. Specifically, they advocated the continuation of anti-imperialism and mass movement. They vowed to fight a "two-front war," battling the CCP on the one hand and the conservatives in the GMD on the other.

Wang's group received an enthusiastic response from the rank and file members of the GMD, most of whom had joined the Party during the radical days of the GMD-CCP cooperation. The radical GMD members, calling themselves the Left GMD, soon challenged the legitimacy of the current Party leadership in Nanjing. In late 1928, Wang's followers founded the clandestine Association for the Reorganization of the Guomindang, which became the central organization of the Left GMD. Wang was its nominal leader, but the most important person behind the association was Wang's protégé Chen Gongbo. Total membership of the association was said to have exceeded 10,000.

From 1929 to 1930, the Left GMD led a series of unsuccessful political and military attacks on Chiang Kaishek's Nanjing government. These included a boycott of the GMD's Third Party Congress and armed revolts in collaboration with various regional militarists. The latter strategy, although practical in the short run, inevitably tarnished the Left GMD's image as principled revolutionaries. In late 1930, the Beiping regime—its last and most ambitious attempt to topple Chiang—again failed. Wang then ordered the dissolution of the Association in early 1931, and the Left GMD gradually lost its appeal as a radical alternative to the conservative rule of Nanjing. Later that year, Wang participated in another anti-Chiang coalition in Canton, but the term "Left GMD" was no longer mentioned. He

merely represented a personal faction.

Wang Ke-wen

References

Eastman, Lloyd E. "Nationalist China during the Nanking Decade, 1927–1937." *The Nationalist Era in China, 1927–1949*, ed. Lloyd E. Eastman. Cambridge, England: Cambridge University Press, 1991.

Wang, Ke-wen. "The Left Kuomintang in Opposition, 1927–1931." *Chinese Studies in History* 20, no. 2 (Winter 1986–87): 3–43.

Lei Feng (1939–62)

Lei Feng was a young Chinese soldier who died accidentally in 1962 and posthumously achieved national prominence as a model for Chinese youth. In March 1963, China's leader Mao Zedong, concerned about the ability of the next generation to sustain his Communist revolution and its goal of national regeneration, urged young people in China to "Learn from Comrade Lei Feng!" Over a thirty-year period, the simple but heroic Lei Feng became a familiar figure to several generations of Chinese. As perhaps the most enduring personification of Communist values (in particular, selfless service to the people and unquestioning obedience to the Communist Party) for Chinese youth, Lei Feng was the focus of an intense nationwide propaganda campaign in 1963 and again in 1977, 1983, and 1990. A recurring figure in Chinese literature and the media, he has in effect become part of popular culture in China.

Lei Feng was reportedly born into a poor peasant family in a village in rural Hunan during World War II. His early life was marked by a series of tragedies: his father was killed during the Japanese occupation of China; his brothers died of disease; and his mother is said to have committed suicide after being raped. Orphaned at the age of six, Lei spent the balance of the civil war period (1946–49) working for a local landlord and living in difficult circumstances. After the Communist victory in China, Lei Feng's situation improved dramatically: by 1956 he had completed his primary school education and become an active member of the Young Pioneers children's organization. He soon entered the work force and became a member of the Communist Youth League (CYL). In 1958, he distinguished himself repeatedly as a model worker and as a young politi-

The "Learn from Lei Feng" campaign. (Xinhua News Agency.)

cal activist, working briefly on a water conservation project and then volunteering to work, during the Great Leap Forward, at a steel factory in northeast China. In 1960, Lei Feng succeeded in joining the People's Liberation Army (PLA), although he did not meet the minimum physical standards, and through his determination became a model soldier (as a truck driver) and a member of the Chinese Communist Party. His military career was distinguished by his diligent study of the works of Chairman Mao, by his willingness to undertake all sorts of extra tasks and by his many "good deeds" on behalf of his fellow soldiers (such as secretly washing their clothes and helping to prepare their meals). Lei Feng died in August 1962 at age twenty-two when a truck, whose driver he was directing, backed into a pole which struck him on the head.

Although Lei Feng died more than thirty years ago, he has remained well-known in China, primarily because he has been periodically the subject of carefully orchestrated national propaganda campaigns. The first and by far the most successful of these mass campaigns occurred in early 1963, but its origins can be traced to the CYL activities in the fall of 1962

involving 500,000 young people in Liaoning, the province in which Lei had been stationed before his death. It was initially aimed at China's youth and was most vigorously conducted by CYL units in schools, the army, and youth organizations. The campaign reached a fever pitch in early March, when Chairman Mao and other Chinese leaders personally endorsed the movement.

Typically, the campaign in each region began with exhibitions about Lei Feng and "report meetings" on his life, followed by interactive CYL-led study sessions. These activities were supported by a mass media blitz about the hero, involving newspapers and magazines, which provided extensive material about the hero (including excerpts from his diary) and about the campaign (and in one case resulted in 30,000 letters from readers in two months); the publication of books and pamphlets; and specially prepared radio broadcasts, newsreels, slide shows, and dramatization. In particular, these materials emphasized Lei Feng's reliance on the writings of Mao Zedong (as his "compass"); his humility ("I am only a drop of water in the ocean"); and his service to the people (as a "rustproof screw"). By the time that the

1963 mass campaign to "learn from Lei Feng" subsided in May, it had involved many millions of Chinese youth in its activities.

In the aftermath of the chaotic Cultural Revolution (1966–76), Lei Feng reemerged as a model for Chinese youth, apparently whenever China's leaders were concerned about the ideological reliability and moral fiber of the next generation. In 1977, interim leader Hua Guofeng invoked Lei Feng to appeal to young people after the death of Chairman Mao and a successful struggle against the Gang of Four. In the early 1980s, Lei Feng's name was linked with campaigns for socialist ethics and against "spiritual pollution." In 1990, the CCP recycled Lei Feng yet again in its post-Tiananmen (1989) effort to deal with the ideological problems of China's youth. In addition, Lei Feng has remained an important figure in children's literature used for moral education in China's schools.

The posthumous treatment of Lei Feng in China has its roots in traditional Chinese history. In Confucian China the power of example (and thus the need to identify proper models for emulation) was a cornerstone of Chinese education. In revolutionary China the process of ideological education became much more intrusive, reflecting Mao Zedong's commitments to revolution and modernization and his ambivalence about the reliability of China's youth to continue his work. The availability of models such as Lei Feng and the Chinese government's nearly total control of the mass media appear to have encouraged the CCP leaders to believe that their vision of China could be inculcated in the young generation.

Martin Singer

Li Dazhao. (Xinhua News Agency.)

References

King, Vincent V. S. *Propaganda Campaigns in Communist China.* Cambridge: Massachusetts Institute of Technology, 1966.

Munro, Donald J. *The Concept of Man in Contemporary China.* Ann Arbor: University of Michigan Press, 1979.

Sheridan, Mary. "The Emulation of Heroes." *The China Quarterly* no. 33 (January–March 1968): 47–72.

Li Dazhao (1889–1927)

Li Dazhao was one of the early Chinese Marxists and co-founder of the Chinese Communist Party. Li was born Shouchang in Leting county, Hebei Province. He had studied law in Tianjin before engaging in the politics of the early Republic in Beijing, and associated himself with the Progressive Party (Jinbudang) under Liang Qichao and Tang Hualong. In 1913, Li went to Japan to study political economics at Waseda University in Tokyo, where he became further acquainted with Western political thought. Upon returning to China in 1916, a Beijing newspaper engaged him as an editor. At first he still worked for Liang and Tang, but he soon broke with them because of his harsh criticism of the Anhui Clique then in power. From this point onward, Li became increasingly radical, both intellectually and politically. He promoted democracy, attacked Confucianism, and became a leading advocate of the New Culture Movement. In 1918, Cai Yuanpei, then president of Beijing University, invited Li to teach economics at the university and to serve as curator of the university library.

During this period, Li came to be deeply impressed with the Bolshevik revolution in Russia and interested in Marxism. His writings in *New Youth (Xinqingnian),* the magazine of which he was editor, praised the revolution as a "victory of the common people" and confirmed the applicability of the Marxist agenda in China. He then participated in the May

Fourth movement in 1919 and debated with liberal reformers such as Hu Shih on the question of "issues versus 'isms.'" Li rejected Hu's plea for a careful study of specific issues concerning China before commitment to any "ism," and suggested instead that the adoption of an overall "ism" is essential to the understanding and solution of China's problems.

Li's enthusiasm for Marxism led to contacts with the Comintern agent Gregory Voitinsky and the establishment of one of the earliest Communist organizations in China, the Beijing Communist Group, in 1920. One of its members was Mao Zedong, then an employee at the library. Following the founding of the Chinese Communist Party (CCP) in 1921, Li was elected as a member of its Central Committee, and became active in coordinating party work and labor movement in north China. He also played a leading role, together with Liao Zhongkai, in establishing the first United Front between the CCP and Sun Yatsen's Guomindang (GMD). In 1922, under the instruction of the Comintern, he reached an agreement with Sun in Shanghai, which allowed CCP members to join the GMD "as individuals" and work with it for an anti-imperialist, anti-militarist "National Revolution." At the GMD's first party congress in Canton in 1924, Li spoke in defense of the necessity and benefits of this alliance. He was then elected to the Central Committee of the Guomindang.

Returning to Beijing, Li led the anti-imperialist student demonstration in the city that resulted in the March Eighteenth Massacre of 1926. He then became wanted by the Beijing government. In April 1927, while hiding in the Soviet Embassy, Li was arrested by the police dispatched by the Manchurian warlord Zhang Zuolin, who controlled Beijing at the time, and was executed at the end of that month.

As a political thinker and activist, Li had an important influence on Mao Zedong, the future CCP leader. His populist and voluntarist interpretation of Marxism is believed to have shaped Mao's early thought, and his contributions to party organization and the United Front were indispensable for the initial development of the CCP.

Wang Ke-wen

References

Dirlik, Arif. *The Origins of Chinese Communism.* Oxford, England: Oxford University Press, 1989.

Meisner, Maurice. *Li Ta-chao and the Origins of Chinese Marxism.* Cambridge, MA: Harvard University Press, 1967.

Li Denghui (Lee Teng-hui, b. 1923)

As president of the Republic of China (ROC) in Taiwan, Li Denghui is the first native Taiwanese president of the Guomindang (GMD) government since its retreat to the island in 1949.

Born in Taibei, Taiwan, Li grew up under Japanese colonial rule. In 1948 he graduated from the economics department at National Taiwan University, among the first to do so after the return of the island to China in 1945. Following a short teaching stint, he went to the United States for graduate studies and received a Ph.D. in agricultural economics at Cornell University in 1968. Li then returned to Taiwan and worked for the provincial government and for the U.S.-ROC Commission on Rural Reconstruction. Up to this time he had not pursued a career in politics. In fact he was under government surveillance because of his early connections with the Taiwanese Communist movement.

In 1972 Li, an agricultural specialist at forty-nine, was recruited by Premier Jiang Jingguo into his cabinet as part of Jiang's attempt to indigenize the GMD regime in Taiwan. Li's loyal and low-keyed service in the 1970s apparently impressed Jiang, and as Jiang succeeded to the presidency in 1978, he appointed Li as mayor of Taibei. Three years later Li was promoted to head the provincial government of Taiwan. Then in 1984, when Jiang's vice-president Xie Dongmin retired, Li, a "dark-horse candidate," was named by Jiang as the Number Two man in the GMD regime. Upon Jiang's death in 1988, Li became president of the ROC, thus ending the forty-year dynasty of the Jiang family on the island.

Li's meteoric rise to power has been viewed with suspicion by some and amazement by all. His lack of political experience seems to have been more than compensated for by self-confidence and a sense of mission. Meanwhile, many mainlanders worry that he may be secretly in favor of an independent Taiwan. In the early 1990s, Li was remarkably successful in removing or subduing his mainlander opponents within the GMD, and in establishing a cordial relationship with the Taiwanese opposition outside of the regime. Under his administration Taiwan has experienced unprecedented democratic reforms as well as a transformation of self-identity, but relations between the island

Li Denghui elected ROC President in Taiwan, 1996. (Courtesy of ROC Government Information Office.)

regime and the People's Republic on the mainland suffered setbacks following Li's high-profile visit to the United States in 1995. In March 1996, Li was reelected, in the first direct presidential election in Chinese history, as the President of ROC.

Wang Ke-wen

References

Tien, Hung-mao. *The Great Transformation: Political and Social Change in the Republic of China*. Stanford, CA: Hoover Institution Press, 1989.

Copper, John C. *Taiwan: Nation-State or Province?* 2d ed. Boulder, CO: Westview Press, 1996.

Li Hongzhang (1823–1901)

Li Hongzhang was a high official of the Qing dynasty, a leading modernizer, and a diplomat. Li came from a gentry family of Hefei, Anhui. Having studied under Zeng Guofan in Beijing,

he became a *jinshi* in 1847, in the same class as Shen Baozhen and Guo Songtao, with whom he had a good working relationship later in life. In 1853 Li, then serving as a Hanlin scholar, was ordered to return to his native province to organize a defense against the Nian and Taiping rebels. Being a pragmatic man more interested in action than in scholarship, he gladly accepted this assignment. His success led to numerous awards and a reputation for military leadership. His activities also gave him the opportunity to work once more with his patron, Zeng Guofan, in the capacity of a personal assistant *(mufu)*. In 1861, acting on Zeng's initiative, he organized a new army of Anhui men to defend the city of Shanghai and establish it as a base for the anti-Taiping campaign. In 1862, at the age of thirty-nine, he was made governor of Jiangsu, the province in which Shanghai was located.

Upon arrival at Shanghai, Li immediately recognized the challenge of the West. A sense of patriotism developed, one that was further fueled by a sense of shame because of China's backward military technology. He was determined to improve the quality of his troops to the level of the foreign-led Ever-Victorious Army, "to strive for self-strengthening," as he put it. His Huai Army *(Huaijun)*, increasingly armed with Western weapons and subjected to Western-style drill, eventually contributed greatly to the Qing victory as it tied down the best Taiping forces and protected the rich resources of Shanghai.

Though Li admired the West for its technology, he distrusted the foreigners' designs on China. He repeatedly refused their request to build railways in China. The telegraph, however, had a simpler technology and bore a lower cost, and he was prepared to have Chinese lines erected if Western demands became irresistible. But highest on Li's priority was the manufacture of modern arms: once the Chinese possessed the knowledge and the facilities for it, they could keep the Westerners at bay. He soon had three small arsenals built—the precursors of the arsenal at Nanjing and the Jiangnan Arsenal at Shanghai, both established in 1865. To insure Chinese mastery of the new science and technology, he had a school and a translation bureau attached to the Jiangnan Arsenal. To bring his efforts to their logical conclusion, Li also proposed to incorporate technology in the civil service examinations, to reorganize the traditional Green Standard Armies, and to replace the outmoded "water force" *(shuishi)* with a modern navy. These proposals proved too progressive for the Qing court.

In the administration of Jiangsu, Li's policies were largely consistent with those of the Tongzhi Restoration. Rehabilitation of war-torn areas and tax-rate reductions were the order of the day. But as his concern with the Western threat grew, he focused increasingly on the ways to develop the state's wealth and power. To that end, he, guided by his sense of realism, was prepared to countenance corrupt officials and plundering troops. But his realism also resulted in a more benign policy toward merchants, as he wanted them to compete more effectively with Western traders and recapture control over profits *(liquan)*.

Between 1865 and 1870, Li held several important posts, but his single most important accomplishment was the suppression of the Nian Rebellion in 1868. Then, two years later, while on his way to relieve the ailing Zeng Guofan, who was having difficulties settling the dispute with the French over the Tianjin Massacre, Li was made Zeng's successor as governor-general of the metropolitan province of Zhili. For a quarter of a century, Li held this all-important post and concurrently the office of the imperial commissioner of trade for the Northern Ports *(Beiyang)*. The powers inherent in these offices and their proximity to Beijing virtually turned Li, who was already experienced in dealing with Westerners and foreign affairs, into China's foreign minister.

Long tenure gave Li a unique opportunity to promote China's search for wealth and power. In 1872, he garnered merchant support to form a joint stock enterprise—the China Merchants' Steam Navigation (CMSN) Company—to challenge Western domination of the coastal carrying trade. Under the *guandu shangban* formula he proposed, the merchants were to enjoy considerable managerial autonomy under general government supervision. In the initial period up to 1883, the company, with Li's support, operated successfully. By 1876, it was in a position to take over the American-owned Shanghai Steam Navigation Company (with the help of Shen Baozhen). The CMSN Company became the model for other modernizing enterprises: the Hubei Coal Mining Company (1875), the Kaiping Mining Company (1877), and the Shanghai Cotton Cloth Mill (1878).

The search for wealth was soon superseded by the need to bolster China's defense as Japa-

Li Hongzhang. (Courtesy of Nationalist Party Archives.)

nese and Russian threats mounted. Li had admired Japan's transformation under the Meiji Constitution, and had wanted to cooperate with it against the West. Even after the Japanese invasion of Taiwan in 1874, Li still tried to come to terms with Japan over Korea, especially as the Russian threat loomed large.

China's inability to repel the Japanese on Taiwan sparked a major policy debate in 1874 and 1875. Li proposed further defense modernization through the purchase of more advanced warships, the manufacture of up-to-date weapons, modern military training, and the replacement of the old land and water forces by a modern army and navy. To improve China's economic base, he proposed mechanized mining of all sorts of minerals, establishment of textile mills, and the building of railways and telegraph lines. These were to be reinforced by examinations based on Western learning and the sending of students abroad. Few of Li's proposals enjoyed support and even fewer were put into practice. The campaign in the Northwest, as well as misplaced imperial priorities, diverted much-needed funds from these modernizing efforts. Nevertheless, some headway was made in the development of a northern fleet, the Beiyang fleet, after

1875 and a naval academy was established under his aegis at Tianjin in 1880.

After the Sino-French War (1884–85), Li's ability to promote industrial modernization suffered as his conservative opponents, the *Qingliu* critics, rose in influence. The CMSN Company was forced to undergo government investigation and reorganization. It declined as it came under bureaucratic influences and its profits were used to underwrite unrelated undertakings. Merchant support for the company quickly dissipated. After 1888, a lack of funds also frustrated Li's efforts at naval development. For the eventual failure to build a stronger naval force, however, Li's bias in favor of a defensive rather than an offensive approach is partly to blame.

After Japan annexed the Ryukyu kingdom in 1879 and posed real threats to Korea, Li adopted a more forceful Korean policy. To prevent the Japanese from gaining exclusive rights in Korea, he had the Korean government establish diplomatic relations with Western countries and, at the same time, build up its defense. Political instability and a palace coup in 1884 afforded Li the opportunity to move troops into Korea and strengthen China's hold on Seoul. In 1885, Li appointed Yuan Shikai as China's resident representative in Korea and, through Yuan, gained control over much of Korea's internal affairs. But the strong policy alienated the Koreans. Continued political instability gave Japan the opportunity to challenge China's position there. The ensuing Sino-Japanese War of 1894 to 1895 was largely fought with Li's resources. China's defeat therefore resulted in the loss of his personal prestige as well as his Beiyang fleet. Further, he was stripped of his honors and his governor-generalship, although he was appointed plenipotentiary to negotiate a peace treaty with the Japanese.

In 1896, Li represented China at the coronation of Czar Nicholas II. In Russia, he allegedly accepted a bribe and ceded to the Russians the right to extend the Trans-Siberian Railway across Manchuria to Vladivostok, thereby saving them a distance of more than 300 miles. After a period of service attached to the Zongli Yamen, Li was relieved of his duties during the Hundred Days Reform of 1898, only to be appointed governor-general of LiangGuang the next year. During the Boxer Uprising (1900), he, along with other southern provincial authorities, refused to follow an imperial order to wage war against the West and, instead, pledged to protect foreigners and their properties in their provinces.

By this act of disobedience, these officials had saved China from an even more disastrous international crisis. Also because of this action, Li became an obvious choice to represent China at the peace negotiations. Soon after signing the Boxer Protocol in 1901, he died.

Li's public life spanned half a century. His political astuteness combined with a sensitivity to the needs of the time made him an important political figure and a progressive reformer. Although a patriot beyond question, Li often allowed his realism to take precedence over Confucian or moral principles. He was willing to employ men without much regard for their moral qualities, and he himself, at least once, sacrificed Chinese interests for personal gains.

David Pong

References

Kennedy, Thomas L. *The Arms of Kiangnan: Modernization in the Chinese Ordnance Industry, 1860–1895.* Boulder, CO: Westview Press, 1978.

Liu, Kwang-ching, and Samuel Chu, eds. *Li Hung-chang: Diplomat and Modernizer.* Special issues of *Chinese Studies in History,* Fall and Winter 1990; Summer and Fall 1991.

Spector, Stanley. *Li Hung-chang and the Huai Army: A Study in Nineteenth-Century Chinese Regionalism.* Seattle: University of Washington Press, 1964.

Li Peng (b. 1928)

Li Peng was the premier of the People's Republic during the Tiananmen Incident of 1989. Born in Sichuan in 1928, Li was the son of Communist writer Li Shouxun, who was executed by the Guomindang government in 1931. Li Peng was then adopted by Zhou Enlai and his wife Deng Yingchao. In 1941, he went to Yan'an to study, where he joined the Chinese Communist Party.

Before his appointment as premier in 1988, Li Peng was involved since 1955 in developing China's national economy through the power industry. Trained as an engineer from 1948 to 1954 in the Soviet Union, Li assumed a variety of provincial-level and central posts in China (undoubtedly assisted by Zhou Enlai) charged with overseeing electrical power generation. Following the Soviet model, Li has always considered development of giant, costly hydroelectric projects as a key to the country's transition to a modern, industrial economy. Since becoming premier, Li has supported construction of the giant Three Gorges Dam on the Yangtze River in Hubei province that, with its planned eighteen million kilowatt capacity and proposed height of 175 meters, will be the largest hydroelectric project in the world and an object of considerable national pride—and expense.

During Li Peng's tenure as premier, China has also increased investment in prestigious military and high technology projects designed to enhance the country's international stature. China has emphasized development of major new weapons systems, such as a second generation hydrogen bomb that was tested in 1990, along with world-class lasers and supercomputers. China has also flexed its international muscle by continuing to sell major quantities of conventional arms on the world market, although its apparent sales of ballistic missiles and proliferation of nuclear material to unstable Third World countries, such as Iran, have come under increased international pressure, especially from the United States. In Li Peng's view, production and export of high technology weapons, rather than adoption of capitalist markets, would enhance China's international economic and political position as an emerging great power. Threats against the United States that failure to pass Most Favored Nation status for China would lead his government to boycott American products, such as Boeing aircraft, were aimed at demonstrating to foreigners—and the Chinese public—the country's growing economic strength in international affairs.

Li Peng has also promoted China's international standing, especially since the military crackdown in June 1989, with frequent travels abroad and invitations to foreign dignitaries to visit the People's Republic of China (PRC). Although still something of an international pariah because of his role in suppressing the 1989 democracy movement, Li has visited various Asian, Middle Eastern, and European countries, where demonstrating students protested his presence. Attendance at the United Nations summit conference in January 1992, where he briefly met with the American President and the Russian President, have all been calculated to associate the premier with China's growing international presence as an economic, political, and military power. Establishment of diplomatic relations with South Korea in 1992, visits to Beijing by British Prime Minister John Major to discuss the Hong Kong issue, and a visit to China by the Japanese emperor, reinforce the impression that during Li's tenure China has gradually emerged from its international isolation brought on by the Tiananmen Incident.

As a political hard-liner, Li Peng has also supported the propaganda campaign to denounce purported Western attempts to subvert China through "peaceful evolution" *(heping yanbian)*. A vitriolic and bold attempt to tap anti-foreign feeling in China, this ideological barrage has dominated much of the official Chinese press since 1989 in its reaction to international criticism of the Chinese Communist government's human rights abuses. Despite the widespread appeal of Western culture and values among average Chinese, Li and other hard-liners have consistently portrayed Western governments—especially the United States—in terms consistent with the Chinese Communist Party's (CCP) long history of anti-imperialism. Official statements condemning past Japanese atrocities committed in China during World War II, further associates Li Peng's government with traditional Communist nationalism. If Li Peng is ever to shed his image stemming from the June Fourth crackdown as the "most hated person in China," such raw appeals to nationalism may insure his political survival.

Lawrence Sullivan

References

Bartke, Wolfgang. *Who's Who in the People's Republic of China.* Armonk, NY: M. E. Sharpe, 1991.

Li Xiannian (1909–92)

A veteran Communist leader, Li Xiannian was president of the People's Republic from 1983 to 1988. A native of Hubei, Li received no formal education and worked as a carpenter before joining the Chinese Communist Party (CCP) in 1927. In the late 1920s and early 1930s, he led a small guerrilla force in Hubei, which later became part of Zhang Guotao's Red Fourth Front Army. Li participated in the Long March (1934–35) as political commissar of a unit under Zhang, who parted ways with Mao Zedong in Sichuan and entered Gansu, only to be attacked and his forces decimated by a local warlord. Li fled to Xinjiang and eventually rejoined Mao's forces in Shaanxi.

During the Sino-Japanese War (1937–45), Li worked to establish and expand the CCP base areas in central China, first in the Dabie Mountains along the Hubei-Hunan border and then in the EYuWanXiangGan (Hubei-Henan-Anhui-Hunan-Jiangxi) border region. He became a member of the Party's Central Committee at the end of the war and served as deputy-commander, under Liu Bocheng and Lin Biao, during the civil war of 1945 to 1949.

After the founding of the People's Republic, Li's first assignment was to consolidate the CCP's control in central China. He served as governor of Hubei and mayor of Wuhan. Then his responsibilities gradually shifted to economic affairs. In 1954, he was appointed minister of finance and then vice-premier in charge of financial and economic policies. Throughout the first Five-Year Plan, the Great Leap Forward, and its aftermath, Li remained in that position. His political fortune was not hurt by the upheavals until the outbreak of the Cultural Revolution in 1966. While only briefly criticized at the beginning of the Cultural Revolution, Li lost much of his power in the Party and government as Lin Biao and the radicals assumed total control. He was not ousted, but could perform only ceremonial functions in the late 1960s and early 1970s. Shortly after Mao's death in 1976, Li sided with his old military colleague Ye Jianying in orchestrating the coup that overthrew the Gang of Four.

During the uncertain post-Mao years, Li mediated between the rivals Hua Guofeng and Deng Xiaoping. When Deng returned to power with Li's assistance, Li was appointed vice-chairman of the State Financial and Economic Commission. In 1983 the CCP decided to reestablish the post of state chairman (president), which had been abolished since the purge of Liu Shaoqi in 1966. Deng selected Li, at 76, to head the Chinese state until he was replaced by Yang Shangkun in 1988.

Wang Ke-wen

References

Boorman, Howard L., and Richard C. Howard, eds. *Biographical Dictionary of Republican China*, vol. 2. New York, NY: Columbia University Press, 1968.

Bartke, Wolfgang. *Who's Who in the People's Republic of China*. Armonk, NY: M. E. Sharpe, 1991.

Li Yuanhong (1864–1928)

Li Yuanhong was the leader of the Wuhan revo-lutionary government in 1911 and president of the Chinese Republic during 1916 to 1917 and 1922 to 1923.

Born in Huangpi, Hubei, Li graduated from the Beiyang Naval Academy in Tianjin and later fought in the first Sino-Japanese War (1894–95). After the war he became a training officer in the New Army established by Zhang Zhidong, governor-General of Hunan and Hubei. When the Wuchang Uprising broke out in October 1911, Li was a brigade commander in the New Army stationed in that city. He accepted the leadership of the mutinying soldiers, with tremendous reluctance, after the uprising had gained initial success. Nevertheless, as head of the revolutionary government at Wuhan, Li emerged as a prominent leader of the Revolution of 1911. In January 1912, he became vice-president of the provisional government of the new Republic at Nanjing.

Li soon associated himself closely with Yuan Shikai, who replaced Sun Yatsen as president of the Republic in February. Later that year, he collaborated with Yuan in killing several Hubei revolutionary leaders. He again sided with Yuan during Sun's Second Revolution against Yuan in 1913. When Yuan attempted to make himself an emperor in 1915, however, Li refused to lend his support. He succeeded to the presidency following Yuan's death in 1916.

As president, Li came into bitter conflict with Premier Duan Qirui, leader of the Anhui Clique, on the issue of China's participation in World War I. In May 1917, Duan tried to coerce the parliament to pass his War Participation Act. Li retaliated by dismissing Duan from office, which provoked open rebellion by Duan's supporters in the provinces. In June, Li summoned the military leader Zhang Xun to Beijing to mediate the conflict. Zhang had his own political agenda. In July, Zhang staged a *coup d'état* against the government and supported the restoration of the deposed Qing emperor. Li took refuge in the Japanese Embassy, and yielded his presidency to vice-president Feng Guozhang. Weeks later, Duan Qirui defeated Zhang Xun and reestablished the Republic. Li, however, had lost his power.

After the first Zhili-Fengtian War (1922), the triumphant Zhili Clique attempted to legitimize its power in Beijing by restoring the old parliament and president before 1917. Cao Kun and Wu Peifu, the clique's leaders, invited Li to return from his retirement in Tianjin and resume the presidency. But Li was merely their puppet. In 1923, he was again forced out of office by the Zhili Clique. Shortly afterward Cao Kun bribed the parliament into electing himself as the president. Li spent his last years in Tianjin.

Wang Ke-wen

References

Boorman, Howard L., and Richard C. Howard, eds. *Biographical Dictionary of Republican China,* vol. 2. New York, NY: Columbia University Press, 1968.

Nathan, Andrew J. *Peking Politics, 1918– 1923: Factionalism and the Failure of Constitutionalism.* Berkeley: University of California Press, 1976.

Li Zongren (1891–1969)

Li Zongren was the leader of the Guangxi Clique and the acting president of the Guomindang (GMD) government in 1949. A native of Guilin, Guangxi province, Li joined the provincial army after graduating from a military academy, and rose steadily in rank during the warlord years of the early Republic. By 1920 he had commanded a significant portion of the Guangxi forces and become a threat to Lu Rongting, the ruler of the province. Relatively progressive in his political thinking, Li allied himself with Sun Yatsen's Guomindang in Canton in 1923. He then collaborated with two other military leaders in the province, Bai Chongxi and Huang Shaoxiong, in defeating Lu and uniting Guangxi under their leadership. Henceforth, Li was known as the leader of the Guangxi Clique, or, in distinction from the old warlord faction under Lu Rongting, of the "New Guangxi Clique."

Li's Guangxi forces marched into Hunan in mid-1926, which started the Northern Expedition of the GMD. As the United Front between the GMD and the Chinese Communist Party (CCP) began to disintegrate during the expedition, Li sided with Chiang Kaishek. In April 1927, he participated in the planning of Chiang's anti-Communist purge in Shanghai and subsequently carried out the purge in the territory under his control. When the GMD regime in Wuhan launched an offensive against Chiang's Nanjing regime later that year, however, Li pressed Chiang to resign and approached Wuhan for a peaceful settlement. In September, the Nanjing-Wuhan split ended after both sides had purged the Communists from their ranks, and Li's Guangxi Clique dominated the Special Committee that supervised the reunification of the GMD. The Committee was soon overthrown by Chiang Kaishek, who returned to power in early 1928.

When the Northern Expedition was completed in late 1928, the Guangxi Clique controlled, in addition to its home province, parts of south, central, and north China and posed a serious threat to the Nanjing government under Chiang. In 1929, Chiang's attempt to reduce the power of the regional militarists through the Disbandment Conference failed, and for the next three years the Guangxi Clique participated in every major military revolt against Nanjing. All of them were defeated by Chiang. Following the collapse of the last of those revolts, the Extraordinary Conference in Canton in 1931, Li retreated to Guangxi and joined with Guangdong in maintaining a *de facto* southwestern autonomy from Nanjing.

During the early 1930s, Li restored peace and order, as well as promoted social and economic development in Guangxi. Like Yan Xishan in Shanxi, Li seemed to believe that national reconstruction should begin at the provincial level—in other words, regionalism was a necessary step toward nationalism. In 1936 Hu Hanmin, the nominal leader of the southwestern autonomy, died. Expecting attacks from Nanjing, Li and the Guangdong leader Chen Jitang staged another anti-Nanjing revolt, known as the Guangdong-Guangxi Incident, using resistance against Japan as a pretext. The revolt soon failed.

With the outbreak of the Sino-Japanese War in 1937, the Guangxi Clique resumed cooperation with Chiang Kaishek and actively participated in the war. As commander of the Fifth War Zone and governor of Anhui, Li was credited with the largest victory won by the Chinese in the war, the Battle of Taierzhuang in 1938. During the last years of the war, however, the Guangxi Clique again kept a distance from Chiang's government in Chongqing. Guilin, like Kunming under the warlord Long Yun, became known as a center of liberal critics of the GMD.

After the war ended, Chiang appointed Li as head of the Beiping branch of the GMD government. While supporting Chiang's civil war against the CCP, the Guangxi Clique quietly competed with Chiang for political influence. In 1948, Li was elected vice-president of the Republic by the first National Congress, much to

Chiang's dismay. As Chiang's popularity declined with the losing of the civil war by the GMD, many viewed Li as a liberal alternative in the Party who might revitalize the GMD government through reforms. In January 1949, Chiang stepped down as president and Li succeeded him in the office. He tried unsuccessfully to negotiate a peaceful settlement with the CCP. In October, Li flew to the United States under the pretext of seeking treatment for his illness. Months later Chiang resumed the presidency in Taiwan, and the Chinese Mainland fell to the Communists.

From 1949 to 1965, Li lived in the United States as a political refugee. Homesickness as well as the appeal of the early reconstructions under the People's Republic eventually persuaded him to return to China in 1965, at the age of 74. He was warmly welcomed by the CCP government, but one year later the Cultural Revolution occurred. Protected by Zhou Enlai from attacks by the Red Guards, Li's health deteriorated. He died in 1969.

Wang Ke-wen

References

Eastman, Lloyd E. *Seeds of Destruction: Nationalist China in War and Revolution, 1937–1949.* Stanford, CA: Stanford University Press, 1984.

Lary, Diana. *Region and Nation: The Kwangsi Clique in Chinese Politics, 1925–1937.* London, England: Cambridge University Press, 1974.

Li, Tsung-jen, and Te-kong Tong. *The Memoirs of Li Tsung-jen.* Boulder, CO: Westview Press, 1979.

Liang Qichao (1873–1929)

Liang Qichao was an essayist, politician, reformer, and arguably the most influential intellectual in modern China. Born in Xinhui, Guangdong, Liang studied with the reform-minded Kang Youwei as a teenager and was deeply influenced by Kang's thought. He followed Kang and participated in the Hundred Days Reform of 1898, then fled to Japan when the reform failed. In Japan, Liang briefly contacted the revolutionaries under Sun Yatsen, but soon became their principal opponent in a series of political debates concerning the future of China. He favored establishing through reform a constitutional monarchy, with the Qing emperor Guangxu at its center, and opposed a violent republican revolution which he believed would lead the country to chaos and foreign domination. His journal, *Xinmin congbao* (The New People Miscellany), competed with the revolutionary *Minbao* (The People's Report) for support among overseas Chinese students.

Following a break with Kang Youwei's Emperor Protection Society *(Baohuanghui)*, Liang organized his Political Information Society *(Zhengwenshe)* in Japan in 1907 in support of the emerging constitutionalist movement back home. When the Revolution of 1911 replaced the Qing dynasty with a republic, Liang returned to China and became a party politician. Under President Yuan Shikai he led the Progressive Party *(Jinbudang)* in the parliament and served as minister of justice. He turned against Yuan in 1915, however, after Yuan announced his plan to make himself emperor. Liang was a major instigator and coordinator behind the successful anti-Yuan revolt in the Southwest, led by his former student Cai E. After Yuan's downfall, Liang returned to Beijing, where he headed the newly organized Association for Constitutional Research, later known as the "Research Clique." He again became active in parliamentary politics before retiring to an academic life at the end of the 1910s.

Liang was one of the major contributors to the introduction of the Western concept of nation to China. Between 1898 and 1903, in his widely read writings, he called the attention of the Chinese to the rebuilding of China on a nation-state model. His most celebrated series of articles, titled "On the New Citizen," suggested that the achievement of an organic society, the key of success to a nation, was founded on the consciousness of its citizens with regard to their rights and obligations to the state. As imperial China, a centralized empire, lacked such civic solidarity, Liang saw the country being fragmented into innumerable units along kinship, geographical, or occupational lines. He called for the creation of a conciousness of the citizenry among Chinese in constructing a genuine Chinese nation.

Liang was, therefore, puzzled and dismayed by the approach to nation-building advocated by the anti-Manchu revolutionaries. The latter put ethnic consciousness before political awareness as the foundation of the nation; they argued that, in order to establish a new Chinese nation, the Manchus would have to be overthrown and their political power returned to the hands of Han Chinese. Liang was ambivalent about this approach at first, but after a trip to the United States in 1903 he decided that citizenry was more important than ethnicity in national formation. Historically, Liang pointed out, citizenry and ethnicity did not necessarily converge. In view of the multiethnic composition of the Chinese nation, and because of the presence of a foreign threat, it made more sense to him to promote a "greater nationalism" among the Chinese than a "lesser nationalism," *i.e.,* anti-Manchuism. For Liang, greater nationalism meant uniting the Han people with ethnic minorities such as the Manchus, the Mongols, and the Tibetans to form the Chinese nation-state. He identified the state structure as the only rational body that could resolve any potential conflict among the country's constituents. In other words, although rejecting ethnic consciousness as the necessary source of a nation, he nevertheless recognized its existence and subjected the individual conciousness of the citizenry to the collective rationality of the state. Liang's greater nationalism was not popular among the revolutionary Chinese during the last decade of the Qing, but the new republic quietly adopted it after 1911.

Liang's pioneering work in introducing Western thoughts and reexamining traditional Chinese culture moved a whole generation of literate Chinese from the 1890s to the 1910s. Although not an active participant in the New Culture movement, to the extent that the May Fourth youth regarded the liberation of the individual as essential to the liberation of the nation, Liang remained their intellectual mentor. In his last years he parted ways with the radical ideological currents of the 1920s, but even Mao Zedong borrowed his term "new people" *(xinmin)* in naming Mao's first revolutionary group in Hunan.

Chiu-chun Lee

References

Chang, Hao. *Liang Ch'i-ch'ao and Intellectual Transition in China, 1898–1907.* Cambridge, MA: Harvard University Press, 1971.

Huang, Philip C. *Liang Ch'i-ch'ao and Modern Chinese Liberalism.* Seattle: University of Washington Press, 1972.

Levenson, Joseph R. *Liang ch'i-ch'ao and the Mind of Modern China,* 2d ed. Berkeley: University of California Press, 1970.

Liang Shuming (1898–1988)

Leading Chinese philosopher, ardent advocate of Confucian relevance to modern society, and promoter of the Rural Reconstruction movement, Liang Shuming, called by some "the last Confucian," defended the importance of Confucian culture when the demand for learning from the West swept the Chinese intellectual scene. Unlike the late Qing conservatives who saw Confucian culture as an indigenous Chinese tradition, Liang Shuming evaluated Confucian culture from a global perspective. He argued that Confucian humanism could enrich the human soul in an increasingly dehumanized technological world.

To some extent, Liang's lifelong defense of Confucian culture was a continuation of where his father, Liang Ji, had left off. Liang Ji stunned the Chinese intellectual world by drowning himself in Beijing's Pure Dharma Lake in 1919. Before his death, Liang Ji was said to have been upset by what he saw in China after the Revolution of 1911. His suicide was widely interpreted as a martyrdom for the dying Confucian culture.

Born to a scholar-gentry family in Beijing, Liang Shuming spent his early years studying Buddhism, not Confucianism. He was first known to the academic world as a Buddhist scholar. Beginning in 1917, he taught Buddhist studies at the prestigious Beijing University for several years and wrote two books on Indian Buddhism.

At the age of twenty-eight, the precocious Liang had already written the first important book in his life: *Eastern and Western Cultures and Their Philosophies (Dongxi wenhua jiqi zhexue,* 1921). Written at a time when the Chinese were concerned about the destructive power of science, Liang devoted his book to discussing the three stages of human development—man's conquest of nature, man's harmony with nature, and man's negation of nature. Liang equated these three stages of human development with three cultures in the world—the Western culture of material acquisition, the Chinese Confucian culture of moderation, and the Indian Buddhist culture of withdrawal. With the bankruptcy of Western science already in sight, Liang proclaimed that the Chinese Confucian culture would soon be the world culture.

Liang Shuming not only theorized about the revival of the Confucian culture but also worked to materialize his vision by engaging himself in rural construction. Between 1929 and 1937, Liang visited rural villages in Hunan and Shandong to establish village communities modeled after ancient Chinese practices. For Liang, the aim of rural reconstruction was not to bring modern conveniences and technical expertise to backward rural areas. Rather, rural reconstruction was a "Confucian modernization" aimed at forming communal organizations among villagers. Such organizations would allow villagers to meet their common needs without reliance on Western technology and government support. A mixture of self-government and pedagogy, the village organizations were to be informal, spontaneous, and spiritually uplifting. Everything would revolve around schools where teachers steeped in Confucian classics would provide the leadership. Although there were still problems to be resolved, Liang proved the plausibility of his version of rural reconstruction in his management of Zouping county in Shandong.

Politically, Liang Shuming adopted the traditional role of a Confucian scholar by serving as an independent critic of the government. During the Sino-Japanese War (1937–45) and the civil war (1946–49), Liang led a bipartisan group to keep the Goumindang and the Communists in dialogue. After 1949, Liang distinguished himself by being a daring critic of Mao Zedong's policies. For his criticism he was heavily attacked by the Chinese Communist Party (CCP) during the mid-1950s and the Cultural Revolution (1966–76). In death, Liang is remembered for his unbounded belief in Confucianism and his noncompliance with political coercion.

Tze-ki Hon

References

Alitto, Guy S. *The Last Confucian: Liang Shu-ming and the Chinese Dilemma of Modernity.* Berkeley: University of California Press, 1979.

Ip, Hung-Yok. "Liang Shuming and the Idea of Democracy in Modern China." *Modern China* 17, no. 4 (October 1991): 469–508.

Liao Zhongkai (1877–1925)

Guomindang leader and financier, Liao Zhongkai was the principal architect of the first Guomindang-Chinese Communist Party (GMD-CCP) United Front in the 1920s. Liao came from an overseas Chinese family. He was born in San Francisco and received his early education in the United States. Returning to China at the age of sixteen, he then went to Japan for university studies. These experiences in foreign lands stimulated a deep sense of nationalism in Liao. He was deeply disturbed, for example, by the anti-Chinese movement in California in the 1880s and 1890s, which led him to believe that only a strong China could protect her people from foreign discrimination. In 1905, he joined Sun Yatsen's revolutionary movement in Japan, but before the Revolution of 1911, his position in the Tongmenghui or in Sun's entourage was not prominent. Not until Sun organized the Chinese Revolutionary Party in Japan, after the failure of his Second Revolution (1913) against Yuan Shikai, did he recognize Liao's loyalty and talent. Liao became Sun's major assistant in financing the revolution and later served as *de facto* finance minister in Sun's Canton regimes in the late 1910s and early 1920s.

A westernized intellectual, Liao was also interested in modern ideological currents. As early as in the Tongmenghui period he had translated articles on Western theories of political economy and anarchism for *Minbao (The People's Report)*. In the May Fourth era he was again active in introducing socialist and democratic ideas into China, mainly through writing articles for Sun's magazine *Jianshe (Reconstruction)* in Shanghai. He engaged in a debate on the ancient Chinese "well-field system" *(jintian)* with Hu Shih and Hu Hanmin. Liao's interest in socialism may have partially accounted for his appointment by Sun, in 1923, as Sun's representative in negotiating an alliance with the Soviet Union and the Chinese Communists. The other reasons for this assignment was Liao's fluency in English and his familiarity with financial matters, which was an important part of the promised assistance from Moscow. Following a lengthy secret meeting between Liao and the Comintern representative Adolf Jaffe in Japan, Liao not only helped design the blueprint of the GMD-CCP United Front but he himself became a leading advocate for this new alliance.

From late 1923 to early 1924, Liao enthusiastically lobbied in the GMD for support for the United Front, and then played a key role in the Party's reorganization and the funding for a new military academy at Whampoa, both under Soviet guidance. He was also in charge of the GMD's new enterprise of labor and peasant movements; this soon gave him the reputation of being the leader of the Party's radical, or "left," wing.

When Sun Yatsen died in March 1925, Liao was a leading candidate for the succession to Sun's leadership. In July he participated in a coup that helped to consolidate the leftists' control over the GMD. Meanwhile, as finance minister, he worked aggressively to centralize the Canton regime's finance at the expense of the independent revenues of local armies. Both of these actions produced enemies for him. In August 1925, Liao was assassinated in Canton, allegedly by conservative GMD leaders in collaboration with army officers. His death provoked a purge of the Party's right wing by the Canton regime, now under Wang Jingwei and Chiang Kaishek, and polarized the Party for many years.

Liao was never a Communist, but his wife, He Xiangning, and son, Liao Chengzhi, later held prominent positions in the People's Republic.

Wang Ke-wen

References

Chan, Gilbert F. "Liao Chung-k'ai, 1878–1925: The Career of a Chinese Revolutionary." *Essays in Chinese Studies Presented to Professor Lo Hsiang-lin on His Retirement from the Chair of Chinese, University of Hong Kong,* 319–48. Hong Kong: University of Hong Kong, 1970.

Wilbur, C. Martin. *Sun Yat-sen: Frustrated Patriot.* New York, NY: Columbia University Press, 1976.

Lin Biao (1907–71)

Lin Biao was the military leader of the Chinese Communist Party (CCP) and Mao Zedong's designated successor during the Cultural Revolution. He was killed in an alleged coup d'état attempt.

Lin Biao was born into a well-to-do merchant family in Huanggang, Hubei. He entered the fourth class of the Whampoa Military Academy, from which he graduated in 1926, just in time to join the Northern Expedition (1926–28). During the expedition he served as a company commander in Ye Ting's famed independent regiment, and it was then that he became a full-fledged member of the Chinese Communist Party. He took part in the Nanchang Uprising staged by the CCP following the split between the Guomindang (GMD) and the CCP at Wuhan in July 1927.

Following the Communist commander

Zhu De, Lin went to join Mao Zedong at the new Soviet base in the Jinggang Mountains in May 1928. Lin fought well in the battles that defended the base against Chiang Kaishek's Bandit-Suppression campaigns and rose to be commander of the First Group Army in 1932. Together with Peng Dehuai, commander of the Third Army, and Dong Zhentang, commander of the Fifth Army, they led the only Red Army in the Jiangxi Soviet. During the Long March of 1934 and 1935, Lin and Peng's troops bore the brunt of the assaults from Chiang's pursuing forces until they made a rendezvous with the Fourth Front Red Army from northern Sichuan.

With the outbreak of the Marco Polo Bridge Incident in 1937, the formation of a second GMD-CCP United Front against Japan became a reality, and the Red Army was reorganized into the Eighth Route Army under the GMD government. Lin commanded the 115th Division, one of the army's three divisions. Lin achieved national fame for his victory over the Japanese army at the Pingxing Pass (along the Great Wall). During September 23 to 30, 1937, Lin's 115th Division scored a major victory by ambushing a Japanese convoy escorted by a force of more than one thousand men, killing almost all and taking only one prisoner.

Upon the Japanese surrender in August 1945, the CCP sent Lin to Manchuria, where he reinforced his army by recruiting from the Communist-held bases and by reorganizing the puppet troops of Manchukuo. He was also aided by the friendly Soviet occupation forces in taking over Japanese equipment and weapons. As a result, he forged a strong Communist force that was able to defeat the GMD in Manchuria, a major factor that led to the downfall of Chiang Kaishek's regime on the mainland.

Being always Mao's man, Lin sided with Mao in all intra-party struggles from the early 1930s to the Great Proletarian Cultural Revolution in the 1960s. When Peng Dehuai fell into disgrace in 1959, Lin took his place as defense minister of the People's Republic. In launching the Cultural Revolution, Mao turned to him for support. The military played a critical role in first assisting the Red Guards and later disarming them. Consequently, not only did Lin consolidate his power in the armed forces, he succeeded in making himself the revolutionary successor to Mao, which was written into the CCP constitution of 1969.

At the Lushan Conference in 1970, Lin bid unsuccessfully for the chairmanship of the State, a position vacated by Liu Shaoqi following Liu's purge in the early days of the Cultural Revolution. Too impatient to wait for natural succession to Mao's leadership, Lin resorted to conspiratorial activities, as evidenced by a document titled the "Outline of Project 571," planning for a military coup d'état and the assassination of Mao. When this attempt failed, according to the official CCP account, Lin flew out of the country with his family, but his airplane crashed near Undur Khan, Outer Mongolia, on September 13, 1971. All of those on board were killed. The incident, details of which remain a mystery to this date, is generally known as the Lin Biao affair.

The melodrama of Lin did not end with his death. His alleged conspiracy against Mao represented not merely a defeat and disgrace for Lin, but it pointed to Mao's failure as well. To many loyal Maoists in the Cultural Revolution, the Lin Biao affair was disillusioning. It revealed to them division and betrayal at the top of the revolutionary leadership. The CCP tried to remedy the damage that the affair had inflicted to its credibility by launching the "Criticizing Lin Biao and Confucius" campaign in the early 1970s. As it turned out, aside from criticizing Lin, the campaign became an innuendo attack on moderate leaders such as Zhou Enlai, Deng Xiaoping, and even Hua Guofeng, by the radicals in the Party. It did not conclude until the death of Mao.

Tien-wei Wu

References

Wu, Tien-wei. *Lin Biao and Gang of Four*. Carbondale: Southern Illinois University Press, 1983.

Lin Biao Affair

See LIN BIAO

Lin Sen (1867–1943)

Veteran Guomindang (GMD) leader and nominal head of the Chinese state from 1932 to 1943, Lin Sen was born in the coastal province of Fujian and received a new-style education in his youth. While working at the Maritime Customs in Shanghai in the early 1900s, he joined the Tongmenghui led by Sun Yatsen. During the Revolution of 1911, Lin led the revolt in Jiangxi and was subsequently elected speaker of the provisional senate when the revolutionary government was founded in Nanjing. In 1913 he was again elected into the first parliament of the Republic, leading the Guomindang that was newly organized on the basis of the old Tongmenghui. When President Yuan Shikai dissolved the parliament, Lin went to Japan and joined Sun Yatsen's Chinese Revolutionary Party in 1914. For the next two years he worked for the Party in America, promoting anti-Yuan activities among overseas Chinese. After the fall of Yuan he briefly returned to Beijing, but soon followed Sun to Canton to establish a regime that challenged the legitimacy of the Beijing government. From 1917 to 1924, he served in various prominent positions in the Canton regime and in Sun's "new" Guomindang.

When Sun reorganized the "new" Guomindang along Leninist lines in 1924, Lin, together with a number of other Party veterans, was deprived of much of was his power and influence to make room for the Party's new ally, the Chinese Communists. Shortly after Sun's death in 1925, Lin and more than one dozen Guomindang leaders organized the Western Hills Meeting in Beijing and openly attacked the GMD Party-government in Canton, then headed by Wang Jingwei, as pro-Communist. These veterans, later known as the "Western Hills faction," soon established their own Party headquarters in Shanghai. Largely inactive during the following year, the faction returned to the center of power in the wake of the Nanjing-Wuhan split during the Northern Expedition. Lin became a member of the Special Committee that presided over the reunification of the Party in 1927 and later vice-head of the Legislative Yuan in the Nanjing government. He cooperated with the Nanjing government under Chiang Kaishek until the Tangshan Incident of 1931, when Chiang placed Party elder Hu Hanmin under house arrest. The incident led to the Nanjing-Canton split, in which Lin was a leader of the Canton opposition. When the two sides of the conflict reached a rapprochement in 1932, Chiang resigned as chairman of the national government and, as a compromise to Canton, named Lin as his successor.

Lin held that prestigious post for eleven years, during which time he saw the GMD government engaged in pacification campaigns against the Chinese Communists, difficult negotiations with Japan, and finally a prolonged anti-Japanese war of resistance; yet he enjoyed little power. He was only a figurehead, while the real leadership in Nanjing, and during the war in Chongqing, was still in the hands of Chiang Kaishek. Lin was injured in a traffic accident in Chongqing in 1943 and died a few months later.

Wang Ke-wen

References

Boorman, Howard L., and Richard C. Howard, eds. *Biographical Dictionary of Republican China,* vol. 2. New York, NY: Columbia University Press, 1968.

Lin Shu (1852–1924)

Lin Shu was a pioneer translator of Western literature in modern China. Born in Fujian province, Lin Shu (Qinnan) received his *juren* degree in 1882 but failed in his attempts to pass the *jinshi* examination. In 1905, after establishing a reputation in literary translation, he became an instructor at the Metropolitan University (*Jingshi daxuetang*). When the institution was reorganized into Beijing University in 1912, he was appointed professor of literature there.

Although ignorant of Western languages, Lin developed an avid interest in the literary works of the Western world that were being brought into China during the late Qing. From the 1890s to the 1910s, he relied on the oral interpretation of others and "translated," in beautiful classical Chinese, more than 170 novels and stories from Europe and America. Among them were Alexandre Dumas's *La Dame aux Camelias,* Sir Walter Scott's *Ivanhoe,* Rider Haggard's *Joan Haste,* Harriet Beecher Stowe's *Uncle Tom's Cabin,* various works by Shakespeare, Dickens and Tolstoy, and such popular works as Aesop's fables and Arthur Conan Doyle's Sherlock Holmes stories.

Lin supported the Reform movement of the 1890s, but became increasingly conservative after the Revolution of 1911. During the May Fourth movement, he was outspoken in defending Chinese tradition and attacking the "New Culture," especially the vernacular literature. Nevertheless, Lin's translations influenced a whole generation of Chinese readers, including such well-known "New Culture" writers as Lu Xun and Shen Congwen. His introduction of Western literary styles and skills had a direct impact on the development of modern Chinese literature. In this sense, Lin played a critical role in the enlightenment of Chinese intelligentsia at the turn of the century.

Wang Ke-wen

References

Boorman, Howard L., and Richard C. Howard, eds. *Biographical Dictionary of Republican China,* vol. 2. New York, NY: Columbia University Press, 1968.

Lin Zexu (1785–1850)

Leading statecraft reformer in the late Qing, Lin Zexu's suppression of opium trade in Canton started the Opium War of 1840 to 1842.

Born in Houguan, Fujian, Lin received the *jinshi* degree at the age of twenty-six and was then appointed a Hanlin scholar. As a young junior official in Beijing, Lin associated himself with the Statecraft School (*jingshi xuepai*) that was influential among Chinese scholars at the time. He also helped organize the Xuannan Poetry Club, whose members included such reformist thinkers as Wei Yuan, Gong Zizhen, and Huang Juezi. After 1820, Lin climbed rapidly the bureaucratic ladder, partly reflecting a trend of increasing Han presence in the provincial bureaucracy of the Qing, and became governor of Jiangsu in 1832. In 1837 he was promoted to the post of governor-general of Hubei and Hunan.

When the issue of opium traffic arose in the 1830s, Lin emerged as a leading advocate for a total prohibition of the drug, as opposed to those who favored its legalization. In view of the financial drain the illegal opium importation was causing the Chinese empire, some officials suggested that China should try to abolish the ban of the drug and replace it with taxation and cultivation, so as to prevent the loss of silver to the West through the opium traffic. Lin, on the other hand, took a moralist approach. Opium was too evil a disease for China, Lin contended, to be treated simply as a financial issue. In addition to suppressing the domestic opium consumption with heavy punishment and forced rehabilitation, Lin proposed strict measures in dealing with foreign opium traffickers. His arguments apparently impressed Emperor Daoguang, who, in December 1838, appointed Lin as imperial commissioner for Frontier Defense with the special assignment of opium suppression in Canton.

Arriving in Canton in March 1839, Lin first tried to persuade by peaceful means the Western merchants there to stop the illegal opium trade. In a letter he wrote to Queen Victoria, Lin appealed to the British monarch with moral arguments. Seeing those efforts as ineffective, Lin ordered the seizure of foreign-owned opium and forced Western merchants to sign a bond promising a discontinuation of the opium traffic. Over 20,000 chests of opium were confiscated and subsequently destroyed in Canton. This hard-line policy led to the British attack in the following year, known as the Opium War.

As China suffered defeat in the early stage of the war, Emperor Daoguang reversed his militant foreign policy and sought compromise with the British by dismissing Lin from office. In July 1840, Lin was condemned to exile in Ili in central Asia. Lin remained in Ili, where he was put in charge of the Chinese colonization of the Northwest, until 1845. He was then restored to high offices and, in 1850, appointed once again as imperial commissioner charged with the task of coordinating the suppression of the rising Taiping Rebellion in Guangxi. Already old and ill, Lin died on his way to his new post.

In nationalist Chinese historiography, Lin is invariably portrayed as a loyal, conscientious, and capable scholar-official who first stood up against Western oppression of China. He has in fact become a symbol of modern Chinese patriotism. This image contains a degree of truth. However, Lin, like most of his contemporaries, was inexperienced in dealing with the West and overly confident of China's strength. In his reports to the emperor, Lin repeatedly predicted that the "barbarians" would not and could not fight against the Chinese empire. Such a view left the Qing ill-prepared for the coming military challenge.

This does not mean that Lin was ignorant of the West. While in Canton, he diligently investigated Western conditions and ordered the translation of many foreign newspapers as well as Vattel's treatise on international law. His *Sizhouzhi (A Survey of Four Continents)*, a partial translation of Murray's *Cyclopedia of Geography*, served as the basis of Wei Yuan's *Haiguo tuzhi (Illustrated Treatise on the Maritime Kingdoms)*. The latter work also used many other materials collected by Lin. Although not publicly advocating the emulation of Western weaponry, Lin purchased two hundred foreign guns to strengthen Canton's coastal defense and studied Western gunmaking. In this sense, he was a pioneer in practicing the late Qing reformist idea of "learning from the barbarians in order to control the barbarians" *(shiyi changji yizhiyi)*.

Wang Ke-wen

References

Chang, Hisn-pao. *Commissioner Lin and the Opium War.* Cambridge, MA: Harvard University Press, 1964.

Polachek, James. *The Inner Opium War.* Cambridge, MA: Harvard University Press, 1992.

Waley, Arthur. *The Opium War Through Chinese Eyes.* London, England: George Allen & Unwin, 1958.

Literature Revolution

The literature revolution was one of the most important events in modern Chinese history. Its impact on literature, and on the social, political, and intellectual outlook of twentieth-century China is beyond calculation.

Scholars usually attribute the origin of the literature revolution to Hu Shih's "A Preliminary Discussion of Literary Reform," which appeared in *New Youth (Xinqingnian)* in January 1917. Indeed, this essay by its most important leader initiated the movement. However, Hu had already formed the essential ideas of the new literature during the latter part of his sojourn at Cornell University (1910–15). The aforementioned essay was a more systematic expression of those ideas.

When the literature revolution first started, it lacked a distinct sense of nationalism. As time went on, nationalistic feeling became more apparent in the thinking of Hu Shih and other proponents of the movement. Initially, Hu's proposals concerning a reform of Chinese literature were prompted by the challenge that came from his conservative Chinese friends studying in the United States. A nationalistic consciousness set in when Hu began to elaborate his own ideas and decided that one of the practical functions of literature was to serve as an instrument of national modernization.

The central spirit of the literature is best expressed in a passage written by the journalist Huang Yuanyong and repeatedly quoted by Hu Shih: "We must endeavor to bring Chinese thought into direct contact with the contemporary thought of the world, thereby to accelerate its radical awakening. . . . The method seems to consist in using simple and simplified language and literature for wide dissemination of ideas among the people." A new literature was, then, to take the place of politics and everything else as the agent to achieve the transformation of China. This nationalistic sentiment inevitably created a utilitarian concept of literature, which had more to do with China's modernization than with literature itself.

As Hu Shih pointed out by quoting Huang Yuanyong, the medium to achieve change for China would be a vernacular language. This explains why "literature revolution" and "vernacular literature" have been synonymous in modern Chinese history. Hu Shih insisted that the history of Chinese literature be "simply a history of metabolism of languages (instruments)." A literature loses its vitality when its medium of expression is no longer capable of expressing the sentiments and ideas of the period in which that literature exists. Then a new medium of expression will rise to take the place of the old. This, Hu said, is what is called "literature revolution." "All the literature revolutions in history have been revolutions in instruments of expression."

The predominant mood of the literature revolution was utilitarian, and the concept of literature held by Hu Shih and his supporters was unsophisticated. Interestingly, however, the literature revolution had an enormous impact on just about every aspect of life in modern China. The adoption of the vernacular language made many endeavors easier: access to education, reception of Western thought, and expression of modern ideas. The new literature, written in the vernacular, carried with it a whole set of new values, views, and outlooks, all of which resoundingly rejected much of the old way. In a word, the literature revolution can be considered a centerpiece of the May Fourth intellectual revolution.

Min-chih Chou

References

Chou, Min-chih. *Hu Shih and Intellectual Choice in Modern China*. Ann Arbor: University of Michigan Press, 1984.

Grieder, Jerome B. *Hu Shih and the Chinese Renaissance: Liberalism in the Chinese Revolution, 1917–1937*. Cambridge, MA: Harvard University Press, 1970.

Liu Shaoqi (1898–1969)

Liu Shaoqi was one of the top leaders of the Chinese Communist Party (CCP), and chairman of the People's Republic of China (PRC) from 1959 to 1969.

Liu was born into a wealthy rural family in Hunan. Like many of his generation, Liu received a traditional education before entering the newly established modern schools. In 1919, Liu went to Beijing to learn French, as part of his preparation for the then popular work-study program abroad. Liu's plan to go to France, however, did not materialize. He soon participated in the activities associated with the May Fourth movement, organizing night schools for workers around Beijing and Tianjin. The winter of 1920 was a turning point in Liu's life: he became a member of the newly organized Socialist Youth, and then went to Shanghai to study Russian in preparation for a trip to Moscow. Between 1921 and 1922, Liu was a student at the Eastern Communist Labor University in Moscow. He joined the Chinese Communist Party (CCP) there in 1921.

Liu returned to Shanghai in 1923 and worked as a secretary in the CCP-led Chinese Labor Congress. He first demonstrated his organizational and strategic skills during the Anyuan Miners' Strike in September. After that he became one of the key CCP leaders in the labor movement, playing a major role in the May Thirtieth demonstrations of 1925 and the Hankou-Jiujiang Incident of 1927. In 1930, after the collapse of the first Guomindang-Chinese Communist Party (GMD-CCP) United Front, the CCP sent Liu to Moscow to attend the Fifth Congress of the International Red Workers. He stayed there for several months and became a member of the CCP's Central Committee at this time. In the fall of 1931, Liu returned to China and headed the Party's Labor Department.

Unlike other CCP leaders who worked in the urban centers, Liu developed flexible and moderate strategies for the mobilization of workers under the GMD rule. In 1932, Liu left the cities for the Jiangxi Soviet, where he was mainly in charge of labor. During the Long March of 1934 to 1935, Liu was one of the main supporters of Mao Zedong at the Zunyi Conference, which brought Mao back to the CCP leadership.

In 1936, Liu was appointed head of the CCP's North China Bureau. He reversed the old radicalism in Party work in that region and implemented the new moderate policy, which supported an anti-Japanese United Front across class and political lines. After the outbreak of the Sino-Japanese War in 1937, Liu demonstrated his ability to work under the United Front by successfully organizing the Anti-Japanese New Army in Shanxi and by creating CCP base areas in north China in a short period of time. In 1938, after Mao's initial attack on Wang Ming's Comintern line, Liu was briefly transferred to the Central China Bureau to enforce Mao's orders there. In the wake of the New Fourth Army Incident in 1941, Liu again headed the Central China Bureau and served as political commissar of the reestablished New Fourth Army. He saved the army and developed the CCP base area there under the most difficult situation.

Liu returned to Yan'an in 1943 to become a member of the CCP's Central Secretariat and vice-chairman of the Military Committee. During the Rectification campaign, Liu was Mao's most important assistant in eliminating Wang Ming's influence within the Party. Consequently, the Party recognized Liu as the model of "correct Party line" in the urban centers during the prewar years. He was chosen to revise the Party constitution, which was then adopted by the Seventh Party Congress in 1945. In the new constitution, Liu promoted "Mao Zedong thought" as the ideological guideline for the CCP. Liu himself was promoted to be Mao's deputy in the Party.

When Mao went to Chongqing to negotiate with Chiang Kaishek in August 1945, shortly after the end of the war, Liu served as acting chairman of the CCP. It was during this time that he helped to formulate an important strategy for the CCP: to move the Party's major forces to northeast China (Manchuria) in preparation for a civil war with the GMD. Throughout most of the civil war, Liu directed the land reform program in north China, which was critical to the securing of peasants' support for the Communist revolution.

Following the founding of the People's Republic, Liu continued his cooperation with Mao and maintained his position as the second-in-command in the CCP. With Mao's support, Liu defeated his intra-party rival, Gao Gang, in the 1950s. He succeeded Mao as chairman of the People's Republic in 1959, when Mao's Great Leap Forward had shown signs of being a disaster. While Mao retreated to the backseat, Liu was in charge of the daily affairs of the Party and the State. At the Lushan Conference of 1959, Liu firmly supported Mao's purge of Peng Dehuai.

By the late 1950s, Liu had been widely considered as Mao's immediate successor. It was also during this time, however, that Mao developed a profound distrust of Liu. In 1962, the Great Leap Forward was clearly a failure. In a speech at a Party conference in 1962, Liu identified human error as the main cause of the current crisis and considered the situation very serious. The speech reminded Mao of Khrushchev's de-Stalinist secret speech in 1956; Mao began to suspect that Liu might attack him one day as Khrushchev had attacked Stalin. Mao also regarded Liu's new economic policy, which reversed Maoist radicalism and promoted individual incentives for production, as capitalistic.

Mao's suspicion of Liu and other senior comrades was compounded by his concern about the problems of bureaucracy within the CCP, and by his anxiety over the loss of his credibility due to the failure of his programs. He soon developed a new theory of "class struggle under socialism," which warned against the threat of "capitalist-roaders within the Party." Still loyal to Mao, Liu tried to follow Mao's radical policies while preventing them from causing too great a damage. During the Four Clean-ups (Socialist Education movement) in 1964 and 1965, Mao saw the main theme of the campaign as a struggle between socialism and capitalism. Liu, however, insisted that the campaign was more complex than purely a class struggle. This disagreement led Mao to distrust Liu totally; he was now convinced that Liu was the leading "capitalist-roader within the Party."

In 1966, Mao launched the Great Proletarian Cultural Revolution to purge Liu and many other CCP leaders at all levels. Caught by surprise, Liu offered little resistance. He was placed under house arrest in 1967 and then sent to a prison in Kaifeng, Henan. In 1968 Liu was expelled from the Party. Lacking proper medical treatment, he died of illness in prison in November 1969. Ten years after Liu's death, and four years after Mao's demise, the CCP formally rehabilitated Liu at the Eleventh Party Congress in 1980. By then, the CCP leadership had been seized by Deng Xiaoping, Liu's close assistant in the early 1960s, whose post-Mao reforms echoed Liu's pragmatic economic policies two decades earlier.

He Gaochao

References

Dittmer, Lowell. *Liu Shao-ch'i and the Chinese Cultural Revolution: The Politics of Mass Criticism.* Berkeley: University of California Press, 1974.

MacFarquhar, Roderick. *The Politics of*

China, 1949–1989. Cambridge England: Cambridge University Press, 1993.

Liu Shipei (1884–1919)

A theoretician of nationalism and internationalism in the Revolution of 1911, Liu Shipei switched his support to the Qing government under circumstances that will probably never be fully clear. In his twenties, Liu attempted to combine a Rousseau-influenced conception of democracy, which evolved into a call for anarchism, with an anti-Manchuism which rested variously on a particularistic theory of Chinese racial identity and the universalistic notion that all peoples need freedom and equality. Liu saw his early projects as an extension of the works of seventeenth-century Ming loyalist Neo-Confucians, and he wrote not just for Chinese but of the human condition as such.

Liu's family had produced distinguished scholars for four generations in Yangzhou. They were leaders in the textual studies movement of the Qing, specializing in the *Spring and Autumn Annals* and with a particular interest in Ming loyalism. Liu's grandfather had edited, in the 1860s, the first collected works of Wang Fuzhi, whose explicitly racist theories stood out in the history of Confucianism. Liu obtained his *juren* degree at the young age of nineteen, but in the following year, 1903, failed the *jinshi* exams. He thereupon traveled to Shanghai just as the *Subao* case was breaking, and he became close friends with Zhang Binglin. Under the name of "Restore the Han (race)" *(Guanghan)*, Liu wrote and co-wrote a number of influential pamphlets and was involved in an assassination plot. He called for the expulsion of the Manchus on the basis that they were a people distinct from Chinese civilization as defined by geography and culture. Following Huang Zongxi, the Ming loyalist, and Rousseau, Liu also attempted to find the roots of democracy in China's ancient philosophy. He thus became one of the leaders of the widespread student radical movement.

A prominent leader of the National Essence movement as well, Liu not only resuscitated parts of the Chinese tradition which he thought people could use, but also used tradition to attack tradition. His utopian tendencies were expressed in his discussion of the pre-imperial Chinese state, and he became an anarchist in Tokyo in 1907 and 1908. However, he returned to China to work for the Manchu governor-general Duanfang at the end of 1908, and after 1911 supported conservative causes, including Yuan Shikai's attempt to become emperor in 1915. He taught at Beijing University, where he became one of the leading opponents of the vernacular movement, from 1917 until his death from tuberculosis.

Combining the roles of radical propagandist and classical scholar between 1903 and 1908, Liu simultaneously attempted to redefine the Chinese tradition by encompassing noncanonical philosophers and to point the way to a future without oppression by conducting a complete revolution. As a founder of China's anarchist movement, Liu criticized anti-Manchu nationalism as too narrow. The Manchus were a source of oppression and had to be expelled, but simply replacing the Qing with a government staffed by Han Chinese would solve no problems. Republicanism was flawed, because as monarchism and other forms of dictatorship rested on sheer force, so-called democracies, with little more subtlety, relied on the power of money, which gave domination to capitalists instead of aristocrats. Rather, a revolution of the whole people ought to replace government with cooperative forms of social organization. Liu and his wife, He Zhen, were perhaps the first Chinese revolutionaries to call for peasants to rise up in cooperation with workers. The origins of inequality lay in class, labor, and gender, but if people shared the process and the fruits of production on an equal basis, these distinctions would wither. They also taught that women's liberation was at root an economic question, though one encumbered with layers of cultural misconceptions. Liu presented a highly activist and voluntarist conception of revolution.

Liu's solution to Manchu oppression and to Western imperialism alike was not to strengthen the government, which would only continue to deprive the people of freedom and equality, but to liberate the energies of the people directly. Again, the destruction of capitalism was key. Anticipating in some respects Lenin's theses on imperialism (1916), Liu supported a pan-Asian populist rebellion which would forge links with Western revolutionaries to overthrow colonial and home regimes simultaneously. The solidarity of the weak would produce the circumstances in which the strong would collapse and allow an anarcho-communist society to emerge. Liu remained skeptical of reformism and republicanism his whole life, but when he turned away from radicalism, in supporting the emperor-system on the grounds that it was most in accord with China's traditions and non-activist government, Liu supported some of the most reactionary elements of Chinese society.

Like Zhang Binglin, Liu left a bifurcated legacy. His scholarship on Chinese literary and textual tradition continues to earn attention from Chinese scholars, while his political influence is a matter for historians to debate. But what to later ages appear to be contradictions between his radical and conservative impulses may be less puzzling when one realizes that to Liu, as to Zhang, politics and culture were inseparable concerns, and his politics were part and parcel of his scholarship.

Peter Zarrow

References

Bernal, Martin. "Liu Shih-p'ei and National Essence." *The Limits of Change: Essays on Conservative Alternatives in Republican China,* ed. Charlotte Furth, 90–112. Cambridge, MA: Harvard University Press, 1976.

Chang, Hao. *Chinese Intellectuals in Crisis: Search for Order and Meaning, 1890–1911.* Berkeley: University of California Press, 1987.

Zarrow, Peter. *Anarchism and Chinese Political Culture.* New York, NY: Columbia University Press, 1990.

Lone Battalion *(Gujun)*

See AUGUST THIRTEENTH INCIDENT

Long March

In October 1934, besieged by Guomindang (GMD) troops under the supreme command of Chiang Kaishek, the Chinese Communist leaders abandoned their central base area in Jiangxi Province. Their retreat to the northwest, lasting for approximately one year, became a seminal watershed in Chinese Communist Party (CCP) history known as the Long March. Of the 90,000 troops and estimated 30,000 civilians who departed from Jiangxi, only 30,000 survived the seven-thousand-mile journey across Hunan, Guangxi, Guizhou, Yunnan, Sichuan, and Gansu, arriving in northern Shaanxi in October 1935.

The Long March was of great importance on at least three counts. First, the sheer persistence of those who survived the retreat and its difficult battles became the Party's talisman during the next critical decade, as large numbers of peasants and intellectual émigrés, inspired by the Red Army's heroism, built a renewed revolutionary movement in the ShaanGanNing (Shaanxi-Gansu-Ningxia) base area, centered at the remote city of Yan'an. Second, it was also during the early phase of the Long March, at the historic meeting at Zunyi in Guizhou province in January 1935, that Mao Zedong secured his top leadership role, becoming CCP chairman. The importance of Mao's victory was that he established a firm foundation for his rural-based strategy for the revolutionary movement, defeating his principal rivals, most of whom had been members of the "twenty-eight Bolsheviks" with strong ties to the Comintern, who believed that the movement should be proletarian and hence, urban-based. Third, strong bonds of loyalty forged among the emerging top-ranking leaders of the CCP during the difficult months of the Long March secured leadership by a tight-knit, yet often internally feuding, group. These bonds, and the feuds which became endemic with them, would later form the foundation and central political dynamic of the new government of the People's Republic of China.

Nationalist aspirations played a key role in the deliberations of top-ranking members of the CCP concerning the strategy and course that the Long March should take. There was disagreement about the ultimate destination of the men and women who left the central base area. But the position that eventually won the day was shaped in large part by the fact that the northwest was rapidly becoming one of the most important points at which a war of resistance could be organized to fight against advancing Japanese troops. Warlord commanders in the northwest were either won over or neutralized *vis-á-vis* the Communists, as they realized the growing importance of the survivors of the Long March, along with their new peasant recruits and the nationalistically-inspired intellectuals who now flocked to Yan'an, in forming a stronger, more determined opposition to the Japanese. These growing sentiments coalesced in the Xian Incident of December 1936, when Chiang Kaishek was detained by a group of his own generals until he agreed to stop his war against the Communists in favor of a new anti-Japanese United Front.

Recent research has also demonstrated the

importance of the resistance efforts established by those left behind in various southern and central Soviet bases as the Long March was launched (with the period now increasingly referred to in CCP history as the "Three-Year War"). Although the men and women left behind faced a myriad of extraordinarily difficult situations, many of them remained staunchly committed to keeping the anti-imperialist, anti-feudal revolution alive, and provided the foundation upon which the CCP would launch its final battles against Chiang Kaishek between 1946 and 1949.

Lynda S. Bell

References

Benton, Gregor. *Mountain Fires: The Red Army's Three-Year War in South China, 1934–1938*. Berkeley: University of California Press, 1992.

Salisbury, Harrison E. *The Long March: The Untold Story*. New York, NY: Harper & Row, 1985.

Wilson, Dick. *The Long March 1935: The Epic of Chinese Communism's Survival*. New York, NY: The Viking Press, 1971.

Lu Xun (Zhou Shuren, 1881–1936)

Lu Xun was a leading writer and man-of-letters in modern China.

Zhou Shuren, pen-named Lu Xun, was born of a declining Zhejiang gentry family in the late Qing era. After briefly enrolling in naval and railway-mining colleges, he went to Japan in 1902 to study medicine. In 1906, he gave up medicine for literature, and later joined the anti-Manchu Restoration Society *(Guangfuhui)* in Tokyo. Returning to China in 1909, he taught biology and chemistry in Hangzhou. After the Revolution of 1911, Lu Xun moved to Beijing to work in the new republic's Ministry of Education.

In 1917, he resigned from the post and joined the editorial staff of the *New Youth (Xinqingnian)*, a leading iconoclast journal of the May Fourth era. He wrote for the journal the first modern Chinese short stories, which established the genre in language and in form. His social commentaries, often in bitterly sardonic tones, were immensely popular. He soon taught at various colleges, including the prestigious Beijing University. In 1926, Lu went south and eventually arrived in Canton, then under the control of the Guomindang-Communist United

Lu Xun. (Xinhua News Agency.)

Front.

When the alliance collapsed during the Northern Expedition (1926–28), Lu was stunned by the Guomindang's (GMD) bloody anti-Communist purges and left for Shanghai, where he spent the rest of his life. Beginning in 1930, Lu Xun headed the League of Chinese Left-Wing Writers, a Communist front, and was enormously influential in China's literary circles. Upon his death-bed, he split with the Communist leaders in the league, but the Chinese Communist authorities have sponsored a "Lu Xun cult" until this day.

Lu Xun is the most written about, yet most misinterpreted, intellectual figure in modern Chinese history. Official historiography in the People's Republic has embedded him in the Communist-led national liberation struggle: he is said to have evolved, intellectually and politically, from "petty bourgeois" evolutionism to the shining path of Marxism. Actually, the pre-1930 Lu Xun displayed a fin-de-siècle intellectual temperament. In his 1907 essays, he criticized nineteenth-century civilization for fostering crass materialism and mass democracy—a sentiment of the European decadents, which was irrelevant to China then. Lu Xun regarded fin-de-siècle thoughts, notably Nietzschean superman philosophy, as "laying the foundation of the twentieth century." He also favored Carlyle's "hero worship," the Byronic cult of genius, and Ibsen's war on the mob. His view of the "Satanic poets" as saviors of their nations smacks of Modernist celebrations of the marginal artist-rebel.

The weak and unstable republic that resulted from the Revolution of 1911 drove Lu Xun to pessimism. He lamented wasting outstanding individuals on a fruitless cause. The theme of "cannibalistic" masses devouring such individuals underlies his "A Madman's Diary" (1918) and "Medicine" (1919), which have since become classics in modern Chinese literature. Using a then fashionable imagery, he likened Chinese culture to a "syphilitic" heredity. "Degeneration," a familiar theme in Western fin-de-siècle literature, also appeared in Lu Xun's stories. He depicted his most famous creation, Ah Q (in "The True Story of Ah Q," 1921), as having "physical blemishes," which symbolized moral bankruptcy. Chinese culture, in his view, had perverted nature for too long. Salvation lay in the revival of "instincts" in order to save, if not oneself, at least the future generation.

Lu Xun's evolutionism suggested a similar fear of racial degeneration. His younger brother, Zhou Jianren, was among China's first eugenicists, whose views he supported. The fin-de-siècle irrationalism of Lu Xun vitiated against any naive belief in progress. This strain emerged most prominently in his early 1920s writings about the dream state, which betrayed symbolist affinities. He also applied Freudian insights to expose Chinese hypocrisy concerning sex. Even on the eve of joining the Communist cause in 1930, he surmised that "darkness" would still be present in the future "golden world."

Lu Xun's self-image was the anti-masses' "lone warrior of the spirit." Upon joining the League of Chinese Left-Wing Writers, he adopted a "Promethean" stance—self-sacrifice for the unworthy masses. The 1930s was the most politicized phase of his career; he combated the GMD government's campaign on "nationalist literature" and the apolitical "third category of people" in China's intelligentsia. He was also involved in the leftist massification campaign that advocated the popularization of Chinese literary form. This was the Lu Xun whom the Communists later glorified. Attack-

ing the dark reality of the GMD rule and helping the Chinese Communist Party (CCP) underground to escape government persecutions, Lu Xun achieved, by the time of his death, icon status in the book of Chinese Communism.

Lung-kee Sun

References

Lee, Leo Ou-fan, ed. *Lu Xun and His Legacy.* Berkeley: University of California Press, 1985.

Sun, Lung-kee. "To Be or Not to Be 'Eaten'—Lu Xun's Dilemma of Political Engagement." *Modern China* 22, no. 4 (October 1986): 459–85.

———. "The *Fin de Siècle* Lu Xun." *Republican China* 18, no. 2 (April 1994): 64–98.

Lytton Commission

When Japan moved into Manchuria following the Manchurian Incident of September 1931, the League of Nations agreed, at Japan's suggestion, to create a commission to investigate the origins of the conflict between Japan and China. It was headed by Lord Lytton of Great Britain and included representatives from France, Germany, Italy, and the United States. The commission spent six weeks in the spring of 1932 conducting its investigation in Manchuria and reported to the league in October, condemning Japan as the aggressor but calling on China to respect Japanese rights. In the meantime, Japan had established the puppet state of Manchukuo in March and had recognized it officially in September. The Lytton report evoked a wave of indignation in Japan; when the league adopted the report in February 1933 (by a vote of 42–1, with only Japan opposing), Japan's delegate, Matsuoka Yqsuke, walked out, and the following month Japan withdrew from the league. The episode stimulated rising nationalism in Japan and further isolated the country from the international community.

James L. Huffman

References

Thorne, Christopher. *The Limits of Foreign Policy: The West, the League, and the Far Eastern Crisis of 1931–1933.* New York, NY: Putnam, 1973.

M

Manchukuo (Manzhouguo)

Japan's puppet state in Manchuria (1932–45). This region had been under indirect Japanese control since the end of the Russo-Japanese War in 1905, when Russian leases were taken over by Japan. As a result, the South Manchurian Railway Company developed vast industrial operations in Manchuria, while the Japanese Guandong army occupied territories around the railway and exerted wide influence in the region.

When the Guandong army attacked Mukden, the largest city in Manchuria, during the Manchurian Incident of September 18, 1931, Japan initiated active plans to create a formal puppet state. The Western powers opposed these plans, and even Inukai Tsuyoshi's civilian government in Tokyo attempted to delay them in order to combat the army's growing independence. But Inukai's assassination on May 15, 1932, crushed government resistance, and, on September 15 of that year, the Saitō Makoto administration recognized Manchukuo as a sovereign state, with Japan assuming responsibility for its internal security and defense.

Under the agreement, Pu Yi, the last emperor of the Qing Dynasty (1644–1912) was made regent, and actual control of the state was placed under the General Affairs Board of the Guandong army, which had responsibility for approving laws and policies proposed by the nominal (Chinese) ministers of state. The General Affairs Board, in turn, worked under the Tokyo government's Manchurian Affairs Board. In 1934, Pu Yi was named emperor of Manchukuo.

The Manchukuo state consisted of the three Chinese provinces (Liaoning, Jilin, and Heilongjiang) that traditionally had made up Manchuria, plus Jehol Province in Inner Mongolia. It had a wartime population of more than 40 million, including 20,000 Japanese immigrant families and 2 million Koreans. From the mid-1930s onward, even its economy was dominated by the military, with the South Manchurian Railway Company losing its interests to the army-backed Manchuria Heavy Industry Company, and metals, minerals, and agricultural products being exported to assist in Japan's war effort. The Soviet Union invaded Manchukuo on September 9, 1945, and Pu Yi abdicated on September 18.

James L. Huffman

References

Duus, Peter, Ramon H. Myers, and Mark R. Peattie, eds. *The Japanese Informal Empire in China, 1895–1937*. Princeton, NJ: Princeton University Press, 1989.

Manchurian Incident

The Japanese attack of September 18, 1931, that led to Japan's occupation of Manchuria (northeastern China) is known as the Manchurian Incident.

As early as 1898, Japanese Prime Minister Yamagata Aritomo had formulated a "continental policy" for expansion into the Asian continent. On the eve of the Revolution of 1911 in China, another Japanese prime minister, Saionji Kinmochi, had formulated a new policy for Japan's sole domination over China. In 1912, Yamagata submitted his recommendation for the Japanese invasion of Man-Mon (Manchuria and Mongolia) as the first step toward continental conquest. Shortly after the outbreak of World War I, Japan presented to President Yuan Shikai of China the Twenty-One

Japanese troops entering Shenyang (Mukden), September 1931.

Demands, the core of which was the permanent occupation of Man-Mon by Japan.

Upon assuming his premiership in 1927, Tanaka Giichi vigorously pursued the policy of annexing Man-Mon, which was embodied in his "Tanaka Memorial." Implementing this policy, Japan intervened in Chiang Kaishek's Northern Expedition in Shandong in the Jinan Incident of May 1928. One month later, Japan's Guandong Army assassinated the Manchurian warlord Zhang Zuolin to prevent Chiang's forces from entering Manchuria. The latter incident, however, aroused criticism from the Japanese public and the Western powers, and the Guandong Army did not proceed to seize Manchuria immediately. Nevertheless, some Japanese historians see the assassination of Zhang as the origin of the second Sino-Japanese War (1937–45).

The Japanese continued to develop a plan for the conquest of Manchuria in the following years. Ugaki Issei, a Tanaka protégé, published his "Outline of My Views Concerning the China Question" in September 1928, and his "Judgment on the Situation in the Sixth Year of Showa" in April 1931, both of which addressed the issue of Man-Mon. Ishiwara Kanji, one of the young officer-plotters of the Guandong Army, wrote "An Outline on the Question of Manchuria and Mongolia" and "Plan for the Guandong Army's Occupation of Man-Mon." The latter two documents served as blueprints of the Manchurian Incident.

In 1931, the Guandong Army redoubled its efforts to make war preparations in Manchuria. In May it engineered the Wanbaoshan Incident over the clash of water rights between Chinese farmers and Korean immigrants near the Sino-Korean border. Then, in June, it exploited the Nakamura affair, in which a Japanese army captain on an espionage mission was killed by Chinese residents in the Xingan Mountains. By September, the Japanese military had decided to move ahead of schedule its original plan of launching the Man-Mon war within a year. To implement the plan, two documents were produced and adopted: "The Disposal of the Nakamura Affair Thereafter" and "Retaliation Measures in Case of the Nakamura Affair Unresolved." Accordingly, the Guandong Army fabricated the Liutiaohu case, claiming that the Japanese-owned railway there had been sabotaged by the Chinese, and initiated a military offensive against Chinese authorities on September 18.

Zhang Xueliang, who had recently succeeded his father Zhang Zuolin as ruler of Manchuria and had pledged his support to Chiang Kaishek's Nanjing government, ordered his troops not to resist, but to withdraw, in the face of Japanese attack. It has since been speculated that he was acting on Chiang's order. Without losing a single soldier, therefore, the Guandong Army seized Shenyang (Mukden), and within four months occupied all of Manchuria. The Nanjing government appealed to the League of Nations and the signatories of the Nine-Power Treaty, which had promised to respect China's political independence and territorial integrity, for mediation. The United States adopted a non-recognition policy but took no action to stop Japan. The league twice passed resolutions condemning Japan's invasion and demanding the withdrawal of her troops. In defying the league's resolutions and the report of the Lytton Commission, which the league dispatched to Manchuria for an investigation, Japan withdrew from the league in March 1933. China was left to deal with Japanese aggression by herself.

Tien-wei Wu

References

Iriye, Akira. *After Imperialism: The Search for a New Order in the Far East, 1921–1931.* Cambridge, MA: Harvard University Press, 1965.

Ogatao, Sadako N. *Defiances in Manchuria: the Making of Japanese Foreign Policy.* Berkeley: University of California Press, 1966.

Mao Zedong (1898–1976)

Leader of the Chinese Communist Party (CCP) and the People's Republic of China (PRC), Mao Zedong was one of the twentieth century's most influential revolutionaries. Mao is best known for his innovative approaches to the two modern Chinese revolutions: the New Democratic Revolution in 1927 to 1949, culminating in the establishment of the People's Republic; and the Socialist Revolution since 1953, culminating in the Cultural Revolution of 1966 to 1976. The leadership of Mao led to great success in the first revolution, but his role in the second was much less positive.

Mao was born in Hunan into the family of a rich peasant and grain merchant. After the Revolution of 1911, Mao briefly joined the Hunan New Army. In 1913, he entered a normal college in the province and received a college education in the midst of China's experiment with constitutional democracy, warlordism, and the New Culture movement. In April 1918, Mao organized a student association, the *Xinmin Xuehui* (New People's Study Society), to discuss urgent social issues. He was further exposed to the ideological debates on liberalism, democratic reformism, utopian socialism and anarchism when he went to Beijing University to work as a library assistant during 1918 and 1919. There he met Chen Duxiu and Li Dazhao, the leading Chinese Marxists of the day.

During the May Fourth movement, Mao was back in Hunan, where he became a leading figure in the local version of the national movement. He published a weekly, the *Xiangjiang Review,* to spread revolutionary ideas, including his newly acquired knowledge of Marxism. With five thousand copies each issue, the journal became the most important vehicle for intellectual liberation in Hunan. Mao also helped to establish the Hunan Student Association, which organized students' strikes against the Beijing government and mobilized a movement to expel the warlord governor, Zhang Jingyao.

In late 1919, Mao went to Beijing again and developed a close relationship with Li Dazhao. He joined Li's Marxist Research Association, and through its activities pursued further reading on Marxism. In 1920, Mao met with Chen Duxiu, who was organizing the Chinese Communist Party in Shanghai and asked for Chen's advice on the possibility of launching a revolution in Hunan. It is generally believed that he became a Marxist during this period. Upon his return to Hunan, Mao organized a Socialist Youth Group and a Communist Group in the city of Changsha. Consequently, he represented the Changsha Communist Group at the First National Congress of the Chinese Communist Party in Shanghai in July 1921, becoming one of the Party's founders.

In 1921 to 1923, Mao concentrated his work on organizing a labor movement in Hunan, then the major focus of the CCP. He then went to Shanghai to work for the Party's Central Committee, of which he became a member in 1924. When the CCP formed the first United Front with the Guomindang (GMD), Mao, as all the other CCP members, joined the GMD. At the First National Congress of the GMD in Canton in 1924, he was also elected a reserve member of the GMD's Central Committee, and later served as the acting head of the GMD's Propaganda Department.

In February 1925, Mao returned to his home village for a "sick leave." The sick leave gave him an opportunity to revisit and reevaluate the rural situations after a long absence. He soon developed an interest in the peasants, who constituted the great majority of China's population. Under Mao's leadership, Hunan became

M

one of the major peasant movement centers in the country, with more than two million peasants organized in peasant associations by the end of 1926. Mao himself was forced by the local government to leave the province in October 1925. He went to Canton and directed the GMD's Training Institute of Peasant Movement. With his newly acquired experience of peasant mobilization in Hunan, he became an expert and advocate of peasant movements in both the CCP and the GMD.

Two important writings which Mao produced during this period, "An Analysis of the Classes in Chinese Society" (December 1925) and "Report of an Investigation of the Hunan Peasant Movement" (March 1927), reflected the emerging theme of Mao's political orientations—relying on peasants as the major force in the Chinese revolution. When the United Front collapsed and the GMD purged the CCP in 1927, Mao participated in the CCP's August Seventh Conference and helped to reformulate the Party's strategy. Supporting the new Party line of land revolution and armed uprising against the GMD, Mao declared at the meeting, "political power grows out of the barrel of the gun!"

After the meeting, Mao returned to Hunan and organized the Harvest Uprising. The failure of that uprising prompted Mao to look for new approaches to revolution. Instead of following the Russian example of attacking urban centers, he decided to develop rural bases with peasant support. His creation of the "revolutionary base" in Jinggang Mountains marked a turning point for Mao and the CCP. Between 1927 and 1931, Mao displayed his creativity in inventing a formula for a mass revolution in China, which combined the use of rural bases, state structure, moderate and flexible land reforms, and guerrilla warfare. The formula was successful. The Jiangxi base under Mao's control became the CCP's Central Soviet Area in 1930.

From late 1931 to early 1935, however, the CCP Central Committee, then dominated by the "Twenty-eight Bolsheviks," or "internationalists," stripped Mao of much of his political and military power. The leadership denounced Mao's moderate land policies as "narrow empiricism" and his military strategies as "guerrilla bad habit." In 1932, they further criticized Mao as being opportunistic and ordered him to take another "sick leave." After the Central Committee moved from Shanghai to the Central Base Area in early 1933, Mao was totally excluded from decision-making in the CCP.

Mao did not regain his power and influence until the Zunyi Conference in January 1935, following the loss of the Jiangxi base to the GMD's Bandit-Suppression Campaigns. At the meeting, held during the CCP's Long March, Mao convinced other CCP leaders that he had a superior military strategy that would guide the Party out of the present crisis. He resumed membership in the Politburo and leadership of the Red Army. The Zunyi Conference was pivotal for the survival of the CCP and for Mao's political career. Thenceforth, his position in the CCP was never seriously challenged.

In 1936, Mao led the CCP to its new base in Yan'an, in northern Shaanxi. As the Japanese invasion in China intensified in the early 1930s, Mao and his comrades adopted the new strategy of organizing a national anti-Japanese united front. The question was how to deal with the GMD government and its leader, Chiang Kaishek. They finally took the position of *lianJiang kangRi* (cooperating with Chiang to resist Japan). When the Xian Incident occurred in December 1936, Mao and his comrades accepted the Comintern's advice and worked for the release of Chiang Kaishek, but they refused to criticize the rebelling generals, Zhang Xueliang and Yang Hucheng. The peaceful settlement of the incident opened a door for the formation of the second United Front between the CCP and the GMD.

The Sino-Japanese War of 1937 to 1945 was a critical period for Mao and the CCP. During the war, the CCP and the GMD joined hands to fight the invading Japanese. Guiding the CCP in the midst of rapidly changing military situations, Mao tried to maintain a balance between launching a revolutionary program to consolidate the Party's mass support and preserving the alliance with other Chinese who supported the war effort. He also struggled to contrast his position to that of the GMD and that of Wang Ming, his pro-Comintern intra-party rival. Mao distinguished the CCP's nationalism from that of the GMD by emphasizing wartime social reform and mass mobilization, and distinguished his line of leadership from that of Wang Ming by emphasizing the strategic interplays between class struggle and class compromise. He accused Wang Ming and the Comintern of supporting the second United Front at the expense of the CCP's revolutionary integrity.

Between 1941 and 1944, Mao launched a Rectification campaign in Yan'an to eradicate bad styles of leadership, dogmatism, bureaucratism, and factionalism within the Party. The main target of the campaign, dogmatism, was actually a code word for blindly following Moscow's instructions. As a result of this campaign, Mao won a total victory over Wang Ming and the Comintern, and consolidated his control of the CCP. In the seventh Party Congress in April 1945, Mao's political thinking was canonized as "Mao Zedong thought," the official guiding principle for the Party. He assumed all top Party positions at this time, which he held until his death.

At the end of the Sino-Japanese War, the CCP and the GMD prepared for a new struggle for the control of China. Under American mediation, Mao went to Chongqing, the wartime capital, in late 1945 to negotiate for peace with Chiang Kaishek. A peace agreement was signed, but neither side truly wanted a peaceful solution for postwar China. During the ensuing civil war, Mao demonstrated his political and military talents by designing a land reform program to mobilize peasant support while directing a series of successful major battles. This eventually turned the tide in the CCP's favor and led to the collapse of the GMD government. On October 1, 1949, Mao pronounced the establishment of the People's Republic of China and became its first chairman.

In the early 1950s, Mao built a solid foundation for the new state: controlling hyperinflation, implementing land reform, eliminating residual opposition to the government, and establishing national institutions. Mao also designed the PRC's basic foreign policy. In December 1949, he visited the Soviet Union, his first trip abroad, and signed a treaty with Stalin. The treaty formalized China's "leaning to one side," toward the socialist camp headed by Moscow, in the Cold War. The most critical foreign relations event Mao faced in the early years of the PRC was the Korean War. Perceiving the American military involvement in the Korean Peninsula and in Taiwan Strait as an immediate threat to the new Communist government, Mao made the bold decision of sending Chinese forces into Korea. The Korean War gave China credibility as a socialist power and brought in the badly needed Soviet aid.

A by-product of the Korean War was that it enabled Mao to launch the "Five-Anti" Campaign and impose greater control over the national bourgeoisie by creating a public consensus on the necessity of the socialization of businesses. The war also allowed Mao to initiate the Thought Reform Campaign in 1951 and 1952 and convert the intellectuals to Marxist doctrines.

Soviet aid was critical to the construction of China's economic infrastructure in the first Five Year Plan of 1953 to 1958, but it also brought the fundamental problems in Soviet-style "command economy" to China. Mao was aware of these problems, and he always tried to find an alternative to Moscow's model of socialist industrialization and development. In the early 1950s, Mao succeeded in transforming the Chinese economy into a socialist system. He carried out agricultural collectivization at a deliberately slow pace, which differed dramatically from Stalin's rapid and violent collectivization in the Soviet Union. The handicraft industries and commercial enterprises in the cities were also gradually and smoothly brought under state ownership.

Mao's innovative approach to socialist development experienced its first setback in the period of 1956 to 1957. Alarmed by Khrushchev's de-Stalinization movement in the Soviet Union, Mao was eager to avoid Stalin's mistakes. The unrest in Poland and Hungary in 1956 also led Mao to sense the need to deal with social discontent. In 1956, Mao delivered a speech on "Ten Major Relations," which outlined his new approach to socialism. He emphasized the importance of decentralization under a command economy and the lenient treatment of political dissenters. Opening public channels for criticism of the Party and the State, he declared, "let a hundred flowers blossom and a hundred schools of thought contend." The Hundred Flowers campaign, however, lasted for only two months in 1957. Some intellectuals' harsh attack on the CCP forced Mao to change his mind. He soon began a nationwide Anti-Rightist campaign to suppress critics. About 550,000 people were classified as rightists and prosecuted.

The Anti-Rightist campaign also intimidated the CCP cadres from thinking independently and speaking out. This unintended result directly affected Mao's next experiment: the Great Leap Forward. In order to speed up China's industrialization and transition to Communism, Mao resorted to what had proven to be the most effective instrument in his past revolutionary career: the mobilization of the Chinese masses. Mao launched the movement in August 1958. Impossible targets of production, exaggerated and false reports by the cadres, and the lack of incentives in the population to work in the people's communes caused a disastrous failure of the campaign. The failure led to huge famines in 1959–62, resulting in the deaths of 20 million people.

By the time the Lushan Conference convened in 1959, Mao had noticed the problems caused by the radicalism of the Great Leap Forward. Yet facing criticisms at the meeting from other Party leaders, such as Peng Dehuai, Mao felt threatened and purged all of his opponents. He especially suspected a possible alliance between his opponents and Moscow, where Khrushchev and his comrades also considered Mao's movement a mistake. Mao's behavior at Lushan was typical of his tendency to put personal power above national interest, although he would consider the two as identical.

In 1960, as the famine became obvious, Mao had to face the failure of the Great Leap Forward and admit his mistakes. He retreated to the "second line" of leadership, allowing Liu Shaoqi and Deng Xiaoping to take over the daily direction of government. Liu and Deng quickly reversed Mao's radical programs and returned to a policy of pragmatic economic development, which Mao considered as not being truly socialistic.

As Mao desisted from direct management of the economy in the early 1960s, he turned his attention to the issue of revisionism. Sino-Soviet relations were deteriorating at the time, and "revisionism" became a code word in China for Khrushchev's foreign and domestic policies. Mao worried that there might be "Chinese Khrushchevs" among top CCP leaders who would turn against him when they had an opportunity. In 1962, Mao called the CCP's attention to the importance of class struggle under socialism. He claimed that not only did the class struggle between proletarians and capitalists still exist in Chinese society, it also existed within the Party itself. A Socialist Education movement, launched in 1963 to eliminate corruption and revisionism among lower level cadres, failed to satisfy Mao.

Mao considered those CCP leaders, such as Liu and Deng, who disagreed with him on economic policy issues, as the most dangerous revisionists within the CCP. He also considered the existing Party and State apparatus as unreliable, because they were controlled by the revisionists. In 1966, Mao launched the Great Proletarian Cultural Revolution to seize power from the "capitalist-roaders within the Party." The Cultural Revolution represented yet another innovation in Mao's lifelong struggle against bureaucratism and capitalism. By mobilizing the Red Guards—mainly students, workers and peasants—to openly attack the establishment, Mao believed that he had found the ultimate democracy. Liu, Deng, and many other top officials were brutally attacked and purged. Taking their places were Lin Biao, the defense minister, Jiang Qing, Mao's wife, and a group of radicals loyal to Mao.

However, the Cultural Revolution quickly degenerated into social chaos. The Red Guards became divided and engaged in a power struggle among themselves. Each faction claimed to be the "real revolutionaries" and competed with others to take over the government. The expected great "social democracy" turned into a great terror. Not until 1969 did the nationwide chaos subside, when Mao ordered Lin Biao's People's Liberation Army, the only state institution still intact, to wrest control from the Red Guards.

The most constructive policy which Mao initiated during this period was to redefine the PRC's international position. In order to balance the increasing threat from the Soviet Union, Mao decided to enter a strategic alliance with the United States, which had been on the opposing side of China in the Vietnam War. At Mao's invitation, President Richard Nixon's 1971 visit laid the foundation for the normalization of Sino-American relations. Mao's rational approach to international relations formed a sharp contrast to his disorderly and tempestuous style in domestic politics.

The restoration of social order in the final stage of the Cultural Revolution precipitated new power struggles within the Party. In 1971, Lin Biao, Mao's designated successor, died in an attempted flight after the failure of his alleged plan to assassinate Mao. Thereafter, Mao had to maintain a power balance between the Gang of Four, the radical group led by Jiang Qing, and the senior and moderate leaders headed by Premier Zhou Enlai and the newly restored Deng Xiaoping. Popular discontent against the Cultural Revolution finally exploded in the first Tiananmen Incident of April 5, 1976. On his deathbed, Mao again removed Deng Xiaoping from power after hearing biased reports about Deng's connection to the incident. Mao died months later, leaving behind a country devastated by the Cultural Revolution.

Mao's last years contributed little positive input to China's development. Yet his concerns about the danger of bureaucratism, and of the oppression of people by power-holders, proved to be insightful. Unfortunately, Mao promoted a revolutionary, rather than democratic, way of treating the issue. His concerns, moreover, were sometimes put into the service of his power struggle against political rivals. Nevertheless, Mao built a unified, independent and reasonably prosperous China during the first half of his career, and, at least for a while, imbued the Chinese people with a spirit of idealism in their struggle for modernization.

He Gaochao

References

Han, Suyin. *The Morning Deluge: Mao Tsetung and the Chinese Revolution, 1893–1954.* Boston, MA: Little, Brown, 1972.
———. *Wind in the Tower: Mao Tsetung and the Chinese Revolution, 1949–1974.* Boston, MA: Little, Brown, 1976.
Terrill, Ross. *Mao: A Biography.* Rev. ed. New York, NY: Touchstone, 1993.

Mao Zedong Thought

Mao Zedong Thought is a political philosophy (broadly defined) developed by the Chinese Communist leader, Mao Zedong. The doctrine is said to represent the creative development of the principles of Marxism-Leninism based on the specific national conditions of China and the concrete practice of the Chinese revolution. Mao Zedong thought became the official ideology of the Chinese Communist Party (CCP) in 1945, and, following the CCP's nationwide victory in 1949, the state ideology of the People's Republic of China. It has also exerted a significant influence on Communist movements in Asia and elsewhere, including the Vietnam Communist Party and the Shining Path in Peru. Today, however, Mao Zedong thought is in decline in China, as Marxism-Leninism is throughout the world.

The origins of Mao's thought (the CCP seldom refers to "Maoism") lie in the theoretical and policy debates between Mao and certain Soviet-trained CCP leaders (for example, Wang Ming) in the early decades of the Party, from the mid-1920s to the mid-1940s. The Soviet-educated leaders argued that Marxist-Leninist theory, and importantly, the practical experience of the Bolshevik revolution of 1917, dictated a fairly quick seizure of power based on the CCP's leadership of the urban proletariat in such key cities as Beijing, Shanghai, and Canton. Mao, on the other hand, argued that in China it would be necessary to base the revolution on the vast peasant population (the "main force"); further, the revolution in China would take a relatively long time, *i.e.*, it would be a protracted struggle over several decades.

Following Mao's ascendancy in the CCP during the Long March (1934–36), his viewpoint came to be accepted as an important reformulation of Marxism-Leninism on the basis of the practical experience of the Chinese revolution. By 1943, Mao and other key party theoreticians, such as Chen Boda, had developed the concept of Mao Zedong thought *(Mao Zedong sixiang),* which was said to represent the sinification *(zhongguohua),* or the nationalization *(minzuhua),* of the original European form of scientific socialism. Following the eclipse of the Soviet-oriented leaders, Mao Zedong thought was designated the CCP's guiding ideology in the new Party constitution of 1945. To give the new term a distinctly Chinese flavor, and to help distance it from Marxism-Leninism, the CCP used the term *sixiang* (thought) rather than *zhuyi* ("ism"), an unmistakably foreign term that had been introduced into China via Japanese translations of Marxist-Leninist texts.

In an effort to form a broad national coalition to resist the Japanese, who invaded China in 1937, Mao put forward the concept of "new democracy" in 1940. He argued that, because of China's specific national conditions, the proletarian revolution would of necessity include the "national bourgeoisie" (mid-level capitalists), as well as the petty bourgeoisie, the proletariat and the peasantry. The national bourgeoisie, which was said to be progressive and patriotic, could help the Communist Party complete the tasks of the "national" (or "bourgeois-democratic") revolution and subsequently play a positive role in building socialism in China. The time-span required was left unclear, other than to note that it would be relatively long.

Following nationwide victory in 1949 (and even earlier), the CCP began to promote Mao Zedong thought (or, usually, Marxism-Leninism-Mao Zedong thought) as the creative development of revolutionary theory in the context of the nationalist, anti-colonial wars of national liberation in Asia, Africa, and Latin America. Further, China's peasant-based, protracted revolution incorporating the concept of new democracy was hailed as the model for all

Third World struggles, just as the Bolshevik revolution served as a model for the developed societies of the West.

Increasingly, from the 1950s on, the Soviet and other Communist parties (especially in Europe) denounced Mao's thought and the Chinese revolutionary model as examples of petty-bourgeois and/or peasant mentality infused with Chinese cultural and nationalist concepts of superiority. After the Sino-Soviet split in the early 1960s, the Chinese had some success in promoting Mao's thought as the theoretical basis of the current stage of the international revolutionary movement, but they had only limited success and the idea was downgraded (though not completely abandoned) after Mao's death in 1976.

In the 1990s, the CCP continues to promote Mao's thought as the ideological guideline of the Party, and the basis of building what is called "socialism with Chinese characteristics." Despite Mao's later failings, especially during the Great Leap Forward (1958–59) and the Cultural Revolution (1966–76), Mao Zedong thought continues to confer a certain degree of nationalist legitimacy on the CCP. Whether this will long remain the case after the passing of the original revolutionary leaders (few are active today) remains to be seen.

Raymond F. Wylie

References
Schram, Stuart R. *The Political Thought of Mao Tse-tung.* London, England: Praeger, 1969.
Starr, John Bryan. *Continuing the Revolution: The Political Thought of Mao.* Princeton, NJ: Princeton University Press, 1979.
Wylie, Raymond F. *The Emergence of Maoism: Mao Tse-tung, Ch'en Po-ta and the Search for Chinese Theory, 1935–1945.* Stanford, CA: Stanford University Press, 1980.

March Eighteenth Massacre

In early 1926, the Fengtian and Zhili forces launched a joint attack against Feng Yuxiang's Guominjun (National People's Army) in north China. A Japanese warship transporting the Fengtian troops was attacked by Feng's forces outside the port of Dagu. Japan, which helped the Zhili-Fengtian side of the war, immediately invited all the signatories of the Boxer Protocol of 1901 to send an ultimatum to the Chinese government in Beijing. The ultimatum demanded

cessation of the military conflict and the removal of the Dagu defense facilities, and threatened military intervention. On March 18, in protest against this ultimatum, an anti-imperialist mass meeting was held at Tiananmen in Beijing. The meeting called for, among other demands, the abolition of unequal treaties, the expulsion from China of the diplomats of the intervening countries, and the withdrawal of all foreign warships from Chinese ports. After the meeting, a crowd of about two thousand marched to the office of Duan Qirui, then provisional executive of the Beijing government, to submit a petition. The guards fired on the crowd with machine guns, killing forty-seven and wounding more than two hundred others. Most of the demonstraters were students.

The meeting and demonstration had been organized by branches of the Guomindang and Chinese Communist Party, then forming a United Front and supporting Feng Yuxiang in the war. After the bloody incident the Beijing government cracked down on the United Front and its leaders, such as Li Dazhao. The March Eighteenth Massacre was one of the largest acts of suppression by the government in the early Republic. It severely discredited Duan Qirui and reinforced the rising tide of anti-imperialism in China.

Wang Ke-wen

References
Strand, David. *Rickshaw Beijing.* Berkeley: University of California Press, 1989.

"March of the Volunteers" (Yiyongjun Jinxingqu)

One of the most popular patriotic songs during the 1930s and 1940s, later becoming the national anthem of the People's Republic. Written by Nie Er with lyrics by Tian Han, the song was originally the theme song of a 1935 movie, *Children of the Storm (Fengyun ernu).* Its music and stirring opening lines—"Arise, all you who refuse to be slaves . . ."—enjoyed instant and continued popularity in the anti-Japanese years of prewar and wartime China. Nie and Tian were members of the Chinese Communist Party, and in 1949 the newly founded People's Republic adopted the song as its national anthem. Although the militant lyrics have largely lost their relevance in the present era of "reform and open-up," they do remind people of the nationalist origins of the Chinese Communist revolution.

Wang Ke-wen

Chinese troops heading for the front in the early months of the second Sino-Japanese War. (Courtesy of Nationalist Party Archives.)

Marco Polo Bridge Incident

On July 7, 1937, the Chinese army clashed with Japanese troops stationed in north China near the Marco Polo Bridge, southwest of Beiping (Beijing). Although the two sides may not have expected it, the incident triggered a full-scale war between the two countries that lasted for eight years.

According to Chinese historians, the incident began when Japanese troops, staging an evening exercise in the Marco Polo Bridge area, demanded a search in the nearby Wanping county under the pretext that they had been fired upon and that one of their soldiers was missing (he later returned to his unit). When the mayor of Wanping rejected the demand, the Japanese sent in reinforcements and besieged the county. On July 8 they launched an attack, and the Chinese forces of the Twenty-ninth Army, commanded by Song Zheyuan, resisted. The conflict soon spread to northern Hebei.

On July 14, the Nanjing government held a discussion meeting *(tanhuahui)* at Lushan, Jiangxi, with other political parties and non-party intellectuals to review national affairs. Chiang Kaishek, head of the government's Military Committee, delivered a major policy speech at the meeting. He recalled a statement he had made in 1935, that he would not give up hope for peace with Japan and called for national sacrifice "unless the final moment has been reached." Chiang suggested that the conflict at the Marco Polo Bridge may have been that "final moment." Nevertheless, Nanjing was still attempting to reach a peaceful settlement with Japan, even while it was ordering reinforcements into the region. Negotiation continued for several weeks without progress, mainly because the Japanese insisted on parleying only with the local authorities (*i.e.,* Song Zheyuan) and not with Nanjing. This strategy aimed at alienating regional military leaders from Nanjing, and in effect repudiated Nanjing's authority over the northern provinces. In late July Chiang decided to resort to war. He instructed Song Zheyuan's army to fight the Japanese with the assistance of Nanjing's own forces. They were not the match of the invaders. By the end of July, Beiping and Tianjin had fallen into Japanese hands. The second Sino-Japanese War had begun.

Historians generally agree that the August Thirteenth Incident in Shanghai, a month after the Marco Polo Bridge Incident, was even more critical than the conflict on July 7 in determining the scale and the unavoidability of the Sino-Japanese War. In the popular Chinese mind, however, the Marco Polo Bridge Incident looms as the most significant symbol of the war of resistance against Japan. Widely publicized by the Chinese government and the media as the "final moment" when the country, after years of humiliation, stood up against the Japanese invader, the incident has been remembered as a shining moment of Chinese nationalism.

Wang Ke-wen

References
Ch'i, Hsi-sheng. *Nationalist China at War:*

Military Defeat and Political Collapse, 1937–1945. Ann Arbor: University of Michigan Press, 1982.

Dorn, Frank. *The Sino-Japanese War, 1937–41: From Marco Polo Bridge to Pearl Harbor.* New York, NY: Macmillan, 1974.

Margary Affair

In the mid-1870s, Great Britain, in an attempt to help her declining trade in Asia, decided to build a railway from Burma to China's southwestern province of Yunnan. The railway, the British believed, would open a new trade route to China's interior.

In 1874, the British government ordered an exploratory mission, led by Colonel Horace A. Browne, to survey the terrain and path from Burma to Yunnan. Meanwhile, the British embassy in Beijing dispatched a young vice-consul, Augustus Margary, to the Southwest to meet the mission. They met at the Burmese town of Bhamo in January 1875, and soon crossed the Sino-Burmese border into Yunnan. On February 21, traveling in the Tengyue area in Yunnan, Margary and five others in the exploratory mission were ambushed and killed by local Chinese.

Although Chinese officials had warned the mission about the risks in the southwestern border area, and according to international law the mission was at its own risk when it chose to expose itself to danger, the British government immediately demanded redress from the Chinese government in Beijing. In addition to indemnity, an official apology, and severe punishment of the local authorities, the British also stipulated a set of other extraneous concessions. In September 1876, the Qing court, under the British threat of breaking off relations with China, concluded the Chefoo Convention (or Treaty of Yantai) with the British to settle the Margary affair. In this agreement the British obtained the opening of four more Chinese ports to Western trade, the expansion of extraterritoriality to interior China, and the waiver of *lijin,* a form of domestic tariff in the treaty ports.

Three other important consequences resulted from the Chefoo Convention: (1) in compliance with the convention, China dispatched an apology mission to Great Britain, led by Guo Songtao, which later became the first resident Chinese delegation abroad; (2) the Chinese negotiator, Li Hongzhang, emerged from the con-

vention as *de facto* foreign minister in the Qing court; and (3) the British were allowed to conduct another exploratory mission from the Chinese capital to India, through Tibet. This last development signified a major step in the realization of Great Britain's territorial ambition over Tibet.

Wang Ke-wen

References

Hsu, Immanuel C. Y. *China's Entrance into the Family of Nations: The Diplomatic Phase, 1858–1880.* Cambridge, MA: Harvard University Press, 1960.

Marriage Law of 1950

One of the first laws promulgated by the People's Republic of China, the marriage law represented a major effort made by the new Communist government to improve the status of Chinese women.

The law abolished such feudal marriage practices as bigamy, concubinage, and child-brides, and replaced them with a "new democratic" system that consisted of monogamy, freedom to choose husband or wife, freedom to seek divorce, and freedom to remarry for widows. With this legislation the parental control of marriage, which had existed in China for thousands of years, came to an end. In name at least, marriage now was to be determined by the free will of the man and woman involved without the interference by any third party. In addition, the law prescribed that "husband and wife are companions living together and shall enjoy equal status in the home." This principle undermined the traditional male-dominated Chinese family and for the first time recognized the rights of female members in the family.

After its promulgation in 1950, the law encountered expected resistance from the Chinese populace. As late as 1953, a campaign for the implementation of the marriage law was still waged by the government. Eventually, the new marriage practices became the norm in the society, and a legal foundation for the enhancement of the status of women was established in China.

Since the late Qing period the issue of women's rights has been closely related to nationalism. To liberate women from the oppressive system of traditional marriage and family was regarded by many Chinese reformers as crucial to the strengthening of the nation's ability to compete with the West and survive in the modern world. Largely motivated by this belief, radical youth in the May Fourth era chose China's traditional marriage and family as their major targets of attack. The Chinese Communist Party inherited this goal, as well as its nationalist rationale, despite apparent contradictions between the latter and the Party's internationalist ideology. "New democratic" marriages had been practiced by the Chinese Communists themselves and introduced in areas under their rule before 1949. The Marriage Law of 1950 finally spread the reform to the whole country. Although it did not result in complete gender equality, it signified a break with the past and the beginning of women's liberation in China.

Wang Ke-wen

References

Gilmartin, Christina, et al., ed. *Engendering China: Women, Culture, and the State.* Cambridge, MA: Harvard University Press, 1994.

Kazuko, Ono. *Chinese Women in a Century of Revolution, 1850–1950,* ed. Joshua A. Fogel. Stanford, CA: Stanford University Press, 1989.

Meijer, M. J. *Marriage Law and Policy in the Chinese People's Republic.* Hong Kong: Hong Kong University Press, 1972.

Marshall Mission

The Marshall Mission (December 20, 1945–January 8, 1947) was the last abortive American effort to resolve the conflict between the Guomindang (GMD) and the Chinese Communist Party (CCP) in pre-1949 China. This American intervention in the Chinese civil war resulted in failure to secure the strategic hold of the United States in East Asia and in alienating the Communists.

Despite the official rhetoric of friendship for China, American policy was not based on altruism or sentimental attachment to the Chinese people, but on American national interests. Aiming to occupy a dominant position in East Asia, the United States required a relatively strong and friendly China capable of counterbalancing the Soviet Union and open to the penetration of American capital. As early as November 1944, Ambassador Patrick J. Hurley began to mediate the power struggle between the GMD and the CCP for fear that a civil war would expand the Soviet influence in China. After Hurley's resignation in November 1945, President Harry S. Truman appointed George C. Marshall to continue the ambassador's task. The official goal of Marshall's mission was to secure an immediate cease-fire, to broaden the basis of the one-party GMD government, and to help create a "strong, united, and democratic China."

Marshall's high prestige, the enormous power of his country, and the anti-civil war sentiment in China produced rapid results. On January 10, 1946, he committed the GMD and the CCP to calling a Political Consultative Conference and an immediate cease-fire. The two major achievements of the Conference during January and February 1946 were a program to establish constitutional government and a military reorganization agreement that demanded massive troop reduction on both sides and the integration of Communist forces into a united national army.

However, the GMD would not grant the CCP equal political power, whereas the Communists resisted the integration of their armies. Because of years of strife, the two antagonists did not trust one another. Secretly, the extremists in both parties found Marshall obstructing victory. Although Marshall's presence kept the GMD and the CCP from ripping apart the façade of cooperation, they ignored the truce once he was out of sight. Large-scale fighting occurred in April 1946, and the resolutions of the Political Consultative Conference remained dreams on paper. In June 1946, Marshall's last cease-fire arrangement expired, and the CCP demanded the withdrawal of American troops from China. By then, the two parties had decided to embark upon a new course of action irrespective of Marshall, whose influence had faded. Inconclusive negotiations nonetheless continued for six more months. Marshall realized that he had failed in his mission and returned to Washington on January 8, 1947, to become the United States secretary of state.

The United States had intervened in a war in which neither the GMD nor the CCP could represent the interests of all the Chinese people. Posing as a peace-maker and an "honest broker," the American government ultimately was resented by both the GMD and the CCP. The GMD blamed Washington for spoiling its optimum chances for destroying the Communists; the latter attacked the United States for ostensibly appearing as a neutral mediator while ac-

M

tually aiding the GMD. The two Chinese parties were embroiled in a life-or-death conflict; the assumption that American mediation might influence its course was illusionary. Marshall, in his farewell message to the Chinese people, said that China's hope lay with the liberals (such as Hu Shih), but they lacked the power to exercise a "controlling influence." In other words, only the politically weak liberals could serve the interests of the Chinese people and those of the United States. In the final analysis, Marshall's failure stemmed from the inability of the United States to bridge the gulf between its own national goals and Chinese realities, and the American mediation created a gleam of false hope for all.

Joseph K. S. Yick

References

Beal, John Robinson. *Marshall in China.* New York, NY: Doubleday, 1970.

Hsu, Immanuel C. Y. *The Rise of Modern China,* 4th ed. New York, NY: Oxford University Press, 1990.

Tsou, Tang. *America's Failure in China, 1941–1950.* Chicago, IL: University of Chicago Press, 1963.

Martial Arts

The martial arts are traditional Chinese techniques of individual combat, said to have originated in the Warring States period (403–221 B.C.). These include forms of boxing, generally known as *quanshu,* and the use of such traditional weapons as spears and swords. Practiced privately, these techniques were sometimes associated with famous Buddhist sects or monasteries. In 1899 and 1900, martial arts, combined with local superstitions, armed the anti-foreign Boxer Uprising in north China. The defeat of the Boxers by foreign armies symbolized the challenge modern military technology posed to the ancient fighting skills. The latter, however, has retained its appeal among the Chinese, and some foreigners, throughout the twentieth century.

In 1909, the famous martial arts expert Huo Yuanjia founded the Jingwu Physical Exercise Association, later renamed Jingwu Physical Education Association, in Shanghai. The association advocated the study of martial arts for the purpose of strengthening the nation and the race. In the ensuing years, branches of the association spread to Zhejiang, Guangdong, Sichuan and Southeast Asia. By 1928, it had a membership of over 400,000 people. Although it also developed programs in the modern sports of soccer, basketball, and wrestling, its focus remained on martial arts. Other similar organizations, such as the Shanghai Chinese Martial Arts Society founded in 1919, also appeared, but Jingwu was widely recognized as the leader.

During the May Fourth era, martial arts caught the attention of cultural conservatives, who saw it as representing a form of "national essence." Several warlords actively promoted it, and the Beiyang government included "new martial arts" in the physical education curriculum of middle schools. In 1928, the Guomindang government formally designated martial arts as the national technique *(guoshu)* and established the Central National Techniques Academy for the training and examination of martial arts teachers. With branches in the provinces and cities, the Academy sometimes competed with Jingwu for influence. At the Fifth National Games in 1933, martial arts were introduced for the first time as a competition sport. This status remained throughout the Guomindang period and has continued into the Communist era, although it never became recognized in the Olympic Games.

Since the 1970s, Chinese martial arts have gained increasing popularity in the West. Bruce Lee, an overseas Chinese actor and martial arts expert, achieved fame by starring in the American television series "Green Hornet" in the 1960s. In the 1970s, he made a series of movies, mostly produced in Hong Kong, which became huge box office hits and attracted global cult followings. Lee died at a young age in 1973, but his impact on Chinese and Western popular culture proved to be profound and long-lasting. His hero image enhanced the cultural and national pride of the Chinese and helped to promote martial arts as a form of self-defense and exercise among people in the West. Since then, martial arts films have developed into a special genre in world cinema, producing numerous Asian and Western stars, and "kung-fu" (martial arts) have become household words in America.

Wang Ke-wen

Marxism-Leninism

Marxism-Leninism is a political philosophy (broadly defined) developed by Karl Heinrich Marx and Vladimir Ilyich Lenin. It became the state ideology of the Soviet Union from 1917 to 1991, the People's Republic of China from

1949 to the present, and of a number of other countries as well. It has also served as the ideological basis of many Communist parties and movements in Asia and throughout the world. Today, Marxism-Leninism is in worldwide decline, although it has had a critical relationship with the development of nationalism in twentieth-century China.

In its original (Marxist) formulation, Marxism-Leninism was hostile to the intense nationalism of nineteenth-century Europe, arguing that nationalism was a form of "false consciousness" by which the international monopoly capitalist class (which had no national loyalties) controlled the petty bourgeoisie, the proletariat and the peasantry of its respective nation-state. According to Marx, an understanding of "scientific socialism" would enable the exploited classes of all countries to realize their common political interests regardless of national identity. This would prepare the way for the proletarian revolution that would overthrow the capitalist world system and lead to a classless global society in which nationalism would gradually disappear.

For his part, Lenin was sensitive to the enormous appeal of nationalism in the anti-imperialist, anti-colonial movements of independence that were emerging in early twentieth-century Asia, particularly China. In 1920, following the Bolshevik revolution of 1917, the Second Congress of the Communist International promulgated a set of theses that recognized the critical role of the "national bourgeoisie" (mid-level capitalists) in spearheading the nationalist, anti-colonial struggles of the "toilers of the East," as represented, for example, by Sun Yatsen in China. The victory of these nationalist struggles for independence (later called wars of national liberation) would complete the national, or bourgeois-democratic, revolution, to be followed by the inevitable proletarian revolution. This would chart the course for the construction of socialism on a national basis, leading eventually to an international communist system in which nationalism, like the nation-state itself, would wither away.

This accommodation between Marxism-Leninism and Asian nationalism, albeit of limited duration, set the stage for cooperation between the Guomindang (GMD) and the Chinese Communist Party (CCP). In the first United Front (1923–27), the two parties joined forces to destroy the warlords and oppose Western imperialism, and in the second (1937–45),

they came together to resist the invading Japanese. The first United Front was largely successful, the second much less so; in any case, these periods of cooperation were marriages of convenience that did not dispel the profound differences between the two parties. Following the triumph of the Communists in 1949, the Revolutionary Committee of the GMD was included along with a number of other small opposition parties in the National People's Congress. But its role was largely symbolic, a token in deference to the concept of "new democracy" that the CCP had been promoting since 1940 in an effort to build a broad national coalition that would appeal to all Chinese regardless of class, including the national bourgeoisie. The ideas behind new democracy were developed largely by the CCP leader Mao Zedong and were soon integrated into Mao Zedong's thought, which was designated the CCP's official ideology in the new party constitution of 1945.

Since then, the theoretical basis of the CCP has been labeled Marxism-Leninism-Mao Zedong thought, or simply, Mao Zedong thought, which is said to represent the "sinification" or nationalization of the original European theory based on the specific national conditions of China, *e.g.*, a predominantly peasant population and a protracted revolutionary struggle. As such, it has been denounced by the Soviet and other like-minded Communist parties as a form of petty-bourgeois and/or peasant mentality in the service of the nationalist aspirations of the new Chinese ruling elite. On the other hand, Mao's reformulation of the original doctrine has had a considerable influence on certain other Communist movements, ranging from the Vietnam Communist Party to the Shining Path in Peru.

In the 1990s, Marxism-Leninism is in worldwide decline, and even in China it is honored more in form than substance. Still, the post-Mao regime claims that it is building "socialism with Chinese characteristics," in what appears to be an ongoing effort to harmonize the relationship between a Western-derived ideology and Chinese nationalist sentiment.

Raymond F. Wylie

References
d'Encosse, Hélène, and Stuart R. Schram. *Marxism and Asia: An Introduction with Readings.* London, England: Allen Lane, 1969.
Meisner, Maurice. *Marxism, Maoism and Utopianism: Eight Essays.* Madison:

University of Wisconsin Press, 1982.

Treadgold, Donald W., ed. *Soviet and Chinese Communism: Similarities and Differences*. Seattle: University of Washington Press, 1967.

Mass Line

It was during his years in the Jiangxi Soviet (1931–34) that Mao Zedong gave the Chinese Communist revolution a uniquely nationalist coloring. He did so by reaching the momentous conclusion that the Chinese Communist Party (CCP) could ignore the city-based proletariat and still gain its revolutionary ends by mobilizing the peasant masses. However, to achieve success, the Party, according to Mao's thesis, had to gain popular legitimacy by integrating itself with the masses. Mao's ideas, concerning the kind of relations the Party had to establish with the masses to prove that it was genuinely responsive to their needs and aspirations, gradually came to be embodied in his "mass line" method of government. Mao gave the concept its definitive formulation in a directive to the Party in 1943. The relevant portion of the directive reads as follows:

> In all practical work of our Party, all correct leadership is necessarily from the masses, to the masses. This means: take the ideas of the masses (scattered and unsystematic ideas) and concentrate them (through study turn them into concentrated and systematic ideas), then go to the masses and propagate and explain these ideas until the masses embrace them as their own, hold fast to them and translate them into action, and test the correctness of these ideas in such action.

The "mass line" approach parallels Lenin's notion of "democratic centralism," which permits the people at the periphery of the Party to discuss issues democratically, before the Party center turns them into unchallengeable decisions. However, Mao's thought differs from Lenin's thinking because the "mass line" extends the so-called democratic process beyond the Party circle to include the masses, and also because, apparently, it seeks the ideas of the masses as inputs for policymaking. In this, the "mass line" may actually be closer to China's tradition which had stressed the need for a good government always to bear in mind the interests of the people, and devote itself to their welfare.

The "mass line" was successful in gaining popularity for the CCP in the relatively uncomplicated political environment of Yan'an, but it lost much of its intrinsic value after the establishment of the People's Republic, when most of the CCP leaders, forced to turn their attention to the vast and complex problems of national development, decided to bring the revolution to a halt. Mao, however, disagreed with these leaders and kept pushing his model for China's modernization; the model was based on the concepts of "permanent revolution," the "mass line," and mass campaigns. Although Mao's experiments (such as the Great Leap Forward and the Great Proletarian Cultural Revolution) with his model failed, and although many of Mao's policies were rejected or reversed after his death, the post-Mao leadership of China has still accepted the "mass line" (now bereft of all content) as a part of the correct Party ideology.

Ranbir Vohra

References

Mao, Tse-tung. *Selected Works of Mao Tse-tung*, vol. 4. New York, NY: International Publishers, 1965.

May Fourth Movement

The historical event that marked the transformation of Chinese nationalism into its twentieth-century form, which is characterized by an emphasis on anti-imperialism and mass mobilization, is known as the May Fourth movement. The name "May Fourth" is derived from a student demonstration held in Beijing on May 4, 1919. On that day, as news arrived from Paris that the post-World War I Peace Conference had decided to turn over former German interests in Shandong to Japan, about three thousand college and high school students in the Chinese capital staged a demonstration at Tiananmen under the leadership of students from Beijing University. They protested against not only the violation of Chinese sovereignty by the foreign powers but the failure of the Chinese government to defend national interests. Following a parade on the streets, the students attacked and burned down the residence of a pro-Japanese official. The police arrested dozens of demonstrators, and the students responded by launching a strike the next day.

The incident triggered the first nationwide

May Fourth demonstration in Beijing, 1919. (Courtesy of Nationalist Party Archives.)

anti-imperialist mass movement in modern Chinese history. In the ensuing weeks similar demonstrations occurred in more than one hundred other cities in China, and the students were joined by workers and merchants. At first taking a hard-line stand, the Beijing government eventually capitulated. By early June the arrested students were released and three pro-Japanese officials were dismissed from office. The Chinese delegation in Paris was ordered not to sign the peace treaty. China's new generation of intellectuals acquired a first-hand knowledge of the power of the masses.

The May Fourth movement is generally viewed as the political expression of a New Culture movement that had emerged before 1919. Historians believe that the New Culture movement, originating in the publication of the cultural critics magazine *New Youth* (*Xinqingnian*) in 1915, had a far reaching impact on the formation of modern Chinese nationalism. Attributing the failure of the Revolution of 1911 in building a strong and democratic state to the suppression of individualism in China's Confucian tradition, the New Culture movement called for a complete reevaluation of Chinese culture. Writings by Chen Duxiu, Hu Shih, and others in *New Youth* advocated the liberation of the Chinese people from the yoke of Confucianism and the adoption of Western culture, especially "Mr. Science and Mr. Democracy." Only by releasing the strength of the individual, they argued, could the nation as a whole be strengthened. It was these messages that had prepared the students for the violent confrontation on May 4.

The significance of the New Culture iconoclasm lies both in its destruction of the authority of tradition and in its stress on the rupture of history. The national identity of China, which had largely remained unchanged through the Revolution of 1911, now underwent a transformation with a new root in the modern context. China was no longer defined by its historical genealogy but by its place in the contemporary world. The May Fourth generation saw the necessity to make the painful, yet inevitable, choice between past and present, culture and state. In other words, in order to secure the survival of the present Chinese state, Chinese culture, indeed the entire Chinese past, had to be recast. Such a recognition, together with the anti-imperialist mass movement, was to be the main theme of Chinese nationalism for the next half-century.

Chiu-chun Lee

References
Chow, Tse-tsung. *The May Fourth Movement: Intellectual Revolution in Modern China.* Cambridge, MA: Harvard University Press, 1960.
Schwarcz, Vera. *The Chinese Enlightenment.*

Berkeley: University of California Press, 1986.

Schwartz, Benjamin I., ed. *Reflections on the May Fourth Movement.* Cambridge, MA: Harvard University Press, 1972.

May Thirtieth Movement

On May 30, 1925, police under the command of a British officer in the international settlement of Shanghai fired on a crowd of demonstrators that had met in Nanking Road to protest the treatment of Chinese workers in Japanese-owned textile mills in the city. Eleven people were killed, and more than twenty others wounded. Within forty-eight hours, large parts of Shanghai were gripped by a general strike aimed chiefly at the British and the Japanese. Under the leadership of local Commu-

An anti-imperialist demonstrator in Beijing during the May Thirtieth movement, 1925. (Courtesy of Nationalist Party Archives.)

nists, such as Li Lisan, Qu Qiubai, and Liu Shaoqi, a General Labor Union was formed, which in turn became the central force in a Federation of Workers, Merchants, and Students that was to become the central coordinating force for the strike. Despite efforts by the Chinese General Chamber of Commerce to moderate the radical demands of the strikers, and the efforts of foreign and Chinese diplomats to settle the affair, it was not until the late autumn of 1925 that the city returned to something like its normal condition.

The movement of protest that spread from the shooting in Nanking Road went far beyond Shanghai, however, sweeping through China's major cities that spring and summer with an extraordinary rapidity, and it has conventionally been seen as the start of the National Revolution. There were outbreaks in Beijing, Nanjing, Hankou, Chongqing, and most important, in Canton, where firing broke out as a Chinese protest march passed opposite the foreign concessions on Shameen Island, leading to the deaths of fifty-three Chinese and one foreigner. The Shameen Massacre, as it was called, was in turn the catalyst for the sixteen-month-long Hong Kong-Canton strike against British interests in south China.

Unlike the May Fourth movement of 1919, the May Thirtieth movement profited from the existence of a small but well-organized Chinese Communist Party and of a Guomindang movement that had already started building a base and a military force in Canton. Membership in both parties grew rapidly as a result of the movement, and the Federation in Shanghai can be seen in some ways as a model United Front organization—a movement cutting across classes and interest groups, seeking to unite patriotic Chinese in a general protest against imperialism, yet a movement that remained to a large extent under Communist influence. It was also instrumental in extracting from the foreign authorities agreements for representation in the governance of the city's international settlement and French concession. Though a combination of factional rivalries and foreign and warlord pressure led to the breakup of the Federation before the end of 1925, its influence, and that of the General Labor Union remained, and would play an important role in the three armed uprisings in 1926 and 1927 that brought Shanghai into the revolutionary camp during the Northern Expedition.

Nicholas R. Clifford

References

Clifford, Nicholas R. *Spoilt Children of Empire: Westerners in Shanghai and the Chinese Revolution of the 1920s.* Hanover, NH: Middlebury College Press, 1991.

Rigby, Richard. *The May Thirtieth Movement: Events and Themes.* Canberra: Australian National University Press, 1980.

Merchant Corps Incident

The Merchant Corps in Canton was a self-defense force organized by the city's business community in 1911. In 1922 the *comprador* of the Hong Kong-Shanghai Bank, Chen Lianbo, who also headed the Canton Chamber of Commerce, assumed command of this force. The corps had a strength of about four thousand men at the time.

In late 1923, after the founding of his third Canton regime and the adoption of an anti-imperialist stance with Soviet assistance, Sun Yatsen clashed with the Western powers in an attempt to control the Canton Maritime Customs. The Western countries, especially Great Britain, whose Hong Kong colony was nearby, viewed Sun's Guomindang (GMD) government with increasing alarm. The Merchant Corps had earlier ordered a large cache of weapons with the approval of the Canton regime. In August 1924, the shipment of weapons arrived at the harbor outside of Canton. Concerned about possible imperialist sabotage, Sun ordered the confiscation of the shipment. The Canton merchants immediately protested and threatened a general strike. The British also sent warships into the harbor as a show of strength and to demonstrate their support for the merchants. Sun, who was directing his Northern Expedition at Shaoguan at the time, appointed Hu Hanmin to negotiate with the merchants.

Hu soon reached an agreement with the merchants, promising the return of a portion of the weapons at the price of some "financial contributions" by the business community to Sun's Northern Expedition. On October 10, however, students and workers parading on the streets of Canton in celebration of the "Double-Ten" National Day, clashed with the Merchant Corps. Dozens of pro-GMD paraders were killed by the corps. In the wake of this conflict, the corps was said to have planned a revolt to overthrow the Canton regime and replace it with a merchants' government. In the face of this crisis, Sun ordered the organization of a Revolutionary Committee in Canton to dispatch the matter by force. He instructed a part of the Northern Expeditionary forces to return from the front and attack the Merchant Corps at Canton. The cadets at the newly established Whampoa Military Academy, commanded by Chiang Kaishek, also joined the battle. The campaign lasted for one day, from the evening of August 14 to the morning of August 15, and the Merchant Corps was thoroughly crushed. Almost half of the city's business district was destroyed in the battle, causing huge losses in lives and property. Chen Lianbo fled to Hong Kong and the corps was permanently disbanded. The incident came to symbolize the militant anti-imperialism of Sun Yatsen and his GMD in the early 1920s.

Wang Ke-wen

References

Loh, Pichon P. Y. *The Early Chiang Kai-shek: A Study of His Personality and Politics, 1887–1924.* New York, NY: Columbia University Press, 1971.

Wilbur, C. Martin. *Sun Yat-sen: Frustrated Patriot.* New York, NY: Columbia University Press, 1976.

Minbao (The People's Report)

Minbao, The People's Report, was the official journal of the Tongmenghui (Revolutionary Alliance), an organization founded in August 1905 by the republican revolutionaries. Its first issue was published on November 26, 1905 in Tokyo, where the Tongmenghui had its headquarters. In October 1908, it was closed down by Japanese police after its twenty-fourth issue, but two additional numbers were published in January and February 1910.

It is commonly thought that the revolutionaries chose their journal's name in order to underline the unifying element in Sun Yatsen's Three Peoples' Principles *(minzu, minzhu,* and *minsheng),* then known as the "three great principles" and widely regarded as the core of revolutionary ideology. But it has been convincingly argued by a leading scholar of *Minbao,* Hung-yuan Chu, that the Tongmenghui leaders were more influenced by general world intellectual trends, especially the idea that an era of monarchy had reached a dead end and a new era of the people was beginning.

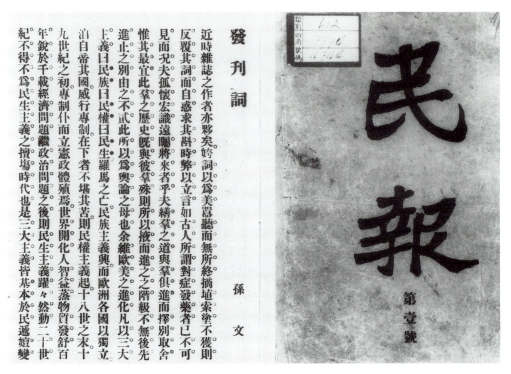

The first issue of Minbao, November 1905. (Courtesy of Nationalist Party Archives.)

This argument is strengthened by the fact that *Minbao* writers concerned themselves not only with China but with the world, and especially with nationalist and democratic struggles in such countries as Russia, Poland, Turkey, Persia, and India, and with patriotic heroes such as George Washington, Guiseppe Mazzini, Giuseppe Garibaldi, and Léon Gambetta. Although the journal was a propaganda organ for the Chinese revolution, it was also a voice for worldwide liberation struggles. *Minbao*'s contents certify that Chinese nationalists felt a kinship with patriots everywhere, and that Chinese nationalism was influenced by the global climate in which it grew.

Writers in *Minbao* included the major intellectuals of the time. Zhang Binglin, who edited the journal for fifteen issues, was its most prolific contributor. Wang Jingwei and Hu Hanmin were also frequent writers for *Minbao*, sometimes collaborating on articles and generally representing the Sun Yatsen wing of the Tongmenghui. Other prominent contributors included Chen Tianhua (who committed suicide only twelve days after *Minbao*'s first issue appeared; his writings were published posthumously through issue number nine), Zhu Zhixin, Song Jiaoren, Liao Zhongkai, and Liu Shipei. On topics related to nationalism, the main writers were Zhang, Chen, and Wang.

Zhang, the oldest of *Minbao*'s writers (he was thirty-seven years old when he became editor in mid-1906), was the revolutionaries' answer to Kang Youwei. A classical scholar of vast erudition, Zhang was also an activist who had virtually invited martyrdom and, as a result, spent three years in jail (1903–06) in the celebrated *Subao* case. His nationalism had a strongly anti-Manchu and racist thrust, but on occasion he voiced an even stronger anti-imperialism; once, for example, he noted that Western domination was a far greater menace than the Manchus were and that China's cause was one with India's against Great Britain and Vietnam's against France.

Chen Tianhua and Wang Jingwei wrote powerful essays in *Minbao* from its very first number. Both employed Social Darwinian ideas to develop a racial interpretation of nationalism, but neither confined his nationalist rhetoric to racial arguments alone, and both were concerned to define the sources of national strength. Wang, for example, argued at length that states organized by people with a common history and culture were more likely to be stronger than non-homogeneous ones, and to enjoy more freedom and equality.

Nationalist rhetoric in *Minbao* frequently lapsed into bitter chauvinism, but many articles probed serious questions about national identity, the right of people to self-determination, and the relationships between race and nation, nation and state, and among nation-states. *Minbao*'s anti-imperialism, like its anti-Manchuism, could at times be fervid, but its statements of basic principles insisted that it stood for world peace, international cooperation, and respect for all treaties and other international obligations.

Minbao writers sought to bring modern Western ideas to bear upon old questions in China's history and on current problems. These ideas were worked out under the pressure of revolutionary activity and, it must be emphasized, in the heat of fractious debate. For some two years *Minbao* was challenged by Liang Qichao in his *Xinmin congbao (The New People Miscellany)*, and their exchanges, although often edifying, at times could not resist the temptation to score debaters' points. All in all, however, *Minbao* represented a new development in Chinese political journalism, and it constitutes a rich source of data on early twentieth-century Chinese nationalism.

Michael Gasster

References

Bernal, Martin. *Chinese Socialism to 1917.* Ithaca, NY: Cornell University Press, 1976.

Gasster, Michael. *Chinese Intellectuals and the Revolution of 1911: The Birth of Modern Chinese Radicalism.* Seattle: University of Washington Press, 1969.

Model Plays *(Yangbanxi)*

The model plays *(yangbanxi)* of the Cultural Revolution were the artistic centerpiece of a political upheaval centrally concerned with the redefinition of Chinese and international culture. The set of works initially proclaimed as models in 1966 were the basis of Jiang Qing's claim to have personally led an unprecedented breakthrough in international proletarian culture. The eight works included in the original set of models represented three highly sophisticated and elite genres of performing art, none of which had an extensive history of revolutionary transformation. The initial works consisted of five Peking operas: *Taking Tiger Mountain by Strategy (Zhiqu Weihushan), Shajia Creek*

(Shajiabang), On the Dock (Haigang), Raid on the White Tiger Regiment (Qixi Baihutuan), and *The Red Lantern (Hongdengji);* two ballets: *The White-haired Girl (Baimaonü)* and *The Red Detachment of Women (Hongse niangzijun);* and a symphony, *Shajia Creek (Shajiabang).* The nine works added to the corpus of models in the early and mid-1970s—a piano concerto, a piano accompaniment for voice, a symphony, two dance dramas and four Beijing operas—were also in elite genres. Among the original and the later models, many of the non-operatic models were transpositions of earlier model operas into foreign or foreign-influenced elite genres.

Each of the original model plays had an earlier and indigenous history, in most cases in a Chinese opera style. Earlier versions of each of these works were repeatedly revised and at some point during the revision stage they were declared to be model plays. Eventually, definitive texts and performance guides were produced, but the works were models not only in this fixed sense but also in the context of exemplifying a politicized creative process recommended for all Chinese—and international proletarian—literature and art.

Toward the end of the Cultural Revolution the model plays and their process of creation were increasingly theoreticized and cited as the basis of a new theory of literature and art. Beginning in 1970, a national movement popularized the revolutionary model plays. Amateur performances of the heroism of these plays was credited as having a transformative effect in the lives of ordinary people. The plays became widely performed in their original versions and were adapted into a steadily increasing number of different opera styles and other performing genres. The end of the Cultural Revolution was accompanied by a repudiation of the policy of promoting the set of model plays—but individual works within the set have continued to be performed and to be popular.

The model plays were a complex fusion of national and international processes and aspirations. Some of the models (in ballet and symphony) represented claims that Chinese revolutionary artists could transform the most intransigent genres of international (and bourgeois) art. This marked a decisive turn away from the earlier Chinese policy on revolutionary literature and art, accepted from the time of Mao Zedong's *Talks at the Yan'an Forum on Literature and Art* (1942), that revolutionary

"Shajiabang"—one of the revolutionary "model plays."

art should use national and folk forms of art to achieve its purposes.

The model plays were all in elite genres, although the prominence of Beijing opera and the national claim for a Chinese breakthrough on the international stage signified an important national dimension to the model plays. This national dimension is also evident in the content of each play. They all concern Chinese political processes and several concern the war of liberation or post-liberation anti-imperialist struggles. In the characteristics of the performance, they all draw heavily upon traditional Chinese performing arts.

Ellen R. Judd

References

Mowry, Hua-yuan Li. *Yang-ban-hsi: New Theater in China.* Berkeley: University of California Press, 1973.

Tung, Constantine, and Colin Mackerras, eds. *Drama in the People's Republic of China.* Albany: State University of New York Press, 1987.

Modern Drama

Chinese modern drama *(huaju)* emerged in the early twentieth century as a form of Western-influenced spoken drama which, from its beginning, was deeply involved in national and leftist political processes. Its most obvious difference from indigenous Chinese drama is formal—it lacks the music, song, dance, acrobatics, and pageantry of the multifaceted Chinese opera, and relies upon spoken dialogue. Its identification as modern drama refers to its significant nonformal features, its involvement in modern historical processes, and its expression of contemporary social and political themes.

Chinese modern drama was first performed by Chinese students in Japan in 1907 as part of an effort to collect funds for flood relief in China. Later the same year, the same students presented a Chinese modern drama adaptation of *Uncle Tom's Cabin* in Japan, and this was also staged the same year in Shanghai. Subsequently, further experimentation in modern drama was made in China, still following Western lines as introduced through Japanese channels. During the May Fourth movement, the development of Chinese modern drama was stimulated by the translation of works by influential European playwrights, such as Ibsen, Shaw, Wilde, and Strindberg. In the 1920s and early 1930s, several major Chinese playwrights produced works of modern drama, most notably Tian Han, Ouyang Yuqian, Cao Yu, and Xia Yan. Their works were characterized by explicit concern with national issues and by leftist political orientation.

Organizationally, many of the leading people in modern drama were actively involved in the League of Chinese Left-Wing Dramatists. Following the outbreak of the Sino-Japanese War in 1937, the modern drama of the coastal cities moved inland and became a vehicle for nationalist mobilization. In this move it partly converged with a similar dramatic current active in the Communist border regions where spoken drama of an agitative and propagandist nature had been imported from the Soviet Union, especially through the work of Li Bozhao, and had been used for mobilizational purposes from the early 1930s. Within the Communist areas, there was subsequently a shift during the Yan'an period toward heavier use of indigenous folk forms, and modern drama was one component in the Yan'an era of dramatic synthesis.

Following the Communist victory in 1949, the government provided a subsidized infrastructure of theaters, troupes, and schools for modern drama (in addition to those for Chinese opera and the other performing arts). Modern drama in the early post-liberation years portrayed the earlier national and revolutionary struggles and served the new national order. It was eclipsed during the Cultural Revolution era, when there was a narrow emphasis on a set of selected model plays, of which none was a modern drama, but became a renewed area of active experimental and international influence in the 1980s. In the 1990s, the substantial influence of Chinese modern drama was especially evident in its important contribution to the Chinese cinema.

Ellen R. Judd

References

Mackerras, Colin. *The Chinese Theatre in Modern Times.* Amherst, MA: University of Massachusetts Press, 1975.

Mongolian Autonomous Government

The Japanese-sponsored regime in Inner Mongolia during the second Sino-Japanese War (1937–45) was called the Mongolian Autonomous Government.

In 1936, following its invasion in western Inner Mongolia, the Japanese Guandong Army supported the Mongolian prince Demchukdonggrub to organize the Mongolian Autonomous Military Government at Coptchil (Dehua). Demchukdonggrub had long been an advocate of Mongolian autonomy within China, but the new regime was firmly under Japanese control.

It employed Japanese as advisers to the various branches of the government and signed agreements with the Japanese puppet state of Manchukuo. After the outbreak of the second Sino-Japanese War in 1937, the Coptchil regime moved with the Japanese troops into the province of Suiyuan and reorganized itself into the Mongolian Federated Autonomous Government, with Prince Yun as its chairman. When Prince Yun died the next year, Demchukdonggrub succeeded his leadership.

In 1939, as the Japanese conquered other parts of Inner Mongolia, the Suiyuan government was combined with two other Japanese puppet regimes in Chahar and Shanxi and formed the Mongolian Borderlands United Autonomous Government. With its capital at Kalgan, the regime continued to depend on Japanese support. Japan, however, never allowed the Kalgan regime to administer eastern Inner Mongolia, which was governed by Manchukuo, or to declare independence. After the establishment of Wang Jingwei's pro-Japanese "National Government" at Nanjing in 1940, the Kalgan regime was nominally brought under Nanjing's jurisdiction, but in reality it remained a separate unit under Japan's scheme of "divide and rule" in China.

The Mongolian regime disappeared in the wake of Japan's surrender in 1945. Although a product of foreign imperialist encroachment, it reflected the problem of ethnic separatism that has plagued the modern Chinese state.

Wang Ke-wen

References

Boyle, John Hunter. *China and Japan at War, 1937–1945: The Politics of Collaboration.* Stanford, CA: Stanford University Press, 1972.

Mongolian Autonomy and Independence

Mongolia was a part of the Manchu (Qing) empire. The Qing government maintained effective military control in Inner (southern) Mongolia, while Outer (northern) Mongolia enjoyed a greater degree of autonomy. Although contacts with Russia were unavoidable due to its geographical closeness, Chinese rule in Mongolia was relatively stable throughout the eighteenth and nineteenth centuries.

After the Russo-Japanese War of 1904 to 1905, Mongolia came to be deeply influenced by Western ideas. The wave of socialism was ushered into Outer Mongolia from czarist Russia. Meanwhile, Inner Mongolian students who returned from Japan brought home ideas of nationalism and national self-determination. In Darhan county, to the south of Chasaketu, there emerged a Mongolian liberation movement led by Ayohsi, which displayed characteristics of a democratic movement and a movement for national self-determination. Thenceforth, the ideologies of socialism, democracy, and nationalism converged and reinforced one another in the politics of Mongolia.

Russia, Great Britain, and Japan used these ideologies to instigate the Mongolians and the Tibetans to challenge Chinese rule in these regions in the early twentieth century, when China was sinking into internal chaos. With the encouragement of Russia and Japan, Mongolia gave birth to a number of separatist movements. During the republican revolution in China, Outer Mongolian separatists demanded an independent Greater Mongolia. They were initially supported by the Chinese revolutionaries under Sun Yatsen, who fervently advocated the expulsion of the Manchus from China proper. Sun and the Mongolians joined hands in denouncing the Qing government, but they had different goals. The Mongolians wanted independence, thus turning their nation into a state; the Chinese revolutionaries, on the other hand, were only concerned about the overthrow of the Manchu domination in China. After the establishment of the Republic of China in 1911, the independence movements in Inner and Outer Mongolia went their separate ways.

Inner Mongolia maintained a close relationship with the new Chinese Republic. During the 1930s, Prince Demchukdonggrub briefly led an autonomy movement that received support from Japan. After Japan's defeat at the end of World War II, Demchukdonggrub restored contacts with the Guomindang (GMD) government of China. On May 1, 1947, the GMD government established the Inner Mongolia Autonomous Region, recognizing the Mongolians' right to self-government. It was the first autonomous region of national minorities in China. In 1949, on the eve of the GMD's defeat in the civil war with the Chinese Communists, Demchukdonggrub telegraphed the GMD government in the name of the "People's Congress of Mongolia," once again proclaiming Inner Mongolia autonomy. The declaration of the congress pointed out that "it is the main trend of the twentieth century that nations demand

freedom, and politics become democratic." The congress also passed a Mongolian Autonomy Act, which cited Sun Yatsen's teachings of nationalism as a source of legitimacy for the Inner Mongolian autonomy.

After the Communist victory in China, Demchukdonggrub fled to Outer Mongolia and was arrested there. He was handed over to the Chinese Communist government and sent to prison in 1952. Thus his movement came to an end. Under the People's Republic of China, Inner Mongolia has maintained its status as an autonomous region. In 1988, the region had a population of 20,939,000, which included 14.7 percent Mongolians, 82.2 percent Han, and 3.1 percent other minorities.

In Outer Mongolia, an independent feudal monarchy emerged in 1911 under the leadership of the Jebtsundamba Khutuktus of Urga VIII. The independence was supported by Russia but not recognized by the new Chinese Republic. After years of negotiations, a Sino-Russian-Mongolian agreement was concluded in 1914 which changed the political status of Outer Mongolia from independence to autonomy within China, but recognized Russian domination of the region. In the wake of the October Revolution in Russia in 1917, Jebtsundamba abolished the autonomy and was soon overthrown by Damding Suhbaatar, a Mongolian nationalist and Communist. Suhbaatar's forces expelled the White Russians and the Chinese from Outer Mongolia and came to power on July 11, 1921, which is regarded as the founding date of the present Mongolian state. The Mongolian People's Republic was officially proclaimed in Outer Mongolia on November 26, 1924, with its capital at Ulan Bator (Urga).

After World War II, the GMD government of China, in exchange for Soviet support for itself in the civil war, formally recognized the Mongolian People's Republic on January 5, 1946. The GMD's position changed, however, after it was defeated by the Chinese Communists and moved to Taiwan. In 1954, the GMD government in Taiwan abrogated the 1945 Sino-Soviet Treaty of Friendship and Alliance and began to block Outer Mongolia's effort to join the United Nations. The Communist government on the mainland, on the other hand, accepted the reality of Outer Mongolian independence.

Since its independence, Outer Mongolia has achieved tremendous success in its nation-building. As of January 1991, it had established diplomatic relations with 107 countries. Before the fall of the USSR, it was under Soviet military protection. During the 1990s, Russian troops finally left Outer Mongolia, and Mongolian president Orchirbat visited the United States for the first time.

Hong-yuan Chu

References

Bawden, C. R. *The Modern History of Mongolia*. London, England: Routledge, Chapman & Hall, 1989.

Ewing, Thomas. *Between the Hammer and the Anvil? Chinese and Russian Policies in Outer Mongolia, 1911–1921*. Bloomington: Indiana University Press, 1980.

Leung, Edwin Pak-wah. "Regional Autonomy Versus Central Authority: The Inner Mongolian Autonomous Movement and the Chinese Response, 1925–1947." *Journal of Oriental Studies* no. 24 (1987): 49–62.

Mukden Incident

See MANCHURIAN INCIDENT

Muslim Uprisings (Southwest, 1856–73; Northwest, 1862–77)

The Muslim revolts in Yunnan, Shaanxi, Gansu, Qinghai, and Chinese Turkestan occurred as unrelated events, except in the context of the general breakdown of the Qing dynasty along with the accompanying lawlessness, including an upsurge of intra-group violence. Muslims arrived in China by the seventh century and settled in various areas over the next millennium. They probably numbered several million by the mid-nineteenth century. Many ethnic groups, such as Turks, Tibetans, Mongols, and Han Chinese *(Dungans)* counted members among the Muslims. Sectarian rivalries and personality disputes similarly divided the Islamic faithful.

The Yunnan Uprising, also known as the Panthay Rebellion, commenced in 1856, when fighting between Han Chinese and Muslims led to the capture of many cities by the latter. For six years, various central government attempts to retake the area failed. Then in 1862, Ma Rulong, a major rebel leader, surrendered and joined the effort to reclaim the province. His actions, along with the selection of more able government commanders in the early 1870s, proved successful by 1873.

The Shaan-Gan Uprisings stemmed from causes similar to those in the south: official corruption, discrimination against the Muslims, and intragroup violence. An additional factor was the sectarian dispute between the old and new teachings. The latter had been introduced in the 1760s by a local pilgrim, Ma Mingxin, who stressed a new and vocal way of praying. Rivalries and disputes lasted for the next century and played a role in the defeat of the Muslim challengers.

The uprising began in 1862, and lasted more than one decade, with bitter fighting and great atrocities on both sides. Little success came until Zuo Zongtang assumed command of government troops in 1868. He laid careful plans and concentrated on two main "new sect" centers, Jinjibao and Suzhou. Zuo declared the new sect as heterodox and thereby deserving of the most ruthless eradication. He offered fair treatment to other groups who would sincerely surrender. Both new sect places fought valiantly but succumbed to superior numbers and weaponry. The carnage was appalling. By 1873, the lands of China proper were clear of Muslim unrest.

Chinese Turkestan, a site of Turkish Islam, had long been outside Chinese authority (750s-1750s). A Manchu force incorporated it into the Qing empire in the 1750s. Various Muslim adventurers plotted and acted unsuccessfully to regain Chinese Turkestan, especially in the early nineteenth century. A revolt broke out in the Ili valley in 1863. This sparked other anti-government efforts, and soon the entire area was under Muslim control or, as in the case of the Ili valley, a Russian protectorate. Ya'qub Beg, an able soldier and politician from west of Chinese Turkestan, marched east and by 1870 commanded much of the region. Soon the British and Russians traded with his government, which was recognized by the Ottoman empire in 1873.

Having defeated the Muslims in Shaan-Gan in 1873, Zuo turned his attention to Chinese Turkestan. After securing governmental support, Zuo surmounted the daunting logistic problems. His troops moved in 1876 and reclaimed the last bastions by 1877. The northern realm fell first, followed by the southern. The death of Ya'qub Beg in mid-1877 facilitated the campaign. Again extensive loss of life occurred.

The Muslim uprisings had resulted from discriminatory policies of the Manchus and Han Chinese, along with the decline and near collapse of the Qing; the latter only whetted the appetites of adventurers such as Ya'qub Beg. The challenge and successful response did ensure that these strategic frontier areas would remain in Chinese control. The Muslims also suffered terrible population losses and remained quiescent until the fourth decade of the twentieth century.

Lanny B. Fields

References

Chan, Wellington K. K. "Ma Ju-lung: From Rebel to Turncoat in the Yunnan Rebellion." *Harvard Papers on China* no. 20 (1966): 86–118.

Fields, Lanny B. *Tso Tsung-t'ang and the Muslims: Statecraft in Northwest China, 1868–1880.* Kingston, Ontario: The Limestone Press, 1978.

Yuan, Tsing. "Yakub Beg (1820–1877) and the Moslem Rebellion in Chinese Turkestan." *Central Asiatic Journal* no. 6 (1961): 134–167.

N

Nanjing-Canton Split

On February 28, 1931, Chiang Kaishek, chairman of the Nanjing government, placed his colleague Hu Hanmin under house arrest in Tangshan. Hu, a senior leader of the Guomindang (GMD) and head of the Legislative Yuan at the time, had been engaged in dispute for months with Chiang over the issue of the constitution. Chiang proposed the promulgation of a "provisional constitution" *(yuefa)* for the current period of political tutelage *(xunzheng),* but Hu, true to the teaching of Sun Yatsen, opposed the idea. The dispute in fact revealed more profound causes for the conflict between the two men. Hu had long been dissatisfied with Chiang's monopoly of power in the Party and government. He regarded Chiang's proposal as a means of further enhancing and legitimizing Chiang's own power.

Hu enjoyed a significant following within and outside of the Nanjing government, most of all among his fellow Cantonese. Enraged by the house arrest, his followers in the government soon left Nanjing in protest. They found an ally in their opposition to Chiang in the Guangdong militarist Chen Jitang. In May they gathered in Canton and, with Chen's support, organized an "extraordinary session of the GMD Central Committees" to challenge Chiang's authority. The "Extraordinary Session" was dominated by Hu's close friends, such as Gu Yingfen and Deng Zeru, but they also enlisted support from various anti-Chiang factions in the country, including the Western Hills faction, Wang Jingwei's Left Guomindang, the Guangxi Clique, and several other regional militarists. In essence, however, the opposition was a Cantonese coalition. Almost all the active participants in the "extraordinary session" were natives of Guangdong, with Chen Jitang's Guangdong Army acting as their major military backing.

The "extraordinary session" immediately established its own "national government" in Canton, which claimed to carry on the legacy of the Canton government before the Northern Expedition (1926–28). The GMD regime was thereby formally divided. Nanjing and Canton, however, tried to avoid a military confrontation. Chiang Kaishek still gave his main attention to the Bandit-Suppression Campaigns against the Chinese Communists, whereas Chen Jitang was unwilling to commit his forces in a war with Nanjing. As the stalemate continued into August, the opposition in Canton began to show signs of internal dissension.

On September 18, the Manchurian Incident occurred. Within days, most of Manchuria fell to the Japanese army. The split between Nanjing and Canton undoubtedly prevented the GMD from making a swift and effective response to the crisis, and the public was angered by the GMD's poor performance. In the face of this national emergency, Nanjing and Canton quickly dispatched representatives to meet in Hong Kong, and in late October they held a formal peace conference in Shanghai.

Describing its goal as "overthrowing dictatorship and restoring democracy," the Canton opposition had been insisting on two conditions for a compromise with the Nanjing government: (1) the release of Hu Hanmin; and (2) the resignation of Chiang Kaishek. On the eve of the Shanghai Conference, Chiang released Hu and allowed his departure to Shanghai. During the two-week conference, Canton pressed for the second condition without success. Eventually, the representatives agreed upon a novel reunification plan. They decided that Nanjing and Canton would convene their separate GMD Fourth Party Congresses and each elect a portion of the new Central Committee. The two would then merge in Nanjing and organize a new government. Upon the establishment of the new Nanjing government, Chiang would step down and the Canton government would dissolve itself. Resolutions on reforms in finance, military organization and government structure completed the agreement.

The peace settlement failed to end the conflict. In late November, Nanjing held its Fourth Party Congress and elected its assigned portion of the Central Committee, but division disrupted the Fourth Party Congress in Canton. Hu Hanmin's followers were displeased with the failure of Canton's representatives to obtain the immediate resignation of Chiang and tried to reject the Shanghai settlement. In protest, two of the leading representatives, Wang Jingwei and Sun Fo, withdrew their factions from the congress. Wang's faction subsequently held its own Fourth Party Congress in Shanghai and, with Nanjing's support, created another portion of the Central Committee. In late December, Central Committee members from Nanjing, Canton, and Shanghai finally merged in Nanjing, and Chiang resigned from the government.

The most immediate impact of the Nanjing-Canton split was its crippling of the GMD at the time of the Manchurian Incident. To a great extent, it contributed to the failure of the Nanjing government's handling of the crisis, and thus seriously damaged the standing of the GMD in the eyes of nationalistic Chinese. The split also led to south China's prolonged autonomy in the first half of the 1930s. Hu Hanmin went to Canton at the end of 1931. For the next five years, he headed the Southwest Political Affairs Committee (*Xinan zhengwu weiyuanhui*) that ruled the provinces of Guangdong and Guangxi in open defiance of Nanjing's authority. This was yet one more mockery of the national unity claimed by the GMD.

Wang Ke-wen

References

Lary, Diana. *Region and Nation: The Kwangsi Clique in Chinese Politics, 1925–1937*. London, England: Cambridge University Press, 1974.

So, Wai-chor. *The Kuomintang Left in the National Revolution, 1924–1931*. Hong Kong: Oxford University Press, 1991.

Nanjing Decade (1927–37)

The ten-year period during which the Guomindang (GMD), under the leadership of Chiang Kaishek, nominally ruled China proper is called the Nanjing Decade.

In 1927, during the Northern Expedition, Chiang Kaishek established his national government at Nanjing. From then, until shortly after the outbreak of the second Sino-Japanese War in 1937, this ancient city in the Lower Yangtze remained the capital of the GMD regime. During this period, Chiang's opponents tried more than once to organize another "national government" in challenging Nanjing's authority, notably the Wuhan regime of 1927, the Beiping "enlarged session" of 1930, the Canton "extraordinary session" of 1931, and the Fujian Rebellion of 1933 to 1934, yet none of them was able to overthrow the Nanjing government.

These challenges, nevertheless, indicate a significant characteristic of the decade, *i.e.,* political disunity and instability. To an extent, Chiang incorporated rather than eliminated warlordism during his Northern Expedition. Many regional militarists chose to declare their support for the Nanjing government in exchange for Chiang's tolerance of their regional autonomy. When Chiang attempted to expand the authority of his national government into their domains during the decade, they resisted by force. In addition, Chiang's rapid ascendancy in the GMD, primarily with the help of the "barrel of the gun," had created for him numerous intra-party enemies. The collaboration between these enemies and the regional militarists explain almost every rebellion noted above.

The rebellions were not the only, or the most serious, problems confronting the Nanjing government during the decade. The Chinese Communist Party (CCP), following the collapse of the first GMD-CCP United Front in 1927, initiated a long struggle against GMD rule, with guerrilla wars in the countryside and underground sabotages in the cities. Chiang apparently took the CCP as the major threat to his power. From 1930 to 1934, he launched five Bandit-Suppression Campaigns against the CCP's rural base in Jiangxi and eventually drove them on its Long March to the Northwest. Meanwhile, beginning with the Manchurian Incident of 1931, the Japanese encroachment on China attracted national attention and consumed enormous energy of the Nanjing government.

Throughout the first half of the 1930s, Japan continued to expand her territorial control into north China. In part realizing China's military weakness and in part upholding the principle of "domestic pacification before external resistance" *(annei rangwai),* Chiang and his partners in Nanjing, such as Wang Jingwei, managed the Japanese threat essentially through negotiation and appeasement. This policy frustrated and alienated many nationalistic Chinese.

Despite all these domestic and foreign threats to its rule, the Nanjing government still managed to accomplish certain tasks of national reconstruction. The tariff autonomy in 1928, the monetary reform in 1935, and the construction of railroads, highways and telegraph lines in some provinces were important examples. Historians sympathetic to the GMD have praised the Nanjing Decade as the golden years of nation-building and lamented the "lost chance" of the GMD, as its work was disrupted by the Sino-Japanese War of 1937 to 1945. The critics, on the other hand, have pointed to the fact that the Nanjing government never fully controlled the whole country during those ten years. Although on the eve of the Japanese invasion the government extended its influence to the Southwest while pursuing the fleeing CCP, the core of Nanjing's rule remained the Lower Yangtze provinces. The other provinces were either in the hands of regional militarists or occupied by Japan. Whatever plans of nation-building the government may have tried to implement, therefore, would have had little nationwide impact. Moreover, critics argue that throughout the decade the GMD displayed little vision in its work. It used most of its resources in civil wars and in military build-up, and it paid little attention to fundamental social and economic reforms that might have improved the lives of the masses.

Controversial as it is, the fact remains that the Nanjing decade was the only time when the GMD could claim to be China's national ruler. But for a brief and chaotic period between the end of the Sino-Japanese War and the civil war of 1945 to 1949, it never had such an opportunity again.

Wang Ke-wen

References

Eastman, Lloyd E. *The Abortive Revolution: China under Nationalist Rule, 1927–1937.* Cambridge, MA: Harvard University Press, 1974.

Tien, Hung-mao. *Government and Politics in Kuomintang China, 1927–1937.* Stanford, CA: Stanford University Press, 1972.

Young, Arthur N. *China's Nation-Building Effort, 1927–1937: The Financial and Economic Record.* Stanford, CA: Hoover Institution Press, 1971.

Nanjing Incident (1927)

On March 23, 1927, the National Revolutionary Army occupied Nanjing. The Guomindang's Northern Expedition, launched less than one year earlier, thereby entered the Lower Yangtze valley.

Under the Guomindang–Chinese Communist Party (GMD-CCP) United Front, the expedition had been not only a military effort to reunify China under one government but a "National Revolution" for the reshaping of the country's domestic and foreign policies. In December 1926, as the expedition swept into central China, leaders of the United Front established a government in Wuhan that adopted as its basic foreign policy a militant anti-imperialist stance, and in January 1927 the Wuhan government orchestrated the forcible recovery of the British concessions in Hankou and Jiujiang. Such actions alarmed the foreign powers, which quickly mobilized and reinforced their troops in the Nanjing-Shanghai area as the expeditionary forces moved down along the Yangtze River.

On March 24, clashes occurred between the incoming National Revolutionary Army (the Second and Sixth Armies) and foreigners in Nanjing. In the chaos a number of Westerners were killed. The British and American gunboats gathering at Xiaguan, the river port outside the city, immediately opened fire upon Chinese troops, causing severe casualties and considerable property damage. The foreign powers then demanded apologies and compensations from the Chinese, as well as punishment of the Chinese offenders.

The incident took place at a critical juncture in the "National Revolution." Chiang Kaishek, commander-in-chief of the National Revolutionary Army, was eager to establish a separate power base to challenge the Wuhan government that had recently reduced his power in the GMD. Chiang used the incident as an opportunity to seek the friendship of the nervous foreign powers in his bid for Party leadership. He displayed a conciliatory attitude during post-incident contacts with the British and the Americans, and blamed the incident on the radicals, *i.e.,* Communists, among his troops. The powers were both impressed and relieved; they saw in Chiang a chance to undermine the anti-imperialist radicalism of the GMD from within. This paved the way for Chiang's purge of the Communists from the GMD in Shanghai, also with foreign support, weeks later.

Wang Ke-wen

References

Borg, Dorothy. *American Policy and the Chinese Revolution, 1925–1928.* New York, NY: Macmillan, 1947.

Wilbur, C. Martin. *The Nationalist Revolution in China, 1923–1928.* Cambridge, England: Cambridge University Press, 1983.

Nanjing Massacre (1937)

Having seized Manchuria in the Manchurian Incident of 1931, Japan continued to escalate her aggression against China with the goal of severing north China from the central government at Nanjing. Eventually, Japan launched a full-scale invasion following the Marco Polo Bridge Incident on July 7, 1937, and China was forced to muster an all-out resistance against Japan. One month later, Japan opened a second front at Shanghai in the August Thirteenth Incident. The battle in Shanghai lasted until November 12, 1937.

The biggest prize for the Japanese army was the capture of Nanjing, the capital of China, which was defended by thirteen Chinese divisions comprising approximately 150,000 men, against the Japanese attacking force of seven-and-a-half divisions numbering nearly 200,000 men. The Shanghai Refugee Shelter had taken in 450,000 Chinese refugees during the battle. Trying to forestall a similar crisis, foreign residents at Nanjing established the International Committee for the Nanjing "safety zone" in mid-November 1937, and negotiated with the Chinese authorities and the Japanese embassy for support. On December 1, Ma Chaojun, mayor of Nanjing, turned over to the committee responsibility for the safety zone, which centered around the American embassy and the Nanjing University, opposite the Japanese embassy. After the fall of the city, the population of the safety zone exceeded 290,000 people.

By December 8, Japanese forces had taken most of the strategic positions of the outer defense of Nanjing. On the morning of December 13, the Japanese took the west gate, followed by the fall of the other gates in quick succession. By 11 A.M., some Japanese soldiers had entered the safety zone. In the presence of George A. Fitcher, an American missionary who served as deputy secretary-general of the zone, they killed twenty refugees. Thus commenced the wanton massacre, rape, looting, and burning that did not abate until March 1938.

The postwar Tokyo Trial confirmed that in the first six weeks after the fall of Nanjing, over 200,000 Chinese civilians and disarmed soldiers were killed, and 20,000 women were raped. Subsequent investigations, including interviews with 1,700 survivors of the Nanjing Massacre, determined that the death toll was actually 340,000, including Chinese men and women of all ages. Apparently, twenty-eight cases of large-scale mass murders had resulted in the deaths of 190,000 people, whereas individual murders had taken about 150,000 lives. Equally shocking was the raping. A recent study has shown that as many as 80,000 women had been raped, many of them then murdered, at Nanjing.

The Nanjing Massacre, also known in the West as the "Rape of Nanking," provoked worldwide condemnation at the time and ranks among the worst wartime atrocities in human history. One of the first reports on the massacre was filed by Tillman Durdin for *The New York Times* on December 18, 1938. In China, the Japanese brutalities enraged the whole population, which now was more than ever determined to continue the war of resistance.

After World War II, little attention has been given to this tragedy by historians writing outside of China. Since the 1970s, the Japanese government has made several attempts, officially or unofficially, to deny the veracity of this occurrence. Despite Chinese protest of these denials the Western countries have been guided in their reactions by the economic success of postwar Japan and by the strategic importance of Japan in the Cold War. Consequently, they have generally tolerated Japanese attempts to whitewash the incident. The Nanjing Massacre has turned into an "alleged" incident in the minds of many Japanese, especially those of the younger generation.

In 1990, a 190-page document prepared by Nazi Germany's embassy in Nanjing was discovered in the Potsdam archives in reunified Germany. The document confirmed the occurrence and extent of the Nanjing Massacre. The discovery was followed by the release in 1991 of photographs taken by an American witness, Mr. Fitcher, and film footages shot by Reverend John Magee, another American. Meanwhile, the Chinese government has completed the construction of a memorial museum dedicated to the victims of the massacre at Nanjing.

Tien-wei Wu

References

Timperley, H. J. *Japanese Terror in China.* New York, NY: Modern Age Books, Inc., 1938.

Nanjing-Wuhan Split

In October 1926, the Northern Expeditionary forces of the Guomindang (GMD) captured Wuhan. Acting upon a previous Party decision, the GMD headquarters and its national government in Canton began their relocation to Wuhan. In December, the first group of GMD leaders arrived in Wuhan and, guided by the Soviet adviser Mikhail Borodin, established a Provisional Joint Council of the GMD Central Executive Committee and the National Government Committee to assume temporary leadership of the Party government. Xu Qian was elected as chairman and Borodin became its adviser.

Chiang Kaishek, commander-in-chief of the Northern Expeditionary forces, was able to persuade the second group of GMD leaders traveling from Canton to Wuhan to remain at his military headquarters in Nanchang. They soon organized the Provisional Central Political Council of the GMD and challenged the legitimacy of the Wuhan council. In the ensuing months, both sides denounced each other as illegal, and a personal conflict erupted between Chiang and Borodin. In March 1927 most members of the Nanchang group rejoined their comrades in Wuhan, where they held the third plenum of the GMD's second Central Executive Committee. In the absence of Chiang and some of his supporters, the plenum nullified most of Chiang's political and military power and replaced it with a form of collective leadership. It also strengthened the United Front with the Chinese Communist Party (CCP). In April, Chiang's intra-party rival Wang Jingwei returned from his exile in Europe and became head of the Party government in Wuhan.

Under the direction of Borodin and the United Front, Wuhan adopted a militant anti-imperialist policy aimed especially at Great Britain. In January 1927, the regime had ordered the forcible recovery of British concessions in Hankou and Jiujiang. Such action naturally alarmed the foreign powers and they saw in Chiang the only leader to counter Wuhan's radical influence. When the Northern Expeditionary forces entered the Lower Yangtze valley in April, Chiang, with the support of the foreign powers, moved against the United Front. On April 12, Chiang launched the bloody "party purification" against the CCP in Shanghai and then established his own Party headquarters and national government in Nanjing. Wuhan immediately expelled Chiang from the GMD. The camp of the "National Revolution" formally split into two rival regimes.

In May, both sides resumed their separate Northern Expeditions against the northern warlords. New pressures from the conservative generals on Wuhan's side, including Feng Yuxiang, who had just joined the GMD, soon forced the GMD in Wuhan to reconsider its position on the United Front. As tension grew in Wuhan, Borodin and the CCP wavered between helping the left wing of the GMD and developing the independent strength of the CCP. In June, the contents of a telegram from Moscow, which ordered the CCP to organize its own armed forces, was revealed to Wang Jingwei by the Comintern representative M.N. Roy. The message further convinced the GMD leaders that their condition was precarious. On July 16, the Wuhan regime announced the termination of the United Front. The CCP was expelled and Borodin returned to the Soviet Union.

Agreement on the United Front issue did not reduce Wuhan's hostility toward Chiang Kaishek, and in late July the regime launched an "eastern expedition" against Nanjing. Two weeks later Chiang was forced to step down (he returned to power in early 1928) and negotiations for the peaceful union of the two regimes began. In late August, the Wuhan leaders decided to move the Party government to Nanjing. In early September, GMD leaders from all factions organized a Special Committee in Nanjing to preside over the Party's reunification. The Wuhan-Nanjing split therewith ended. In its wake, however, the "National Revolution" abandoned its initial anti-imperialist stance as well as its radical agenda to seek fundamental changes in China.

Wang Ke-wen

References

Jordan, Donald A. *The Northern Expedition: China's National Revolution of 1926–1928*. Honolulu: The University Press of Hawaii, 1976.

North, Robert C., and Xenia J. Eudin. *M. N. Roy's Mission to China: The Communist-Kuomintang Split of 1927*. Berkeley: University of California Press, 1963.

Wilbur, C. Martin. *The Nationalist Revolution in China, 1923–1928*. Cambridge, England: Cambridge University Press, 1983.

National Bourgeoisie

The concept of the "national bourgeoisie" is the product of Chinese Communist political theory and historiography. The "national bourgeoisie" is distinguished from the "*comprador* bourgeoisie" and/or "bureaucratic bourgeoisie" and is tied to the analysis of Chinese society in the late nineteenth and early twentieth centuries as semicolonial and semifeudal. According to this theory, the bureaucratic and *comprador* bourgeoisie colluded with the imperialist powers in preserving China's semifeudal, semi-colonial economy. The "national bourgeoisie," however, had a dual character. On the one hand, it was oppressed by foreign and *comprador* capitalists; on the other hand, it had economic ties to the forces of imperialism and feudalism. Hence politically, the national bourgeoisie sometimes supported nationalist revolutionary movements, as in the Revolution of 1911 and the Northern Expedition of 1926 to 1927, but sometimes it supported counterrevolution, as in the period from 1927 to 1931. It suffered under Chiang Kaishek's regime as the bureaucratic capitalists increased their control of China's modern economy. During the Sino-Japanese War of 1937 to 1945, the Communists, with some reservations, included the national bourgeoisie as part of the United Front in support of the "new democracy."

This Chinese Communist interpretation has been recently challenged by Western historians, and circumvented by some Chinese scholars. Marie-Claire Bergere, in her study of the Chinese bourgeoisie, and Parks Coble, in his study of the Shanghai capitalists, have pointed out that the distinction between national bourgeoisie and *comprador* bourgeoisie was political, not economic. Bergere asserts that the term "'national bourgeoisie' . . . came to mean those

who were willing to collaborate with the Communist Party. Those who rejected it were dubbed '*compradors*.' Roles varied according to political fluctuations." Coble writes that in the Chinese Communist view, any capitalist supporting Chiang's counterrevolution was *ipso facto* a comprador bourgeois, irrespective of his economic interests. This interpretation was obviously developed to fulfill political needs. In their 1985 study of "capitalist sprouts" in China, Xu Dixin and Wu Chengming implicitly rejected the political distinction between bureaucratic and national capitalists by treating the category solely as an economic concern. They pointed out that many enterprises had investments from both groups and that the relationship between the two was fluid. Pinpointing the specific sources of capital in any given enterprise over time would require further analysis, they claimed.

Although rejecting the concept of the national bourgeoisie *per se*, Bergere, Coble and others agree that bourgeois nationalism did exist in early-twentieth-century China. Exactly when and why certain elements of the bourgeoisie supported national movements varied depending on historical circumstances, not because of a distinction between a national bourgeoisie as opposed to a *comprador* or bureaucratic bourgeoisie.

Andrea McElderry

References

Bergere, Marie-Claire. *The Golden Age of the Chinese Bourgeoisie, 1911–1937*. Trans. Jane Lloyd. Cambridge, England: Cambridge University Press, 1989.

Coble, Parks M. *The Shanghai Capitalists and the Nationalist Government, 1927–1937*. Cambridge, MA: Harvard University Press, 1980.

"National Character"

"National character" discussions in China began with the birth of modern nationalism in the 1890s. Yan Fu, a social evolutionist trained in England, compared the Chinese character unfavorably to the dynamic Western ethos. Chinese ecumenism waned after 1900, and Confucian reformers such as Liang Qichao turned to nation-building. Liang lamented the underdevelopment of Chinese political capabilities, making them slavish subjects, not modern citizens. After 1902, reformers and revolutionaries alike stressed the need for a modern Chinese nationhood through the forging of psychological cohesion. The "national psychology" discourse, of German and French origins, inspired their debates on the urgency of national education and the feasibility of national revolution.

The fall of imperial China in 1912 impelled Liang to reaffirm Chinese cultural values as a means to ensure stability. Yet the republic soon became a fiasco, causing Chinese and Japanese intellectuals to wonder if the Chinese were prone to chaos and despotism. They regarded the Chinese nation as either infantile or senile. Attempts at monarchical restoration prompted the iconoclast journal, *New Youth,* to attack Chinese despotic mentality, which it believed to have been fostered by Confucianism. The New Culture movement that *New Youth* and its followers promoted was countered by the Eastern Culture camp, which defended the superiority of the Chinese cultural spirit.

More corrosive critiques of the Chinese national character came from the proponents of "decadence" and "degeneration" views, then popular in the West but disguised as "evolutionism." Echoing Nietzsche's condemnation of Christianity as two millennia of decadence, Lu Xun charged that, inasmuch as the Chinese people had gone against nature since antiquity, their vital forces had become perverted. This perversion was embodied in the pathetic figure of Ah Q, the protagonist of Lu Xun's most famous story, published in 1921. Lu Xun also likened Chinese culture to a syphilitic inheritance. Such sentiments were shared by eugenicists, notably Zhou Jianren. Degeneration theories also inspired Chen Duxiu, founder of the Chinese Communist Party, and the theorists of the Chinese Youth Party.

With Marxism waxing after 1925, degeneration theories became a minor intellectual current in China. From the 1920s to the 1930s, the notion of degeneration was wedded to a geographical viewpoint. Since the north-south split was central to the republican era, discussions of degeneration often reflected southern snobbery. Pan Guangdan affirmed the American geographer-eugenicist Ellsworth Huntington's position on north China's racial degeneration. He attributed it to the unfavorable conditions which influenced the process of natural selection in that region. Zhang Junjun, another Huntington follower, averred that calamities had driven the best stock of north China to the South, where they were enervated by the subtropical climate, resulting in the combination of a feeble northern intelligence contained in a weak southern physique. Lin Yutang's *My Country and My People* (1935) turned north-south tension into a dialectic struggle between nature and decadence: the vigorous northern barbarians periodically rejuvenated the overly mature Chinese civilization. The north-south historical schism later resurfaced in John K. Fairbank's view of "continental China" versus "maritime China."

In postwar America, the Research in Contemporary Cultures at Columbia University conducted large-scale studies on national characters. Freudian in spirit, the Americans projected their own anxieties about the "absent father," the "castrating mother," and the loss of virility onto the "Chinese personality." Later, Lucian Pye and Richard Solomon replaced "mother" with "father" as the emaciating agency in forming the Chinese authoritarian personality. They also shifted the emphasis from the "sapping of virility" to the "inability to manage aggression." American views were parroted in a 1971 symposium on Chinese character by Taiwan's Academia Sinica.

In postwar Taiwan, the rebel Li Ao and the cynic Bo Yang took up the critique of national character as a means of venting their discontent with the sociopolitical status quo. Their approach was literary rather than theoretical. Li ridiculed Taiwan's gerontocratic power structure and revived the syphilitic imagery of Chinese tradition. Bo recycled another of Lu Xun's imagery, namely, that Chinese society is a "jar for marinating human flesh."

The failed Maoist revolution reactivated the critique of national character among Chinese intellectuals, first by Sun Longji's structuralist *The Deep Structure of Chinese Culture* (1983) in Hong Kong, then followed by mainland intellectuals. The latter touched on a variety of themes, from despotism to the lack of virility in Chinese males, but they were still confined by the Marxian concept of feudalism. The critique culminated in the 1988 television series, "River Elegy" ("Heshang")," which reintroduced the north-south, continental-maritime split to support the "special economic zones" experiment in south China.

Lung-kee Sun

References

Sun, Lung-kee. "Contemporary Chinese Culture: Structure and Emotionality." *The Austrialian Journal of Chinese Affairs* no. 26 (July 1991): 1–41.

———. "Social Psychology in the Late Qing Period." *Modern China* 18, no. 3 (July 1992): 235–62.

National Emergency Conference

The National Emergency Conference was convened by the Guomindang (GMD) government in the wake of the Manchurian Incident of September 1931 for the purpose of examining major national policies. The Manchurian Incident was a severe blow to the GMD's status as the national leader. It occurred while the Party was paralyzed by the Nanjing-Canton split and the government offered no effective defense or strategy to prevent northeast China (Manchuria) from falling into Japanese hands. Under popular pressure and in an attempt to salvage popular support, the GMD decided, during its Fourth Party Congress at Nanjing in November, to convene a National Emergency Conference *(Guonan huiyi)* with representatives from outside the government. In January 1932, the government formally announced its plan to invite "reputable men with knowledge and experience" from various sectors of society to the conference, which would "seek ways of national self-reliance." One hundred and eighty-nine such people received the invitation, many of them known critics of the GMD.

The January Twenty-Eighth Incident in Shanghai, however, soon forced the government to move its seat from Nanjing to Loyang and postpone the conference. Meanwhile, the new GMD government under Chiang Kaishek and Wang Jingwei was alarmed by the declared intention of some of the invited delegates to criticize the GMD's political tutelage at the conference. As a precautionary measure Wang and Chiang added about two hundred GMD delegates to the conference and shifted the subjects of discussion from "all matters relating to the national emergency" to policies of national defense, disaster relief, and bandit suppression.

Angered by this new measure, many invited delegates decided to boycott the conference. When the conference was finally held at Loyang on April 7, only one hundred and forty-four delegates attended—about one-third of the total number invited—and most of them GMD members. Nevertheless, the conference passed resolutions urging the speedy transition of the GMD government from political tutelage to constitutional democracy, and the organization of a national representative assembly under political tutelage. It rejected a proposal for the formation of a coalition government, but not before causing serious disputes among the delegates.

The GMD government did not put these resolutions into practice. The conference failed to serve the GMD's purpose of displaying popular support for the government and fostering national solidarity in the face of Japanese aggression. It in fact reflected widespread discontent with the Party's rule in China, even within its own ranks.

Wang Ke-wen

References

Eastman, Lloyd E. *The Abortive Revolution: China under Nationalist Rule, 1927–1937.* Cambridge, MA: Harvard University Press, 1974.

National Essence

As an idea, national essence *(guocui)* refers to the entirety of Chinese culture, especially traditional literature, philosophy and art. As a movement, between the late 1890s and the 1920s, it helped to define the goals of Chinese nationalists: it linked the preservation of the nation and race with the preservation of its civilization. Intellectuals associated with the national essence supported the Revolution of 1911 and were anti-monarchist as well as anti-Manchu. However, the national essence became increasingly tied to conservative politics, and during the May Fourth era after 1919, as nationalism became associated with both political radicalization and cultural iconoclasm, the national essence drifted away from the mainstream of Chinese nationalism.

Originally a Japanese neologism *(kokusui)*, national essence was in part an East Asian defense against the onslaught of Western culture. Emerging in the late 1880s, national essence thinkers criticized the unreflective westernization policies of the Meiji government and sought to define a unique Japanese spirit. In China, however, it grew naturally out of the Han learning tradition of the Qing dynasty, which had subjected the classics to new scrutiny, challenging many accepted interpretations and datings. Its first eminent spokesmen included the philologists and classicists Zhang Binglin, Liu Shipei, Huang Jie, Chen Quping and Liu

Yazu. Organizations active before the Revolution of 1911 included the Society for the Protection of National Studies, which published the rather academic *National Essence Journal,* and the Southern Society, which published poetry and prose anthologies and resuscitated much Ming loyalist literature.

The National Essence movement assimilated a visceral anti-Manchuism to a firm commitment to keeping Chinese culture alive. Political and cultural interests were occasionally mixed with social radicalism, as a new concern with the common folk was becoming widespread. Yet one motive behind the effort to preserve Chinese culture, clearer after the revolution, was fear of adulteration of the high scholarly traditions by popular culture. It is hairsplitting to try to determine whether the national essence scholars were more committed to the nation-state (government, territory, race) or culture (language, philosophy, literature), for it was precisely their point that the two categories intrinsically overlapped. On the one hand, a people could exist without a state but would perish without a culture. On the other hand, culture was a means to preserve the nation-state.

National essence scholars differed openly and sometimes acrimoniously on questions of political involvement in the disturbed years that followed the Revolution of 1911. Beijing University became the home of both iconoclastic radicals and many of the increasingly conservative (anti-reform) national essence scholars. Southeastern University in Nanjing, however, became the actual center of national essence thought in the May Fourth era. There, Wu Mi and Mei Guangdi, among others, founded the *Critical Review* in 1922. Wu regarded himself as a disciple of Huang Jie, and both Wu and Mei had studied with the humanist Irving Babbitt at Harvard University. By this time, however, national essence had come for many to signify old-fashioned views, if not reactionary positions. Articles in the *Critical Review* deliberately defended the traditional high Chinese culture and also introduced a conservative view of Western culture: from classical Greek philosophy to Renaissance humanism to Babbitt.

Wu and Mei emphasized that, for all of their respect for Western culture, it too was in crisis. World War I had shown the failure of Western values, and they thought the West had something to learn from China. But they perhaps became better known for what they opposed: Marxism and communism, vernacular literature, liberalism, the search for Chinese nationhood in folk culture, and the entire New Culture movement. They believed that some kind of essential quality is inherent in Chinese culture, and they increasingly identified this with "aristocratic" culture. The *Critical Review* did not last past the 1920s, and with its demise the National Essence movement came to an end. Zhang Binglin ran a private National Studies Seminar in the 1930s, and the identification of national identity with traditional culture continues even today. The movement, however, died with the splintering of traditional culture, a process in which national essence scholars themselves had played a role.

National essence thinking contributed to the development of Chinese nationalism by accepting the notion that China constituted not "all under heaven" *(tianxia)* but one great cultural tradition among several. Its adherents supported certain features of westernization as variously desirable and inevitable, while also picking and choosing from among the options of traditional Chinese culture in a new way. A latent radicalism thus lay within the national essence school as long as alternative traditions could be used to critique the present. Its emphasis on the heroic knight-errant or the poet-scholar activist also provided an agent of change. The school was conservative, however, in several senses of the term. The search for an undying "essence" denied that Chinese identity was ultimately subject to historical evolution or any but the most basic conditions, such as ancient geography. Furthermore, national essence scholars before 1911 criticized the Manchus and appealed to disinterested public-mindedness *(gong)* to attack monarchical despotism in general, but saw republicanism in this light less as a civic virtue than as a politics of selfishness *(si)*. After 1912, therefore, national essence scholars offered little support to the makeshift institutions of the Republic.

Since national essence was the historical expression of the Chinese genius, any attempt to uproot this heritage would result in incalculable loss in political as well as cultural terms. "Mainstream" Chinese nationalism assumed a much more iconoclastic form, explicitly denying the validity of at least the high traditions of Chinese culture. Yet national essence scholarship contributed even to this view, both because national essence scholars trained many of its leading exponents (Lu Xun, Zhou Zuoren, Qian Xuantong) and because even iconoclasm had to know what it was rejecting. More to the point, many, probably most, educated Chinese fell neither into the iconoclastic nor the conservative camps, but instead favored fundamental changes while finding a source of pride in China's rich cultural traditions.

Peter Zarrow

References

Bernal, Martin. "Liu Shih-p'ei and National Essence." *The Limits of Change: Essays on Conservative Alternatives in Republican China,* ed. Charlotte Furth, 90–112. Cambridge, MA: Harvard University Press, 1976.

Schneider, Laurence A. "National Essence and the New Intelligentsia." Ibid. 57–89.

National People's Army (Guominjun)

See FENG YUXIANG

National Protection Movement

The National Protection movement, (Huguo Yundong) a military revolt, overthrew Yuan Shikai and his monarchical attempt in 1916.

In December 1915 Yuan Shikai, first president of the Chinese Republic, announced his plan of reverting the country to monarchy and enthroning himself as Emperor Hongxian on January 1, 1916. The announcement enraged those who supported the Republic. Cai E, a Yunnan military leader then serving in Yuan's government in Beijing, secretly returned to his home province and staged a revolt. Cai secured assistance from the military governor of Yunnan, Tang Jiyao, the former Guomindang general Li Liejun, and his mentor, Liang Qichao. On December 25, Cai, Tang, and Li declared the independence of Yunnan in opposition to Yuan's monarchical plan, taking as their example the cessation of the provinces during the Revolution of 1911. Tang retained his governorship in Yunnan, while Cai and Li assumed command of the anti-Yuan National Protection Army *(Huguojun).* On January 1, 1916, they again issued a manifesto calling for the military overthrow of the "traitor of the Republic," and launched an attack on Yuan's Beiyang forces in the neighboring provinces of Sichuan and Hunan.

The anti-Yuan movement received nationwide sympathy and dealt a severe blow to Yuan's legitimacy. Soon the provinces of Guizhou, Guangxi, Guangdong, Zhejiang, Shaanxi, Sichuan, and Hunan also declared their independence. Yuan was forced first to postpone the enthronement and then, on March 22, to cancel the entire plan. But he still tried to keep his presidency. The National Protection forces refused to compromise. In May, the independent provinces organized a national regime at Zhaoqing, Guangdong, and elected Tang Jiyao as their military leader. The regime was supported by the Jinbudang (Progressive Party), and Sun Yatsen's Chinese Revolutionary Party also joined the anti-Yuan movement.

Faced with strong opposition, and dissension within his own camp, Yuan and his government quickly collapsed. On June 6, Yuan died of illness and was succeeded by his vice-president, Li Yuanhong. In July, Li reestablished the provisional constitution and the parliament that Yuan had abolished, and the Zhaoqing regime dissolved. Cai E himself died of illness at the end of that year, but the National Protection movement which he had initiated helped to save the young Republic from Yuan's dictatorship and imperial ambition.

Wang Ke-wen

References

Sutton, Donald S. *Provincial Militarism and the Chinese Republic: The Yunnan Army, 1905–25.* Ann Arbor: University of Michigan Press, 1980.

Young, Ernest P. *The Presidency of Yuan Shih-k'ai: Liberalism and Dictatorship in Early Republican China.* Ann Arbor: University of Michigan Press, 1977.

National Revolution *(Guomin Geming)*

The proclaimed mission of the Nationalist Party or Guomindang (GMD) in China, "national revolution" *(guomin geming)* first appeared in Sun Yatsen's *Design for Revolution (Geming fanglue)* of 1906, in which Sun coined the term to distinguish his republican revolutionary movement from the "revolution of heroes" *(yingxiong geming)* of the past. The term was defined simply as a joint effort by all people in China, who fought for the principles of "liberty, equality, and fraternity." In that spirit, Sun repeatedly used the term "national people" *(guomin)* to name his organizations after the founding of the Republic. In 1919, for example, Sun reorganized his Chinese Revolutionary

Party *(Zhonghua gemingdang)* into the Chinese Guomindang (literally National People's Party, but the popular English translation has been Nationalist Party).

By then, however, the term had assumed some new meanings, or rather implications. After the success of the Bolshevik revolution in Russia, the Comintern called for national revolutions by colonial or semicolonial societies to overthrow imperialism and achieve national independence. The translation of "national revolution" into *guomin geming* by Sun Yatsen and his followers in the early 1920s was apparently intentional, because Sun was forming an alliance with the Soviet Union at the time. A convergence of aims would be conducive to this new alliance. Under Soviet guidance, Sun's Guomindang established the first United Front with the young Chinese Communist Party (CCP) in 1923, and for the next few years national revolution became the common goal of both parties.

The exact connotation of the term, however, was never fully resolved. All in the United Front agreed that the nature of their "national revolution" was anti-imperialist and anti-militarist (as the warlords were now regarded as domestic agents of imperialism), serious disagreement arose concerning the socio-economic dimensions of the effort. The CCP and the left wing of the GMD believed that the revolution should pursue a socialist reconstruction of Chinese society. The right wing of the GMD rejected such a view. During his lifetime, Sun was never clear in his own interpretations. After his death in 1925, the controversy was intensified by a power struggle, as the CCP attempted to use the radical interpretation to increase its own influence within the GMD. Dai Jitao's *National Revolution and the Chinese Guomindang* of 1925 represented a right-wing response to the radical interpretation. Dai Jitao argued for class harmony instead of class struggle, and suggested that Sun Yatsen's political philosophy was based not on Marxism but on the Confucianist concept of humanity *(renai)*.

As the Northern Expedition began in 1926, differences in the understanding of the nature of national revolution led to conflicting policies in the territories newly recovered by the United Front, precipitating a split between left and right. In 1927, Chiang Kaishek launched his anti-Communist purge and terminated the United Front. Dai Jitao's conservative interpretation became the ideological rationale of his action.

In the years immediately following the completion of the Northern Expedition, as the CCP abandoned the term "national revolution" and launched its own socialist revolution in China, the GMD continued to debate this issue. The Left GMD, led by Wang Jingwei and Chen Gongbo, lamented the fact that the Northern Expedition had failed to accomplish the anti-imperialist, anti-militarist and noncapitalist goals of the "national revolution." The anarchists who supported Chiang Kaishek, on the other hand, insisted that "national revolution" simply meant a revolution by all the people *(quanmin geming)*, potentially including militarists and capitalists, against their common enemy, imperialism. Chiang himself never admitted the abolition of anti-imperialism, or even the noncapitalist approach to national reconstruction, as long-term objectives of the GMD, yet his government in effect sought to maintain the domestic and external *status quo* in China. As Chiang gradually consolidated his power in GMD China, the intra-party debate subsided. After 1930, "national revolution" came to be identified with the nominal reunification of China in the Northern Expedition and the subsequent GMD rule.

Wang Ke-wen

References

Bedeski, Robert E. *State-building in Modern China: The Kuomintang in the Prewar Period.* Berkeley: University of California Press, 1981.

Wilbur, C. Martin. *The Nationalist Revolution in China, 1923–1928.* Cambridge, England: Cambridge University Press, 1984.

National Revolutionary Army

The formal title of the Guomindang army from 1926 to 1949 was the National Revolutionary Army (NRA). In May 1926, during the first Guomindang–Chinese Communist Party (GMD-CCP) United Front, the GMD government in Canton unified all the armed forces under its control into the National Revolutionary Army, so named because of the mission of "National Revolution" *(guomin geming)* which the United Front claimed. The NRA comprised the former armies of Guangdong, Hunan, Jiangxi, and Guangxi, as well as the Whampoa Training Corps. Chiang Kaishek became its commander-in-chief. Two months later, the NRA launched the Northern Expedition against the warlords. Along the way, the NRA absorbed defeated warlord forces. By April 1927, it had swelled from eight (July 1926) to more than forty armies. In the final phase of the campaign, the NRA was reorganized into four army groups commanded separately by Chiang Kaishek, Feng Yuxiang, Yan Xishan, and Li Zongren. Again, it incorporated Feng's Guominjun and Yan's Shanxi Army into its ranks. The NRA's rapid growth ensured the GMD's power and legitimacy as China's national ruler, but it also diluted the ideological commitment and political loyalty of the GMD military forces. During the Nanjing Decade (1927–37) that followed the completion of the Northern Expedition, many NRA units turned against Chiang's Nanjing regime and waged civil wars.

When the Sino-Japanese War (1937–45) began and the second GMD-CCP United Front was formed, the CCP's Red Army was absorbed into the NRA. Under this unified title, the Chinese forces fought against the invading Japanese in a long war of resistance, symbolizing China's unity and independence. After the conflict, the civil war between the GMD and the CCP erupted. In 1947, when the GMD government adopted a constitution, it renamed the NRA as the Chinese Army.

Wang Ke-wen

References

Liu, F. F. *A Military History of Modern China, 1924–1949.* Princeton, NJ: Princeton University Press, 1956.

National Salvation Association

In 1935, Japan stepped up its invasion of China. Following the signing of the secret Qin-Doihara Agreement in June and the He-Umezu Agreement in July, Japan turned north China (including Hebei, Chahar, Beiping, and Tianjin) into its "semi-colony" through virtual control over the Hebei-Chahar Political Affairs Committee established by General Song Zheyuan in December. North China was becoming another Manchukuo. Pursuing the policy of exterminating the Communists before engaging in external resistance, the Guomindang government made one territorial concession after another, seemingly unwilling to face up to Japanese aggression.

The failure of the Guomindang to resist Japan engendered a mood of militant nation-

"Any attempt to sabotage the anti-Japanese movement is an act of counter-revolution!"—A wall poster in Shanghai in the early 1930s. (Courtesy of Nationalist Party Archives.)

alism among the urban elites. The student demonstrations in Beiping at the end of that year, known as the December Ninth movement, hastened the rapid growth of a national salvation movement. This began with the founding of the Cultural Circle's National Salvation Association in December 1935, when intellectuals along with business and labor groups throughout urban China organized themselves into various National Salvation Associations (*Jiuguohui*) to demand an immediate war against Japan.

On May 31, 1936, in an effort to create a unified national salvation movement, seventy representatives of over sixty National Salvation Associations from eighteen provinces and cities met in Shanghai to form the All-China Federation of National Salvation Associations. It elected a board of forty directors that included such prominent political and cultural figures as Soong Qingling, He Xiangning, Shen Junru, Zou Daofen, and Li Gongpu, and it published a weekly, *National Salvation News,* to voice its anti-Japanese agenda. The federation's inaugural manifesto criticized the government's weak-kneed policy toward Japan and appealed to all patriotic parties in China, including especially the Guomindang and the Chinese Communists, to stop their civil war and instead form a united front of "mighty force" against Japanese imperialism.

The federation was generally well-connected with the political establishment, but it lacked a mass base. To mobilize grassroots support, the federation organized the commemoration of the fifth anniversary of the Manchurian Incident in September 1936; in November, it led an anti-Japanese mass procession through downtown Shanghai on the occasion of the funeral of writer Lu Xun; and in the same month it helped in the fundraising and public relations for a series of labor strikes at Japanese-owned cotton mills in Shanghai and Qingdao.

The Guomindang government in Nanjing then took steps to suppress the national salvation movement. The chief victims of Nanjing's show of force were the seven respected leaders of the federation: Shen Junru, Zou Daofen, Zhang Naiqi, Shi Liang, Sha Qianli, Li Gongpu, and Wang Zaoshi. On November 23, the government arrested these "seven gentlemen" (*qi junzi*), as they were later referred to in the press, and prepared to transport them to Nanjing for a military trial. But the arrest evoked massive protests throughout the country, which forced the government temporarily to detain the "seven gentlemen" in Suzhou. The public outrage soon subsided when Chiang Kaishek was kidnapped by Zhang Xuelinang in Xian in December. The Xian Incident and its dramatic conclusion enabled the second United Front to be formed between the Guomindang and the Chinese Communists. China finally rallied in a national resistance against Japan. After the Sino-Japanese War broke out in July 1937, the "seven gentlemen" were freed.

During the war, the federation moved with the government to the interior and, since its patriotic demand was basically fulfilled, it merged into the China Democratic League when the latter was formed in 1939. In the chaotic postwar era, when the country again languished in the grip of civil war and foreign harassment, the federation changed its name to the Chinese People's National Salvation Association and once more sought to liberate China from the yoke of imperialism and dictatorship.

Poshek Fu

References

Coble, Parks M. *Facing Japan,* Cambridge, MA: Harvard University Press, 1991.

Fu, Poshek. *Passivity, Resistance, and Collaboration.* Stanford, CA: Stanford University Press, 1993.

National Socialist Party of China
See CHANG, CARSUN

Native Place Associations

Native place associations, commonly *huiguan* (prior to the twentieth century) or *tongxianghui* (usually the twentieth century) were formed by sojourners from other parts of China who organized themselves in Chinese cities according to native province, prefecture or county for mutual aid and protection and in pursuit of common economic, social, and cultural interests. Native place associations were influential economic and cultural centers in urban areas and often featured prominently in the anti-foreignism and early nationalist social mobilization that developed at the end of the nineteenth century and in the early republican period.

Tension between native place associations and Westerners began as foreign authorities attempted to expand their concession areas in Chinese treaty ports. In nineteenth century commercial cities, native place associations were among the largest Chinese corporate landholders and could easily mobilize sectors of the Chinese community in defense of their interests.

Huiguan were at the core of the first major social conflicts between Chinese and foreigners in late nineteenth-century Shanghai, the largest Chinese commercial city and treaty port. In the Ningbo Cemetery Riots (1874 and 1898), sojourners from Ningbo prefecture (Zhejiang province) rioted to prevent French encroachments on Ningbo burial grounds in Shanghai. The killing of Chinese by French troops in 1898 led to an anti-foreign strike by Ningbo people in Shanghai, stopping shipping and impairing foreign trade. Sectors of the Ningbo community also boycotted French goods.

Such conflicts soon acquired new meaning as symbols of a Chinese national struggle against imperialism. Activists incorporated and built on native place sentiments in popular anti-imperialist movements in the first years of the twentieth century. In December 1904, when drunken Russian soldiers accidentally killed a Ningbo sojourner in Shanghai, thirty thousand Ningbo sojourners protested, persuading their native place association to demand redress from foreign authorities in the city. This became a *cause célèbre* in the radical press, which identified the Ningbo people's struggle as a national struggle.

Coalitions of sojourning merchant associations helped to mobilize and implement the anti-American boycott and the Mixed Court Riot (both in 1905). Merchant-led associations were also active in the railway and mining rights recovery movements preceding the Revolution of 1911. In revolutionary mobilization itself, these associations served as important funding and recruitment networks.

A new form of native place association which rejected the older name *huiguan* and called itself *tongxianghui* emerged during the time of the revolution. This self-consciously modern, somewhat more democratic and explicitly nationalist type of native place organization grew in numbers and popularity during the republican period. *Tongxianghui,* together with the older *huiguan,* were important in the social mobilization underlying the May Fourth movement (1919), particularly in Shanghai. After the May Fourth movement, the relative political significance of native place associations diminished as new forms of political and occupational associations developed. *Tongxianghui* in Shang-

hai grew again in membership and significance in the 1930s, as other forms of associational life were constrained by the Guomindang government. Several of the more powerful *Tongxianghui* participated in the production of anti-Japanese propaganda and fundraising efforts, as well as in sheltering anti-Japanese activists. In the course of Japanese attacks on Shanghai in 1932 and 1937, native place associations played a major role in housing and caring for war refugees, transporting many back to their native provinces.

Bryna Goodman

References

Belsky, R. D. "Bones of Contention: Siming Gongsuo Riots of 1874 and 1898." *Papers on Chinese History* 1, no. 1 (Spring 1992): 56–73.

Goodman, Bryna. "New Culture, Old Habits: Native-Place Organization and the May Fourth Movement." *Shanghai Sojourners,* ed. Frederic Wakeman, Jr. and Wenhsin Yeh. Berkeley: University of California Press, 1992.

Nativist Literature

The Nativist Literary movement *(Xiangtu wenxue yundong),* the first wave of ethnic consciousness in post-1949 Taiwan under Guomindang (GMD) rule, was launched when Taiwan experienced a series of political setbacks on the international scene: the Diaoyutai controversy in 1970, withdrawal from the United Nations in 1971, Nixon's visit to the People's Republic of China (PRC) and the severance of diplomatic relations with Japan in 1973. A prevailing sense of crisis at Taiwan's future soon culminated in a large-scale intellectual movement calling for a reexamination of various aspects of Taiwan society.

In an ideological-moralistic vein, the proponents of the movement identified the Western-influenced modernist literature which had emerged on the island since the 1960s as their prime target of criticism. They considered the introspective and obscure orientation of Taiwan's modernist literature as elitist, decadent, and socially irresponsible, symptomatic of the self-exile mood propagated by the émigré government and of the island's endangered cultural identity caused by the neocolonial imperialism of the capitalist West. The movement provided an opportunity for native intellectuals to express a long-subdued discontent with the power structure of Taiwan's political, socioeconomic and cultural system. In retrospect, the movement represented a contestation of spaces between different interest groups on the island in the 1970s: high and low literature/culture, the urban and the rural, capitalism and socialism, the bourgeoisie and the working class, and mainlanders and Taiwanese.

The term *Xiangtu wenxue* was first used in 1930 by a group of Taiwanese writers, who advocated an extensive use of Taiwanese dialect and the depiction of the plight of Taiwanese under the Japanese occupation. Although focusing on homeland or village-earth *(xiangtu)*, the movement at the time was not intended to be exclusively regional or rural. It was rather nationalistic in nature, an expression of Chinese consciousness against Japanese colonial rule. In the 1970s, when the Nativist movement resurfaced in a new milieu, the legacy of Taiwanese forebears was charged with new implications and profound ramifications, particularly as to what the term *xiangtu* may mean. Writers such as Wang To and Yang Qingchu redefined *Xiangtu wenxue* as exposé literature of social evils. They created a tragic image of the lower social strata Taiwanese, exploited by the rich and the powerful.

In addition to this exploiter/exploited polarizing intent, their fiction is also deliberately regional; they eulogize folk tradition and rural culture, identifying them as the Taiwanese ethnic heritage. In contrast to this Taiwan-centered trend, Chen Yingzhen's fiction defined *xiangtu* in the context of Chinese nationalism, and this proclaimed cultural affinity to China immediately made him a controversial figure among the *xiangtu* advocates who were mostly anti-Chinese. Reminiscent of his predecessors' romantic notion of a mother China in the colonial period, Chen's nationalism is infused with a personal vision of a cultural critic who is primarily concerned with the postcolonial impact of Western hegemony in various guises on the Third World.

Still other writers, such as Huang Chunming and Wang Zhenhe, who received high acclaim from the *xiangtu* advocates, refused to be labeled as *xiangtu* writers. Both writers, each in his own way, used regionalism as an expression of universality; their tragicomic world of the downtrodden Taiwanese is a microcosm of the human condition. The conscious line-drawing between themselves and the *xiangtu* activists signifies their resistance of turning the term *xiangtu* into a slogan.

The movement reached its climax in 1977, when a series of heated debates erupted. Attacks came from academic liberals, modernist writers as well as pro-government émigré writers, who opened fire at the *xiangtu* advocates' proletarian emphasis and class consciousness. On the other hand, *xiangtu* advocates also met with sympathy and support from certain prominent émigré scholars of the older generation, who saw in the movement a rebirth of the May Fourth movement spirit. The debates ended in 1978 when the mainland-based authorities, threatened by the mass appeal of the movement, intervened by issuing warnings against ethnic separatism (a sentiment suspected of promoting Taiwan independence) and against any ideological linkage with Marxism. In the name of artistic autonomy and social harmony, the government condemned nativist literature as heretical. In late 1978, the *Xiangtu wenxue* entered its last phase as a literary movement when some of its key figures exited from the literary scene and continued their oppositional journey in the political arena.

Although short-lived, the movement had significant impact not only on the development of Taiwan's creative literature, but more importantly, on the island's political, social, and cultural life in general, which has been veering toward indigenization since the 1980s.

Li-fen Chen

References
Lau, Joseph S. "Echoes of the May Fourth Movement in Hsiang-tu Fiction." *Mainland China, Taiwan, and U.S. Policy,* ed. Hung-mao Tien, 135–150. Cambridge, MA: Oelgeschlager, Gunn & Hain, 1983.
Wang, Jing. "Taiwan Hsiang-t'u Literature: Perspectives in the Evolution of a Literary Movement." *Chinese Fiction from Taiwan: Critical Perspectives,* ed. Jeannette L. Faurot, 43–70. Bloomington: Indiana University Press, 1980.

New Army

The New Army was a modernized national army founded by the Qing government as part of its reform program in the 1890s to the 1910s. The first unit of the new-style armed force, called Dingwu Army, was established in north

China following China's defeat in the first Sino-Japanese War (1894–95). It was soon taken over by Yuan Shikai and renamed the Newly Created Army *(xinjian lujun),* or "New Army." Around the same time, the governor-general of LiangJiang (Jiangsu and Zhejiang), Zhang Zhidong, organized another "New Army" that was also called Self-Strengthening Army *(ziqiangjun).* In 1901, Yuan expanded his "New Army" into Beiyang Army, which in 1905 absorbed Zhang's Self-Strengthening Army. Later, the Qing government unified all armed forces in the country into the Chinese Army, with two-thirds of it coming from Yuan's Beiyang system, but the Chinese Army was still generally referred to as the "New Army."

In the early 1900s, a large number of patriotic youth in China went overseas, especially to Japan, in pursuit of military studies. They were motivated by a desire to strengthen China's military so that the country could effectively defend itself against imperialist encroachments. Many of them subsequently turned to anti-Manchuism and joined the revolutionary organizations in Japan or Europe. After returning to China, these well-trained young men often found employment in the New Army but still worked secretly for the anti-Manchu cause. After 1906, Sun Yatsen's Tongmenghui (Revolutionary Alliance) shifted its attention from the secret societies to the New Army as the potential "arms of the revolution." Indeed, the Wuchang Uprising in October 1911 that eventually overthrew the Qing Dynasty was initiated by revolutionary officers and soldiers in the New Army in Wuhan. On the other hand, the Beiyang portion of the New Army was to become the foundation of Chinese warlordism during the early years of the Republic.

Wang Ke-wen

References

Fung, Edmund S. K. *The Military Dimension of the Chinese Revolution: The New Army and Its Role in the Revolution of 1911.* Vancouver: University of British Columbia Press, 1980.

Hatano, Yoshihiro. "The New Armies." *China in Revolution: The First Phase, 1900–1913,* ed. Mary C. Wright, 365–82. New Haven, CT: Yale University Press, 1968.

Powell, Ralph L. *The Rise of Chinese Military Power, 1895–1912.* Princeton, NJ: Princeton University Press, 1955.

New Confucianism *(Xin Rujia)*

New Confucianism is a twentieth-century intellectual movement that seeks to revitalize Confucian philosophy as China's cultural foundation.

Since the May Fourth movement, the mainstream of Chinese intellectual thought has been iconoclasm and westernization. Confucianism has been regarded, especially by the youth, as outdated and reactionary. Several attempts by the republican leaders, from Yuan Shikai to Chiang Kaishek, to use Confucianism as the ideological rationale for their conservative political causes further discredited this intellectual tradition in the public eye. To counter this current, believers of Confucianism began to advocate a reexamination—and modernization—of the philosophy in order to reassert its dominant position in the country's culture and society.

The movement began in the 1920s under the leadership of Liang Shuming and Xiung Shili, and later was guided by Feng Youlan, He Ling and Carsun Chang (Zhang Junmai). Emphasizing the universal significance of Confucianism, the New Confucianists expanded on the themes of Song-Ming neo-Confucianism while supplementing them with the analytical framework of Western metaphysics. In his landmark work, *Eastern and Western Cultures and Their Philosophies (Dongxi wenhua jiqi zhexue),* Liang Shuming compared the Western, Indian, and Chinese civilizations and concluded that the revival of Chinese (essentially Confucian) culture was not only the future fate of China but the destiny of the world. Among the early New Confucianists He Ling was probably the most nationalist in his arguments. Writing during the second Sino-Japanese War (1937–45), He identified Confucianism as the national philosophy *(minzu zhexue)* and linked the revival of Confucianism with national revival.

In 1958, after the Communist victory on the mainland, a group of New Confucianists, Carsun Chang, Tang Junyi, Mou Zongsan, and Xu Fuguan, issued "A Manifesto to the World on Chinese Culture" *(Wei Zhongguo wenhua jinggao shijie renshi xuanyan)* in Hong Kong. It reaffirmed the vitality of the humanist tradition of Chinese culture, *i.e.,* Confucianism, but admitted the need of this tradition to incorporate Western science and democracy in order to continue its development in the modern world. Implicitly anti-Communist, the manifesto represented the view of a new generation of New Confucianists. Through teaching and writing, their thinking influenced the Chinese intellectuals in Taiwan and Hong Kong during the following decades. The movement remains active today, with new vitalities injected into it by Tu Wei-ming (Du Weiming) and others.

Wang Ke-wen

References

Chang, Hao. "New Confucianism and the Intellectual Crisis of Contemporary China." *The Limits of Change: Essays on Conservative Alternatives in Republican China,* ed. Charlotte Furth, 276–302. Cambridge, MA: Harvard University Press, 1976.

Munro, Donald J. "Humanism in Modern China: Fung Yu-lan and Hsiung Shih-li." *Nothing Concealed: Essays in Honor of Liu Yu-yun,* ed. Frederick Wakeman, Jr., 179–192. Taibei: Chinese Materials and Research Aids Service Center, 1970.

New Culture Movement

See MAY FOURTH MOVEMENT

New Democracy

"New democracy" *(Xin minzhuzhuyi),* a political concept developed by the Chinese Communist leader Mao Zedong, became a central plank of the Chinese Communist Party (CCP) in 1940. The concept was formulated to build a broad national coalition under the leadership of the Communist Party by providing a role for the "national bourgeoisie" (mid-level capitalists) as well as the petty bourgeoisie, the proletariat, and the peasantry in the revolutionary movement. It was said to represent the creative development of Marxism-Leninism based on the specific national conditions of China.

The central ideas behind the new-democracy concept date to the early 1920s, when the Communist International (Comintern) determined that a "united front" between the CCP and the Guomindang (GMD) would be necessary in order to complete the national, or bourgeois-democratic, revolution in China. The role of the Communist Party was to cooperate with non-Communist, nationalist elements in the creation of a broad national coalition to destroy the warlords and oppose Western imperialism (First United Front, 1923–27) and to resist the Japanese invasion of China (Second United Front, 1937–41). The first United Front was relatively successful in achieving its goal, the second much less so; both ultimately broke down amid mutual acrimony and bloodshed.

Following his ascendancy in the CCP during the Long March (1934–36), Mao Zedong worked with a small group of party theoreticians (*e.g.*, Chen Boda) to develop a comprehensive ideological framework for the CCP. The core idea behind this effort was the sinification, or nationalization, of Marxism-Leninism, based on the concrete practice of the Chinese revolution. A key element in this reformulation of Marxist doctrine was the concept of new democracy, which Mao elaborated in an important work in January 1940. Due to its relative backwardness, he argued, Chinese society had yet to complete the national, or bourgeois-democratic, revolution; it therefore followed that in China, unlike in czarist Russia, the Communist Party could not move directly into the socialist phase of the revolution. Rather, the Party would necessarily have to build a broad coalition of national bourgeoisie, petty bourgeoisie, proletariat, and peasantry in order to unite the country to overthrow the "big" or *comprador*/bureaucrat bourgeoisie (*i.e.*, the top GMD leaders and their financial backers), expel the Western imperialists, and destroy the Japanese invaders.

These goals having been accomplished, the CCP next turned to build a new-democratic republic on the basis of a "united dictatorship of several classes" that would serve as a moderate, half-way house on the way to the higher stage of building socialism under a proletarian dictatorship. The duration of the new democratic stage of development was left unclear, although it was said to be relatively long. New democracy, which encompassed the Three Peoples' Principles of the late GMD leader Sun Yatsen, was later integrated into what came to be known as Mao Zedong thought, which was written into the CCP's new constitution of 1945 as the official Party ideology.

New democracy did much to broaden the CCP's nationalist appeal in China during the second Sino-Japanese War until 1945, and during the subsequent civil war of 1946 to 1949. It also influenced the Party's policies in the first decade of the new regime, and was reflected in the new national flag, a red field displaying a large yellow star symbolizing the CCP, and four small stars representing the new democratic coalition of national bourgeoisie, petty bourgeoisie, proletariat, and peasantry.

Internationally, the CCP claimed that new democracy, as developed in China, was equally applicable to the emerging revolutionary movements throughout the Third World of Asia, Africa, and Latin America. That is to say, Mao Zedong thought and the Chinese revolutionary model—and not Marxism-Leninism and the Soviet model—were to be the appropriate guides for revolutionary struggles in the less-developed "countryside" of the world. Not surprisingly, the Russian and other like-minded Communist parties, especially in Europe, rejected these claims.

The ideas behind new democracy were given short shrift by Mao during the radicalization of Chinese politics in the Hundred Flowers and Anti-Rightist campaign (1956–57) and the Cultural Revolution (1966–69), when sharp class struggle became the order of the day. Under the more moderate post-Mao regime, however, the general principles of new democracy have been revived in effect under the rubric of building "socialism with Chinese characteristics." The term encompasses a broad, nationalist conception of socialism that includes many elements of new democracy, especially its emphasis on a multiclass coalition, including the national bourgeoisie and the pursuit of relatively moderate policies with broad national appeal.

Raymond F. Wylie

References

Mao, Tse-tung. *Selected Works of Mao Tse-tung,* vol. 3. New York, NY: International Publishers, 1965.

Uhalley, Stephen, Jr. *A History of the Chinese Communist Party.* Stanford, CA: Hoover Institution Press, 1988.

Van Slyke, Lyman P. *Enemies and Friends: The United Front in Chinese Communist History.* Stanford, CA: Stanford University Press, 1968.

New Fourth Army

See NEW FOURTH ARMY INCIDENT

New Fourth Army Incident

The New Fourth Army Incident was the armed conflict between the Guomindang (GMD) and the Chinese Communist Party (CCP) which in effect ended their United Front during the Sino-Japanese War (1937–45).

On January 4, 1941, the CCP-led New Fourth Army evacuated its headquarters, with about nine thousand combat men, from southern Anhui to north of the Yangtze. Instead of moving northward, the troops were directed southward by their commissar Xiang Ying. After two days on the march, they found themselves encircled and attacked by a GMD force that was six to eight times more numerous. The fighting lasted for eight days, and the New Fourth Army unit eventually collapsed; fewer than two thousand men survived and fled north of the Yangtze River. During the fighting the headquarters had its leadership reshuffled. Deputy commissar Rao Shushi and the non-Communist commander Ye Ting took over control of the unit and charged Xiang Ying and his chief-of-staff Zhou Zikun of deserting the army. Rao then ordered Ye to make an overture to the GMD for a truce. Ye was subsequently detained by the GMD until the end of the war; Rao managed to escape from captivity. Xiang Ying and Zhou Zikun refused to go north with the troops and were killed by their personal guards.

The GMD government in Chongqing portrayed the New Fourth Army Incident, also known as the "Southern Anhui Incident," as a matter of military discipline, yet it was in fact an anti-climax of two years' intensifying frictions and conflicts between the GMD and the CCP. After the outbreak of the Sino-Japanese War in 1937, the CCP forces in south China were reorganized into the New Fourth Army, under the GMD government, as part of the arrangement of the second United Front. The two parties initially maintained a cordial relationship, but in early 1939 the decline of the Japanese offensive brought an end to the honeymoon period. The two parties began to engage in a power struggle behind the Japanese lines. Directed and coordinated by Liu Shaoqi, the secretary of the newly created Central China Bureau of the CCP, the New Fourth Army and the Eighth Route Army moved toward the area east of the Jinpu Railroad, south of the Longhai Railroad, and north of the Yangtze River. The GMD general Han Deqin, claiming exclusive authority over Jiangsu province, launched a series of attacks on the intruding Communist troops to stop them from entrenching themselves. But he suffered one humiliating defeat after another. Following a decisive battle in Huangqiao in October 1940, Han's only field army was wiped out and his field commander perished in an attempt to flee for safety. Hence the New Fourth Army replaced Han's army as the most important anti-Japanese force in the Lower Yangtze.

In response, Chiang Kaishek toughened his position in his negotiation with the CCP, which had started in the summer of 1940. Late in 1940, in the wake of the Japanese signing of a tripartite treaty with Italy and Germany, the American and British governments decided to bolster Chiang's anti-Japanese war efforts in China. Encouraged by its improved international standing, Chiang's government demanded that all Communist forces, including the New Fourth Army, be moved north of the Yellow River by a certain date. The CCP refused to evacuate its troops from between the Yellow and the Yangtze rivers, but as a propaganda gesture of conciliation, promised to evacuate them from south of the Yangtze. Exasperated by Han Deqin's defeat in northern Jiangsu and boldened by Western support, Chiang personally ordered the New Fourth Army to depart from southern Anhui by the end of the year. Commissar Xiang Ying, who was also the secretary of the South China Bureau, was not enthusiastic about the CCP's decision to contest north Yangtze. He used the evacuation as an excuse to acquire extra appropriations and ammunition from Yan'an. Unable to control Xiang, Mao Zedong compromised but persistently urged Xiang to lead his troops north, lest Chiang Kaishek attack him.

By the time Xiang Ying realized that his procrastination might play into Chiang's hands and incur a disaster, he had already missed the deadline by four days. When he moved his troops, he further decided on his own to defy the GMD's wish concerning the evacuation route. Rather than taking an eastern or a northern route, as the GMD had stipulated earlier, he took a southern detour to Huang Mountain. Xiang's behavior enabled Chiang to justify his ambush in terms of military discipline. Although the attack destroyed only one-tenth of the New Fourth Army and left the north Yangtze New Fourth Army intact, Chiang ordered the whole New Fourth Army to disband on January 17.

Either unaware of or unfamiliar with the GMD-CCP frictions behind the Japanese lines, the Chinese people seemed to have been caught by surprise. Japanese imperialism loomed as their paramount concern. Public opinion, both inside and outside of unoccupied China, tended to blame the GMD government for the problem and urged it to exercise self-restraint. Franklin Roosevelt and Joseph Stalin joined the call for Chiang Kaishek to suspend any further anti-Communist activities.

The incident provided a chance for the Chinese Communists to flaunt their anti-Japanese commitment. CCP propaganda transformed the military defeat into a vindication of its patriotism. It portrayed the incident as a plot by some pro-Japanese GMD officers to push Chiang into capitulating to the Japanese. The accusation was baseless but plausible to most anti-Japanese Chinese, particularly after the much publicized Communist offensive of the Battle of Hundred Regiments in 1940. Seizing Chiang's embarrassment, the CCP adopted a high political posture. It not only defied Chiang's order and reestablished the New Fourth Army's headquarters in north Yangtze, but also boycotted the People's Political Council convened by the GMD government. The Party demanded Chiang's public apology and punishment of responsible officers, and requested the release of captured soldiers and political prisoners. Under the pressure of public opinion, Chiang reiterated his determination to maintain a peaceful relation with the CCP. Yet the harm had been done; the anti-Japanese public now sympathized with the CCP and identified it more closely with nationalism.

Within the CCP, the incident had serious implications for the composition of its leadership. In late 1938, Mao Zedong had won the Comintern's recognition of his Party leadership but had been unable to completely discredit the "Internationalist" Party line of 1931 to 1935. One major obstacle had been Xiang Ying, a genuine proletarian who supported the "Internationalist" leader Wang Ming. Before the incident, Liu Shaoqi's direction of the New Fourth Army's entrenchment in central China, and his replacement of Xiang as the Party chief in the region, had already increased Mao's leverage in dealing with Wang Ming. The incident further undermined Wang's conciliatory policy toward the GMD government. Mao thus labeled Wang's wartime policy as opportunistic and criticized Xiang's lack of enthusiasm for expanding into northern Jiangsu as an endorsement of Wang's viewpoint. This criticism made it easier for Mao to discredit Wang Ming and his "Internationalist" Party line.

Yung-fa Chen

References
Benton, Gregor. *The Origins and Early Growth of the New Fourth Army, 1934–*

1941. Berkeley: University of California Press, forthcoming.

Chen, Yung-fa. *Making Revolution: The Communist Movement in Eastern and Central China, 1937–1945.* Berkeley: University of California Press, 1986.

New Life Movement

The New Life movement was a social movement promoted by Chiang Kaishek in the early 1930s that reflected the ideological stance of the Guomindang (GMD) and the Nanjing regime.

Chiang announced the New Life movement *(Xinshenghuo yundong)* in a speech delivered at Nanchang in February 1934, when he launched the fifth Bandit-Suppression campaign against the Chinese Communist Party's (CCP) Jiangxi Soviet. It was based on his belief that the anti-Communist effort was not only a military struggle but also an ideological-political one. The goal of the movement, as its name suggests, was to create a new lifestyle for the people, especially those in the areas formerly under Communist control, that would restore order and stability in society. Chiang proposed four central criteria for the new lifestyle; they were the traditional Confucian virtues of propriety *(li)*, righteousness *(yi)*, honesty *(lian)*, and sense of shame *(chi)*. Putting them in practice, one was to follow the principles of cleanliness, orderliness, simplicity, frugality, and rapidity in daily activity. Chiang hoped that these guidelines would lead to a "militant, productive, and artful" lifestyle for the Chinese, which in turn would help to revitalize the country.

An Association for the Promotion of the New Life Movement, organized in Nanchang in March, soon had branches in other cities and provinces. In July a national headquarters of the association was founded at Nanjing, with Chiang himself as chairman and most of the leading officials in the GMD government as directors. The government heavily promoted the movement throughout 1934 and 1935, with pamphlets, school programs, mass meetings, and parades. Various government agencies, as well as GMD factions such as the Blue Shirts *(lixingshe)*, were mobilized for the cause. By 1936, branches of the association had been established in twenty provinces and most major cities, even overseas. But the movement also began to lose momentum and become bureaucratized. Although in name it persisted into the Sino-Japanese War (1937–45), in reality it had ceased to have any impact on society after the first three years.

The New Life movement, however, was a historically significant phenomenon. It was symbolic, and symptomatic, of the GMD's approach to national reconstruction under Chiang Kaishek. The movement displayed Chiang's ideological syntheticism; it was a mixture of Confucianism, fascism, and Christianity— YMCA style. The Confucianist element of the movement can be found not just in its vocabulary but in its basic premise. The underlying assumption of the movement was that ideological indoctrination, enforced through the cultivation of certain behavioral patterns, was more effective than socioeconomic improvements in eliminating the Communist appeal to the populace. At the same time, Chiang openly praised contemporary Germany and Italy as China's models. He was impressed by the militaristic values of the fascist countries, although those values are also reminiscent of the legalist ideals in ancient China. The attention to mild social reform and the Western flavor of the "new life," on the other hand, resembled the work of the Christian missionaries. Madame Chiang (Soong Meiling), an American-educated Christian, played a major role in the movement.

To the extent that the movement envisioned a strong and united China, one that would be ready to face external challenges, it was indeed nationalistic. Yet it failed to deal with the fundamental ills in Chinese society, such as poverty, oppression and inequality, that were fomenting the Communist revolution. Instead it demanded loyalty and obedience from the people. The movement, therefore, could not help but become simplistic and formalistic. A "New Life" banner in a small county, according to one report, asked the people to use soap in their daily washes, overlooking the fact that few in the county could afford that modern item. Examples such as this indicated both the superficiality of Chiang's understanding of the deep-rooted problems of his country, and the distance between his urban, Westernized regime and the masses in rural China.

Wang Ke-wen

References

Chu, Samuel C. "The New Life Movement before the Sino-Japanese Conflict: A Reflection of Kuomintang Limitations in Thought and Action." *China at the Crossroads: Nationalists and Commu-*

nists, 1927–1949, ed. F. Gilbert Chan, 37–68. Boulder, CO: Westview Press, 1980.

Dirlik, Arif. "The Ideological Foundation of the New Life Movement: A Study in Counterrevolution." *Journal of Asian Studies* (August 1975): 945–80.

Eastman, Lloyd E. "The Kuomintang in the 1930s." *The Limits of Change: Essays on Conservative Alternatives in Republican China,* ed. Charlotte Furth, 191–210. Cambridge, MA: Harvard University Press, 1976.

N

Liang Qichao. (Courtesy of Nationalist Party Archives.)

New People Miscellany (Xinmin Congbao)

Xinmin congbao, a semi-monthly journal published by Liang Qichao in Yokohama, Japan, for the promotion of reformist ideas, was founded in February 1902 and closed in November 1907, publishing a total of ninety-six issues. It was a sequel to Liang's *Qingyibao (Pure Discussion Journal).* Liang was editor-in-chief; other reformers, such as Ma Junwu, Huang Yuzhi, Wu Zhongyao, and Liang's mentor, Kang Youwei, were regular contributors. In its "Publication Note" the journal made the following declarations: (1) It is necessary to create new people in order to build a new nation; (2) To accomplish the fore-mentioned goal, education should take precedence ever politics; (3) Public interest and public well-being should always be the most important consideration.

Adopting the format of a general magazine, the journal published news, novels, and scholarly essays, as well as political commentaries. The primary theme of its content, nevertheless, was the introduction of Western ideas and the discussion of the current situation in China. It clearly reflected the political stance of the reformers under Kang and Liang, who advocated a constitutional monarchy and supported Emperor Guangxu. The journal was therefore opposed to the call for revolution by Sun Yatsen and his followers. After the publication of *Minbao (The People's Report)* as the organ of Sun's Tongmenghui in Tokyo in 1905, the two journals engaged in a fierce debate on the proper solution to China's crisis. *Xinmin congbao* harshly criticized *Minbao*'s revolutionary programs and its anti-Manchu nationalism. An ethnic revolution against the Manchus, it argued, was narrow-minded and divisive. Moreover, under the current circumstances in China, a violent overthrow of the government would certainly lead to disintegration and foreign intervention. China's only viable option was an orderly reform within the framework of the Qing monarchy. In a sense, Liang's camp was arguing for the replacement of traditional Han nationalism by a modern Chinese nationalism.

Toward the end, *Xinmin congbao* seemed to be losing momentum in the debate as the cause of revolution became increasingly popular among the young and idealistic Chinese students in Japan, yet its articles, often written in Liang's unique and eloquent style, exerted a significant impact on those youths. Reformers and revolutionaries alike were informed and enlightened by the journal. In the 1900s, it served as a major medium for the infusion of nationalist concepts to the Chinese, and as the forum for a serious analysis and critique of the Tongmenghui's proposals.

Wang Ke-wen

References

Chang, Hao. *Liang ch'i-ch'ao and Intellectual Transition in China, 1890–1907.* Cambridge, MA: Harvard University Press, 1971.

Huang, Philip C. *Liang Ch'i-ch'ao and Modern Chinese Liberalism.* Seattle: University of Washington Press, 1972.

New Tide Society

On November 18, 1918, about twenty young students organized the New Tide Society *(Xinchaoshe)* in Beijing. The students had been inspired by Hu Shih, Li Dazhao, and Zhou Zuoren, their professors at Beijing University, and many had enrolled in the latter's class, "The History of European Literature." The society published the monthly journal *New Tide (Xinchao),* the country's fourth vernacular-language periodical and the second most important in the May Fourth movement. The journal specialized in introducing Western thought to China and aimed to emancipate the mind of China's youth from the rigid conventions of the past. Society members were mostly in their twenties, but they closely affiliated themselves with the publishers of the teachers' journal *New Youth (Xinqingnian),* and targeted middle school students as their reading audience.

Many members of the New Tide and the Citizen *(Guominshe)* societies actively participated as important leaders of the May Fourth movement. The chief editor of *New Tide,* Fu Sinian, acted as the marshal of the demonstration held on May 4, 1919. This nationalistic movement called for the ouster of traitors in the Beijing government, and strongly opposed foreign imperialism. The fervor of nationalism was best represented by a famous manifesto drafted by Luo Jialun, who later succeeded Fu Sinian as *New Tide*'s chief editor. Luo and his compatriots swore that, should China's sovereign territory be conquered, it would never be ceded without a fight, and that even though the Chinese people might encounter bloody warfare, they would never capitulate.

Interestingly, few, if any, articles in *New Tide* overtly encouraged nationalism. Instead, their authors tended to expound lofty idealistic theories often without regard for practical realities. It was also ironic that, in a way, the *New Tide* writers were even more radical than those of the *New Youth* journal in criticizing Chinese traditions. And, they advocated revolution following the Russian model, albeit their understanding was limited to a vague smattering of socialism and democracy.

The New Tide Society's ardent iconoclasm toward Chinese tradition reached the point where some followers began to assert that "the West and China can be equated with right and wrong, [respectively]," and that "it is acceptable to become totally Westernized" (Fu Sinian). Contrary to the standard definition of "nationalism"—*i.e.,* the positive glorification of a nation's heritage—the New Tide Society posited a negative attack against Chinese traditions and values. In their place, the importation of whatever Western ideas and teachings might be needed to bolster national strength was deemed acceptable. This posture has amazed many scholars, and in the 1950s a major critic, Xu Fuguan, concluded that "in all the world there was nothing more strange than the May Fourth youths who championed nationalism by means of washing away the history and culture of their nation."

New Tide ceased publication in March 1922 after only twelve issues. The main reason for its stoppage stemmed from the fact that most of its key contributors had gone to study in America and Europe. Afterward, Sun Fuyuan and Li Xiaofeng transformed the society into a study and publishing organization. The name of the Beixin publishing company is in fact an abbreviation of Beijing University (Beida) and New Tide (Xinchao). Its prestigious reputation as a publisher of intellectual thought carries on its inheritance from the New Tide society.

The political orientations within the New Tide group eventually split to highlight sharp differences. Fu Sinian and Luo Jialun favored the ruling Guomindang, whereas Tan Pingshan, Zhang Shenfu, and others sympathized with the Chinese Communist Party. Despite this divided aftermath, nationalism remained a major concern for most of these men. For example, Fu, who founded Academica Sinica's Institute of History and Philology in 1928, was dismayed that the forefront of sinological research was based in Paris and Berlin, and not in Beijing. He hoped "to bring the center of sinology back from Paris and Berlin to China." This sentiment was echoed by many eminent scholars at the Institute of History and Philology. Since the 1930s, the institute has become one of the leading facilities for Chinese historical, philological, and archaeological studies in the world.

New Tide members who went on to enjoy success as writers included Ye Shaojun, Zhu Ziqing, Yu Pingbo, and Kang Baiqing. Others became leading academicians, such as Fu Sinian and Gu Jiegang in history, Wang Jingxi in psychology, and Feng Youlan in the history of philosophy.

Fan-shen Wang

References
Chow, Tse-tsung. *The May Fourth Move-*

ment: *Intellectual Revolution in Modern China*. Cambridge, MA: Harvard University Press, 1960.

Schneider, Laurence A. *Ku Chieh-kang and China's New History*. Berkeley: University of California Press, 1971.

Schwarcz, Vera. *The Chinese Enlightenment: Intellectuals and the Legacy of the May Fourth Movement of 1919*. Berkeley: University of California Press, 1986.

New Youth

New Youth (Xinqingnian) was the most influential magazine published in China in the pre-1949 period. Its founding in 1915 by Chen Duxiu launched the New Culture movement. The magazine advocated science and democracy and promoted new ideas and literature. It exerted a seminal influence on most of the early leaders of the Chinese Communist Party (CCP) and played a key role in establishing the reputations of such major Chinese intellectual figures as Hu Shih and Lu Xun and in awakening the national consciousness of a whole generation of Chinese youth.

The original title of the magazine was *Youth (Qingnian)*. Chen Duxiu established the journal to create an ideological awakening among the young people of China and to warn them against the stagnant traditions of China's past. He discussed and translated a whole range of Western authors and thinkers, including Turgenev, Ibsen, Wilde, Schopenhauer, Franklin, Mill, Nietzsche, and Tolstoy. In its early years, its pages championed the ideas of science and democracy. After Chen joined the faculty of Beijing University in 1917, he relocated the editorial headquarters of the journal from Shanghai to the capital and changed the magazine's name to *New Youth*. Many prominent members of the Beijing University faculty, such as Hu Shih, Lu Xun, and Li Dazhao, began to contribute regularly to *New Youth*.

The magazine's strident attacks on Confucianism and its advocacy of the use of the vernacular in Chinese writing attracted the attention of many Chinese intellectuals. The magazine is usually given credit for having launched the vernacular movement in China. Students throughout China were influenced by *New Youth* to form organizations for reform and study. Numerous other journals and papers imitating *New Youth* began to publish in the period from 1915 to 1924. Not long after the magazine moved to Beijing, contributors to the publication formed a New Youth Society *(Xin qingnianshe)*, and in 1919 they issued a New Youth Manifesto, calling for the abandonment of irrelevant ideas and advocating mass movement and social reconstruction.

When Chen founded the magazine he declared it to be nonpolitical, but it became involved in political issues from the start: attacking Yuan Shikai's abortive attempt to become emperor, opposing warlordism, and advocating China's participation in World War I. In September 1920, Chen established a new New Youth Society for editing and writing the paper in Shanghai where he had now moved. This omitted many of the older Beijing-based liberal contributors to the journal, who in any case were becoming increasingly alienated as the editorial policy of the magazine moved close to that of the CCP. In 1921, after the magazine was suppressed by authorities in the French concession, Chen moved it to Canton and converted it into a CCP organ. Published irregularly after April 1925, it ceased publication altogether on July 25, 1926.

Lee Feigon

References

Chow, Tse-tsung. *The May Fourth Movement: Intellectual Revolution in Modern China*. Cambridge, MA: Harvard University Press, 1960.

Feigon, Lee. *Chen Duxiu: Founder of the Chinese Communist Party*. Princeton, NJ: Princeton University Press, 1983.

Liu, Chun-jo. *Controversies in Modern Chinese Intellectual History*. Cambridge, MA: Harvard University Press, 1964.

Nian Rebellion

The Nian Rebellion, which has been somewhat over-shadowed by the Taiping Rebellion, falls both within the pattern of peasant rebellion of pre-modern China and the more recent nationalistic movements of the nineteenth and twentieth centuries. Motivating factors that the Nian shared with their peasant rebellion forerunners included incompetent and/or corrupt officials who neglected their duties, economic hardship, and general insecurity in society. To this list the Nian added a nationalistic element and guerrilla warfare. The latter, pioneered by the Nian, foreshadowed the People's Liberation Army at least in terms of gaining and sustaining support from the Chinese peasantry by utilizing a code of conduct which proscribed mistreatment of the masses.

The name "Nian" probably refers to either the torchlights made of twisted oiled paper that were sometimes carried on raids, or to the Nian's grouping in a band consisting of a few men or of several score. Geographically, the Nian's base was the area between the Huai and the Yellow rivers. This locale, which is comprised of parts of Henan, Anhuei, and Jiangsu provinces, contained vast expanses of land unsuitable for rice cultivation. Frequent floods and droughts added to the rather miserable life of the peasantry. In addition, several rather unique aspects of the region benefited the Nian. The river systems frequently created marshy areas around the villages, which were used to their advantage by the Nian, who were much more familiar with the topography than were pursuing government troops. Also, the earthen or brick walls of the larger villages in the locale provided protection. Next, the region possessed an abundant supply of horses, which allowed for the development of mobile cavalry units. And finally, there was a vigorous salt-smuggling trade in the area. This activity, which supposedly involved brave and aggressive men prepared to flout authority, was the chosen profession of several Nian leaders.

The history of the Nian may be divided into four relatively distinct stages. The first, dating from the late eighteenth century to 1852, was localized, decentralized, and sporadic as far as the rebellions are concerned. Prompted by several years of bad harvests, a large number of men from the region between the Huai and the Yellow rivers had earlier joined existing rebel sects. When the government was finally able to disband these, the men, made arrogant and bold by their previous adventures, turned to a life of drinking and gambling. Soon they organized into small bands and engaged in salt-smuggling, pillaging, kidnapping, and looting to support their new lifestyle. Incompetent and/or corrupt officials in the area ensured the continuation of this activity.

The second phase, covering the period from 1852 to 1855, marked the transition of the Nian from a small, unstructured pillaging movement of roaming bandits to a substantial nationalistic enterprise. The contributing factors to this transformation appear to be twofold. Widespread famine in the area in 1851 and 1852 greatly increased the number of men who claimed Nian membership. In February 1853,

the Taipings took Anqing and released the Nian rebels held prisoner there by the government. These newly freed rebels returned to Nian bastions full of praise for their liberators. Shortly thereafter the Nian and Taipings established connections. This linkage resulted in the rapidly growing Nian becoming avowedly anti-government and anti-Manchu. As an outward display of this nationalistic evolution, the Nian began the practice of keeping their hair long.

The third era of the Nian occurred between 1856 and 1864, when Nian units fought alongside the Taipings as separate entities. The relationship was more an alliance than an amalgamation. The Nian retained their independence and their unique form of warfare. Relying on a strong cavalry and skillful guerrilla tactics, the Nian, who numbered somewhere between 30,000 and 50,000, won numerous victories against much larger Qing forces. The local peasantry's support, fostered both by a widespread resentment against the Manchu regime and by the Nian practice of treating the masses fairly, also aided the Nian's success.

The end of the Nian came between 1865 and 1868. Superior opposition forces and a combination of tactical mistakes, such as organizing huge regiments and splitting them into two groups, which campaigned far beyond their home base, caused the demise. The Qing troops, led by Zeng Guofan and Li Hongzhang, were larger and better fed, led, and paid. They eventually surrounded and then eliminated the Nian. After the rebellion was suppressed, the government required the registration of peasants in the former Nian areas and conducted the election of new village heads. These measures prevented a reemergence of the movement.

Gerald W. Berkley

References

Chiang, Siang-tseh. *The Nian Rebellion.* Seattle: University of Washington Press, 1954.

Perry, Elizabeth J. *Rebels and Revolutionaries in North China, 1845–1945.* Stanford, CA: Stanford University Press, 1980.

Teng, S. Y. *The Nian Army and Their Guerilla Warfare, 1851–1868.* Paris: Mouton, 1961.

Nineteenth Route Army

See FUJIAN REBELLION; JANUARY TWENTY-EIGHTH INCIDENT

Nishihara Loans

The Nishihara loans were negotiated and signed between the Beijing government and Japan from 1917 to 1918. After resuming the post of premier in 1917, Duan Qirui was intent on reunifying the country by force. In order to do so, he needed much more financial resources than his government could afford. He therefore acquired a total of 386 million yen in loans from Japan. Some 145 million yen were negotiated between Nishihara Kamezo, adviser to Japan's Terauchi Cabinet, and Cao Rulin, the Chinese Minister of Communication. The amount included two Communication Bank loans, a wired telegraph loan, three railway loans, a gold mines and forests loan, and the War Participation Loan. They were known collectively as the "Nishihara Loans."

While in name most of these loans were issued for the purpose of developing China's natural resources and communication systems, little if any of them were in fact used in those venues. They represented the political support which Japan provided to Duan's government, which used the funds to strengthen its military and political capabilities. The War Participation Loan, especially, helped Duan to establish a War Participation Army that was equipped and trained by the Japanese. Ostensibly organized to prepare for China's entrance into World War I, this army, comprising three divisions and four mixed brigades, posed a formidable threat to the Canton government in the South and to other regional militarists who refused to cooperate with Beijing. Meanwhile, through these loans Japan greatly enhanced her economic control in Manchuria and north China and broadened her political influence over the Beijing government. Patriotic Chinese regarded the loans as a national disgrace and an evidence of the pro-Japanese stance of Duan Qirui's government.

Wang Ke-wen

References

Chi, Madeleine. "Ts'ao Ju-lin (1876–1966): His Japanese Connections." *The Chinese and the Japanese: Essays in Political and Cultural Interactions,* ed. Akira Iriye. Princeton, NJ: Princeton University Press, 1980.

Jansen, Marius B. *Japan and China: From War to Peace, 1894–1972.* Chicago, IL: Rand McNally College Publishing Co., 1975.

Normalization of Sino-American Relations

See SHANGHAI COMMUNIQUÉ

North China Autonomy

Also known as the "specialization of north China" *(Huabei teshuhua),* the term "north China autonomy" refers to a series of events in the early 1930s that represented Japan's attempt to carve out the northern provinces of China as a special area of its influence and control. These events eventually caused the outbreak of the second Sino-Japanese War in 1937.

Following the Manchurian Incident of 1931, Japan's Guandong Army took control of Manchuria and established the puppet state of Manchukuo. It soon expanded its influence to the Great Wall under the pretext of protecting Manchukuo. In early 1933, the Japanese occupied the Inner Mongolian province of Jehol and continued their invasion of the eastern part of Hebei province (both provinces were adjacent to Manchuria). Unwilling to confront Japan in a war, the Guomindang (GMD) government in Nanjing sought a peace settlement of the conflict. The Tanggu Truce, concluded in May, recognized Japan's occupation of Jehol in exchange for China's possession of Hebei.

In order to negotiate the Tanggu Truce, Nanjing had established a Political Reorganization Committee in Beijing as its representative in north China (essentially Hebei). The committee enjoyed a semi-autonomous status, so that the government could maintain its superficial claim of not directly negotiating with Japan. The Japanese welcomed the move because they too wanted an autonomous, pro-Japanese regime in north China, which could potentially become the second Manchukuo. Huang Fu, an experienced bureaucrat from the Beiyang era, a non-GMD member with ties to Japan, and a close friend of Chiang Kaishek, was appointed as head of the committee. Huang's pro-Japanese potential was a key factor that persuaded Japan to accept the Tanggu Truce.

In May 1935, the Guandong Army demanded the withdrawal of Nanjing's political and military presence from Hebei. As a result, Nanjing made two more concessions, the He-Umezu Agreement and the Qin-Doihara Agreement, to comply with Japanese demands. Having succeeded in this first step, the Japanese searched for a pro-Japanese leader to guide the North China Autonomy movement that they now promoted.

N

Inasmuch as Huang Fu refused to cooperate with Japan any longer, Nanjing abolished Huang's committee in August 1935 and appointed Song Zheyuan, commander of the Twenty-Ninth Army, to command the Beijing-Tianjin area. Song was an ex-follower of Feng Yuxiang and his troops were the former Guominjun under Feng; the Japanese therefore did not consider him part of the Nan-jing establishment. In November the Guandong Army pressured Song to declare the "high-level self-rule" (gaodu zizhi) of the five northern provinces of Hebei, Shanxi, Chahar, Suiyuan, and Shandong. Song hesitated. A few days later, the Japanese established the puppet organization Eastern Hebei Anti-Communist Self-Rule Committee, headed by Yin Rugeng, which in effect placed the eastern part of Hebei under Japanese control.

In response to this crisis, Nanjing reached an agreement with Song and allowed him to organize a Hebei-Chahar Political Affairs Committee in December. All of the members of this committee were militarists or politicians with little connection to Nanjing. During the next year and a half, Song's committee made compromises with the Japanese and at least nominally satisfied Japan's scheme of a north China autonomy. Song, however, maintained close contact with Nanjing and rejected Japan's further demand of establishing a north China autonomous government. This delicate and ambivalent situation remained until the Marco Polo Bridge Incident in July 1937, when Song's troops clashed with Japanese forces and triggered the second Sino-Japanese War.

Throughout the early 1930s, Nanjing's underlying policy toward the crises in north China was resistance while negotiating (yimian dikang yimian jiaoshe). The policy was decided jointly by Chiang Kaishek, head of the Military Committee, and Wang Jingwei, head of the Administrative Yuan (premier); Huang Fu, He Yingqin, and Song Zheyuan shouldered the task of its implementation. It was a policy necessitated by Chiang's overall strategy of domestic pacification before external resistance (xian annei hou rangwai), but it conflicted with contemporary Chinese nationalist sentiment and reduced the government's popularity.

Wang Ke-wen

References

Coble, Parks M. Jr. *Facing Japan*. Cambridge, MA: Harvard University Press, 1991.
Israel, John. *Student Nationalism in China, 1927–1937*. Stanford, CA: Stanford University Press, 1966.

Northeast Anti-Japanese Volunteer Army

Although the Japanese army seized the three northeastern provinces (Manchuria) within four months after the Manchurian Incident on September 18, 1931, it occupied and controlled only the railway lines and large cities, leaving the vast countryside to Chinese partisan forces, which at their height reached over 300,000 men. This posed a great threat to the Japanese rule in Manchuria.

The initial stage of the partisan activity in Manchuria was marked by the dominant role played by the remaining forces of Zhang Xueliang's Northeast Army. At the time of the Manchurian Incident, Zhang's troops numbered about 190,000 in Manchuria: 50,000 from Liaoning province withdrew inside the Great Wall, 80,000 defected to the Japanese and were reorganized into the newly-created Manchukuo Army, and the rest became the backbone of the anti-Japanese partisan forces. However, in northern Manchuria, at least five regular brigades of the Northeast Army remained intact and were swelled with new volunteers. Now led by Ma Zhanshan, they adopted the title Northeast Anti-Japanese Volunteer Army (Dongbei kangRi yiyongjun) and fought some fierce battles against the Japanese and puppet troops, notably at the Nen River Bridge, an engagement which drew worldwide attention. By December 1932, Ma was largely defeated. With other partisan leaders, such as Su Bingwen, Li Tu, Zhang Tianjiu, and Wang Delin, along with three thousand troops and seven hundred refugees, he took the trans-Siberia train and returned to China via Moscow.

Ma's defeat did not end Chinese guerrilla activities in southern Manchuria. The origins of the guerrillas may be traced to the defense of Jinzhou in late 1931, when Huang Xiansheng, a confidant of Zhang Xueliang, organized a guerrilla force of nearly 50,000 men with the help of the Northeast National Salvation Society. Some of those guerrilla leaders were intellectuals, such as Miao Kexiu and Deng Tiemei. Others were officers of the Northeast Army. By early 1933, they were also defeated. Some of them, as in the case of Feng Zhanhai and Tang Juwu, successfully broke through the enemy lines and reached Jehol.

The second phase of the partisan movement in Manchuria was characterized by the leadership of the Chinese Communists. With the capture of Jehol province by the Japanese, culminating in the Great Wall battles in early 1933, the partisan forces were sharply reduced in numbers. At that time the Chinese Communist Party had about two thousand members in the region, mainly scattered throughout Harbin, Shenyang, and Dairen. The Party instructed these members to join the partisan forces, which were organized into five armies, commanded by Yang Jingyu, Zhao Shangzhi, Wu Detai, Li Yanlu, and Zhou Baozhong. Further reorganization of the partisan forces took place in 1936, resulting in the merger of the first and second Anti-Japanese Allied Armies *(Kang-Ri lianjun)* into the First Route Army and the recruitment of many Koreans.

The last stage, during the Sino-Japanese War of 1937 to 1945, witnessed the most difficult time of the partisan movement in Manchuria. In 1939, the partisan forces were reduced from 30,000 to 2,000 men, with the result that many of them sought sanctuary in the Soviet Union. The Soviet military established two camps for them, one near Khabarovsk and the other near Ussurisk. In 1942, the Soviets organized them into a brigade of four battalions, with Zhou Baozhong as brigadier. It was this Chinese Communist force that first returned to Manchuria in early September, immediately after the Japanese surrender.

Tien-wei Wu

References

Lee, Chong-sik. *Revolutionary Struggle in Manchuria: Chinese Communism and Soviet Interest, 1922–1946.* Berkeley: University of California Press, 1983.

Northern Expedition

The military campaigns launched by the Canton regime to reunify the country in the 1920s were known as the Northern Expedition. There were three such attempts, the first two led by Sun Yatsen, and the third fought by Chiang Kaishek's National Revolutionary Army. The entire process lasted one decade.

In August 1917, Sun Yatsen led the Chinese parliament to Canton, where he established a military government. He decided to launch a Northern Expedition against the Beiyang warlords who controlled the Beijing government. The campaign, however, was aborted because of the lack of support from the Guangxi and Yunnan militarists upon whom Sun depended at the time. In December 1921, following the founding of another Canton regime, Sun at last implemented his plan. He established his military headquarters *(dabenying)* at Guilin, Guangxi, and ordered his troops to attack the provinces of Jiangxi and Hunan. The campaign was sabotaged by Chen Jiongming's coup d'état in Canton six months later, and Sun was forced to go to Shanghai.

When the Jiangsu-Zhejiang War broke out in September 1924, Sun, then administering his third Canton regime, found it an opportunity to launch yet another Northern Expedition. He moved his military headquarters to Shaoguan, Guangdong, and dispatched troops into Jiangxi. After initial victories, the campaign ended without any accomplishment because Sun's main force, the Yunnan Army, refused to leave its lucrative base in Canton. The failure of all these Northern Expedition attempts taught Sun a lesson. He realized that in order to be successful, he must first organize an armed force of his own. He soon began the planning of the establishment of a military academy.

The most well-known "Northern Expedition" was the campaign led by the Guomindang (GMD) government in Canton after Sun Yatsen's death. In 1926, the Canton regime decided to launch the Northern Expedition in order to fulfill the wish of its late leader. On June 6, the GMD appointed Chiang Kaishek as commander-in-chief of the Northern Expeditionary forces, titled the National Revolutionary Army (NRA). On July 9, the campaign formally began. The NRA, totaling eight armies, was divided into three groups. It marched northward along three lines: Hunan-Hubei, Fujian-Zhejiang, and Jiangxi. The battle cry of the NRA, "Overthrow Foreign Powers and Eliminate Warlords," mirrored the May Fourth slogan of "Resist Foreign Domination and Eliminate Domestic Traitors" and embraced the rising tide of nationalism among the Chinese.

The Northern Expedition therefore progressed rapidly with popular support. By the end of 1926, Wu Peifu had been driven out of Wushengguan and the NRA had occupied Hubei. The campaigns in the Fujian-Zhejiang area were also successful because the enemy forces, commanded by Sun Chuanfang, were concentrated in Jiangxi. Soon both provinces fell to the NRA. In Jiangxi, the NRA took

Nanchang in November after some hard-fought battles. Sun Chuanfang's main forces were wiped out. Advancing eastward along the Yangtze River, the NRA took Nanjing on March 24 and Shanghai on March 26, 1927. As the NRA was entering Nanjing, an anti-foreign riot (the Nanjing Incident) occurred, which created complications in the relations between the Northern Expedition and the foreign powers.

Further complicating the political situation at this time was the escalating conflict within the Guomindang–Chinese Communist Party (GMD-CCP) United Front, which had directed the Northern Expedition thus far, and within the GMD. The conflict eventually caused Chiang Kaishek's purge of the Communists in Shanghai and led to the Nanjing-Wuhan split from April to September. On August 12, Chiang's intra-party rivals forced him to resign, and the Northern Expedition was interrupted. Not until early 1928 was the conflict resolved and the GMD reunified. Having terminated the United Front and crushed the CCP, the GMD decided to resume the Northern Expedition in February 1928. Chiang had returned to his command in January. The GMD now appointed him as chairman of the government's Military Committee and commander of the NRA's First Army Group. The other three army groups were commanded by Feng Yuxiang, Yan Xishan, and Li Zongren.

The second half of the Northern Expedition formally commenced on April 5. Again, the NRA marched northward along three lines: the railways of Tianjin-Pukou, Beijing-Hankou, and Zhengding-Taiyuan. The advance was briefly disrupted by the Japanese in Shandong in May, known as the Jinan Incident. Despite popular anti-imperialist sentiment which the incident provoked, Chiang Kaishek avoided a confrontation with Japan and continued the war against the warlords. By early June, the NRA had besieged Beijing from the south and the west. Zhang Zuolin, the warlord who controlled the Beijing government at the time, hastily retreated to his base in Manchuria. He was killed by the Japanese on the way. On June 8 the NRA entered Beijing. One week later, leaders of the GMD and the NRA paid their respect to Sun Yatsen at the Western Hills outside the city, where Sun's body temporarily rested, and announced the successful completion of the Northern Expedition. Later that year, Zhang Xueliang succeeded his father Zhang Zuolin as ruler of Manchuria and declared his support for the GMD government in Nanjing in December. Nominally at least, the decade of warlordism had ended and China had been reunified by the GMD.

Lu Fang-shang

References

Jordan, Donald A. *The Northern Expedition: China's National Revolution of 1926–1928.* Honolulu: The University Press of Hawaii, 1976.

Wilbur, C. Martin. *The Nationalist Revolution in China, 1923–1928.* Cambridge, England: Cambridge University Press, 1985.

One Country, Two Systems

"One country, two systems" was the general scheme proposed by the People's Republic of China (PRC) as a framework for its reunification with Hong Kong and Taiwan.

The substance of the scheme was introduced by Ye Jiangying, then chairman of the PRC's National People's Congress, in 1981. In his appeal to the Guomindang-ruled Taiwan for a peaceful reunification with the mainland, Ye promised that the island would be able to maintain its current social and economic systems, as well as its military, as a "special administrative district with high-degree autonomy" after its incorporation into the PRC. In 1982, Deng Xiaoping suggested a similar arrangement for Hong Kong during his talk with the British prime minister Margaret Thatcher on the scheduled return of that British colony in 1997. Deng called this principle "one country, two systems" *(yiguo liangzhi)*. It allows the coexistence of two different social and economic systems, *i.e.*, socialism (PRC) and capitalism (Taiwan and Hong Kong) under a single Chinese (PRC) sovereignty. The principle indicated a major political and ideological concession by the Communist government on the issue of national unification.

Since then the PRC has consistently promoted this principle in its call for reunification with Hong Kong and Taiwan. The Basic Law of Hong Kong, drafted by the PRC in the late 1980s and to be implemented after 1997, represents an attempt to codify this political concept. It permits the continuation of lifestyle, private ownership of property, legal system, and capitalist economy in Hong Kong for at least fifty years after 1997. Taiwan, however, has thus far rejected this scheme as a basis of its

possible reunification with the PRC.

National unity, defined as the preservation of China's territorial and ethnic composition at the time of her first confrontation with the West in the mid-nineteenth century, has always been a primary objective of modern Chinese nationalism. Although the PRC's scheme of "one country, two systems" is often seen by outsiders, including many in Hong Kong and Taiwan, as a propaganda ploy, it nevertheless reflects the Communist government's desire to achieve national unity. As the PRC began to dismantle its own socialist system in the 1980s, the compromise in ideology it offers in the scheme may in the end prove irrelevant.

Wang Ke-wen

Open Door Policy

The Open Door policy was a collective foreign effort to maintain access to China's fabled markets. As the country with the largest share of the trade, Great Britain long favored open markets, but it was the United States that issued the formal declaration of the Open Door policy. The United States secretary of state John Hay's Open Door Notes, sent to Great Britain, Russia, France, Germany, Italy, and Japan in September 1899, sought assurances that, within their Chinese spheres of influence, these powers would not interfere with the economic concessions or interests of the others. The "notes" also asserted that harbor and railroad charges be the same for all and that the Chinese tariffs be collected by the Chinese within each sphere.

Although the powers responded evasively to the initiative, Hay declared in March 1900 that all had assented. On July 3, 1900, the secretary sent a second Open Door Note, which solicited no formal reply, to the same six governments, plus Austria-Hungary. Prompted by the threat of a partition of China by foreign military forces sent to quell the Boxer attack on the Western delegations in Beijing, this circular extended the Open Door concept to include respect for China's possession and control of its own territory. The Open Door policy did not have the force of a treaty agreement until the signing of the Nine Power Treaty in Washington in 1922, a vague convention pledging the signatories to respect the Open Door in China.

The Open Door policy had conflicting implications for Chinese nationalism. On the one hand, it aimed to prevent the dismemberment of a weak China by aggressive foreign powers and to maintain respect for China's territorial and administrative "entity" or "integrity," the terms generally used to refer to China's sovereignty. Pragmatic considerations of the balance of power and not the Open Door Notes prevented China's partition in 1900, but the concept of China's survival became part of twentieth-century diplomacy in East Asia. China signed the Nine Power Treaty, and when Japan overtly violated that agreement with the seizure of Manchuria in 1931, the United States responded with its so-called nonrecognition doctrine, which was a reassertion of the Open Door policy. The refusal of the United States to tolerate Japan's disregard for China's integrity remained a persistent issue and became a cause of the Japanese-American war in the Pacific.

Despite the seeming benevolence of the Open Door policy, it also had its aggressive implications. Hay's formulation in 1899 and 1900 did not include the Chinese government, whose officials were not consulted nor even notified about the dispatch of the Open Door Notes. The policy accepted the existence of spheres of influence and was designed to continue the advantages of equal opportunity that the foreign countries enjoyed in China under the most-favored-nation provisions of the unequal treaties. The invocation of the Open Door policy in the big-power diplomacy of the 1920s and 1930s was aimed more at checking the Japanese threat to Western interests than at defending China.

David L. Anderson

References

Anderson, David L. *Imperialism and Idealism: American Diplomats in China, 1861–1898.* Bloomington: Indiana University Press, 1985.
Fairbank, John King. *The United States and China,* 4th ed. Cambridge, MA: Harvard University Press, 1983.

Open-Up Policy

During the early years of the People's Republic, China maintained political and economic ties only with her socialist allies, *i.e.,* the Soviet Union and eastern European countries. After the Sino-Soviet split in the late 1950s, the country was further isolated in the world community, with the exception of a few Third World countries in Asia, Latin America, and Africa as friends. The 1972 visit of United States president Richard Nixon to China finally changed the situation. Since then, China has gradually resumed contacts with the capitalist countries in the West.

In 1978, at the third plenum of the CCP's Eleventh Central Committee, the new Party leadership under Deng Xiaoping terminated the Maoist seclusion of the past thirty years and opened the country to the outside world. Described by the Chinese as open-up *(kaifang)* or reform and open-up *(gaige kaifang),* the new policy aimed at introducing foreign technology, capital and management skills to expedite China's four modernizations. The "open-up" policy had several major components: foreign trade, foreign investment, scholarly exchange, and tourism.

By the early 1980s, over 90 percent of China's foreign trade was conducted with nonsocialist countries. Since then, China's major trading partners have been Japan, the United States, and Hong Kong. Initially China imported raw materials, such as agricultural products and chemicals, but the focus soon shifted to the acquisition of industrial machinery and manufactured goods. China's primary items of export included oil, textiles and light industrial products. Since the late 1980s, China has also become an active participant in international arms sales. In order to compete in the world market, China improved her own product quality, devalued her currency, and studied capitalist business practices. Through expanding trade, the country's foreign currency reserve increased rapidly and ranked among the world's largest in the 1990s.

To attract foreign capital and investments in China, Deng Xiaoping's government in 1979 established four "special economic zones" in

The "Special Economic Zone" of Shenzhen in the late 1990s. (Xinhua News Agency.)

the coastal areas (Shenzhen, Zhuhai, Shantou, and Xiamen), where foreign businesses enjoyed preferential treatment in taxes and other forms of government assistance. A number of coastal cities were also allowed to receive foreign investments under conditions similar to those provided in the "special economic zones." Shortly thereafter, Beijing allowed local authorities to negotiate their own foreign investment deals. Meanwhile it constructed, for the first time since 1949, a legal system to regulate and protect foreign businesses throughout China.

As diplomatic and business relations between China and the West strengthened, contacts among the people increased as well. Since the late 1970s, most of the foreigners who traveled to China have been tourists, whereas Chinese travels to the outside world have been mostly scholarly visits, especially students seeking advanced education abroad. Foreign study has been a strong current among China's educated elite since the beginning of the twentieth century, but it was completely halted during the 1960s and early 1970s. As China desperately needed advanced knowledge in science, technology, and business for her "four modernizations," the dispatch of students to foreign countries again became an urgent undertaking. At first the government funded nearly all of these students, but this quickly changed as domestic

economic reform enabled more families to support their children's overseas study. By the 1990s, the overwhelming majority of Chinese students studying abroad were privately funded. The country that attracted the largest number of Chinese students is the United States. Between 1979 and 1990 more than 100,000 Chinese students and scholars went to America. In contrast, the number of foreign students studying in China has been insignificant, compared to that of foreign tourists. Tourism provided an important source of income for China, totaling over 2 billion dollars on the eve of the Tiananmen Incident in 1989.

The "open-up" policy was a drastic reversal of the "self-reliance" strategy advocated by Mao Zedong. While profits in trade and foreign capital created economic prosperity and rising living standards, China now became increasingly dependent on the world market. All of the new windows to the outside world, moreover, produced far-reaching repercussions in China. Western fashions, lifestyle, and values flowed into China, together with foreign products and tourists. The Chinese students overseas, like their predecessors in the first half of this century, often became influenced by the culture of their host countries and returned, if they did, with new perspectives and mentalities. After decades of isolation, the Chinese found the popular culture as well as the intellectual thought of the West refreshing and exciting. The Western impact under the "open-up" policy soon became the catalyst of dramatic social and cultural changes in China. Alarmed by the potential of these changes to trigger a political one, the Chinese Communist Party (CCP) government launched the campaign against spiritual pollution in 1983 and attacked bourgeois liberalism in 1986. Beijing's worry was not unfounded. The Tiananmen Incident of 1989 was to a great extent the result of a decade of Western cultural influence.

There has been another important by-product of the "open-up" policy. As increased Western contacts and successful economic reform led to a better business environment in China, overseas Chinese became a major source of outside investment and trade contacts. Following the political liberalization in Taiwan at the end of the 1980s, people on the Guomindang-controlled island also began to play a role in the new policy. Mainland China is currently among the largest trading partners of Taiwan, and Taiwan among the most important investors in China's coastal provinces. The "open-up" policy thus indirectly contributed to the economic, if not political, integration of "Greater China."

Wang Ke-wen

References

Ho, Samuel P. S., and Ralph W. Huenemann. *China's Open Door Policy: The Quest for Foreign Technology and Capital.* Vancouver: University of British Columbia Press, 1984.

Orleans, Leo A. *Chinese Students in America: Policies, Issues, and Numbers.* Washington, DC: National Academy Press, 1988.

Tsao, James T. H. *China's Development Strategies and Foreign Trade.* Lexington, MA: Lexington Books, 1987.

Opium War

The Opium War, a Sino-British conflict, signified China's entrance into the modern world and resulted in the formation of anti-imperialist nationalism in the Chinese.

Dissatisfied with the restrictions the Canton system placed on the Sino-foreign trade, and thus on her potential profit from the China market, Great Britain made several diplomatic attempts to negotiate this matter with the Qing empire after the late eighteenth century. Most notable among those attempts were the Macartney Mission in 1793 and the Amherst Mission of 1816. All of them failed because the Qing, upholding the traditional Chinese belief of China's economic self-sufficiency and cultural superiority, refused to consider the "barbarians'" demand of changing its trade practices. By the early nineteenth century, the British moved toward the use of force to solve this problem.

By that time, Great Britain and a few other Western countries had also begun to sell opium to China as a means to balance their trade deficit with the Qing empire. Opium, used initially as a form of medicine by the Chinese, became a popular addictive drug in China at the turn of the nineteenth century. The Western suppliers both exploited and encouraged this trend. Since the Qing government had long outlawed the sale, consumption, and import of opium, Western merchants smuggled the drug into China, often with the assistance of Chinese smugglers, along her southern coast. The British were the most aggressive among all Westerners in this illegal opium trade. During the 1830s, British opium imports reached 35,000 chests (approximately 135 pounds per chest) a year. The British government in India collected about 10 percent of its revenues from taxes on opium export.

As opium addiction created devastating social and economic problems in the Chinese society, and the illegal opium trade reversed the balance of Sino-foreign commerce, the Qing government became increasingly concerned with the drug's source of supply. In 1839, after issuing numerous edicts concerning the prohibition of opium use and transaction, Emperor Daoguang dispatched Lin Zexu to Canton as imperial commissioner on opium suppression. Lin's initial appeal to the British government on the opium problem, based on moral arguments, failed to produce any response. Lin then ordered the suspension of Sino-foreign trade and the blockade of foreign factories in Canton, forcing Western merchants to surrender their opium and sign a bond guaranteeing the ending of opium smuggling. All of the Western merchants eventually complied. The British traders, however, turned over their opium first to Charles Elliot, the British government's chief Superintendent of Trade in Canton, who then handed it to Lin. This arrangement transformed the seizure into a matter between the Chinese and the British governments.

Viewing the issue as an opportunity to

teach China a lesson about cooperation in foreign trade, London quickly decided to retaliate against the Qing empire by force. It claimed that Lin's high-handed measures had insulted the queen of England and ordered the British fleet in India to go to China and deliver a letter to Emperor Daoguang. In mid-1840 the British expeditionary force arrived and attacked Canton. It soon sailed upward along the coast, engaging in skirmishes with Chinese troops at various points. The British finally delivered the letter at Tianjin, and the alarmed Emperor Daoguang agreed to open a negotiation with the British at Canton. In January 1841, the Chuanbi Convention was signed between Elliot and the Manchu official Qishan. Neither London or Beijing, however, was pleased with this settlement. Qishan was immediately dismissed, and Elliot recalled.

The British felt that they had to demonstrate their military might once again in order to extract more concessions from the Chinese. During the following months, the expeditionary force destroyed the Chinese naval defense and held Canton for ransom, then occupied Xiamen, Dinghai, Ningpo, and Zhenjiang along the southeast coast, threatening the major Yangtze city of Nanjing. The Chinese defense proved to be utterly incompetent. In panic, Emperor Daoguang sought a peaceful settlement again. The resulting Treaty of Nanjing, signed by the Chinese representative Qiying and the British representative Henry Pottinger in August 1842, was the first "unequal treaty" concluded between China and the modern West.

According to the treaty, the Qing government agreed to abolish the Canton system and open five ports (Canton, Xiamen, Fuzhou, Ningpo, and Shanghai) for Sino-British trade; it also allowed the British to station consuls at those ports, who could communicate with the Chinese officials on an equal basis. In addition, the Chinese island of Hong Kong was ceded to the British, the Chinese had to pay to the British an indemnity of 21 million Mexican silver dollars (plus 6 million as ransom for Canton), and the tariff on China's imports and exports was set on a fixed low rate. In the supplementary agreements signed in 1843, the British further obtained the privileges of extraterritoriality and "most-favored nation" status. The latter would automatically grant Great Britain any concession China might extend to other countries in the future. As a clear indication of China's defeat in the conflict, her main concern, opium, was not even mentioned in the settlement.

Although the Opium War attracted only limited elite attention in China at the time, it has since become a landmark in Chinese history. Historians generally regard the incident as a symbol of China's forced encounter with the intruding West, commencing a century of humiliating experience under foreign imperialist assault. By the same token, the Opium War is also described as the origin of modern nationalist consciousness of the Chinese. Although the West sometimes described the conflict as a trade war, to many Chinese it was about the moral issue of opium smuggling and suppression. The victory of the British in the war left in them a bitter sense of injustice about the international community which China was being introduced into. This feeling, which was not entirely unjustified, had a lasting impact on the Chinese perception of, and relations with, the outside world. Nevertheless, through this conflict, the Chinese elite came to realize the existence of a world of nations, many of which possessed technologies and institutions more advanced than those in China. A mixed desire to protect the Chinese state against foreign threat, and to explore the strength of foreigners so as to enhance China's ability in self-defense, gradually emerged. It was to shape Chinese nationalism throughout the nineteenth and twentieth centuries.

Wang Ke-wen

References

Chang, Hsin-pao. *Commissioner Lin and the Opium War.* Cambridge, MA: Harvard University Press, 1964.

Fay, Peter W. *The Opium War, 1840–1842.* Chapel Hill: University of North Carolina Press, 1975.

Wakeman, Frederic, Jr. "The Canton Trade and the Opium War." *The Cambridge History of China,* ed. John K. Fairbank, vol. 10, 163–212. Cambridge, England: Cambridge University Press, 1978.

Overseas Chinese (Huaqiao)

The first wave of Chinese emigrants to Southeast Asia took place in the fifteenth century when the Ming dynasty (1368–1644) launched several maritime expeditions across the Indian Ocean. After the founding of the Qing dynasty

(1644–1912), however, the Manchu government closed the southeast coast and prohibited
the overseas emigration of Chinese. Not until
the nineteenth century did large numbers of
southern Chinese, driven by economic difficulties and attracted by new contacts with the
West, travel to Southeast Asia and America at
the risk of government sanctions. Settling in
foreign lands, the Chinese emigrants often
worked in lowly professions and suffered discrimination by the local people. In general, the
Chinese in Southeast Asia fared better than
those in North America or elsewhere in the
Western world. By the end of the nineteenth
century, there were around 90,000 Chinese
overseas, excluding those in Hong Kong and
Macau.

Although living outside of China, these
Chinese emigrants maintained their national
identity and their concern about conditions at
home. In a sense, they were even more interested and active in Chinese politics than their
compatriots in China, because of the stimula-
tion they received by observing foreign political systems and the freedom they enjoyed in
voicing political opinions. Faced with contempt
and harassment in foreign societies, moreover,
they were eager to see a strong and united
China, one which might better protect their
interests and dignity. From the 1890s to the
early 1900s, overseas Chinese were a main
source of support for the republican revolutionary movement led by Sun Yatsen, himself an
overseas Chinese. During the same period,
other political movements, such as the constitutional reformers under Kang Youwei and
Liang Qichao, rivaled Sun for political and financial assistance from the overseas Chinese
communities. Connections with the Hong
League gave Sun the upper hand. When the
Revolution of 1911 occurred, for example, the
Hong League in North America (or Homen
Zhigongtang) raised funds from overseas Chinese to purchase aircrafts for Sun's revolutionary government. In recognition of the political
significance of overseas Chinese, the new republican government in 1912 reserved a number of
seats for them in its parliament.

Overseas Chinese continued to play important political roles in the early Republic. Praised
by Sun Yatsen as "Mother of the Revolution,"
they generally supported Sun against Sun's various political rivals. In addition to Sun, a few
other overseas Chinese, such as Liao Zhongkai,
Eugene Chen (Chen Youren), and the Soong

family, rose to prominence in the Guomindang
(GMD) government of the 1920s to the 1940s.
During the second Sino-Japanese War (1937–
45), overseas Chinese, then numbering around
eight million, made enormous financial contributions to the war effort. The Chinese government established an "Overseas Chinese News
Agency" in 1941 to 1948 for the sole purpose
of informing overseas Chinese about the motherland and consolidating their support. Also
during the war, however, overseas Chinese began to be divided by the emerging conflict between the GMD and the Chinese Communist
Party (CCP).

After 1949, both the CCP government on
the mainland and the GMD government in
Taiwan tried to win the allegiance of overseas
Chinese, although the CCP's effort was less
consistent than that made by the GMD. The
GMD government, for example, still reserves
seats for overseas Chinese in its national representative bodies. Because the People's Republic
of China (PRC) was isolated by the West in the
1950s and 1960s, and because many Taiwanese students went to the West for advanced
studies during that period, for a long time Taibei
was more successful than Beijing in gaining the
support of the Chinese communities in the
West. But there were contentions in Southeast
Asia. When the PRC reestablished contacts with
the West in the early 1970s, many overseas
Chinese shifted their loyalty to Beijing, and a
new wave of Chinese immigrants arrived from
the mainland. The overseas competition between the GMD and the CCP regained momentum, until Beijing and Taibei reached a rapprochement in the late 1980s.

Under the current economic reforms and
"open-up" policy, overseas Chinese have become a major source of external investment and
trade contacts for the growing mainland market. Motivated by profits as well as patriotism,
Chinese abroad often generously finance the
development of their home towns. The
Tiananmen Incident of 1989 provoked angry
protests from Chinese around the world, but
did not stop their effort to assist China's economic transformation.

More than 30 million Chinese reside overseas in the 1990s. Their (Chinese) nationalist
sentiment, fostered by a deep-rooted cultural
pride and by the experience of external oppression in the modern times, has testified to the
strength of China's national solidarity, yet has
also proved to be an obstacle to their assimila-

tion with the new societies in which they chose to live. In Southeast Asia, the ambivalent loyalty of the Chinese communities has led to ethnic conflict and government persecution. Although the Chinese national, if not cultural, identity usually disappears after two or three generations in foreign lands, the constant outflow of Chinese emigrants in the past two centuries has kept this "overseas nationalism" alive. It has been a tremendous political and economic asset to the Chinese state.

Wang Ke-wen

References

Pan, Lynn. *Sons of the Yellow Emperor: A History of the Chinese Diaspora*. Boston, MA: Little, Brown, 1990.

Tsai, Sih-shan Henry. *The Chinese Experience in America*. Bloomington: Indiana University Press, 1986.

Yen, Ching Hwang. *The Overseas Chinese and the 1911 Revolution: With Special Reference to Singapore and Malaya*. Kuala Lumpur: Oxford University Press, 1976.

O

P

Pan-Asianism

As a concept of regional alliance, Pan-Asianism has a built-in ambiguity which makes it susceptible to diverse interpretations. There are two types of "pan-" movements. One constitutes an alliance of weak states sharing a common cultural or racial background, whose relationship is based on the principle of equality. The other is built upon the domination of a group of countries by a strong power that imposes itself on others in the name of racial, cultural, and/or geographical bondage. In the late nineteenth century, Japan subscribed to the second type of Pan-Asianism built upon her strength, whereas China, as a weak country, had tended to interpret it along the lines of the first type.

As modern Chinese nationalism was largely a reaction to Western imperialist encroachments, Pan-Asianism, which appealed to the Chinese people's regional identity, as distinct from that of the West, was compatible with this nationalist strain. Since the late Qing, Chinese perception of the regional alliance has gone through several changes. At first, the Chinese approach to the idea of regional alliance had a cultural rather than a political connotation. In 1907, when Japan, a new member of the imperialist camp, was poised to entrench its power in China, the Chinese revolutionary Zhang Binglin organized the Asian Harmony and Friendship Assembly in Tokyo. It looked to India and China, both victims of Western imperialism despite their distinguished cultural heritage, rather than to Japan, as joint leaders of the Asian alliance in resisting the West. Later, facing rising Japanese hegemony in East Asia, China became more wary of Pan-Asianism.

On the eve of the May Fourth movement, Li Dazhao proposed "New Asianism" as a substitute for "Pan-Asianism." This suggested that while the Chinese did not reject the idea of a regional alliance, they suspected Pan-Asianism as being associated with Japanese imperialist expansion in the region. Meanwhile, the realization that China and Japan shared some common interests prompted many Chinese to continue embracing Pan-Asianism in words, if not in deeds. From the Twenty-One Demands of 1915 to the creation of Manchukuo in 1931, and to the invasion of China in 1937, Japanese militarists and nationalists had used Pan-Asianism to justify their expansionism in the region. While Pan-Asianism served the interests of Japanese imperialism, it was also exploited by the Chinese to facilitate Chinese nationalism.

In the history of the Republic of China, Pan-Asianism had been associated with two names: Sun Yatsen and Wang Jingwei. Sun made comments on this subject three times. The first was related to an article "On China's Survival" *(Zhongguo cunwang wenti)*, written in 1917 by the Guomindang (GMD) ideologue Zhu Zhixin but attributed to Sun. The second and the third involved two speeches which Sun delivered in Kobe, Japan, on his way to Beijing shortly before his death in March 1925. In summary, Sun stressed three points regarding Pan-Asianism: (1) the relationship between China and Japan was one of symbiosis; (2) Eastern and Western civilizations differed in that one followed "the way of right," the other "the way of might." Japan, being an Eastern country, should choose "right" over "might"; and (3) Japan should help to release China from the shackles of unequal treaties. In view of China's weakness at the time, these remarks represented more of an appeal to the Japanese people than a demand issued to the Japanese government.

The power imbalance between the two countries became even more pronounced in 1940, during the second Sino-Japanese War, when Wang Jingwei used Pan-Asianism to rationalize his collaboration with the Japanese conquerors and claimed that in so doing, he was carrying out the death wish of the late Party leader. Pan-Asianism thus interpreted was posed not as an alternative to nationalism, but as its underpinning. However, the fact that Japanese militarists had used it to propagate the Greater East Asian Co-Prosperity Sphere, a regional alliance presupposing Japan's domination in the region, made it difficult for Chinese collaborationists, devoid of political autonomy and any plausible claim to equality, to convince their fellow countrymen that Pan-Asianism was indeed compatible with the aspirations of Chinese nationalism.

Luo Jiu-jung

References

Beasley, W. G. *Japanese Imperialism, 1895–1945*. Oxford, England: Oxford University Press, 1987.

Iriye, Akira. "Toward a New Cultural Order: The Hsin-min Hui." *The Chinese and the Japanese: Essays in Political and Cultural Interactions,* ed. Akira Iriye, 254–274. Princeton, NJ: Princeton University Press, 1980.

Jansen, Marius. *The Japanese and Sun Yat-sen*. Cambridge, MA: Harvard University Press, 1954.

Party Purification (Qingdang)

Party purification was the purge of the Chinese Communists from the Guomindang, which in effect terminated the first Guomindang–Chinese Communist Party (GMD-CCP) United Front (1924–27).

As the Northern Expedition swept into the Yangtze River valley in late 1926, dissension in the United Front and within the GMD deepened. GMD elements who were dissatisfied with Chiang Kaishek's rapid rise to Party leadership collaborated with the CCP members and seized control of the new GMD headquarters and its national government in Wuhan. They soon tried to dismantle Chiang's military and political power. Feeling threatened, Chiang, then directing campaigns in Jiangxi, became increasingly hostile toward the Wuhan regime and the United Front upon which it was based.

From late 1926 to early 1927, Chiang's troops clashed with pro-Wuhan GMD branches and CCP-led labor unions in a number of recently taken Yangtze cities.

In March 1927, with the help of general strikes organized by the CCP, Chiang's forces entered Shanghai. Now in direct contact with the foreign and Chinese business interests in the Lower Yangtze area, which were alarmed by the radical policies of the United Front, Chiang found new support for his opposition to the Wuhan regime. He quietly met with potential allies in the Party and the military to plan for an open break with Wuhan. A group of GMD veterans in the Party's Central Supervisory Committee (CSC) agreed with Chiang's plan and provided him with the necessary institutional basis to challenge Wuhan's authority. On April 2 they held a CSC plenum in Shanghai which urged the Party to take extraordinary actions against the Communists, who they claimed were subverting the GMD. One week later, these CSC members issued a circular telegram denouncing the pro-Communist tendencies of the Wuhan regime.

Throughout this period, Chiang's forces were competing with the CCP-led workers in controlling Shanghai. On April 12, Chiang's 26th Corps, assisted by the local underworld Green Gang, launched a surprise attack on the Shanghai General Labor Union and disarmed its pickets. In protest against this action, the workers organized a mass demonstration on the next day, which was brutally suppressed by the troops. Massive arrests and executions of suspected Communists and leftists followed and continued for weeks, resulting in the deaths of about five thousand workers, students, and CCP members in that city. Meanwhile, Chiang's followers took similar actions in Jiangsu, Zhejiang, Anhui, Fujian, Guangdong, and Guangxi.

Wuhan summarily relieved Chiang from all of his posts and expelled him from the GMD. Chiang, backed by conservative Party veterans, several of his military commanders, and the foreign powers, established his own GMD headquarters and national government in Nanjing on April 18. The Nanjing regime formally terminated the United Front and ordered the arrest of leading Communists. A Central Party Purification Committee, organized by the regime on May 7, had the task of ousting Communists as well as "local bullies and evil gentry, venal officials, opportunists, and all corrupted and degenerated elements" from the Party. The

Committee then appointed local committees in fourteen provinces and four cities to carry out the work, but they were active only in areas under Chiang's control.

In July, the GMD leaders in Wuhan, facing increasing political and military isolation and an imminent Communist takeover, also decided to end the United Front. The purge of Communists and leftists from the GMD thereupon spread into most of south and central China. By the end of 1927, the CCP had been driven underground with a loss of 80 percent of its membership. The GMD was seriously affected as well. The regimes at Wuhan and Nanjing were reunified in early 1928, with Chiang Kaishek as the Party's leader. The radical trend that had been guiding the Party for the past three years was suppressed. The new government of China now turned from the Soviet Union to the capitalist West for assistance and guidance.

Wang Ke-wen

References

Wilbur, C. Martin. *The Nationalist Revolution in China, 1923–1928.* Cambridge, England: Cambridge University Press, 1983.
Wu, Tien-wei. "Chiang Kai-shek's April 12 Coup of 1927." *China in the 1920's: Nationalism and Revolution,* eds. Gilbert F. Chan and Thomas H. Etzold, 147–59. New York, NY: New Viewpoints, 1976.

Peace Movement

See WANG JINGWEI; WANG JINGWEI REGIME

Peasant Movement

Romantics to the contrary, it is not easy for a peasantry to engage in sustained rebellion. Peasants are especially handicapped in passing from passive recognition of wrongs to political participation as a means for setting them right. The factors that make this so are numerous. First, peasants tend to work alone or in small groups. Second, the peasant's workload is such that even momentary alterations of routine threaten his ability to survive. Third, mutual aid provided by such groups as secret societies tend to cushion peasant discontent. Finally, the isolation of the village often deprives the peasantry of the knowledge needed to articulate their interests with appropriate forms of action.

Given that peasants are slow to rise, what special circumstances exacerbated peasant conditions in early twentieth-century China so that the peasantry were willing to participate on a massive scale in revolutionary activity? Several not necessarily exclusive answers have been put forth. The first argues that the involvement of the Chinese peasantry in the revolutions of the twentieth century was the result of three great crises: demographic, ecological, and governmental. The demographic crisis is most easily depicted in bare figures. China's population in 1775 was 265 million. By 1900 it was around 600 million. The ecological crisis involved a stepped-up capitalization of rent which resulted in the transfer of resources from those unable to keep up to those able to pay. In addition, capitalist mobilization of resources was reinforced through the pressure of taxation, of demands for redemption payments, and through the increased needs for industrially produced commodities on the part of the peasantry itself. Finally, both the demographic and ecological crises converged in the crisis in authority. Both the Qing and the Guomindang governments proved incapable of effectively leading the country.

The second theory that has been presented to explain Chinese peasant involvement in the events of twentieth-century China is nationalism. In *Peasant Nationalism and Communist Power,* Chalmers Johnson made the argument that the peasants supported the Chinese Communist Party after 1937, not because of its social programs aimed at addressing the three crises mentioned earlier, but because the Communists led a war-energized, radical nationalist movement, with socialist ideology merely an adjunct to Chinese nationalism. Johnson argues that before the Japanese invasion in 1937, the major Communist appeals of land redistribution and justice for the poor failed to gain substantial peasant involvement in the revolution. The Japanese invasion of China created two related conditions which finally enabled the Communists to gain power through peasant mass mobilization. First, because of the invasion the situation in rural areas degenerated. Gentry fled. Poverty worsened. Second, the particularly harsh practice of the Japanese against the Chinese peasantry encouraged the formation of spontaneous local self-defense units. The Communists then took advantage of this situation, abandoned their social and economic programs, and adopted a nationalist, anti-Japanese one instead. Under the banner of nationalism the Communists organized, coordinated, and led the peasant movement of resistance against the invading Japanese.

Johnson's once influential thesis has since been disputed by other scholars of modern China, who proposed yet a number of other explanations of the peasant support for the Communist revolution, ranging from the appeal of the Communist reform programs to the organizational skills of the Communists. These new explanations, often based on detailed studies of the Communist base areas, have seriously weakened the link between the Chinese peasantry and nationalism previously assumed by Johnson.

Although generalization is difficult, the most probable explanation for the massive involvement of the Chinese peasant in the revolutionary movement of the twentieth century may include all of the factors mentioned above. A combination of demographic, ecological, and governmental crises, anti-Japanese feelings, and effective Communist strategies led the peasantry to revolution. The myth about "peasant nationalism" as the most important driving force behind the phenomenon, however, has largely been dispelled.

Gerald W. Berkley

References

Gillin, Donald G. "'Peasant Nationalism' in the History of Chinese Communism." *Journal of Asian Studies* 23, no. 2 (February 1964): 269–89.

Johnson, Chalmers. *Peasant Nationalism and Communist Power: The Emergence of Revolutionary China, 1937–1945*. Stanford, CA: Stanford University Press, 1962.

Little, Daniel. *Understanding Peasant China: Studies in the Philosophy of Social Science*. New Haven, CT: Yale University Press, 1989.

Peng Dehuai (1898–1974)

Peng Dehuai was a military leader in the Chinese Communist Party (CCP) and the People's Republic, the commander-in-chief of the Chinese forces in the Korean War, and a critic of Mao Zedong during the Great Leap Forward.

A native of Hunan province, Peng was a rebellious youth and was expelled from his home at the age of nine. He wandered through a number of jobs until enlisting in the local army in 1916. As a soldier in the warlord armies he experienced first-hand the hardship of the poor and the underclass. By 1926 he had become an officer; he joined the Guomindang

(GMD) forces and participated in the Northern Expedition.

In 1928, after the collapse of the first GMD-CCP United Front, Peng joined the CCP and followed Mao Zedong to the Jiangxi Soviet, thus beginning his life-long association with Mao. In the following years, his skill in battlefield command was tested in the defense of the Soviets against the GMD's Bandit-Suppression Campaigns, and he rose to second in command (under Zhu De) in the Red Army. His leadership was again critical to the survival of the Red Army in the Long March. During the Sino-Japanese War of 1937 to 1945 Peng played an important role in the CCP's anti-Japanese effort in north China. He was in charge of the Battle of Hundred Regiments in 1940. Then in the civil war of 1945 to 1949, his main responsibility was to conquer northwestern and western China for Mao.

Following the founding of the People's Republic, Peng helped to restore order and establish the administration of the Northwest region, much as what Lin Biao did in the South, Chen Yi did in the East, and Gao Gang did in the Northeast. When the Korean War broke out in 1950, Peng commanded the Chinese "People's Volunteers" who fought against the United Nations forces in Korea. After returning to Beijing in 1953, he became minister of defense and *de facto* chief of the People's Liberation Army. As the Korean War increased the domestic support for the new CCP government, Peng's popularity also rose.

Then came the turning point in Peng's career: the Lushan Conference in 1959. The conference was held during the disaster of Mao's Great Leap Forward, yet few in the CCP leadership were willing to risk their own political fortune by openly criticizing the campaign. Peng, known for his candor and friendship with Mao, was almost alone in launching a bold attack on Mao's policy at the conference. Mao was furious. He labeled Peng's comments on the Great Leap Forward (included in a long memorandum submitted to him) as a planned and organized "rightist opportunist" activity. The other leaders duly followed Mao's direction. The conference denounced Peng as the leader of an anti-Party group and placed him under house arrest.

In 1962, Peng wrote a long letter of self-criticism to Mao, as the product of his "repentance" over the past two years. The letter, however, showed that he remained convinced of some of his initial comments on Mao's policy.

This led to more criticism and punishments; he was formally removed from all positions in the Party and the government. In 1965, Mao ordered Peng to take over a minor task in the Southwest.

It was widely believed that the play *Hairui's Dismissal from Office*, which started the debate that served as a prelude to the Cultural Revolution of 1966 to 1976, was an implicit attack on Mao's purge of Peng. Unsurprisingly, therefore, Peng became a major target of Jiang Qing and the radicals during the Cultural Revolution. He was brought back to Beijing and subjected to repeated mental and physical abuse at the hands of the Red Guards, until his death in 1974.

Wang Ke-wen

References

Bartke, Wolfgang. *A Biographical Dictionary and Analysis of China's Party Leadership, 1922–1988.* New York, NY: K. G. Saur, 1990.

The Case of P'eng Te-huai, 1959–1968. Hong Kong: Union Research Institute, 1968.

Klein, Donald W., and Ann B. Clark, eds. *Biographical Dictionary of Chinese Communism, 1921–1965.* Cambridge, MA: Harvard University Press, 1971.

People's Communes

Under the Chinese Communist Party's (CCP) program of "transition to socialism," China commenced agricultural collectivization in 1953. By 1956, advanced producer cooperatives had been formed throughout the country. In 1958, during the Great Leap Forward, Mao Zedong urged the merger of these cooperatives into People's Communes. Mao's goals were to outgrow the Soviet-style Five Year Plan by promoting decentralization, even rural/urban development, and a labor-intensive strategy for industrialization. Further collectivizing agriculture, Mao believed, would also increase capital accumulation and state revenue.

The first experimental commune appeared in Henan in April 1958. As the organization spread rapidly in north China, the Maoist propagandist Chen Boda first used the term "people's commune" in July to imply a transition into communism. A CCP Politburo session in August approved the commune's nationwide implementation, but defined its basis as collective ownership and socialist distribution. It was also to merge with the rural administration of *xiang* and became an all-comprehensive economic, social, political, cultural, and military unit in rural China.

Before the year's end, larger-size communes, totaling 26,000 people each, appeared, engulfing the entire rural population. The movement entered into its most radical phase in the summer and fall of 1958, when many communes went communist and dissolved the family units of their members. However, peasant resistance, food shortages caused by labor diversion to nonagricultural projects, and breakdown of centralized planning soon led to a decline of the movement. In December, the CCP took a step backward by devolving ownership and accounting of the communes downward to the sub-commune "production brigades." Mao also resigned from the state chairmanship.

Severe natural calamities in 1959 undermined the communes further. Floods, drought, and famine ravaged the country. Although Mao triumphed in the intra-party struggle over the commune policy at the Lushan Plenum in July–August, when Peng Dehuai was punished for his criticism of Mao, harsh reality forced the Party to further retreat from communization. It gradually reintroduced material incentives and private markets in the countryside. Within the communes, ownership and accounting were further lowered to the "production team" level in 1961. The Party also reduced the size of communes.

Mao nonetheless maintained his utopian vision of communization. In 1964, he presented the Dazhai brigade in Shanxi as a model for rural development. During the early stage of the Cultural Revolution (1966–69), the commune's size waxed again. Meanwhile, revolutionary committees at the commune level assumed Party, management, and military functions. In many rural areas, attempts were made to abolish private plots and farm markets and to ban sideline occupations. Despite all the sound and fury, the workpoint system remained socialist, instead of "communist," and the accounting unit stayed with the production teams. In 1969, an experiment to make the brigade or commune "the unit of account" failed.

After 1972, China's countryside returned to the 1962 to 1965 pattern of mixing material incentives with collectivization. The commune was eroded further after Mao's death in 1976. In 1978, several provinces broke the production team up into smaller neighborhood "work groups." By the end of 1980, a new system of fixing quotas of agricultural production directly to each peasant household, *i.e.,* the "responsibility system," became widespread. About 20 percent of the peasant households were included in this system, and they also managed farmland as individual plots. The 1982 State Constitution finally ended the all-comprehensive communes and reestablished township as the basic rural administrative unit. Communes gradually became corporate business ventures.

Lung-kee Sun

References

Meisner, Maurice. *Mao's China and After: A History of the People's Republic.* New York, NY: The Free Press, 1985.

People's Liberation Army

The People's Liberation Army (PLA) has been the military arm of the Chinese Communist Party (CCP) since 1946 and the national army of the People's Republic of China (PRC) since 1949.

The People's Liberation Army was reorganized on the basis of the CCP forces during the Sino-Japanese War (1937–45), primarily the Eighth Route Army and the New Fourth Army, at the beginning of the civil war (1945–49). It performed excellently in the civil war by winning almost every battle until the Guomindang (GMD) government was driven out of the mainland. Since the founding of the PRC, the PLA fought several wars against foreign enemies: the Korean War of 1950 to 1953 (under the title of "Chinese People's Volunteer Army"), the Sino-Indian border conflict of 1962, the Sino-Soviet border conflict of 1969, and the Sino-Vietnamese War of 1979. In the first and last wars it suffered enormous casualties. Along the coast of Fujian province, the PLA engaged, until the early 1990s, in a prolonged stalemate with the GMD forces on the islands of Quemoy (Jinmen) and Matsu (Mazu) and in Taiwan.

The PLA, established in late 1946 with Zhu De as commander and Peng Dehuai as deputy-commander, was initially a ground force of 2.5 million men. By the end of 1949, its size had grown to more than 5 million, and with the absorption of the defeated or surrendered GMD forces, it also had a navy and an air force. During the first decade of the PRC, the PLA was equipped only with conventional weapons, mostly Russian-made. This was improved gradually, and in the late 1960s it began to acquire nuclear weapons, making it one of the

People's Liberation Army in parade—the slogan in the background reads: "Build a modernized army with Chinese characteristics." (Xinhua News Agency.)

most powerful armed forces in the world. The PRC, however, has maintained that the PLA's nuclear capability is for deterrent purposes only.

The PLA has been acclaimed by the CCP as a proletarian army dedicated to the cause of Marxism-Leninism and Mao Zedong thought. In theory and in practice, it is under the total control of the Party. Partly because of such a control, perhaps, there has not been a military coup under the PRC, but the PLA has intervened in politics in other ways. In the early 1960s the PLA, then under the command of Lin Biao, was in the vanguard of the Study Mao Zedong Thought campaign and the creation of a personal cult of Mao. Later, during the Cultural Revolution, the PLA served as Mao's instrument to restore order in society and consolidate power for the leftists. The country was under *de facto* military rule from 1969 to 1971.

In the post-Mao era the PLA has undergone significant changes. Deng Xiaoping, in an effort to redirect China's resources to economic development, reduced the size of the PLA by over one million men in the 1980s. In the Tiananmen Incident of 1989, the PLA carried out the suppression of the demonstrators in Beijing, thereby tarnishing its reputation among the Chinese people. The Incident and the rapid economic reforms have lowered the status as well as the morale of the PLA in the 1990s, although its military technology has become quite advanced and is making a profit for the PRC in the world market. Presently, the PLA is generally viewed as a conservative force in Chinese politics.

Wang Ke-wen

Mao Zedong accepting the state emblem of the People's Republic of China in 1950. (Xinhua News Agency.)

References

Joffe, Ellis. *The Chinese Army After Mao.* Cambridge, MA: Harvard University Press, 1987.

Nelsen, Harvey W. *The Chinese Military System: An Organizational Study of the Chinese People's Liberation Army.* Boulder, CO: Westview Press, 1977.

People's Political Council

In response to the Japanese invasion, which began in the summer of 1937, the Guomindang government desperately needed popular support and national unity. An anti-Japanese united front resulted when the ruling Guomindang (GMD) reached agreements with the Chinese Communist Party (CCP) and other minority parties and groups in China. The People's Political Council (PPC) was then established to symbolize popular participation in state affairs and to whip up the national struggle against an overpowering enemy.

Although frequently referred to as China's "wartime parliament" by Chinese and foreign news media during the war, the PPC never acquired the power and status of a parliamentary body. However, the urgent need of wartime unity pressured the enfeebled GMD government to accord the PPC due respect and the opinions of its members with tolerance. The PPC had a nine-year life-span (July 1938–June 1947), divided into four successive councils, with a total of thirteen sessions. It played a relatively effective role during the Sino-Japanese War. The PPC had a membership of 200 in the beginning, and it increased eventually to 362 during the final session of the fourth council. However, the proportion of the non-GMD councillors had declined, an indication of a reverse trend from the government's initial liberal position.

From the outset the PPC was given a host of nominal powers. In fact, however, only its power of hearing reports from government ministers, of interpellation, and of investigation carried some weight. This was mainly because government officials were subject to criticism by "public opinion," as expressed by the councillors. In spite of the limited power the PPC enjoyed, the body discussed virtually all major wartime problems. Motivated by a strong sense of patriotic duty, many councillors, particularly the non-GMD ones, often boldly criticized government policies or the misconduct of some government officials and military commanders.

The most important contribution of the PPC was to uphold national unity in China. During the early phase of the war, the PPC gave the wartime government its unswerving support. It lifted the morale of the populace and strengthened its will of resistance. China's wartime unity faced a dangerous test in early 1939 when Japan launched a "peace offensive" which enticed Wang Jingwei, the second-ranking GMD leader and the speaker of the PPC, to desert the wartime government and announce his desire to pursue peace negotiations based on Japan's proposed conditions. The PPC immediately objected to Wang's action and affirmed its support of Chiang Kaishek and the continued resistance to Japanese aggression. One year later, when Wang formed his Nanjing regime, the PPC condemned him and his followers as traitors, and called upon the soldiers and people of China to resist Japan to the last.

A second, more ominous threat to China's wartime unity was the precarious GMD-CCP United Front. With the bitter memory of one decade of armed rivalry, the two parties distrusted each other. Once the Japanese pressure lessened in 1939, cracks appeared in the United Front. The situation was made worse by the weakening of the GMD's military and the simultaneous expansion of the CCP's influence in north and central China. As the Communists established guerrilla base areas behind the Japanese lines, clashes between the two parties occurred in increasing frequency and intensity. PPC councillors became gravely concerned about this development. The non-GMD councillors in particular worked hard to prevent the breakdown of the United Front, and finally were able to bring the two sides to the conference table. The PPC was often used as a forum for the GMD and the CCP to exchange their views. Although unable to resolve their differences, the effort did avoid an open split between the two parties for the rest of the war.

In their effort to maintain national unity and to urge the adoption of a democratic constitution, many non-GMD councillors in the PPC seceded to form a new political association in late 1939. This association eventually evolved into the China Democratic League in October 1944, and its members viewed themselves as representing the "third force" in China. The Democratic League became politically active from 1944 to 1948, when it tried unsuccessfully to bring about a non-military solution to China's national problems.

Lawrence N. Shyu

References

Eastman, Lloyd E. *Seeds of Destruction: Nationalist China in War and Revolution, 1937–1949.* Stanford, CA: Stanford University Press, 1984.

Shyu, Lawrence N. "China's 'Wartime Parliament': The People's Political Council, 1938–1945." *Nationalist China during the Sino-Japanese War, 1937–1945,* ed. Paul K. T. Sih. Hicksville, NY: Exposition Press, 1977.

People's Republic of China

On October 1, 1949, following its triumph in the civil war, the Chinese Communist Party (CCP) established the Central People's Government in Beijing and announced the founding of a new state, named the People's Republic of China (PRC). Mao Zedong became its first chairman. At the time the defeated Guomindang still controlled the provinces in the Southwest. By the end of that year, all the Guomindang forces on the mainland had been eliminated, although Chiang Kaishek and his supporters found refuge on the island of Taiwan. Since then the People's Republic has never been able to claim effective control over all of China, and in the international community it has had to compete with the Republic of China in Taiwan for representation and legitimacy.

Other than Taiwan (and the Pescadores), the People's Republic extends its sovereignty to most of the territory which the Republic of China had initially inherited from the Qing empire in 1912. This included Tibet, which the Communist government liberated in 1951. Outer Mongolia, on the other hand, was allowed to become independent by the Guomindang government in 1946 and thus is not part of the People's Republic. From the very beginning, the People's Republic has been under the total control of the CCP, although other democratic parties have been allowed a nominal existence. Party comes before the state, and socialism is the declared principle for the organization of the state and the economy.

Mao stepped down as chairman of the state in late 1958, during his disastrous Great Leap Forward program, and was succeeded by Liu Shaoqi. Seven years later Mao initiated the Great Proletarian Cultural Revolution that nearly destroyed the state apparatus. Liu was arrested, and later died in prison. The state Chairmanship remained vacant throughout the turmoil. Not until 1983 was the position reestablished and held by Li Xiannian.

In foreign affairs, the People's Republic sided closely with the Soviet Union during the 1950s. After the Sino-Soviet split in the early 1960s, it was isolated from most of the developed countries in the world, yet was able to become a nuclear power on its own. In the early 1970s it improved relations with the United States and, as a result, gained diplomatic recognitions from many countries that had formerly recognized the Republic of China in Taiwan. The People's Republic is now a permanent member of the Security Council of the United Nations.

At one of the preparational meetings for the founding of the People's Republic, Mao declared that "the Chinese people have now stood up!" In the sense that Western and Japanese imperialist encroachments on China were terminated after 1949, this statement contained a degree of truth. Nationalism was certainly one of the major factors that contributed to the success of the Chinese Communist revolution. Yet the People's Republic was at least for more than a decade under the dominant influence of the Soviet Union. Only after the mid-1960s did China become an independent power. Since the post-Mao reforms in the late 1970s, the country has also been recognized as a potential economic giant.

Wang Ke-wen

References

Meisner, Maurice. *Mao's China: A History of the People's Republic.* New York, NY: The Free Press, 1977.

Political Consultative Conference

Convened shortly after the end of the second Sino-Japanese War, the Political Consultative Conference aimed at finding a peaceful solution to China's political crisis and realizing democratic reform under the Guomindang (GMD) government. Chiang Kaishek and Mao Zedong, at the end of their meeting in September–October 1945, proposed the Conference as a possible alternative to the imminent Guomindang–Chinese Communist party (GMD-CCP) civil war. From January 10 to 31, 1946, the conference was held in Chongqing and was attended by thirty-eight representatives of the various political parties or groups in China, including the GMD, the CCP, the Chinese Youth Party, and the Democratic League.

Under pressure from the oppositions, the GMD pledged at the conference to protect the basic freedoms of the people, respect the legal status of the opposition parties, hold nationwide elections and release political prisoners. After lengthy discussions the conference decided on major issues concerning the country's postwar political structure, such as the drafting of a constitution, the organization of a national assembly, and the nationalization of the military. As to the future central government of China, the conference agreed on the establishment of a coalition government in the form of a multiparty State Council with executive and legislative powers. The GMD would control half of the council's forty members, but any of its resolutions would require a two-thirds majority. Through this and other arrangements, the conference attempted the peaceful transformation of the GMD's one-party dictatorship into a constitutional democracy, satisfying the demands of the CCP while protecting the independence of the minor parties. George C. Marshall, the American special envoy mediating the GMD-CCP conflict in China at the time, praised the conference resolutions as "liberal and forward-looking."

The hope of peace that the conference projected, however, soon evaporated. In July, the GMD government announced its decision to convene the national assembly before the formation of a coalition government, in open disregard of the conference resolutions. The CCP and the Democratic League retaliated by boycotting the assembly, and the coalition government never materialized. The conference thus failed to prevent the outbreak of a civil war between the GMD and the CCP; China's future was still decided by force. Upon its victory in the civil war in September 1949, the CCP organized its own Chinese People's Political Consultative Conference at Beijing to legitimize its new regime. This conference met for twelve days and approved the basic organization and platform (Common Program) of the CCP's People's Government. Since then, the conference has been a regular institution under the People's Republic, symbolizing the united front between the ruling CCP and other democratic parties in the country. It has served largely as a rubber-stamp consultative organ for the CCP dictatorship.

Wang Ke-wen

References

Tsou, Tang. *America's Failure in China, 1941–50.* Chicago, IL: University of Chicago Press, 1963.

Political Tutelage *(Xunzheng)*

The theoretical basis of the Guomindang's (GMD) Party rule in China was known as political tutelage.

Upon the completion of its Northern Expedition, the GMD proclaimed in 1928 the commencement of the period of political tutelage *(xunzheng)*. The term was taken from Sun Yatsen's *Fundamentals of National Reconstruction (Jianguo dagang)* of 1924, although the concept could be traced to his *Design for Revolution (Geming fanglue)* of 1906. In the 1924 work Sun prescribed three consecutive stages of the GMD's National Revolution: the period of "military rule" *(junzheng),* the period of "political tutelage," and the period of "constitutional democracy" *(xianzheng).* Military rule, according to Sun, would begin as soon as the revolutionary uprising had succeeded in taking control of a county. When an entire province has been "pacified," *i.e.,* controlled by the "revolutionaries" (GMD), it would then be put under political tutelage. During this stage, the focus of reconstruction would be at the county level, where the county government under the GMD would train the populace to exercise its right of self-government. Not until this training had been completed would the county be allowed to elect its representative assembly, which would in turn organize a new county government. After all counties in a province had organized their new governments, a provincial assembly would be elected to produce the new provincial government. The process would then be repeated at the national level. The last step would also signal the country's transition into constitutional democracy. Sun suggested that this stage-by-stage approach to revolution and reconstruction could prevent a premature advancement to democracy, which he believed had caused the failure of the early Republic. Following Sun's blueprint, the GMD thus defined the Northern Expedition as the stage of military rule and the completion of it the beginning of political tutelage.

In October 1928, the GMD government promulgated an "Outline of Political Tutelage," according to which the government at all levels were placed under the supervision of the GMD. The Party's Central Executive Committee was entrusted with the power to guide the national government, but a Central Political Council was created to link the Party and the government and to decide major policies. This last arrangement was not a prescription of Sun Yatsen, whose program was vague in details, and soon became a subject of controversy. In the early years of political tutelage, an intraparty debate arose concerning the meaning of Party rule. Some GMD members contended that the term meant simply "rule by Party principles." In other words, as long as the government upheld Sun's Three Peoples' Principles in its policies, it should be considered as being under GMD supervision. Others insisted on a strict definition of the term "rule by Party members." All government officials, in their view, had to come from the GMD. The debate was more than a theoretical one. The latter group was apparently dissatisfied with the inclusion of non-GMD members in the new "Party government" and in the expedient Central Political Committee. As Chiang Kaishek, the leader of the GMD, needed the assistance of many non-GMD bureaucrats in running his government, the former group won the debate with Chiang's support.

There were more problems in the "Party rule" at the provincial and local levels. Throughout the Nanjing Decade of 1927 to 1937, the GMD presided over only a nominally unified country, with a majority of the provinces still in the hands of former warlords or new militarists in the GMD. These provincial rulers had little interest in allowing the GMD organizations to supervise their governments. The general pattern, therefore, was for the existing provincial or local ruler to assume control, if not the actual leadership, of the comparable GMD branches and turn them into their own instruments of power. The ideal chain of command under the political tutelage was thus reversed: instead of the Party directing the government and the military, the military was now directing the government, which in turn directed the Party. Under the name of political tutelage, the reality of military rule continued.

Nevertheless, the theory of political tutelage provided a rationale for the GMD to monopolize political power *vis-à-vis* other political groups in China, and to restrict the people's basic freedoms. Censorship, secret police, and party privileges characterized the GMD rule. Sun Yatsen had indicated that the period of political tutelage would last six years. The GMD accordingly announced in June 1929 that this would be the duration of its Party rule. When the end of that six-year period arrived in 1935, the GMD government drafted a constitution, which was promulgated the following year, in preparation for the transition into a constitutional democracy. The transition, however, did not occur until the late 1940s.

A main reason for the postponement of constitutional democracy was the outbreak of the Sino-Japanese War in July 1937, but there were other factors that prevented the GMD from concluding its political tutelage on time. During the Nanjing Decade, the primary task of Chiang Kaishek's government was the suppression of domestic rivals, including regional militarists and the Chinese Communists, and after 1931 it also faced the external threat of Japanese imperialism. The GMD thus had little attention left for the supposed training of the populace for self-government. Moreover, Chiang considered the concentration of power in the hands of the GMD, especially in the hands of its leader, as necessary for China's reconstruction. In the early 1930s, he was clearly impressed by the fascist models of Germany and Italy and tried to emulate them. To a degree, the domestic and external threats served as excuses for his government to prolong and strengthen Party rule at the expense of the development of democracy in China. When the GMD eventually terminated political tutelage in May 1948, it was largely a political tactic in aid of its civil war with the CCP, and the constitutional democracy it implemented was soon superseded by a martial law that returned all power to the GMD.

The political tutelage of the GMD was criticized by other political groups, as well as by liberal intellectuals, in the 1930s and 1940s. The Party often justified its monopoly of power with nationalist arguments such as national unity and loyalty to the state, but its practice of dictatorship and suppression inevitably alienated the populace and fueled the opposition. At least in urban areas, many educated Chinese preferred the CCP's promise of "new democracy" over the GMD's reality of political tute-

lage during the civil war of 1945 to 1949.

Wang Ke-wen

References

Bedeski, Robert E. *State-building in Modern China: The Kuomintang in the Prewar Period.* Berkeley: Center for Chinese Studies Publications, University of California Press, 1981.

Tien, Hung-mao. *Government and Politics in Kuomintang China, 1927–1937.* Stanford, CA: Stanford University Press, 1972.

Prince Gong (1833–98)

Leader of the Qing government during the Tongzhi Restoration and the Self-Strengthening movement (1860s-1880s), Prince Gong, Yixin, was the sixth son of the Qing emperor Daoguang. He had eight brothers and ten sisters, of whom only he and Princess Shouan were born to Empress Xiaojingzheng, a concubine of Daoguang. However, the empress took care of Daoguang's fourth son, Yiju (the heir prince), after Yiju's own mother died in 1840. Yiju and Yixin thus were brought up together and established a close relationship.

Following Prince Yiju's enthronement as Emperor Xianfeng in 1851, Yixin was granted a special imperial title, that of Gong Zhong Qing Wang (Respectfully Loyal Prince), popularly known as Gong Wang (or Prince Gong). As the highest ranking prince in the Qing court, he was entitled to direct access to the emperor on state affairs. Prince Gong's growing power at court and occasional arrogance toward his emperor brother, however, soon bred jealousies. In 1855, under the pretext that Prince Gong had mismanaged the funeral service for Empress Dowager Xiaojingzheng, Emperor Xianfeng deprived Prince Gong of all his posts in the government and ordered him to return to study in the Palace School for Princes.

In the meantime, the government experienced internal and external crises. Internally, the Taiping Rebellion was on the rise and threatened the survival of the Qing dynasty. Externally, the Western powers were dissatisfied with the implementation of the Treaty of Nanjing (1842) and demanded more open ports in south China. Emperor Xianfeng desperately needed Prince Gong's advice and support. In 1857, Prince Gong was recalled and appointed commanding general of the palace guards and director of the Grand Council. In 1859, Prince Gong also assumed his position as senior chamberlain of the Imperial Forces in Beijing.

By then, China was too weak to cope with these crises, even with the competent Prince Gong in control. The British-French Joint Expeditionary Forces pressed aggressively into Tianjin and Beijing in the summer of 1860. Emperor Xianfeng had to flee the city and take refuge in Jehol. Prince Gong, left alone in Beijing to deal with the allied forces under Lord Elgin of Great Britain and Baron Gras of France, secured a peace treaty (the Beijing Convention) in November 1860. The treaty opened China to the West diplomatically, and also liberated the conservative mind of Prince Gong. Recognizing the military superiority of the Western powers, he became the first High Manchu Prince to adopt a realistic attitude toward the West and seek realistic policy changes.

Meanwhile, in Jehol Emperor Xianfeng died. The emperor had been surrounded by ultra-conservative officials, such as Sushun, who detested Prince Gong's "pro-Barbarian" policy. They prepared to challenge the new treaty upon their return to Beijing. The politically ambitious Empress Dowager Cixi, mother of the new infant emperor Tongzhi, exploited the power struggle between Prince Gong and the ultraconservatives to enhance her own power. In late 1861, she sided with Prince Gong and launched a *coup d'état,* which successfully ousted all ultra-conservatives from the government.

The alliance of Prince Gong and Empress Dowager Cixi created an atmosphere of openness in the 1860s and 1870s that brought new strength to China. Prince Gong recruited Han Chinese leaders, such as Zeng Guofan, Zuo Zongtang, and Li Hongzhang, and supported their self-strengthening programs in south China. The outstanding results included the Fuzhou Shipyard, the Jiangnan Arsenal, the Tongwenguan, the appointment of Robert Hart as inspector-general of Chinese maritime customs, and the establishment of the Zongli Yamen. With the support of Zeng, Zuo and Li, the Taiping Rebellion was finally suppressed in 1864, and the Muslim Uprisings quelled by 1873. Prince Gong's prestige and power, however, were short-lived. Empress Dowager Cixi began to suspect that Prince Gong had become too pro-Han and "pro-Barbarian" in his policies, and questioned his loyalty to the Manchu imperial household.

Allied with Woren, a powerful Manchu conservative at court, Cixi harshly attacked Prince Gong's alleged mishandling of the Ili Crisis in 1871 and 1879. Some Han Chinese officials, such as the *Qingyi* leaders Zhang Zhidong and Zhang Peilun, also criticized his leadership. Prince Gong became increasingly timid and unsure of himself, which further eroded his political power in Beijing. Finally, in 1884, he was forced to retire to private life and left the empress dowager to rule the Qing court by herself. His defeat seriously weakened China's Self-Strengthening movement.

Anthony Y. Teng

References

Fairbank, John K., ed. *The Cambridge History of China,* vol. 10. Cambridge, England: Cambridge University Press, 1978.

———. *The I.G. in Beijing: Letters of Robert Hart.* Cambridge, MA: Harvard University Press, 1975.

Wright, Mary C. *The Last Stand of Chinese Conservatism: The T'ung-chih Restoration, 1862–1874.* Stanford, CA: Stanford University Press, 1957.

Progressive Party *(Jinbudang)*

Established in Beijing in 1913, the Jinbudang was organized by former bureaucrats and constitutionalists of the late Qing period in an attempt to continue their political influence under the new Republic. During its brief existence until 1915, the party generally supported the presidency of Yuan Shikai and competed with the early Guomindang for control of the parliament.

Following the election of the first parliament in April 1913, three minor conservative parties, the Gonghedang (Republican Party), the Minzhudang (Democratic Party), and the Tongyidang (Unification Party) joined hands to form a new party to counter the Guomindang, the majority party in the parliament. The new party emphasized statism *(guojia zhuyi),* strong government, constitutionalism, and peace in its platform. Its leaders included Li Yuanhong (who served as head of the party), Liang Qichao, Tang Hualong, Zhang Jian, and Wu Tingfang. The party was said to have received financial support from President Yuan Shikai.

After the Second Revolution of 1913, which outlawed the Guomindang and thus in effect paralyzed the parliament, the party still supported Yuan as China's "strong man" and favored the election of a formal president (Yuan) before the promulgation of a constitution. When Yuan announced his plan to make himself emperor in 1915, however, most Jinbudang leaders opposed him. Liang Qichao strongly supported the National Protection movement *(Huguo yundong)* led by Cai E in Yunnan and Guizhou. The party then disintegrated and devolved into two minor groups, the Association for the Study of the Constitution under Liang and the Association for Discussing the Constitution under Tang Hualong. The former group then became the Research Clique and remained active after the downfall of Yuan.

Wang Ke-wen

References

Young, Ernest P. *The Presidency of Yuan Shih-k'ai: Liberalism and Dictatorship in Early Republican China.* Ann Arbor: University of Michigan Press, 1977.

Provisional Constitution *(Yuefa)*

Promulgated by the provisional government under Sun Yatsen on March 11, 1912, following the abdication of the Qing dynasty, the provisional constitution, with seven chapters and fifty-six articles, claimed to have "the same effect as the Constitution before the implementation of a formal constitution." It declared that the sovereignty of the country belonged to its people and that the people were entitled to the basic freedoms. It also defined the central political structure of the Chinese Republic on the model of Western democracy, with a clear division of power among the executive, legislative, and judicial branches.

The provisional constitution was drafted by the government's Legislative Bureau, headed by Song Jiaoren, shortly before Sun Yatsen yielded the presidency to Yuan Shikai. In order to balance Yuan's power as president, the document effectively restricted the presidential power with a strong cabinet and parliament. This intention did not escape Yuan's attention. Shortly after his suppression of Sun's Second Revolution in 1913, Yuan abrogated the provisional constitution and dissolved the parliament. He then organized a Provisional Constitution Conference for the purpose of drafting a new document. On May 1, 1914, the conference completed and promulgated a "new provisional constitution," which concentrated all power in the hands of the president. In the re-

vised political structure, the president enjoyed not only unlimited terms but also the right to name his own successor.

As Yuan was soon overthrown by the National Protection movement of 1916, his "new provisional constitution" had almost no impact on the early Republic. The original one, however, continued to be a subject of political conflict. Because the post-Yuan government in Beijing refused to adhere to the old constitutional order represented by the provisional constitution, Sun Yatsen launched the Constitution Protection movement *(Hufa yundong)* and established an anti-Beijing regime in Canton from 1917 to 1923.

Wang Ke-wen

Puyi, Henry (1906–67)

The last emperor of the Qing (Manchu) dynasty, Puyi became a Japanese puppet during the 1930s and 1940s; he died in the 1960s as a gardener in Beijing.

Puyi was only three years old when he succeeded to the throne, with the reign title Xuantong, in 1908. His father, Prince Chun, acted as the regent. Three years later the Qing dynasty was overthrown by the Revolution of 1911. After his abdication, Puyi was allowed to remain in the Forbidden City in Beijing and continued to enjoy imperial privileges. In 1917, he briefly returned to the throne when the warlord Zhang Xun launched the aborted attempt to restore the Qing. Puyi's life in the imperial palace finally ended in 1924. Following the second Zhili-Fengtian War, Feng Yuxiang drove the deposed Qing court out of the Forbidden City, calling it the Capital Revolution. Puyi found temporary refuge at the Japanese embassy in Beijing.

From 1925 to 1932, Puyi lived in the Japanese concession in Tianjin. Now in his twenties, he had developed a degree of understanding and interest in politics. He was naturally bitter about the Han people and the Republic, and he saw the Japanese as his true friends. In 1931, the Japanese took over Manchuria in the Manchurian Incident, then invited Puyi to return to his homeland and head the new state of Manchukuo (Kingdom of the Manchu). He accepted the invitation. For the following thirteen years, until the end of World War II, Puyi was the nominal ruler (Emperor Kangde) of Manchuria. His government was under the total control of the Japanese Guandong Army and he had almost no say in policymaking, but at least he was an emperor again.

When the Japanese surrendered in August 1945, Puyi again abdicated from the throne. Days later he was captured by the advancing Soviet Army. He subsequently served as a witness at the Tokyo War Trial and then was returned to China in 1950. The new Communist government imprisoned him at a reform camp for war criminals in Fushun, in former Manchuria. After nine years of "re-education and repentance," he was released and allowed to work at the Beijing botanical garden. In his memoir, written in his last years, Puyi praised lavishly the benevolence of the Communist rule and denounced his earlier anti-Han feelings. He died in the first years of the Cultural Revolution.

Wang Ke-wen

References

Power, Brian. *The Puppet Emperor: The Life of Pu Yi, The Last Emperor of China.* New York, NY: Universe Books, 1988.

Pu Yi, Henry. *The Last Manchu: The Autobiography of Henry Pu Yi, Last Emperor of China.* Trans. Kuo Ying Paul Tsai. New York, NY: Putnam, 1967.

Qin-Doihara Agreement

In June 1935, under the pretext that the Chinese forces in the Inner Mongolian province of Chahar had briefly detained four Japanese military agents (known as the Zhangbei Incident), the Guandong Army protested and demanded a series of new concessions from the Chinese. Meanwhile, Japanese aircraft sent to the Beiping area and units of the Guandong Army to the Jehol border threatened military actions. Under pressure, Qin Dechun, head of the Department of Civil Administration of the Chahar provincial government, reached an agreement with Doihara Kenji, chief of the Japanese military intelligence in Manchuria and north China, on June 27. The Chinese government agreed to (1) apologize to the Japanese Army and dismiss responsible officials; (2) guarantee Japanese citizens right of free movement in Chahar; (3) abolish all Guomindang organizations in Chahar; (4) replace Song Zheyuan as governor of Chahar; and (5) remove Song's 29th Army from eastern Chahar and create a demilitarized zone in that region. The Japanese also presented a number of other demands, involving Chinese support for the establishment of Japanese control over Mongolia, but the Chinese have since denied that they were accepted.

The Qin-Doihara Agreement resembled the He-Umezu Agreement reached in Hebei around the same time; both assisted the Japanese Army to extend its control into north China and Mongolia. As in the He-Umezu Agreement, Qin Dechun only sent a note to Doihara indicating his acceptance of the Japanese demands, and thereby avoided the signing of a formal document. Nevertheless, the Guomindang government did comply with all the items in the agreement and allowed the Japanese to set the stage for an autonomous Mongolia. To nationalistic Chinese, this was yet more evidence of Japan's unlimited ambition toward China and of the Chiang Kaishek government's weak-kneed policy in facing that threat.

Wang Ke-wen

References

Coble, Parks M. *Facing Japan.* Cambridge, MA: Harvard University Press, 1991.

Kahn, Winston. "Doihara Kenji and the North China Autonomy Movement, 1935–1936." *China and Japan: Search for Balance Since World War I,* ed. Alvin D. Coox and Hilary Conroy. Santa Barbara, CA: Clio Press, 1978.

Qing Dynasty

The Qing dynasty was founded in 1644 and ruled China for 268 years, until its overthrow by the Revolution of 1911. A total of ten emperors reigned over the Qing empire.

Several aspects of the Qing dynasty were closely related to the development of nationalism in modern China. The dynasty was founded by the Manchus, a northeastern non-Han ethnic group whom the Han people traditionally regarded as barbarians. The Manchu conquest of China, during 1644 to 1683, encountered strong resistance from the Han people, and the Manchus often retaliated with massacres. Although the Qing rule was generally effective and benevolent in the next two centuries, the Manchus were segregated from the Han Chinese and many of them enjoyed the status and privileges of a ruling class. The shadow of "barbarian rule," therefore, was never completely cleared from the minds of some Han Chinese.

This anti-Manchu dimension was to become an important characteristic of the emerging Chinese nationalism in the late nineteenth and early twentieth centuries.

The Qing established, for the first time, the size and shape of the territory that was later inherited by the Republic and then by the current Chinese state. This territory included Manchuria, Mongolia, Chinese Turkestan (Xinjiang), Tibet, and Taiwan. Much of these territories were incorporated into the Qing empire because, at least in part, of the advantageous position and background of the Manchus as a non-Han minority. Such a legacy helped create the multiethnic composition of the modern Chinese state and embedded the concept of a multiethnic *Zhonghua minzu* (Chinese race) as the focus of modern Chinese national identity.

During the last one-third of its rule, from Emperor Daoguang (ruling 1821–50) to Xuantong (ruling 1908–12), the dynasty was confronted with an unprecedented threat from the West. Its failure to manage the crisis and defend the integrity and interests of China provoked nationalistic Chinese to direct their attacks not only on the imperialist West (and later Japan) but also on the "Manchu barbarians." Many Han Chinese believed, during the final years of the dynasty, that the Qing rulers were unable—and unwilling—to defend China because they themselves were not Chinese. This line of thought eventually shaped the Revolution of 1911, which forced the Qing to abdicate in early 1912.

Wang Ke-wen

References

Ho, Ping-ti. "The Significance of the Ch'ing Period in Chinese History." *Journal of Asian Studies* 26, no. 2 (February 1967): 189–95.

Smith, Richard J. *China's Cultural Heritage: The Ch'ing Dynasty, 1644–1912.* Boulder, CO: Westview Press, 1983.

Qing Restoration Attempt

After the Revolution of 1911, a number of former officials in the military and in the government remained loyal to the Qing. The political chaos of the early Republic further convinced them that a Qing restoration was not only possible but desirable. Zhang Xun, a senior officer in the former Qing army, was one such Qing loyalist. Zhang had been a protégé of Yuan Shikai and commander of the Qing forces in the Lower Yangtze area before 1911. When Yuan became president of the new Republic, Zhang was appointed a general of the Chinese army, but was known to have displayed his loyalty to the former dynasty by ordering his troops to retain their queues. He did not support Yuan's attempt to make himself emperor in 1915, yet he took no action to oppose it. Following Yuan's failure and death, Zhang saw himself as the new leader of the Beiyang system and engaged in rivalry with other possible successors to Yuan, especially Duan Qirui.

In 1916 and 1917, Zhang hosted a number of meetings of the military governors *(dujun)* in his base, Xuzhou, to promote the restoration cause. As the post-Yuan Beijing government was paralyzed by a bitter conflict between President Li Yuanhong and Premier Duan Qirui, Zhang perceived opportunities to realize his own political ambition. In June 1917, he led his troops into Beijing at the request of Li to mediate Li's dispute with Duan. While there, he staged a coup to expel Li from office and place the deposed Qing emperor, Puyi, back on the throne. Assistance to Zhang's effort included the support of Kang Youwei, former leader of the Hundred Days Reform (1898).

During the following weeks, the restored Qing emperor resumed his reign of Xuantong and began to organize a new imperial government while Duan Qirui, backed by the majority of the Beiyang commanders and another former leader of the 1898 reform, Liang Qichao, launched a military expedition from Tianjin. By mid-July, Zhang's "queue army" was defeated and Zhang took refuge in the Dutch embassy in Beijing. The Qing emperor abdicated once again. Duan, now the hero who reestablished the Republic, assumed complete control over the new Beijing government.

To an extent, the abortive Qing restoration was merely a farcical episode. Some claim that it was manipulated by Duan Qirui in the president-premier power struggle. Yet it also symbolized the political uncertainty and desperation of the early Republic. Frustration over the lack of positive effects of the Revolution of 1911 was a sentiment shared not just by the Qing loyalists. The nationalistic goal of a strong and unified China seemed still beyond reach, and restoring the Qing dynasty was simply one of the many remedies that proved to be unfeasible and counterproductive.

Wang Ke-wen

References

Ch'i, Hsi-sheng. *Warlord Politics in China, 1916–1928*. Stanford, CA: Stanford University Press, 1976.

Power, Brian. *The Puppet Emperor*. New York, NY: Universe Books, 1988.

Qingyi Movement

Qingyi literally means "pure discussion" and can more properly be understood as "critical elite opinion." It represents a form of political activity that dates at least to the Han dynasty (202 B.C.–A.D. 220) and implies a coherent opposition movement working outside the center of power to effect changes in perceived incorrect and ineffective policies. The most well-known example of the phenomenon in the late Qing—the Qingyi movement of the 1870s and 1880s—made a major contribution to the rise of nationalism in modern China.

This Qingyi movement was a crucial part of the opposition during the era of Li Hongzhang and the Self-Strengtheners. Through a series of memorials and policy debates, opponents to Li's self-strengthening programs proposed their alternatives, which stressed a variety of internal reforms ranging from expanding the right to memorialize the throne, to fighting corruption, to improving education. Leading members of the movement included such prominent officials as Zhang Peilun and Weng Tonghe.

One way the movement contributed to the rise of nationalism was its emphasis on populism. The *qingyi* called for a moral revival that would unite all the people of China into a grand national effort to solve internal problems and shake off foreign domination. One of its frequently proclaimed goals was "to unite those above with those below." Similarly, "what the barbarian has always feared," they stressed, was "the consolidation of the hearts of the Chinese people."

The *qingyi's* other contribution to nationalism was through its militant opposition to Western control and influence, for the movement opposed everything Western save, perhaps, for weaponry that could be used against the foreigners themselves. One reason why the *qingyi* was so hostile to Western influences and self-strengthening was its sense that Li Hongzhang was emphasizing economic innovation as the key to China's problems precisely in order to avoid the consequences of broad-based politics and fervent nationalism. As one member wrote, "the superiority of China over foreign lands lies not in reliance on equipment, but in the steadfastness of the minds of the people." In times of confrontation with foreigners, as with France in 1884 and Japan in 1895, the *qingyi* represented the war party.

The Hundred Days Reform of 1898 grew directly out of the *qingyi*. Historians often miss this link because of the tendency in the twentieth century to equate Chinese radicalism with the desire to borrow from the West rather than seeking internal change and national unity. The Reform movement ended *qingyi* disdain toward Western learning, while keeping its emphasis on internal reform and militant nationalism. On the other hand, the official support for the Boxer Uprising of 1900 may have been encouraged by *qingyi* members who had not changed their attitude toward borrowing from the West.

John Schrecker

References

Schrecker, John. *The Chinese Revolution in Historical Perspective*. New York, NY: Praeger, 1991.

Qiu Jin (1875 [1877?]–1907)

Prominent woman revolutionary in the late Qing, Qiu Jin, a native of Shaoxing, Zhejiang province, is widely known as a martyr of the anti-Manchu revolution. The beloved daughter of a scholar-official family, she was taught to read and write as a child. As an adult she took up fencing, riding, and drinking, and named herself Jingxiong (meaning "competing with males") and Jianhu Nuxia (The Knight Errant of Lake Chien). In 1900, the Boxer Uprising and the Allied expedition to Beijing devastated China and further exposed the corruption and ignorance of the Manchu government. Qiu, deeply concerned about the survival of the country, gradually transformed herself from a reformer to a revolutionary. In 1904, she left her husband and children to study in Japan. There she became involved in revolutionary activities and joined several revolutionary organizations, including the Triads, Mutual Love Society, Guangfuhui (Restoration Society), and Sun Yatsen's Tongmenghui (Revolutionary Alliance). When the Russians occupied Manchuria in 1905, Chinese students in Japan felt outraged and organized the Anti-Russia Volunteer Army to fight the Russians. Qiu participated in their activities and translated a book on nursing for the women volunteers.

Qiu Jin. (Courtesy of Nationalist Party Archives.)

In that same year, the Japanese Ministry of Education issued the regulations to restrict Chinese students. Qiu returned to China after Chen Tianhua had committed suicide to protest the Japanese government's action. Qiu taught school, published a women's magazine, and assumed a leading role in the Guangfuhui branch in her native province. In 1907, Qiu formed an alliance with secret societies and organized the Restoration Army *(Guangfujun)* to prepare for an uprising. She drafted an important document for the coup: "Declaration for the Righteous Rising of the Restoration Army," summoning all Chinese to rise against the Manchu government and to sacrifice for the salvation of the Chinese (Han) race. While engaged in planning a local uprising, she and some fellow conspirators were arrested. During interrogation Qiu refused to say, write, or sign anything. Once under great pressure she wrote: "Amidst autumn winds and autumn rains, I am moved to profound sorrow." Qiu was executed by decapitation in Shaoxing.

Chia-lin Pao Tao

References

Rankin, Mary B. "The Emergence of Women at the End of the Ch'ing: The Case of Ch'iu Chin." *Women in Chinese Society,* ed. Margery Wolf and Roxane Witke, 39–66. Stanford, CA: Stanford University Press, 1975.

Quemoy-Matsu Incident

Quemoy (Jinmen) and Matsu (Mazu) are among the several offshore islands in the Taiwan Strait. Although within 1.5 miles and 10 miles, respectively, of the Chinese mainland, they are occupied by the Guomindang government in Taiwan. Quemoy and Matsu had thus become the flashpoints in the continuing Chinese civil war since 1949. The Quemoy-Matsu Incident, also known as the Taiwan Strait Crisis, refers to military attacks and heavy bombardments by the Communist regime against the Guomindang troops on the offshore islands in 1954 to 1955 and 1958.

Within weeks after the People's Republic of China (PRC) was established, the People's Liberation Army (PLA) started a military campaign to seize the offshore islands. This was undoubtedly part of the Communists' ambition to unify the country, including Taiwan. Although the initial effort was unsuccessful, more attempts were planned. The sudden outbreak of the Korean War in 1950, however, changed the strategic planning of the PLA. With the American Seventh Fleet now patrolling the Taiwan Strait, it seemed almost impossible to "liberate" Taiwan, even if the Communist regime could seize Quemoy and Matsu. Instead of attempting to take over all the offshore islands and ultimately Taiwan, the new strategy was to pose a constant threat to Quemoy and Matsu in order to gain military and diplomatic leverage over the United States-Taiwan relations.

In 1954 and 1955, as the United States and the Republic of China (Taiwan) were about to conclude a mutual defense treaty, the PRC initiated the first Taiwan Strait Crisis by launching an intensive artillery barrage against the offshore islands. The action was intended to send a strong message to the United States about the inherent danger of making a security commitment to Taiwan. As the crisis escalated, the two countries faced the possibility of another major military confrontation after the Korean War. China received nuclear threats from the United States.

The crisis did not abort the U.S.-ROC Mutual Defense Treaty of 1954, nor did it cause a military showdown, but it did force some diplomatic contacts to be established between Washington and Beijing. In April 1955, at the

Bandung Conference, Chinese Premier Zhou Enlai offered to negotiate with America to reduce the tensions in the Taiwan Strait. In May, Zhou issued a formal statement declaring that the PRC would "strive for the liberation of Taiwan by peaceful means as far as it is possible." Washington responded positively, which quickly led to the opening of ambassadorial-level talks between the United States and China at Geneva in August 1955.

In August 1958, at the beginning of a nationwide economic mobilization (the Great Leap Forward), the PRC triggered a second Taiwan Strait crisis by launching thousands of artillery shells on Quemoy and Matsu, aimed at cutting off the offshore islands' supply lines. Along with the shelling, amphibious assaults and air strikes were also attempted. The official Chinese statement justified the military action as a severe warning to the Guomindang troops who were harassing the Chinese coastal areas. But observers found other reasons more compelling. The crisis might have been intended to force Washington to resume the ambassadorial talks that were suspended in December 1957. Mao Zedong might also have wanted to renew tension in the Taiwan Strait to pressure Khrushchev, who was seeking to improve Soviet relations with the United States.

Alarmed by Mao's reckless thinking about war, Khrushchev refused to commit himself to China's goal of liberating Taiwan. The Chinese blockade of the supply lines was soon broken by the American Seventh Fleet, but both sides managed to resume their talks in Warsaw. The artillery shelling continued for the next ten years, although with a regular schedule (odd days of the month) and prior warnings. Only the Sino-American rapprochement in 1972 gradually led to a replacement of explosive shells with those of propaganda leaflets and greeting cards. As Mainland China and Taiwan slowly began unofficial contacts and negotiations in the recent decade, tension over the Taiwan Strait has been reduced to a minimum and the shelling has finally stopped.

Shi-ping Zheng

References

Garver, John W. *Foreign Relations of the People's Republic of China.* Englewood Cliffs, NJ: Prentice-Hall, 1993.

Harding, Harry. *A Fragile Relationship: The United States and China since 1972.* Washington, DC: Brookings Institute, 1992.

Stolper, Thomas E. *China, Taiwan, and the Offshore Islands.* Armonk, NY: M. E. Sharpe, 1985.

Quotations From Chairman Mao

Issued on the eve of the Great Proletarian Cultural Revolution (GPCR, 1966–69), the "little red book" entitled *Quotations from Chairman Mao* quickly became a worldwide best-seller for a few short years in the late 1960s. Consisting of short excerpts and aphorisms from Mao's writings from 1929 to 1964, the volume had the intention of establishing Mao as the primary source of political wisdom. Mao used the book as a tool in his successful effort to become a charismatic leader. He needed to rally mass support behind his effort to recapture policy control from his opponents in the party.

The book encompassed most aspects of Mao's thought, *e.g.,* voluntarism, dialectical materialism, anti-intellectualism, class struggle, egalitarianism, guerrilla war tactics, and Leninist principles of political organization. Much of the volume consisted of epistemology and methodology for implementing a national revolution. Uniquely Chinese characteristics received little emphasis. Perhaps this explains the book's popularity in translation.

Considering that this volume became the "bible" for the GPCR, its verbiage is surprisingly restrained. The selections did not justify the later violence of the GPCR; rather, the emphasis fell on education and persuasion. The contents also failed to foreshadow the jingoistic rhetoric that left China diplomatically isolated during the GPCR. Only in the last few pages is there any direct attack on the Soviet leader Nikita Khrushchev and revisionism.

The nationalism reflected in the work was that of proletarian internationalism combined with patriotism. It defined patriotism as the struggle against foreign and domestic enemies of the socialist state. Mao supported socialism in all countries and called for a "peoples' war of national liberation" to free Third World countries from the yoke of imperialism. Narrow nationalism was equated to racism and denounced at home and abroad. Abroad, Mao suggested, such tribal nationalism hindered class struggle; at home it fostered greater Han chauvinism against China's minority peoples. He condemned "great power chauvinism" and pledged China never to behave in such an imperialistic fashion. But he repeatedly stressed the need to prepare for war and expressed full confidence in its triumphant outcome.

A strikingly prescient passage from a 1964 article predicted that Chinese Communism would face a major threat from "peaceful evolution." Revisionists and imperialists would await a gradual counterrevolution, which would see the third or fourth generation of Chinese leadership depart from the Marxist road. The GPCR was intended in part to prevent such a historical change, yet its excesses and human suffering in fact hastened the process. After the Tiananmen Incident in 1989, the Deng Xiaoping leadership resurrected Mao's message. The threat or promise of "peaceful evolution" is certainly much greater now than at the time when Mao penned his words.

Harvey Nelsen

References
Schram, Stuart R. *The Thought of Mao Tse-tung.* New York: Cambridge University Press, 1989.
Starr, John Bryan. *Continuing the Revolution: The Political Thought of Mao Zedong.* Princeton, NJ: Princeton University Press, 1979.

R

Railway Protection Movement

After the first Sino-Japanese War (1894–95), the educated Chinese gradually realized the importance of railway construction to the modernization of their country. In the following decade, a number of railways were built with foreign loans, but gentry and merchants in the provinces soon developed an interest in the projects and demanded local control over the construction and ownership of new railways. In 1905, as part of the Rights-Recovery movement led by gentry and merchants, the right to build and manage the Canton-Hankou Railway and the Sichuan-Hankou Railway were obtained by the people of Guangdong, Hunan, Hubei, and Sichuan.

In May 1911, however, the government announced its policy of nationalizing China's main railways, including the Canton-Hankou and Sichuan-Hankou lines. The policy was in part motivated by Beijing's concern over increasing provincial autonomy, which would be strengthened by provincially owned railways, and in part by its need of foreign loans. Following the announcement, the government concluded a new loan with a four-power banking consortium (Great Britain, Germany, France, and the United States) that used the railway rights as a loan guarantee. The government's action caused an uproar among the gentry and business elite in these provinces. Although their fundraising efforts for the railways had not been successful, these provincial investors resented the recentralization of Beijing's power and the further intrusion of foreign economic influence in China, in addition to the loss of their investment. They immediately organized railway-protection leagues and voiced their protest against the Qing policy through the newly established provincial assemblies. They also experimented with mass movements. Demonstrations and strikes were staged in Changsha; people in Canton boycotted government banknotes; delegations presented petitions at the capital.

In July, the Qing government provided compensations to the private investors in the provinces, yet the indemnity offered to Sichuan was drastically lower than that offered to other provinces. As a result the Railway Protection movement in Sichuan escalated. Led by the provincial assembly, the Sichuan elite employed nationalist as well as provincialist arguments in their attack on Beijing. Their Railway Protection League, with a membership of several hundred thousand, mobilized students for the cause. By August, the protest had grown violent. On August 11, a huge rally in Chengdu, the provincial capital, was followed by a strike. In panic, the governor-general, Zhao Erfeng, ordered the arrest of gentry leaders. His troops soon clashed with the demonstrators in Chengdu, resulting in the killing of thirty-two people. Angered by the massacre, the people mounted massive anti-government riots, which spread to the entire province, and public order broke down.

The gentry-merchant elite consisted mostly of "constitutionalists," not revolutionaries, but as the Qing suppressed their protests, their opposition became radical and their anti-Manchu feelings grew. Members of Sun Yatsen's Tongmenghui in Sichuan, in collaboration with local secret societies, exploited the situation and launched their own uprisings. The latter succeeded in taking control of a few counties. In September, the Qing government ordered the New Army in Wuhan to move into Sichuan and suppress the riots. This gave the revolutionaries in Wuhan an opportunity to stage the Wuchang Uprising in October. The Sichuan Railway Crisis thus triggered the Revolution of 1911.

Wang Ke-wen

References

Gasster, Michael. "The Republican Revolutionary Movement." *The Cambridge History of China,* ed. John K. Fairbank and Kwang-ching Liu, vol. 11, 463–534. Cambridge, England: Cambridge University Press, 1980.

Lee, En-han. *China's Quest for Railway Autonomy, 1904–1911: A Study of the Chinese Railway-Rights Recovery Movement.* Singapore: Singapore University Press, 1977.

Rape of Nanking

See Nanjing Massacre

Rectification *(Zhengfeng)*

Rectification is a major organizational device frequently used by the Chinese Communist Party (CCP) to correct any ideological, organizational, or policy operational deviations among Party members. Chinese official scholars tend to make a distinction between rectification *(zhengfeng)* and Party consolidation *(zhengdang)*. The former is said to deal with ideological and behavioral problems only, whereas the latter also includes disciplinary measures or purges.

Rectification is usually carried out on a large scale—in the form of political campaigns. Party rectification campaigns may vary in their targets, focus, and length, yet they often include the following phases. First, important speeches are made by Party leaders, which are to identify the major problems and to emphasize the significance of the rectification. Then small groups conduct an intensive political study of Party documents and writings by Marx, Lenin, and Mao. This is the "study" phase, which will be followed by the "criticism and self-criticism" phase. During the second phase, participants in small groups engage in a tense process of pinpointing and analyzing their own problems and mistakes, while others interact to build up the pressure. After a full self-exposure and interrogation by peers in the small group, the rectification enters the third phase, "self-examination," in which everyone is required to write down his/her thoughts or confessions. Those

identified as the main targets are isolated, sometimes even jailed, and subjected to public struggle meetings. Finally, at the "organizational rectification" phase, disciplinary actions are taken accordingly and a great rectification victory is declared.

The first such large-scale rectification campaign was orchestrated by Mao Zedong from 1942 to 1944 in Yan'an, the base area of the CCP during China's anti-Japanese war years. The declared targets of this rectification were subjectivism (the so-called dogmatists), sectarianism (those engaged in factional struggles), and Party formalism (those who were responsible for use of political jargons in the Party's propaganda work). Aimed particularly at Soviet-trained leaders in the Party leadership and at urban intellectuals, this rectification served to consolidate Mao's ideological and political dominance in the CCP.

Since the Yan'an campaign, rectification has become institutionalized into the organizational culture of the CCP. It came to be seen as the most effective way of tackling major problems. In post-1949 China, major Party rectification campaigns included: (1) the Party rectification in 1950 to educate newly recruited Party cadres of various family backgrounds against "commandism," and tendencies of bureaucratism; (2) the Three Anti-Campaign in 1952 against "waste, corruption, and bureaucratism"; (3) the Socialist Education movement in 1962 against rural Party and government officials; (4) the Cultural Revolution of 1966 to 1969 against so-called revisionism, which purged the majority of Party officials; and (5) the Party rectification of 1983 to 1987.

As each rectification campaign inevitably produced thousands upon thousands of victims (only to be rehabilitated and cleared of the accusations later), serious doubts emerged about the wisdom of this organizational device. Consequently, rectification has become increasingly ineffective and counter-productive. The last effort by the Party leadership to launch a rectification campaign to discipline the Party was made after the bloody crackdown in the Tiananmen Incident of 1989. Yet, without much support from Party members, this rectification campaign was aborted. Today, the problems of privileges, abuse of power, corruption and crimes are plaguing the CCP organization. Despite serious warnings from some Party leaders, the Party seems beyond rectificaton.

Shi-ping Zheng

References

Bennett, Gordon. *Yundong: Mass Campaigns in Chinese Communist Leadership*. Berkeley: University of California Press, 1976.

Teiwes, Frederick C. *Politics and Purges in China: Rectification and the Decline of Party Norms, 1950–1965*. Armonk, NY: M. E. Sharpe, 1979.

"Red and Expert"

The slogan, "red and expert," connotes the goal of the Chinese Communist Party that all cadres and, ideally, all citizens should combine a high level of ideological consciousness and political commitment ("redness") with technical knowledge and specialized abilities ("expertise"). To be both red and expert, Party cadres are expected to strive constantly to enhance their knowledge and upgrade their skills. Intellectuals, managers, technicians, and other kinds of experts are called upon to learn more of Marxism-Leninism and to become more politically active.

The red-expert dichotomy was first popularized in remarks made by Liu Shaoqi in 1957, although the idea is closely related to earlier formulations by Mao Zedong on contradictions, leadership methods, and the mass line. The concept stemmed from the belief that, although expertise was necessary to promote China's modernization, redness was essential to ensure that modernization remained consistent with socialist precepts and Party rule. The red-and-expert ideal was first meant to apply to elite groups, such as Party cadres and intellectuals. It was soon extended to the masses in general as part of the Maoist goal to forge a new socialist human being who would be politically aware and highly educated.

The simultaneous pursuit of redness and expertise has been a constant principle of contemporary Chinese Communism; but the relative weight assigned to one quality or the other has shifted during various periods of CCP rule. In the Great Leap Forward (1958–61) and the Cultural Revolution (1966–76), political correctness was strongly favored over technical competence as a priority in decision-making; during these radical periods, intellectuals and other experts were often denigrated or even physically persecuted. In times of economic liberalization, including the post-Mao era, greater value has been placed on expertise as the major criterion for the allocation of authority and for career advancement. Redness, however, has always been considered the dominant part of the duality, because it is that quality which undergirds the Party's claim to exercise the "leading role" in Chinese society.

Although the goal has been that individuals should be both red and expert, conflicts between those who are primarily red and those who are primarily expert have frequently been the source of severe political tensions in Chinese organizations. For example, friction over lines of authority between the factory Party secretary (the "red") and the factory manager (the "expert") continues to plague many Chinese industrial enterprises. In this sense, the ideal of red and expert has often turned into a political struggle of red versus expert.

William A. Joseph

References

Meisner, Maurice. *Marxism, Maoism, and Utopianism: Eight Essays*. Madison: University of Wisconsin Press, 1982.

Red Army

The full title of the Red Army was the Chinese Worker and Peasant Red Army. It was the armed forces of the Chinese Communist Party (CCP) during the Nanjing Decade (1927–37). Following the collapse of the first Guomindang–Chinese Communist Party (GMD-CCP) United Front in 1927, the CCP-led forces initially adopted the title of "Chinese Worker and Peasant Revolutionary Army." From 1928 to 1930, as the CCP reestablished centralized control over its party and military apparatus, those forces were gradually renamed the Red Army and given serialized unit numbers. Not only was this title copied from the Soviet Union but its basic organization, including the system of commissars, also followed the Soviet model. At the Gutian Conference in 1929, Mao Zedong reaffirmed the principle of "absolute Party control over the military," which prevented the CCP from falling under military domination as the GMD had.

In the early 1930s, the Red Army was organized into three "Front Armies" as well as several individual units. It was the "barrel of the gun," as Mao called it, on which the CCP relied for the establishment of the Jiangxi Soviet and other smaller Soviet regimes in central, southern, and northwestern China. In 1934 and 1935, after the loss of the Jiangxi Soviet to the GMD forces, the main body of the Red Army protected the CCP in its Long March to Shaanxi. It fought heroically, but also suffered enormous losses along the way. According to one calculation, only 5,000 of the original 100,000 (including some civilians) survived the journey. The total strength of the Red Army throughout the country, meanwhile, shrank from more than 300,000 men (1933) to about 30,000 (1936).

Shortly after the outbreak of the Sino-Japanese War in 1937, the CCP formed the second United Front with the ruling GMD. In accord with their agreement, the Red Army in Shaanxi was reorganized as the Eighth Route Army of the GMD's National Revolutionary Army (NRA). The Red Army guerrilla units that remained in central and southern China were reorganized into the NRA's New Fourth Army. The Red Army thereby ceased to exist.

Wang Ke-wen

Red Guards

The political organizations called Red Guards were composed of middle-school students whom Mao Zedong mobilized in the initial phase of the Great Proletarian Cultural Revolution (1966–69). Their task was to attack Chinese traditions, Western influence, and those accused of "taking the capitalist road" in the Party and government hierarchies.

The Red Guard movement began when a group of student activists at Qinghua Middle School in Beijing wrote posters in May 1966 to criticize the school authorities. They agreed to sign their posters with a revolutionary name— "Red Guard." In July, at a local meeting, the Qinghua Red Guards approached Jiang Qing, Mao Zedong's wife, and asked her to present two copies of their posters to Mao. On August 1, Mao responded to the Qinghua Red Guards, expressing his warm support for their activities.

During the next three months, between August 18 and November 26, Mao appeared at eight mass rallies in Tiananmen Square attended by students who had come to Beijing from all over China either on a free train ride or by foot—following in the footsteps of their revolutionary heroes in the Long March thirty years earlier. Wearing an army uniform and a Red Guard armband, Mao reviewed a total of 11 million Red Guards who were waving their copies of the "little red book" *(Quotations from Chairman Mao)* and chanting slogans such as "Long Live Chairman Mao!" Newspaper pho-tos and films of the mass rallies soon led to a nationwide Red Guard frenzy.

The initial targets of the Red Guard movement were the so-called Four Olds—old idea, old culture, old custom, and old habit. These ranged from books to temples, shoes to hairstyles, street names to forms of address, and Confucius to Beethoven. People who fell victim to attacks by the Red Guards included teachers, writers, artists, actors, professors, and academic authorities. They were paraded, beaten, and humiliated, their apartments searched and personal properties confiscated. Mao's real targets, however, were those in power whom Mao had distrusted as revisionists. With the endorsement from Mao and his radical associates, Red Guards shifted their attacks in October 1966 to focus on senior Party leaders, such as Liu Shaoqi and Deng Xiaoping.

As the power struggle intensified, debates over who should be qualified as Red Guards and who should be the real targets of the Cultural Revolution split the Red Guard movement into many factions. Manipulated by the political cliques within the top leadership, Red Guard factionalism quickly turned into bloody internecine armed struggles. In August 1967, seeing no further value in the Red Guards as an instrument for achieving his political goals and worried that the youths were getting out of hand, Mao began to suppress the Red Guard movement. A few Red Guard leaders were arrested, some escaped to Hong Kong, and in 1968 many were sent to the countryside to receive "reeducation" from the peasants. The Red Guard as a student organization continued to exist for a few more years, but it had lost its revolutionary zeal or political appeal.

The Red Guard movement was a crucial episode in the Cultural Revolution, during which millions of enthusiastic Chinese youths rose to Mao's call, only to find themselves betrayed later. The Red Guard generation, now often referred to as the "lost generation" for its loss of a decade of formal education, or the "wounded generation" for its alienation from the Communist regime, is nevertheless an important force in post-Mao China. Some of the former Red Guards, who became totally disappointed with Communist politics, have made successful careers as writers or businessmen. Others have chosen to promote reforms within the Communist Party. There are others still who have become strong critics of the Communist system.

Shi-ping Zheng

References

Chan, Anita. *Children of Mao: Personality Development and Political Activism in the Red Guard Generation.* Seattle: University of Washington Press, 1985.

Harding, Harry. "The Chinese State in Crisis." *The Cambridge History of China,* ed. Denis Twitchett and John K. Fairbank, vol. 14. Cambridge, England: Cambridge University Press, 1991.

Red Spear Society

The Red Spear Society *(Hongqianghui)* was an organization formed to protect life and property in rural areas of China during the chaotic decades between 1920 and 1950. The name is derived from the tasseled spears that members typically used as weapons. "Red Spear" is often used generically, as well, to refer to numerous similar societies such as the White Spears, Black Spears, Blue Tassels, Five Dragon Society, Son of Heaven Society, Great Immortals, and numerous others. Members of all of these societies practiced various types of martial arts, and subscribed to metaphysically based beliefs that ostensibly provided legitimacy and protection. Initiates learned certain rites for spiritual purification and were taught to believe that by swallowing magic charms, wearing protective amulets, and reciting esoteric incantations, they would be impervious to enemy weapons. Red Spear initiation ceremonies were more or less rigorously observed, depending on the particular group; some units were highly exclusive, initiating only those who had proven themselves worthy, whereas others coercively recruited virtually every able-bodied adult in a village.

The village was the basic unit of the Red Spear organization. Most units were organized and led by members of the local landed elite. In times of crisis, separate village units often formed alliances. In the mid-1920s, for instance, the Red Spear chieftain Lou Baixun led an alliance of as many as 300,000 members, drawn from several counties, against the warlord forces of Yue Weijun. Cooperation among units was the rule, but each had its special interests, and armed conflicts among them were not unusual.

The main purpose of all of the Red Spear-type societies was to defend the rural populace from the depredations of warlords, bandits, and venal officials who had seized local political power following the collapse of the imperial institution in 1911. By 1924, there were over 200,000 feuding warlord troops in Henan province alone. Supplementary and miscellaneous taxes levied to support their activities became an increasingly heavy burden, exacerbated by the uncontrolled plunder of ill-paid warlord troops. Rural hardship in north China became almost unbearable in the early 1920s, when a series of floods and droughts ravaged the area. Hundreds of thousands of people died and countless numbers of rural males resorted to banditry, preying on farming communities and market towns. Organization of societies, such as the Red Spears, was a response by those who had property to protect.

The specific origins of the Red Spears are obscure, but the phenomenon of the rise of such protective societies is as old as China itself. The twentieth-century movement probably began in Shangdong province in the late 1910s and quickly spread to nearby Henan, Hebei, Shanxi, and Shaanxi provinces. Chapters were formed elsewhere as well, but the majority remained concentrated in those five provinces. It is estimated that by 1927 there were over three million members.

Red Spear influence reached its epitome during the Northern Expedition (1926–28) led by the Guomindang (GMD). Some units fought against the GMD, but most supported their efforts to defeat the warlords and reunify the country. Once in control, however, the GMD began to suppress the Red Spears because the latter, typically, put their local advantages above the national interests of the new government and resisted the increasing imposition of new taxes. The movement was in serious decline by the mid-1930s, but it revived in the early years of the Sino-Japanese War (1937–45) when GMD power in north China declined in the face of Japanese aggression. The activities of various Red Spear organizations during the war are not well researched. Some studies credit the organization as a whole with valiant resistance to the Japanese, but there is considerable evidence that many units cooperated, and even officially collaborated, with the Japanese. The major determining factors seem to have been leadership disposition and local interests.

The attitude of the Chinese Communist Party (CCP) toward the Red Spears was ambivalent in the years before the establishment of the People's Republic. On the one hand, they were valued as allies against warlords and the

R

GMD government. On the other hand, as an organization characterized by feudal, superstitious beliefs, led by representatives of the landed elite, and dedicated to preserving local interests and traditional values, the Red Spears were incompatible with the CCP's revolutionary nationalism. The ultimate triumph of Communist nationalism in 1949 doomed the inherently localistic Red Spear movement.

Peter J. Seybolt

References

Perry, Elizabeth J. *Rebels and Revolutionaries in North China, 1845–1945*. Stanford, CA: Stanford University Press, 1980.

Slawinski, Roman. "The Red Spears in the Late 1920s." *Popular Movements and Secret Societies in China, 1840–1950*, ed. Jean Chesneaux. Stanford, CA: Stanford University Press, 1972.

Reorganization Loan

In April 1913 the republican government under Yuan Shikai concluded an agreement with a five-power consortium, representing banks of Great Britain, Germany, France, Russia and Japan, to secure a loan of 25 million pounds. The "reorganization loan" was issued at an annual interest rate of 5 percent and was to be repaid in forty-seven years. China's (salt) gabelle, custom duties and central taxes collected in the four provinces of Zhili (Hebei), Henan, Shandong, and Jiangsu were used as guarantees for the loan.

The rationale for this loan was to enable the government to manage the aftermath of the Revolution of 1911 (thus the Chinese title of the loan, *shanhou*), but in fact its purpose was to provide Yuan, the new president, with necessary funds for his imminent military actions against the Guomindang (Nationalist Party). The relationship between Yuan and this majority party in the parliament had deteriorated rapidly since the assassination of the party's leader Song Jiaoren in March 1913, allegedly by Yuan's men. Yuan therefore signed the loan agreement without the formal approval of the parliament. Armed with this new loan, he soon outlawed the Guomindang and mobilized his troops for an attack on the provinces in the South that were controlled by Guomindang governors.

The reorganization loan was the largest among the thirty-three foreign loans Yuan obtained during his presidency. All of them furthered the young Republic's financial weakness and increased the foreign powers' economic and political exploitation of China.

Wang Ke-wen

References

Young, Ernest P. *The Presidency of Yuan Shih-k'ai: Liberalism and Dictatorship in Early Republican China*. Ann Arbor: University of Michigan Press, 1977.

Republic of China

The Republic of China was founded after the Revolution of 1911. On January 1, 1912, the revolutionaries established their new government in Nanjing, which took the form of Western-style republic—the first in East Asia. Sun Yatsen was elected as its provisional president. On February 12, the Qing court (Emperor Xuantong) abdicated, thus leaving the Republic as the sole legitimate government representing China. Although founded as a result of an anti-Manchu revolution, the Republic soon minimized the emphasis of the revolution on Han nationalism and instead promoted a commonwealth *(gonghe)* of the major ethnic groups currently residing in China, including Han, Manchus, Mongols, Tibetans, and Muslims.

During the next decade, the Republic survived two attempts on its life—first in 1915 and 1916, when Yuan Shikai tried to make himself an emperor, and then in 1917, when Zhang Xun tried to restore the Qing monarchy. From 1917 to 1926, the Republic was paralyzed not only by warlordism but by the existence of two regimes, the Beiyang government in Beijing and the anti-Beiyang government, sometimes headed by Sun Yatsen, in Canton. Both claimed to represent the Republic and accused the other of being illegitimate. In 1928, the southern government, controlled by the Guomindang, reunified the country after two years of the successful Northern Expedition. The Guomindang government continued to use the name Republic of China in the world community. In the early 1930s, the Chinese Communists briefly established a Chinese Soviet Republic at their base in Jiangxi, but its existence received no international recognition.

After the outbreak of the Sino-Japanese War in 1937, the Guomindang government moved its seat from Nanjing to Chongqing and remained there throughout the war. When Wang Jingwei formed his pro-Japanese regime in occupied Nanjing, he also claimed to represent the Republic, and his regime was recognized by Japan and her allies. With the defeat of Japan in 1945, the Chongqing government under Chiang Kaishek again reunified the country. Only four years later, however, Chiang's government was overthrown by the Chinese Communists in a bitter civil war. In 1949 the Chinese Communists established the "People's Republic of China" in Beijing, which was soon recognized by the Soviet bloc and by Great Britain.

Chiang Kaishek and his followers took refuge on the island of Taiwan. Since 1949, Chiang's regime in Taiwan has called itself the Republic of China and insisted that it is the sole legitimate government of whole China, including the "lost territories" on the mainland. With the support of the United States, the regime did retain diplomatic recognition of its claim from most of the countries in the world until the early 1970s. During the 1970s it lost its seat in the United Nations and many of its diplomatic recognitions, including that of the United States, to the People's Republic. Following the death of Chiang (1975) and his son Jingguo (1988), the Republic of China has been increasingly identified, official proclamations notwithstanding, as representing only Taiwan.

Wang Ke-wen

References

Sheridan, James E. *China in Disintegration: The Republican Era in Chinese History, 1912–1949*. New York, NY: The Free Press, 1975.

Republicanism

Republicanism, the demand for the establishment of a republican government, has been inseparable from modern nationalism in China since both emerged as visible political forces in the late nineteenth century. Advocates and defenders of republicanism have been among China's staunchest nationalists, and to a great extent republican ideas and institutions have been bent to the service of Chinese nationalism.

Republicanism in China owes much to the example of Western societies, notably the United States. Western missionaries first introduced to China ideas about representative government, probably beginning with Robert Morrison around 1819. By the 1830s, Chinese scholars were compiling their own accounts, and as early as 1841 these included references to the United States' Constitution and structure of government that were soon afterward used by Wei Yuan in his *Haiguo tuzhi* (1844). Such scattered materials were improved upon by translations of Western works in the 1860s and by accounts written by Chinese who went abroad in the second half of the nineteenth century. A major work on the United States published in China in 1889 included the fullest description of its political system written in Chinese up to that time.

It is not clear to what extent the earliest Chinese republicans were aware of such works, but it is important to note that the question of representative government was under wide discussion among Chinese intellectuals for some years before republicanism emerged as a political movement and an identifiable body of ideas. This only took place after 1895. By about 1890, demands for some kind of representative government were being increasingly heard in China. Concepts such as popular sovereignty and the social contract were becoming familiar at around the same time that concerns arose about China's inability to resist imperialism and about the signs of breakdown in the Chinese political system. The same reformers who were pursuing the question of how to make China militarily stronger and economically more developed were also probing issues of political thought and institutions.

Out of such a reformist and increasingly nationalistic climate in the 1890s came men such as Sun Yatsen, who took the lead in establishing China's first republican revolutionary organization in 1894 and who attempted to formulate a plan for the transition to a republican form of government. Sun and the many others who fought for republicanism did so for a variety of reasons, but surely no goal they had was higher than to make China strong, prosperous, and free of foreign domination—to put China in the first rank of world powers. To the republicanists, no charge against the Qing monarchy was more serious than the dynasty's failure to resist imperialism and maintain China's independence and honor.

Republicanism drew supporters for other reasons, notably its opposition to autocracy, cited by one leader as "the first concern of those who wish to establish a new political order." But however strong their belief in justice and equality, most saw republicanism as a way to make China strong, united, and respected in the world. They admired the United States mostly because it was the rising world power, and they viewed its political system as a major reason for its rise. They also respected a system that could maintain unity in a diverse and divided land, but they pointed to many flaws and weaknesses in the republican structure that required adaptation to China's own needs and conditions.

Republicanism was so much in the air around the turn of the century that one of Sun's most prominent rivals, Liang Qichao, had imbibed it and said he was abandoning it (in favor of constitutional monarchy) only with sorrow: "For ten years I have been drunk on it, I have dreamed of it, I have sung its praises. . . . Now I must take leave of it." But before doing so, he suggested to Sun that republicanism might best be realized by first supporting the emperor and later converting the monarch to president of a republic. Ironically enough, Liang turned against the Qing early in 1911, and although he did not declare for the Republic even after many of his followers already had, preferring instead to try one last time to promote a constitutional monarchy, he accepted the Republic soon after it was founded. Moreover, he quickly joined the new political fray.

Before long, republicanism in China broke down. It did so for complex reasons that have mostly to do with powerful long-term political and social forces that gave it little chance to succeed. In particular, the militarization of Chinese politics and the pressures of foreign relations, together with the many social problems involved in early industrialization and the major cultural transformation China was undergoing, proved far too great a burden for hastily formed new political institutions to bear. Parliaments and constitutions proved all too susceptible to the manipulation of political parties and leaders whose main concern was the strengthening of China, not the preservation of republican institutions.

Republicanism in China has thus been commonly viewed as an experiment that failed, with little to show for its defenders' efforts. And yet it may be asked whether comparison with the history of other modern republics warrants so negative a conclusion, or at least whether such judgments are premature. The record of republicanism in France, for example, where three republican revolutions over some eighty years brought royalists to power in the first three French Republics, is at least as checkered as it is in China; and indeed, nowhere has it been even close to untroubled. Perhaps more to the point, in recent years republicanism has taken on new life in Taiwan, where the name "Republic of China" survives and a pluralist politics is beginning to show inklings of the principles of republicanism, what James Madison called "the authority of the people themselves" and "the capacity of mankind for self-government." Taken together with the survival against all odds of the spirit of self-government in mainland China, a spirit that is now more than one hundred years old in China, Taiwan's new political experiments suggest that the history of republicanism in China may still be in an early stage.

Michael Gasster

References

Gasster, Michael. *Chinese Intellectuals and the Revolution of 1911: The Birth of Modern Chinese Radicalism.* Seattle: University of Washington Press, 1969.

Grieder, Jerome B. *Intellectuals and the State in Modern China: A Narrative History.* New York, NY: Macmillan, 1981.

Schiffrin, Harold Z. *Sun Yat-sen and the Origins of the Chinese Revolution.* Berkeley: University of California Press, 1968.

Resist America and Assist Korea Campaign (kangMei yuanChao)

Following the outbreak of the Korean War on June 25, 1950, the United States immediately announced its support for South Korea in the conflict. By September, the United Nations forces (essentially American forces) had launched a successful counterattack on behalf of South Korea and conquered most of North Korea. The situation deeply alarmed the newly established People's Republic under the Chinese Communist Party (CCP), which was hostile toward the United States and most of the Western countries. As the American forces approached the Sino-Korean border, Beijing repeatedly issued warnings, but Washington did not take these seriously.

In October, the Chinese People's Liberation Army, in the guise of the "Chinese People's Volunteer Army," crossed the Yalu River that divides northeast China from North Korea and entered the war. Commanded by Peng Dehuai, the one million "volunteers" replaced the defeated North Korean troops and mounted five major offensives against the American forces. They took the Americans by surprise and

A "Resist America, Assist Korea" rally in Beijing, 1951. (Xinhua News Agency.)

quickly drove them back to the thirty-eighth parallel. After that, a seesaw battle dragged on along that former dividing line with neither side gaining much ground from the other. Meanwhile, a fervent "Resist America, Assist Korea" campaign waged back home calling for financial as well as other contributions to the war effort by the Chinese people. In July 1951, at the suggestion of the Soviet Union, peace negotiations began while fighting continued. A cease-fire agreement finally signed in July 1953 by the two Koreas, China, and the United States, restoring the situation to that of pre-June 1950. The "volunteers" killed or captured more than one million enemy troops (including 390,000 Americans) during the three-year conflict, but also suffered enormous losses themselves. Their withdrawal from the Korean peninsula was not completed until late 1958.

The Korean War was a distraction and a diversion of resources for the young CCP regime. It is generally believed that Moscow encouraged the regime to participate in the war with a promise of full material assistance. The Soviet Union did not fulfill that promise and later asked Beijing to pay for the aid it had offered during the war. This betrayal partially caused the Sino-Soviet split in the late 1950s. Yet the "Resist America, Assist Korea" campaign also strengthened the CCP regime in significant ways. For the first time since the Opium War of the 1840s, China fought a major Western power to a standstill, which in itself was a kind of victory. Moreover, China fought the war to assist one of her neighbors, a former tributary state, and thus reasserted her dominant position in East Asia.

In 1954, China sat with the United States, Great Britain, France, and the Soviet Union at the Geneva Conference to discuss the problems of Korea and Vietnam, her major power status now recognized even by the hostile West. These accomplishments helped to reinforce the CCP's nationalist claim, which was at once anti-imperialist and imperialist. As is usually the case in a country engaging in external war, patriotism enhances the allegiance of the populace to the current regime. The CCP used the campaign to mobilize popular support for some of its domestic programs, such as the Three-Anti and Five-Anti campaigns, and consolidated its power.

Wang Ke-wen

References

Mineo, Nakajima. "Foreign Relations: From the Korean War to the Bandung Line." *The Cambridge History of China,* ed. Roderick MacFarquhar and John K. Fairbank, vol. 14, 259–289. Cambridge, England: Cambridge University Press, 1987.

Whiting, Allen S. *China Crosses the Yalu: The Decision to Enter the Korean War.* Stanford, CA: Stanford University Press, 1968.

Responsibility System

Alternatively called "household responsibility," "management responsibility," and "production responsibility system," the term "responsibility system" was popularized during the late 1970s and 1980s in China. During this time, far-reaching changes were taking place in the organization of China's economic system, among them the reduced role played by central economic planning institutions and the increased role played by free-market forces. This change necessitated the decentralization of economic decision-making and the creation of autonomous economic units (farms, township and village enterprises, large industrial enterprises, and financial institutions).

The economic reforms in China shifted much of the responsibility for economic decision-making from the central planners to individual agents. This shift began in 1978 with the introduction of the "household responsibility system," which ended the communal organization of Chinese agriculture by redistributing and leasing land to households on the basis of family size. Households were given the responsibility for making the economic decisions previously made by the central planners.

At first, a compulsory grain system required farmers to deliver a certain quantity of grain to the government. Surpluses could then be sold either to the government or on the free market. By 1985 a contract system enabled farmers to negotiate contractual agreements with the government, and any surplus could be sold on the free market. Additional commercial reforms were also introduced that allowed sideline production and rural enterprise, all of which became profitable. The rewards and risks of production thereby accrued to individual farmers.

The purpose of these changes was not only to spur agricultural productivity but also to revitalize peasant enthusiasm and support for the socialist goals of the post-Mao, post-Cultural Revolution regime. They are reminiscent of the mutual aid teams and lower-stage agricultural cooperatives introduced during the 1950s in order to enlist peasant support and initiative. The rural reforms, therefore, may be viewed as consistent with many earlier rural development policies.

The spread of economic reform to urban industry resulted in the "management responsibility" system. An ever-widening range of commodities came under the influence of free-market forces as the influence of the national economic plan diminished. The reform movement in industry culminated with the passage of the Law on Industrial Enterprises Owned by the Whole People in 1988. To accomplish these changes, enterprise managers, instead of central planners, were given the responsibility to make economic decisions, and enterprises were granted at least nominal autonomy.

The reward of making right economic decisions is profit, most of which now came under the control of enterprise management. The risk of autonomous management takes the form of lower profits or losses. The ultimate cost of making wrong decisions is bankruptcy, a concept that had never been made generally effective in the People's Republic of China.

Peter M. Lichtenstein

References

Howard, Pat. *Breaking the Iron Rice Bowl.* Armonk, NY: M. E. Sharpe, 1988.
Parrish, William L., ed. *Chinese Rural Development.* Armonk, NY: M. E. Sharpe, 1985.
Riskin, Carl C. *China's Political Economy.* Oxford, England: Oxford University Press, 1987.

Restoration Society (Guangfuhui)

The origin of the Guangfuhui may be traced to the Association for National Military Education, which was formed in Japan after the disbandment of the Anti-Russia Volunteer Army in May 1903. Gong Baoquan, one of the radical students who organized a secret assassination corps in Tokyo, returned to Shanghai in 1904 and founded the Guangfuhui, with Cai Yuanpei as chairman. Its goal was exclusively nationalistic, as revealed by the fact that each new member had to take an oath upon admission, pledging to "restore the Chinese race and recover the country."

While most of the society's members were intellectuals from Zhejiang, Anhui, and Jiangsu, some of its leaders, such as Gong Baoquan, had close connections with local secret societies. Fascinated with the activities of the Russian populists, Cai Yuanpei and many of his fellow members favored the revolutionary tactic of assassination. Wu Yue, a Guangfuhui member, carried out the attack on five Qing officials at the Beijing railway station on September 24, 1905, and announced in his posthumous writings the beginning of "the age of assassination" in China.

Unlike the Xingzhonghui (Revive China Society) or the Huaxinghui (China Arise Society), the Guangfuhui continued to exist after the formation of the Tongmenghui (Revolutionary Alliance) in 1905. Most of its leading members joined the new organization. In 1907, Xu Xiling launched the Anqing Revolt in the name of the Guangfuhui. The revolt ended in the assassination of Enming, governor of Anhui, and Xu's own death. Qiu Jin, the famous woman revolutionary, was also involved in the episode and was executed in Shaoxing, Zhejiang. After the failure of yet another revolt, Xiong Chengji's mutiny at Anqing in 1908, Guangfuhui activities in central China temporarily subsided.

Within the Revolutionary Alliance, the Guangfuhui faction led by Tao Chengzhang and Zhang Binglin became more critical of Sun Yatsen and the Cantonese group as a result of their differences in geographical background, philosophy, and strategy. In 1910, Tao and Zhang left the Revolutionary Alliance and reconstituted the Guangfuhui in Tokyo. Thereafter the two revolutionary societies competed for funds and membership in Shanghai, Japan and Southeast Asia. In a brief cooperation, the Restoration Army collaborated with the forces of the Revolutionary Alliance to defeat the Qing army at Shanghai and Nanjing after the outbreak of the Revolution of 1911. But the rivalry remained. Tao Chengzhang was assassinated in Shanghai in January 1912, allegedly by an agent of the Revolutionary Alliance. The Guangfuhui disintegrated after Tao's death.

Henry Y. S. Chan

References

Laitinen, Kauko. *Chinese Nationalism in the Late Qing Dynasty: Zhang Binglin as an Anti-Manchu Propagandist.* London, England: Curzon Press, 1990.

Rankin, Mary. *Early Chinese Revolutionaries: Radical Intellectuals in Shanghai and Chekiang, 1902–1911.* Cambridge, MA: Harvard University Press, 1971.

Wong, Young-tsu. *Search for Modern Nationalism: Zhang Binglin and Revolutionary China.* New York, NY: Oxford University Press, 1989.

Returned Students

The term "returned students," a loose translation of *liuxuesheng,* refers to those Chinese young people who have come back to China after a period of study and/or research abroad. These returnees, perhaps totaling 100,000, have played a very important role in modern Chinese history. At the beginning of the twentieth century, they assumed a critical role in the birth of Chinese nationalism and then supplied much of the leadership for the Nationalist and Communist phases of the Chinese revolution. During the republican and Communist periods, their reintegration into Chinese society was frequently problematic. Nonetheless, "returned students" have been the principal conveyors of Western technology and culture to China and have thereby facilitated its modernization.

The "returned student" phenomenon in China dates to the mid-nineteenth century and therefore cuts across three distinct historical periods. Modern China received its first "returned student" during the late Qing dynasty (1644–1912). Yung Wing, a Guangdong native who returned to China in 1855 after ten years of study in the United States, joined the staff of regional leader and reformer Zeng Guofan in 1863. Yung was the architect of the groundbreaking Chinese Educational Mission to the United States that began in 1872. Under the sponsorship of Zeng and then Li Hongzhang, the mission brought a total of 120 young boys, all between the ages of twelve to fifteen and mostly from Guangdong, to New England for fifteen years of study abroad at Chinese government expense. The mission was recalled prematurely in 1881 because conservative Confucian officials feared that the increasingly Americanized young men were losing their Chinese identity.

Notwithstanding their eventually successful careers (mostly in government, the navy, mining and railways, and the telegraph service), "China's First Hundred" returned to a country that was still tradition-bound and, at least initially, regarded them with suspicion and disdain. During the next two decades perhaps an additional hundred students returned from study in Europe (England, France and Germany), sponsored for the most part by the Fuzhou Naval Dockyard.

It was only in the first decade of the twentieth century, after China's defeat in the first Sino-Japanese War (1894–95), the failure of the Hundred Days Reform of 1898 and Western intervention against the Boxer Uprising (1898–1901), that leading moderate reformers such as Zhang Zhidong were able to argue effectively for the expansion of overseas studies. They suggested that in order to strengthen the country with Western learning, it was necessary to enact sweeping educational reforms, including the implementation of a much larger study abroad program, particularly in nearby Japan. Once Zhang succeeded in persuading the Qing government to abolish the two-thousand-year-old Confucian examination system in 1905, thousands of Chinese students (estimates vary, ranging from 18,000 to 30,000 prior to the Revolution of 1911, the majority of whom were sponsored by their home provinces) traveled to Japan, mostly for short-term, non-degree courses of poor quality in specially established schools.

Concentrated in one district in Tokyo, exhilarated by their sudden freedom from the constraints of traditional Chinese society, impressed with Japan's successful modernization, and concerned about the very survival of China, these students became more and more politicized, increasingly anti-Manchu, and supportive of revolutionary organizations such as the Tongmenghui (Revolutionary Alliance). When they returned from Japan to their native provinces, most of these students were not very well trained in their particular fields of study, but they brought with them a new nationalism, heightened political sensitivity and a sympathy for revolution. In later years, many of these individuals enjoyed successful careers in education, government and the military.

During the republican period (1912–49) the profile of China's "returned students" changed dramatically in three ways. Because of a reduction in government support for study abroad after 1911, "returned students" were frequently from wealthier provinces and families. In addition, because the Chinese government was less involved in the study abroad movement, returnees had generally enjoyed more freedom abroad, both in terms of field selection and their everyday lives. Perhaps the biggest change was that, rather than being concentrated in Japan, Chinese students abroad were now more widely scattered, with the largest numbers returning from Japan, the United States, and France, and smaller but significant numbers from the Soviet Union, England, and Germany. For a variety of geographical, cultural, linguistic, and financial reasons, Japan continued to be the most popular destination for study abroad for Chinese students until the Second Sino-Japanese War (1937–45). Nevertheless, increasing tensions between China and Japan, instances of Japanese discrimination against Chinese students, and questions about the quality of Japanese education encouraged many students to study elsewhere.

During and immediately after World War I, France welcomed as many as six thousand Chinese students, mostly through the work-study program (qingong jianxue). These students became exposed to a variety of radical political doctrines in Europe. Upon their return to China, a number of them became active in the newborn labor movement, the anarchist movement and the fledgling Chinese Communist Party. As well, a significant number of Chinese students abroad chose the United States, particularly after 1908, when the American Boxer Indemnity began to fund scholarships for more than one thousand Chinese students to study in America, with emphasis on engineering and the social sciences. Despite discriminatory immigration legislation which affected Chinese students, the United States apparently became the most popular destination of privately sponsored Chinese students during the republican period. After they returned from the United States, many of these students achieved prominence in the government and academia. During World War II, some Chinese students were stranded in the United States, where restrictions on their employment were lifted and they received additional financial assistance. At the time of the Communist victory in China, some returned home, while others elected to remain in America or were prohibited from returning to China because of the strategic importance of their fields of specialization.

Since 1949 the People's Republic of China, reflecting its commitment to accelerate the modernization process, has sent a very large number of students abroad (nearly 100,000 between 1949 and 1989, according to some reports) and also welcomed back a significant number of "returned students," perhaps as many as 50,000. It is clear that a certain number of patriotic students who were studying abroad during the civil war (1945–49) returned to China at the time of the Communist victory. Between 1950 and 1963, China sent a significant number of students and scholars (figures range from 7,500 to 11,000 to 16,000) to the Soviet Union and Eastern Europe, mostly for advanced training in science and technology. It appears that upon their return to China, these academics were typically assigned positions in universities, research institutes, and industry. In the aftermath of the Cultural Revolution, nearly two thousand Chinese students were sent abroad to forty-nine countries between 1972 and 1977, particularly for language training.

By far the largest wave of Chinese students and scholars has been sent abroad as part of China's "open-up" policy since 1978. Reportedly, some 80,000 students and visiting scholars had been sent abroad between 1978 and 1989, and most had studied or were still studying engineering, natural sciences, management, medicine, and agriculture in at least sixty-three countries, with the largest numbers concentrated in the United States, Japan, Germany, England, Canada, and France. By 1989, as many as 30,000 of these students and scholars had returned to China, where they helped to transform Chinese science and technology, and the Chinese economy and society, but where they also encountered a range of professional and personal problems. Another 50,000 were abroad at the time of the Tiananmen Incident of 1989, which provoked Western governments to facilitate a delay in the return of these Chinese academics, many of whom genuinely feared for their safety in China, whereas others merely seized the opportunity to remain abroad. A number of these Chinese academics, particularly in the United States and Canada, have since declared their desire to become permanent residents abroad.

The scholarly literature suggests some common themes for an analysis of China's "returned students" during the three historical periods described above. The motivation of many returnees was clearly patriotism and a desire to serve their country, although sometimes these intentions became distorted by their impatience and their exaggerated sense of ability to effect significant change. But it appears that in two decades, the 1930s and the 1980s, self-interest increasingly replaced patriotism as the motivating factor for many "returned students."

The reception accorded to many returnees was not always friendly: in the nineteenth century they were greeted with disdain by most members of the Confucian elite; in the 1920s they were ridiculed for the irrelevance of their training; in the 1960s they were regarded with suspicion because they had been exposed to "Soviet revisionism"; in the late 1980s their commitment to Communist values was frequently questioned. The employment situation of "returned students" was problematic in all three periods: the first returnees initially found few careers in their areas of specialization; in the republican period many returnees became teachers rather than practitioners in their special fields and they clustered in urban coastal universities where they were more comfortable, but research facilities were inadequate; in the 1980s returnees increasingly complained about inadequate research facilities and funds, low salaries, and limited career opportunities. These problems notwithstanding, some returnees achieved national and even international prominence in their respective specialties.

The tendency for many returnees to insist on applying Western solutions and/or models to Chinese problems without regard to Chinese conditions often has been attacked by their contemporaries. The decision of some of them to remain abroad and not return to China has also invited criticism. Yung Wing himself, for example, became a United States citizen and married an American woman. As soon as restrictive American immigration laws were eased in favor of China, a growing number of Chinese academics chose to establish permanent residence in the United States. This trend has been especially noteworthy since the recent Tiananmen Incident. Nevertheless, many "non-returned students" have maintained their ties with China and played an important role from abroad in China's modernization.

What, then, is the legacy of "returned students" in modern Chinese history? Clearly influenced by their experiences abroad, returnees have played an important role as leaders of the Chinese revolution in the twentieth century. Many of the Guomindang leaders had studied in Japan and the United States, while leaders of the Chinese Communist Party had often studied in France and the Soviet Union. In fact, among the first generation of Communist leaders, only Mao Zedong had not studied abroad in his youth. In addition, "returned students" have brought back to China a better understanding of such alien concepts as nationalism, modernization, progress, revolution, democracy, and human rights; and they have also transmitted to China new ideologies, such as pragmatism, anarchism, socialism, and communism. These new concepts and ideologies have provided a framework and a vocabulary for the

Chinese revolution. As well, "returned students" have brought back information about the world outside China that slowly but inexorably has raised popular expectations and provided an international context for China's modern transformation. Finally, "returned students" have developed and maintained foreign ties, which have linked China with the outside world and enhanced China's international standing. In short, "returned students" have served as relentless agents of change in modern China.

Martin Singer

References

Hayhoe, Ruth, and Marianne Bastid, eds. *China's Education and the Industrialized World: Studies in Cultural Transfer.* Armonk, NY: M. E. Sharpe, 1987.

La Fargue, Thomas E. *China's First Hundred.* Pullman: State College of Washington, 1942.

Wang, Y. C. *Chinese Intellectuals and the West, 1872–1949.* Chapel Hill: University of North Carolina Press, 1966.

Revive China Society (Xingzhonghui)

Sun Yatsen's first anti-Manchu revolutionary organization, the Revive China Society (Xingzhonghui) was founded by Sun in Honolulu during his visit to Hawaii in November 1894. The manifesto of the society, which condemned the corruption of the Manchu government and encouraged the revival of China in indirect terms, was more reformist than revolutionary. After returning to Hong Kong the next year, Sun joined forces with Yang Quyun and his Furen Literary Society to form the Hong Kong Xingzhonghui with a clear anti-Manchu objective. Their plan to start a revolt in Canton fell through when the local authorities discovered the plot. Sun fled to Japan and organized a branch of the society in Yokohama. In subsequent years, branches were established in Taiwan, Southeast Asia, South Africa, and the Americas. Sun refined and expanded the society's programs to include three major principles: expulsion of the barbarians, restoration of China, and establishment of a republican form of government.

The Xingzhonghui may be described as a transitional party which bore characteristics of traditional and modern political organizations. It was a secret society with revolutionary programs. Led by a small group of Western-educated intellectuals who spent most of their time abroad, the society never took root in China. Membership was open to foreigners, but it failed to attract overseas Chinese, partly because of the radicalism of Sun's political ideas and partly because it failed to address issues that affected the interests of overseas Chinese.

In 1899, Sun founded the Xinghanhui (Revive Han Society) to strengthen the ties between the Triads in southern China and the Elder Brothers Society (Gelaohui) in central China, in order to promote coordination in future uprisings. The next year, *Zhongguo ribao (China Journal)* was started in Hong Kong as Xingzhonghui's propaganda organ. After the outbreak of the Boxer Uprising in 1900, some Xinghanhui members joined Tang Caichang's loyalist army in the Yangtze region, but Sun was unable to win the cooperation either of Li Hongzhang, governor-general of Guangdong and Guangxi, or of Kang Youwei, leader of the Emperor Protection Society (Baohuanghui). Supported by some Japanese *shishi* (men of purpose) and Triads members, Sun launched an uprising in Huizhou (Waichow), Guangdong, with initial success, but the revolutionaries were finally defeated because of the shortage of supplies.

After 1900, the Xingzhonghui continued to lose its members to the Baohuanghui. Sun's visits to the United States in 1903 and 1904 hardly improved the situation. When the Tongmenghui (Revolutionary Alliance) came into existence in 1905, most Xingzhonghui members joined the new organization and the society gradually disappeared.

Henry Y. S. Chan

References

Armentrout Ma, and L. Eve. *Revolutionaries, Monarchists, and Chinatowns.* Honolulu: The University Press of Hawaii, 1990.

Schiffrin, Harold. *Sun Yat-sen and the Origins of the Chinese Revolution.* Berkeley: University of California Press, 1970.

Yu, George T. *Party Politics in Republican China: The Kuomintang, 1912–1924.* Berkeley: University of California Press, 1966.

Revolution of 1911

The Revolution of 1911 overthrew the Qing dynasty (1644–1912) and ended a more than two-thousand-year-old imperial system. It did much to foster the growth of nationalism in China, but it did so in diverse and perhaps even contradictory ways.

The revolutionary movement took shape in the 1890s, a time of rapidly developing crises. Major internal problems and serious assaults from abroad had beset China for decades, weakening the central government and undermining political unity and authority. Attempts at reform were undertaken at national and local levels. Many aimed chiefly at parochial needs and issues, but by the 1890s most sought to address the increasingly urgent question of China's survival as a unified state. A new sense of nationalism, dedicated to resisting imperialism and deepening reform, began to emerge.

The nationalist revolutionaries argued that the moderate reforms favored by the government were inadequate and that the Qing had forfeited its claim to rule by failing to resist imperialism and to defend China's sovereignty. Moreover, they argued that as foreign conquerors, the Manchus were inherently incapable of defending China's interests. Only a new government organized differently could restore national unity and strengthen China sufficiently to confront imperialism.

In the course of their involvement, the revolutionaries articulated many new ideas involving nationalism. They examined China's cultural heritage and its national distinctiveness, they analyzed the problems of a multiethnic state and society, and they debated questions of popular sovereignty that broke new ground for social mobilization. A broad coalition was forged that took strong stands against Qing tyranny and imperialist domination of China. The revolutionaries also demanded the full restoration of China's economic rights, fighting especially hard to keep railway building under Chinese control.

At the same time, however, the organization and the course of the revolutionary movement revealed the contradictions that existed at this early stage in the development of modern Chinese nationalism. The movement was divided by social, ideological, and geographical forces and lacked strong leadership and direction. Such unity as it managed to achieve for brief periods could not be sustained. Indeed, the revolution itself was scarcely more than a series of local and provincial independence movements. The shaky coalition that formed to oppose the Qing came apart even as the dynasty was falling.

The revolutionaries' anti-imperialism was also compromised by their appeals for foreign help, sympathy, and protection. The revolutionary movement had a certain foreign orientation from its earliest days. Its first major organization, the Xingzhonghui (Revive China Society), was founded in Hawaii, and its commitment to republicanism drew on the United States as a model. Its core of support remained in Hawaii and other overseas Chinese communities, such as Hong Kong. Additional support came from Japanese sympathizers. The movement broadened in the early 1900s, with the founding of indigenous revolutionary groups such as Huaxinghui (China Arise Society) and Guangfuhui (Restoration Society), but when they joined with the Xingzhonghui in 1905 to form the Tongmenghui (Revolutionary Alliance), it was Sun Yatsen, the Xingzhonghui leader, who became director of the new organization. The choice of Sun was dictated chiefly by his experience abroad and his presumed talent for dealing with foreigners.

As the movement carried its efforts into China with attempted military uprisings, propaganda, and underground organizational work, it retained ties to its many branches abroad—in Tokyo, Hong Kong, Singapore, and other cities in Southeast Asia, as well as in Europe and the western hemisphere. In China, the revolutionaries took refuge in foreign concessions in cities such as Shanghai and Wuhan. By 1911 the movement had become sprawling and diffuse, with only the most tenuous links holding it together.

Inside China, the movement had from the first forged ties with secret societies, which were instrumental in most of the early revolutionary uprisings. Over time, the movement gained two other key elements. First, through agitation and organization, it won many adherents and sympathizers among the officers and enlisted men of the New Army. Second, as political reforms gave dissidents a forum in the newly elected provincial assemblies, dissent turned into active protest, heightened demands, and revolutionary tendencies among various elites.

By the fall of 1911, therefore, serious discontent was spreading to more and more people, and uprisings much like those that a few years earlier had been easily suppressed, now ignited army mutinies and major defections among provincial assembly leaders as well as secret societies. A broad anti-Qing coalition came into existence, as one city and province after another declared independence. With the additional assistance of Yuan Shikai, the revolutionaries brought the Qing down in early 1912. But a movement so lacking in organization, leadership, and mass support, and so hastily amalgamated, proved a fragile base for the new Republic.

The Revolution of 1911 had aimed at creating a stronger and more unified government that could promote the country's development, resist imperialism, and regain full sovereignty and international standing. Its immediate and most visible results fell far short of these goals. For at least a decade-and-a-half after 1911, the Republic created by the revolution was weaker, more divided, and less respected in the world than China had been under the Qing. In the long run, however, the Revolution of 1911 contributed to the revival of China's national spirit. A broader movement to build a strong, unified, fully sovereign, and internationally respected nation-state emerged on its basis.

Michael Gasster

References

Gasster, Michael. "The Republican Revolutionary Movement." *The Cambridge History of China,* ed. John K. Fairbank and Kwang-ching Liu, vol. 11, 463–534. Cambridge, England: Cambridge University Press, 1980.

Wright, Mary C., ed. *China in Revolution: The First Phase, 1900–1913.* New Haven, CT: Yale University Press, 1968.

Revolutionary Alliance (Tongmenghui)

The Tongmenghui was the coalition of revolutionary groups that led the anti-Manchu movement during the early 1900s, culminating in the Revolution of 1911 which ended the Qing rule.

In August 1905, leaders of the revolutionary Xingzhonghui (Revive China Society), Huaxinghui (China Arise Society), Guangfuhui (Restoration Society) and a few other groups met in Tokyo, Japan, and agreed to form a unified organization. This new organization, called Zhongguo Tongmenghui (Chinese Revolutionary Alliance, or The China Federal Association), elected Sun Yatsen, formerly head of the Xingzhonghui, as its leader *(zongli)*. Other principal officers of the Tongmenghui included Huang Xing, Wang Jingwei, Song Jiaoren, Chang Ji, and Deng Jiayan, most of whom were Chinese students in Japan. The alliance not only forged the regionally based anti-dynastic groups into one force, but also signified an expansion of revolutionary influence into the new Chinese intelligentsia.

The Tongmenghui proclaimed its goals to be "expelling the Manchus, restoring Chinese (Han) rule, establishing a republic, and equalizing land rights." Anti-Manchu nationalism was clearly the main theme of its revolutionary appeal, as well as the common ground for cooperation among the participating groups. On that basis Sun Yatsen introduced his ideas of republicanism and moderate socialism, which were suggested by the last two proclaimed goals. From 1906 to 1908, Sun and his associates further drafted the *Design for Revolution (Geming fanglue),* a total of thirteen documents that provided plans for the various aspects of future revolutionary uprisings.

With headquarters in Tokyo, the Tongmenghui established secret branches in major cities in China (Shanghai, Chongqing, Yantai, and Hankou) and public branches overseas (Hong Kong, Singapore, Brussels, San Francisco, and Honolulu). Its organ, *Minbao (The People's Report),* began publication in Tokyo in November 1905, and soon engaged in a fierce debate with the monarchist journals, especially Liang Qichao's *Xinmin congbao (The New People Miscellany).* From 1906 to 1911, the Tongmenghui organized nine uprisings in central and south China with the help of its members in the government's New Army. All of them failed.

Meanwhile, the "revolutionary alliance" itself was threatened by internal division. Personality conflict and differences in revolutionary tactics caused several former Guangfuhui leaders to split with Sun Yatsen and reestablish their society in 1907. Then in 1911, a group of former Huaxinghui members, led by Song Jiaoren, became dissatisfied with Sun's south China-centered uprisings and his dictatorial style of leadership. They organized the virtually independent Central China Branch *(zhongbu zonghui)* of Tongmenghui in Shanghai. It was this latter group that played an assisting role in the Wuchang Uprising later that year, which eventually toppled the Qing dynasty.

Following the founding of the Republic, Song Jiaoren argued that the mission of the Tongmenghui had shifted from overthrowing the Qing with revolutionary uprisings to guiding the Republic through parliamentary politics. Under his leadership, the Tongmenghui joined forces with four other political parties and formed the Guomindang (Nationalist Party) in August 1912.

Wang Ke-wen

References

Gasster, Michael. *Chinese Intellectuals and the Revolution of 1911: The Birth of Modern Chinese Radicalism*. Seattle: University of Washington Press, 1969.

Lee, Ta-ling. *Foundations of the Chinese Revolution, 1905–1912: The Historical Record of the T'ung-meng Hui*. New York, NY: St. John's University Press, 1970.

Revolutionary Diplomacy

The principal line of foreign policy adopted by the Guomindang (GMD) government in the second half of the 1920s, "revolutionary diplomacy" was aimed at abolishing the unequal treaties.

The destruction of the unequal treaty system that had been forced upon China by the Western powers and Japan since the mid-nineteenth century was a major goal of the "National Revolution" *(Guomin geming)* led by the GMD. Under the First United Front with the Chinese Communists, the Party took a militant anti-imperialist stance and regarded the abolition of the unequal treaties as an urgent and important task. The term "revolutionary diplomacy" *(geming waijiao)* was first introduced by Eugene Chen (Chen Youren), foreign minister of the GMD government from June 1926 to August 1927. During that period, the GMD, following the success of the Northern Expedition, moved its seat from Canton to Wuhan. In line with the radicalism of the time, Chen promoted the recovery of China's rights from foreign hands, in open defiance of the existing treaties, by means of militant mass movements. The most notable example of Chen's radical policy was the seizure of the British concessions in Hankou and Jiujiang in January and February 1927.

Following the collapse of the Wuhan government and the reintegration of the GMD under the Nanjing government in late 1927, Chen's forceful methods were replaced by the mild approach of his successors. Wu Chaoshu, Nanjing's foreign minister (April 1927–February 1928), and Wang Zhengting, who later took over the post (June 1928–September 1931), sought to revise the unequal treaties through peaceful negotiations with the powers. They no longer relied on mass movements, which the new anti-Communist leadership of the GMD regarded as potentially subversive, but tried instead to appeal to the foreign governments with reason and patience. Under the guidance of Wu and Wang, the Nanjing government, now the national government of China, initiated a series of negotiations with the United States, Great Britain and France during 1928 to 1931 concerning the restoration of tariff autonomy and the abolition of extraterritoriality. The negotiations resulted in agreements that partially abrogated the unequal treaties, especially with respect to China's tariff rights, yet their full implementation was soon disrupted by the Manchurian Incident of 1931.

The crisis in Sino-Japanese relations overshadowed everything else in China's external relations in the 1930s, as Japan became the focus of anti-imperialist nationalism in China. Revolutionary diplomacy, primarily directed at the West, gradually ceased to be the main theme of China's foreign policy.

Wang Ke-wen

References

Burns, Richard D., and Edward M. Bennett, eds. *Diplomats in Crisis: U.S.-Chinese-Japanese Relations, 1919–1941*. Santa Barbara, CA: ABC-Clio, 1974.

Cavendish, Patrick. "Anti-imperialism in the Kuomintang, 1923–8." *Studies in the Social History of China and Southeast Asia: Essays in Memory of Victor Purcell*, ed. Jerome Ch'en and Nicholas Tarling, 23–56. London, England: Cambridge University Press, 1970.

Richard, Timothy (1845–1919)

One of the most influential Western missionaries in modern China, Timothy Richard was born in South Wales, Great Britain. He became a minister of the Baptist Church in 1869 and was sent to China as a missionary the same year.

In China, Richard traveled to Shandong, Shanxi, and Manchuria and soon befriended a number of Chinese officials through his participation in famine relief activities. He became deeply interested in the domestic situation in China and in 1882 published a long essay in *Wanguo gongbao (Review of the Times)*, the leading missionary journal in China, wherein he proposed technological and institutional reforms. At the time he was also giving regular lectures on Western sciences to officials and the gentry in Shanxi. In 1890, Li Hongzhang invited Richard to become the editorial writer of the Tianjin newspaper *Shibao (The Times)*, for which he wrote a series of commentaries on Chinese affairs. Later these writings were republished as a volume, titled *Shishi xinlun (New Commentaries on Current Affairs)*. The next year he left *Shibao* and assumed the post of secretary in the Guangxuehui (Society for the Diffusion of Knowledge), then the largest Christian cultural enterprise in China. He held that post until 1916.

Following the outbreak of the first Sino-Japanese War of 1894 to 1895, Richard paid several visits to Zhang Zhidong and Li Hongzhang, both powerful regional officials, and suggested closer ties between China and Great Britain in order to counter the threat of Japan. His proposal would have in fact turned China into a British protectorate.

Having been rejected by Zhang and Li, Richard turned his attention to the Reform movement led by Kang Youwei. His Chinese translation of Robert Mackenzie's *The Nineteenth Century: A History,* published in 1895, was immensely popular among the reformers. He soon joined the reformist Qiangxuehui (Society for the Study of National Strengthening) and Liang Qichao became his personal assistant. In late 1895, Richard met Weng Tonghe, head of the Zongli Yamen and tutor of Emperor Guangxu, to whom he suggested wide-ranging reforms in education, morality, and the economy. He no longer proposed a British monopoly of China, but instead advocated an international tutelage of the Chinese government.

When the Hundred Days Reform began in June 1898, Richard was an active participant. Kang Youwei submitted Richard's translation of Mackenzie, together with his own writings, to Emperor Guangxu, and the emperor soon appointed Richard as his imperial adviser. By mid-September, the Reform movement was on the verge of collapse in the face of the counterattack by Empress Dowager Cixi. Richard again suggested that the Chinese government be placed under the joint control of Great Britain, the United States and Japan. Before this proposal could be considered, however, the *coup d'état* occurred. After appealing in vain to foreign legations in Beijing for intervention, he went to Shanghai.

In 1899, Richard published a series of translations on *Wanguo gongbao* which introduced Marxist ideas to the Chinese; he was among the first foreigners to do so. During the Boxer Uprising of 1900, he strongly advocated international intervention and the suppression of the Boxers by force. In 1901, he negotiated with Li Hongzhang on the terms of the post-Boxer settlements in Shanxi, which included the establishment of a Western-style school in that province. The school was subsequently established and Richard supervised its Western Learning branch until 1911.

In 1896 and 1900, Richard had twice met with Sun Yatsen and tried to persuade Sun to abandon his plans for revolution. During and after the Revolution of 1911, therefore, Richard did not favor the revolutionaries. In the early years of the Republic, he supported Yuan Shikai, his old friend in the Qiangxuehui. When Yuan's monarchist attempt failed in 1916, Richard was apparently disillusioned. He left China that year and returned to England. He died three years later.

Wang Ke-wen

References

Cohen, Paul A., and John E. Schrecker, eds. *Reform in Nineteenth-Century China.* Cambridge, MA: Harvard University Press, 1976.

Kwang, Luke S. K. *A Mosaic of the Hundred Days.* Cambridge, MA: Harvard University Press, 1984.

Rights-Recovery Movement

In the early 1900s, many educated Chinese recognized the destructive impact that foreign economic exploitation was exerting on China's industrialization and modernization. Beginning in 1903, a movement to recover China's economic resources from foreign control gradually emerged in the provinces under the leadership of the local gentry and business elite. In 1905, the provincial elite in Hunan, Hubei, and Guangdong persuaded Zhang Zhidong, the governor-general of HuGuang, to redeem the right of constructing the Canton-Hankou Railway from the American-owned China Development Company. The Hubei section of the railway then came under the management of the provincial government, whereas private investors gained the rights to the Hunan and Guangdong sections. Meanwhile, the gentry and merchants in Sichuan organized their own company and obtained the right to build a railway from Hankou to their province. The success of these rights-recovery actions encouraged other provinces in China to follow their example. Soon gentry and merchants in Zhejiang and Jiangsu founded the Railway Protection societies to petition the recovery of the Shanghai-Hangzhou-Ningpo Railway from British control, and the Hebei and Henan provincial elite raised similar demands on the Tianjin-Pukou Railway.

In addition to railways, the provincial elite also wished to recover control over China's mineral resources. In 1907, the Baojin (Protecting Shanxi) Mining Company in Shanxi declared that it would accept only Chinese subscriptions to its shares and refuse foreign ones. It hoped that this would eventually lead to exclusively Chinese ownership of the mines in that province. Many other provinces soon made similar attempts. The gold mines in Heilongjiang, the coal mines in Fengtian, Shandong, and Hubei, the oil fields in Shaanxi, and the silver, copper, and tin mines in Yunnan were but the most notable instances. The movement received tacit and cautious support from the Qing government, which appreciated the popular agitation against foreign encroachment but worried that the drive might get out of control.

The Rights-Recovery movement tried to put into practice the theories of war of commerce *(shangzhan)* that were delineated by reformist thinkers such as Wang Tao and Zheng Guanying. It was no coincidence that Zheng himself was a leader of the movement in Guangdong and served as chief manager of the Guangdong section of the Canton-Hankou Railway in 1906. Although these efforts were often crippled by financial difficulties, as the provincial gentry and merchants were unable to replace foreign capitals with sufficient local funds, they nevertheless represented a new awareness among the Chinese of the need for economic independence. The movement also preceded and partly overlapped the Constitutional Movement of 1906 to 1911. Many leaders in the rights-recovery actions, such as Tang Shouqian in Zhejiang, later became prominent constitutionalists. The specific goals of the two movements clearly differed: one was economic and the other political, but they displayed remarkable similarities in organization, tactics, and social base. Both movements, moreover, supplemented nationalist appeals with provincial or regional sentiments, and thus simultaneously enhanced Chinese nationalism and provincialism.

Wang Ke-wen

References

Chan, Wellington K. K. "Government, Merchants and Industry to 1911." *The Cambridge History of China,* ed. John K. Fairbank and Kwang-ching Liu, vol. 11, 416–462. Cambridge, England: Cambridge University Press, 1980.

Li, En-han. *China's Quest for Railway Autonomy, 1904–1911: A Study of the Chinese Railway-Rights Recovery Movement.* Singapore: Singapore University Press, 1977.

Wright, Timothy. *Coal Mining in China's Economy and Society, 1895–1937.* New York, NY: Cambridge University Press, 1984.

Rural Reconstruction

See LIANG SHUMING; YEN, JAMES

Ryukyu Incident

The Ryukyu Incident, also known as the Formosa Incident, led to the annexation of the Ryukyu Islands by Japan in the 1870s.

In 1871, a boat carrying Ryukyu fishermen was shipwrecked in northern Taiwan (Formosa), where fifty-four of the men were killed by Taiwanese aborigines. The island kingdom of Ryukyu had been a tributary state to the Chinese empire since 1372 but had also been a vassal to the Satsuma Han of Japan since 1609. The new Meiji government in Japan now seized this opportunity to assert exclusive control over the islands. In 1873, it demanded compensations on behalf of the Ryukyuans from the Qing government in China, as Taiwan was recognized as part of China.

The Chinese government rejected the Japanese demand on the ground that the Ryukyu kingdom was under Chinese suzerainty, and thus beyond the legitimate concern of Japan. In 1874, Japanese forces launched a "punitive expedition" against Taiwan, which the Chinese forces stationed in Fujian repelled. Later that year, Great Britain, France, and the United States jointly pressured the Qing government to negotiate with the Japanese over the Ryukyu issue. In a special treaty signed between the two countries in Beijing, China recognized Japanese sovereignty over the Ryukyu Islands and offered compensations to the Japanese government. The treaty provided a legal basis for the Japanese government to force the Ryukyu kingdom to terminate her status as a tributary state to the Chinese empire in 1875, and to annex the kingdom by military conquest in 1879. The Japanese subsequently renamed the islands Okinawa.

From the Chinese perspective, the incident signaled the first major diplomatic failure vis-à-vis Japan in the nineteenth century. The Qing government displayed a degree of ignorance and clumsiness in managing this crisis, which encouraged Meiji Japan to make further moves to replace China as the dominant power in East Asia.

Wang Ke-wen

References

Sakai, Robert K. "The Ryukyu Islands as Fief of Satsuma." *The Chinese World Order,* ed. John K. Fairbank, 112–34. Cambridge, MA: Harvard University Press, 1968.

Ch'en, Ta-tuan. "Investiture of Liu-ch'iu Kings in the Ch'ing Period." Ibid., 135–64.

S

Sanyuanli Incident

In mid-1841, the Opium War resumed after the Chuanbi Convention of January was rejected by both the Chinese and the British governments. In May, the British expeditionary force besieged Canton and held it for a ransom of $6 million Mexican silver dollars.

While waiting for the Chinese authorities to deliver the ransom, British troops destroyed local temples, looted Chinese homes, and raped Chinese women. The most serious incident occurred around Sanyuanli, a village less than two miles north of Canton. Enraged by the foreigners' brutalities, several thousand Sanyuanli peasants attacked a British patrol on May 29. The next day, the local gentry, encouraged by this initial success, organized a larger group of peasants under the banner of "Pacify the British Corps" *(pingYingtuan)* and escalated the attack. Armed with hoes, mattocks, spears, and knives, the peasants, who eventually numbered over ten thousand, inflicted some casualties on the British. Fearing British retaliations, the Chinese authorities soon ordered the local gentry to suspend the assaults, and the peasants withdrew on May 31.

The incident was insignificant in determining the outcome of the war, yet in subsequent Chinese historiography and legends it has become a symbol of popular resistance against Western imperialism. Some Chinese accounts claim that the people in Canton could have won the war had the cowardly Qing officials not intervened on behalf of the foreigners. This pattern of popular, often gentry-led, militancy versus official restraint was to be repeated many times in the later foreign crises of the Qing dynasty. Such militant actions themselves were expressions of anti-imperialist nationalism, which also led to a discontent with the government's conciliatory policy toward the foreigners. This discontent reinforced latent anti-Manchu sentiments among the (Han) Chinese and contributed to the growth of Han nationalism during the late Qing.

Wang Ke-wen

References

Wakeman, Frederic, Jr. *Strangers at the Gate: Social Disorder in South China, 1839–1861*. Berkeley: University of California Press, 1966.

Scar Literature

Scar literature *(Shanghen wenxue),* the first radical departure in Chinese creative literature launched after the death of Mao Zedong, projected a tragic image of contemporary Chinese society. It contributed to the transformation of Chinese patriotic values in the period 1977 to 1980, when the country was just beginning its "open-up" policy. Also translated as "wound literature" or "literature of the wounded," the term *Shanghen wenxue* is sometimes used broadly, as in Taiwan, to identify all the literature in the 1980s People's Republic of China (PRC) that was critical of Communist society. But in the PRC, where the term originated, it refers only to the post-Mao works written prior to 1981, because by then literary taste and daring had quickly surpassed "scar" standards.

Scar literature takes its name from a short story, "The Scar," authored by Lu Xinhua and published August 11, 1978, in *Wenhuibao*. A young girl regrets having sided with the Maoist leadership rather than with her own mother during the Cultural Revolution, when the ultraleftists, for political expediency, labeled her mother a traitor. The first recognized prototype of the genre, however, is Liu Xinwu's *"Banzhuren"* ("The Home-Room Teacher," or "Form Master"), published in November 1977. It excuses the misbehavior of a juvenile delinquent and faults the ideological dogmatism of a Communist Youth League member. These stories and others by noted young and middle-aged authors, such as Kong Jiesheng, Wang Yaping, and Wang Meng, explicitly expose the tragedies and evils of the Cultural Revolution (1966–76), with a focus on the "scarred" generation of young people. They portray the youths as being misled by the ultra-leftists into the excesses of the Red Guard movement, only to become victims after being exiled to the countryside in the aftermath.

The hallmark of true scar literature is its primitive but bitter social exposure, conveyed by a simplistic characterization of people and politics; it blames all evils on policy aberrations perpetrated by Lin Biao and the Gang of Four rather than on wider Maoist, Communist, or national habits and traditions. In retrospect, scar literature is a transitional genre, quite as stereotypical as Maoist socialist realism, but with the heroes and villains of the latter reversed and with a tone of reproach and melancholy instead of optimism about the future under class struggle.

Scar literature symptomized the weakening sense of the Chinese people, particularly of the youth, that China was the world's most politically correct state. It redefined Chinese patriotism as something other than blind obedience to the Communist leaders in power. This led the way to the development of a world-class literature that was freed of political dogma, and which was permeated by a new and less uniform basis for articulating Chinese nationalism. This new literature was less tied to Marxist conceptions of proletarian internationalism and relied more on conventional nationalistic images of a Chinese character rooted in culture, geography, history, and ethnicity.

Jeffrey Kinkley

Second Revolution

The Second Revolution was a struggle led by Sun Yatsen and his followers in 1913 to oppose the dictatorship of Yuan Shikai. It occurred shortly after the anti-Manchu Revolution of 1911, and consequently has been generally referred to as the "Second Revolution."

The assassination of Song Jiaoren and the "reorganization loan" were the direct causes of the Second Revolution. On March 20, 1913, Song, leader of the parliamentary Guomindang, was assassinated at the Shanghai railway station. Song had been advocating the adoption of the cabinet system by the new Republic, and his assassination was believed to have been ordered by President Yuan Shikai, who feared losing his power under that system. The assassination provoked nationwide anger and verbal attacks on Yuan, especially from the Guomindang. Yuan, in order to secure foreign political and financial support for himself, concluded a 25 million pound "reorganization loan" with a five-power banking consortium (Great Britain, France, Germany, Russia, and Japan) on April 26. The Guomindang opposed this loan.

The Song assassination caused a Guomindang split on the issue of anti-Yuan strategies. Sun Yatsen proposed armed uprisings; Huang Hsing and others favored legal resorts. Having arranged the "reorganization loan," Yuan decided to settle his dispute with the Guomindang by force. In June, he dismissed the Guomindang governors in Jiangxi, Anhui, and Guangdong (Li Liejun, Bo Wenwei, and Hu Hanmin, respectively), and ordered his Beiyang forces to attack the South. The Guomindang resisted. On July 12, Li Liejun declared the independence of Jiangxi in Hukou. On July 15, Huang Hsing announced his anti-Yuan uprising in Nanjing. These were followed by Guomindang-led revolts in Shanghai, Anhui, Guangdong, Fujian, Hunan, and Sichuan. Yuan's military strength, however, was far superior to that of the Guomindang, and little coordination or solidarity existed among the rebelling provinces. As a result, the Guomindang's anti-Yuan effort collapsed after only two months. Sun Yatsen and his followers again went into overseas exile, and Yuan extended his influence into the provinces south of the Yangtze River.

The Second Revolution symbolized a confrontation between the traditional and modern influences, as well as between the northern and southern forces, in Chinese politics after the Revolution of 1911. Although the traditional/northern establishment gained the upper hand in this instance, it soon collapsed under the weight of various challenges. The open conflict cleaving Yuan Shikai and the Guomindang was but the beginning of a long period of chaos and disturbances in China.

Lu Fang-shang

References

Wilbur, C. Martin. *Sun Yat-sen: Frustrated Patriot.* New York, NY: Columbia University Press, 1976.

Yu, George T. *Party Politics in Republican China: The Kuomintang, 1912–1924.* Berkeley: University of California Press, 1966.

Secret Societies

Most of Chinese history has been dominated by two major, distinct ideological currents. The first, often presented as orthodoxy, advocated a hierarchical, authoritarian, patriarchal society. The second, often presented as heterodoxy, promoted an anarchistic, individualistic, egalitarian society. The former appealed to the Chinese elite, and, as a result, became the norm. The latter pleased the less fortunate members of Chinese society. Secret societies provided an organized means by which peasants and artisans could express a broad range of non-elite beliefs, needs, and frustrations.

In *Primitive Revolutionaries of China: A Study of Secret Societies in the Late Nineteenth Century,* Fei-Ling Davis listed five characteristics that informed a secret society. First, membership in a secret society was voluntary, which meant that participation was not based on ascriptive qualifications. Social pressure was frequently a factor in the decision to join a secret society. Second, a secret society's existence, rituals, and the identity of its members were usually hidden from outsiders. This served as a protective shield and as a way of differentiating the secret society from the rest of the world. Third, secret societies have either a cellular type or a communal type of organization. Fourth, secret society members act jointly and obey the directives of the society. Fifth, a secret society must either conform to or be alienated from the host society. It cannot exist in a void.

In China, secret societies came into existence as a non-elite means of expressing a broad range of beliefs, needs, and frustrations. They most often appeared in times of bureaucratic inadequacy and/or repression. As early as 203 B.C. a secret society-type of rebellion erupted against the Qin Dynasty, which had attempted to impose bureaucratic centralization. In 184 A.D., the Yellow Turban Rebellion caused the dissolution of the Later Han dynasty and the splintering of China into three separate states known as the Three Kingdoms era (A.D. 220–80). Many Chinese secret societies cite this period as their date of origin.

Incipient defensive nationalism emerged as a secret society ingredient during the Southern Song dynasty (c. 1125), in response to the invasions by Genghis and Kublai Khan, and later by the Manchus. According to legend, the Tiandihui (Heaven and Earth Society) was founded in 1674 in a monastery near Fuzhou by militant Buddhist monks who had been victimized by corrupt officials. Under the slogan "overthrow the Qing and restore the Ming," they developed an elaborate secret ritual and became a blood brotherhood, whose members swore to exterminate Manchu rule.

The validity of the early Qing anti-Manchu origins of the Heaven and Earth Society has been questioned. There is no doubt, however, that Sun Yatsen found the account useful to stress the nationalistic aspects of secret societies in his efforts to overthrow the Manchu (Qing) dynasty. This unsubstantiated linkage between secret societies and modern Chinese nationalism also proved valuable to those who have argued that secret societies were revolutionary in nature and that nationalism redirected their activities from the central government toward the West.

Gerald W. Berkley

References

Chesneaux, Jean. *Secret Societies in China in the Nineteenth and Twentieth Centuries.* Ann Arbor: University of Michigan Press, 1971.

Davis, Fei-Ling. *Primitive Revolutionaries of China: A Study of Secret Societies in the Late Nineteenth Century.* Honolulu: The University Press of Hawaii, 1977.

Ownby, David, and Somers Heidhues, eds. *"Secret Societies" Reconsidered: Perspectives on the Social History of Modern South China and Southeast Asia.* New York, NY: M. E. Sharpe, 1993.

Seeckt, Hans von (1866–1936)

From 1927 to 1938, Chiang Kaishek's Guomindang government employed a large group of German advisers in an effort to strengthen China's military establishment. The highest in rank, and most well-known, among them was General Hans von Seeckt.

Born to an aristocratic family in Prussia, Seeckt was the architect of the post-World War

I reform of the German military. He had a prominent career, serving as chief of staff and then commander-in-chief of the National Defense Forces, before retiring in 1926. In 1933, at the age of sixty-seven, he made his first trip to China and presented a proposal to the Guomindang government for the reform of the Chinese army. The proposal was much valued by Chiang Kaishek, who invited Seeckt back the following year to head the German Advisory Group in China. During 1933 to 1935, Seeckt played a major role in the training and reorganization of the Guomindang troops, and in the planning and execution of Chiang's fifth Bandit-Suppression Campaign against the Chinese Communists. Later he also helped to negotiate a 100 million German mark loan to the Guomindang government for the purchase of weaponry. Seeckt resigned and returned to Germany in 1935. He died the next year.

Seeckt and his German colleagues, including Max Bauer, Hermann Kriebel, Georg Wetzell, and Alexander von Falkenhausen, may be the least controversial among all foreign advisers in republican China. Unlike Mikhail Borodin before them and Joseph Stilwell who came later, the German officers apparently cooperated with Chiang Kaishek well and accomplished their mission in China successfully. To a degree, this may have been due to the technical nature of their assignments, yet their technical advice sometimes had far-reaching political implications. Seeckt, for example, advised Chiang to avoid external conflict as much as possible before completing domestic military reforms, which was an important factor in the formation of Chiang's appeasement policy toward Japan in the 1930s. The success of the German advisers in China also reflected the overall friendly relations between the two countries at the time. Most of the advisers were supporters of the Nazi government in their own country and could not help but to be impressed by Chiang's admiration and imitation of the European Fascist movement in the early 1930s. They were not directly involved in the rise of Chinese Fascist organizations, but their presence alone contributed to the popularity of the German political model in Guomindang China.

Wang Ke-wen

References

Liu, F. F. *A Military History of Modern China, 1924–1949*. Princeton, NJ: Princeton University Press, 1956.

Kirby, William. *German and Republican China*. Stanford, CA: Stanford University Press, 1984.

Self-Reliance

Self-reliance is one of the fundamental doctrines formulated by Mao Zedong, which calls for the Chinese to rely on their own efforts to achieve their political and economic goals—"regeneration through one's own efforts." The principle of self-reliance has underlain Chinese foreign and domestic policies since the late 1950s.

Mao first suggested the idea of self-reliance in December 1935 when he called for a national united front against the invading Japanese. Mao stressed at that time: "We the Chinese have the spirit to fight the enemy to the last drop of our blood, the determination to recover our lost territory by our own efforts, and the ability to stand on our own feet in the family of nations."

From the founding of the People's Republic in 1949 to the mid-1950s, when China implemented the First Five-Year Plan, Mao's principle of self-reliance lost much of its relevance as China adopted the policy of "leaning to one side," that is, relying on Soviet economic and technical assistance. Beginning with the Great Leap Forward in 1958, however, Mao began to reemphasize the idea of self-reliance as China attempted to move away from the Soviet model. He criticized the Stalinist development strategy of focusing on heavy industry at the expense of light industry and agriculture as unsuitable to the Chinese situation. In 1960, amid the deteriorating economic situation in China caused by natural as well as man-made disasters, Moscow suddenly withdrew its Soviet technical advisers and cancelled all the projects in retaliation against Mao's deviation from Soviet guidance. This convinced Chinese leaders, especially Mao, that China should never again become dependent upon a foreign country. They perceived self-reliance to be the only viable way for China to maintain its autonomy and national sovereignty.

The pursuit of self-reliance reached its peak during the initial phase of the Cultural Revolution (1966–69), when China condemned both the United States and the Soviet Union and reduced its trade relations with the outside world. Self-reliance came to mean depending on China's own experiences and resources, emphasizing revolutionary zeal over science and management, reducing China's indebtedness (from time to time, the government proudly announced that China had no foreign or domestic debts), and encouraging indigenous technological innovation as a substitute for the import of foreign technology. The policies of political isolation and economic autarky remained in effect until China and the United States began a gradual rapprochement process in 1972.

In post-Mao China, the principle of self-reliance is quoted only infrequently. Under Deng Xiaoping's economic reform and "open-up" policy, the Maoist rhetoric of self-reliance seems lost in a vast sea of joint ventures, special economic zones, foreign investments, and China's booming trade relations with other countries. One may still find some correlation between the idea of self-reliance and China's independent foreign policy since the 1980s. Yet here lies an important difference. If self-reliance in the form of self-imposed isolation and autarky in the late 1960s reflected China's weakness and poor status in the international community, then China's independent foreign policies in the 1980s represented China's increasing confidence in its economic strength and national power.

Some Chinese may also wonder if it is wise for a big country, like China, to become dependent upon foreign capital and the global market. Nevertheless, as the Chinese people have greatly benefited from an increasing integration into the world economy, this nationalistic concern is diminishing.

Shi-ping Zheng

References

Riskin, Carl. *China's Political Economy: The Quest for Development since 1949.* Oxford, England: Oxford University Press, 1988.

Starr, John Bryan. *Continuing the Revolution: The Political Thought of Mao.* Princeton, NJ: Princeton University Press, 1979.

Self-Strengthening Movement

The Self-Strengthening movement refers to the activities of Chinese leaders in the imperial government and the provinces, beginning in 1861 and extending into the late 1890s, to strengthen military forces, related sectors of the economy, education, and diplomatic machinery in order to suppress domestic rebellions and resist the intrusions of foreign powers.

Diplomatic self-strengthening commenced in 1861 following the British-French occupation of Beijing in the fall of 1860. A new agency, the Zongli Yamen headed by Prince Gong, was established to conduct China's relations with the foreign powers.

In the early 1860s, self-strengthening broadened to include military activities. As resurgent Taiping forces advanced on the foreign treaty port at Shanghai in 1861 and early 1862, provincial leaders in the Yangtze valley, Zeng Guofan, Li Hongzhang, and Zuo Zongtang, became so impressed by the efficacy of British and French weapons and steamships that they decided to purchase them and establish production facilities in China. Over the next three decades, they and other Chinese officials established the Jiangnan Arsenal and Shipyard in Shanghai (1865), the Fuzhou Naval Dockyard (1866), and more than twenty provincial arsenals employing steam-powered machinery and foreign technicians. These plants supplied the newly organized provincial armies: the Hunan Army which subdued the Taiping Rebellion (1851–64) and the Huai Army which pacified the Nian Rebellion (1853–68). The anti-imperialist intent of the arsenals was signified by their production of steamships and heavy coastal defense guns to fortify China's harbors and coastlines against foreign intrusion.

Educational self-strengthening was evident in the establishment of foreign language education and the study of international affairs at the Tongwenguan (College of Foreign Languages) (1861) and a similar institution in Shanghai, the Guang fangyanguan (1863). These measures foreshadowed the dispatch of China's first diplomatic mission to the court of St. James (1878), and of educational missions to the United States (1872–81) and Europe (1875–92).

In 1872, self-strengthening was extended to economic activities. The China Merchant's Steam Navigation Company (1872), the Kaiping Coal Mines north of Tianjin (1877), and the Shanghai Cotton Cloth Mill (1878) were government-supervised merchant-operated enterprises (*guandu shangban*) established by Zhili governor-general Li Hongzhang to compete with the growing imperialist control of China's domestic economy.

After 1875, the Chinese government organized its naval forces into regional fleets. The failure to coordinate these fleets against the French attack on the Fuzhou Naval Dockyard (August 1884) resulted in their destruction and in China's defeat in the Sino-French War (1884–

85). The postwar establishment of a Board of Naval Affairs (1885) financed by provincial levies intended to unify command of China's fleets and coastal defense installations. Naval development was stymied, after 1889, by the diversion of defense funds for the refurbishing of the summer palace for Empress Dowager Cixi's birthday celebration. The Sino-Japanese War (1894–95), fought principally for the control of Korea, was decided largely by naval warfare. China suffered another humiliating defeat.

Although China's self-strengthening measures proved inadequate to withstand the onslaught of Japan's superior naval forces, the technological, military, diplomatic, educational, and economic changes introduced opened the way for further modernization in the twentieth century. Self-strengthening was limited by the resurgence of traditional practices in education, government finance, and personnel administration during the Tongzhi Restoration (1862–74), and by the dispersal of political power and leadership. Even more inhibiting was the renewed pressure of the imperialist powers on China's borders after 1870. It distracted the principal attention of the self-strengtheners and undercut their efforts at achieving a balanced industrialization.

The Self-Strengthening movement has been regarded by some historians as an early manifestation of anti-imperialist nationalism. However, it may also be viewed as a movement to introduce foreign technology and weaponry *(yangwu yundong)* to suppress rebellion and prolong a dynasty that had capitulated to the imperialist powers. The latter interpretation emphasizes only one domestic aspect of the movement and its political consequences, and overlooks the abundant evidence of anti-imperialist intent and the long-term contribution to China's national growth made by the technology introduced during Self-Strengthening.

Thomas L. Kennedy

References

Kennedy, Thomas L. "Self-Strengthening: An Analysis Based on Some Recent Writings." *Ch'ing-shih wen-t'i* 3 no. 1 (November 1974): 3–35.

Kuo, Ting-yee, and Kwang-Ching Liu. "Self-Strengthening: The Pursuit of Western Technology." *The Cambridge History of China,* ed. John K. Fairbank, vol. 10, 491–542. Cambridge, England: Cambridge University Press, 1978.

Shakee Massacre

See CANTON-HONG KONG STRIKE

Shandong Question

The "Shandong question" refers to the controversy over the disposition of Japanese holdings in Shandong province in the wake of World War I, and as such proved a major stimulus to the burst of Chinese nationalism associated with the May Fourth movement.

In 1898, Germany established the colony of Jiaozhou at Qingdao and received railway and mining privileges aimed at making Shandong into a German sphere of influence. As it turned out, China proved extremely successful in limiting German political and economic power. At the start of World War I, however, Japan joined the Allies and seized the German possessions, subsequently amassing much more influence in the province than the Germans had held. During the war, Japan strengthened its hold on the German possessions by forcing agreements, such as the Twenty-One Demands, on the Chinese government and by negotiating secret treaties involving China with the Allied Powers. In 1917, China too entered the war against Germany, partially in order to establish her case for regaining the German holdings once the *Reich* was defeated. The Wilsonian mirage of the national self-determination of peoples also encouraged China's expectations of ousting Japan.

Nonetheless, when the Versailles Peace Conference convened in early 1919, it became evident that Japan had prepared the way for Allied support of the status quo in Shandong. Japan's position was further strengthened when it made public an agreement of September 1918, in which the Beijing government had "gladly agreed" to maintain Japan's privileges in exchange for a 20 million yen loan. On April 18, 1919, the conference officially confirmed Japan's presence in Shandong over Chinese objections.

This development turned the "Shandong question" into a potent symbol of the twin evils that seemed to be destroying China—warlordism and imperialism—and of their interconnection. On May 4, the momentous student demonstration against the treaty erupted in Beijing. Ultimately, the May Fourth demonstration and the upsurge of nationalism that it unleashed helped to shift the New Culture movement in a political direction. The fact that a new Bolshevik government in Russia supported China against the Allies in the so-called Karakhan Proposals also contributed to the rise of Communism in China.

After the decision at Versailles, the Chinese delegates walked out and refused to sign the treaty. Not until 1922, at the Washington Conference, did Japan agree, with suitable compensation, to return Jiaozhou and the Qingdao-Jinan Railway to China, and to turn over the mines to a joint Sino-Japanese company.

John Schrecker

References

Chow, Tse-tsung. *The May Fourth Movement: Intellectual Revolution in Modern China.* Cambridge, MA: Harvard University Press, 1960.

Hsu, Immanuel C. Y. *The Rise of Modern China.* 3rd ed. New York, NY: Oxford University Press, 1983.

Shanghai Communiqué

The Shanghai Communiqué was a joint communiqué issued in Shanghai by the People's Republic of China (PRC) and the United States on February 28, 1972, at the end of President Richard Nixon's historic visit to China. First among several major documents governing Sino-American relations, the Shanghai communiqué not only established the official basis for normalizing relations between the two countries, but also highlighted a practical approach to existing problems.

Since the Korean War (1950–53), the PRC and the United States had been extremely hostile toward each other. While the United States resolutely supported the Guomindang regime in Taiwan and blocked the PRC from entering the United Nations, the PRC condemned the United States as the "Number One enemy of the Chinese people" and frequently tested the American nerve by bombing the offshore islands controlled by Guomindang troops. The Sino-Soviet tension, which gradually escalated in the 1960s and ultimately exploded into the Sino-Soviet border conflict in 1969, forced Chinese and American leaders to reconsider their relationship.

In July 1971, after several months of sending, receiving, and interpreting often ambiguous signals, Henry Kissinger, President Nixon's National Security Adviser, completed a secret trip to China during which the basic terms of a Sino-American rapprochement were worked out. In February 1972, photos of President Nixon shaking hands with Chinese premier Zhou Enlai at Beijing Airport informed the world that the two largest, but culturally and politically different, countries had finally learned how to get along.

The joint communiqué, whose phrases had been carefully and painstakingly negotiated by Zhou and Kissinger, outlined the principal agreements as well as the fundamental differences between the two countries. The two governments identified their common interests in conducting their relations on the "five principles of peaceful co-existence," opposing Soviet hegemony in Asia, reducing the danger of international military conflict, and facilitating people-to-people contacts and exchanges in science, technology, culture, sports, and journalism. More important, the two sides had committed themselves to promoting the normalization of their relations.

In separate statements within one document, the PRC and the United States had reassured their respective allies in Asia of their commitments and continuous support. On the much thornier issue of Taiwan, the two sides agreed to disagree. While the PRC reaffirmed its position that there is only one China, that Taiwan is a province of China and that the PRC solely represents China, the United States declared that it does not challenge the position that "all Chinese on either side of the Taiwan Strait maintain there is but one China and that Taiwan is a part of China." The PRC insisted that the liberation of Taiwan was China's internal affair and no other country should interfere; the United States reaffirmed its interest in a peaceful solution to the Taiwan issue and pledged to withdraw all American forces under the circumstances of decreasing tension in the Taiwan Strait.

Soon after the document was signed, liaison offices were established in Beijing and Washington. Although the official diplomatic relationship did not materialize until 1979, the door was now open. The communiqué was a historical turning point in Sino-American relations. Since 1972, the succeeding Chinese leaderships and American administrations have all promised to follow the spirit, if not the exact letters, of the Shanghai communiqué.

Shi-ping Zheng

S

U.S. President Richard Nixon and his wife, accompanied by Zhou Enlai, in Beijing in 1972. (Xinhua News Agency.)

References

Garver, John W. *Foreign Relations of the People's Republic of China.* Englewood Cliffs, NJ: Prentice-Hall, 1993.

Harding, Harry. *A Fragile Relationship: The United States and China since 1972.* Washington, DC: Brookings Institute, 1992.

Shen Baozhen (1820–79)

Confucian reformer, administrator, modernizer, and high official of the Qing empire, Shen Baozhen was born into a scholar-gentry family in Fuzhou, Fujian, and was brought up by his parents and teachers to adhere to the noblest of Confucian principles and to apply these in the tradition of the Statecraft *(Jingshi)* School. In 1839, the year Shen passed his provincial examinations, he married the daughter of Lin Zexu. Shen eventually earned his *jinshi* degree in 1847, entered the Hanlin Academy, and received a series of appointments in the imperial capital. In 1854, he was made a supervisory censor for Jiangsu and Anhui, which were being bitterly contested between the Taiping rebels and government forces. His censorial memorials, incisive and critical of the government's management of military affairs and the wartime economy, betrayed a strong reformist bent as well as a courage born out of loyalty to the throne.

During his early years, Shen was influenced not only by the poignant anti-British sentiments of one of his teachers but also by his father-in-law, who played a central role in the Opium War (1840–42). Lin's continued dedication to the dynasty after his exile may also have left a deep imprint on Shen. Shen's loyalty to the throne and the dynasty was given an ultimate manifestation when he and his wife, with only a small number of troops, refused to abandon his prefectural seat of Guangxin, Jiangxi, in the face of a strong rebel onslaught. After the siege was raised by the arrival of reinforcements, Zeng Guofan commended Shen for his loyalty and unswerving adherence to Confucian principles. Shen became a legend in his own time.

Rapid promotions followed. In early 1862, at the age of forty-one, he became the governor of Jiangxi. Although the province was often threatened by the Taipings, Shen, along with his superior Zeng Guofan, now governor-general of the LiangJiang provinces, introduced a series of tax rate reductions. Shen himself also started Jiangxi on the road to rehabilitation. As a result, his province was able to contribute substantially to Zeng's military efforts. But Zeng's demands were great and Shen, unable to meet his needs, became estranged from him.

As governor of Jiangxi, Shen became exposed for the first time to the presence of the West. One unfortunate encounter involved the destruction of properties of the Roman Catholic church and its Chinese followers by the local population. That the anti-missionary riots were allowed to take place was often attributed to Shen's anti-foreignism. But if his handling of foreign affairs is examined as a whole, it becomes evident that his overriding concern was with China's territorial and administrative integrity. In fact, he was generally fair-minded and was ready to acknowledge the advantages of such Western inventions as the telegraph and the steamship.

Shen was an able governor, but just as circumstances were beginning to improve after the defeat of the Taipings, he had to retire to his native Fuzhou to mourn his mother's death in 1865. It was there, in 1866, that Zuo Zongtang persuaded him to accept the director-generalship of the Fuzhou Naval Dockyard, which was then being planned. Out of a sense of patriotism and the need to tend to his aging father at Fuzhou, Shen sacrificed a promising career and took a post that many viewed as unworthy.

For eight years (1867–75) Shen headed China's first full-scale naval dockyard and academy. Despite the stigma attached to this utilization of Western shipbuilding technology, made even less appealing by the presence of a large contingent of French engineers and technicians, Shen directed the naval dockyard with unusual energy and dedication. He encouraged members of his gentry-staff to acquaint themselves with modern science and technology, and created opportunities for job specialization among them. Schools were established to train young Chinese in modern naval warfare, construction, and navigation. Chinese workers and apprentices were also given instruction in modern shipbuilding. The vessels built were used to suppress pirates, rescue merchant ships in distress, and, in 1874 and 1875, to help defend Taiwan during a Japanese invasion. Initially designed to build only fully rigged, steam-powered wooden vessels, the navy yard, under Shen's leadership, quickly moved to building the next generation of warships—composite gunboats with compound engines—immediately after the contract with the Europeans expired in 1874. Graduates of the Naval Dockyard School were also sent to Europe for advanced studies.

The Japanese invasion of Taiwan jolted the Qing court into reexamining its policy of defense modernization. One result was the appointment of Shen to the all-important post of governor-general of the LiangJiang provinces, and the concurrent office of Imperial Commissioner for the Southern Ports. Shen was thus charged not only with the administration of the provinces of Jiangsu, Anhui, and Jiangxi, but also the defense and foreign affairs of the southern coastal provinces. In carrying out the latter duties, his efforts were repeatedly frustrated by the shortage of funds and, worse, by the lack of central planning and decisive leadership from Beijing. Despite his larger powers, therefore, he was unable to implement most of the reforms he had been advocating since the mid-1860s: modernizing the curriculum of the civil service examinations, encouraging the scholar-gentry to study science, centralizing budgeting, and creating a modern naval force. Under these circumstances, Shen had to resort to the rather negative approach of curbing further Western incursions in order to defend China's territorial and administrative integrity. His purchase and destruction of the Wusong (Woosung) Railway, often misunderstood, is a case in point. He was not opposed to the railway *per se,* but to an unauthorized, foreign-owned railway in China.

Shen's administration of the LiangJiang provinces began most promisingly. He worked hard to restore the quality of government and made substantial progress in the reconstruction of the post-Taiping economy. But before the full benefits of his efforts could be felt, the provinces were devastated by successive years of locust plagues which, in turn, were aggravated by the prolonged drought and famine in north China. His own failing health also adversely affected his administration, which came to an abrupt end with his death in 1879.

Shen was an administrator of unimpeachable probity and dedication. He combined Confucian principles with practicality. His patriotism led him to an unusual career path. As a modernizer, he not only gave the Fuzhou Naval Dockyard the most successful period of its entire history, he also used his position in it to acquaint himself with Western technology and to introduce the first modern coal mine and telegraph lines in China. Throughout his career, however, his reforms and modernizing efforts were frequently thwarted by imperial indecision and conservative obstruction. Then, toward the end, his poor health and untimely death also prevented him from leaving a stronger legacy for modern China.

David Pong

References

Pong, David. "Confucian Patriotism and the Destruction of the Woosung Railway, 1877." *Modern Asian Studies* 7, no. 4 (1973): 647–76.

———. *Shen Pao-chen and China's Modernization in the Nineteenth Century.* Cambridge, MA: Harvard University Press, 1993.

———. "The Vocabulary of Change: Reformist Ideas of the 1860s and 1870s." *Ideal and Reality: Social and Political Change in Modern China, 1860–1949,* ed. David Pong and Edmund S. K. Fung. Lanham, MD: University Press of America, 1985.

Shen Congwen (1902–88)

A pioneer of China's modern vernacular literature following the May Fourth movement, Shen Congwen was one of China's eminent writers until silenced by the Communist revolution in 1949. One of his many specialties was stories about the Miao and other mountain tribal minorities of southwest China, in which he tried to impel Chinese nationalism in a cultural, multiethnic direction, as a counterpoint to China's Confucian cultural universalism and to the predominant modern nationalism of his day, which stressed pride in the accomplishments of China's dominant Han ethnic group.

Born in the late Qing into a declining military gentry family in Fenghuang, West Hunan, a mountainous cultural border area inhabited by Han soldier immigrants, Miao tribespeople, and sinicized people of pure and mixed Han, Miao, Tujia, and other tribal ancestry, Shen Congwen was himself of mixed Tujia, Han, and Miao blood, although this was a family secret. He never finished primary school, but in adolescence entered a regional army as a footsoldier, was promoted to clerk, and then to librarian of West Hunan's major independent warlord.

Inspired by the Literature Revolution and the New Culture movement, Shen moved to Beijing about 1922, began writing fiction and essays, and in the 1930s emerged as a professor of literature and writing and as a famous writer. Most observers considered him to be among the half-dozen leading writers of his day, and some regarded him as one of the finest Chinese prose stylists of all time. When his literary reputation was restored in the 1980s after the fall of Maoism (Shen had attempted suicide in 1949 and took refuge in art history for the rest of his life), he became one of the few Chinese authors whom the Swedish Academy seriously considered for a Nobel prize in literature.

Many of Shen's works were rarified and philosophical tales, about urban and erotic themes, and many others were idylls or tragedies with psychological and symbolic overtones. His characters were ordinary Chinese peasants and townspeople, as portrayed in his masterwork, *The Border Town.* Shen Congwen also created one of modern China's earliest and most fully developed regional literatures, dedicated to West Hunan, which he depicted as culturally and morally distinct from the rest of China and Hunan. No more than any other Chinese intellectual did he regard regionalism as antithetical to national unity, but some of his works, including the novel *Long River,* revealed sectionalist pride and advocated West Hunanese autonomy. Regional autonomy in modern China was closely related to warlordism, and as an ex-soldier, Shen also wrote many stories celebrating militarism.

Above all, Shen's stories about the Miao elaborated on the romantic image of the southwestern minorities. Not unlike the historian Gu Jiegang, Shen implied that Chinese culture had originated from the national minorities rather than from an apotheosized Han ethnic group. Although Shen Congwen inevitably simplified and romanticized the southwestern tribal culture and moral ethos, he helped to redefine the

Chinese nation as a multicultural body.

Jeff Kinkley

Shen Jiaben (1840–1913)

Shen Jiaben was the chief architect of the late Qing legal reforms. One of the main excuses of the Western countries in forcing the unequal treaties upon Qing China was the backwardness of the Chinese legal system, hence the introduction of extraterritoriality and other protections of foreign nationals on Chinese soil. Japan, which had suffered a similar fate as China did in the mid-nineteenth century, quickly recognized this fact and successfully reformed her legal system after the Meiji Restoration. The Qing government was slow in comprehension and action. Only after the disastrous Boxer Uprising did the Qing government decide to revise its laws and judicial administration. Shen Jiaben was appointed to take charge of this difficult and critical task.

Born in Zhejiang province in 1840, Shen obtained his *iinshi* degree in 1883 and spent most of his career as an official of the Board of Punishments. In 1902, he and Wu Tingfang headed an official commission to reexamine the Code of the Qing Dynasty. Shen soon suggested to the government the adoption of Western laws in order to obtain "complete control of our territory." As a result, the government abolished a number of cruel penalties, the practice of torture, and collective responsibility, and replaced physical punishments (such as public flogging) with fines in 1905. In 1907, it decreed a new system of courts, separated at the lower level from the administrative system. It also reorganized the Board of Punishments into the Ministry of Justice, in which Shen served as vice-minister. In addition, Shen helped to establish a law school, with foreign teachers, in Beijing.

With the assistance of Japanese legal specialists, Shen then drafted new legal codes for the dynasty. By 1908 a draft of the criminal code, modeled on the Japanese one, had been completed, but other officials severely criticized it for its failure to reflect Confucian social and family morality. It was then revised and promulgated, but not enacted, by the government on the eve of the Revolution of 1911. Drafts of the commercial and civil codes were also completed, but the dynasty fell before their promulgation. The Republic subsequently accepted Shen's draft of the criminal code as its law, which was not revised until 1928.

Shen himself was forced to leave the Ministry of Justice in 1910 because of criticisms of his draft codes. He served briefly as vice-president of the national assembly *(zizhengyuan)* before retiring from politics.

Unquestionably, Shen's enthusiasm for legal reform was motivated by a strong sense of nationalism. By incorporating the Western concepts of equality and the independence of the judiciary into the Chinese legal system, Shen's reforms represented a significant attempt to reshape China into a modern state.

Wang Ke-wen

References

Meijer, Marinus J. *The Introduction of Modern Criminal Law in China.* Batavia: De Unie, 1950.

Tao, L. S. "Shen Chia-pen and Modernization of Chinese Law." *Shehui kexue luncong* no. 25 (September 1966): Taibei, 275–90.

Sheng Xuanhuai (1844–1916)

A leading industrial official in the late Qing, Sheng Xuanhuai, a native of Jiangsu, became a protégé of Li Hongzhang while still in his twenties. His talents in management soon received Li's attention and, in the following decades, he was appointed to various important posts at the government-supervised merchant-operated enterprises *(guandu shangban)* controlled by Li, including the China Merchants' Steam Navigation Company, the Chinese Telegraph Bureau, and the Shanghai Cotton Cloth Mill. In 1896, Sheng took over the management of the iron mine in Hanyang, Hubei, the iron foundry in Daye, Hubei, and the coal mine in Pingxiang, Jiangxi, which became the basis of the Han-Ye-Ping industrial complex he founded in 1908. At the same time, he assumed control of a new railway company, and in 1897 helped to establish the Chinese Commercial Bank and the Nanyang School (later the Communication University) in Shanghai. Such extensive experiences made Sheng the personification of the *guandu shangban* policy during the last years of the Qing dynasty.

A shrewd and well-connected bureaucrat, Sheng was active in regional and national politics as well. During the Boxer Uprising in 1900, he was a principal architect of the Southeast Autonomous movement *(dongnan hubao)* led by the governor-generals Zhang Zhidong, Liu Kunyi, Li Hongzhang, and Yuan

Shikai. In 1911, as Minister of Posts and Communications, Sheng persuaded the Qing government to nationalize the country's main railways and to use them as guarantees for a new loan from the four-power banking consortium. This policy, although probably realistic and even farsighted for the Qing, soon backfired. It provoked the Railway Protection movement in the Middle Yangtze provinces, which in turn led to the Revolution of 1911. In order to placate the opposition, the government dismissed Sheng, but by then it was too late to save the dynasty.

After the fall of the Qing, Sheng fled to Japan. In 1912, as chief manager of the Han-Ye-Ping industrial complex, he concluded an agreement with the Japanese to share the ownership of Han-Ye-Ping with them. The action again caused nationalist attacks and he was forced to give up the post for a while. However, Sheng's long-time friendship with Yuan Shikai, now president of the Republic, quickly secured a rehabilitation. In 1913, upon his return to China, Sheng resumed control over the China Merchants' Steam Navigation Company and the Han-Ye-Ping industrial complex. He subsequently provided critical assistance to Yuan during Yuan's suppression of the Second Revolution. In 1916, in the midst of the national upheaval created by Yuan's aborted monarchical attempt, Sheng died of an illness in Shanghai.

Wang Ke-wen

References

Feuerwerker, Albert. *China's Early Industrialization: Sheng Hsuan-huai (1844–1916) and Mandarin Enterprise.* Cambridge, MA: Harvard University Press, 1958.

Sichuan Railway Crisis

See RAILWAY PROTECTION MOVEMENT

Sino-American Mutual Defense Treaty

On October 1, 1949, the Chinese Communists established the Central People's Government of the People's Republic of China (PRC) in Beijing. By December 1949, the PRC had virtually conquered the mainland of China, and the government of the Republic of China (ROC) had moved to Taibei, Taiwan. On January 5, 1950, American President Harry Truman stated at a press conference that the United States had no intention of interfering in the Taiwan situation and would not provide military aid and/or advice to the "Chinese (ROC) forces on Formosa (Taiwan)."

On June 25, 1950, North Korea invaded South Korea, which prompted the United States to change its policy on Taiwan. Two days later, President Truman declared that he had "ordered the Seventh Fleet to prevent an attack on Formosa," and in the meantime he requested the ROC government in Taiwan to cease military operations against the mainland. With the signing of the Korean Armistice Agreement on July 27, 1953, the PRC again began to prepare an attack on Taiwan, which had been postponed by the PRC's intervention in Korea between late 1950 and mid-1953.

In late 1953, the ROC and the United States exchanged their views on the security problems facing both countries. They entered into negotiations on a mutual defense treaty in early 1954. In mid-October 1954, the PRC began to fire on the ROC-controlled Dachen Islands (250 miles northwest of Taiwan); later, sea and air battles were fought between PRC and ROC forces near these islands. Amid this PRC military action against the ROC, the United States and the ROC signed the Mutual Defense Treaty on December 2, 1954.

The essence of the treaty is reflected in the following articles: Article V—Each party recognizes that an armed attack in the West Pacific Area directed against the territories of either of the parties would be dangerous to its own peace and safety and declares that it would act to meet the common danger in accordance with its constitutional processes. Any such armed attack and all measures taken as a result thereof shall be immediately reported to the Security Council of the United Nations. Such measures shall be terminated when the Security Council has taken the measures necessary to restore and maintain international peace and security. Article VI—For the purposes of Articles II and V, the terms "territorial" and "territories" shall mean, in respect of the Republic of China, Taiwan and the Pescadores; and in respect of the United States, the island territories in the West Pacific under its jurisdiction. The provisions of Articles II and V will be applicable to such other territories as may be determined by mutual agreement. Article VII—The government of the Republic of China grants, and the government of the United States accepts, the right to dispose such United States land, air, and sea forces in and about Taiwan and the Pescadores as may be required for their defense, as determined by mutual consent.

The treaty was accompanied by a December 10, 1954, exchange of notes, wherein the ROC agreed not to use force without "joint agreement," except in a clear case of self-defense. On January 29, 1955, the United States Congress adopted a resolution authorizing the president to employ the American armed forces to protect Taiwan, the Pescadores, and related positions and territories of that area.

On December 15, 1978, President Jimmy Carter announced that the United States and the PRC would establish diplomatic relations on January 1, 1979. He also declared that he would sever diplomatic relations with the ROC on that date, and terminate the Mutual Defense Treaty with the ROC one year from that date. On December 31, 1979, the Mutual Defense Treaty was terminated, but the substance of its terms was replaced by the United States Congress' "Taiwan Relations Act" of 1979.

Hungdah Chiu

References

Chiu, Hungdah, ed. *China and the Question of Taiwan: Documents and Analysis.* New York, NY: Praeger, 1973.
———. *China and the Taiwan Issue.* New York, NY: Praeger, 1979.

Sino-British Agreement On Hong Kong

In 1984, after some 140 years as a British colony, Hong Kong found itself on the verge of the most drastic political change in its history. Sino-British negotiations on the future of Hong Kong commenced in that year. After a period of conflict, they signed an agreement on December 19, 1984, to restore China's sovereignty over Hong Kong on July 1, 1997.

This date was necessitated by the expiration of the New Territories' 99-year lease. Through this lease Great Britain had expanded its Hong Kong domain by pressuring the Chinese (Qing) government in the international "scramble for concessions" in 1898. As a matter of fact, Hong Kong coming under British rule stemmed directly from modern China's humiliation by Western imperialists. China's defeat in the first Opium War led to the 1842 Treaty of Nanjing, which ceded the island of Hong Kong to the British in perpetuity. Then China's defeat in the second Opium War again yielded the peninsula of Kowloon to the British in perpetuity under the 1860 Beijing Convention. The three parcels of domain that constituted the British Colony of Hong Kong were all products of the unequal treaties that impaired Chinese national sovereignty. In this sense, Hong Kong under British rule remains an obstacle to China's drive toward national reunification and sovereignty redemption.

In view of the 1997 expiration date for the New Territories, which constituted some 90 percent of Hong Kong's total land area, British prime minister Margaret Thatcher visited Beijing in September 1982 to start negotiations with Chinese paramount leader Deng Xiaoping. The British originally proposed an extension of their colonial administration for 50 years after 1997. But this was rejected by Beijing, which was keen to resume sovereignty over the entire Hong Kong domain on July 1, 1997. Recognizing Hong Kong's unique status and vital economic contribution to the Chinese mainland, Deng proposed a "One country, two systems" formula for the retrocession of Hong Kong's sovereignty. After two and a half years of secret negotiations between London and Beijing, but without the participation of the Hong Kong people, in September 1984 they reached an agreement, commonly known as the 1984 Sino-British Joint Declaration, on the future status of Hong Kong.

This agreement was formally signed in Beijing on December 19, 1984, by prime ministers Margaret Thatcher and Zhao Ziyang. It stipulates that the whole of Hong Kong, not just the New Territories, would be returned to China on July 1, 1997. The government of the People's Republic of China (PRC), under the "One country, two systems" formula, would establish a Hong Kong "special administrative region (SAR)," which would preserve Hong Kong's existing social, economic, and legal systems for 50 years, until 2047. China would enact a basic law for the Hong Kong SAR to codify the provisions in the joint declaration, to specify the relations between the SAR and the central government, and to provide a constitutional framework for the SAR.

The sovereignty retrocession has ushered in a British decolonization process and also brought forth a process of democratization and localization of the administration of Hong Kong. It has also led to Sino-British-Hong Kong discord on the political front. The joint declaration calls for a post-1997 legislature constituted entirely by election and an executive arm headed by an elected chief executive, with all major government departments and branches headed by local Chinese. However, it is over the pace, scope, and actual implementation of electoral reform and constitutional change that has pitted the Hong Kong people against the British colonial regime and against the PRC government since the late 1980s. Their sharply differing stances on democratization have created much tension in the Beijing-Hong Kong-London relationship, thus rendering a smooth transition in the long term highly problematic. As a matter of fact, the 1984 joint declaration has politicized the people of Hong Kong and drawn much international attention to the uncertain prospects of Hong Kong.

Ming K. Chan

References

Chan, Ming K., ed. *Precarious Balance: Hong Kong Between China and Britain, 1842–1992.* Armonk, NY: M. E. Sharpe, 1994.
———, and David Clark, eds. *The Hong Kong Basic Law: Blueprint for "Stability and Prosperity" Under Chinese Sovereignty?* Armonk, NY: M. E. Sharpe, 1991.

Sino-French War

Fought between China and France, the Sino-French War began as strife over their respective interests in Annam (Vietnam) and ended with hostilities along the China coast. It was China's first major military setback since the second Opium War (1857–60). As a result the Qing dynasty lost Annam as a tributary state, and its modern Fuzhou Naval Dockyard and Squadron were badly damaged.

Trouble began when the French, having established control over southern Annam (Cochin China) in 1862, took steps to extend their influence over northern Annam. Their goal was to gain access to south China via the Red River. In 1874 they imposed a new treaty on the Nguyên dynasty, whereby they obtained the right to direct Annamese foreign relations, and to navigate the Red River.

For more than two thousand years, the Annamese had been strongly influenced by the Chinese. During the Qing period, some fifty tribute missions were sent to China, thereby confirming Annamese acceptance of Chinese suzerainty. The notion of an independent or a French-influenced Annam, therefore, was anathema to the Chinese, who refused to recognize the treaty of 1874. However, beset with other foreign crises (the Ryukyu Incident and the Margary affair), the Qing government took no action.

After a period of relative quiet, the French, under their new expansionist premier, Jules Ferry, adopted a strong policy in 1880. In the next year, an armed expedition sent to Tongking had orders to annex the whole of north Annam. But the French soon met with resistance: the Black Flag Army of Liu Yongfu. Liu, a former Triads member and Taiping rebel in China, had established himself in the region with the blessings of the Annamese government. As the French moved into the area, Liu cooperated with the Annamese in opposing them. Still, the French managed to seize Hanoi with a small naval force in April 1882.

Since the summer of 1879, local and central officials in China had become increasingly concerned with French activities in Annam. But until the French capture of Hanoi, the Chinese had had no policy on Annam. After that, they moved some troops to Tongking from the border province of Yunnan. Meanwhile, Zeng Jize, China's minister to France and Great Britain, lodged a strong protest in Paris. When an attempt to avert armed conflict through negotiations collapsed, Chinese resistance became more determined. Chinese troops were moved to more advanced positions in Tongking. The Chinese navy in Guangdong was also ordered to move into Annamese waters. Inside China, the *Qingyi* literati clamored for war. Meanwhile Chinese troops were moved to the South, arsenals stepped up their production, and Li Hongzhang was ordered to proceed posthaste to Guangdong. Then, in May 1883, Captain Henri Rivière, who had become a French national hero following the capture of Hanoi, was killed by the Black Flag Army. The French, too, wanted war.

Li Hongzhang, however, was reluctant to go to the South and fight. He felt that China's military modernization had not reached a point where it could challenge the French. Besides, he knew that his power base in the North would suffer if he got bogged down in a war in the South. When an opportunity arose in Shanghai for him to negotiate with the French *envoyé extraordinaire*, Arthur Tricou, he welcomed it. Again, the negotiations collapsed, as the *Qingyi* cry for war reached a fever pitch.

Both sides prepared for war. When the Chinese did not comply with the French demand that they withdraw their forces in Annam, the French took action. In late August 1883, the French seized Hué, imposed a new treaty on the Annamese, and reduced their country to a French protectorate. In December, they captured Son-Tay, twenty-some miles upstream from Hanoi, and defeated the Black Flags in the process. Bac-Ninh fell in early 1884, despite the numerical superiority of Chinese and Black Flag forces. This humiliating defeat gave the Empress Dowager Cixi the pretext to purge the Grand Council and the Zongli Yamen of moderates, replacing them with advocates of war. Prince Gong was relieved of his offices while the bellicose Prince Chun, the emperor's father, was to take part in all major policy discussions. The change of leadership in Beijing did not result in turning back the advancing French troops in Tongking. Soon Li Hongzhang found himself at the negotiating table again, this time with the French naval captain François Fournier.

Having effected the preconditions for negotiation, which included the recall of Zeng Jize as minister to France, Li met with Fournier at Tianjin in May 1884. The resultant Li-Fournier Convention called for the immediate withdrawal of all Chinese troops in Tongking to within China's borders. In addition, China was to recognize all treaties signed or to be signed between France and Annam, and there was to be free trade along the entire Chinese-Annamese border. Although the French did not exact an indemnity, and they promised to refrain from expressions injurious to China's national prestige in their treaties with Annam, the convention was highly favorable to the French.

During the negotiations, the Chinese were constantly under threat of a French naval attack on the China coast. Li therefore could not have done better. Yet in signing the convention, he had conceded more than the throne had allowed. Li was therefore more vulnerable than ever before to *Qingyi* attacks. In reporting to the throne, he failed to mention the provision for immediate troop withdrawal from Tongking. In his own communication to the commanders in north Annam, Li did inform them of the provision for withdrawal, but he indicated that they should stay put.

Li had hoped that the French would not be in a position to take over Chinese military positions by the deadline. When the French forces approached the Chinese-held Lang-Son, fighting broke out. In the ensuing three-day battle,

the French lost nearly one hundred men and failed to take the town. The defeat outraged Jules Ferry's government. And when an attempt to settle the dispute failed, the French navy first opened fire on Jilong (Keelung) in northern Taiwan, and then attacked the nascent Fuzhou Squadron on August 23, 1884, sinking or damaging eleven of the thirteen ships, and bombarded the Fuzhou Naval Dockyard. The French subsequently attacked Jilong again, seized the Pescadores, and blockaded the island of Taiwan, the Yangtze River, and major ports along the coast and preventing tribute grain from going north.

The Chinese countered by attacking the French in Tongking, mainly to divert their energies from China. Honors were showered on Liu Yongfu of the Black Flags as Beijing ordered him to attack. Despite some successes, including the capture of Lang-Son, military activities were brought to a halt as news of an armistice arrived in April 1885. The final peace agreement, signed in June, reaffirmed Annam as a French protectorate, allowed free trade at designated ports along the Chinese border, and provided for French technical and material assistance should the Chinese choose to request it when they decided to build railways.

Throughout the hostilities in Tongking and on the China coast, war was never declared by either side. Historians differ on the effect of the war. Some consider it a signal of the end of the twenty-odd-year-old effort at defense modernization and the end of the tributary system. Others feel that China, despite its antiquated equipment and poor training, had fought the French to a standstill. Although the Chinese suffered major losses, the setbacks were never one-sided. They denied the French an indemnity, the wish for exclusive rights to supply materials and personnel for China's future railway construction, and access to natural resources in China. Because China was not soundly defeated, the Chinese government failed once again to commit itself to greater reform and modernization. In the last analysis, the Chinese came out of the war relatively unscathed, because the French objectives were largely localized in north Annam and they had limited resources with which to pursue them.

David Pong

References

Eastman, Lloyd E. *Throne and Mandarins: China's Search for a Policy During the*

S

Sino-French Controversy, 1880–1885. Cambridge, MA: Harvard University Press, 1967.

Sino-Indian Border Conflict

During the first decade of the People's Republic of China (PRC), Sino-Indian relations were generally friendly. The Indian government under Nehru, following a policy of non-alignment, sometimes even acted as an intermediary between the PRC and other Asian countries. Yet there had been long-standing disputes between the two Asian giants concerning their common borders. A section of the Sino-Indian border was based on the so-called McMahon Line, a British-Indian version of the border that was imposed on the Tibetan authorities at the Simla Conference of 1913 and 1914. The line runs along the crest of the mountain ranges between Tibet and India, instead of, as the Chinese maintain, running along the bottom of the ridge on the Indian side. The Chinese government, from that of Yuan Shikai to that of the Beiyang warlords, to that of the Guomindang, had never recognized such an arrangement. In the 1950s the Communist government again indicated to India its intention to negotiate on this matter, but Nehru was not interested.

In 1957, the PRC began to construct a road through the disputed area of Aksai Chin to improve communications between Tibet and Xinjiang. The Indian government did not take notice of this activity until 1959, and then issued a strong protest against the construction, claiming that the road infringed on Indian territory. The matter was not resolved because the Tibetan uprising occurred later that year. As large numbers of Tibetans, including the Dalai Lama, fled to India and found political asylum there, tension along the Sino-Indian border increased and relations between the two countires worsened. In 1962, the Indian government ordered its border troops to move forward and occupy the entire disputed area.

On October 20, 1962, Chinese troops launched a counterattack. They swiftly defeated the Indian army and within days took control of the northeast border of India. It appeared that they were in a position to encircle and destroy the whole Indian army in that region. However, having established their military superiority, and thus their ability to settle the dispute by force, the Chinese forces quickly withdrew and returned to the McMahon Line. A humiliated India accused China of aggression, but her status as the leader of Asia and the Third World suffered a severe blow. Nehru was also effectively intimidated from intervening in Tibetan affairs.

The quick victory dramatically enhanced the international prestige of the PRC. Many South and Southeast Asian countries, such as Pakistan and Indonesia, now looked to Beijing for support. Some African countries were impressed by China's military performance and willing to improve their relations with the new Communist power. The brief Sino-Indian conflict, to a degree, contributed to the rise of the PRC as a leader of the Third World. It also precipitated the deterioration in Sino-Soviet relations because Moscow, despite the conflict, continued to show solidarity with India.

Wang Ke-wen

References

Maxwell, Neville. *India's China War.* London, England: Cape, 1970.

Sino-Japanese Peace Treaty (1952)

Signed by Japan and the Guomindang government in Taiwan on April 28, 1952, the Sino-Japanese Peace Treaty symbolized Japan's support for the Nationalist side in the continuing civil war in China rather than the reestablishment of peaceful relations between China and Japan.

Shortly after the surrender of Japan that ended the Sino-Japanese War and World War II, China was engulfed in a bitter civil war between the ruling Guomindang and the Chinese Communists. By the time the international peace conference was convened in San Francisco in 1951, the Chinese mainland had become the People's Republic of China (PRC) ruled by the Chinese Communists, whereas the Guomindang had taken refuge on the island of Taiwan, still calling itself the Republic of China (ROC). One year before the peace conference, the Korean War had broken out, signaling the beginning of the Cold War in Asia and placing the United States and the PRC on opposite sides of the conflict. As a result, the United States decided to support the Guomindang government in Taiwan in a policy of "containment" against the Communist bloc in Asia, and recognized the ROC as the sole legitimate government of China. As a *de facto* protectorate of the United States in the immediate postwar years, Japan naturally followed in the American footsteps.

Neither the PRC nor the ROC signed the San Francisco Peace Treaty that formally ended the war, but shortly after the conclusion of that treaty, the United States pressed Japan to negotiate a separate peace treaty with the ROC and not with the PRC. Secretary of State John Foster Dulles warned Japanese prime minister Yoshida Shigeru that unless Japan fully committed itself to the Guomindang government in Taiwan, the United States Senate might not approve the San Francisco Peace Treaty. Yoshida, who had hoped for relations with both the ROC and the PRC, had to capitulate.

The Sino-Japanese Peace Treaty formally terminated Japan's control over Taiwan, the Pescadores and the South Pacific islands. The ROC gave up its right to demand any war indemnity from Japan—it was, at any rate, in no position to make such demands. Diplomatic relations between the two governments were established, and trade and communication agreements soon followed. The treaty defined Japan-ROC ties for the next twenty years, until Japan shifted its diplomatic recognition to the PRC in 1972. The establishment of Japan-PRC relations should have nullified the peace treaty of 1952, but unofficial and close ties still have existed between Japan and Taiwan.

Wang Ke-wen

References

Jansen, Marius B. *Japan and China: From War to Peace, 1894–1972*. Chicago, IL: Rand McNally, 1975.

Sino-Japanese Rapprochement

Since the end of the Sino-Japanese War and World War II, Japan had followed the United States in recognizing the Republic of China (ROC), *i.e.*, the Guomindang regime in Taiwan, instead of the People's Republic of China (PRC) established in 1949. In 1952, Japan signed a peace treaty with the ROC and not with the PRC, thus in theory continuing the state of belligerence between itself and the Communist government on the mainland. Trade and unofficial contacts, however, gradually developed between the PRC and Japan. After the PRC sundered its Soviet and East European ties in the 1960s, Japan in fact became the PRC's most important trading partner. Both sides became interested in improving official relations. The final, and most decisive, impetus came in 1971, when the American President Richard Nixon announced his plan to visit the PRC. Perceiving that as a signal of an imminent change in American policy toward China as well as overall strategic considerations in East Asia, the Japanese government decided to move rapidly in shifting

Japanese Prime Minister Tanaka Kakuei (center) touring the Great Wall in 1972. (Xinhua News Agency.)

its diplomatic recognition from the ROC to the PRC.

In September 1972, Japan's new prime minister Tanaka Kakuei visited Beijing. Negotiations between Tanaka and Zhou Enlai, the Chinese premier, went smoothly and led to the establishment of full diplomatic ties between the PRC and Japan. Their joint statement formally ended the abnormal state of affairs between the two governments. Japan expressed regret for the sufferings inflicted on China before 1945, whereas the PRC renounced, as the ROC did twenty years earlier, any claim to a war indemnity. In 1978 the two countries signed a Sino-Japanese Peace and Friendship Treaty, which included, at Chinese insistence, an anti-hegemony clause aimed at the Soviet Union. A series of agreements on trade, travel, and communications were also concluded in the late 1970s.

Wang Ke-wen

References

Jansen, Marius B. *Japan and China: From War to Peace, 1894–1972.* Chicago, IL: Rand McNally, 1975.

Sino-Japanese Treaty of Peace and Friendship (1978)

See Sino-Japanese Rapprochement

Sino-Japanese War, 1894–95

The first war in modern times between China and Japan, the Sino-Japanese War of 1894 to 1895, was fought over their respective interests in Korea. An easy victory quickly catapulted Japan into near big-power status, whereas China's unexpectedly swift defeat brought upon her the sobriquet of "the sick man of Asia," the loss of large parts of the Qing empire to the imperialist powers in the form of "spheres of influence," to be followed by yet another round of unsuccessful reforms, the Hundred Days Reform of 1898.

The war originated in Japan's growing interest in Korea. Appropriately dubbed the "hermit kingdom," Korea was reluctant to establish diplomatic relations with other countries. Its only foreign relations were with China, whose suzerainty it accepted and to whose emperor its king paid tribute. In 1871 to 1873, several Japanese leaders plotted a punitive expedition to invade Korea on the pretext that it refused to recognize the new Meiji government (notwith-standing the humiliating language the Japanese used when announcing their new regime). They subsequently abandoned the expedition, however. Instead, the Japanese resorted to the use of gunboats in 1876 to impose the Treaty of Kanghwa on the Koreans. The treaty opened three ports to trade and, more importantly, described Korea as independent. This latter provision threatened Chinese overlordship in Korea, while it gave Japan a noble-sounding pretext to intervene on Korea's behalf. The Zongli Yamen's failure to protest against this provision weakened China's position further.

Even before 1876, the Chinese had considered opening Korean ports to the imperialist powers in order to forestall any one country from establishing an exclusive foothold there. With the Treaty of Kanghwa and the Japanese annexation of Ryukyu in 1879, the Chinese, reversing the Zongli Yamen's weak policy, set out to counter Japanese influence in Korea. The Qing government thereupon took the management of Korean relations from the Board of Rites and gave it to Li Hongzhang. By this time, the Japanese had already successfully encouraged the creation of a pro-Japanese faction at the Korean court in Seoul and had induced bright Korean youths to study in Japan. Li responded with a two-pronged offensive: (1) he had the Korean government sign commercial agreements with the United States, Great Britain and Germany in 1882, and (2) he strengthened China's ties with the Korean royal family. The latter gesture led to the emergence of a pro-Chinese faction stronger than the one that favored Japan.

Factional conflicts at the Korean court, aggravated by the Sino-Japanese rivalry, soon produced a coup d'état led by the king's father, the Tai Wön Kun, against Queen Min, who had employed Japanese officers for military reforms. In the ensuing violence the Japanese minister was forced to flee and his legation was destroyed. Fearing Japanese retaliation, the Chinese sent three thousand troops to Seoul, restored peace, and took the Tai Wön Kun to China. Difficulties with Japan were settled by the Korean willingness to indemnify Japanese losses and to allow Japanese troops to be stationed at their legation. The Japanese right to send troops to Korea aggravated Sino-Japanese rivalry.

Following the turbulence of 1882, Li Hongzhang exerted China's authority by placing his men in positions that would influence Korean affairs on all fronts—trade, military,

The outbreak of first Sino-Japanese War, 1894. (Courtesy of Nationalist Party Archives.)

diplomatic, and political. He also had Korea sign an exclusive treaty with China to underscore China's overlordship, which ranked the Korean king at the same level as China's commissioner of trade for the Northern Ports (Li's office). This move marked the transition from a tributary to a colonial relationship between the two countries.

Despite certain progressive features, this unequal relationship, exacerbated by Chinese official high-handedness, provoked Korean hostility, especially from the pro-Japanese faction. The latter, incited by the Japanese minister, staged a *coup d'état* in late 1884. It was quickly put down by the Chinese. But the Chinese, in the midst of a war with France, and the Japanese, plagued by financial problems at home, were ready for a settlement. The Tianjin Convention signed between Li Hongzhang and Ito Hirobumi provided for the withdrawal of troops by both sides. The signatories also agreed that, in future, either party would notify Korea and each other when dispatching armed forces to deal with any serious disturbances there. The agreement gave the Japanese a status that virtually equaled that of China in Korea. Japanese incitement of the coup was never condemned.

Following this difficult-to-explain diplomatic flop, Li Hongzhang doubled his effort to strengthen China's position. He made Yuan Shikai China's representative in Korea to direct its internal and external affairs. For a while, the Japanese and the British, fearful of Russian designs on Korea, thought that the Chinese in-

tervention would help thwart Russian expansion. They were therefore willing to countenance a stronger Chinese presence. But Yuan's arrogance and domineering policy provoked the hostility of the Koreans, who became more eager for independence. An overriding concern with political control also blinded Yuan to Korea's need for broad reforms. The Chinese, whose main objective was not territorial expansion, but to use Korea to curb further imperialist inroads in East Asia, ended up by alienating the Koreans and thereby opened the door to Japanese aggression.

The immediate causes of the Sino-Japanese War are to be found in the assassination of a pro-Japanese Korean leader, probably by Yuan Shikai's agents, and in the Tonghak uprising and its suppression in 1894. In an attempt to liquidate the latter, which the government branded as a heterodox movement, the Koreans had requested Chinese military help. The Japanese, having first encouraged the Chinese to intervene, then found ample reason to send their own forces to Korea, as the Li-Ito Agreement of 1884 provided. The war underscored Japanese superiority in equipment and tactics. Having dealt a crushing blow to the Chinese troops at Pyongyang, they inflicted an even more disastrous defeat on the Chinese naval forces. Poor preparation, undue reliance on diplomacy, inadequate training, and a mismatch between weapons and munitions were the oft-cited reasons for China's defeat. The fact that the war was fought largely with Li Hongzhang's forces, with little support from the rest of China, was a further cause for the Japanese victory.

The Treaty of Shimonoseki brought the war to an end. Signed on April 17, 1895, by Ito and Mutsu Munemitsu on the Japanese side and by Li Hongzhang on the Chinese, the treaty provided for Korea's independence, China's payment of an indemnity of 200 million taels, the cession of Taiwan, the Pescadores, and the Liaodong peninsula, the opening of four Chinese ports, and Japanese rights to build and operate factories in China. Thanks to the intervention of Russia, Germany, and France (the Triple Intervention), Japan was forced to give up the Liaodong peninsula in exchange for an additional thirty million taels from China. Taiwan and the Pescadores, however, were taken over by the Japanese after local resistance movements were eliminated. These islands reverted to China after World War II.

David Pong

References

Chu, Samuel, and Kwang-ching Liu, eds. *Li Hung-chang and China's Early Modernization.* Armonk, NY: M. E. Sharpe, 1994.

Bealsey, W. G. *Japanese Imperialism, 1894–1945.* Oxford, England: Oxford University Press, 1987.

Sino-Japanese War, 1937–45

An eight-year war of resistance *(kangzhan)* fought by the Chinese against Japanese invasion, the Sino-Japanese War of 1937 to 1945 led to, and became part of, World War II in Asia.

Although some Chinese historians date the war from the Manchurian Incident of 1931, the generally accepted chronology regards the Marco Polo Bridge Incident of 1937 as the starting point of the war. The origins of the Sino-Japanese conflict, however, may be traced at least to the early 1930s. Following the Japanese conquest of northeast China in the Manchurian Incident, Japan continued her expansion inside the Great Wall. During the first half of the 1930s, the Japanese attacked Shanghai, invaded Inner Mongolia, and conspired to make north China independent of the Chinese government at Nanjing. The Nanjing government, under the Guomindang (GMD), made a series of compromises with the Japanese in order to concentrate on domestic problems.

On July 7, 1937, clashes between the Chinese and Japanese forces at the Marco Polo Bridge near Beiping erupted into a full-scale military conflict. Despite initial hesitation on the part of the Nanjing government, war became inevitable when the Japanese launched another attack on Shanghai on August 13. Chiang Kaishek, leader of the GMD government, hoped that a stiff Chinese resistance in Shanghai would attract the attention and sympathy of the Western powers, and end the war through mediation. This, however, did not occur as the Western countries were worried about their own crisis in Europe. By the end of 1937, Shanghai and Nanjing fell to the Japanese. The Rape of Nanking in December further aroused Chinese hatred toward Japan and enhanced their determination to continue the resistance by force. Yet the Japanese troops were clearly superior in weaponry and in organization. Moving across the north China plain southward and along the Yangtze River westward, they soon occupied most of the major cities and railway lines in eastern and central China. Even a deliberate flooding of the Yellow River by the Chinese government failed to stop them.

Shortly after the outbreak of the war, the GMD government formed an anti-Japanese alliance with the Chinese Communist Party (CCP), known as the Second United Front. In the face of a foreign aggression, the two parties suspended their civil war and joined forces to fight the invader. The GMD government first retreated to Wuhan and, after the fall of that city in October 1938, to the southwestern city of Chongqing in Sichuan province. Together with the government, most of the industries, businesses, and schools in the coastal areas also moved westward to the "great rear" *(dahoufang)* in one of the largest internal migrations in the country's history.

From 1939 to 1944, a stalemate persisted between the Chinese and the invading Japanese, with a vertical line extending from Beiping to Wuhan to Canton as the approximate division between the Japanese occupied territories and free China. After a major counterattack in late 1939 ended in failure, the Chinese could only "trade space for time," waiting and hoping for the arrival of Western assistance. The Japanese, on the other hand, were caught in a "China quagmire"—to further their conquest and occupation in China would exceed their limited strength, yet to withdraw without obtaining significant benefits from the Chinese would be humiliating. In late 1938, Wang Jingwei, Chiang Kaishek's deputy in the GMD government, left Chongqing and went to Hanoi to initiate a peace movement between the two countries. He subsequently signed a peace treaty with the Japanese in Shanghai and established a regime in Japanese-occupied Nanjing. Both the peace movement and the Nanjing regime, however, failed to end the war; most Chinese viewed Wang's actions as treasonous. The Japanese soon abandoned their plan of ignoring Chiang and negotiating peace with other Chinese leaders.

As it was beyond the ability of the Japanese army to control more than major cities and railways in the so-called occupied territories, the vast rural areas in north and east China became a political vacuum after the flight of the GMD government in 1938 and 1939. The situation created a golden opportunity for the CCP to extend its influence behind the enemy lines. With the effective use of guerrilla warfare, the implemention of socioeconomic reforms, and an appeal to anti-Japanese nationalism, the CCP forces built a number of anti-Japanese base areas, known as the "border-region" governments, throughout the occupied territories on the basis of peasant support. The success of the CCP operations resulted in a dramatic increase in its party membership, military strength, and territorial base during the war.

The expansion of the CCP alarmed the GMD government in Chongqing. As the Japanese advances slowed down, the old animosity between the two parties resurfaced. In early 1941, the GMD attacked and decimated a CCP force behind the Japanese line (New Fourth Army Incident), in effect terminating the Second United Front. From then on, until the end of the war, the GMD government imposed a blockade on the CCP central base at Yan'an; the two parties fought separately against the Japanese—and occasionally against each other.

The GMD government itself maintained a difficult existence in Chongqing. Having been cut off from its prewar political and financial base in the coastal provinces, the regime had to cooperate with the militarists and landlords in the Southwest and survived on diminishing resources. Japanese air raids posed a constant and serious threat to the city, as evidenced in the Chongqing tunnel tragedy of June 1941. This dire situation was finally over when the Pacific War broke out on December 7, 1941. With the United States becoming its major ally in the war against Japan, the GMD government began to receive American military and economic assis-

tance. Preserving and strengthening the Sino-American alliance was now a critical task for Chongqing during the remainder of the war. While jealously guarding the American aid against any attempt by the CCP to share it, the GMD eventually had to yield to American pressure and agreed to a rapprochement with CCP toward the end of the war.

In early 1944, active campaigns returned with the launching of "Operation Ichigo" by the Japanese. The main target of the Japanese offensive was southwest China. By the end of that year, the Japanese army had not only taken Hunan but advanced into Guangxi and Guizhou, thereby threatening Chongqing itself. The offensive then stopped because of the Allied victory in the Pacific, but it clearly demonstrated the ineffectiveness of the GMD military. In fact, the last years of the war was a period of increasing demoralization and corruption for the GMD. Dependent on American support, many GMD leaders now paid more attention to their own comfort than to the war effort. Rampant inflation, political repression, and brutal military conscription characterized GMD rule, presenting a sharp contrast to the vigorous and populist atmosphere in the CCP base areas. A gradual shift of popular support from the GMD to the CCP was taking place.

Against this background the war suddenly ended on August 15, 1945. The Japanese surrender, following the atom bombing of Hiroshima and Nagasaki by the United States, caught China by surprise. On September 3, the GMD government formally accepted the Japanese surrender at Nanjing, but a competition between the GMD and the CCP forces for the recovery of formerly occupied territories was underway.

At once devastating and inspiring, the second Sino-Japanese War was arguably the most significant event in the history of twentieth-century China. More than 20 million Chinese died in the war, with an estimated loss of $60 billion in properties. For nearly a decade the country was submerged in the terror and chaos of massive destruction and flight. Meanwhile, a whole generation of Chinese grew up in an environment of national resistance against aggression, enduring the hardship of war or foreign occupation, and learning the meaning of patriotism in real life situations. The war also brought the urban Chinese in the coastal areas closer to the life of their peasant compatriots in the hinterland, and the Chinese peasants closer to the world of national politics. A new political consciousness was created in both as a result. In the years to come, the nationalist fervor that had been created by the war, and vindicated by the final victory, was to be capitalized on by the CCP and its People's Republic. On the other hand, the exhausting war disrupted the nation-building effort of the GMD and weakened its foundation, in the end sealing its fate as China's ruler.

Wang Ke-wen

References

Ch'i, Hsi-sheng. *Nationalist China at War: Military Defeats and Political Collapse, 1937–1945.* Ann Arbor: University of Michigan Press, 1982.

Eastman, Lloyd E., et al. *The Nationalist Era in China, 1927–1949.* Cambridge, England: Cambridge University Press, 1991.

Hsiung, James C., and Steven I. Levine, eds. *China's Bitter Victory: The War with Japan, 1937–1945.* Armonk, NY: M. E. Sharpe, 1992.

Sino-Russian Secret Alliance

After the first Sino-Japanese War (1894–95), some Chinese officials saw Russia as a potential ally in China's attempt to resist Western and Japanese imperialism. Their leader was the Qing government's paramount diplomat, Li Hongzhang, whose view gained the approval of the powerful Empress Dowager Cixi.

China's interest in establishing an alliance with Russia coincided with the desire of the Russian empire to extend the Trans-Siberian Railway across Manchuria and reach the port of Vladivostok. This of course required Chinese consent. In 1896, the Qing government sent Li Hongzhang to St. Petersburg as China's emissary for the coronation of the new czar, Nicholas II. At St. Petersburg, Li conducted lengthy negotiations with Count Witte. Witte promised Li Russian military assistance in case of an emergency in China and argued that a Russian railway in Manchuria would facilitate such assistance. Li was convinced and reached an agreement with Witte: China would permit Russia to construct the Chinese Eastern Railway across Manchuria, which would be owned and operated by Russia but could be redeemed by China after thirty-six years. In return, Russia agreed to defend China against any attack from Japan. A formal treaty, signed at the Rus-

sian capital, sealed the secret alliance.

Although paying a high price in terms of China's sovereignty and territorial integrity, Li viewed the Sino-Russian agreement as a diplomatic victory. China was again able to "use barbarians to control barbarians" *(yiyi zhiyi)*. Yet the secret alliance failed even in the short run to protect China from increasing foreign encroachment, as the "scramble for concessions" in the following years attested.

Wang Ke-wen

References

Lensen, George Alexander. *Balance of Intrigue.* 2 vols. Honolulu: The University Press of Hawaii, 1982.

Witte, Sergei Iul'evich. *The Memoirs of Count Witte,* trans. and ed. Abraham Yarmolinsky. New York, NY: H. Fertig, 1967.

Sino-Soviet Split

A gradual process of strained relationships between China and the Soviet Union in the 1960s that ultimately led to the military confrontations along the border in 1969, the Sino-Soviet split was caused by historical, ideological, and economic factors.

The relationship between the two Communist parties was never an easy one. The Soviet-imposed revolutionary strategy with a focus on the urban areas cost the Chinese Communists dearly in 1927, when Chiang Kaishek's troops seized the cities and massacred tens of thousands of Communists. Stalin's unbalanced support for the Guomindang regime in the 1940s and his disrespect for Mao Zedong was no secret. Mao in turn had relentlessly purged his Moscow-trained opponents in the Chinese Communist Party leadership.

After the Communists took over mainland China, Mao decided to "lean to one side" by concluding a friendship treaty with Stalin in 1950. Although uncomfortable with Beijing's reliance on Moscow, Mao had no choice because the Soviet Union was the only country to which China could turn for economic and military assistance. After Stalin died in 1953 and Khrushchev became the new leader in Moscow, Sino-Soviet tensions reemerged over ideological and economic issues. In 1957, during his second and final trip to Moscow, Mao managed to obtain Khrushchev's promise to continue Soviet technical support for China's industrial development, including assistance to develop atomic weaponry. Yet signs of differences between Mao and Khrushchev over the issues of Stalin, war, and global Communist strategies were already evident.

The Sino-Soviet alliance began to disintegrate in 1958, when Mao launched the Great Leap Forward—an attempt to achieve China's economic growth through mass mobilization. By then Mao had concluded that reliance upon the Soviet Union was damaging Chinese national interests. As China grew increasingly independent of Soviet control, Khrushchev became openly critical of Mao's deviationist tendencies. He was further irritated when Mao initiated military attacks against Guomindang troops in Quemoy without first informing Moscow. The Taiwan Strait Crisis of 1958 was a purely domestic matter for Mao, but for Khrushchev, it was jeopardizing his efforts to improve relations with the United States, because the two superpowers might be dragged into a war on behalf of their respective allies on the mainland and on Taiwan. Khrushchev's refusal to support Mao's military adventures and subsequent decision to renege on the promise to help China's nuclear program convinced Mao that the Soviets could not be trusted.

In anger and frustration, Mao in April 1960 approved the publication of an article in Chinese newspapers on the occasion of the 100th anniversary of Lenin's birth, which condemned the "modern revisionist," *i.e.,* Khrushchev. In June, at a meeting attended by the Communist parties from many countries, the Chinese and Soviet representatives exchanged fierce verbal attacks. On July 16, 1960, Khrushchev suddenly announced the withdrawal of all Soviet advisers and technicians from China, and the cancellation of all Soviet-assisted projects in China. This severe blow came amidst China's worsening economic situation caused by a combination of human errors and natural disasters. For the next four years, the two Communist parties engaged in open polemics.

Although Khrushchev was ousted from office in 1964, Sino-Soviet tensions did not abate. The territorial disputes that began in 1962 prompted both sides to launch massive troop mobilizations along the border. In 1969, small incidents escalated into several military confrontations along the border. Only the danger of a full-scale war, possibly involving nuclear weapons, forced the two countries to cool down. Yet for the twenty years that followed, the two Communist giants remained hostile toward each other, until Mikhail Gorbachev shook hands with Deng Xiaoping during his official visit to Beijing in May 1989.

Shi-ping Zheng

References

Garver, John W. *Foreign Relations of the People's Republic of China.* Englewood Cliffs, NJ: Prentice-Hall, 1993.

Schram, Stuart R. "Mao Tse-tung's Thought from 1949–1976." *The Cambridge History of China,* eds. Roderick MacFarquhar and John K. Fairbank, vol. 15, 1–104. Cambridge, England: Cambridge University Press, 1991.

Zagoria, Donald. *The Sino-Soviet Conflict, 1956–1961.* Princeton, NJ: Princeton University Press, 1962.

Sino-Soviet Treaty of Friendship, Alliance and Mutual Assistance (1950)

See "LEANING TO ONE SIDE"

Sino-Soviet Treaty of Friendship and Alliance (1945)

The Sino-Soviet Treaty of Friendship and Alliance between the Guomindang government and Stalin's Soviet Union granted independence of Outer Mongolia from China as one of its most important consequences.

At the Yalta Conference in February 1945, the United States and Great Britain agreed to Stalin's requests concerning Manchuria and Mongolia in exchange for the Soviet participation, after the surrender of Germany, in the war against Japan. Following the conference, the United States pressured the Chinese government under the GMD to conclude a treaty with the Soviet Union to that effect. In June, Chiang Kaishek dispatched his premier T. V. Soong and his son Jingguo to Moscow for negotiating the treaty. Stalin offered a thirty-year alliance with China against Japan and his support for the GMD government as China's legitimate leader, and demanded special influence in Manchuria and the self-determination of Outer Mongolia in return.

They reached agreements on Manchuria relatively smoothly. China agreed to a Sino-Soviet joint control of the Chinese Eastern and the Southern Manchurian Railways (for thirty years), and to partial Soviet control over the strategic ports of Port Arthur (Lushun) and Dairen. The Soviet Union promised to withdraw her forces completely from Manchuria three months after the defeat of Japan. The Mongolian issue, however, was difficult to resolve. Chiang Kaishek's image as a nationalist leader would be undermined if he allowed the independence of Outer Mongolia, even though Chinese rule over that region had been nominal. Stalin, however, would not yield on this issue.

As the negotiation became protracted, the war situation altered rapidly. On August 6, the Americans dropped the first atom bomb on Hiroshima; two days later, the Soviet Union entered the war against Japan. On August 9, another atomic bomb fell on Nagasaki, and the next day Japan surrendered. Faced with such a swift ending of the war, the GMD government shifted its attention to its renewed civil war with the Chinese Communists. Chiang Kaishek's most urgent concern now was GMD control over Manchuria, which he claimed was the *raison d'être* of the war of resistance against Japan, and the prevention of Soviet assistance to the Chinese Communist Party (CCP). These new considerations forced him to compromise on the Mongolian issue in order to ensure Stalin's support for his government in the impending civil war. On July 30, T. V. Soong, who allegedly opposed the compromise, resigned as Chiang's representative and was replaced by Foreign Minister Wang Shijie. After securing Stalin's promise of non-intervention in Xinjiang, Wang signed the treaty with his Soviet counterpart Molotov on August 14.

The Sino-Soviet Treaty of 1945 might have been unavoidable under the circumstances, but it severely damaged the GMD's claim to Chinese nationalism. While Chiang's government celebrated its victory in an eight-year war with Japan and hailed the recovery of the formerly occupied territories, it peacefully and permanently surrendered another huge piece of Chinese land to the Soviet Union. Outer Mongolia soon declared its independence by means of a plebiscite, and the resulting Mongolian People's Republic became a Soviet satellite.

In addition, the 1945 treaty granted the Soviet Union all the special rights and interests in Manchuria that czarist Russia had lost to Japan after the Russo-Japanese War of 1904 and 1905. In a sense, the treaty virtually nullified the Chinese victory in the Sino-Japanese War. The promises Chiang obtained from Stalin in the treaty in the end did not materialize.

During their postwar occupation of Manchuria, the Soviet troops found ways to assist the CCP in competing with the GMD for control of the region. When the People's Republic was proclaimed in 1949, Moscow was the first country in the world to offer its diplomatic recognition. After its defeat and retreat to Taiwan, the GMD unilaterally abrogated the treaty, but its successor in China, the new government under the CCP, had to accept its consequences.

Wang Ke-wen

References

Garver, John W. *Chinese-Soviet Relations, 1937–1945.* Oxford, England: Oxford University Press, 1988.

Levine, Steven I. *Anvil of Victory: The Communist Victory in Manchuria, 1945–1948.* New York, NY: Columbia University Press, 1987.

Liang, Chin-tung. "The Sino-Soviet Treaty of Friendship and Alliance of 1945: The Inside Story." *Nationalist China during the Sino-Japanese War, 1937–1945,* ed. Paul K. T. Sih. New York, NY: Exposition Press, 1977.

Sino-Vietnamese War

During the Vietnam War of the 1950s to the 1970s, the People's Republic of China (PRC) offered moral as well as material support to North Vietnam. Chinese weapons and advice were crucial to the early victories of the Vietnamese in their war against the French. In the American stage of the war, China provided around 300,000 technicians and troops, and more than $15 billion in economic aid to Hanoi. When the war ended in 1975, however, the new Socialist Republic of Vietnam accepted the friendship and alliance of China's bitter rival, the Soviet Union.

In December 1978 Vietnam, under Moscow's patronage, launched an invasion of her communist neighbor Cambodia, and by January 1979 the Vietnamese army had conquered Cambodia and destroyed the Chinese-backed Pol Pot regime. The invasion was at least in part a reaction against the normalization of relations between the PRC and the United States on January 1, 1979. The PRC regarded the invasion and the Soviet-Vietnamese alliance as an act of betrayal by Vietnam and an attempt by the Soviet Union to establish her hegemony in Asia. From late January to early

February, China's new leader, Deng Xiaoping, visited the United States. He apparently obtained American consent to China's forthcoming actions against Vietnam. A week after Deng's return to Beijing, Chinese troops crossed the border and invaded Vietnam.

China claimed that her invasion was in retaliation against Vietnam's repeated incursions into Chinese territory, but in fact it was a punishment for the recent Vietnamese actions. The PRC tried to conduct the war on the model of the Sino-Indian border conflict of 1962, with a swift victory and a quick withdrawal, but this time it underestimated its enemy. The thirty-year war with the French and the Americans had hardened the Vietnamese, and they now possessed the best American as well as Soviet arsenals left from that war. A total of 250,000 Chinese troops, equipped with tanks and fighter planes, mounted a massive attack in mid-February. It was successful in the beginning, taking four Vietnamese provincial capitals within one week. The Chinese advance, however, soon bogged down. Experienced in guerrilla warfare, the Vietnamese avoided major confrontations with the invader and opted for skirmishes and harassments. As Chinese hopes for a quick victory faded, the danger of Soviet intervention loomed large. In early March, after a hard-fought victory at Lang-Son, the PRC called for a ceasefire and announced the withdrawal of its troops. Hanoi agreed, and Chinese troops completed their withdrawal from Vietnam in mid-March.

During the seventeen-day war China succeeded in occupying almost all the major cities in northern Vietnam. Beijing claimed to have accomplished its objectives in the war; it had taught the ungrateful former ally a lesson. Yet the war also taught China a lesson. China suffered 46,000 casualties and lost much equipment. Moreover, the Chinese discovered that they lacked modernized military technology. The over $1 billion cost of the war had a negative effect on the PRC's "four modernizations," but the leaders in Beijing now keenly recognized their country's need for strengthening its military establishment.

Wang Ke-wen

References

Hood, Steven J. *Dragons Entangled: Indochina and the China-Vietnam War.* Armonk, NY: M. E. Sharpe, 1992.

Lawson, Eugene K. *Sino-Vietnamese Conflict.* New York, NY: Praeger, 1984.

Ray, Heman. *China's Vietnam War.* New Delhi: Radiant, 1983.

Social Darwinism

The origin of Social Darwinism can be traced to the Enlightenment idea of progress. However, whereas the idea of progress related mostly with the normative of the evolutionary process and its connection to the universe, Social Darwinism focused on its implications in human affairs and organizations. It was this focus that attracted the attention of the late-nineteenth-century Chinese intellectuals, who were searching for a nationalistic solution to China's problems.

Yan Fu was the first person to introduce Social Darwinism to China. In 1895, when China was defeated by Japan in the first Sino-Japanese War, Yan called on his countrymen to examine the key of success in the West. The awareness of the life-and-death competitive process in the universe, Yan contended, prescribed the Westerner to seek for ways to survive in this malevolent world. The consequence of their efforts was the formation of an organic society in the modern times. To avoid deterioration or distinction, Yan suggested that China should reorganize its own society on the Western model.

The organic view of society was in fact a notion of proto-national society. Yan's call for a reexamination of the traditional idea of society in China challenged the Confucian order. It pointed to a new direction of thinking for Chinese reformers, who had been concerned only with issues of technology and political institution. Once enlightened by Yan, however, reformers rode the mounting tide of reform in China beyond Yan's initial formulation. The reformers took one step further in identifying the specific agent for the task of reconstructing Chinese society. Their differing views on what the best agent might be in the Darwinist world drew the line between the constitutionalists and the revolutionaries during the last decade of the Qing dynasty.

For the constitutionalists, preserving the Qing dynasty was necessary for further reforms in China. Crucial to their position was the belief that the state is the only possible agent for social progress in the Darwinist evolutionary process. Liang Qichao, the most outspoken leader of the constitutionalist camp, argued that in the present world the states were the principal units in the competition among human beings for survival. This was the result of the development of human society from the "savage" to the "civilized" condition—in other words, the state is the highest expression of human civilization to date. In order to survive and also to be a civilized person, therefore, an individual had no alternative but to submit to the sovereignty of the state.

Liang's statist view of Social Darwinism was refuted by the naturalist view of the revolutionaries. The revolutionaries, such as Wang Jingwei and Zhang Binglin, opposed the imposition of the state upon the individual. Instead, they stressed that competition in the present world existed among national societies formed on the basis of ethnic homogeneity. Ethnicity provided a cultural ground for individuals to build a natural society from the bottom up, rather than having one imposed from the top down. The revolutionaries' arguments proved to be more persuasive than those of the constitutionalists among China's younger generation. It not only appealed to their longing for individual liberation, but supplied a rationale for their anti-Manchu sentiments.

Social Darwinist influence in China gradually declined after World War I. The outcome of the Great War disappointed many Chinese intellectuals, who had believed that either competition among the states or among the natural societies would bring progress to human civilization. Now it seemed that the expansion of national power had instead led to self-destruction among the Western countries. After the war, Chinese intellectuals sought frameworks that would permit cooperation among peoples of different identities. The most noteworthy example of such collaboration was the Communist movement, which advocated an alliance of the oppressed classes regardless of their ethnic or national backgrounds.

In addition to the class approach, anti-imperialism during the 1920s also suggested the conclusion of an alliance among the oppressed countries in the world. While it still adhered to the idea of progress, the anti-imperialist framework had moved away from the notion of natural selection and given a new context for the discourse on ethnicity. After the 1920s Social Darwinism ceased to be an important component in the Chinese concept of the nation-state.

Chiu-chun Lee

References

Chang, Hao. *Liang Ch'i-ch'ao and Intellectual Transition in China, 1890–1911.* Cambridge, MA: Harvard University Press, 1971.

Schwartz, Benjamin I. *In Search of Wealth and Power: Yen Fu and the West.* Cambridge, MA: Harvard University Press, 1964.

Socialism with Chinese Characteristics

China's economic reforms began several years after the arrest of the Gang of Four in 1976, which symbolized the end of Cultural Revolution ideology and of Maoist economic theory and practice. The much-heralded economic reforms began with a series of local rural experiments approved by the third plenum of the Eleventh Central Committee of the Chinese Communist Party (December 1978) and led to the de-collectivization and comprehensive reorganization of China's agricultural sector.

Several years later, the reforms spread to the urban industrial, financial, and banking sectors. Enterprise management, labor allocation, capital investment, foreign trade, property ownership, and price determination were all dramatically modified to encourage decentralized decision making, enterprise autonomy, and freedom of economic choice. Fewer and fewer commodities were produced, allocated, and priced by the national economic plan. More and more fell under the influence of free-market forces.

The Chinese leadership under Deng Xiaoping did not regard these reforms as replacing socialism with free-market capitalism, but as an attempt to make the planning system more flexible and efficient by narrowing its scope. This was a euphemism for decentralization and depoliticization of economic decision making. "Making planning more efficient" meant the introduction of economic rationality and competitive market institutions into an otherwise socialist economy. Economic reform implied a pragmatic shift from "putting politics in command" to "putting economics in command," but the general goal of building socialism in China remained.

To make the reforms compatible with Marxist principles, Deng's leadership argued that China in the late 1970s had not yet attained the stage of a "true," or "advanced," socialism, mainly because the prerequisite economic foundations had yet to be established. It was therefore essential for China to undergo an extra stage of development, called the "primary stage of socialism," during which interval these economic foundations could be prepared. "Advanced socialism," according to this analysis, is the final stage prior to communism, when socialist principles are fully operational. But the economic and social prerequisites set forth by Marx have to be securely established during the primary stage.

The primary stage is an amendment of sorts to orthodox Marxist development theory. It stipulates the introduction of free markets and other capitalist-type institutions into China's economy. The resulting economic configuration, which has been called "socialist commodity production," reflects the Marxist definition of a commodity as a product which is produced for the purpose of being sold in the market. That is, commodities are goods which are produced to meet the demands of the marketplace rather than the commands of the central planners. It involves not only the use of markets but also the decentralization of economic decision-making.

During the 1980s and 1990s, this view of socialist commodity production became the theoretical basis for the reformist economic development strategy. This newly conceived Chinese road to socialism was thought to reflect more accurately the actual conditions existing in China, and hence came to be known as "socialism with Chinese characteristics."

The term signifies an intense desire by the Chinese leadership to sinify—to make uniquely Chinese—the economic reforms and experiments undertaken since the death of Mao Zedong. It reflects the mixture of strong nationalistic sentiment with political economic ideology, theory and practice. The term also suggests that true socialism would take a long time to achieve, an idea that resembles Mao's own thoughts prior to 1955.

Peter M. Lichtenstein

References

Harding, Harry. *China's Second Revolution: Reform After Mao.* Washington, DC: Brookings Institution Press, 1987.

Hsu, Robert C. *Economic Theories in China, 1979–1988.* Cambridge, England: Cambridge University Press, 1991.

Riskin, Carl. *China's Political Economy.* Ox-

ford, England: Oxford University Press, 1987.

Society for the Study of European Affairs (Oushi Yanjiuhui)

After the failure of the Second Revolution (1913) against Yuan Shikai, Sun Yatsen and his followers fled overseas. In 1914, Sun organized the Chinese Revolutionary Party *(Zhonghua gemingdang)* in Japan to continue his anti-Yuan effort. Because the new Party demanded absolute personal loyalty to Sun, many of Sun's former followers refused to join. These revolutionaries established the Society for the Study of European Affairs *(Oushi yanjiuhui)*, which became their own organization in Japan. It was so named because the alleged purpose of the society was to discuss the possible impact of the European war (World War I) on China.

Leading members of the society included Li Genyuan, Li Liejun, Niu Yongjian, Zou Lu, and Chen Jiongming. They supported Huang Hsing, then in America, as their leader, but the actual moving force behind the society was Li Genyuan. When Japan presented the Twenty-One Demands to Yuan Shikai's government in January 1915, the society judged it necessary to side with Yuan in this foreign crisis. Yuan, they argued, after all represented the Chinese national interest in this incident, and Japan posed a threat to all Chinese. The society believed that a solidarity with Yuan would, if not strengthen Yuan's position in his negotiation with the Japanese, at least show the patriotism of the anti-Yuan revolutionaries during a national crisis. The society acted in sharp contrast to the position of Sun Yatsen's party. The latter insisted on opposing Yuan at all cost. Later that year, Yuan began his effort of proclaiming himself emperor of China. Members of the society quickly resumed their anti-Yuan activities, but the society ceased to function as a group. Li Liejun played a major role in the National Protection movement *(Huguo yundong)* in Yunnan that eventually overthrew Yuan's government.

Wang Ke-wen

References

Hsueh, Chun-tu. *Huang Hsing and the Chinese Revolution.* Stanford, CA: Stanford University Press, 1961.

Yu, George T. *Party Politics in Republican China: The Kuomintang, 1912–1924.* Berkeley: University of California Press, 1966.

Society for The Study of National Strengthening (Qiangxuehui)

See KANG YOUWEI; STUDY SOCIETIES

Song Jiaoren (1882–1913)

Anti-Manchu revolutionary and leader of the parliamentary Guomindang during the early Republic, Song Jiaoren was born to a gentry family in Taoyuan, Hunan province, and received a classical education as a youth. After earning a *shengyuan* degree, however, he enrolled in a new-style school in Wuchang in 1902. Song was influenced by anti-Manchu ideas early in life. He was briefly involved in Tang Caichang's Zilijun (Independent Army) Uprising in 1900. In 1903, when his fellow-provincial Huang Hsing returned from Japan to organize revolts in Hunan, Song became a leading member of Huang's Huaxinghui (China Arise Society). The Qing government soon discovered their revolutionary plot, and Song was forced to flee to Japan in 1904.

In Japan, Song studied at Waseda University and founded a revolutionary journal, *Twentieth-Century China*. His writings in the journal suggested a deep appreciation of Japanese nationalism and militarism, but the Japanese government suppressed the journal because of its anti-Manchu stance. In 1905, Sun Yatsen returned to Tokyo. Together with Huang Hsing, Song agreed to merge the Huaxinghui with other revolutionary groups and form the Tongmenghui (Revolutionary Alliance), with Sun as its leader. *Twentieth-Century China* was revived under the new name of *Minbao* and served as an organ of the Tongmenghui. During a trip to the Chinese-Korean border in 1907, to enlist local bandits in staging revolts in Manchuria, Song uncovered Japan's attempt to falsify border lines in order to incorporate parts of Manchuria into Korea. He subsequently incorporated his findings into a book and revealed its contents to the Qing government. This information assisted the Qing to reject Japanese territorial demands.

Song returned to China in early 1911. After writing briefly for the revolutionary newspaper *Minlibao* (People's Independence) in Shanghai, he participated in the Canton Uprising in April. The failure of that uprising furthered Song's dissatisfaction with Sun Yatsen's leadership, and he soon organized the Central China branch of the Tongmenghui, which in effect was independent of the Tokyo headquarters. When the Wuchang Uprising erupted later that year, Song joined Huang Hsing in leading the revolutionaries and planning for a republican government. By this time Song had become an advocate of the parliamentary system, which conflicted with the presidential system proposed by Sun Yatsen. In January 1912, Sun became provisional president of the Republic; he appointed Song to head the Legislative Bureau in the new government. Months later, Sun yielded the presidency to Yuan Shikai, who then appointed Song as minister of agriculture. The provisional constitution that Sun promulgated before leaving office, however, was drafted by Song's bureau and included many features of a parliamentary system.

In order to lead the Republic onto the path of parliamentary democracy, Song merged the Tongmenghui with several smaller political groups to form a new party, the Guomindang. The party elected Sun as chairman and Song as its acting chairman. Song openly criticized Yuan Shikai, whose commitment to the Republic he questioned, and believed that only a strong parliament could restrain Yuan's power. In late 1912, the Guomindang won the first general election of the Republic and became the majority party in the new parliament. It was likely that Song would be the next premier. In March 1913, on his way to Beijing to meet with Yuan, Song was assassinated at the Shanghai railway station. The evidence suggests that the killing was ordered by Yuan himself.

Wang Ke-wen

References

Liew, K. S. *Struggle for Democracy: Sung Jiao-ren and the 1911 Revolution*. Berkeley: University of California Press, 1971.
Price, Don C. "Sung Chiao-jen, Confucianism and Revolution." *Ch'ing-shih wen-t'i* 3, no. 7 (November 1977): 40–66.

Soong Meiling (b. 1897)

Soong Meiling (Madame Chiang Kaishek), the younger sister of T. V. Soong, Soong Ailing (wife of H. H. Kung), and Song Qingling (Madame Sun Yatsen), was one of the most powerful women in the republican era.

Meiling's family came from Hainan Island, but she was born in Shanghai where her father, Charles Jones Soong, had become a successful missionary and businessman. Because of her father's American training and connections,

Meiling grew up in a highly westernized environment. At the age of eleven, she went to the United States with her sister Qingling. She became fluent in English and eventually graduated from Wellesley College in 1917. Upon returning to Shanghai, she did church and social work.

In 1927, through the arrangement of her sister Ailing, Meiling married the Guomindang (GMD) general Chiang Kaishek. Chiang, who was ten years older, already had two wives and a concubine at the time. He formally divorced his first wife (Mao Fumei) and the concubine (Yao Yecheng) and sent the second wife (Chen Jieru) to the United States before marrying Meiling. The marriage had significant, and intended, political effects. It occurred in the midst of the Northern Expedition, and Chiang had just resigned from his position as commander-in-chief of the National Revolutionary Army due to the Nanjing-Wuhan split. Marrying a member of the powerful Soong family not only gave Chiang the prestige of being the late Sun Yatsen's brother-in-law, won him the support of T. V. Soong and H. H. Kung (with their valuable influence in Shanghai's financial circles), but also brought him Western friendship. In order to persuade Meiling's mother to agree to this marriage, Chiang promised to convert to Christianity—which he did in 1930. The alliance between Chiang and the Soong family vastly increased Chiang's political strength and contributed to his return to political power in early 1928.

During the Nanjing Decade (1927–37), Meiling directed women's work in the GMD and the government, served as a member of the Legislative Yuan, and helped establish a modern Chinese air force. At times she also acted as Chiang's interpreter and adviser. But the most important task she performed was to enhance Chiang's ties with Westerners in China and the Western countries. The fact that Chiang had an American-educated wife, and that both of them were Christian, created an extremely positive impression of Chiang and the Nanjing government in the American missionary community in China. Through the propaganda of such supporters as the publisher Henry Luce, this impression was passed on to the American public in the 1930s and continued to be popular in that country during World War II.

During the Xian Incident in 1936, Meiling, together with the Australian adviser W. H. Donald (whom she introduced to Chiang), played key roles in the negotiation that resulted in the release of Chiang. She later published a book in English about the incident, *Sian: A Coup d'État*. When the second Sino-Japanese War broke out in 1937, Meiling helped mobilize and train Chinese women for the war effort as director of the Women's Advisory Committee of the New Life movement. Later in the war, she again took the responsibility of securing Western, especially American, assistance for Chiang's government in Chongqing. She wrote articles and gave speeches in English, published such works as *This Is Our China* (1940) and *China Shall Rise Again* (1941) for Western audiences. In 1942 and 1943 Meiling visited the United States, where she became the first Chinese and the second woman ever to address the joint session of the United States Congress. Her international prestige reached its peak during this trip. The woman who once reportedly declared, "the only thing Oriental about me is my face," now became, in the words of an American commentator, "the personification of Free China." In 1943, she accompanied Chiang to the Cairo Conference.

At the same time, Meiling's relatives became notorious for their corruption and lavish lifestyle during the war. Both T. V. Soong and H. H. Kung came under attack by other factions in the GMD; this naturally had a negative effect on Meiling's reputation and her relationship with Chiang. Shortly after the Japanese surrender, the Guomindang–Chinese Communist Party (GMD-CCP) civil war began. This time, American public opinion and government aid were not as easy to win by the GMD as in the past. During 1948 to 1950, Meiling was on another mission to the United States to obtain support for Chiang's government, but her mission proved unsuccessful. By the time she left the United States, the GMD had been driven out of the mainland by the Chinese Communists and had retreated to the island of Taiwan.

In Taiwan Chiang still, and probably more than ever, needed American support. During the precarious months in 1950, Chiang appointed Meiling's protégé, the American-educated Wu Guozhen, as governor of Taiwan in order to impress the United States. Meanwhile Meiling founded and headed the Chinese Women's Anti-Communist League. She paid several unofficial visits to the United States in the 1950s and 1960s, acting as Chiang's personal envoy. It is believed that she and her family, many of whose members now resided in the United States, played an important part in supporting the influential "China Lobby" in America.

In the 1970s, it became clear that Chiang decided to pass his power in Taiwan to his son Jingguo (born by his first wife). Meiling was not on good terms with Jingguo, who had arrested her nephew for black-marketing in Shanghai in 1948 and had ousted Wu Guozhen from Taiwan in 1953. As chairperson of the GMD's Central Advisory Committee, she was in no position to compete with Jingguo for Party or government leadership. Shortly after Chiang Kaishek died in 1975, Meiling left Taiwan for the United States and took permanent residence in Long Island, New York. In 1986 until 1991 she returned to Taiwan for a long visit. During that period Jingguo died. As the aging matriarch of the ruling family, she gave her blessing to Jingguo's successor Li Denghui.

Wang Ke-wen

References

Hahn, Emily. *The Soong Sisters*. New York, NY: Doubleday, 1941.
Seagrave, Sterling. *The Soong Dynasty*. New York, NY: Harper & Row, 1985.

Soong Qingling (1893–1981)

Soong Qingling, Madame Sun Yatsen, was a supporter of the Chinese Communist Party (CCP) and leader of the People's Republic.

Born in Shanghai, Qingling was the second of the three Soong (Song) sisters: Ailing, Qingling, and Meiling. She went to the United States in 1908, together with Meiling, for a college education. Upon graduating from Wesleyan College in 1913, Qingling returned to China. That year, Sun Yatsen fled to Japan following the failure of his Second Revolution against Yuan Shikai. Ailing, who was Sun's secretary in Japan but now about to marry H. H. Kung, turned her job over to Qingling. Qingling went to Japan immediately. One year later, she married Sun, who was twenty-six years her senior and already had a wife, a mistress and two children. The marriage was said to have been opposed by both the Soong family and some of Sun's followers.

For the next decade, Qingling was Sun's close companion and assistant. She accompanied Sun in the founding of three successive Canton regimes—and the collapse of two of them. During Chen Jiongming's *coup d'etat* against Sun in 1922 Qingling bravely protected

Sun Yatsen and Madame Sun (Soong Qingling) in the early 1920s. (Courtesy of Nationalist Party Archives.)

Sun at the risk of her own life and safety. She suffered a miscarriage as a result. When Sun reorganized his Guomindang under the new alliance with the Soviet Union and the CCP in 1923, Qingling was a firm supporter of this radical line. In 1925 she went to Beijing with Sun for a conference with the leaders of the Beijing government. Sun became ill and died in Beijing in March. On Sun's death-bed Qingling helped him draft an English letter to the Soviet Union, which was then accepted as one of Sun's last testaments.

After Sun's death Qingling became a member of the GMD's left wing. During the Nanjing-Wuhan split in 1927, she was a leader of the pro-United Front Wuhan regime. When that regime also terminated the United Front, she broke off with the GMD leadership, accusing the party of betraying the wish of its former leader, her late husband. Frustrated by the decision of her brother (T. V. Soong) to join the anti-Communist government in Nanjing and by Meiling's plan to marry the leader of that government, Chiang Kaishek, Qingling left for the Soviet Union and stayed abroad for nearly four years. The self-imposed exile was interrupted only by a brief trip to China in 1929 to attend the state funeral of Sun Yatsen in Nanjing. While in Berlin, Qingling supported the effort of Deng Yanda, another former member of the GMD's left wing, to organize the Third Party. The Third Party, later adopting the name Provisional Action Committee of the Guomindang, continued to uphold the radical line of the GMD-CCP United Front but presented itself as an alternative to the two existing parties.

Qingling returned to China in June 1931, shortly before the Manchurian Incident, and soon organized popular support for the Chinese resistance against Japan during the January Twenty-Eighth Incident (1932) in Shanghai. She continued to oppose Chiang Kaishek's Nanjing regime, which all of her sisters and brothers now worked for. Angered by the arrest and execution of Deng Yanda by Chiang in late 1931, Qingling organized the China League for Civil Rights (Zhongguo minquan baozhang tongmeng) with the help of Cai Yuanpei and Yang Xinfo. The league helped rescue and defend dissidents, mostly Communists, who had been arrested by Nanjing. It became such an annoyance to Nanjing that Chiang's men assassinated Yang in 1933, allegedly in an attempt to intimidate Qingling. Qingling was undaunted; she remained active politically and maintained contacts with a group of leftist Western journalists and writers in Shanghai.

Following the outbreak of the Sino-Japanese War in 1937, Qingling moved to Hong Kong. She founded the China Defense League (Baowei Zhongguo tongmeng) there for the purpose of China's wartime relief and children's welfare, but the league also supplied medical aid to the CCP base areas in the hinterland. Wartime nationalism led to a temporary rapprochement between Qingling and Chiang Kaishek, as well as other members of her family. In 1940, she flew with Ailing and Meiling to Chongqing, where the Soong sisters cooperated in wartime relief work and in the promotion of industrial cooperatives, or the Gung Ho movement. In 1945, she accompanied T. V. to Moscow for the negotiation of the Sino-Soviet Treaty of Friendship and Alliance—she was considered a leading pro-Soviet figure in China at the time. During the GMD-CCP civil war of 1945 to 1949 Qingling revived her attack on Chiang's government. She briefly participated in an abortive attempt to organize another third party, but in 1949 accepted Mao Zedong's invitation to attend the Chinese People's Political Consultative Conference in Beijing, and soon became vice-chairman of the CCP's new government.

In the People's Republic, Qingling was honored with a number of ceremonial posts with no real power or responsibilities. Hailed by the CCP as a model of Chinese women and of non-Party "democrats," she symbolized both the legacy of Sun Yatsen and national unity under the CCP. She also worked to attract international friendship for the Beijing government, joining several official delegations to Eastern Europe and South Asia in the 1950s and 1960s. During the Cultural Revolution of 1966 to 1976 her house in Shanghai was ransacked and she was denounced by the Red Guards, but thanks to the protection of Zhou Enlai she was saved from further persecutions or purge. Qingling lived to see the end of the Mao era and the post-Mao reforms under Deng Xiaoping. She was named honorary chairman of the People's Republic and inducted into the CCP shortly before her death in 1981.

Wang Ke-wen

References

Chang, Jung (with Jon Halliday). *Madame Sun Yat-sen*. New York, NY: The Viking Press, 1986.

Hahn, Emily. *The Soong Sisters*. New York, NY: Doubleday, 1941.

Snow, Helen Foster. *Women in Modern China*. New York, NY: Humanities Press, 1967.

Soong, T. V. (Song Ziwen, 1894–1971)

T. V. Soong was a financier, a diplomat, a major figure in the Guomindang government, a strong promoter of economic modernization, and an advocate of close ties with the Western powers.

Born in Shanghai to a highly Americanized, Christian family, T. V. Soong received his B.A. from Harvard University in 1915, studied at Columbia University, and worked briefly on Wall Street before returning to Shanghai in 1917. Soong's career shifted from business to politics, largely through the connections of his sisters. His eldest sister Soong Qingling married

S

Chinese revolutionary leader Sun Yatsen in 1914; his youngest sister Soong Meiling married Chiang Kaishek in 1927.

Through these ties and with his strong background in banking and business, Soong became a leading figure in the GMD government. First in Canton in 1925 and later in Chiang's Nanjing regime, Soong served as minister of finance and founder of the Central Bank of China. In these posts Soong proved invaluable to Chiang by raising funds on the Shanghai bond market to cover the deficits generated by Chiang's military campaigns. Soong also created the National Economic Council to foster China's economic development.

Despite his importance to the government, or perhaps because of it, Soong's relationship with Chiang and other family members was not always smooth. After the Manchurian Incident in 1931, Chiang advocated appeasing the Japanese and fighting the Chinese Communists, whereas Soong not only favored stronger resistance to Japan, but felt unable to fund the increasingly costly anti-Communist campaigns. This disagreement, and pressure from Tokyo, led Chiang to replace Soong as minister of finance in 1933 with their mutual brother-in-law, H. H. Kung, the husband of Soong Ailing. Soong's dismissal did not mean a complete withdrawal from public affairs. He remained active in the National Economic Council and founded the semi-private China Development Finance Corporation. In March 1935, when Kung decided to bring the Bank of China (China's largest bank) under tighter government control, he appointed Soong as the new director. From these positions Soong played an active public and a semi-private role in China's business and banking. Also, during the Xian Incident of December 1936, Soong flew to the beleaguered Chiang, acting in conjunction with his sister Soong Meiling.

Following the Japanese invasion of China in the summer of 1937, Soong became more involved in diplomatic affairs. His fluency in English and broad knowledge of the United States prompted Chiang to send him to America as his personal representative. From 1940 to 1942, he helped to arrange American aid to Chongqing. After Pearl Harbor, Soong became foreign minister and then head of the Executive Yuan (premier) of the Chongqing government. In 1945, he went to Moscow to negotiate the Soviet Union's entry into the war against Japan, but later he refused to sign the Sino-Soviet Treaty of Friend-

ship and Alliance because it recognized the independence of Outer Mongolia. He resigned as premier in 1947 amid attacks on his policies as well as his personal integrity. His last official position, during the Guomindang-Chinese Communist Party (GMD-CCP) civil war, was governor of Guangdong.

Throughout his long career, Soong could claim many accomplishments as a nationalist—modernization of China's currency and banking system, development of industry and commerce, and the fostering of resistance to Japan. Despite this distinguished career, however, Soong's reputation has remained tarnished. In the People's Republic, Soong's extensive investment in private enterprises, and his apparent use of government position to obtain personal financial benefits, have led to frequent denunciations of him as a bureaucratic capitalist. Among American writers, Soong also acquired a reputation for corruption. The widely read, if seriously inaccurate work by Sterling Seagrave, *The Soong Dynasty* (1985), has fixed a negative image of Soong in the West. Even in Taiwan, Soong has received only limited praise. Perhaps because of his less than smooth relations with other family members, Soong did not join Chiang in Taiwan but retreated to the United States, where he died in 1971.

Parks M. Coble

References

Coble, Parks M. *The Shanghai Capitalists and the Nationalist Government, 1927–1937.* 2d ed. Cambridge, MA: Harvard University Press, 1986.

T. V. Soong Papers, Archives of the Hoover Institution on War, Revolution, Peace. Stanford, CA.

Southeast Autonomous Movement (Dongnan Hubao)

During the Boxer Uprising of 1899 to 1901, a group of regional officials under the Qing decided not to support the government's attack on foreigners. In June 1900, when the Qing court of Empress Dowager Cixi declared war on all foreign powers, the provincial authorities in southeast China—Li Hongzhang at Canton, Liu Kunyi at Nanjing, Zhang Zhidong at Wuhan, and Yuan Shikai in Shangdong—collectively refused to accept the imperial decree. These governors-general or governors described the war declaration by Beijing, as well as the subsequent instruction that they should organize the Boxers to fight the foreign invaders, as illegitimate orders *(luanming)* issued under the improper influence of reactionaries. On the suggestion of Sheng Xuanhuai, Director of Railways and Telegraphs, Zhang Zhidong and Liu Kunyi entered into an informal pact with the foreign consuls in Shanghai, guaranteeing the safety of foreign lives and properties within their jurisdictions in exchange for the promise by the foreign powers of not sending troops into their provinces. Li Hongzhang, Yuan Shikai, and the governors-general of Fujian and Zhejiang soon joined this pact. During the following two months, until the defeat of the Qing court by the Allied forces in August, the pact was upheld in the entire southeast of China with the support of local gentry and business elites. The areas that were affected by the Boxer catastrophe were thus limited to north and northeast China.

The Southeast Autonomous movement, or "Mutual Protection Pact of the Southeastern Provinces" *(dongnan hubao)*, had significant implications in the emergence of modern Chinese nationalism. It represented a rational attitude toward the outside world. The regional officials regarded the war against all foreign powers as hopeless and, indeed, foolish. All of them were leaders of technological and (to a degree) institutional reforms in China, and they believed that such efforts of self-strengthening could not succeed without the pursuit of peaceful relations with other countries. At the same time, the autonomy of the Southeast both reflected and reinforced the trend of political decentralization that had begun in mid-nineteenth century China. Zhang, Liu, Li, and Yuan apparently saw independent actions taken at the provincial level as a viable option for the protection of the empire in the case of disorder or incompetence at the center. The fact that they were all Han Chinese may further explain their alienation from the Manchu court. Their unprecedented action in 1900, therefore, paved the way for the declaration of independence by the provinces during the Revolution of 1911 and the regionalist politics in the 1910s and 1920s.

Wang Ke-wen

References

Purcell, Victor C. *The Boxer Uprising.* Cambridge, England: Cambridge University Press, 1963.

Southern Society

The Southern Society (Nanshe) was an elite literary club during the late Qing and early Republic. Its founders included Chen Qubing, Gao Xu, and Liu Yaze, all famous poets and radical anti-Manchu intellectuals in the Lower Yangtze region. The society was formally established in Suzhou in 1909; its name implied a loyalty to the "southern" (Ming) identity and an opposition to the "northern court" of Manchu. Most of its seventeen original members also belonged to the revolutionary Tongmenghui. In fact, Liu Yaze once described the society as the "cultural arm" of the Tongmenghui.

The activity of the society, however, was only implicitly political. Through private gatherings in which they composed poems and exchanged literary criticisms, the Southern Society poets hoped to foster and reinforce Han nationalism. One of the main themes of their works was praise for such heroes as the anti-Manchu revolutionary Qiu Jin. By the time of the Revolution of 1911, membership of the society had increased to more than one thousand, with branches throughout the region. Among its well-known members were Ma Junwu, Su Manshu, and Cai Yuanpei. It became one of the most influential cultural groups in China. After the founding of the Republic, the society became gradually divided on political and ideological issues. Some members supported Yuan Shikai, others joined the following of Sun Yatsen. In the late 1910s, the society found itself on the conservative side, upholding traditional literary forms and cultural values against the currents of iconoclastic "New Culture" of the May Fourth movement.

The society was part of the movement in defense of "national essence" *(guocui)* and represented a form of cultural, although not necessarily political, conservatism. Nationalist and elitist, it entertained the idea of a Chinese state that was closely associated with Han and Confucian heritages. Yet the tide of "New Culture" eventually tore the society apart. The Southern Society was forced to disband by internal disputes in 1923.

Wang Ke-wen

References

Schneider, Laurence A. "National Essence and the New Intelligentsia." *The Limits of Change: Essays on Conservative Alternatives in Republican China,* ed. Charlotte Furth, 57–89. Cambridge, MA:

Harvard University Press, 1976.

Rankin, Mary B. *Early Chinese Revolutionaries: Radical Intellectuals in Shanghai and Chekiang, 1902–1911.* Cambridge, MA: Harvard University Press, 1971.

Southwest Associated University (Xinan Lianda)

After the outbreak of the second Sino-Japanese War in 1937, many institutions of higher education in the coastal provinces moved inland to avoid Japanese attack and occupation. Three of the country's best universities, Beijing, Qinghua, and Nankai, all in the Beijing-Tianjin area, followed the Guomindang (GMD) government to southwest China. Faculty, staff, and students, along with some equipment, endured long and hazardous journeys in order to continue their education in Chinese territory. On October 25, 1937, these three universities combined and formed the Changsha Provisional University at Changsha in Hunan province. As the war approached there in early 1938, they were again forced to relocate themselves to Kunming, the provincial capital of Yunnan. On May 4, 1938, the three universities formally established their new joint organization at Kunming and renamed it the Southwest Associated University *(Xinan lianda)*.

The *Xinan lianda* was governed by a standing committee that included the presidents of the three constituting universities, and the president of Qinghua, Mei Yiqi, served as its chairman. The university had twenty-six departments located in five colleges: liberal arts, natural sciences, engineering, law and business, and normal. Its faculty, most of which it inherited from the old Beijing, Qinghua, and Nankai universities, represented the academic elite in wartime China. Between 1938 and 1946, more than 2,500 students graduated from the university, among them future leading intellectuals and Nobel Prize winners. In the early 1940s, the university became a political hotbed, fomenting liberal critics of the GMD government as well as supporters of the Chinese Communist Party (CCP) in its faculty and student body. Long Yun, the provincial ruler of Yunnan, tolerated this political dissent as a way of strengthening his regional power against the control of Chiang Kaishek's wartime government in Chongqing. In 1946, the year after the end of the war, the university disbanded, and the three constituent universities returned to their original sites in north

China. For members of the *Xinan lianda*, however, the institution forever symbolized a period of patriotism, idealism, and wartime solidarity.

Wang Ke-wen

References

Eastman, Lloyd E. "Regional Politics and the Central Government: Yunnan and Chungking." *Nationalist China during the Sino-Japanese War, 1937–1945*, ed. Paul K. T., Sih, 329–62. Hicksville, NY: Exposition Press, 1977.

Israel, John. "Southwest Associated University: Survival as an Ultimate Value." Ibid., 131–54.

Sphere of Influence

A sphere of influence is a specific territorial area in which a country claims to possess special interests and influence over the claims of other countries. After Japan forced China to cede part of its territory in the Treaty of Shimonoseki in 1895, the way seemed open for other ambitious powers to take possession of parts of China. The so-called Triple Intervention by Russia, Germany, and France returned part of this territory, the Liaodong Peninsula, to the Qing government, but the price of this assistance was high. In 1897 and 1898, these countries and others demanded and received substantial administrative and economic concessions from the feeble Chinese empire that produced foreign spheres of influence in vital areas. Germany leased Jiaozhou Bay for ninety-nine years and obtained railroad routes in Shandong province. Russia acquired Port Arthur, Dalian, and the entire Liaodong Peninsula. France leased Guangzhou Bay and asserted preeminence in Guangdong, Guangxi, and Yunnan. Not to be left out, Great Britain secured paramount power in Weihaiwei and in Kowloon adjacent to Hong Kong. The British also forced China to grant them exclusive economic rights (termed nonalienation) in the Yangtze valley, and Japan made a similar arrangement in Fujian province. By 1899, each European power and Japan had its own sphere of influence in eastern China in which the authority of Beijing as well as the rights of other countries were restricted.

The sphere of influence system delivered a serious blow to China's sovereignty, and the danger of China being dismembered and forced into a colonial or semicolonial status appeared real. The concession scramble prompted the

Open Door policy of the United States (which had not claimed a sphere). This policy accepted the existence of the spheres, but sought to prevent them from becoming an outright partitioning of China. Within China, the creation of the foreign concessions produced a crisis that led to the abortive Hundred Days Reform in 1898. This limited attempt at self-strengthening and its defeat by conservatives in the Qing government left the sphere question unresolved. In fact, it deepened China's domestic divisions and increased her vulnerability.

The spheres of influence were a profound stimulus to the growth of Chinese nationalism, and they became targets for both xenophobic and revolutionary nationalists. They produced resentment, urgency, and a nascent patriotism as the Chinese recognized that the existence of the spheres exposed China to more encroachment, perhaps even extinction.

David L. Anderson

References

Hsiao, Kung-chuan. *A Modern China and A New World: K'ang Yu-wei, Reformer and Utopian, 1858–1927.* Seattle: University of Washington Press, 1975.

Langer, William L. *The Diplomacy of Imperialism, 1890–1902.* New York, NY: Knopf, 1951.

Statecraft School

In the early nineteenth century, domestic rebellions and the problems resulting from contacts with Europeans indicated to some Chinese intellectuals symptoms of dynastic decline. The deepening social and political crises led them to reevaluate their scholarship, and many concluded that a change in the direction of their intellectual pursuit was necessary in order to meet the challenge of the time. They especially criticized the Neo-Confucian tradition of metaphysics and moralism, and believed that more attention should be given to practical matters that would be of use to the world *(zhiyong),* i.e., to the improvement of government and society. Most of these new thinkers were from Hunan province, and all were influenced by the Gongyang studies of "new text" Confucianism, which emphasized institutional reform as a main theme of Confucian philosophy.

Among the first group of new thinkers were Gong Zizhen and Wei Yuan. Both were born at the end of the eighteenth century, but reached their maturity of thought during the early nineteenth century. Gong's writings commented extensively on the political and economic problems at the time and offered various reform proposals. Wei paid special attention to the issue of coastal defense and later to the necessity of learning from the West. In the 1820s, Wei received an invitation from He Changling, another advocate of the new scholarship, to compile the multivolume work *Huangchao jingshi wenbian (Collected Writings on Statecraft of the Reigning Dynasty).* The work, divided into sections on customs, military affairs, administration, laws, agriculture and public works, etc., called the attention of contemporary scholars to current affairs *(shiwu).* It reflected the thinking of Wei and his friends. Thereafter, numerous similar works, all titled *jingshi* (statecraft), were compiled and published. This new kind of scholarship was therefore commonly referred to as the "Statecraft School" *(jingshi xuepai).*

As the representative of an energetic intellectual current, the Statecraft School prepared Wei Yuan and those who followed to face the central issue of the current affairs in the mid-nineteenth century, i.e., the intrusion of the West. The school's influence may be clearly traced in the attitude and scholarship of many reformist thinkers after the Opium War, including Feng Guifen, Xue Fucheng, Ma Jianzhong, Wang Tao, and Zheng Guanying. Leaders of the anti-Taiping campaigns and the Self-Strengthening movement, such as Zeng Guofan and Zuo Zongtang, were also followers of the school. As late as in the 1890s, Kang Youwei and Tan Sitong still used the Gongyang philosophy to justify their support for the Hundred Days Reform. To the extent that these later reformers broadened the mind of the Chinese to realize their place in the modern world and to the new ways of defending China against foreign encroachment, the Statecraft School contributed significantly to the rise of modern Chinese nationalism.

Wang Ke-wen

References

Hao, Yen-p'ing and Wang Erh-min. "Changing Chinese Views of Western Relations, 1840–95." *Cambridge History of China,* ed. John K. Fairbank and Kwang-ching Liu, vol. 11, 142–201. Cambridge, England: Cambridge University Press, 1980.

Jones, Susan Mann, and Philip A. Kuhn.

"Dynastic Decline and the Roots of Rebellion." *Cambridge History of China,*
ed. John K. Fairbank, vol. 10, 107–162.
Cambridge, England: Cambridge University Press, 1978.
Wakeman, Frederick, Jr.. "The Huang-ch'ao
ching-shih wen-pien." *Ch'ing-shih wen-
t'i* (February 1969): 8–22.

Stilwell, Joseph Warren (1883–1946)

In January 1942, "Vinegar Joe" Joseph Stilwell, on the recommendation of General George Marshall, was selected to serve as the Chief of the General Staff to Chiang Kaishek. Stilwell first served in China as a United States army language officer, and during his second tour he was characterized by one officer as the one person who knew "China and the Far East better, in my opinion, than any other officer in the service."

As Chiang's Chief of the General Staff, Stilwell was charged to "supervise and control all United States defense-air affairs for China" and "improve, maintain, and control the Burma Road in China." Stilwell was also to improve the combat effectiveness of the Chinese soldiers, enabling them to make better use of American aid.

Almost immediately upon Stilwell's arrival, differing personalities and conflicting wartime agendas created tension between Chiang and Stilwell. Stilwell held Chiang Kaishek in low esteem. He saw Chiang as either the cause or a symptom of China's problems, claiming that the "cure for China's troubles is the elimination of Chiang Kaishek." When President Franklin Roosevelt asked him what he thought of the Chinese leader, Stilwell replied: "He's a vacillating, tricky, undependable old scoundrel who never keeps his word."

Stilwell advocated concentrating on the land war, retaking Burma, and the use of Chinese Communist forces in the prosecution of the war. General Claire Lee Chennault, a strong American supporter of Chiang Kaishek, favored an intensified air war against the Japanese. Chiang agreed with Chennault, preferring to keep his soldiers in reserve for what he believed was the impending civil war against the Chinese Communists. This was a central dispute, reflecting the Communist desire to have all Chinese fight the Japanese, and the Guomindang's (GMD) plan to hold their best troops in reserve for the civil war. Many observers became con-

Chiang Kaishek, Madame Chiang (Meiling Soong) and Joseph Stilwell in Chongqing, 1942. (Courtesy of Nationalist Party Archives.)

vinced that the Communists addressed the needs of Chinese nationalism by resisting the Japanese with much more consistency than did the GMD armies. By supporting Chiang, the United States alienated itself from the more credible representatives of Chinese nationalism, which hurt its credibility in the postwar years.

A turning point in the conflict between Stilwell and Chiang came in late 1943, when the air offensive against the Japanese turned into a disaster. Roosevelt decided to reevaluate American activity in China. The decision was influenced by the calamity and by Chiang's refusal in April 1944 to send troops to Burma after Stilwell returned to China to fight the Japanese. Chiang finally relented in the face of Roosevelt's threat to terminate aid, but he continued to use his best troops to blockade against the Communists.

On this issue, Chiang defied Stilwell and Roosevelt by resisting any attempts to preempt his leadership or to use the GMD troops against the Japanese in any sustained way. Convinced that the situation had become untenable, Roosevelt dispatched Vice-President Henry Wallace to China to investigate. Wallace's report cast doubt on the viability of the GMD and their leader: "Chiang, at best, is a short-term investment. It is not believed that he has the intelligence or political strength to run post-war

China." By July 4, 1944, Roosevelt had approved a telegram to Chiang requesting that Stilwell be given command of American and Chinese forces. Meanwhile, Chiang requested the president to send someone to China to help improve his relations with Stilwell.

President Roosevelt's envoy, former Secretary of War Patrick J. Hurley, arrived in the wartime capital of Chongqing on September 6, 1944. As Chinese armies took a pounding from the Japanese in Guilin, Stilwell exploded: "It's a mess . . . what they ought to do is shoot the G-mo [Chiang] . . . and the rest of the gang." Just then, he received a telegram from Roosevelt asking Chiang to turn over to him the command of all troops. Stilwell's elation was short-lived. Chiang and T. V. Soong convinced Hurley to oppose the move. The latter sent a telegram to the president supporting Chiang, who eventually triumphed. On October 18, 1944, Roosevelt recalled Stilwell.

The recall ended the period of overt friction between Guomindang China and the United States. Stilwell's criticisms of Chiang were echoed by subsequent observers, and their accuracy has been proven by history. Yet at the same time, Stilwell reflected American culture, American preoccupations, and American agendas. Chiang, a man determined to survive and to take China in a particular direction of his own choosing, resisted Stilwell when the Americans' agenda threatened his position. The final result was not a misunderstanding, but rather that ultimately the United States would wed itself to Chiang; this in turn resulted in the animus that characterized the relationship between the United States and the People's Republic of China prior to the normalization of relations in 1979.

Edwin Clausen

References

Schaller, Michael. *The United States Crusade in China, 1938–1945*. New York, NY: Columbia University Press, 1979.

Stilwell, Joseph. *The Stilwell Papers*, ed. Theodore H. White. New York, NY: William Sloane, 1948.

Tuchman, Barbara. *Stilwell and the American Experience in China, 1911–1945*. New York, NY: Macmillan, 1971.

Street Drama

"Street drama" *(jietouju)* served as a powerful propaganda device in China before and during the Sino-Japanese War (1937–45). During the Battle of Shanghai in 1937, for example, thousands of writers and artists were organized into drama troupes to stage plays on the street and in residential alleys to drum up support for the war effort.

As a sub-genre of Chinese modern drama *(huaju)*, "street drama" originated in the early 1930s as an experiment to spread the message of national salvation. Ever since the Manchurian Incident of 1931, Chinese intellectuals had endeavored to mobilize public opinion against the Guomindang government's policy of "domestic pacification before external resistance," which concentrated all of the government's resources to fight the Communists while making territorial concessions to the invading Japanese. The intellectuals called for an immediate war to ward off the foreign invaders, and "street drama" was one mobilization strategy they employed.

They produced plays to be performed on the street, or sometimes in school auditoriums, to call attention to the Japanese aggression. The patriotic messages of these plays were invariably clear and straightforward and their language was formulaic. The plays usually consisted of single episodes and required simple props. Stressing active interaction between the actors and the audience, performers applied little makeup and wore ordinary clothes, identifying themselves with members of the audience who were encouraged to shout and chant during the performance. Audience participation helped to create a sense of immediacy that was absent in professional theatre.

Among the score or so of "street dramas" produced in the 1930s, including *Let's Fight Back to Home (Dahui laojia qu)* and *The Posterity of Traitors (Hanjian de zisun)*, the most popular one was *Put Down Your Whip (Fangxia nide bianzi)* by Chen Liting. First written in 1931, the play was performed numerous times and went through many revisions—usually made *ad hoc* at each performance to suit the needs of various conditions. Its plot involves a father who whips his daughter to force her to be a street singer for money. A young worker (seemingly coming from the gathering audience) intervenes. The father then explains (to the worker and the audience) that they were driven out of their home in Manchuria by the Japanese and that now they were destitute. As the audience is moved by the plight of the father and daughter, the worker (with the help of other "secret performers" in the audience) leads the audience into an emotional outburst of nationalistic fervor, shouting anti-Japanese slogans.

As a way of propagating nationalist messages among a still largely illiterate population, "street drama" proved to be ingenious and effective. It helped to mobilize the Chinese for the war of resistance, and played a special role in the rise of popular nationalism in modern China.

Poshek Fu

Student Movement

The modern Chinese student movement was shaped to a significant extent by the students' nationalistic desire to strengthen and modernize China. Emerging as a distinctive social group in the early twentieth century, modern students shared a sense of mission and self-importance in effecting political, social, and educational changes which they believed would bring about China's salvation through national strengthening and modernization. From the collapse of the Qing to the founding of the Communist regime in 1949, students saw the attainment of these goals frustrated by domestic political divisions and imperialist exploitation. Anti-warlordism and the demand for national unity, as well as anti-imperialism—the struggle to regain China's lost sovereign rights and resistance to foreign encroachment—constituted the two interacting themes of the student movement during that period.

An organized and sustained movement began with the May Fourth Incident of May 4, 1919, when students in Beijing protested the Japanese occupation of former German concessions in Shandong. The 1920s witnessed the alliance of many students, frustrated by the inability of the May Fourth movement to effect meaningful changes. The Guomindang (GMD) and the Communists not only captured the nationalistic aspirations of students in their call for revolution, but also provided students with military power and bases of operation outside the campuses. Manifestations of student activism ranged from localized incidents to nationwide movements, such as the May Thirtieth movement of 1925.

Student activism contributed greatly to the success of the GMD in unifying parts of China by 1928. Despite the Nanjing government's attempt to control the students, Japanese aggression in Manchuria in 1931 caused a resurgence of student activism which targeted not only Japan but also the government's failure to protect China's territories and sovereign rights. The war years of 1937 to 1945 witnessed the defection of many students, disillusioned by the inability of the GMD to create a strong and independent China, to the Communist camp. The four-year struggle after Japan's surrender further eroded the GMD's support. Many students identified the civil war as the chief cause of the country's economic problems, and American support of the GMD as a contributing factor to China's continual political fragmentation. By 1949, the student movement had seriously undermined the authority and legitimacy of the GMD regime and helped to pave the way for the Communist victory.

After 1949, the Communists hoped to ensure student support of their new regime's political, social, and ideological goals through thought reform and control. Student protests against the Party's domination of intellectual life, however, surfaced briefly during the Hundred Flowers campaign in 1957. During the Cultural Revolution of 1966 to 1976, the new student generation responded to Mao's call to revolution, but many youths also became victims of the ensuing terror and disorder as well as the factional strife among Party leaders. By the late 1970s, with the government launching new economic policies, students and intellectuals increasingly demanded more political and intellectual freedoms, which they deemed vital to the success of China's modernization. Their frustration with the government's inaction led to the intensification of the democratic movement. A series of demonstrations in the late 1980s culminated in the confrontation in Tiananmen Square in June 1989, when the government used force to crush student dissent. Without organized allies and means of coercion, the student movement has proved to be particularly vulnerable to government suppression.

Ka-che Yip

References

Yang, Winston L. Y., and Marsha L. Wagner, eds. *Tiananmen: China's Struggle for Democracy.* Baltimore: School of Law, University of Maryland, 1990.

Yip, Ka-che. "Student Nationalism in Republican China, 1912–1949." *Canadian Review of Studies in Nationalism* 9, no. 2 (Fall 1982): 247–61.

Study Societies (Xuehui)

Study societies were a form of elite organization that emerged in the Reform Movement at the end of the nineteenth century and continued to play a major role in Chinese culture and politics of the early twentieth century.

In the 1890s, leaders of the Reform movement, such as Kang Youwei and Liang Qichao, promoted the organization of study societies *(xuehui)* as a way of educating and mobilizing China's gentry elite for the cause of reform. Through these societies, the reformers hoped, advanced Western learning might be introduced to the intellectuals (degree-holders) and then propagated through them in the society. At the same time, the gentry elite would form a certain amount of political consensus and solidarity through these organizational ties, in support of the movement.

These societies were often organized on a geographical basis or on the basis of intellectual specialty. Examples of the former type included the Guangdong Study Society *(Yuexuehui)*, the Fujian Study Society *(Minxuehui)*, the Sichuan Study Society *(Shuxuehui)*, and the Shaanxi Study Society *(Guanxuehui)*, all established in 1898; of the latter type there were the Economic Study Society *(Jingji xuehui)*, the Society for Critical Examination of the Classics *(Jiaojing xuehui)* and the Public Law Study Society *(Gongfa xuehui)*. Some study societies were organized explicitly for political purposes, such as the Society for the Study of National Strengthening *(Qiangxuehui)*, founded by Kang Youwei himself.

Established in Beijing and Shanghai in 1895, the Society for the Study of National-Strengthening was the earliest and most famous reformist organization of this period, and it set the standard for all the subsequent late-Qing study societies. The society published periodicals and provided facilities, such as publishing houses, libraries, and museums, for the discussion of current affairs by its members, which included leading scholars at the time. It also exemplified some of the weaknesses of the elite organizations. The Beijing and Shanghai branches of the society later became undermined by factional divisions resulting from personality conflicts as well as ideological differences.

The failure of the Hundred Days Reform in 1898 sealed the fate of the first group of study societies established by the reformers. As a form of elite organization, however, the study societies continued to prosper and received occasional official support. During the Rights-Recovery movement and the Constitutional movement in the early 1900s, gentry and business elites in the provinces organized numerous study societies on the model of those in the 1890s. They were increasingly formal in organization, with by-laws and officers and expanding memberships. From 1895 to 1898, for example, the total membership of study societies throughout the country numbered fewer than 10,000, but in 1909 educational societies alone, which totalled 723, had in excess of 48,000 members. These societies constituted a major force behind the social and political changes in the last years of the Qing.

As a late-Qing phenomenon, the study societies reflected both traditional and modern mentalities. They clearly regarded the leadership of the gentry as necessary in China's transformation. As reformers such as Kang and Liang explained, degree-holders were the middle class in China who could bridge the gap between the government and the people. They possessed greater knowledge and influence than any other group in Chinese society, and therefore held the special responsibility of guiding and representing the populace in public affairs. This traditional sense of superiority and mission shaped the elitist character of the study societies. At the same time, the study societies indicated, to some extent, a recognition of popular sovereignty. By rallying non-official members in the society for political causes, these organizations challenged the traditional cosmological concept of legitimacy in imperial China. Although they never intended to function as an opposition to the government, the very fact that they were independent of the government made them significantly modern. Moreover, their organizational features as well as their instruments of operation differed sharply from those of the traditional gentry groupings. Together with new-style schools and a modern press (including newspapers), the study societies helped to create a new political consciousness among the educated elite in late Qing China.

After the founding of the Republic, the formation of study societies surged to new heights during the May Fourth era of the late 1910s and early 1920s. Geographically based study societies declined in number, but explicitly political-oriented groups became extremely popular among the new generation of students. Their titles varied from "study societies" to "associations" *(hui)* or "societies" *(she)*, but the general purposes and organizational features of these student groups remained similar to those of the gentry organizations in the late Qing. The new awareness of the importance of the masses in culture and politics did not prevent the May Fourth intellectuals from organizing elitist groups among themselves. Even high school students at teenage level began to engage in such activity. The New People's Study Society (Xinmin xuehui) in Hunan became well known because its membership included young Mao Zedong; however, it was but one of the thousands of student groups during that era.

One of the largest and most important May Fourth study societies was the Young China Association (Shaonian Zhongguo xuehui) of 1918 to 1925. Claiming as its goal the "creation of a young China with scientific spirit and social activism," the association attracted into its ranks many future leaders of the Chinese Communist Party (CCP), the Chinese Youth Party, and the Guomindang (GMD). Like the Society for the Study of National-Strengthening more than two decades earlier, however, this once influential group eventually terminated because of ideological and personal clashes among its members.

There were more durable organizations, of course. The Nineteen-Sixteen Society (Bingchen xueshe), later renamed the Chinese Society for Scholarship and Arts (Zhonghua xueyishe), lasted from 1916 to 1958. The connection to regular publications of the May Fourth study societies was even closer than that of their late-Qing predecessors, partly as a result of the popularity of vernacular literature. Many student groups were in fact centered around a particular journal, such as the New Tide Society (Xinchaoshe).

As the nature of the May Fourth study societies was often explicitly political, some of them soon evolved into political factions or were in fact organized with that purpose in mind. In the 1920s a few factions within the GMD originated in study societies. Notable cases included the New China Study Society (XinZhong xuehui) at Beijing University and the Sun Wenist Association (Sun Wen zhuyi xuehui) at the Whampoa Military Academy. In the CCP, the Trotskyite groups, such as the October Society (Shiyueshe) and the Proletariat Society (Wuchanzheshe), both founded in 1930, may be seen as the socialist variations of study societies.

In the meantime, the study societies with a focus on special venues of academic or social interest continued to exist and gradually developed into modern professional associations. The Chinese Geological Society, established by V. K. Ting (Ding Wenjiang) in 1922 and the Chinese Association for the Promotion of Mass Education established by James Yen (Yan Yangchu) in 1923 were major examples. By the 1930s, such professional associations had become a common feature in the Chinese academic world.

In the late Qing and in the early Republic, the study societies represented a response to the national crisis by China's social and intellectual elites. Motivated by the desire to save the country from foreign oppression, they believed that private and voluntary associations might enhance national solidarity, enlighten the government and the people, and effect modernizing changes. In this sense, the study societies not only articulated Chinese nationalism but also helped in the creation of public sphere in modern China.

Wang Ke-wen

References

Chang, Hao. "Intellectual Change and the Reform Movement, 1890–8." *The Cambridge History of China,* ed. John K. Fairbank and Kwang-ching Liu, vol. 11, 274–338. Cambridge, England: Cambridge University Press, 1980.

Gasster, Michael. "The Republican Revolutionary Movement." *The Cambridge History of China,* ed. John K. Fairbank and Kwang-ching Liu, vol. 11, 463–534. Cambridge, England: Cambridge University Press, 1980.

Tse-tsung, Chow. *The May Fourth Movement: Intellectual Revolution in Modern China.* Cambridge, MA: Harvard University Press, 1960.

Subao Case

In 1903, the Qing government sought to arrest and try on sedition charges several writers for *Subao (Jiangsu Gazette).* Criticism of the government for caving in to Russian and French encroachments had reached a peak among the student community, and *Subao* published a number of explicitly anti-Manchu articles in May and June. The accused lived in Shanghai's international settlement, however, and the British-dominated Municipal Council agreed only to issue arrest warrants in July on the understanding that the men would be tried by the Mixed Court, giving ultimate decision-making power to a British magistrate.

The long, public, and ultimately unsuccessful attempt to extradite the accused made the Qing government appear weak, which gave radicals further opportunity to express their views. The December trial was anti-climactic. The British agreed that the accused were guilty of *lèse majesté*, but into May 1904, the Qing continued to insist on life imprisonment for the accused. The Qing accepted lighter sentences only after the British threatened to free the men. The government's main targets were Cai Yuanpei and Wu Zhihui, both of whom left Shanghai before their arrests, Zhang Binglin, who allowed himself to be arrested, and Zou Rong, who followed Zhang. In the end, Zhang and Zou were given prison terms of three and two years with hard labor (minus time served), respectively; other persons originally arrested were released. Zou died in prison, amid rumors that the Manchus had poisoned him, and Zhang emerged a hero in 1906.

The *Subao* case was a turning point on the road to the Revolution of 1911 because it helped to define the precise difference between reform and revolution. Nationalism would increasingly assume anti-Manchu overtones. The case spotlighted the radicalization of the intelligentsia and the ardent patriotism of students who feared the "carving up of China" and indeed the "extinction of the Chinese race."

The Chinese Educational Association and its Patriotic School were founded in Shanghai in 1902; from its beginning the school was a center for discussing Western political theory and organizing public meetings. The Qing's continued refusal to resist more militantly the Russian presence in southern Manchuria and French machinations in Guangxi fueled such opposition. The *Subao*, originally founded as a business journal, was bought in 1900 by a reformist publisher, Chen Fan. Chen began printing articles by Patriotic School students and faculty at the end of 1902. Zhang Shizhao, a student, became editor in May 1903. Under Zhang, the paper openly called for revolution.

Since the Qing treated as equally treasonable reformers who wanted to replace Empress Dowager Cixi with Emperor Guangxu and revolutionaries calling for the overthrow of the dynasty, the line between reform and revolution had been quite uncertain. The *Subao* case gave Zhang Binglin especially the opportunity to define revolution in anti-Manchu terms while gaining broader sympathy. His polemic with the reformer Kang Youwei and his praise for Zou Rong's *Revolutionary Army (Gemingjun)* highlighted the inadequacy of attempting to restore the emperor to power. *Revolutionary Army* had been an enormously successful pamphlet containing a frank appeal to abolish the monarchy and wipe out the Manchus. In his rebuttal to Kang (partly published in *Subao*), Zhang called the emperor "a little clown" and used his personal name, a taboo character. Fundamentally, Zhang argued that the Manchus were incapable of instituting significant reform, whereas a revolution stemming from and encouraging popular nationalism would be constructive.

A number of key Chinese officials hampered the government's crackdown by alerting the targets of arrest and giving all of them, including Zhang and Zou, time to get away. Such officials were not traitors but early examples of what became a fairly common phenomenon in the last years of the dynasty: men who hoped that the government would conduct thorough reforms but who were still sympathetic to revolutionaries. Great Britain had no right to try Chinese subjects under the treaties; however, the execution of political dissidents since 1898 only strengthened the determination of the Shanghai foreign community to try the men by Western standards, even against the initial instincts of their own diplomats. Ironically, the *Subao* case thus formed a chapter in the rise of international settlements to *de facto* autonomy and augmented the scope of imperialism in China.

The *Subao* case contributed to the downfall of the Qing, which was made to appear weak and vindictive. Radical organizations suffered in the short run, and enmities between former allies in the Chinese Educational Association hardened. Nonetheless, the cause of the revolutionaries was furthered through propaganda and martyrdom. Above all, the *Subao* case linked revolution to Chinese nationalism.

Peter Zarrow

References

Lust, John. "The *Su-pao* Case." *Bulletin of the School of Oriental and African Studies* 27, no. 2 (1964): 408–29.

Rankin, Mary Backus. *Early Chinese Revolutionaries: Radical Intellectuals in Shang-*

hai and Chekiang, 1902–1911. Cambridge, MA: Harvard University Press, 1971.

Wang, Y. C. "The Su-pao Case: A study of Foreign Pressure, Intellectual Fermentation, and Dynastic Decline." *Monumenta Serica* no. 24 (1965): 84–129.

Sun Chuanfang (1885–1935)

A principal warlord in the early Republic and a native of Shandong, Sun Chuanfang had been a member of Sun Yatsen's Tongmenghui while attending military school in Japan in the early 1900s. During the chaotic years following the Revolution of 1911, he served in the Beiyang Army and rose steadily in rank. He fought for the Zhili Clique in the Zhili-Anhui War of 1918 and the first Zhili-Fengtian War of 1922. As his clique triumphed in both wars, Sun was eventually awarded with the province of Fujian. In 1924, the Jiangsu-Zhejiang War broke out; Sun assisted the Jiangsu warlord Qi Xieyuan, a fellow member of the Zhili Clique, to defeat the Zhejiang warlord Lu Yongxiang. The war triggered the second Zhili-Fengtian War, in which the Zhili Clique lost, but Sun survived and expanded his control to Zhejiang. Then in 1925, he defeated Zhang Zongchang, Qi Xieyuan's successor in Jiangsu. With the five provinces of Zhejiang, Jiansu, Fujian, Anhui, and Jiangxi as his domain, Sun became the most powerful Zhili warlord in the country. In fact it was with his help that Wu Peifu, his former boss, was able to stage a political comeback in the Upper Yangtze provinces in 1925.

During his brief tenure in the Lower Yangtze region, Sun appointed capable persons to administrative posts, such as the scholar V. K. Ting (Ding Wenjiang) as mayor of Shanghai. In 1926, Chiang Kaishek's Guomindang forces defeated Sun in the Northern Expedition. Sun appealed to the Fengtian Clique of Zhang Zuolin for help, but suffered more defeats in 1927 and 1928, resulting in the total destruction of his troops. Under the Guomindang government, Sun first sought refuge in Manchuria under the protection of Zhang Xueliang, son of Zhang Zuolin, and then moved to the foreign concession in Tianjin after the 1931 Manchurian Incident. He was assassinated in 1935.

Wang Ke-wen

References

Boorman, Howard L., and Richard C. Howard, eds. *Biographical Dictionary of Republican China,* vol. 3. New York, NY: Columbia University Press, 1970.

Sun-Jaffe Manifesto

The Sun-Jaffe Manifesto was an agreement negotiated by Sun Yatsen and the Soviet diplomat A. A. Jaffe (also Joffe, Yoffe, Ioffe) in Shanghai in January 1923, which established the basis for Guomindang-Soviet cooperation in the Chinese revolution of 1923 to 1927. The intention of the manifesto was to exchange Soviet arms and advisers for Sun's recognition of the Soviet state.

After World War I, Sun sought a "Lafayette" in his quest to control warlord-ridden China. The Western powers were contented with the existing situation. Shortly after the October Revolution, the Soviets sought someone who would carry the revolution to China. More than once, Soviet representatives had visited and evaluated Sun, but also considered such warlords as Zhang Zuolin, We Peifu, and Chen Jiongming, for such a task. All of them were found wanting as standard-bearers of Soviet interests at that time.

In August 1922, the diplomatically isolated Soviet Russia sought foreign recognition, whereupon Jaffe appealed in Beijing to establish formal diplomatic relations with the Beijing government. Jaffe also carried instructions from the Executive Committee of the Comintern, in accord with the decisions of its recently concluded Fourth Congress, which had decided that the colonial world was not yet ready for Communism and that for the time being Soviet interests could be best served by supporting each country's leading national bourgeoisie.

Jaffe was to secure recognition for the Soviet Union from the Beijing government and also to work for its overthrow. The immediate goal was the former task. The Beijing regime showed no interest in Jaffe's scheme. Jaffe also maintained contact with Sun in Shanghai during the fall and early winter of 1922. When it became apparent that Beijing would not recognize the Soviet regime, Jaffe began to pay increasing attention to Sun. The only problem was that Sun lacked a geographically focused unit with which relations could be established. In December, it appeared as though that problem might be solved shortly.

On January 16, 1923, Sun's military allies, who had been expelled from Canton earlier, reclaimed the city. This provided Sun with the required geographical base. On January 17, Jaffe arrived in Shanghai, and the next day he met Sun for the first of several negotiating sessions, out of which the Sun-Jaffe Manifesto emerged. According to the joint statement, released on January 26, the two parties agreed that China was not ready for the Soviet system and that, for now, the most important task was to establish Chinese national unity and independence, in the pursuit of which, "China would receive the warmest sympathy of the Russian people and could depend on the aid of Russia." The manifesto, which also included sections on the status of the Chinese Eastern Railway and Inner Mongolia, formatted the Politburo's decision in March 1923 to dispatch arms and political and military advisers to Sun in Canton and to receive Sun's military assistant, Chiang Kaishek, in Moscow later that year.

Dan N. Jacobs

References

Brandt, Conrad, Benjamin Schwartz, and John K. Fairbank, eds. *A Documentary History of Chinese Communism.* Cambridge, MA: Harvard University Press, 1952.

Jacobs, Daniel N. *Borodin: Stalin's Man in China.* Cambridge, MA: Harvard University Press, 1981.

Wilbur, C. Martin, and Julie Lien-ying How, eds. *Missionaries of Revolution: Soviet Advisers and Nationalist China, 1920–1927.* Cambridge, MA: Harvard University Press, 1989.

Sun Yatsen (Sun Zhongshan, 1866–1925)

Revered posthumously as "Father of the Republic," Sun Yatsen devoted his entire life to fighting for a new China that in the end evaded him. His revolutionary career, however, displayed far greater complexity and ambiguity than the official histories of both the Guomindang and the Communists admit. This is especially true regarding his positions on nationalism.

Sun was the son of a peasant family in Xiangshan, Guangdong province. At age twelve he emigrated with his mother to Hawaii, where his elder brother had established a business, and enrolled in a local missionary school. In 1884, he continued his Western-style education in Hong Kong and eventually graduated from the College of Medicine for Chinese in 1892. This uncommon foreign experience had imbued Sun with extraordinary ideas early in his life. He had become a Christian as a teenager and was greatly attracted to Western political institutions. Since childhood he also had admired the Taipings, whose rebellion ended two years before his birth; and during a brief schooling in Canton, he had made friends with classmates who had connections in the secret societies. The seeds of anti-Manchuism and American-style republicanism had been planted in his mind, although he was not yet a revolutionary at this time.

At first, Sun practiced medicine in Macao and Canton, but his real ambition and interests were in politics. For a while he associated himself with the gentry-reformers in Guangdong and in 1894 wrote a letter to Li Hongzhang, then commissioner of the northern ports, suggesting further reforms in China's technologies and institutions. Failure to impress Li deepened Sun's frustration, which he must have already felt as an "outsider" to the traditional sociopolitical establishment. He soon turned from reform to revolution.

In late 1894 in Honolulu Sun founded his first revolutionary organization, the Xingzhonghui (Revive China Society), which advocated the expulsion of the Manchus from China and the establishment of a republic. Initial supporters of the society were mostly marginal members of Chinese society, like Sun himself. In 1895, the Xingzhonghui's first attempt at revolt in Canton was aborted; Sun escaped to Japan. For the next sixteen years, he was wanted by the Qing government and unable to return to China. While visiting England in 1896, Sun was kidnapped by the Chinese embassy in London, which planned to return him to China for execution. He was finally released with the help of his former teacher, Dr. Cantlie. The incident gained for Sun international fame as China's leading revolutionary, which was to become his greatest political asset.

During these years Sun developed the basic ideas of his Three Peoples' Principles, a combination of Han nationalism, republicanism, and moderate socialism. After 1897, Sun moved his base of operation to Japan, where he received assistance from Japanese politicians and *shishi* (men of purpose) who saw the need for a strong China to be Japan's ally in resisting Western imperialism. Following the failure of the Hundred Days Reform of 1898, the Baohuanghui (Emperor Protection Society), organized by Kang Youwei and Liang Qichao, be-

Sun Yatsen and his Japanese friends, 1899. (Courtesy of Nationalist Party Archives.)

came Sun's major rival in attracting support from overseas Chinese. The financial and political bases of the Xingzhonghui in Japan, Hawaii, and the United States were seriously threatened. In 1900, Sun organized another revolt in China and again failed.

The Boxer catastrophe of 1900 helped revive Sun's revolutionary movement from limbo. As the Qing government was fatally discredited by the incident, Sun's prestige among overseas Chinese rose and eventually surpassed that of the monarchists. After 1905, when the Qing abolished the civil service examinations, the number of young Chinese studying in Japan increased dramatically; many of them became Sun's followers. In 1905 Sun won the support of two other revolutionary groups in Japan, the Huaxinghui (China Arise Society) and the Guangfuhui (Restoration Society) and formed the Tongmenghui (Revolutionary Alliance) in Tokyo. He was elected as its chairman.

The Tongmenghui signified an expansion of the basis of Sun's movement to China's future elite, the modern intelligentsia. Between 1906 and 1910, the Tongmenghui organized eight more uprisings in China—none of them successful, but the revolutionary momentum was gathering. Its organ in Tokyo, *Minbao,* debated fiercely with Liang Qichao's publications on the issue of reform or revolution for China. The "revolutionary alliance" itself, however, was split by internal division. After 1907, many Guangfuhui members and some Huaxinghui members broke with Sun.

When the Revolution of 1911 began, it was launched by groups with no direct connections to Sun, who was in the United States at the time. Upon learning the news, Sun traveled to China by way of Europe, and on his way persuaded the Western governments to maintain their neutrality in the revolutionary war. When he returned to Shanghai, delegates of the independent provinces elected him as provisional president of the revolutionary government in Nanjing. As head of the new Republic, Sun abandoned his former anti-Manchu stance and advocated the creation of a "commonwealth" *(gonghe)* of the five major ethnic groups in China: Han, Manchus, Mongols, Tibetans, and Muslims. This was to be the ethnic framework of the modern Chinese state.

In April 1912, Sun yielded the presidency to Yuan Shikai, premier of the Qing government, in exchange for Yuan's support for the revolution. Before leaving office Sun promulgated a provisional constitution, which he hoped would restrain Yuan's power under the Republic. He was then elected director-general of the Guomindang, a parliamentary party organized on the basis of the old Tongmenghui. In 1913, Song Jiaoren, the *de facto* leader of the Guomindang, was assassinated by Yuan's men. This drove Sun to openly oppose Yuan's government, yet the anti-Yuan Second Revolution soon failed. Once again Sun escaped to Japan, where he reorganized the Guomindang into the Chinese Revolutionary Party. When Japan presented the Twenty-One Demands to Yuan's government in 1914, Sun was said to have secretly accepted those demands on the condition that Japan support him.

In 1916, Yuan died in the midst of his aborted monarchical attempt. The country sank into warlordism. Sun returned to China and led a Constitution Protection movement that was to defend the provisional constitution against the illegitimate rule of the Beiyang warlords. From 1917 to 1923, Sun launched three attempts to found a national government in Canton to challenge the Beiyang government in Beijing. The first two attempts failed due to opposition from the southern militarists upon whom he relied; his aspiration for national leadership conflicted with the regionalist schemes of the warlords in Guangdong and Guangxi. In between these Canton regimes, Sun reshaped his political following and reorganized the Chinese Revolutionary Party into a new Guomindang. In 1923, he reached an agreement with the Soviet Union by accepting Chinese Communists into his Guomindang in exchange for Russian assistance to his anti-Beijing cause.

The new alliance with Russia resulted in part from Sun's frustration over rejections by the Western powers to his plea for help, and in part from his new appreciation of the Russian model of revolution. Sun and his followers were touched by the trend of radicalization of China's intelligentsia in the post-May Fourth era. Following the founding of the third Canton regime in 1923, Sun worked closely with his Soviet adviser Mikhail Borodin to reorganize the new Guomindang into a Leninist party, and to reinterpret his Three Peoples' Principles along anti-imperialist and socialist lines. His views on *minzu zhuyi*, which had become a standard Chinese translation for "nationalism," emphasized the need to liberate China from her status as a "subcolony" of the foreign powers. The Canton regime thus adopted a hostile attitude toward the West, especially Great Britain.

Meanwhile, Sun continued to form alliances with the various warlord factions in the country in the hope of toppling the Beijing government. In late 1924, his warlord allies Duan Qirui and Feng Yuxiang captured Beijing. At their invitation Sun went to Beijing for a conference on national reunification. He fell ill on the way and, shortly after arriving, died there in March 1925.

During his lifetime, Americans often described Sun as the "George Washington of China"; when he died his followers praised him as "China's Lenin." As contradictory as these titles may sound, they point to one fact about Sun's career—his interest in using foreign models, and foreign aids, for the building of a new China. As a politician Sun demonstrated vision and resilience that surpassed those of most of his contemporaries, yet he never hesitated to accept foreign assistance for his cause, sometimes at the cost of national interests. Japan was one of the primary sources of Sun's foreign support ever since his anti-Manchu revolutionary years. In one of his last public speeches, given in Japan during his trip to Beijing, Sun still promoted Sino-Japanese friendship under the framework of Pan-Asianism. At various stages of his career he promised generous rights to China's resources to the Americans and the Germans, before finally turning to the Russians, to solicit their help in overthrowing China's current government. In 1919 he issued an invitation for the "international development of China" and made numerous concessions to foreign powers that contradicted his later stance on anti-imperialism.

Nevertheless, the most important legacy that Sun left was his unfinished anti-imperialist "National Revolution" of the 1920s, which was to be claimed by both the Guomindang and the Chinese Communists in the ensuing decades. The two parties often evoked Sun's name and ideas as a common ground for their cooperation with each other and for national unity. In death, Sun has become a greater symbol of Chinese nationalism than he was when alive.

Wang Ke-wen

References

Schiffrin, Harold. *Sun Yat-sen and the Origins of the Chinese Revolution.* Berkeley: University of California Press, 1968.

Sharman, Lyon. *Sun Yat-sen: His Life and Its Meaning.* Stanford, CA: Stanford University Press, 1968.

Wilbur, C. Martin. *Sun Yat-sen: Frustrated Patriot.* New York, NY: Columbia University Press, 1976.

T

Taiping Rebellion

One of the largest rebellions in Chinese history, the Taiping ("Great Peace") movement was a complex expression of Chinese nationalism.

Originating in the Guangdong-Guangxi area, the Taiping Rebellion was at once shaped by anti-Manchu nationalism, Hakka ethnic solidarity, Confucian utopianism, and a distorted form of Christian millenarianism. Its leader, Hong Xiuquan, turned toward ideological and political heterodoxy after being repeatedly rejected in the civil service examinations. One of the main themes of his dissident thought was the hatred of Manchu rule in China. Refuting the legitimacy of the Qing dynasty not only offered a convenient justification for his failure in seeking a place in its officialdom, but could exploit the latent Han nationalism that was still powerful in south China, especially among the lower classes. But Hong encased his anti-Manchu message in a sinicized Christian framework, describing himself as God's "second" son with a divine mission to expel the Manchu "devils" from China.

Hong's rebellious intent was assisted by the volatile environment in the southern provinces of Guangdong and Guangxi in the mid-nineteenth century. Economic depression and unemployment, resulting from long-term trends such as population growth and silver shortage, and recent developments such as the loss of Canton's monopoly of foreign trade, led to rampant disturbances along the Pearl River. Government corruption and oppression made the situation worse. In the midst of this crisis, the ethnic conflict between the Hakka minority and native southerners also intensified. A Hakka himself, Hong founded the Society of God Worshippers in 1843. It soon became a rallying point for the militant Hakkas to join hands in self-protection. The society's religious appeal further provided an exotic messianic vision for its members to engage in collective political action, much like the function of folk religions in the Chinese peasant revolts of the past.

The Taiping Rebellion, which erupted in 1851, capitalized on this social disorder in south China and on popular discontent with the Qing government in the wake of China's defeat in the Opium War (1840–42). With Hakkas as its core, Hong and his rebels attracted an enthusiastic following from the local poor (miners, workers, and peasants) who shared their political and religious purposes. As a symbolic gesture of their challenge to Manchu domination, Taiping males refused to wear the Manchu hairstyle of queues ("pig-tails") and were referred to by their contemporaries as the "long hair."

After capturing Nanjing as the capital of his Heavenly Kingdom of Great Peace in 1853, Hong promulgated the *Land System of the Heavenly Dynasty (Tianchao tianmu zhidu)* as the blueprint of the rebels' social, economic, and political reconstruction. The document, although never fully implemented under the Taiping regime, revealed a coherent vision of the ideal society. Its prominent features included the abolition of private property, communal farming, militarization of the population, restructuring of grass-roots organizations, equality between men and women, and unity of religion and government. Some of these new institutions were clearly inspired by the Confucian classic *The Rites of Zhou (Zhouli)*, whereas others were influenced by the Christian Old and New Testaments. The Taipings also enforced a puritanical lifestyle, forbade opium-smoking, footbinding, and prostitution.

Eventually it was these radical programs and policies that provoked the greatest opposition to the Taipings from mainstream Chinese society. The Confucian gentry elite, shocked by the Taipings' ambitious attempt to demolish the traditional order, came to the aid of the faltering Qing government and organized their own resistance against the rebellion. The gentry-led forces, especially the (Hunan Army) *Xiangjun* and Huai Army *Huaijun*, took over the main responsibility for suppressing the Taipings after 1860. With the help of the Western powers, these armies in the end defeated the rebels. Nanjing fell to the Hunan Army in 1864.

The ideological and political choices made by the Taipings and the Chinese gentry were intriguing. The Taipings, adopting a Western religion in support of their opposition to the Manchu rule, did not feel that their Han nationalism was compromised by the foreign origin of their religious-ideological belief. While this may suggest a degree of cosmopolitanism, the Taipings were incapable of formulating a foreign policy that could gain support, or at least neutrality, from the Western countries. Their unorthodox Christianity, ignorance of the outside world, and refusal to recognize the existing foreign privileges in China produced such a negative impression among Westerners that the foreign powers soon decided to back the Qing in the civil war.

On the other hand, the anti-Taiping gentry, all of them Han Chinese, offered their allegiance to a non-Han regime in order to preserve the Chinese—essentially Confucian—way of life. Although the Taipings were also Han Chinese, and some of their institutions derived from the Confucian classics, the "barbarian" appearance of their overall religious-ideological appeal was tremendously alarming to the gentry. The "Chineseness" of China, to the gentry elite, was defined by the Confucian worldview and the existing social and political systems allegedly based on that worldview. The legitimacy of the Qing dynasty came from its support of those Confucian systems, and in this sense, a "civilized" Manchu regime was superior to a "barbarous" Han one. To an extent the gentry were simply protecting the Chinese socioeconomic status quo, in which they themselves had significant vested interests, but their loyalty to the Confucian cultural tradition was certainly a principal factor behind their political stance. So strong was that loyalty, in fact, that they were willing to enlist Western military assistance in the war against fellow Han Chinese.

The Taiping Rebellion lasted fourteen years and affected more than half of the Chinese empire. A total of 20 million people lost their lives. The chaos and political uncertainty it created stirred uprisings in other parts of China that often outlived the Taipings, such as the Nian, the Muslim, and Miao rebellions. None of these revolts in the end succeeded in overthrowing the Qing. The suppression of the Taipings actually led to a restoration of the Manchu regime in the 1860s and 1870s. But the rebellion did help to transfer political power from the Manchus to the Han under the Qing, albeit unintentionally. The long civil war waged by the Taipings proved the incompetence of the Qing military establishment and forced the Qing court to rely on the Han gentry elite for continuing the anti-Taiping campaign. Upon the defeat of the rebels by the gentry-led forces, the gentry leaders were rewarded by being appointed as regional or provincial rulers. With their personal armies, as well as the financial independence they acquired during the civil war, these gentry-officials (Zeng Guofan, Li Hongzhang, and Zuo Zongtang) played a major role in Qing politics during the second half of the nineteenth century. The power of the Manchu regime in Beijing thus gradually devolved to the Han governors in the provinces.

The historical importance of the Taiping Rebellion also lies in its impact on later revolts and revolutions in China. Its anti-Manchuism and egalitarian ideal inspired the republican revolutionaries as well as the Chinese Communists in the twentieth century. Sun Yatsen, founder of the Republic, later integrated some of the Taipings' ideas into his Three Peoples' Principles, and historians in the People's Republic today still praise the rebellion as the first peasant revolution in modern China.

Wang Ke-wen

References

Jen, Yuwen. *The Taiping Revolutionary Movement.* New Haven, CT: Yale University Press, 1973.

Kuhn, Philip A. "The Taiping Rebellion." *The Cambridge History of China,* ed. John K. Fairbank, vol. 10, 264–350. Cambridge, England: Cambridge University Press, 1978,

Shih, Vincent Y. C. *The Taiping Ideology: Its Source, Interpretations and Influences.*

Seattle: University of Washington Press, 1967.

Taiwan Minzhuguo

Strictly speaking, "Taiwan Minzhuguo" refers to the short-lived republic inaugurated in Taibei, Taiwan, on May 25, 1895, by Tang Jingsong, former Qing governor of that province, with the strong support of local Chinese merchants and gentry. Historians generally agree that this, Asia's first republic, began as a diplomatic ploy to prevent Japanese occupation of Taiwan in accordance with the Treaty of Shimonoseki, signed in April by representatives of China and Japan, and to secure foreign intervention to force a return of the island to China. Nevertheless, scholars recognize the significant impact that this formal declaration of political autonomy had on consolidating islandwide Taiwanese resistance, which challenged the Japanese military for another four months.

Analysis of official Qing documents and diplomatic records shows that Zhang Zhidong and Wang Zhichun, Qing diplomats in Paris, provided Tang with the notion of "popular will" as a basis in international law to reject the cession of Taiwan to Japan; that they also encouraged its use by Taiwan officials in 1895 is without doubt. Secondly, the long awaited arrival of two French steamers in Taiwan waters on May 19 and the hint of French aid if Taiwan would only declare its independence persuaded Tang and the local gentry to seek political separation from China. The May 23 declaration that announced the new republic, in its establishment of a democratic government with elected officials and legislators, clearly exceeded the intent of Zhang and other sympathetic Qing officials. However, the direct connection between the declaration of self-reliance and the anticipated foreign intervention in the minds of Tang Jingsong and his gentry supporters meant that official resistance to the Japanese occupation would be weak and limited.

Despite these apparent weaknesses, the establishment of the Taiwan Minzhuguo is evidence of the acceptance and use of the concept of "popular will" by local elites in Taiwan. Furthermore, the sustained resistance to the Japanese takeover, led by Liu Yongfu (former leader of the Black Flag Army) and local gentry figures in central and south Taiwan, shows that militia leaders had accepted local responsibility for the defense of the island. Their refusal to submit peacefully to Japanese rule and their identification with Taiwan and Taiwanese affairs comprised an important legacy for the later Taiwanese nationalist movement.

Douglas Fix

References

Lamley, Harry. "A Short-Lived Republic and War, 1895." *Taiwan in Modern Times,* ed. Paul K. T. Sih, 241–316. New York: St. John's University Press, 1973.

Taiwan Relations Act

On December 15, 1978, President Jimmy Carter announced that the United States would recognize the People's Republic of China (PRC) on January 1, 1979, and sever diplomatic relations with the Republic of China (ROC) in Taiwan from that date. Once formal relations with the ROC were severed, President Carter indicated that "the American people and the people of Taiwan will maintain commercial, cultural, and other relations without official government representation and without diplomatic relations." As a result, he would seek adjustment to American laws and regulations to maintain such relations. On January 29, the Carter administration sent a bill to Congress and, after extensive discussions and modifications, Congress adopted the Taiwan Relations Act by an overwhelming majority on March 29. It was signed into law by President Carter on April 10.

The Taiwan Relations Act has 18 sections. It states that, since the president had terminated governmental relations between the United States and Taiwan, Congress found the Act necessary to help maintain peace, security, and stability in the western Pacific and to promote the friendship between the United States and the people of Taiwan. It also stipulates that the United States dealings with Taiwan would be conducted through an instrumentality established by Taiwan (later on known as the Coordination Council for North American Affairs, and since August 1994, as Taibei Economic and Cultural Representative Office), "which the president determines has the necessary authority under the law applied by the people on Taiwan to provide assurances and take other actions on behalf of Taiwan in accordance with this Act."

Under the Taiwan Relations Act, the United States nominally accepted the PRC's three con-

ditions for establishing diplomatic relations—
severance of diplomatic relations with Taiwan,
abrogation of the Sino (ROC)-American Mutual
Defense Treaty of 1954, and withdrawal of
troops from Taiwan; but in fact, the first two
conditions were replaced effectively by the Act.

Hungdah Chiu

References

Bader, William B., and Jeffrey T. Bergner, eds.
*The Taiwan Relations Act: A Decade of
Implementation.* Indianapolis, IN:
Hudson Institute, 1989.

Chiu, Hungdah. *The Taiwan Relations Act
and Sino-American Relations.* Baltimore: University of Maryland School of
Law, Occasional Paper Series, 1990.

Wolff, Lester L., and David L. Simon, eds.
*Legislative History of the Taiwan Rela-
tions Act.* Baltimore: University of Maryland School of Law, Occasional Paper
Series, 1982.

Taiwanese Independence Movement

Taidu (Taiwanese Independence movement)
generally refers to the post-1949 activities of a
disparate group of Taiwanese activists and organizations that have been promoting a sovereign and independent Taiwan, whose ultimate
future would be determined solely by the inhabitants of the island. Their demand for political
autonomy has been based on the uncertain legal status of Taiwan after World War II, the
historical separation of Taiwan from China, the
inability of the Guomindang (GMD) to speak
for the interests and needs of the Taiwanese, the
unique historical experiences of the Taiwanese
people, and the right to self-determination guaranteed by the United Nations charter. Taidu
leaders have employed several strategies to at-
tain their objective, including mobilizing Taiwanese support for independence, appealing
internationally for a United Nations trusteeship
and plebiscite to decide Taiwan's future, lobby-
ing foreign governments for recognition, publicizing Taidu interpretations of the "Taiwan
question," and physically attacking GMD officials and facilities.

The Taidu *qua* movement originated soon
after the suppression of Taiwanese discontent
with GMD rule, expressed in the February
Twenty-Eighth Incident of 1947, although demands for independence from Japanese colonial
rule had surfaced earlier. In 1949, Thomas Liao

(Liao Wenyi), head of the Formosan League for
Reemancipation in Hong Kong, called for immediate Supreme Command of the Allied Powers (SCAP) occupation of Formosa and the
Pescadores, the organization of a provisional
Taiwanese government and legislature, and a
national plebiscite. Liao soon moved to Japan,
where he established a political party, inaugurated a provisional government in 1955, and
lobbied for international support for independence.

In 1964, Peng Mingmin, Xie Congmin,
and Wei Tingchao attempted to circulate within
Taiwan a "Declaration of Formosan Self-Salvation," which criticized GMD rule, called for a
new democratic government, and promoted
independence from China. Their arrests prevented distribution of the manifesto, but Peng's
escape overseas in 1970 increased support for
the movement.

When Liao and officials in his provisional
government defected to the GMD in 1965, the
control of Taidu shifted to younger activists in
Japan affiliated with the Formosan Youth Association, whose organ, *Taiwan Seinen* (Taiwan
Youth), helped to cultivate a broad network of
supporters in Japan, the United States, Europe,
and Taiwan. The association promoted Taiwanese consciousness, self-determination, and independence via its publications, demonstrations,
and aid to political prisoners in Taiwan.

A worldwide network emerged in November 1966, when remnants of Liao's provisional
government and the United Young Formosans
for Independence in Tokyo, the United Formosans in America for Independence, the United
Formosans in Europe for Independence, and the
Canadian Committee for Human Rights in
Formosa made a unified appeal in *The New
York Times* for Formosan self-determination.
This cooperation precipitated the establishment
of the World United Formosans for Independence four years later.

With more Taiwanese students studying
abroad after 1970, and growing concern about
the international status of the Republic of China
(the GMD government in Taiwan) after 1971,
Taidu manifested two new tendencies: broader
overseas Taiwanese support for self-determination and violent militancy by some activists. The
attempted assassination of Jiang Jingguo in the
United States in 1970, the postal bombing of
Xie Dongmin in 1976, and attacks on GMD
offices abroad following the Gaoxiong Incident
of 1979 exemplified the destructive capabilities

of the radical faction. These actions ultimately harmed support for Taidu's aims.

Open calls for independence surfaced in Taiwan in the 1970s. In 1977, the Taiwan Presbyterian Church urged the Guomindang to "take effective measures whereby Taiwan may become a new independent country." The publicized trials of defendants in the Gaoxiong Incident case encouraged private discussion of Taiwan's sovereignty, while a heated debate over the nativist literature *(Xiangtu wenxue)* sparked discussion of Taiwanese cultural identity. In 1986, the Democratic Progressive Party publicly declared that "Taiwan's future should be determined by all residents of Taiwan according to the principles of freedom, self-determination, universality, justice, and equality." Five years later, the Party promised "to build a Taiwanese republic with independent sovereignty."

This activity precipitated initiatives by overseas Taidu organizations to move back to Taiwan as early as 1986. By the early 1990s, several radical proponents of Taiwanese independence had resurfaced in Taiwan, making it the new center of pro-independence activities.

Douglas Fix

References

Martin, Joseph. *Terrorism and the Taiwan Independence Movement*. Taibei: Institute on Contemporary China, 1985.

Mendel, Douglas. *The Politics of Formosan Nationalism*. Berkeley: University of California Press, 1970.

Tan Kah Kee (Chen Jiageng, 1874–1961)

Overseas Chinese entrepreneur and philanthropist, Tan Kah Kee was a supporter of Sun Yatsen's republican revolution in the 1900s and Mao Zedong's Communist revolution in the 1940s.

A native of Fujian province, Tan went to Singapore as a youth to help his father's business in that British colony. In 1910, already a successful businessman in rice, fresh produce, rubber, and shipping, he joined Sun Yatsen's Tongmenghui and contributed financially to Sun's revolutionary movement. This contribution continued after the founding of the Chinese Republic in 1912. During the 1910s and 1920s, Tan's business in Singapore expanded rapidly, and he established schools, libraries, hospitals, and other public service facilities in his home-town of Jimei, Fujian. In 1921, he founded the Xiamen University. In 1924, he became the publisher of a newspaper, *Nanyang shangbao* (Chinese Journal of Commerce), in Singapore.

After the Manchurian Incident of 1931, Tan became concerned about Japanese aggression in China. His involvement in China's crisis deepened when the Sino-Japanese War broke out in 1937. He raised funds for China's war chest, sponsored relief activity for the country's war refugees, and became a member of the People's Political Council under the wartime Chinese government. Meanwhile, Tan's political loyalty shifted. After a trip to China in 1940, during which he visited Chongqing and Yan'an, Tan found himself disillusioned with the Guomindang (GMD) and sympathetic to the Chinese Communist Party (CCP). In 1946, he published *Nanqiao ribao* (Southern Overseas Chinese Daily), which harshly criticized the GMD. When the People's Republic was founded in 1949, Tan was invited to attend the Chinese People's Political Consultative Conference sponsored by the CCP and soon joined the CCP government. After that, he spent most of his time in China, and finally renounced his British citizenship in 1957. He died in Beijing in 1961.

Upholding his Chinese identity throughout his life and moved by a strong sense of Chinese nationalism, Tan was hailed by the CCP as a model of patriotic overseas Chinese.

Wang Ke-wen

References

Yong, C. F. *Tan Kah-kee: The Making of an Overseas Chinese Legend*. Singapore: Oxford University Press, 1987.

Tan Sitong (1865–98)

Scholar, philosopher, reformer, martyr of the Hundred Days Reform, Tan was a native of Hunan province but spent his childhood in Beijing, where his father was an official. At the age of twelve his mother and two siblings died in an epidemic which almost killed Tan. Emotionally close to his mother and distant from his father, Tan was deeply marked by this tragedy.

In his youth, Tan dutifully studied for the civil service examinations; he ultimately failed six times at the provincial level. He came to despise the orthodox curriculum and developed an adventurous, questing spirit. His early thinking was shaped toward Han nationalism by the writings of the seventeenth-century scholars

Wang Fuzhi and Huang Zongxi. He took up swordsmanship and made loyal friends in the non-literati world of self-styled knights-errant. When his father was stationed in Gansu, he rode and hunted on the frontiers with carefree companions. In his twenties he served briefly with Liu Jintang, the governor of Xinjiang. His extensive travels gave him a broad view of China's difficulties and hatred for social oppression.

China's defeat by Japan in 1895 coincided with a personal crisis for Tan, who had just failed the examinations for a fifth time. Stimulated by Kang Youwei's eclectic scholarship and driven by his own search for universal truth, he avidly sought inspiration from Western science, Huayan Buddhism, the teachings of Jesus, and a broadly spiritual interpretation of the Confucian heritage. In his *Study of Humanity* (*Renxue*, 1898), he expounded a syncretic philosophy that was at once personal and national. He affirmed the individual's freedom from the three bonds and five constraints of orthodox Confucianism, and he castigated autocratic rule, the tyranny of the family, arranged marriage, concubinage, footbinding, and the examination system. He also attacked the Manchus and called for nationalism and republicanism as the foundation of China's renovation.

During the same period, Tan worked passionately for reform. From 1897 to 1898 he was in Hunan, where progressive scholars and officials organized schools, study societies, newspapers, and commercial enterprises. He believed that a reformed Hunan could become a center for national rejuvenation if China were dismembered by the powers. When the reform movement shifted to the capital in the summer of 1898, Tan was summoned for an audience with Emperor Guangxu, who appointed him a secretary in the Grand Council. For the last weeks of the Hundred Days Reform he became one of the emperor's confidants. As tensions grew between the reformers and Empress Dowager Cixi, both sides sought support from Yuan Shikai, whose modern troops held the balance of military power around the capital. On September 18, Tan visited Yuan in a late night appeal to aid the emperor. But Yuan betrayed Tan's scheme and three days later the Empress Dowager's *coup d'état* terminated reform. Tan refused to flee, and on September 28 he was executed with five others in a deliberate act of martyrdom. Tan's intense patriotism, radical views, and disdain for death made him

a revered model for later revolutionaries.

Charlton M. Lewis

References

Chang, Hao. *Chinese Intellectuals in Crisis.* Berkeley: University of California Press, 1987.

T'an, Ssu-t'ung. *An Experiment of Benevolence: The Jen-hsueh of T'an Ssu-t'ung,* trans. Chan Sin-wai. Hong Kong: Chinese University Press, 1984.

Tang Shaoyi (1860–1938)

Late Qing diplomat and early republican political leader, Tang Shaoyi was born in Tangjiacun (Tang Family Village) in Xiangshan, Guangdong province. He was related to Tong King-sing (Tang Tingshu), the leading entrepreneur during China's early industrialization. In 1871, the Qing government assigned Tong King-sing to select 120 youths to be sent to study, under the supervision of Yung Wing, as the first Chinese Educational Mission to the United States. Tang Shaoyi joined the mission in 1874 as a member of the third detachment of forty students. He first lived with the Eugene Gardiner family in Springfield, Massachusetts, where he completed his elementary education and then moved to Hartford, Connecticut, for high school. After graduating with honors, he enrolled in Columbia University and had completed only one year in college when the mission was recalled.

On his return to China, Tang was sent by the government to Korea, where he eventually joined Yuan Shikai's staff in the Chinese residency. Tang used the knowledge and skills he had acquired in the West to help establish Chinese supremacy over Korea. He served as Yuan's chief diplomatic consultant and assumed charge of Chinese affairs when Yuan fled to Tianjin on the eve of the first Sino-Japanese War (1894–95).

Tang's career in China began in 1900 as head of the Shandong Bureau of Foreign Affairs in the administration of Governor Yuan Shikai. He devoted his energies and talents to countering the thrust of foreign encroachment and securing recognition of Chin's sovereign rights. Until 1911, Tang's fortunes were closely linked to those of Yuan. With Yuan's promotion to governor-general of Zhili and commissioner of the northern ports in 1901, Tang became Tianjin Daotai and Customs Superintendent, a key diplomat in the conduct of Chinese foreign policy. He was the chief liaison for Western diplomats in their dealings with the Chinese government and served as Yuan's confidential interpreter and assistant in discussions with foreign envoys and private individuals.

In 1905, the Qing appointed Tang as Chinese plenipotentiary to negotiate with the British in India over the status of Tibet in the aftermath of the Younghusband Expedition and the signing of the Lhasa Convention. Tang successfully concluded the Beijing Adhesion Agreement in 1906, which tried to supplant British influence in Tibet and make Tibet an integral part of China. On his return from India in 1905, Tang assumed the junior vice-presidency of the Board of Foreign Affairs in Beijing and remained a central government official until 1907. He spearheaded the effort to assert Chinese sovereignty more actively, to restrict the imperialist privileges previously conceded in railway and mining affairs, and promote the Rights-Recovery movement. Tang also played a leading role in the opium suppression movement by pressuring foreigners to cooperate in ending the opium trade. In addition, he launched the initiative to end the independent status of the Maritime Customs Service and to bring it more firmly under Chinese control.

When the Qing government reorganized northeast China in April 1907, Tang Shaoyi became the first governor of Fengtian province. His area of responsibility, however, remained diplomacy, and he served as the chief negotiator for all of the Three Eastern Provinces (Manchuria). In Fengtian, Tang consistently countered the expansion of the Japanese presence.

Tang's career suffered a severe setback in 1908 with the death of Empress Dowager Cixi and Yuan Shikai's forced retirement. He reemerged during the Revolution of 1911 as Yuan's representative in the North-South peace negotiations held in Shanghai. After Sun Yatsen resigned in favor of Yuan Shikai as provisional president of the Republic of China, Tang became Yuan's first prime minister. Tang's government resigned after three months, however, when Yuan demonstrated his willingness to sacrifice China's sovereignty to foreigners to bolster his own position.

Tang subsequently emerged as a respected elder statesman in the Guomindang and in Sun Yatsen's Canton regimes of 1917 to 1922, but exercised little actual power or responsibility. After the Northern Expedition (1926–28), he briefly participated in the 1931 Canton opposition against Chiang Kaishek's Nanjing government. Tang remained dedicated to Chinese national interests and ultimately made the supreme sacrifice. He was assassinated in 1938 in the French concession in Shanghai on Chiang's orders to cover up the peace initiative Tang had made to the Japanese at Chiang's request.

Louis T. Sigel

References

Li, Chien-nung. *The Political History of China, 1840–1928.* Stanford, CA: Stanford University Press, 1967.

Sigel, Louis T. "Ch'ing Tibetan Policy (1906–1910)." *Harvard Papers on China* no. 20 (1966): 117–201.

Sigel, Louis T. "The Diplomacy of Chinese Nationalism, 1900–1911." *Myth and Reality: Social and Political Change in Modern China, 1860–1949,* ed. David Pong and Edmund Fung. Lanham, MD: University Press of America, 1985.

Tanggu Truce

Following the Manchurian Incident of 1931, Japanese troops occupied the Inner Mongolian province of Jehol in 1933 and continued to invade north China. In May, the Chinese defense along the Great Wall collapsed and the Japanese forces reached the Beijing-Tianjin area. Japanese occupation of those cities would have been a serious blow to the prestige of the ruling Guomindang and would have forced Chiang Kaishek to stop his campaign against the Chinese Communists. To avoid such outcomes, the Nanjing government negotiated a peace settlement with Japan and signed a truce at Tanggu, east of Tianjin, on May 31.

According to the settlement, the Chinese agreed to withdraw their forces to western Hebei (which included Beijing and Tianjin), and the Japanese, to the Great Wall. It created a demilitarized zone in eastern Hebei, but the Japanese troops that had been permitted by the Boxer Protocol of 1901 were to remain in that zone. Law and order within the zone would be maintained by Chinese police units "that were not hostile to the Japanese." In addition, Chinese forces in the truce area were forbidden to engage in any "provocative or disturbing actions," a vague statement that the Guandong Army could use to instigate future Sino-Japanese conflicts.

The truce was signed by Nanjing's Xiong

Bin and the Guandong Army's Okumura Yasuji, but the Chinese side of the negotiations was conducted by Huang Fu. Huang was head of the Political Reorganization Committee at Beijing, an *ad hoc* organization established by Nanjing on May 3 to deal with the Japanese threat in north China. Although the committee enjoyed a semi-autonomous status, Huang was in close contact with Nanjing throughout the negotiations.

In Nanjing, the decision to appease Japan was agreed upon by Chiang Kaishek and Wang Jingwei. Chiang, then directing anti-Communist campaigns in Jiangxi, successfully distanced himself from the settlement and left Wang and Huang to take the public responsibility for it. Yet the Tanggu Truce was a major step in realizing Chiang's overall policy of "domestic pacification before external resistance." In effect it recognized the Japanese occupation of Manchuria and Jehol and gave Japan free access to parts of north China and Inner Mongolia. Although some of the humiliating political arrangements in the settlement were kept secret at the time, the truce aroused immediate attacks by many Chinese as amounting to a surrender to Japanese aggression.

Wang Ke-wen

References

Coble, Parks M. *Facing Japan.* Cambridge, MA: Harvard University Press, 1991.
Israel, John. *Student Nationalism in China, 1927–1937.* Stanford, CA: Stanford University Press, 1966.

Tao Xingzhi (1891–1946)

Prominent educator in modern China, Tao Xingzhi is known principally for the innovative pedagogy he developed to educate the common people.

Tao's own education included a grounding in the Chinese classics, acquired at a traditional Chinese school, followed by study of English, mathematics, and medicine at two Protestant missionary schools, then literature and philosophy at Nanjing University, after which he traveled to the United States to study political science briefly at the University of Illinois, and finally education and philosophy with John Dewey at Columbia University Teachers' College.

While at Nanjing University, Tao was so impressed by the theory of the Ming dynasty neo-Confucian philosopher Wang Yangming that "knowledge and action are one," that he changed his name from Tao Wenjun to Tao Zhixing (Tao Knowledge-Action). It was the similarity, and the difference, in the epistemology of Wang Yangming and that of John Dewey that attracted Tao to Columbia. Both philosophers agreed on the unity of knowledge and action, but whereas Wang had asserted that "knowledge is the beginning of action, action is the completion of knowledge," Dewey reversed the formulation, asserting that knowing is based on experience, in other words, that action is the beginning of knowledge.

Armed with Dewey's theories, Tao returned to China in 1917 to take a faculty position at the Nanjing National Teachers College (later Southeastern University) where, eventually, he succeeded in transforming the curriculum to emphasize teaching students how to learn rather than stuffing them full of static facts. He was instrumental in bringing Dewey to China for a series of lectures between 1919 and 1921, and in promoting Deweyan ideas in the new journal, *New Education (Xinjiaoyu).*

The work for which Tao is best known began in late 1921 with the formation of the Chinese National Association for the Advancement of Education. In 1923, he and James Yen (Yan Yangchu) launched the first Mass Education movement, a literacy campaign structured on "people's reading circles" in factories, shops, temples, homes, on the docks, among rickshaw pullers, and so on. The text was a thousand-character basic reader that he and James Yen compiled. The campaign spread with remarkable speed and success from Nanjing to every part of the country until it was suppressed in 1927 by regional warlords and conservative officials in the new Guomindang government, who found its emphasis on promoting "literacy for democracy" too radical and threatening.

Having had his activities curtailed in urban areas, Tao turned his attention to the countryside. In March 1927, he and Zhao Shuyu established a teacher training school at Xiaozhuang near Nanjing. The pedagogy he developed at this school anticipated almost all of the educational reforms later promoted by Mao Zedong. Teachers and students lived and worked together, physical labor was combined with classroom study, learning was a process of mutual interaction between teacher and student and was to be derived from practical, everyday problems, moving from near to far, concrete to abstract.

It was at Xiaozhuang that Tao reformulated Dewey's approach to learning by declaring that "life is education," "society is school"—rather than the other way around—as Dewey had it. Tao now began to promote the concept of "schools without walls." The Xiaozhuang movement spread rapidly to other areas, but again, its success led to its ultimate failure. Conscious of the implications of Tao's pedagogy for radical change, the national government in Nanjing shut the Xiaozhuang school in 1930 and discouraged similar projects. It was at about this time that Tao Zhixing changed his name again, to Tao Xingzhi (Tao Action-Knowledge), declaring that Wang Yangming had it backward when he said, "knowing is difficult, doing is easy." Tao knew what to do, but was not allowed to do it. By emphasizing that "doing" is what is difficult, Tao also reaffirmed Dewey's proposition that knowledge follows naturally from experience, and again anticipated Mao's similar contention that in the acquisition of all true knowledge, practice precedes theory and then is deepened, enriched, and transformed by theory in an unending dialectical process.

Tao remained active in various education projects in China and abroad following the suppression of the Xiaozhuang experiment, but he was always inhibited by the power of established authority. In 1932, he set up work-study groups for workers in Shanghai and elsewhere, which again focused on literacy, but the content was changed to emphasize what Tao now believed was China's most urgent issue—the growing imposition of Japanese imperialism. Tao became a champion of a patriotic movement that he called "education for national crisis." During most of the Sino-Japanese War (1937–45), Tao was in southwest China, where he established a school for talented orphans. After the war he returned to Shanghai and founded Social University, a school for working-class youth. He dedicated what other time he had to promoting democracy and seeking a peaceful solution to the differences between the Guomindang and the Communists. True to his pedagogical principles, Tao combined the theory and practice of democracy at Social University by having the student body elect the administrators and trustees of the school. Tao's activities, including serving on the Standing Committee of the Democratic League, again aroused the suspicion and animosity of the Guomindang. When two of his fellow Democratic League associates were assassinated, Tao was convinced that there would be a "third bullet" for him. Disregarding his high blood pressure, Tao drove himself to settle his affairs. He died of a stroke on July 25, 1946, at age fifty-five.

Tao Xingzhi's contribution to nationalism in China is patent. According to a biography, his colleagues often described Tao as the "most thoroughly Chinese" of the students who had returned home after study abroad. His search for ideas in foreign lands was motivated by a desire to change and strengthen his native land. For him, education was a tool to free the common Chinese people from oppression, both domestic and foreign.

Peter J. Seybolt

References

Boorman, Howard L., and Richard C. Howard, eds. *Biographical Dictionary of China*, vol. 3. New York, NY: Columbia University Press, 1968.

Seybolt, Peter J., ed. "Tao Xingzhi." *Special Issue of Chinese Education* 7, no. 4 (Winter 1974–75).

Tariff Autonomy

After the Opium War (1840–42), Qing China was forced to relinquish control over her own tariff, or maritime customs, in a series of unequal treaties. Not only was the tariff rate set at a certain limit (around 5 percent) and the Chinese government was not allowed to change it, but the management of China's Maritime Customs Service was also given to the foreign powers. At that time, the concept and the institution of maritime customs were new to the Chinese, and the consequences of such an arrangement were not fully appreciated by the Qing. As years passed and China began to introduce Western-style industry into the country, the devastating effect of a fixed and foreign-controlled tariff on China's economic development was gradually understood by its political leaders and intellectuals.

Outcries against foreign control of the Chinese tariff and demands for its return to Chinese hands had been voiced by nationalist Chinese since the late nineteenth century, yet no change had occurred. In the wake of the anti-imperialist May Thirtieth Movement in 1925, the Beijing government under Duan Qirui held a Special Tariff Conference with the foreign powers for the purpose of negotiating the return of tariff rights to China. Twelve foreign countries sent delegates to this conference, which commenced in Beijing in October, and China's representative Wang Zhengting submitted the demand of tariff autonomy on behalf of Duan's government. Meanwhile, the Guomindang government in Canton mobilized workers and students throughout the country for mass demonstrations against the conference. The demonstrators questioned the sincerity of Duan Qirui's government and rejected the peaceful approach to regaining China's independence.

At the conference, the foreign powers paid lip service to China's tariff rights, but insisted that this right could not be returned to China before China abolished *likin (lijin)*, an internal transit tax on goods collected by the Chinese government since the mid-nineteenth century, and before anti-imperialist propaganda and activity in China were suppressed. The difficulty in realizing these conditions in effect undermined the Chinese proposal, and the conference ended in July 1926 without a resolution of the problem.

Shortly after the Guomindang's (GMD) nominal unification of China, the new national government at Nanjing pressed the foreign powers on this issue again. Wang Zhengting, now Nanjing's foreign minister, continued his effort of 1925 and 1926 under the new framework of revolutionary diplomacy. In July 1928, Wang announced that all of the unequal treaties signed by the previous Chinese governments would be either abrogated or replaced with new ones by the Nanjing government. This implied the unilateral abolition by China of two of the most important foreign privileges in the country: extraterritoriality and tariff control. As a goodwill gesture to the new GMD regime, which the West regarded as modern and pro-Western, the foreign powers adopted a conciliatory stance. The United States took the lead in reaching an agreement with Nanjing by returning tariff rights to China on January 1, 1929. Other major foreign powers soon followed suit. The Nanjing government subsequently raised the tariff rate to increase its revenue, and by 1931 maritime customs duties had become its largest source of revenue.

Wang Ke-wen

References

Cavendish, Patrick. "Anti-Imperialism in the Kuomintang, 1923–8." *Studies in the Social History of China and Southeast Asia: Essays in Memory of Victor Purcell*, ed. Jerome Ch'en and Nicholas Tarling, 23–56. London, England: Cambridge University Press, 1970.

Third Party

See DENG YANDA

Three Peoples' Principles

The Three Peoples' Principles are the political doctrines of Sun Yatsen for the reconstruction of China. The "three principles" refer to "Peoples' National Consciousness" *(minzu),* i.e., nationalism; "Peoples' Rights" *(minquan),* i.e., democracy; and "Peoples' Livelihood" *(minsheng),* i.e., socioeconomic well-being. Sun often compared them to Lincoln's famous expression, a government "of the people, by the people, and for the people."

Sun first constructed the doctrines during his brief stay in Europe, following his first aborted Canton revolt in 1895. After 1905, Sun and his followers elaborated and propagated these ideas in *Minbao,* the organ of Tongmenghui. In its original content, "nationalism" emphasized anti-Manchuism, whereas "socioeconomic well-being" showed traces of moderate measures in capital regulation and land equalization. After the Revolution of 1911 and the failure of the early Republic, Sun's political ideas became increasingly radical. By the early 1920s, he had been influenced by the Bolshevik revolution in Russia and the ideology of Marxism-Leninism. As a result, the specific contents of the doctrines were modified. "Nationalism" assumed greater anti-imperialist character, as the goal of anti-Manchuism had been accomplished and the foreign powers were now regarded as the principal menace to China's independence, and "socioeconomic well-being" came to be identified closely with socialism and Communism. Even the doctrine of democracy, although still upholding the principle of constitutionalism, now allowed a preparatory stage of political tutelage that resembled the Leninist party dictatorship.

The Three Peoples' Principles never appeared in a detailed written form. The only draft Sun was said to have written about them was destroyed during the *coup d'état* of Chen Jiongming in 1922. In 1924, Sun gave a series of lectures, still unfinished at the time of his death, on these doctrines in Canton. His followers accepted the lectures as the final version of the doctrines. This final version was to a large extent shaped by the First United Front between his party and the Chinese Communists, and thus displayed radical tendencies. The Communists have since called this version the "New Three Peoples' Principles" that reflected Sun's truly progressive ideas, while the Guomindang has tried hard to modify its radical tones and to bring them closer in line with Sun's earlier, more moderate, programs.

From 1928 to 1949, when the Guomindang was in power in China, the Three Peoples' Principles were the country's official ideology, providing rationales (if not actual guidelines) for government policies and the basic content of political education in schools. This practice continued after the government's retreat to Taiwan in 1949.

Wang Ke-wen

References

Chang, Sidney H., and Leonard H. D. Gordon. *All Under Heaven: Sun Yat-sen and His Revolutionary Thought.* Stanford, CA: Hoover Institution Press, 1991.

Sharman, Lyon. *Sun Yat-sen, His Life and Its Meaning.* Stanford, CA: Stanford University Press, 1968.

Three-Self Patriotic Church

The Three-Self Patriotic Church represented the People's Republic's unique attempt to deal with the problem of how to indigenize and thus make truly Chinese an alien Western religion—Christianity. The problem of how to adapt Christianity to Chinese society and culture was one that Catholic and Protestant missionaries had recognized since the time of the Jesuit pioneer Matteo Ricci and the English Presbyterian exemplars working in Fujian and then Taiwan in the 1850s and 1860s. One issue was organizational and centered around the following three questions: First, who should control the congregations? Second, who should support them, the foreign mission board or the local church members? And third, who should train the local ministers? Another issue was theological: How far could a given church go to adapt its belief system to Chinese mores and to Chinese culture and still be recognizably Christian to the Roman Catholic Church or to the mainline evangelical/pentecostal denominations? These were all thorny issues that Chinese Christians and their Western missionary mentors dealt with, with varying degrees of success.

From the end of the Boxer Rebellion in 1901 to the final victory of the Chinese Communist Party (CCP) in 1949, such questions became paramount. When the new regime took over, some important theologians were in place and ready to confront these issues.

The new regime was radically socialist, intensely nationalistic, and strongly anti-imperialist. It demanded that church authorities create a Chinese Christianity that reflected these core tenets of the new state. The CCP leadership found in Y. T. Wu (Wu Yaozong) and his junior compatriot, K. H. Ting (Ding Guangxun), men whom they could trust to implement the changes that would transform Western-centered Christianity into a Chinese-centered belief system.

The major architect of the body that became the Three-Self Patriotic Church was Y. T. Wu. Wu was born into a Cantonese non-Christian family. He converted as a young adult after hearing a dynamic and inspired leader of the liberal and social gospel-oriented Student Volunteer movement. He became the secretary of the Beijing YMCA in 1920, and four years later traveled to the United States to study theology and philosophy at Union Theological Seminary and Columbia University. When he returned to China, he assumed a major role at the YMCA headquarters in Shanghai, served in various posts and in 1946 organized the periodical, *Tianfeng* (Heaven's Wind). This journal remains the voice of the church in China to this day in the 1990s.

Y. T. Wu's radical sensibility evolved slowly over the course of the 1930s and 1940s. By the time of the CCP victory he was clearly pro-Communist in his political ideology. Because of his stature in the Chinese church community, because of the increasingly anti-missionary stance of his essays and his speeches, and because of the liberal/radical form of Christianity he embraced, he was chosen by the regime to create a new and ultra-nationalistic form of Chinese Christianity. In this effort he was joined by a number of other church leaders, including the man who now heads the church, K. H. Ting.

The first step was the publication of the *Direction of Endeavor for Chinese Christianity in the Construction of the New China.* This was more a political than a theological statement that set the tone and the agenda for what would soon take place and anticipated the creation of a unified, patriotic, and anti-Western Chinese Protestant church. In 1951, with Y. T. Wu as its head, the Three-Self Patriotic Church took shape. The core ideas of the new body—self-government, self-support, and self-propagation—were each adopted from ideas developed and publicized by the YMCA that Y. T. Wu had helped to lead before 1949.

During the first seven years, the Three-Self Patriotic Church acted as a central governing body for the various denominations that actively supported it, and served as an overview body for the many evangelical and pentecostal churches that did not. With the radicalization of Chinese society that accompanied the Great Leap Forward, the denominations were phased out and the leaders of the Three-Self Church attempted to create a markedly homogeneous interdenominational form of Protestantism. This meant obliterating differences in style of worship, in patterns of organization, and in systems of belief to which the various churches had clung in the manner of their Western contemporaries. It also meant creating a more socialist and therefore more politically correct type of Protestantism—a form of Christianity that Y. T. Wu was ready to formulate and embrace.

Part of this process also involved self-denunciation and denunciation of the more evangelical and pentecostal belief systems and churches. This was a divisive and painful process to many of those involved, but it did serve to legitimize Three-Self Church members and leaders in the eyes of the political authorities. Many Western observers and Chinese church leaders in Hong Kong and in Taiwan openly criticized such self-criticism and high-level integration, but the multileveled transformation process acted as a survival mechanism during the Cultural Revolution, when Christianity came under sharp attack by the Red Guards.

Since the late 1970s, the CCP has liberalized its policies toward religion and its study. Scholars of Christianity in China have been able to travel to the West for graduate training and for participation in conferences. Church leaders such as Bishop Ting have been able to hold major conferences in Nanjing and to come to the West and meet with American and European church leaders. Key figures in the Catholic order Maryknoll and the China Program division of the Churches of Christ are involved in this renewed dialogue with the Three-Self Church. In China the houses of worship conducted by the Church are usually full. Independent evangelicals have also seen a resurgence of their own churches, though they are still suspect in the eyes of the authorities.

As the history of the Three-Self Patriotic Church suggests, the survival of Christianity in a radical, totalitarian China is due in large measure to the work of those Christian leaders willing to deal with the state authorities and to mold a Protestantism that is indigenous, patriotic, and true to socialist and Christian core values.

Murray A. Rubinstein

References

Luo, Zhufeng, ed. *Religion Under Socialism in China.* Armonk, NY: M. E. Sharpe, 1991.

MacInnis, Donald F., ed. *Religion in China Today: Policy and Practice.* Maryknoll, NY: Orbis Books, 1989.

Whitehead, Raymond L., ed. *No Longer Strangers: Selected Writings of K. H. Ting.* Maryknoll, NY: Orbis Books, 1989.

Ti-Yong Theory

In the late nineteenth century, as China suffered military defeats and her territory was partitioned by foreign powers, Chinese scholar-officials recognized the need for reform. Although they agreed that the country had to be strengthened by learning from the West, they disagreed on how much and how fast the learning should be. Whereas the radicals demanded sweeping reforms and fundamental changes, the conservatives decried the loss of Chinese uniqueness and the crumbling of the Chinese traditional system. The ti-yong theory emerged in this debate on reform as a synthetic alternative. It was the moderate reformers' umbrella formula for balancing the demand for learning from the West with the need to preserve the essence of Chinese culture.

The ti-yong theory consists of two key concepts: *ti* (substance) and *yong* (function). Originally a pair of metaphysical concepts in neo-Confucianism, *ti* and *yong* jointly signified the organic and inseparable link between an object's hidden potentialities *(ti)* and its manifest capabilities *(yong)*. For neo-Confucian thinkers, an object's potentialities and capabilities are ontologically identical. They are interpenetrative and interlocked like two faces of the same coin.

In the late nineteenth century, however, *ti* and *yong* assumed different meanings. They did not signify the state of being, but the state of learning. They connoted the division of the body of learning *(ti)* and the field of functional learning *(yong)*. The field of substantial learning was concerned with moral judgments, cultural predilections, and social divisions, whereas the field of functional learning focused on technical conveniences and tactical adjustments. Seen in this light, *ti* and *yong* were no longer equal parts of the single process; they became two separate parts of different importance. As an end, *ti* was always primary and essential. It set the priority and direction for the entire society. As a means, *yong* was always secondary and supportive. It only provided the technical supports to achieve the intended social goals.

For the moderate reformers in the late nineteenth century, the new ti-yong theory was their ideological justification for finding a common ground between the radicals and the conservatives. They identified the Chinese learning as *ti* and the Western learning as *yong*. Armed with this ti-yong bifurcation of Chinese learning and Western learning, the moderate reformers reproached the radicals by asking them to relate their demands for reform to the existing structure of the Chinese system. Conversely, the moderate reformers kept the conservatives at bay by telling them that the Western reforms in China were merely technical and nonessential.

Among the late-nineteenth-century reformers, Zhang Zhidong gave the new ti-yong theory its most articulate form. In his *Exhortation to Learning* (1898), Zhang offered the Chinese reformers a dictum: "Chinese learning for fundamental principles; Western learning for practical applications" *(zhong xue wei ti, xi xue wei yong)*. He further classified Chinese learning as inner learning and Western learning as outer learning. Whereas the inner learning formed the core of the body of learning, the outer learning implemented the core with technical details.

Although being criticized by some contemporary scholars as a half-hearted measure of reform, the ti-yong theory did provide the Chinese reformers with a working agenda for bringing reforms to China. The effectiveness of the theory lay in its deliberate imprecision of meaning. Although the relative roles of Chinese learning and Western learning were specifically defined in the ti-yong theory, the exact contents on Chinese learning and Western learning changed accordingly. In the 1850s, when the dominant concern at the time was strengthening Chinese defenses, the meaning of Western learning was confined to armaments and military technologies; Chinese learning covered all areas except the military. In the Self-Strengthening movement of the 1860s and 1870s, when the dominant concern was to establish China's economic and financial infrastructure, the meaning of Western learning was expanded to include commercial enterprises and industrial technologies. Correspondingly, the meaning of Chinese learning was shifted to social behaviors and moral codes. In the Hundred Days Reform (1898), when the dominant concern was political institutions, Western learning was understood as constitutional monarchy and the parliamentary system. Concomitantly, the meaning of Chinese learning was changed to the imperial system and social hierarchy. In short, the *ti-yong* theory was the Chinese reformers' framework for negotiating their different concerns and their different reform strategies.

Tze-ki Hon

References

Levenson, Joseph R. *Confucian China and Its Modern Fate: A Trilogy*. Berkeley: University of California Press, 1968.

Tiananmen Incident of 1976

The 1976 Tiananmen Incident took place in Tiananmen Square, Beijing, on April 5, 1976. It symbolizes an emotion-packed period in China's political leadership succession crisis.

In 1969, during the Cultural Revolution, Marshal Lin Biao became Chairman Mao Zedong's handpicked successor. On the other hand, Mao allowed his wife Jiang Qing and three of her followers (Mao called them the "Gang of Four") to compete with Lin Biao for power. Premier Zhou Enlai remained the most senior and well-respected statesman. Though seriously ill, he continued to try to steer the country to a peaceful future. Mao had to rely on Zhou for maintaining domestic law and order and in conducting diplomacy with the two superpowers—the United States and the Soviet Union.

Mao's worst surprise came when Lin Biao plotted to assassinate him and failed in 1971. Lin was killed while trying to escape to the USSR. As a result, Zhou Enlai and the newly reinstalled Deng Xiaoping became the principal rivals of the Gang of Four in the leadership succession struggle. The gang feared that Deng

Zhou Enlai in 1974. (Xinhua News Agency.)

would lead the moderates in the Party to succeed Mao, especially if Mao should die before Zhou. Zhou, then hospitalized, had left Deng in charge of the government, and Deng held a position in the Party second only to Mao and Zhou. The anti-Confucius campaign in 1974 to 1976, organized by the Gang, was aimed to prevent both Zhou and Deng from becoming Mao's successor. Mao appeared to still have confidence in Deng. He was fully aware that Zhou might soon die and Deng would be the only leader capable of maintaining law and order throughout the realm. In 1975, Deng drafted many major policy documents promoting the "four modernizations," which were strongly supported by the sick Premier Zhou.

Zhou died on January 8, 1976, eight months earlier than Mao did. The entire nation was in mourning over Zhou's departure. The people were consoled by the expectation that Vice-Premier Deng would succeed Zhou as the new premier. The residents of Beijing wanted to express their grief by large gatherings, but their wish was frustrated by the Gang of Four, who did not allow the media to endorse such activity. Populace viewing of Zhou's body was also denied. These restrictions angered the students, intellectuals and ordinary citizens in Beijing, who were further shocked by the sudden disappearance of Deng from the press the day after he delivered Zhou's funeral speech. Meanwhile,

Mao handpicked Hua Guofeng as acting premier without approval of the Politburo. Mao's decision stunned the country, but it also denied the Gang of Four the new premiership. He apparently did not trust his estranged wife.

The fifth day of April is the annual Spring Memorial Day. As the day approached, Beijing residents daily placed flowers in Tiananmen Square in memory of "the beloved Premier Zhou," but at night the government had the flowers removed. The people's fury and grief reached the boiling point, ready to explode. On April 5, 1976, less than three months after Zhou's death and Deng's disappearance, students and citizens gathered at the square for a memorial service and to protest against the government. Trouble developed between soldiers and the demonstrators. Burning, death and arrests followed. Mao took advantage of this chaotic situation to formally appoint Hua Guofeng as premier and as first vice-chairman of the Party, therefore his official successor. The irony of it all was that the official media, controlled by the Gang of Four, accused the missing Deng Xiaoping of being the chief instigator of the incident. Deng was soon dismissed from office. Two years later, after Mao's death in September 1976, and after Hua Guofeng (then simultaneously Party chairman and premier) lost majority support in the Party, a resolution cleared Deng from the charge of instigator of the 1976 Tiananmen Incident.

David Wen-wei Chang

References

Chang, David Wen-wei. *Zhou Enlai and Deng Xiaoping in the Chinese Leadership Succession Crisis.* Lanham, MD: University Press of America, 1983.

Tiananmen Incident of 1989
The 1989 Tiananmen Incident comprised the student-led demonstrations centered at the Tiananmen Square in Beijing, from mid-April to early June, 1989, which ended in the bloody government crackdown on June 4.

Aside from democracy and corruption, no issue evoked more conflict between the student-led mass movement and the Chinese Communist government than nationalism. Before the military crackdown in Beijing and other cities, student demonstrators insisted on labeling their movement as patriotic. After the massacre, the government attacked the counterrevolutionary

Student demonstration at Tiananmen, 1989.

rebellion with equal vociferousness as foreign-inspired. Both sides claimed to uphold the patriotic mantel and defend the national interest to legitimize their actions in the eyes of the Chinese people.

Following the crackdown, the government stressed its role in saving China from what it described as an international conspiracy to overthrow the Communist Party and China's socialist system. In an official report on the turmoil delivered to a session of the National People's Conference convened in July (1989), Beijing mayor Chen Xitong clearly established the foreign origins of the movement. Although he acknowledged the role of domestic problems in the outbreak of the demonstrations, Chen claimed that from the beginning of the mass movement which followed Hu Yaobang's death on April 15, "political forces in the West" had supported Chinese students as part of a larger strategy to "make socialist countries, including China, give up the socialist road. . . ." In the conspiratorial terms that would typify Chinese government accounts of the democracy movement, Chinese students and sympathetic intellectuals in and outside the government were portrayed as having "colluded with foreign forces" (which supposedly included "a high-

ranking official" in Taiwan and a New York-based Chinese student "reactionary organization groomed by the Guomindang") in order to destroy the "true" defender of China's national interest—the Chinese Communist Party (CCP).

During the later stages of their occupation of Tiananmen Square, students had constructed a "Goddess of Democracy"—ironclad evidence to the CCP leadership's mind that the students "took American-style democracy and freedom as their spiritual pillar." Citing purported financial assistance to the students from abroad (Taiwan, Hong Kong, and the United States), along with sympathetic treatment of the student movement in the foreign press and the Voice of America, Chen Xitong portrayed the People's Liberation Army's action on June 3 and 4 as the only way to preempt the "battle" that a "small handful" of democracy movement leaders and "hostile forces overseas" had planned against the Chinese state.

Casting the democracy movement as a "puppet" of foreign interests made obvious political sense to the Chinese government. What better way to defuse the Chinese students' appeal to the common people than to picture foreign intrigue as the sinister "black hand" behind the movement? On every subsequent anniversary of the Tiananmen crackdown, the Chinese government has, in fact, invoked traditional nationalist, anti-imperialist themes, such as China's victimization during the mid-nineteenth century Opium Wars, to drive home to the Chinese public the link between the democracy movement and the unending conspiracy of foreign interests in China unbroken for over a century.

Yet, there is more to this nationalistic appeal than meets the eye: It also tacitly acknowledges that the students had elicited considerable national sympathy through their own appeals to national interests and patriotism. During the demonstrations before the crackdown, the students and their supporters consistently cast their movement as patriotic and insisted, as a major demand, that the government label it so. This was particularly effective when through their hunger strike students dispelled popular notions about their personal selfishness—a theme effectively exploited by the government during earlier student demonstrations in Shanghai and Beijing in 1986. No other action, indeed, mobilized more popular sympathy than the students' apparent willingness to die for the country in the face of government intransigence. At the height of the demonstrations and hunger strike in May, it was the students—not the government—who had captured the patriotic label and effectively used it to outmaneuver the CCP leadership. That the government was so emphatic in linking the students to foreigners and traditional enemies of China—Japan, Great Britain, and the United States—demonstrates just how successful the students in 1989 had been in mobilizing nationalist sentiments *against* the Chinese Communist government.

Lawrence Sullivan

References

Ogden, Suzanne, et al., eds. *China's Search for Democracy: The Student and Mass Movement of 1989.* Armonk, NY: M. E. Sharpe, 1992.

Saich, Tony, ed. *The Chinese People's Movement: Perspectives on Spring 1989.* Armonk, NY: M. E. Sharpe, 1990.

Tianjin Incident

The Tianjin Incident was a delayed reaction to the process of Western missionary expansion in late imperial China. Finding an opening in the wording of the Treaty of Nanjing, missionaries began to establish stations in the coastal treaty ports. Then using to their advantage their roles as translators and diplomatic intermediaries, missionaries included a toleration/mission protection clause in the Treaty of Tianjin and the Beijing Convention. These opened the way to the evangelization of the hinterland areas, evangelization and church planting that was guaranteed through the protection of the Qing officialdom.

This evangelization by Catholics and Protestants forced members of the Chinese elite to consider the challenge posed by a militant and expansionist Christianity, one that had entered China under the protection of Western arms. Meanwhile, the missionaries proceeded to establish a variety of benevolent institutions, including schools, clinics, hospitals, and orphanages. A dispute over an orphanage and what took place within its walls led directly to the Tianjin Incident of 1870.

The Confucian-trained scholar-gentry *(shenshi)* felt threatened by this missionary invasion and by the direct challenge that Christianity, in its basic forms, posed to the Confucian thought system that was the gentry's core ideology. Their fears were well justified, because the missionaries openly attacked Confucianism in many of their writings and did so with considerable ferocity. Furthermore, they attacked Confucianism in the Western press as a means of justifying their cultural battle with the Chinese elite. The scholar-gentry rose to the battle and sought ways to stem the Christian tide. Many thought that they had to mobilize the common people by making them aware of the threat that Christianity presented to Chinese society and religious culture.

Falling back on the formal Qing proscription of the religion, a crisp statement of policy informed by the widely stated Chinese belief in the conflict between orthodoxy and heterodoxy, key figures within the gentry republished Ming literati attacks on expansionist and "heterodox" Catholicism. They also published two types of new materials. One consisted of manifestos, pamphlets, and posters, which were intended to foster a general hatred of Christianity. In the second category were placards, handbills, and notices. These were targeted to specific instances and circumstances, and were used to focus the generalized anger of the commoners and urge them to take direct action. Both types of material were highly agitative and contained illustrations and slogans that the masses could readily understand and respond to.

This scholar-gentry battle was carried out on many fronts throughout the Qing empire. In Taiwan in 1868, for example, violent gentry-incited opposition forced English Presbyterian missionaries to leave their station in the city of Tainan and find safety among the Western merchants farther south in the city now known as Gaoxiong. They did return to their mission station and their evangelical and education efforts, but it was over a year later.

The most diplomatically damaging of the anti-missionary incidents was the one that took place in Tianjin in June 1870. The spring of that year had been a difficult one and an epidemic raged. One facility hit hard by the epidemic was an orphanage, Notre Dame des Victoires, conducted by French nuns. Rumors to the effect that the nuns gathered in terminally ill infants to baptize them before they died, thus making them Catholic, were circulated by the gentry through the various means discussed earlier. Officials investigating the accusations found no grounds for the rumors, but the anti-missionary agitation grew, nevertheless.

The spark flared when the French consul fired at the investigating Qing officials. The orphanage was destroyed, as was the French consulate. The mob attacked those working there as well as others within the French diplomatic and religious communities. Altogether, ten nuns, the French consul and his chancellor, four other French citizens, a number of Russians, a Chinese priest, and some of the orphans were killed. To make matters even worse, the bodies of most of the slain foreigners were mutilated. Accounts of the massacre in the port that served the capital, Beijing, spread and spurred other anti-Christian/anti-mission demonstrations in Shandong, Zhili, Jiangxi, Jiangsu, and Guangdong.

The Qing government paid dearly for this act of gentry-inspired commoner action. It was forced to pay a high indemnity to the French government and to the authorities of the French Catholic Church. Furthermore, its hopes to renegotiate treaties that would modify the nature of Western extraterritoriality in China were frustrated. Violent, xenophobic, anti-missionary agitation proved to be a costly way of dealing with the threat of Western religious imperialism.

Murray A. Rubinstein

References

Cohen, Paul A. *China and Christianity*. Cambridge, MA: Harvard University Press, 1964.

———. "Christian Missions and Their Impact." *The Cambridge History of China*, ed. Dennis Twitchett and John K. Fairbank, vol. 10, 543–590. Cambridge, England: Cambridge University Press, 1978.

Tianjin Massacre

See TIANJIN INCIDENT

Tianxia

Tianxia—"All under heaven" is the traditional term used by the Chinese in referring to China. Before the nineteenth century, the Chinese government and elite believed the "celestial empire" *(tianchao)* to be the most civilized place in the world, indeed the only place on earth that could be regarded as fully civilized. The Chinese monarch, referred to as the "son of heaven" *(tianzi)*, possessed the power and authority to rule the entire civilized world, *i.e.,* China, and to influence the not-yet-civilized areas. Such a belief was based on two premises: first, that Chinese civilization was the only form of civilization that could be recognized as such, and secondly, that political power and authority derived from superiority in degrees of civilization. No concept of national sovereignty is suggested here, and for centuries the Chinese empire viewed and treated other states that came into contact with China as cultural and political inferiors.

To a degree, this Chinese perception was supported by historical reality. China was the origin and center of East Asian civilization; throughout most of traditional history, her political and economic strength did enable her to dominate that region. Although not always engaging in territorial expansion at the expense of the smaller states around it, the Chinese empire generally expected other peoples or societies, whom it described as "barbarians," to recognize its leadership by paying homage to the Chinese ruler. The tributary system *(chaogong)* that originated in the first century was a clear example of this. In this system, other peoples and societies came to the Chinese capital, brought gifts, and paid respect to the Chinese emperor. In return they were granted the privilege of trading with China and receiving Chinese political or military protection.

It was this concept, and conviction, of China as a universal empire that was challenged and eventually undermined during the nineteenth century. The coming of the industrialized Western countries proved to the Chinese that their empire was not superior to that of the new "barbarians" in technology, institution, or culture. With the increase in geographical and historical knowledge, they also realized the existence of a family of nations, as well as civilizations, of which China was only one. Although the new term that the Chinese came to use in referring to their country, *Zhongguo,* still means the "middle kingdom" and thus is a reminder of the old self-image and worldview, it nevertheless includes the word *"guo"* (kingdom, state) and implies an equal status held by China and other states or *guo.* The demise of *tianxia* was therefore an essential step toward the recognition of a Chinese state, and thus toward the emergence of modern Chinese nationalism.

Wang Ke-wen

References

Fairbank, John K., ed. *The Chinese World Order: Traditional China's Foreign Relations.* Cambridge, MA: Harvard University Press, 1968.

Tibetan Independence Movement

The kingdom of Tibet had been a tributary state to the Chinese empire since the eighteenth century. When the tide of nationalism spread from the West to the rest of the world in the nineteenth century, Tibet also received its impact. Just as Mongolia and Manchuria were manipulated by Russia and Japan to separate themselves from China, Tibet was under the instigation of Great Britain to do the same. Great Britain was interested in controlling Tibet so as to protect her colony, India, from the Russian influence in central Asia. As early as in 1890, Great Britain had forced Qing China to cede an area along the Tibetan-Indian border to India.

In the late nineteenth century, the Tibetan leaders had become influenced by the new trends of thought in the West. With British and other Western countries' support, a number of these leaders began to oppose the Chinese rule. Shortly before the turn of the twentieth century, the thirteenth Dalai Lama (1896–1933) took over the reigns in Tibet and announced the region's right to self-determination. In 1904, British troops, commanded by Francis Younghusband, invaded the Tibetan capital Lhasa, and the Dalai Lama briefly took refuge in Mongolia and China. From then on, Tibet entered an era of uncertainty as a pawn between two powers: Great Britain and China. In 1910, the Chinese reasserted their authority over Tibet by force. This time the Dalai Lama fled to India and called for a separation from China.

Under the influence of the global tide of nationalism, separatists in Outer Mongolia and Tibet, together with the Chinese revolutionaries led by Sun Yatsen, expressed support for each other and fervently advocated the expulsion of the Manchus from China. They shared a common enemy, the Qing government, but had different goals. The former two wanted "national" independence, building a state on the basis of their respective ethnic groups. The latter did not support such "national" revolutions; all they desired was to overthrow the Manchu rule in China and replace the monarchy with a republic. Sun's vision of the new Chinese Republic was that it would be controlled by the Han people but would still include the Mongolian, Manchurian, and Tibetan minorities.

When the Revolution of 1911 occurred in China, the thirteenth Dalai Lama took advantage of the political turmoil and expelled Chinese officials and soldiers from Tibet. In foreign relations, he allied himself first with Russia to resist Great Britain, and then with Great Britain in order to be separated from China. In 1913, he further proclaimed four resolutions that attempted to expel all Chinese from Tibet with the help of Great Britain. In the Simla Conference of 1913 and 1914, the Dalai Lama signed an agreement with the British which declared the full autonomy of Outer (western) Tibet. In a public statement he asserted that "Tibet has never been a vassal state to China and will not, in the future, maintain this relationship with China." The Chinese republican government refused to recognize this British-Tibetan agreement.

The Simla Conference also recognized the special influence enjoyed by the British in Tibet. After a British attack on Tibet from Nepal, however, the Dalai Lama became aware of Tibet's vulnerability and the need for Chinese assistance. In 1929, he set up representative offices in the Chinese capital, Nanjing, and agreed to allow the Guomindang government to supervise Tibet's defense, transportation, and foreign affairs. But Tibet enjoyed autonomy in handling its internal affairs. It still wished to keep a distance from China and, as its long-time isolation had been broken, to open to non-Chinese influence.

The fourteenth Dalai Lama formally assumed his leadership in Tibet upon coming of age in 1950, forty days after the Chinese Communist troops marched into Tibet on November 17. The next year, he appointed Nga-phod Ngag-dband 'jigs-med to head a delegation to Beijing, the new Chinese capital, to negotiate and sign the "Agreement on Measures for the Peaceful Liberation of Tibet." In this agreement, it was made clear that the Chinese Communist government would be the supreme authority in Tibet, controlling its defense and foreign affairs. In the meantime, Beijing guaranteed to maintain the existing political condition and the Dalai Lama's status in Tibet, that is, not to interfere with Tibetan internal affairs such as religion and customs.

Five years after the agreement, however, the situation changed. In 1955, Mao Zedong personally told the Dalai Lama during the latter's visit to Beijing that "religion is poison," which "hinders the progress of the country." Mao's real concern, as a Chinese nationalist, was of course the territorial integrity of the Chinese state. In 1959, armed rebellions against Chinese rule broke out all over Tibet. An organization called the Enlarged Congress of an Independent Tibet asked the Tibetans to "expel the Han people." In the midst of the chaos, the Dalai Lama and most of his followers escaped across the Himalayas and entered India. India allowed the Dalai Lama to reside in Mussoorie, in a northern province. There he started a new stage of the Tibetan Independence movement under foreign protection.

In Tibet, after the suppression of the rebellions in 1962, Beijing replaced the Tibetan government with Chinese military rule. Beijing's tight control intended to mold Tibet in the pattern of the rest of Communist China. It demolished Tibetan social, economic, and religious structures, destroying slavery and nobility, confiscating private property, and suppressing the Lamaist Church. Between 1963 and 1971, no foreign visitors were allowed to enter Tibet, and only a few Nepalese traders remained. The Tibetan peasants were organized into peasant associations in preparation for collectivization and communization. A large number of Chinese military as well as civilians immigrated from Mandarin-speaking areas into Tibet. They settled down and began to integrate with the local Tibetans. In 1967, the People's Republic of China (PRC) formally established the Tibetan Autonomous Region, with Nga-phod Ngag-dband 'jigs-med as its chairman.

Since the 1960s the fourteenth Dalai Lama has formed his government-in-exile in India. Although he received support from a number of foreign countries, the Dalai Lama realized, after thirty years of overseas activity, that he had made little progress. He also realized that there were many problems among the 100,000 Tibetan refugees in India, the most serious one being a crisis of cultural identity. Many of these Tibetans not only had lost their ability to write and speak the Tibetan language, but also had gradually felt distant to their own heritage. The eighteenth-century-like condition of the old Tibet, moreover, made them ill-prepared for the twentieth-century world. As time passed, they found it difficult to maintain their cultural values. The Dalai Lama had to adopt a realistic policy. Since 1980, he has engaged in contacts and dialogues with the Communist government of China. In recent years, the Dalai Lama visited Europe, the United States, and Taiwan and advocated the European model of a multinational alliance based on practical needs. He has modified his original idea of a Tibetan nation-state, but he still regards Tibet as "a state independent of the People's Republic of China."

Thus, although the Tibetan diasporas have inherited the legacy of Tibetan nationalism, their aspiration for political independence is becoming weaker and weaker. Meanwhile, the Tibetans who remain home are constrained by Beijing's military forces and, through marriage, education, and close inhabitation, are mixed with the Han people and culture.

Hong-yuan Chu

References

Lamb, Alastair. *Britain and Chinese Central Asia: The Road to Lhasa 1767 to 1905*. London, England: Routledge and Kegan Paul, 1960.

Goldstein, Melvyn. *A History of Modern Tibet, 1913–1951: The Demise of the Lamaist State*. Berkeley: University of California Press, 1989.

Ting, V. K. (Ding Wenjiang, 1887–1936)

V. K. Ting was a leading intellectual and the first Western-trained geologist in modern China. Known to many as "the Chinese Huxley," Ting took it upon himself to educate his countrymen in the principles of the scientific method. Conjoining science and nationalism, Ting used his professional knowledge to demonstrate the importance of science in China's national rejuvenation.

Born in rural Jiangsu of gentry parents, Ting spent his childhood studying the Chinese classics with the intention of passing the civil service examinations. But as the late Qing government was increasing its efforts to bring Western technologies to China, Ting's parents capitalized on the reform environment by sending Ting to Japan in 1902. After remaining in Japan for two years, Ting traveled to Great Britain and studied geology at the University of Glasgow.

The experience in Scotland was pivotal in Ting's intellectual development. When he first arrived in Glasgow, like many Chinese he was drawn to science primarily for utilitarian reasons. Science was considered to be the Western key to making China strong. Among the different disciplines of science, geology particularly attracted Ting because of its nationalistic importance. Lack of mining was one of China's weaknesses. In Ting's day, mining in China was practically a Western monopoly operated by foreign firms and protected by foreigners' special rights. With his geological training, Ting believed that he could reclaim China's lost territorial and economic rights from foreign powers. But the more Ting learned about science, the more he realized that his previous utilitarian training was deficient. He discovered that science was more than a technique; it was a world view encompassing all aspects of human life. In science Ting found a rational mode of thinking and an empirical attitude, both of which were essential in reforming Chinese society.

Ting left Great Britain in 1911 and returned to China shortly after the Revolution of 1911. The newly established republican government took Ting's special training seriously. In 1916 Ting became the founding director of the Geological Survey of China, a new branch under the government's Ministry of Commerce and Industry. Under Ting's leadership, the Geological Survey became one of China's internationally renowned scientific institutions. The Geological Survey served as a teaching and as a research institution. As its director, Ting trained many Chinese geologists and published scholarly papers in its two journals: *Bulletin of the Geological Survey of China* and *Paleontologica Sinica*.

In 1921, Ting left the Geological Survey to enter private business. He became the managing director of Beipiao Coal Mine in Manchuria, thereby fulfilling his early dream of breaking the Western monopoly of Chinese mining. In 1926, Ting was invited by the warlord Sun Chuanfang to participate in his administration of Shanghai and negotiate with foreign powers for the abolition of the Sino-Foreign Mixed Court in the city. In his spare time, he continued his academic research. In the 1920s, he published two pamphlets on Chinese mining: *Mining in China During the Past Fifty Years* (1922), and *Materials for a History of Foreign Capitalized Mining* (1929).

As a well-known geologist, Ting became a leader in his own discipline and an advocate for the modernization of China through science. For Ting, practicing science was more than a professional vocation; it was the means to bring about a strong and independent China. For this reason, on various occasions he fervently defended the value of science in national renewal. The most famous case occurred in 1923 when Ting and Carsun Chang (Zhang Junmai) engaged in a hot "debate about whether or not science could offer a view of life." This became known as the debate on science and philosophy of life. Ting challenged Chang's observation that science could not offer much to people's spiritual life. In his bold statement, "the omnipotence of science," Ting argued that the rational thinking of science provided human beings with the means to know what is humanly knowable. Therefore, scientific thinking could potentially resolve all human problems, including those concerning human society and life.

Although friendly with many liberal thinkers in China, Ting harbored a strong dose of elitism in his political thinking. His political writings published in the 1930s supported the establishment of an enlightened dictatorship in China and state planning of the Chinese economy. For Ting, the effective way to modernize China was to place all decisions in the hands of a selected few. He envisioned a political system not unlike that of the USSR, which he visited in 1933. Politically, Ting the scientist was a social engineer.

Tze-ki Hon

References

Furth, Charlotte. *Ting Wen-chiang: Science*

and China's New Culture. Cambridge, MA: Harvard University Press, 1970.

Tongzhi Restoration

In 1862 Emperor Tongzhi, aged seven, succeeded to the throne as the ruler of the Qing empire. His father, Emperor Xianfeng, had died in the previous year in Jehol, when the capital was under British-French occupation. Shortly after Tongzhi's accession in Jehol and before his return to Beijing, his mother, Empress Dowager Cixi, and his uncle, Prince Gong, staged a *coup d'état* and eliminated the eight regents appointed by the late Xianfeng to guide the young emperor. From then on the court came under the joint control of Cixi and Prince Gong. Cixi was to remain in power for the rest of the nineteenth century.

Although Tongzhi never became the major policymaker in his court, the decade of his reign (1862–74) was known as the Tongzhi Restoration. The term "restoration" *(zhongxing)* was often used by Chinese historians to describe the revival of national strength or the restoration of political order in the middle of a dynasty. It applies to the Tongzhi reign essentially for two reasons. First, it was under Emperor Tongzhi that the Taiping Rebellion (1851–64) was finally suppressed. The rebellion davastated most of south and central China and seriously weakened the power as well as the legitimacy of the Qing dynasty. Throughout the reign of Tongzhi, the Qing painstakingly reconsolidated its rule over China and gradually recovered from the military, financial, and economic blows it had suffered at the hands of the Taipings. Secondly, the Anglo-French occupation of Beijing, resulting from the *Arrow* War (or the second Opium War) of 1858 to 1860, shocked the Qing into the reality of the Western threat. In the 1860s and 1870s, a number of Han officials who had defeated the Taipings, in particular Zeng Guofan, Li Hongzhang, and Zuo Zongtang, initiated a series of military, institutional, and technological reforms in the provinces, based on Western models. These reforms, known as the Self-Strengthening movement, were supported and coordinated by Prince Gong. For a while, at least, they represented the hope of a modernization effort from the top down.

Yet most of the Tongzhi policies were traditional remedies for dynastic crises: relief and public work projects, land reclamation, water control, tax reduction, modification of the examinations, and the like. These measures failed to solve the unprecedented problems China was facing at the time. Foreign policy crises also distracted the government. At first the West adopted a relatively tolerant attitude toward the young emperor, giving China a breathing space for reform; however, conflict soon reemerged with the Tianjin Incident in 1870. An additional hindrance to the Tongzhi reign was the gradual loss of political power and authority by the center to the provinces. This trend toward regional autonomy had begun with the effort to suppress the Taiping Rebellion, and neither Cixi nor Prince Gong was able to reverse the course now.

In historical perspective, the Tongzhi Restoration proved to be a temporary rejuvenation of the Manchu rule. Some of the self-strengthening reforms continued after the death of Tongzhi in 1874 and did increase the dynasty's ability to manage its foreign and domestic challenges. But in the end those challenges proved to be too profound and complex for the Qing government to comprehend and overcome. The empire disintegrated less than forty years later.

Wang Ke-wen

References

Liu, Kwang-ching. "The Ch'ing Restoration," in *The Cambridge History of China*, ed. John K. Fairbank, vol. 10, 409–490. Cambridge, England: Cambridge University Press, 1978.

Wright, Mary C. *The Last Stand of Chinese Conservatism: The T'ung-chih Restoration, 1862–1874*. Stanford, CA: Stanford University Press, 1957.

Trade Associations

The modern version of traditional Chinese guilds *(hanghui)*, trade associations *(tongye gonghui)* first appeared at the turn of the twentieth century. They adopted two forms: voluntary associations based on contractual agreements on production and sale, often called *lianhesuo* or *yingyesuo*; and compulsory, monopolistic associations, which controlled entire trades.

The earliest *tongye gonghui* was organized by the flour industry in Shanghai in 1904, partly as a mediating and arbitrating agency for internal disputes, and partly as a response to foreign competition. It coordinated and facilitated the purchase of wheat for the participating factories. Similar associations were then formed by leather and fur industries, fire insurance companies and florists. After the Revolution of 1911, the Beiyang government encouraged this trend by ordering the formation of associations in all trades. Many of the newly organized trade associations, however, came under control by gangsters. When the Guomindang came to power in 1928, it reorganized and reregistered the existing *tongye gonghui*, but continued the Beiyang policy of encouraging such formations.

As the traditional guilds further declined in the 1920s and 1930s, modern trade associations continued to grow in number and influence. Government promotion was certainly a contributing factor, but a more important cause may have been the world depression and the foreign economic penetration of China. Facing external threat, China's emerging industries and businesses sensed the need for solidarity and cooperation among themselves. On the eve of the second Sino-Japanese War (1937–45), more than two hundred *tongye gonghui* operated in Shanghai alone.

One of the most prominent activities of these trade associations, therefore, was their struggle against foreign competition. The porcelain industry in Shanghai, for example, effectively defeated Japanese imports by organizing a *yingyesuo* in the late 1920s. It also helped to develop overseas markets for Chinese porcelains in the following decades. In general, *tongye gonghui* played a major role in the promotion of native products and the revival of indigenous industries in modern China.

The monopolistic trade associations emerged mostly during the Sino-Japanese War, in areas under Japanese occupation. In an effort to mobilize and exploit the economic resources of China for the Japanese war machine, the occupation authorities forced the organization of new trade associations, called *lianhehui*, to replace the old ones. These control-oriented associations were abolished with Japan's defeat in the war. *Tongye gonghui* then briefly revived themselves in the late 1940s, but the Communist victory in 1949 again sealed their fate. They perished when the Communist government socialized the country's industries and eliminated commercial enterprise in the early 1950s.

Wang Ke-wen

Treaty of Aigun

The Treaty of Aigun was signed between China and Russia in 1858. Imperial Russia's ambitions and objectives in China during the nineteenth century differed from those of the maritime Western countries. As an Asian land power with one of the world's longest land borders between herself and China, Russia sought territorial expansion rather than trade and missionary activity in China. After the Opium War of 1840 to 1842, Russia gradually extended her control in eastern Siberia into the Amur River basin, south of the Sino-Russian border defined by the Treaty of Nerchinsk (1689). During the *Arrow War* (the second Opium War) in 1858, as the Qing government was facing a joint Anglo-French attack in south China, Count Muraviev, the Russian governor-general of Eastern Siberia, launched an invasion into the northeast. His troops defeated the Chinese frontier forces and on May 28 forced the Manchu general Yishan to sign a treaty in the Chinese city of Aigun. The treaty recognized Russian control over the area north of the Amur River, a total exceeding 230,000 square miles, and placed the area between the Amur and Ussuri Rivers and the Pacific Ocean under Sino-Russian joint control. It also allowed only Chinese and Russian ships to use the Amur and Ussuri rivers. This was one of the largest territorial losses suffered by China in modern times.

Shortly after the signing of the Treaty of Aigun, Russia sent Count Putiatin to Beijing to ensure a Russian share of the British and French gains in the Treaty of Tianjin (1858). This resulted in the signing of a separate Treaty of Tianjin between Russia and China in June 1858. The Qing government tried to use this opportunity to repudiate the Treaty of Aigun, particularly with regard to the joint-control area. As the trouble between China and the maritime West continued, Russia was always able to exploit the situation to her advantage. In 1860, during negotiations for the Beijing Convention, the Russian envoy Ignatiev presented himself as a mediator between China and her enemies England and France, and persuaded Prince Gong to sign an agreement (Treaty of Beijing) that not only confirmed the Sino-Russian treaties of Aigun and Tianjin but ceded the entire joint-control area to Russia, which soon became the latter's Maritime Province.

Wang Ke-wen

References
Clubb, O. Edmund. *China and Russia: The "Great Game."* New York, NY: Columbia University Press, 1972.

Quested, R. K. I. *The Expansion of Russia in East Asia, 1857–1860*. Kuala Lumpur: University of Malaya Press, 1968.

Treaty of Nanjing
See OPIUM WAR

Treaty of St. Petersburg
See ILI CRISIS

Treaty of Shimonoseki
See SINO-JAPANESE WAR (1894–95)

Treaty of Tianjin
See ARROW WAR; TREATY OF AIGUN

Treaty of Wangxia
Signed by China and the United States in 1844, the Treaty of Wangxia represented the first extension of the British gains from the Opium War to another Western country. Shortly after the Opium War (1840–42), the Americans requested a sharing of the British privileges in China. Some Qing officials regarded the request as an opportunity to court favors with the "American barbarians" in their attempt to control the "English barbarians." As a result, the United States government sent Caleb Cushing, commanding a fleet of three ships, to Macao in early 1844. There, with the help of the local American doctor Peter Parker, he negotiated with Qiying, the imperial commissioner of the Qing court.

A treaty was signed in Wangxia, a small village near Macao, in July. It permitted the United States to enjoy all the benefits that the British had obtained in the Sino-British Treaty of Nanjing (1842) and its supplementary agreements. These benefits included extraterritoriality, negotiated custom duties, trading at the five opened ports, and most-favored-nations treatment. In addition, the treaty prohibited opium trade, gave Americans the right to maintain churches and hospitals in the five ports, and allowed American warships to anchor, for no more than two days at a time, at ports other than the five designated ports. The two governments also agreed to review the treaty for possible revision in twelve years.

The treaty thus peacefully established an unequal relationship between the United States and China, for the like of which England had fought a war. To an extent, this reinforced the American perception of itself as a "friend of the Chinese," and foreshadowed the introduction of the Open Door policy several decades later.

Wang Ke-wen

References
Gulick, Edward. *Peter Parker and the Opening of China*. Cambridge, MA: Harvard University Press, 1973.
Hunt, Michael. *The Making of a Special Relationship: The United States and China to 1914*. New York, NY: Columbia University Press, 1985.

Treaty of Whampoa
The Treaty of Whampoa was the first unequal treaty signed between China and France in modern times. In essence it was a copy of the Sino-American Treaty of Wangxia (1844), which peacefully extended to the United States the privileges which China had granted to the British after the Opium War (1840–42). One month after the signing of the Treaty of Wangxia, the French government sent Theodore de Lagrene to Macao and pressed for a similar agreement with the Qing. Backed by a fleet of eight ships, Lagrene succeeded in entering negotiations with the Chinese imperial commissioner Qiying. In October 1844, Lagrene and Qiying signed a treaty on board a French battleship anchored in the port of Whampoa. In addition to enjoying all the benefits that had been given to England and the United States since 1842, including extraterritoriality, negotiated custom duties, trading at the five opened ports and most-favored-nations treatment, the French were given special permission to propagate Roman Catholicism. As in the case of the Treaty of Wangxia, the Chinese generally saw this new Sino-French relationship as part of their strategy of "controlling barbarians with barbarians," and failed to appreciate its damaging impact on the sovereignty of China.

Wang Ke-wen

References
Fairbank, John K. *Trade and Diplomacy on the China Coast: The Opening of the Treaty Ports, 1842–1854*. Cambridge, MA: Harvard University Press, 1953.
Grosse-Aschhoff, Angelus. *The Negotiations Between Ch'i-ying and Lagrene, 1844–*

1846. New York, NY: Franciscan Institute, 1950.

Treaty Ports

Treaty ports were coastal and riverine cities in China opened to foreign trade, as stipulated in treaties concluded between various foreign powers and the Qing government. The first five treaty ports, Canton, Xiamen (Amoy), Fuzhou, Ningpo, and Shanghai, were opened as a result of the Treaty of Nanjing, 1842. Sixteen more were opened before 1896, and another twenty-eight between 1896 and 1911. Of these, Shanghai, Tianjin, Canton, and Hankou became the major entrepôts.

The treaty ports had a dual role in the development of Chinese nationalism. On one hand, they were the seats of foreign power in China and hence represented imperialist encroachment on the Chinese. Opened as a result of "unequal treaties," they were protected by foreign land and naval forces. The existence of "concessions," areas administered by foreigners, in a number of the treaty ports represented an abridgement of national sovereignty. From their stations in various treaty ports, treaty power consuls exercised judicial authority over their own nationals (extraterritoriality). Foreign economic interests congregated in the treaty ports and, from a nationalist point of view, the treaty ports thus served as bases for imperialist economic exploitation of China.

On the other hand, the treaty port environment nurtured nationalism and nationalists. Treaty ports brought Chinese officials, businessmen, and intellectuals into firsthand contact with Western technology, methods, and ideas, including nationalism. And they also provided security from internal upheavals and established an orderly business environment. As a result, Chinese settled in large numbers in these areas, which became crucibles for social, economic, and political change. Shanghai is an example. Here the international and French concessions came to comprise most of the modern city of Shanghai. In the early years after the port was opened in 1843, the foreign settlements contained only 1 percent of Shanghai's population, but by 1942, when they were occupied by the Japanese army, the concessions contained 62 percent of the population. This growth was primarily due to Chinese immigration, beginning with the Taiping Rebellion (1851–64). Capital as well as people flowed into the con-

cessions which became centers for Chinese commerce, finance, and modern industry. In the early twentieth century, Shanghai and other large treaty ports saw the emergence of a bourgeoisie and a proletariat, which espoused nationalism and other modern values.

Treaty ports also sheltered nationalist reformers and revolutionaries. In the years before the Revolution of 1911, most radical intellectuals stayed in large cities abroad or, when in China, congregated in the foreign areas of the major treaty ports. The Chinese Communist Party was founded in Shanghai's French concession. Along with Hong Kong, the treaty port concessions offered a ready escape from Chinese authority. And, no doubt, many of the nationalist tracts inveighing against foreign imperialism were penned under foreign protection in the treaty ports.

Andrea McElderry

References

Gasster, Michael. "The Republican Revolutionary Movement." *The Cambridge History of China*, ed. John K. Fairbank and Kwang-ching Liu, vol. 2, 463–534. Cambridge, England: Cambridge University Press, 1980

Murphey, Rhoads. "The Treaty Ports and China's Modernization." *The Chinese City Between Two Worlds*, ed. Mark Elvin and G. William Skinner, 17–71. Stanford, CA: Stanford University Press, 1974.

Wright, Stanley. *Hart and the Chinese Customs.* Belfast: Wm Mullan, 1950.

Triads

Also known as the Hong League *(Hongmen)* or the Three Harmonies Society *(Sanhehui),* the Triads was the largest and most influential secret society in south China from the seventeenth to the early twentieth century. The name of the society is said to have derived from the reign title of the founding emperor of the Ming dynasty (1368–1644), which the society vowed to restore. After the Manchu conquest of China and the establishment of the Qing dynasty (1644–1912), loyalists to the former Ming (some believed to be the followers of Zheng Chenggong, or Koxinga, in Taiwan) formed the society for the purpose of continuing their anti-Manchu activities underground. During the eighteenth century, branches of the society spread from Taiwan and Fujian to Guangdong,

Guangxi, and the Yangtze valley. Some well-known secret societies in these areas, such as the Elder Brother Society *(Gelaohui)* and the Heaven and Earth Society *(Tiandihui)*, were identified as regional varieties of the Triads.

The internal organization of the Triads was modeled on that of the Liangshan bandits as described in the traditional Chinese novel, *The Water Margin (Shuihuzhuan)*, with lodges *(tang)* as its principal sections or branches. Members of the society mostly came from the lower classes, united by a sense of brotherhood, strictly enforced discipline, and Han nationalism. Under the slogan of "overthrowing the Qing and restoring the Ming," the Heaven and Earth Society led several uprisings in the southern provinces and indirectly contributed to the rise of the Taiping Rebellion of 1851 to 1864. A Lower Yangtze offshoot of the Triads, the Small Sword Society *(Xiaodaohui)* staged an uprising and briefly took control of Shanghai during the Taiping disturbance. After the second Opium War of 1858 to 1860, the Triads was also active in the anti-missionary riots, directing its nationalist attack on both the Manchu ruler and the Western intruders.

When large numbers of southern Chinese emigrated overseas in the nineteenth century, mostly to North America and Hawaii, those areas established branches of the Triads. In North America it adopted the name Hongmen Zhigongtang, with lodges in many major cities of the United States and Canada. This overseas Chinese organization was a main source of political and financial support for the anti-Manchu revolutionary movement led by Sun Yatsen. In fact, Sun allegedly imitated the organizational structure of the Hongmen Zhigongtang in constructing his Tongmenghui (Revolutionary Alliance) in 1905.

After the fall of the Qing and the founding of the Republic, the Triads gradually lost its political purpose and evolved into a mafia-type organization. The overseas Hongmen Zhigongtang was reorganized in 1925 into a political party, the Chinese Zhigongdang, which subsequently opposed the rule of Chiang Kaishek. After 1949, the People's Republic accepted the Chinese Zhigongdang as one of the democratic parties, but the domestic Triads found it difficult to survive under the Chinese Communist Party (CCP) and moved its base to Southeast Asia and North America. In recent decades, the Triads has virtually become a generic term in Western vocabulary for the Chinese overseas underworld.

The Triads may have ceased to be a unified society today, but its various successors still engage in criminal activities on an international scale. The (Han) nationalist origin of the society has long been forgotten.

Wang Ke-wen

References

Chesneaux, Jean, ed. *Popular Movements and Secret Societies in China, 1840–1950*. Stanford, CA: Stanford University Press, 1972.

Trotskyism

Trotskyism is the ideology that sprang from a number of oppositionist groups formed among Marxists who considered themselves followers of the ideas of the Soviet Communist leader, Leon Trotsky. They generally have wanted to depend less on the peasantry and more on the urban proletariat in carrying out the Chinese revolution than the dominant wing of the Chinese Communist Party (CCP). They also have been strong advocates of inter-party democracy and have tended to emphasize the internationalist aspects of the Communist revolution.

Trotskyist groups first formed among Chinese students studying in Moscow in the late 1920s. In 1929, Chen Duxiu, the former secretary general of the CCP, became attracted to some of their ideas. After Chen and his supporters were expelled from the CCP in 1929, he helped to organize a unified Leftist Opposition among the various Trotskyist groups.

The Leftist Opposition argued that the Communist Party had to stop following what it considered to be an "adventurist" policy and instead work on regaining the support of the masses. The most expeditious way to do that was through the use of democratic slogans which would expose the sham nature of Guomindang rule. Following Trotsky, most members of the Leftist Opposition ultimately agreed that the best way to accomplish this goal was to call for the establishment of a national assembly. They also concurred with Trotsky on the need for more democracy within the Party. Furthermore, most agreed that the Guomindang had destroyed the remnants of feudal rule in China and that it would be possible to complete the bourgeois revolution by relying on an alliance of the proletariat and the poor peasantry. Finally, it was the opinion of the Trotskyists that the revolution, once successful, could immediately move toward the creation of a socialist state as part of an international revolution.

The unity among Trotskyist groups did not last long. Police raids and internal bickering shattered them, especially after Chen Duxiu was imprisoned in the fall of 1932. Nonetheless, prominent members, such as Peng Shuzhi, one of the original founders of the CCP, and Wang Fanxi, whose writings in exile attracted the attention of many young Chinese in the 1980s, managed to escape imprisonment. The group remained a small but viable force until 1949. Those few who remained behind in China were imprisoned in December 1949. Throughout the 1980s, many young Chinese dissident intellectuals began to view Trotskyism as the road not taken in Chinese politics, one that might have led to a more humane, urban-oriented Communism. Young intellectuals especially admired the writings of Wang Shiwei, who was executed by the CCP as a Trotskyist in the 1940s for his insistence on the need for the independence of literature from Party control.

Lee Feigon

References

P'eng, Shu-tse. *The Chinese Communist Party in Power*. New York, NY: Monad Press, 1980.

Wang, Fan-hsi. *Chinese Revolutionary: Memoirs, 1919–1949*, trans. Gregor Benton. Oxford, England: Oxford University Press, 1980.

Twenty-One Demands

Shortly after the outbreak of World War I, Japan declared war against Germany and dispatched troops to occupy the German "sphere of influence" in the Chinese province of Shandong. Taking advantage of the Western countries' preoccupation with the war in Europe, Japan decided to expand her influence in China to a degree which no other power had attempted before. In January 1915, Japan presented to the Chinese government a total of twenty-one demands, arranged in five groups:

1. Transference of German rights in Shandong to Japan, making the province a Japanese "sphere of influence";

2. Recognition of Japan's dominant position in southern Manchuria and eastern Inner Mongolia, allowing the Japanese to lease or own land, to trade or manu-

Japan presenting the Twenty-One Demands, 1915. (Courtesy of Nationalist Party Archives.)

facture, and to hold exclusive rights in mining and railroad construction there;

3. Sino-Japanese joint operation of China's largest industrial complex, the Hanyeping Iron and Steel Works in Hubei, as well as Japanese exclusive mining rights in that area;

4. Promise by China of not ceding or leasing her coastal area to any power other than Japan;

5. Employment of Japanese political, financial, and military advisers by the Chinese government; partial Japanese control of Chinese police and arsenals; Japanese first right to provide loans and arms to China; Japanese exclusive right to invest in Fujian and to build railroads between Hubei, Jiangxi, and Guangdong.

If accepted by China, these demands would have in effect reduced China to a protectorate of Japan. After months of secret negotiations, Japan pressed China to accept the demands with an ultimatum on May 7, 1915. The Chinese government, under Yuan Shikai, managed to persuade Japan to drop, at least for the time being, the fifth group of demands, but had to accept the rest on May 9. The Chinese have since remembered the date as the National Humiliation Day *(guochi)*. News about the Twenty-One Demands led to nationwide anti-Japanese protest in China; the nationalistic outburst briefly enhanced popular support for Yuan's government. Meanwhile, Yuan's chief political opponent, Sun Yatsen,

who was in Japan at the time, was discredited for his ambivalent position on this issue. Later Chinese historians, however, have accused Yuan of capitulating to the demands in order to obtain Japan's support for his monarchical attempt.

The incident marked a turning point in the history of Sino-Japanese relations. Since the late Qing, and especially since China's defeat in the first Sino-Japanese War of 1894 to 1895, the Chinese had looked up to Japan as a model of westernizing reform. Thousands of Chinese youth had gone to Japan to study her methods of self-strengthening, viewing Japan's success in competing with the West with envy and admiration. The Twenty-One Demands drastically changed this perception. As Western dominance of East Asia declined after World War I, the Chinese found Japan replacing the Western countries as the most serious threat to China's survival. Thereafter Chinese anti-imperialist sentiments shifted to aim at Japan, and Chinese nationalism became synonymous with a hatred for Japan. This anti-Japanese feeling was to last until the end of World War II.

Wang Ke-wen

References

Jansen, Marius B. *Japan and China: From War to Peace, 1894–1972.* Chicago, IL: Rand McNally, 1975.

Young, Ernest P. *The Presidency of Yuan Shih-k'ai: Liberalism and Dictatorship in Early Republican China.* Ann Arbor: University of Michigan Press, 1977.

U

Unequal Treaties

The series of treaties which China concluded with the Western countries and Japan during the late Qing and the early Republic are known as the "unequal treaties." The first incidence and principal example of such treaties was the Sino-British Treaty of Nanjing, signed after the Opium War of 1840 to 1842. That treaty and its supplements established the foundation of China's inferior status in the world community she was now forced to join, namely, extraterritoriality and negotiated tariffs. These two principles were imposed on China but not on Great Britain, and there was no statement made in the treaty indicating a mutual respect of the integrity of sovereignty and a recognition of equal status between the two signatories. The treaties China subsequently concluded with other powers, such as the Treaty of Wangxia with the United States (1844) and the Treaty of Whampoa with France (1844), automatically accepted this unequal practice.

The Nanjing treaty also imposed on China the payment of war indemnities and cession of land, which were often repeated in the treaties which China signed as the result of her defeat in wars during the next half century, including the Beijing Convention (1860) following the second Opium War, the Treaty of Shimonoseki (1895) following the first Sino-Japanese War, and the Boxer Protocol (1901). Russia did not directly engage in wars with China before 1900, yet it managed to exploit the external crises which China faced in this period and gained territories from China in peaceful settlements, *e.g.,* the Treaty of Aigun (1858). During the "scramble for concessions" in the last years of the nineteenth century, all agreements which China concluded with the powers, yielding to them Chinese territorial and economic rights, may be regarded as unequal treaties as well.

After the Revolution of 1911, the new Republic not only inherited the old unequal treaties from the Qing dynasty but concluded new ones, the most notorious being Japan's Twenty-One Demands in 1915. By then, however, the term and concept of unequal treaties had become common knowledge among educated Chinese. To them, the treaties marked the oppression and exploitation of China by the foreign powers, which undermined China's independence and impeded economic development. It became the hated target of the rising tide of modern Chinese nationalism and, in the 1920s and after, closely linked to the anti-imperialism movement. Abolishing the unequal treaties was the main goal of the "National Revolution" of the 1920s, but the Guomindang (GMD) government that emerged from the revolution failed to accomplish the goal with its "revolutionary diplomacy." In fact, during the early 1930s, the government had to sign a series of agreements with Japan that resembled, both in content and in spirit, the unequal treaties of the past. Not until World War II, when China, as an ally of most of the Western countries in war with Japan, did the powers finally agree to abolish their unequal treaties with China. This was realized in 1943, a full century after the conclusion of the Treaty of Nanjing.

Wang Ke-wen

References

Etzold, Thomas H. "In Search of Sovereignty: The Unequal Treaties in Sino-American Relations, 1925–30." *China in the 1920s: Nationalism and Revolution,* ed. F. Gilbert Chan and Thomas H. Etzold,

The signing of Sino-British Treaty of Nanjing, 1842. (Courtesy of Nationalist Party Archives.)

176–196. New York, NY: New Viewpoints, 1976.

United Front, 1923–27

The cooperation between the Guomindang (GMD) and the Chinese Communist Party (CCP) under Soviet guidance, known as the United Front, helped to consolidate the revolutionary regime at Canton and to carry out the initial phase of the Northern Expedition.

The United Front resulted from the alliance between Sun Yatsen and the Soviet Union in the early 1920s. In a sense, the United Front included three partners—the GMD, the CCP, and the Comintern. In late 1921, the Comintern representative Hendricus Sneevliet (Maring), who had just assisted in the founding of the CCP, met with Sun at Guilin. An initial proposal for cooperation was discussed but no immediate action taken. Not until his expulsion from Canton by Chen Jiongming in mid-1922 did Sun turn his attention to the possible new alliance. Shortly after arriving in Shanghai, Sun met with CCP leaders, including Li Dazhao and Chen Duxiu, for a discussion on the reorganization of his own party, the GMD. In January 1923, Sun met with the Soviet envoy Adolf Jaffe in Shanghai and announced the Sun-Jaffe Manifesto, which affirmed the new alliance. The following month, Sun returned to Canton to establish his new Canton regime and soon received assistance from Moscow and the CCP.

Sun had expressed a degree of interest in, and admiration for, the success of the Bolshevik revolution in Russia, yet the primary motive behind his decision to collaborate with the Soviet Union was the need for material assistance. Seeking foreign support had been a constant effort in Sun's revolutionary career. After being rejected by all the major Western powers, Sun found the Soviet Union to be the most likely ally. Moscow and the Comintern had decided in the early 1920s to undermine the capitalist countries by aiding anti-imperialist national revolutions in colonial or semicolonial societies. In China, they had approached Wu Peifu and Feng Yuxiang, in addition to Sun Yatsen, for that purpose, but in the end focused their support on Sun. Their military and financial assistance to Sun, however, came with an important condition: Sun had to form a United Front with the newly organized CCP. At Sun's insistence, the United Front took a peculiar form; instead of allying with the CCP, the GMD absorbed the CCP, admitting all of its members into its ranks. In the GMD, therefore, the United Front was referred to as the policy of "admitting the Communists and allying with Russia" *(lianE rongjong)*.

Under the guidance of principal Soviet adviser Mikhail Borodin and with the support of CCP members, Sun and his party accomplished a series of major tasks in Canton in 1924: the reorganization of the GMD on the Leninist model, the establishment of a military academy at Whampoa for the training of a revolutionary armed force, and the adoption of anti-imperialism and mass movement as the guidelines of the Canton regime. The alliance, especially the Soviet aid, quickly built a vigorous revolutionary base in Guangdong province. The GMD and the CCP both grew under the United Front. The CCP was especially active and influential in the mass movement. The problem, however, was that the CCP not only grew faster than the GMD but that it grew within the GMD. Retaining their CCP membership while working in the GMD, these "dual members" soon drew suspicion and hostility from other GMD members. During the early days of the United Front, a confident Sun suppressed several complaints against the new alliance, but relations between the two parties deteriorated soon after Sun's death in March 1925.

After mid-1925, the controversy concerning "dual members" was galvanized by a power struggle within the GMD for the succession to Sun's leadership. In November, a group of anti-Communist GMD veterans gathered at the Western Hills near Beijing, where Sun's coffin temporarily rested, and held a Party meeting. They decided to terminate the United Front but to maintain the alliance with Moscow. The action was denounced as illegal by the GMD leadership at Canton, which reaffirmed its legitimacy by strengthening the United Front. In March 1926, the GMD leadership in Canton itself divided. Chiang Kaishek, head of the Whampoa Military Academy, expelled the leader of the Party-government, Wang Jingwei, with a *coup d'état*. Chiang had suspected an illicit collaboration involving Wang, the Soviet advisers, and the CCP. He placed the latter two groups under restraint, but declared his support for the United Front once Wang was purged. Chiang realized that Soviet aid was still indispensable for the Canton regime.

In July 1926, Chiang initiated the Northern Expedition to reunify the country. Guided by the United Front and supported by the CCP-led mass movement, the campaign progressed smoothly. By the end of that year, the expeditionary forces had advanced into the Yangtze valley, but tension within the United Front also heightened. There is no denying that the Comintern and the CCP regarded the National Revolution, the self-proclaimed mission of the GMD, as only the first step toward their eventual goal of socialist revolution in China. The latter task would have to be shouldered by the CCP alone, which meant that eventually the GMD would be brushed aside.

The success of the initial phase of the Northern Expedition brought the United Front closer to that eventual parting. Throughout late 1926 and early 1927, Communists in Moscow and China debated on when and how to transform the current revolution into a socialist one, and the GMD was increasingly alarmed. In early 1927 the GMD split on the issue of the United Front and Party leadership, resulting in the formation of two rival camps: one situated in Wuhan, the other in Nanjing. In April, Chiang, after receiving promises of support from the Western powers and from Chinese financiers, launched his party purification (*qingdang*) in Shanghai, purging the CCP from the GMD in a bloody massacre. Feeling insecure, the CCP at Wuhan intensified the mass movement in order to create its own power base. The CCP action antagonized the GMD in Wuhan and in July the Wuhan regime also announced its break with the CCP. Borodin was sent back to the Soviet Union and the CCP soon resorted to armed uprisings. The four-year GMD-CCP alliance ended in chaos for both parties.

Wang Ke-wen

References

Van Slyke, Lyman P. *Enemies and Friends: The United Front in Chinese Communist History.* Stanford, CA: Stanford University Press, 1968.

Wilbur, C. Martin. *The Nationalist Revolution in China, 1923–1928.* London, England: Cambridge University Press, 1983.

United Front, 1937–45

The United Front of 1937 to 1945 was an anti-Japanese alliance between the Guomindang (GMD) and the Chinese Communist Party (CCP) during the second Sino-Japanese War.

After the Long March (1934–35), the CCP had to completely reassess its political strategy. Although its troops had won several victories over the enemy and therefore gained a respite for themselves, it needed to find ways to deter the GMD army from its hot pursuit. Meanwhile, the Comintern representative Lin Yuying (Zhang Hao) arrived in northern Shaanxi with Moscow's instructions for the formation of an anti-Japanese united front in China. In late December 1935, the CCP Politburo meeting at Wayaobao decided to accept the new Moscow line. During the following months, the CCP softened its policy regarding land revolution, while stepping up its attempts to identify itself with the anti-Japanese cause. It sent Liu Shaoqi to revive the underground Party in north China by assisting the student demonstrations in the December Ninth Movement, and Feng Xuefeng to Shanghai to drum up the intellectuals' anti-Japanese sentiment in central China. Both missions aimed at attracting popular support for the Party's anti-Japanese stance, so that the GMD government would be pressured into suspending its annihilation campaign against the remaining Communist troops in northern Shaanxi.

Initially, the GMD government under Chiang Kaishek was unmoved by the CCP's new strategy. In February 1936, the Red Army, driven by Chiang's attacks and the poverty of the loess plateau in northern Shaanxi, crossed the Yellow River and invaded Yan Xishan's Shanxi. The failure of this operation persuaded the Communist leaders to seek peace with potentially anti-Chiang forces within the GMD ranks, especially the Northeast Army under Zhang Xueliang and the Northwest Army under Yang Hucheng. By the early summer of 1936, the CCP had signed secret agreements of mutual assistance with both armies. The CCP also softened its attitude toward Chiang Kaishek for a number of reasons. First, Zhang Xueliang had a high esteem for Chiang and asked the Communists to endorse an anti-Japanese alliance with Chiang as its Fascist leader. Second, the Guangdong-Guangxi Rebellion against Nanjing crumbled in July 1936, much more rapidly than the Communists had expected; the Party found that it should not underestimate Chiang's political and military capability. Third, the Comintern telegrammed and urged the CCP to make further concessions to Chiang in order to push him into active resistance against Japanese aggression. Secret contacts between representatives of the CCP (Zhou Enlai) and the GMD (Chen Lifu) had begun in early 1936, although they did not convince Chiang to abandon his policy of domestic pacification before external resistance.

In October 1936, the Japanese instigated the separatist movement of Inner Mongolia and the Mongolian attack at Suiyuan. The incident galvanized anti-Japanese public opinion and popular discontent with the continuing GMD-CCP civil war. Yet Chiang still pushed for his anti-Communist campaigns and arrested several anti-Japanese war advocates in Shanghai. The Xian (Sian) Incident in December finally changed his mind. At first, the CCP leadership urged Zhang Xueliang to submit Chiang to a public trial at Xian. But Moscow's response soon made the Party realize that Stalin did not approve of the kidnapping. The Party therefore returned to its earlier policy of including Chiang in an anti-Japanese united front and worked to end the incident peacefully. The Xian Incident thus paved the way for a new GMD-CCP rapprochement. After Chiang's release, the two parties agreed to end their civil war. Chiang, however, insisted that the Communists give up their control over the Red Army, while the CCP sought to preserve its military and political autonomy within the framework of a unified China under Chiang's nominal leadership.

Before the negotiations ended, the Marco Polo Bridge Incident in July 1937 led to a full-scale war between China and Japan. This new crisis forced Chiang Kaishek to accept the CCP as a partner in the war of resistance, even though the Communists still refused to abandon their autonomous status. The Second United Front formally came into existence in August. The CCP forces were renamed the Eighth Route Army (in north China) and the New Fourth Army (in south China). They became a part of the national military but remained under CCP command. Meanwhile, CCP members were invited into the GMD government's wartime organizations, such as the Military Commission, in Wuhan and later in Chongqing. When the People's Political Council *(Guomin canzhenghui)* was established in July 1938 as a prototype parliament, the CCP also sent delegates to participate in it. Wang Ming and Zhou Enlai were the principal CCP representatives in its alliance with the GMD.

At the beginning of the war, the Communist forces accepted strategic coordination with the GMD in their fight against the Japanese, but after the Japanese occupation of Taiyuan in September 1937, the CCP began to emphasize independent guerrilla warfare aiming at establishing base areas behind the Japanese lines. The United Front was thereby transformed into a framework within which the CCP and the GMD competed with each other for supremacy.

When the Japanese offensive ceased in late 1938, skirmishes and conflicts between the two parties' armies intensified. The GMD was especially worried about the CCP's successful operation in establishing base areas, or border-region governments, in the Japanese-occupied territories. In January 1941, the GMD forces ambushed and destroyed the CCP's New Fourth Army in southern Anhui, in effect terminating the Second United Front. The CCP delegates withdrew from the People's Political Council in protest, and communications between the two parties were suspended for a long time. The GMD accused the CCP of using the war to expand its own power, whereas the CCP criticized the GMD for ineffective resistance and capitulating to Japan.

Neither of the two parties, however, wanted a civil war at this time. The GMD soon imposed a blockade on the CCP central base at Yan'an, and the CCP reestablished its "New Fourth Army" without the government's authorization, but superficially at least, they continued the anti-Japanese war. Not until the Japanese surrender in August 1945 did the two parties formally discard the façade of a United Front and renew their civil war.

Yung-fa Chen
Wang Ke-wen

References

Kataoka, Tetsuya. *Resistance and Revolution in China: The Communists and the Second United Front.* Berkeley: University of California Press, 1974.

Van Slyke, Lyman P. *Enemies and Friends: The United Front in Chinese Communist History.* Stanford, CA: Stanford University Press, 1968.

U

Vernacular Literature
See LITERATURE REVOLUTION

Versailles Peace Treaty
The Versailles Peace Treaty ended World War I. The peace conference convened in January 1919, amid high hopes in Japan and around the world. The Japanese delegation, led by Saionji Kinmochi, hoped to obtain Japanese control over the territories Japan had taken from Germany in China's Shandong Province, as well as over Germany's Pacific islands north of the equator. They also sought ratification of a racial-equality clause as an antidote to discrimination that Asian immigrants had experienced in Western countries. The Chinese delegation, led by Wellington Koo, sought recovery of Chinese rights which had been ceded to Germany. Despite U.S. President Woodrow Wilson's inspiring preconference rhetoric, the treaty itself disappointed both the Chinese and the Japanese.

Japan gained a permanent seat in the League of Nations, had its Shandong holdings confirmed, and had Germany's Pacific islands (the Carolinas, Marshall, and Marianas) mandated. But, even though China, Italy, France, and Great Britain had earlier agreed to support Japan's territorial claims, Wilson resisted and went along only when Japan threatened not to sign the treaty. Moreover, China's government refused to ratify the treaty, in response to the anger that swept that country on May 4, 1919, in reaction to Japan's territorial acquisitions, among other things. Most distressing to many Japanese was the American and British opposition to the racial-equality clause. Although a clear majority favored it, the Americans and the British (joined by Poland, Romania, and Brazil) blocked it. A final disappointment was the American failure to join the League of Nations.

James L. Huffman

References

Murakami, Hyoe. *Japan: The Years of Trial, 1919–52*. Tokyo: Japan Culture Institute, 1982.
Nish, Ian. *Japanese Foreign Policy, 1869–1942*. London: Routledge and Kegan Paul, 1977.

Wang Jingwei (1883–1944)

A revolutionary hero who ended his career as a puppet of the Japanese invader, the name of Wang Jingwei (zhaoming) has become synonymous with "traitor" *(hanjian)* in the popular Chinese mind; yet his controversial life suggests the complexity and ambiguity of modern Chinese nationalism.

Born in 1883 to a poor scholarly family at Canton, Wang received a classical education and passed the provincial examination with distinction before going to Japan on a government scholarship in 1904. While in Japan, Wang came into contact with the emerging revolutionary movement among overseas Chinese students, and in 1905 he became a leading member of Sun Yatsen's Tongmenghui. In the subsequent polemic between the revolutionary journal *Minbao* and the constitutionalist publications, Wang was a major spokesman for the anti-Manchu nationalist cause. In 1910, he led an abortive attempt to assassinate the Manchu regent prince in Beijing and was arrested and jailed by the Qing government. The incident made him a national hero.

Released shortly after the outbreak of the Revolution of 1911, Wang worked for a compromise between the revolutionaries and Yuan Shikai. When a settlement was reached and Yuan became the first president of the new republic, Wang withdrew from politics and devoted his attention to cultural and educational activities. In 1917 he returned to the entourage of Sun Yatsen and helped Sun organize a regime at Canton in opposition to the Beijing government. For the next seven years, Wang was a principal assistant to Sun, and in 1924 he became a member of the Central Executive Committee of the reorganized Guomindang (GMD).

Sun's death in 1925 made Wang a leading contender for the succession to GMD leadership. He was elected head of the party and the Canton government in July, and as such continued Sun's policy of allying with the Soviet Union and cooperating with the Chinese Communists. In March 1926, he was ousted by Chiang Kaishek after the Zhongshan Gunboat Incident. He stayed in Europe for nearly one year and returned in early 1927, during the Northern Expedition, to head the leftist Wuhan regime. The confrontation between Wang's Wuhan regime and the Nanjing regime under Chiang Kaishek was brought to an end in August as both sides purged the Communists from the GMD. In the following struggle for leadership of the reunified GMD, however, Wang again lost to Chiang.

From 1928 to 1931, while spending most of his time in overseas exile, Wang led an opposition to Chiang's new Nanjing government. He became known as the leader of the "Left GMD," an ideological-political movement claiming to represent the Party's radical line of 1924 to 1927. With the assistance of his factional followers and some anti-Chiang militarists, he directed a series of unsuccessful attacks aimed at toppling Chiang. In early 1932, in the wake of the Japanese invasion in Manchuria, Wang finally decided to cooperate with Chiang, and from 1932 to 1935, he served as head of the administrative Yuan (*i.e.*, premier) in Nanjing, interrupted only by a leave from late 1932 to early 1933.

As one of the top policymakers in the Nanjing government, Wang gave his main attention to the crisis in Sino-Japanese relations. Once an advocate of militant anti-imperialism, Wang was much more moderate now in actually conducting the country's foreign policy. He shared Chiang's view that domestic problems, especially the status of the Communists, should be settled first before turning to the external threat of Japan. Under his guidance, a series of territorial concessions were made to Japan in north China, an action which nationalistic Chinese severely criticized.

Meanwhile, Wang's power in the party and the government was being undercut by Chiang. In late 1935 Wang was wounded in an assassination attempt and soon resigned. He took another trip to France and did not return until shortly before the outbreak of the second Sino-Japanese War in 1937. During the first year of that war, Wang served under Chiang in the GMD's wartime government. In part disappointed by his continued loss of power to Chiang, and in part pessimistic about China's ability to fight against Japan, Wang soon became involved in a secret effort to end the war through negotiation. In December 1938, he left the wartime capital of Chongqing and went to Hanoi, where he announced his peace movement, and then went to Shanghai to negotiate a separate peace with Japan. In March 1940, with the help of the Japanese, he established a new "national government" in Japanese-occupied Nanjing. For the next four years, Wang tried to restore effective Chinese rule over the occupied territories, while limiting the military and economic domination of these territories by the Japanese army. Neither of these efforts was successful, and Wang's regime was generally regarded as a Japanese puppet.

Wang was fortunate enough to die in 1944, of an illness caused by the wound he had received in the 1935 assassination attempt. He was thus spared the humiliation and severe punishments suffered by his followers in the peace movement after the war. The complete picture of the motivations of his wartime defection, which literally ruined the reputation of a lifetime, has remained an enigma to his contemporaries as well as to historians. Wang himself would have undoubtedly agreed with the claim made by some of his followers during the postwar trials that he was a patriot trying to save the country from almost certain defeat and destruction. The fact that he miscalculated the course of the war does not make his cause any less noble. In a sense, it could be argued that Wang was a nationalist throughout his life. To preserve the Chinese nation at all costs was a goal he shared with other nationalistic Chinese. The

point of departure lay in their understanding as to what kind of Chinese nation, or state, that was worthy of preservation.

Wang Ke-wen

References

Boorman, Howard L. "Wang Ching-wei: A Political Profile," in *Revolutionary Leaders of Modern China*, ed. Chun-tu Hsueh. Oxford, England: Oxford University Press, 1971.

Bunker, Gerald E. *The Peace Conspiracy: Wang Ching-wei and the China War, 1937–1941*. Cambridge, MA: Harvard University Press, 1972.

So, Wai-chor. *The Kuomintang Left in the National Revolution*. Hong Kong: Oxford University Press, 1992.

Wang Jingwei Regime

The Wang Jingwei regime was the "national government" established by Wang Jingwei, with Japanese support, during the second Sino-Japanese War.

Between 1940 and 1945, there were two Nationalist (Guomindang) governments in China, one in Chongqing, the other in Nanjing; each claimed to be the legitimate government of China. This was not the first time that such an event occurred; in 1927, 1930 and 1931, China briefly had more than one Guomindang (GMD) government. However, the 1940 split of the GMD government was fundamentally different from the previous incidents. The GMD government in Nanjing was established in March 1940 under the aegis of the Japanese, then engaged in an all-out invasion against China. In spite of itself, the Nanjing government was by definition a collaborationist regime, whose fate had been inextricably bound up since its inception with that of the Japanese imperialists.

The Wang Jingwei regime was launched on March 31, 1940, well over a year after Wang Jingwei fled Chongqing to embark on peace negotiations with the Japanese in response to the overtures of the then Japanese prime minister Konoe Fumimoro. The delay was mainly due to opposition within the Japanese leadership concerning the wisdom of supporting Wang, a yet unknown factor, lest this move forestall any chance of reconciliation with Chiang Kaishek in Chongqing. According to Wang, the establishment of a rival government to Chongqing was not part of his original plan either. He made the decision only after Zeng Zhongming, his confidential secretary and close friend, was assassinated by Chongqing secret agents in Hanoi on March 20, 1939.

Styled as a replica of its namesake in Chongqing, the GMD government in Nanjing retained all the symbolism pertaining to Chongqing, including the tri-color national flag but with a yellow triangular pennant attached, bearing the slogan "Peace, National Construction, and Anti-Communism." As far as its political organization was concerned, the Wang regime copied the Chongqing establishment with only minor revisions. A Central Political Council was created, allegedly superseding the old Central Political Committee in Chongqing as the main decision-making body, to which the five ministries were responsible. The regime dismissed the GMD and its government in Chongqing as illegal on the grounds that members of the party leadership there had come under Chinese Communist control. It based its claim to political legitimacy on the Sixth National Congress of the GMD held in Shanghai on August 28, 1939, a haphazard gathering of dubious party members and others. Through Japan's mediation, it received diplomatic recognition from nine Axis countries. Ironically, Japan did not extend its formal recognition to the regime until November 30, 1940.

The Wang regime incorporated the existing "provisional government" in Beijing and the "reformed government" in Nanjing, formerly set up by the Japanese North China Despatch Army and Central China Despatch Army, respectively. While the "reformed government" was absorbed into Wang Jingwei's government, the "provisional government" was transformed into the North China Political Council, and remained beyond the control of the Wang regime. The territory over which Nanjing had some measure of control was mainly confined to southeast China. Even there, it had access only to cities, leaving large portions of the rural areas to guerrilla troops of Chongqing and the Communists.

Wang himself served as acting chairman and premier of his regime, with Lin Sen, recognized chairman of the GMD government in Chongqing, as its top leader until Lin's death in 1943. After Wang's own demise in 1944, his positions were succeeded by Chen Gongbo. Chen announced the dissolution of the regime when Japan surrendered in August 1945.

Luo Jiu-jung

Wang Jingwei. (Courtesy of Nationalist Party Archives.)

References

Boyle, John Hunter. *China and Japan at War, 1937–1945: The Politics of Collaboration.* Stanford, CA: Stanford University Press, 1972.

Bunker, Gerald E. *The Peace Conspiracy: Wang Ching-wei and the China War, 1937–1941.* Cambridge, MA: Harvard University Press, 1972.

Morley, James W., ed. *The China Quagmire: Japan's Expansion on the Asian Continent, 1933–1941.* New York, NY: Columbia University Press, 1983.

Wang Ming (1904–74)

See INTERNATIONALISTS

Wang Tao (1828–97)

Reformist writer and thinker, Wang Tao was one of the first journalists in modern China. Born as Wang Libin in Sozhou, Jiangsu province, Wang was the son of a village tutor. In 1845, he passed the first level of the examination system and received the *shengyuan* degree, but soon abandoned the traditional career through examinations and went to work for a publishing house owned by a British missionary in Shanghai. The experience and knowledge he obtained during the next thirteen years in Shanghai changed his worldview and his life. An ambitious and intelligent young man, Wang began to write to local officials on the defense and foreign policies of post-Opium War China. In 1862, when the Taiping Rebellion swept across the Yangtze provinces, Wang (using the name "Huang Wan") wrote a letter to a rebel general advising him on strategies. The Qing government discovered the letter and Wang had to flee to Hong Kong. His prospect of an official career under the Qing was thereby doomed.

In Hong Kong, Wang assisted the British missionary James Legge in translating Chinese classics into English. When Legge returned to Scotland in the late 1860s, he invited Wang to travel to Europe and continue the translation project. Between 1867 and 1870 Wang visited Great Britain, France, and Russia; he may have been the first Chinese intellectual from nineteenth-century China to have made such a private tour. The trip greatly impressed him. Not only did he recognize the obvious technological advances of the modern West, he also discovered that the Western cultural tradition was no less developed than that of Confucian China. Upon his return to Hong Kong, he translated a book on the Franco-Prussian War, which found an enthusiastic audience in both China and Japan.

In part motivated by his trip to Europe, Wang launched a career in publishing and journalism to propagate his views. In 1873 he founded a publishing company and in the following year began the publication of the *Xunhuan Daily,* one of the first modern-style Chinese newspapers, in Hong Kong. His commentaries in the *Xunhuan Daily* were widely read, and the newspaper became extremely successful. In 1884, with the tacit approval of Li Hongzhang, Wang finally returned to Shanghai. He became the editor-in-chief of *Shenbao,* the city's leading newspaper, and founded another publishing company. In his last years, Wang met the young Sun Yatsen and supported Sun's effort to present his reformist ideas to Li Hongzhang.

In many ways, Wang was ahead of his time. His first-hand observation of the West was unparalleled among his contemporaries, and he experimented with newspapers as a vehicle of voicing opinions. He strongly supported the Self-Strengthening movement led by Li Hongzhang and others, but the scope of his reform proposals far exceeded that of the movement, which was limited to military technology and foreign policy. One example was Wang's advocacy of Western methods in commerce and industry. His own business experiences enabled him to see the critical role played by private capital in the accumulation of national wealth, and he criticized the Confucian bias against merchants. He did, however, favor a degree of mercantilism in China's international trade, an idea that resembled the concept of war of commerce *(shangzhan)* promoted by Zheng Guanying at the time. Furthermore, Wang saw a need for political and institutional reforms. He argued for a fundamental change in the examination system and suggested a new regimen of public education.

Wang often compared the family of nations in the modern world to the situation of the Warring States era (403–221 B.C.) in ancient Chinese history. China was but one country among many, he emphasized, and she was neither "all under the heaven" *(tianxia)* nor the "middle kingdom." Shocking as this view was to many of his readers, it represented an important step toward the emergence of modern Chinese nationalism. These ideas placed Wang in the forefront of China's reformist thinkers during the late Qing, and, through his prolific and eloquent writings, his influence on contemporary intellectuals was profound.

Wang Ke-wen

References

Cohan, Paul A. *Between Tradition and Modernity: Wang T'ao and Reform in Late Ch'ing China.* Cambridge, MA: Harvard University Press, 1974.

McAleavy, Henry. *Wang T'ao: The Life and Writings of A Displaced Person.* London, England: The China Society, 1953.

War of the Central Plains

See DISBANDMENT CONFERENCE

Warlordism

Warlordism was a political condition that emerged in early republican China, in which individual military commanders exercised autonomous political power by virtue of the actual or threatened use of the military force under their personal control. The immediate context for the rise of warlordism was a lack of a political consensus following the Revolution of 1911 on the form of government that should replace the imperial system, as well as a lack of an agreement on who should have power in this new government. Military force was ultimately applied to resolve these conflicts, leading to a series of civil wars: the Second Revolution in 1913, the National Protection movement in 1916, the military mobilization against the Qing Restoration attempt in 1917, and a series of military conflicts associated with the outbreak of the Constitution Protection Movement in 1917. Rather than leading to any lasting political solution, these aggressions served to increase the political influence of the military commanders who participated in them. These commanders then used this political influence to extend their control over central, provincial, and local governments. A political fragmentation of the country among these competing "warlords" resulted.

The warlord period, the height of the military's political dominance, has been conventionally dated from 1916, when Yuan Shikai's death ended the attempt to establish centralized bureaucratic control over the provinces, to 1926, when the Northern Expedition provided a new basis for the reunification of the country under the Guomindang. In fact, the emergence of warlordism was not a uniform process that can be easily confined within these parameters. Some military commanders began to exhibit the politically independent behavior characteristic of warlordism as early as the Revolution of 1911. In some areas, military commanders did not establish their political dominance until some time after Yuan Shikai's death. Likewise, despite the nominal reunification of China after the Northern Expedition, many individual military commanders retained a large degree of political autonomy, resulting in a condition that may be called "residual warlordism."

The emergence of warlordism shattered nationalist dreams that the Revolution of 1911 would pave the way for the creation of a strong, unified Chinese state. Political and military fragmentation hindered China's ability to resist foreign threats. National defense was neglected as military commanders devoted their armies to domestic struggles for political power. As warlords monopolized state finances to support their growing armies, they deprived the country of funds needed for educational development and economic construc-

tion. Frequent civil wars disrupted agriculture and commerce throughout wide areas. The Chinese state in the early republican period was in many ways weaker than it had been under the late Qing dynasty, and the rise of warlordism was to a large degree responsible for this situation. Although most warlords claimed to be inspired by nationalism, and some were perhaps sincere in this claim, the existence of warlordism became an important domestic obstacle to Chinese nationalist aspirations. The May Fourth movement of 1919 combined anti-warlordism with anti-imperialism as the two main goals of Chinese nationalism. The Guomindang and the Chinese Communists adopted this formulation and made the elimination of warlordism a key element of their nationalist programs.

Edward A. McCord

References

Ch'i, Hsi-sheng. *Warlord Politics in China, 1916–1928*. Stanford, CA: Stanford University Press, 1976.

Sheridan, James E. *Chinese Warlord: The Career of Feng Yu-hsiang*. Stanford, CA: Stanford University Press, 1966.

Sutton, Donald S. *Provincial Militarism and the Chinese Republic: The Yunnan Army, 1905–25*. Ann Arbor: University of Michigan Press, 1980.

Washington Conference

Through its three major treaties and associated resolutions, the Washington Conference (November 1921–February 1922) reformulated international foreign policy in East Asia after World War I by bringing limited disarmament and a degree of multilateral cooperation among the major powers with interests in the western Pacific. It served as a basis for Japanese-Western relations until the London Naval Conference of 1930.

The Four Power Treaty confirmed Japan as the leading military power in East Asia by guaranteeing naval superiority in its home waters and by prohibiting the great powers from constructing new naval bases in the Western Pacific. The Five Power Treaty created a 5:5:3 ratio of capital ships for Great Britain, the United States, and Japan and limited the potential for a disastrously expensive naval race at a time when the Japanese economy was weakened. The Nine Power Treaty pledged respect for the sovereignty, independence, and territorial integrity of China. From the perspective of the United States, it also ended the Lansing-Ishii Agreement that had recognized Japan's special Manchurian interests.

Japan's actions at the conference culminated a struggle between military and diplomatic advocates and temporarily enhanced the position of the civilian leadership in foreign policy. The agreements confirmed cooperation with Western powers and demonstrated that national defense based on arms control and treaties could benefit Japan by providing security and by reducing military costs. They also increased economic ties and improved Japanese-American relations.

Yet, the Washington agreements also irritated many Japanese. Japanese nationalists complained of the humiliating capitulation to London and Washington and objected to the limitations on capital ships, which compromised Japan's independence, and to the undermining of Japan's legitimate special mission on the Asian mainland.

After 1925, particularly as tensions increased in China, it became increasingly difficult for Japanese leaders to accept the Washington system of international cooperation, even though most argued that the agreements only slightly affected Japanese special interests and that Japan retained freedom of action in Manchuria. Tanaka Giichi of the Friends of Constitutional Government Party, in particular called for a positive foreign policy to strengthen Japan's position in Manchuria. Yet, even Shidehara Kijuro of the rival Constitutional Democratic Party, who preferred operating more within an international framework, could not appear to sacrifice Japanese national interests. By the end of the decade, advocates for a Japanese-dominated economic bloc, encompassing Manchuria, Mongolia, and China's maritime provinces, and advocates of territorial expansion were clearly challenging international cooperation reflected in the Washington agreements.

Robert D. Fiala

References

Iriye, Akira. *After Imperialism: The Search for a New Order in the Far East, 1921–1931*. Cambridge, MA: Harvard University Press, 1965.

Nish, Ian. "Japan and Naval Aspects of the Washington Conference." *Modern Japan: Aspects of History, Literature and Society,* ed. W. G. Beasley. Berkeley: University of California Press, 1975.

Wei Yuan (1794–1857)

Wei Yuan was a late Qing reformist thinker and an early advocate of the westernization of military technology.

Born to a family of officials in Hunan, Wei befriended such noted scholar-officials as Lin Zexu and Gong Zizhen while studying "new text" Confucianism in Beijing. A leading member of the Statecraft School *(jingshi xuepai),* Wei helped his friend He Changling, an official in Jiangsu, to compile *Huangchao jingshi wenbian (Collected Writings on Statecraft of the Reigning Dynasty)* in the 1820s. He subsequently served on the personal staff *(mufu)* of two successive governors-general of LiangJiang and drafted various proposals for institutional reform. In 1831 he moved to Yangzhou, a city known for its tradition of practical scholarship. After receiving the degree of *jinshi* in 1844, Wei became an official in Jiangsu province. During the Taiping Rebellion, he assisted the Qing court to suppress the Taipings, but died of illness before the Rebellion ended.

Wei was best known for his work, *Haiguo tuzhi (Illustrated Treatise on the Maritime Kingdoms),* which he began in 1841 at the request of the then governor-general of Guangdong and Guangxi, Lin Zexu, and which he completed in 1852. Totaling one hundred volumes in its final form, the work provided one of the first introductions to Western science, technology, and geography in modern China. It was based on Lin's earlier work, *Sizhouzhi (A Survey of the Four Continents),* but it was much greater in length and depth and had a new focus on technology. The message in *Haiguo tuzhi* is clear—in Wei's own words, "to imitate the best skills of the barbarians in order to control the barbarians."

Writing during the years between the first (1840–42) and the second (1858–60) Opium Wars, Wei was convinced that China could not protect herself against the new Western threat without learning the West's key military technologies and organizations. There is no unchanging *tao* (way), he argued, and China must modify the ancient ways to fit the needs of the present situation. This evolutionist view pioneered the reformist thought of the late Qing. In addition to serving as an intellectual precursor of and guide to the Self-Strengthening movement of the 1870s and 1880s, *Haiguo tuzhi* was said to have exerted tremendous influence in mid-nineteenth-century Japan.

Nationalist sentiments may be discerned not only in the self-strengthening message of *Haiguo tuzhi* but also in Wei's *Shengwuji (Record of Imperial Military Achievements)*, written in the wake of the first Opium War. The latter book, which examines the military successes of the early Qing emperors, was aimed at arousing self-confidence in his countrymen, as well as calling their attention to the importance of the military, in the face of the new tasks confronting national defense. Although Wei's understanding of China's problems may appear limited in hindsight, his propagation of Western knowledge and his advocacy of reform were indeed revolutionary for his time.

Wang Ke-wen

References

Leonard, Jane Kate. *Wei Yuan and China's Rediscovery of Maritime World*. Cambridge, MA: Harvard University Press, 1984.

Mitchell, Peter. "The Limits of Reformism: Wei Yuan's Reaction to Western Intrusion." *Modern Asian Studies* 6, no. 2 (April 1972): 175–204.

Wenxiang (1815–76)

Leading reformist official during the Self-Strengthening movement and the son of a Manchu official, Wenxiang launched his career in the Board of Works after receiving his *jinshi* degree in the 1840s. Distinguished performance led to rapid promotions in the 1850s, and by 1859 he had become grand councillor and vice-president of the Board of Revenue at the court of Emperor Xianfeng. During the second Opium War (1858–60), when British and French forces occupied Beijing and the court fled to Inner Mongolia, he was appointed deputy to Prince Gong in conducting peace negotiations with the foreign troops in the capital. He proved to be capable in managing "barbarian affairs," and soon became an important member of the newly established Zongli Yamen.

Experience in dealing with Western countries led Wenxiang to a realistic reassessment of the defense and foreign policies of the Qing empire. In the 1860s and 1870s, he became a key supporter in the central government for the

Self-Strengthening movement; and he assisted Prince Gong to obtain imperial approval for the military and industrial projects initiated by Han officials in the provinces. Wenxiang's understanding of the West may have been limited, but he clearly recognized the superiority of Western military technology and believed that it should be introduced into China. He favored the idea of using foreign troops to suppress the Taiping Rebellion, and was a leading advocate for the founding of the Tongwenguan in 1867. Foreign observers at the time described Wenxiang as "the most advanced and patriotic man in the government." His death from illness in 1876 dealt a severe blow to Prince Gong's political strength at the court and to the Self-Strengthening movement.

Wang Ke-wen

References

Wright, Mary C. *The Last Stand of Chinese Conservatism: The T'ung-chih Restoration, 1862–1874*. Stanford, CA: Stanford University Press, 1966.

Whampoa Military Academy

Founded in Canton in 1924, the Whampoa Military Academy was a product of the first Guomindang–Chinese Communist Party (GMD-CCP) United Front. It provided early training for many future leaders of the Guomindang and the Chinese Communist Party, and later served as an important power base for its commandant, Chiang Kaishek.

The official name of the academy was the Army Academy of the Chinese Nationalist Party (Guomindang). It came to be known as the "Whampoa Academy" because of its location at Whampoa (Huangpu) Island near Canton. In the early 1920s, after repeated setbacks in his revolutionary career because of opposition from the militarists, Sun Yatsen keenly felt the need to control an armed force of his own. One of his conditions in forming the new alliance with the Soviet Union in 1922 was Soviet support for the establishment of an army loyal to his cause. In 1923, Sun dispatched Chiang Kaishek, his military assistant, to the Soviet Union. Part of Chiang's mission was to study the training and organization of the Red Army. Shortly after that, the Guomindang decided to establish a military academy as the training school for the officers of a revolutionary army. With key efforts made by Liao Zhongkai,

Chiang Kaishek and the Russian adviser Mikhail Borodin, the academy was formally established in June 1924. Most of its initial funding came from Moscow.

Before his death in March 1925, Sun Yatsen held the honorary title of director (zongli) of the Whampoa Academy. He appointed Chiang Kaishek as commandant and Liao Zhongkai as Party representative (commissar). The academy was modeled on the Soviet Red Command Schools, with an emphasis on political and ideological indoctrination. In addition to basic military skills, students were taught such subjects as Sun's Three Peoples' Principles, socialism, imperialism, and the revolutionary history of the Soviet Union. Prominent members of both parties in the United Front were employed as political instructors. The Communist Zhou Enlai, for example, was head of the academy's Political Department. The military instructors were mostly graduates of the prestigious Baoding Military Academy.

Whampoa's training course was short, about six months for each class. From its founding until the beginning of the Northern Expedition (1926–28), the academy produced four classes of graduates. The first class had 645 graduates; the size of the fourth class had increased to 2,654. These young men were recruited from all over China, with the largest numbers from Guangdong and Hunan. During the first two years of the academy's existence, the students had to fight for the revolutionary regime in Canton even before graduation. The suppression of the Merchants' Corps (late 1924), the two eastern expeditions against Chen Jiongming (early and late 1925), the campaign against the Yunnan and Guangxi militarists (mid-1925), and the assistance to the Canton-Hong Kong Strike (mid-1925 to late 1926) required almost constant involvement of the Whampoa students in military actions, and their performance was impressive. In October 1924, the academy organized its training corps (jiaodaotuan) on the model of the Soviet Red Army. This was soon to be copied by the National Revolutionary Army. By the time Canton launched its Northern Expedition, the graduates as well as the organizational principles of Whampoa had become the backbone of the United Front's military strength.

By then, however, the academy itself was no longer a united force. As the United Front deteriorated after the death of Sun Yatsen and the assassination of Liao Zhongkai in 1925, the Whampoa instructors and students were also divided by the GMD-CCP conflict. Two student organizations, the leftist Chinese Young Soldiers Association (Zhongguo qingnian junren lianhehui) and the rightist Sun Wenist Association (Sun Wen zhuyi xuehui) appeared in that year and soon engaged in bitter struggle. Chiang Kaishek initially tried to mediate between the two factions in order to maintain the solidarity of his military following, but by the time of the Zhongshan Gunboat Incident of March 1926 he himself began a shift to the right.

Shortly after the incident, the Whampoa Academy was reorganized and expanded into the Central Military Political Academy. Following the progress of the Northern Expedition, branches of the academy were established in Chaozhou, Nanjing, Changsha, and Wuhan. In April 1927, the United Front moved the academy's main campus to Wuhan, and after Chiang purged the CCP from the GMD, he moved it again to Nanjing. The original Whampoa Academy ceased to exist.

During the following decades, the early Whampoa cadets played a significant role in the Chinese revolution. Most of the GMD cadets became Chiang's loyal followers and senior officers. They upheld personal ties with the commandant that resembled the relationship between Zeng Guofan and the Hunan Army or Yuan Shikai and the Beiyang Army. Their CCP classmates led the revolutionary war for the Communists and some, such as Lin Biao, eventually assumed military leadership in the People's Republic.

Both groups were motivated by a strong sense of nationalism. In the era of warlordism, the Whampoa Academy represented an effort to place the military under the guidance of a revolutionary force that worked for national unity and independence. This nationalist appeal attracted thousands of patriotic and ambitious youth to Canton and to the United Front. They did accomplish their immediate goal by defeating the warlords in the Northern Expedition. Yet in the long run, these cadets became instruments in the GMD-CCP civil war that seriously weakened and divided China before 1949.

Wang Ke-wen

References

Landis, Richard B. "Training and Indoctrination at the Whampoa Academy." *China in the 1920s: Nationalism and Revolution*, ed. F. Gilbert Chan and Thomas H.

Etzold. New York, NY: New Viewpoints, 1976: 73–93.

Liu, F. F. *A Military History of Modern China, 1924–1949*. Princeton, NJ: Princeton University Press, 1956.

MacFarquhar, Roderick L. "The Whampoa Military Academy." *Harvard Papers on China* 9 (1955): 146–72.

Woren (1804–71)

A leading conservative official and thinker in the late Qing and a native of Mongolia, Woren succeeded in the examination system and climbed quickly up the ladder of officialdom in Beijing. When the first Opium War (1840–42) broke out, he was already the chief justice at Emperor Daoguang's court. Although he shared his colleagues' sense of crisis that resulted from the new threat from the West, Woren saw no need to alter China's traditional ways or to adopt any part of the Western civilization in order to defend the "celestial empire." A devout student of Song neo-Confucianism, he proposed instead a "rectification" of the moral order of the country as the fundamental solution to China's domestic and external problems.

In the 1860s, when the Self-Strengthening movement commenced under the leadership of Prince Gong and Zeng Guofan, Woren was grand secretary and tutor to Emperor Tongzhi. From such influential posts he vehemently opposed many of the self-strengtheners' plans, including the establishment of government schools (*i.e.,* Tongwenguan) to introduce Western sciences. To follow the "barbarian ways" was not only dangerous but unnecessary, Woren argued, as the foundation of a society lies not in technologies but in its people's heart. He became the leader of a conservative faction in the government that engaged in a long and fierce debate with the self-strengtheners led by Prince Gong. The fact that the latter eventually gained the imperial sanction for their efforts seemed to have little effect on Woren's political career, which remained successful until his death.

In the mid-nineteenth century, Woren's position was representative of a conservative response to the unprecedented challenge that China faced. He and his supporters found it impossible to distinguish the Chinese nation from her cultural tradition, which was embodied in her beliefs and institutions. To change any of these, in their view, would amount to a negation of what had made the Chinese Chinese. In

this sense, Woren, a Manchu, was no less nationalistic than his reform-minded contemporaries, even though his understanding of "nation" profoundly differed from its meaning in the modern world. As China's weakness became increasingly apparent under foreign encroachment in the 1870s and 1880s, however, Woren's position was doomed. In the end, it was a question of how much of China's tradition needed to be changed, not if it should be changed at all, that became the main concern of China's political and intellectual elite.

Wang Ke-wen

References

Chang, Hao. "The Antiforeignist Role of Wo-jen, 1804–1871." *Harvard Papers on China* no. 14 (1960): 1–29.

Work-Study Movement *(Qingong jianxue yundong)*

The Work-Study movement (a condensing of the Diligent-Work Frugal-Study movement) in its modern version went through several manifestations from the beginning years of the twentieth century until the 1920s. Encouraged by Li Shizeng, Wu Zhihui and Cai Yuanpei, the Work-Study movement had its most visible moment between 1919 and 1921, when over 1,600 Chinese youths traveled to France. The objective of the Work-Study movement was to encourage young Chinese to work in the undermanned post-World War I French factories. With their frugally saved wages, the Chinese worker-students aspired to a French education. This Western education was to be used in the goal of national salvation, by developing skills that would spur modernization.

The Work-Study movement went through a cycle of tremendous enthusiasm during the first eighteen months, but as successive waves of Chinese arrived, the reality of French inflation and unemployment was reflected in the difficulty of placing young Chinese in French factories. Other problems also existed, such as lack of language proficiency and technical training. Students lived in conditions of poverty and underemployment. The year 1921 saw three Chinese political movements in France that ended in the repatriation of 104 Chinese worker-students to China. Some Chinese left voluntarily, whereas a great number remained in France. But the momentum of the Work-Study movement had essentially ended. There were those who remained and worked, and those who formed political parties that included the European branch of the Chinese Communist Organizations (1922), the Chinese Youth Party (1923), and the European branches of the Guomindang (1923).

Although it was related to overseas activities, the Work-Study movement played a significant role in shaping Chinese nationalist politics. The Work-Study movement dynamically reflected the emerging "New Culture" nationalism. Although the Chinese who sojourned in France had different political perspectives and group affiliations, most were united by their goal of national salvation. On the other hand, the downswing of the Work-Study movement ushered in a relatively new form of Chinese nationalist activity, the political party. Almost half a dozen Chinese political parties formed in Europe after 1922. The breadth of political agitation, theoretical exposure, and recruitment activities provided significant political training for many key leaders in the Chinese revolution, such as Zhou Enlai, Deng Xiaoping, Zhu De, Nie Rongzhen, Zeng Qi, and Li Huang. As an illustration, when the People's Republic of China was proclaimed in 1949, three leaders stood on the podium: Mao Zedong, Zhou Enlai and Zhu De. Two of these revolutionaries had adopted Marxism in Europe. Indeed, the Work-Study Movement was an important crucible of Chinese nationalism.

Marilyn Levine

References

Bailey, Paul. "The Chinese Work-Study Movement in France." *China Quarterly* no. 115 (September 1988): 441–61.

Levine, Marilyn. *The Found Generation: Chinese Communists in Europe During the Twenties.* Seattle: University of Washington Press, 1993.

Revolution of 1911. Vancouver: University of British Columbia Press, 1980.

Wu Peifu (1874–1939)

Wu Peifu was a major warlord in the early republican era and leader of the Zhili Clique. A native of Shandong province, Wu had received the *shengyuan* degree in the examination system before enrolling in the military academies of the late Qing. When the Revolution of 1911 broke out he was an officer in the Beiyang Army under Cao Kun. Cao and Wu played critical roles in assisting Yuan Shikai to consolidate his power during the revolution and the ensuing years. They were rewarded with repeated promotions.

After Yuan's death, Wu became identified as a leading figure in the emerging Zhili Clique. He participated in the campaigns against Zhang Xun's Qing restoration attempt and then against Sun Yatsen's Canton regime. As the rivalry between the Zhili Clique and the ruling Anhui Clique intensified, Wu declared his opposition to Premier Duan Qirui's policy of unifying the country by force and proposed a peace negotiation between Beijing and Canton. In 1920, Wu and Cao Kun joined hands with the Fengtian Clique and ousted Duan from the Beijing government (the Zhili-Anhui War). For the next two years the two victorious factions jointly controlled the central government in Beijing while competing with each other for the expansion of their influence into the Yangtze River area. This conflict eventually led to the first Zhili-Fengtian War in 1922, in which Cao and Wu's Zhili forces triumphed. Later that year, through bribery and intimidation, Wu helped the election of Cao to the new presidency of the Republic. Wu was appointed commissioner (governor) of the Zhili-Henan-Shandong provinces, but in many ways was the *de facto* leader of the Zhili Clique and its government.

As national leader, Wu reversed the pro-Japanese foreign policy of the Anhui Clique and adopted a conciliatory stance toward other political forces in the country, including that of Sun Yatsen. For a while he tolerated Communist labor unions in his territories, but that tolerance ended after the Beijing-Hankow Railway Strike in 1923. The same year Sun returned to Canton and the new Canton regime, under Soviet influence, also became hostile to Wu.

In 1924, the second Zhili-Fengtian War began. This time, Wu was fatally crippled by the defection to the Fengtian side of one of his commanders, Feng Yuxiang, and suffered a disastrous defeat. He retreated into Hunan for recuperation and reorganization. In late 1925, Wu staged a political comeback with the support of his former subordinates. He succeeded in dominating the middle and upper Yangtze River provinces and soon collaborated with his former rival, the Fengtian Clique, in an attack against Feng Yuxiang. While this war was still in progress, the Guomindang launched its Northern Expedition from Canton. In late 1926 Wu was again defeated by Chiang Kaishek's

Guomindang forces and fled to Sichuan.

During the following decade of the Guomindang rule, Wu retired from politics and lived in Beijing. After the Manchurian Incident of 1931, he repeatedly rejected Japanese offers of leading a pro-Japanese political force in north China. During the Sino-Japanese War Wu stayed in occupied Beijing. In 1939 he died after a dental surgery; the death was rumored to have been arranged by the Japanese.

Wu once declared his principles as "not assuming the post of military governor, not living in foreign concessions, not collaborating with foreigners, and not receiving foreign loans." These words were aimed mainly at criticizing the behaviors of his political opponents, especially the Anhui Clique; he did uphold most of them in deeds throughout his life. After his death, the Guomindang government, then in Chongqing, publicly praised his patriotism and his anti-Japanese stance.

Wang Ke-wen

References

Wou, Odoric Y. K. *Militarism in Modern China: The Career of Wu P'ei-fu, 1916–39.* Dawson, Australia: Wm. Dawson & Sons, 1978.

Wu Tingfang (1842–1922)

Wu Tingfang was a leading diplomat and civilian politician in the early Republic. Born to a Cantonese family in Singapore, he received his education in Hong Kong and Great Britain. In 1880, he became the first Chinese member of Hong Kong's legislative council. By then he had already been active in the colony's Chinese newspapers and in association with such reformers as Wang Tao and Ho Kai, the latter being also his brother-in-law. In 1882, he returned to China and worked for Li Hongzhang, thus beginning an illustrious career in government and the diplomatic service.

At the time China was making her first entrance into the modern international community, and Wu's knowledge and background proved to be of tremendous use to the Qing government. As an assistant to Li Hongzhang, Wu participated in the difficult negotiations that followed the Sino-French War (1885) and the first Sino-Japanese War (1894–95). From 1896 to 1902, he was China's minister to the United States, Spain, and Peru, and again in 1907 to 1909 served as minister to the United

States, Mexico, Peru and Cuba. In the years between these two assignments he was in Beijing, first assisting the government to conclude new commercial treaties with Great Britain, the United States, and Japan, and then working to reform China's legal code.

During the Revolution of 1911, the reform-minded Wu sided with the revolutionaries. He soon represented the republican government of the South in the North-South negotiations that led to the abdication of the Qing emperor. In 1912, he became minister of justice in Sun Yatsen's provisional government in Nanjing; from then on he always supported Sun politically. Under Yuan Shikai's presidency Wu temporarily retired from public office; he returned to government as soon as Yuan died. In 1917, he followed Sun to the South to establish a government that challenged the Beiyang government of the North. He subsequently served as foreign minister in Sun's first (1917–19) and second (1920–22) Canton regimes. In 1921, he also took over the post of minister of finance. The rebellion of Chen Jiongming against Sun in June 1922 dealt a severe blow to Sun's career and apparently deeply frustrated Wu, who had hoped to see China reunified under Sun. He died a week later. Wu's son, Chaoshu (C. C. Wu), later also became foreign minister in the Guomindang government.

As the first generation of modern Chinese diplomats, Wu sought to protect China's rights and interests in the face of increasing foreign encroachments while promoting domestic reforms in order to achieve an equal footing with the West. In this sense he was a nationalist. Sadly, however, his last years were spent in the chaotic conflict of the warlord era, which did little to improve the country's reputation and strength.

Wang Ke-wen

References

Pomerantz-Zhang, Linda. *Wu Tingfang (1842–1922): Reform and Modernization in Modern Chinese History.* Hong Kong: University of Hong Kong Press, 1992.

Wu Zhihui (1864–1953)

Combining a remarkable number of careers over his long life, Wu Zhihui was best known first as a revolutionary propagandist and later as a conservative power in the Guomindang. As Confucian, anarchist, and conservative, Wu supported a modernization program that would include technological progress and educate the Chinese people in the principles of science.

Wu was born into a declining gentry family in Jiangsu. Passing the *juren* exams in 1891, he became a cautiously reformist teacher, but after the Boxer Uprising of 1900 Wu developed a more radical stance. His yardstick for proper behavior was to support the people against the monarchy, students against teachers (a constant issue in the late Qing), and the younger generation against the older. In this era, when the intelligentsia was forming an anti-Manchu ideology on the basis of the Qing court's failure to resist imperialist incursions, Wu's brushes with authority became more frequent. Deported from a brief stint of study in Japan, Wu returned to Shanghai in 1902 to join the radicals around the Chinese Educational Association, the Patriotic School, and their organ, the *Subao*. This turned Wu into a revolutionary. Escaping arrest with the help of authorities, he fled to England and France, where he lived until the Revolution of 1911.

Wu was a fervent (and scatological) anti-Manchu publicist even as he advocated anarchism with Li Shizeng out of Paris after 1906. The theory of revolution that Wu and Li developed emphasized the role of education and evolution in producing true, thoroughgoing change. Anarchist revolution would produce an international system based on a universal, scientific morality shared by all humans. But Wu made particularly clear his support for an anti-Manchu revolution as a legitimate first step toward true revolution. Wu attacked the Qing not only for ceding territory and bringing Chinese under the sway of foreign powers, but for supporting Confucianism and keeping China backward.

Increasingly, Wu's major concern was for China to join the march of progress he saw the advanced countries of the world pursuing. After the Revolution of 1911, Wu and Li organized a number of associations designed to promote personal morality and improve society. Their Society for Frugal Study in France *(Liu-Fa jianxue hui)* arranged to send Chinese students there on work-study programs. Wu was also an early supporter of the nascent labor movement. The spectacle of Europe tearing itself apart during World War I seems to have disillusioned him on the subject of international humanitarianism without affecting his faith in a scientific worldview. During the May Fourth movement (1919) Wu became something of the grand old man of cultural iconoclasts. He firmly supported a younger generation that was attacking Confucianism, whereas he himself urged rapid industrialization to strengthen China and to improve the lives of the people. He supported the vernacular movement and particularly hoped to improve mass literacy by developing a phonetics system.

In terms of the splits within the old revolutionary camp, Wu had been allied with Sun Yat-sen against Zhang Binglin. His ties with Sun then brought Wu into the Guomindang (GMD) in the 1920s. Wu moved away from support for revolution but continued to insist that he believed in anarchist principles. He therefore refused to accept any government positions, but he came to believe in change from the top down and accepted Party jobs. After Sun's death in 1925, Wu soon gave firm support to Chiang Kaishek, the Northern Expedition, and the anti-Communist purge. Wu, who had never been attracted to violence, criticized the Marxist notion of class struggle on the grounds that industrialization would enlarge wealth without destruction.

Emphasizing a leftist reading of Sun Yatsen's Three Peoples' Principles, Wu attempted to turn the GMD in an anarchistic direction in 1927 and 1928, hoping that anarchism would replace Communist labor organizations. The Labor University he helped establish in Shanghai was designed to combine education with social activism; however, the program was not a success and the GMD turned against all forms of radicalism. In the process, Wu was co-opted into Chiang's more conservative interpretation of the Three Peoples' Principles. Wu (and other former anarchists) became members of the rightist "senior statesmen" clique of the GMD. Wu was useful to Chiang for his ties with Sun, which reflected legitimacy onto Chiang, and as a firm anti-Communist with progressive credentials. From his informal influence with the Nanjing government in the 1930s, then, Wu attempted to promote technical education, industrialization, and fiscal reform. He hoped to solve China's social problems through material progress, in other words, resisting attempts to promote social change.

Wu died in Taiwan after he retreated with the GMD to that island in 1949.

Peter Zarrow

References

Dirlik, Arif. *Anarchism in the Chinese Revolution.* Berkeley: University of California, 1991.

Zarrow, Peter. *Anarchism and Chinese Political Culture.* New York, NY: Columbia University Press, 1990.

Wuchang Uprising

The Wuchang Uprising was the first revolt in the Revolution of 1911, leading eventually to the fall of the Qing Dynasty and the founding of the Chinese Republic in 1912.

In 1911, after the failure of the Canton Uprising in April, the revolutionaries decided to shift their focus to the Yangtze provinces. In July, Song Jiaoren established the Central China Branch of the Tongmenghui in Shanghai. Shortly afterward, the Sichuan Railway Crisis occurred. As large portions of the New Army in Wuhan (the tri-city of Wuchang, Hankou, and Hanyang) were ordered by the Qing government to enter Sichuan for the suppression of the Railway-Protection riots, revolutionaries in that tri-city saw an opportunity for action. Two local revolutionary groups, the Literary Institute *(Wenxueshe)* and the Progressive Association *(Gongjinhui),* collaborated in preparing for an uprising on October 10. On October 9, however, the authorities captured a few of their leaders and discovered the plot. In a tense atmosphere, several officers and soldiers in the New Army in Wuchang, who had connections with the revolutionary groups, staged a mutiny on the evening of October 10. As they swiftly took control of strategic points in the city, revolutionaries in other New Army units quickly joined the revolt. After a day of fierce fighting, the government troops were defeated. By October 12, Hankou and Hanyang also fell into the hands of the revolutionaries. They established a military government in Hubei on October 11 and supported (some say forced) a New Army officer,

Li Yuanhong, to become governor. The military government declared the founding of the Republic of China and called for other provinces to support the revolution.

From mid-October to late November, the revolutionaries fought a hard battle with the superior Qing forces dispatched by the court in Beijing. Huang Hsing, the Tongmenghui leader, came to Wuhan and assumed command of the revolutionary army in early November. Although in late November the revolutionaries were driven out of Hankou and Hanyang, they were able to hold out at Wuchang until the declaration of independence by most provinces in south and central China, and until the successful conclusion of the revolution in February 1912. The Wuchang Uprising has since become a landmark in the history of the Chinese revolution, symbolizing the triumph of anti-Manchuism and republicanism. The date of the uprising has been celebrated as the "National Day," or "Double-Tenth," by the Guomindang government.

Wang Ke-wen

References

Dutt, Vidya Prakash. "The First Week of Revolution: The Wuchang Uprising." *China in Revolution: The First Phase, 1900–1913,* ed Mary C. Wright, 383–416. New Haven, CT: Yale University Press, 1968.

Fass, Josef. "Revolutionary Activity in the Province Hu-pei and the Wu-ch'ang Uprising of 1911." *Archiv Orientalni* 28 (1960): 127–49.

Fung, Edmund S. K. *The Military Dimension of the Chinese Revolution: The New Army and Its Role in the Revolution of 1911.* Vancouver: University of British Columbia Press, 1980.

Xian Incident

After the Manchurian Incident in 1931, the Northeast Army under the command of the young marshal Zhang Xueliang was still 200,000 men strong when it was dispatched to Shaanxi to fight the Red Army, which had just completed its seven-thousand-mile Long March in October 1935. Despite its initial victory over the Northeast Army, the Red Army and the newly established Soviet base remained far from secure, because Chiang Kaishek was determined to eradicate the Red Army before taking up the struggle with Japan in pursuance of his policy of domestic pacification before external resistance *(annei rangwai)*.

The young marshal had always hated civil war, especially since his personal tragedy—his father was murdered and he himself was driven out of Manchuria by the Japanese. His primary concern was how to fight the Japanese and recover his homeland, certainly not to suppress the Red Army with his remaining forces. On his own initiative, he reached a rapprochement with the Red Army in November 1935. In the meantime, the Chinese Communist Party (CCP) also approached General Yang Hucheng, leader of the Northwest Army of Shaanxi, whose friendly relations with the CCP dated to the 1920s and who had also reached a truce with the Red Army. The Northeast and the Northwest armies tried to smooth their strained relations in order to bring about a triune alliance between them and the Red Army, which was cemented with the Yan'an Conference between Zhang Xueliang and Zhou Enlai on April 8, 1936.

Unless Chiang accepted their appeal for suspension of the civil war and formation of a united front against Japan, for Zhang and Yang there was really no way of return. In spite of being aware of the precarious situation at Xian, Chiang went there in early December 1936 for a high-level military conference with a view to launching his *coup-de-grace* campaign against the Red Army and drastically reshuffling his command headquarters by appointing Jiang Dingwen to replace the young marshal, whose army was to be transferred to the east. Unexpectedly, on the eve of his departure from Xian, Chiang was seized and put under house arrest by Zhang and Yang, who presented eight demands: (1) reorganize the Nanjing government and admit all parties to share the joint responsibility of saving the nation; (2) stop all kinds of civil war; (3) immediately release the patriotic leaders arrested in Shanghai; (4) release all political prisoners throughout the country; (5) emancipate the patriotic movement of the people; (6) actually carry out the will of Sun Yatsen; (7) safeguard the political freedom of the people to organize and call meetings; and (8) immediately call a national salvation conference.

While the Nanjing leaders were divided on how to save Chiang, his wife Soong Meiling and his brother-in-law T. V. Soong flew to Xian. Their personal diplomacy, with the help of W. H. Donald, Chiang's Australian adviser, succeeded in bringing about Chiang's release. After Chiang verbally accepted the aforementioned demands, Zhang Xueliang, in spite of much opposition, particularly from Yang Hucheng who insisted that Chiang must give a written promise, set Chiang free. Most dramatically, Zhang escorted Chiang back to Nanjing only to be taken prisoner by Chiang, thus changing his role from captor to captive, for which Zhang paid dearly. Zhang was to be under strict surveillance for half a century; he was released on June 4, 1990, his ninetieth birthday.

The CCP had neither foreknowledge of the incident nor did it play a decisive role in the decision to release Chiang. Nevertheless, Zhou Enlai mitigated opposition to Chiang's release by persuading Yang Hucheng to accept Chiang's promise without a written pledge. Certainly, the CCP was the greatest beneficiary of the incident, which saved the Red Army from being annihilated by Chiang.

Tien-wei Wu

References

Wu, Tien-wei. "New Materials on the Xi'an Incident: A Bibliographic Review." *Modern China* 10, no. 1 (January 1984): 115–141.

———. *The Sian Incident: A Pivotal Point in Modern Chinese History.* Ann Arbor: University of Michigan Press, 1976.

Xu Jiyu (1795–1873)

Xu Jiyu was a late Qing reformist, official, and scholar. A native of Shanxi province, Xu received his *jinshi* degree in 1826 and subsequently served in the local governments in Guangxi and Fujian. During the Opium War (1839–42), Xu was in charge of coastal defense in Fujian, where his conciliatory attitude toward the British was criticized by Lin Zexu. After the war, Xu continued his career in the southeast and in 1847 became governor of Fujian, whose responsibilities included the management of foreign trade in Xiamen (Amoy), one of China's first treaty ports. Xu's observations and contacts with Westerners in Xiamen led him to develop a profound interest in the outside world. Assisted by foreign missionaries, Xu completed the pioneering work *Yinghuan zhilue (A Brief Survey of the Maritime Circuit)* in 1848. In 1867, Xu was appointed head of Tongwenguan, the school of Western learning established by the Qing government as part of its self-strengthening programs.

Yinghuan zhilue contributed greatly to modern Chinese intellectual development. The book, with forty-four maps, introduced world geography to Chinese readers. Its presentation of the political, economic, and cultural information on the Western countries was more accurate and organized than that of Wei Yuan's *Haiguo tuzhi (Illustrated Treatise on the Maritime Kingdoms),* completed at the same time. Both works fundamentally changed the Chinese worldview and suggested the country's need to adopt Western technologies.

Wang Ke-wen

References

Drake, Fred W. *China Charts the World: Hsu Chi-yu and His Geography of 1848.* Cambridge, MA: Harvard University Press, 1975.

Xu Shichang (1855–1939)

A protégé of Yuan Shikai, Xu Shichang rose to become the only civilian president in the warlord era of the early Republic.

Born and raised in Henan, Xu received his *jinshi* degree in 1886 and soon served as Yuan Shikai's chief-of-staff in establishing and training the New Army. He became identified as a senior member of the Beiyang group. On the eve of the Revolution of 1911, Xu was governor-general of Manchuria. When the Revolution broke out, he persuaded the Qing court to reinstate Yuan from retirement, which gave Yuan the opportunity to manipulate the situation and eventually to become the first president of the Republic.

Xu briefly retired from public office after the fall of the Qing but was appointed by Yuan as secretary of state in 1914. Xu enjoyed little real power and he shrewdly kept his distance from Yuan's monarchical attempt in 1915 and 1916. After the death of Yuan in 1916, the Beiyang group was divided by a bitter succession struggle between Feng Guozhang's Zhili Clique and Duan Qirui's Anhui Clique. In 1918, Xu, a compromise candidate for the two rival groups, was elected new president.

During his presidency, Xu was confronted with the opposition of the South, where Sun Yatsen had founded his own national government in 1917. The North-South peace conference in Shanghai that Xu had pinned his hopes on lasted from 1919 to 1920, but in the end failed to reunify the country. In 1919, Xu witnessed the outburst of nationalist protests in the May Fourth movement, whose targets included many high officials in his government. Xu's reaction to and treatment of the demonstrating students, compared to those of his successors in modern China, were moderate.

The most serious weakness of Xu's government was its inability to control the warlords. In many ways, he was a puppet of China's divided military, especially the Anhui Clique and its civilian branch, the Anfu Club. In 1922, following the Zhili victory in the first Zhili-Fengtian War, Xu was forced out of office. He devoted his last years to scholarship and published a number of works in philosophy and religion. He died in the early years of the second Sino-Japanese War.

Wang Ke-wen

References

Nanthan, Andrew J. *Peking Politics, 1918–1923: Factionalism and the Failure of Constitutionalism.* Berkeley: University of California Press, 1976.

X

Y

Yalta Conference

As World War II wound down in Europe and Germany's defeat appeared imminent, the Allies focused on the aftermath in Europe and the defeat of Japan. To facilitate the latter, the United States decided to attack Japan directly, eschewing any idea of launching the attack from the Chinese mainland. With this strategy in mind, Joseph Stalin, Franklin Roosevelt, and Winston Churchill gathered at Yalta in the Soviet Crimea from February 4 to February 11, 1945.

When they met there were four basic agenda items: the future of what was then called the "Far East," the future governments of Poland and other Eastern European countries, the future of Germany, and the organization of the United Nations. While there was much disagreement over the fate of Poland and German reparations, less confrontational was the topic of East Asia. Countries in East Asia were not represented during the meeting, even though some, like China, were part of the Allied war effort. Roosevelt had earlier come to the conclusion that Soviet participation in the defeat of Japan in East Asia was necessary. Roosevelt also wanted to set the conditions for Soviet participation, to try to induce the Soviet leader to help maintain a Guomindang China, and to reduce the possibility of direct support to the Chinese Communist Party. For Roosevelt, the rationale of enlisting Soviet assistance involved the question of American lives and neutralizing Soviet influence in East Asia. In this way he hoped to continue to influence events in China to accommodate American ideological, political, and economic interests.

Stalin and Roosevelt hammered out the agreement with little input from the British prime minister. Roosevelt accomplished his objective, committing the Soviet Union to war against Japan within three months of Germany's defeat. The USSR also agreed to support Chiang Kaishek as the leader of China, a move which continued the Soviet Union's intrusion into China's internal affairs. Additionally, Stalin agreed that the USSR would respect Chinese sovereignty in Manchuria and begin to evacuate Soviet troops within three weeks after Japan's defeat.

Stalin's support was conditional; he had divulged his price for war against Japan six weeks prior to the conference. When the Allies reached agreement at Yalta, the Soviets defined their stipulations in the "Draft of Marshall Stalin's Political Conditions for Russia's Entry in the War Against Japan." The Kuril Islands would be transferred to the USSR, the Soviet Union would control Outer Mongolia, and territory lost to Japan in 1905 at the end of the Russo-Japanese War would be returned to Russia. The Allies also agreed that the port at Dairen would be internationalized, while safeguarding Russia's "preeminent interest," that Russia's lease of Port Arthur as a naval base would be restored, and that there would be a joint Soviet-Chinese operation of the Chinese Eastern and South Manchurian railroads.

Although Roosevelt died on April 12, 1945, implementation of the terms of the Yalta Conference involved negotiations with Chiang Kaishek, who sent T. V. Soong to Moscow to negotiate the details of an agreement. Stalin basically affirmed what had been decided while he was in Yalta. But before the final documents were signed, Stalin left for the conference at Potsdam.

Then the international climate changed dramatically. By July 26, 1945, the completion of the atomic bomb led some American policy-makers to conclude that the Soviet Union's participation was not crucial to Japan's eventual defeat. They also believed that perhaps the use of such a terrifying weapon would serve notice to the USSR of American power and resolve, even though they realized that, short of war, Soviet involvement in the war could not be stopped. Therefore on August 8, two days after the first atomic bomb was dropped on Japan, Soviet forces entered the war. The Yalta agreements were then affirmed by the Sino-Soviet Treaty of Friendship and Alliance on August 14.

The Yalta Conference witnessed the positioning of the three major postwar powers with regard to East Asia. The point was not only to assure Japan's defeat, but also to ensure the interests of the United States, Chiang Kaishek, and the USSR. The domestic realities of China were ignored and the United States slowly continued to move from seeking China's cooperation in the war against Japan to assuring that Chiang and his Guomindang did not fall to the Chinese Communists and that the Soviet Union did not support the latter. Stalin was perfectly content to eschew support for the Chinese Communist Party as long as the interests of the Soviet Union were kept intact.

Edwin Clausen

References

Clemens, Diane. *Yalta*. New York, NY: Oxford University Press, 1970.

Feis, Herbert. *The China Tangle: The American Effort in China from Pearl Harbor to the Marshall Mission*. Princeton, NJ: Princeton University Press, 1953.

Yan Fu (1854–1921)

Translator, writer, sociopolitical thinker, and leading intellectual in the late Qing. Yan Fu is best known as the person who introduced the ideas of Charles Darwin, Herbert Spencer, Adam Smith and John Stuart Mill to modern China. Although he supported gradual reform, his writings influenced Chinese reformers and revolutionaries alike.

A native of Fujian province, Yan received a classical education before entering the Fuzhou Naval School in 1866. After graduation, he studied naval technology in England for two years (1877–79). The overseas experience inspired Yan to investigate the causes of China's present weakness as well as the key to the strength of the West. In 1895, the year China suffered humiliating defeat in the first Sino-Japanese War, Yan published a series of essays on his findings about Western, in particular British, society. He praised the Western "public spirit" that converged individual and national interests. China needed to learn this from the West, Yan suggested, if she desired to survive in the modern world.

During the following years Yan translated, or rather interpreted in the form of translation, Thomas Huxley's *Evolution and Ethics,* Adam Smith's *Wealth of Nations,* John Stuart Mill's *On Liberty* and *Logic,* Herbert Spencer's *A Study of Sociology,* and Montesquieu's *The Spirit of the Laws.* These works, together with his own writings, informed his countrymen on a number of major trends in modern Western social and political thought. Among them the most influential was the Social Darwinist idea of natural selection *(wujing tianze),* or the "survival of the fittest." In the evolution of the universe as well as in human history, Yan explained, competition for existence is not only a necessity but the source of progress. In the current world this competition took the form of struggle among nations. Yan argued that the West is winning the struggle because it is able to generate its collective resource by releasing the energy of the individuals through a free society and democratic institutions. Since the latter was lacking in the Chinese tradition, China had no alternative but to abandon her tradition and embrace the Western systems and values.

Yan was dean of the Beiyang Naval Academy and founder of the *Guowenbao (National News Daily),* both at Tianjin, at the time. While his translations and writings exerted revolutionary impacts on China's intellectual circles, his political stance remained conservative. He was close to Kang Youwei and Liang Qichao, but was not involved in the Reform movement of 1898. His belief in the process of evolution, moreover, caused him to disagree with the radical proposal of a republican revolution. The Chinese people, in Yan's opinion, was not yet prepared to move into the stage of republican democracy.

Yet the revolution eventually came, and in many ways proved to be a failure. During the early Republic, Yan became increasingly disillusioned with the country's political condition, which in part explains his support for Yuan Shikai's attempt to make himself an emperor in 1915. Yan also became conservative in his cultural attitude. Although his attack on Chinese tradition was a precursor to May Fourth iconoclasm, and he briefly served as president of the Beijing University in 1912, in his final years Yan found himself in the opposing camp to the "New Culture" youth.

Yan Fu's place in the history of Chinese nationalism is significant. His study and propagation of Social Darwinism were motivated by strong nationalistic concerns. Even his advocacy of Western liberalism was aimed at the building of collective strength, *i.e.*, national wealth and power. In his discussions he generally downplayed Han-Manchu antagonism and stressed China as a single unit participating in the process of global struggle. All of these views shaped the minds of a generation of Chinese and contributed to the emergence of modern China's national consciousness.

Wang Ke-wen

References

Schwartz, Benjamin I. *In Search of Wealth and Power: Yen Fu and the West.* Cambridge, MA: Harvard University Press, 1964.

Yan Xishan (1883–1960)

Ruler of Shanxi province and one of the most enduring warlords in the republican era, Yan Xishan was born to a well-to-do family in Wutai county, Shanxi, and attended a military academy in his home province in his teens. In 1904, he went to Japan for advanced military study and training and joined Sun Yatsen's Tongmenghui the next year. He also became a member of the revolutionary military group, the Dare-to-Die Corps. Returning to China in 1909, he served in the Shanxi Army but secretly worked for the revolutionary cause.

When the Revolution of 1911 erupted, Yan led his troops and staged an anti-Manchu uprising in Taiyuan, the provincial capital. His plan to join forces with Wu Luzhen, another revolutionary commander in Shanxi, and thereby undermine Yuan Shikai's control of north China, was aborted by the assassination of Wu later that year. After assuming the presidency of the new Republic, Yuan nevertheless appointed Yan as governor of Shanxi. Thus began Yan's rule of the province that lasted as long as the Republic itself.

During the early years of the Republic, Yan managed to survive both the dictatorship of Yuan Shikai and the ensuing strife among the warlord factions. Participating occasionally in the warlord wars, such as the expedition against Sun Yatsen's Constitution Protection movement in 1917, Yan always stressed his priority of securing and consolidating his control over Shanxi.

In 1927, Chiang Kaishek's Northern Expeditionary forces swept into the Yangtze region and posed an enormous threat to the northern warlords. Yan again decided to join the winning side. Together with Feng Yuxiang in the Northwest, Yan declared his support for the Guomindang (GMD) as well as for Chiang's purge of the Communists from the Party. He then participated in the last phase of the Northern Expedition against the Fengtian Clique. In return, Chiang not only recognized Yan's rule in Shanxi but allowed Yan to expand his influence into Hebei.

In the years immediately following the completion of the Northern Expedition, as various regional militarists revolted against Chiang's Nanjing government, Yan demanded greater power in north China from Chiang as a condition of his neutrality in the conflicts. In 1930, however, fearing that Chiang might soon move against him, Yan collaborated with Feng Yuxiang, the Guangxi Clique and the anti-Chiang GMD factions in launching a major rebellion. The opposition established a new government in Beiping (known as the "Enlarged Session"), which lasted only four months. By the end of that year, the opposition had been crushed by Chiang and Yan took refuge in the Japanese-controlled Dairen.

In 1931, Yan returned to Shanxi. After the Manchurian Incident, Chiang again tolerated Yan as the ruler of that province. Yan promulgated his "Ten-Year Plan" for provincial reconstruction, and for the next few years developed the industry, agriculture, transportation, and educational systems in Shanxi. Especially noteworthy was his policy of village government *(cunzhi),* which increased governmental control at the grass-roots level and considerably reduced the traditional power of the gentry elite. As a result the economy of Shanxi improved, although much of it became a government monopoly, and law and order generally prevailed. Shanxi came to be known as a "model province."

In 1936, the Chinese Communist Party (CCP), with its base in the neighboring Shaanxi province, extended its influence into Shanxi. In an effort to control the Communists, Yan formed a coalition, the Anti-Japanese Sacrifice Alliance, with them. A "New Army" organized by the alliance included mainly Communist forces. Soon the Sino-Japanese War started and north China, including parts of Shanxi, fell to the Japanese. Yan was appointed by Chiang Kaishek as commander of the "second war zone," and he retreated to the western part of the province. Aware that the growing New Army had become a threat to his power, Yan in late 1939 negotiated a secret truce with the Japanese and turned against the CCP. In 1941, he concluded another peace agreement with the Japanese, and for the remainder of the war he largely stayed out of the conflict.

After the war, Yan supported Chiang's government in the civil war against the CCP. In June 1949, Chiang appointed him head of the Administrative Yuan (premier) of the so-called "wartime cabinet." Some days later Yan left Shanxi, and the CCP captured the province. Many of his followers committed suicide. Yan's premiership did not last long; he eventually followed Chiang to Taiwan. He spent his last years on the island writing treatises on subjects such as "the way to great unity."

Wang Ke-wen

References

Gillin, Donald G. *Warlord: Yen Hsi-shan in Shansi Province, 1911–1949.* Princeton, NJ: Princeton University Press, 1967.

Van Slyke, Lyman P. *Enemies and Friends: The United Front in Chinese Communist History.* Stanford, CA: Stanford University Press, 1967.

Yang Du (1875–1931)

Constitutionalist in the last Qing period and adviser to Yuan Shikai during the early Republic, Yang Du became a member of the Guomindang and the Chinese Communist Party in his last years.

A native of Xiangtan, Hunan, Yang was a child prodigy known for his mastery of the classics. He studied with Wang Kaiyun, the distinguished Hunanese scholar, until 1902, when he went to Japan for the new-style education. Convinced of the importance of reform, he cooperated with Huang Hsing and Yang Shouren to start a monthly, *Youxue yibian (Overseas Students' Translations),* to introduce new knowledge to Chinese students. For the promotion of education in nationalism, he also established the Hunan Compilation and Translations Society *(Hunan bianyishe),* which published textbooks for use in Chinese schools. He soon emerged as a student leader, and was elected general secretary of the Chinese Students' General Association in Japan in 1904.

Between 1905 and 1911, Yang Du played an active role in the Constitutional movement. He offered his assistance to Duanfang in studying Western constitutional systems and making recommendations to the Manchu court. In 1907, he founded *Zhongguo xinbao (New China Journal)* and published a series of articles entitled "The Principles of Gold and Iron" *(Jintie zhuyi),* in which he offered a prescription for national revival. Yang argued that economics and militarism would project the country to wealth and power, and that the Qing government would eventually be replaced through the pressure of public opinion as constitutionalism gained ground.

At the outbreak of the Revolution of 1911, Yang, then in Beijing, collaborated with Wang Jingwei to form the Association for Assisting National Affairs *(Guoshi gongjihui)* in an attempt to mediate between the constitutionalists and revolutionaries. But neither side appreciated their efforts; the society dissolved shortly after. Yuan Shikai appointed Yang a member of the committee representing the Qing government in the peace negotiations in late 1911.

During this period, Yang Du considered Yuan Shikai a strong leader indispensable to the new China. In 1915 he headed the Society to Plan for Stability *(Chouanhui)* to support Yuan's plan for a monarchy. After Yuan's death, the republican government ordered Yang's arrest for his role in the monarchical attempt. He sought asylum in Qingdao and stayed there for two years.

Yang reemerged in 1918 and switched his support to Sun Yatsen. He helped to establish dialogues between Sun and the warlords and eventually joined the Guomindang in 1926. In his last years, he sided with the Communists. When Li Dazhao was arrested in 1927, Yang appealed to the warlords for his release but to no avail. He became a member of the Chinese Communist Party in 1930 and died the next year in Shanghai.

Yang Du has been criticized for his association with Yuan Shikai, yet he was a nationalist whose ultimate concern was China's revival through a prosperous economy and a strong government, as summarized in his "Principles of Gold and Iron." The political choices he made in his last years probably reflected a similar concern.

Henry Y. S. Chan

References

Boorman, Howard L., and Richard C. Howard, eds. *Biographical Dictionary of Republican China*, vol. 4. New York, NY: Columbia University Press, 1971.

Yang Shangkun (b. 1907)

A veteran Communist leader, Yang Shangkun was president of the People's Republic of China from 1988 to 1993.

Born to a wealthy family in Tongnan, Sichuan, Yang joined the Communist Youth as a high school student and became a member of the Chinese Communist Party (CCP) while studying at Shanghai University in the mid-1920s. From 1927 to 1930, he studied at the Sun Yatsen University in Moscow and associated himself closely with Wang Ming (Chen Shaoyu), then the powerful "boss" of the Chinese Communists in the Soviet Union. In 1931, he returned to China with Wang and others, known as the pro-Moscow "twenty-eight Bolsheviks," and immediately took over the leadership of the CCP and the Jiangxi Soviet.

For several years, these "internationalists" successfully sidelined Mao Zedong and brought the Party closer to the line advocated by Stalin. During the Long March of 1934 and 1935, in which Yang took part, they were blamed for the collapse of the Jiangxi Soviet and again lost power to Mao. Yang subsequently held minor positions throughout most of the Sino-Japanese War (1937–45), until appointed to the CCP's North China Bureau in 1943. In 1945, the year the war ended, he became head of the general office of the CCP's Central Committee—signaling his full political rehabilitation. He held that post until the outbreak of the Cultural Revolution in 1966.

Under the People's Republic, Yang initially played a key role in solidifying the alliance between China and the Soviet Union. He was a member of the Chinese delegations that visited Moscow in the 1950s and in the early 1960s, even after the Sino-Soviet split. Such a background, and his prominent position in the Party bureaucracy, made him a natural target in the Cultural Revolution. Yang was among the first group of high Party officials to be "struggled against" in the mass rally in Beijing in 1966. He spent the next decade in "labor reform" and did not reappear in public until 1978. Following Deng Xiaoping's return to power, Yang was appointed chairman of the Guangzhou Revolutionary Committee and vice-governor of Guangdong, working closely with his old friend Ye Jianying. In the 1980s, he became vice-chairman of the CCP's Military Commission (under Deng Xiaoping) and president of the National People's Congress. As one of the "old guards" in the Party and Deng's second-hand man in controlling the "barrel of the gun," Yang helped to maintain the loyalty and stability of the People's Liberation Army (PLA) in the midst of Deng's risky economic reforms.

In 1988, Yang succeeded Li Xiannian as state chairman (president) of the People's Republic. The following year the Tiananmen Incident occurred. It is widely believed that during the incident Yang was a major proponent, within the top leadership of the CCP, of suppressing the demonstrations by force. His own experiences during the Cultural Revolution would not have made him a sympathizer of protesting students. The purge of the reformers in the Party in the wake of the incident greatly enhanced Yang's political influence. Together with his younger brother, Yang Baibing, chief political commissar of the PLA and secretary-general of the Military Commission, and his nephew Yang Jianhua, who commanded the army that carried out the massacre in Beijing, the Yang family was regarded as especially powerful in the military. Even Deng Xiaoping was said to have felt threatened. When Yang stepped down as president in 1993, Deng also removed his relatives from office.

Wang Ke-wen

References

Bartke, Wolfgang. *Who's Who in the People's Republic of China*. Armonk, NY: M. E. Sharpe, 1991.

Ye Mingchen (1809–59)

Governor-general of Guangdong and Guangxi during the *Arrow* War, Ye Mingchen was captured by the British in the war and died in captivity in India.

Ye received his *jinshi* degree in 1835. After that he rose with remarkable speed in the Qing bureaucracy, and by 1848 had become governor of Guangdong. Four years later, he was promoted to governor-general of Liang-Guang. In Guangdong, Ye vigorously suppressed the increasing local disturbances that were being encouraged by the rising Taiping Rebellion. At the same time, he continued his predecessor's policy of resisting the British demand to enter the city of Canton, which had been promised by the Qing government after China's defeat in the Opium War.

When the *Arrow* Incident occurred in early October 1856, Ye displayed inclinations for a peaceful solution, but the British were eager to find an excuse to force a full implementation of the post-Opium War settlement. In late October, the British occupied the naval forts outside of Canton, besieged and bombarded the city. Ye ordered the suspension of foreign trade and directed a successful counterattack, which destroyed the foreign factories near the city. Unaware of London's intentions, Ye sent a glowing report to Emperor Xianfeng, boasting a total victory over the "barbarians."

The next year, the Anglo-French joint expeditionary force arrived on south China's coast. London was determined to teach the Qing empire, and the people of Canton, a lesson about Western military might. In December 1857, the expeditionary force launched an attack on Canton, which Ye's troops proved utterly incapable to defend. In January 1858, the Anglo-French forces captured the city. Ye was taken prisoner. Lord Elgin, commander of the British forces, ordered Ye's exile to Calcutta, where he died in 1859. Ye did not live to see the end of the entire conflict in 1860. Canton was not restored to Chinese rule until 1861.

Ye's hard-line policy in Canton has been described by many as unrealistic and xenophobic. It should be noted, however, that his position was strongly supported by the local gentry elite (such as the *Shengping shexue*), and generally reflected popular sentiment. After the fall of Canton, Beijing blamed Ye for the disaster, but earlier it had also supported his militant policy. To an extent, Ye's experience at Canton mirrored that of the Qing empire at the time, when the emerging Chinese nationalist feelings were frustrated by an increasing awareness of the country's military weakness and ignorance of the outside world.

Wang Ke-wen

References

Wakeman, Frederic, Jr. *Strangers at the Gate: Social Disorder in South China, 1839–1861.* Berkeley: University of California Press, 1966.

Wong, J. Y. *Yeh Ming-ch'en: Viceroy of Liang Kuang (1852–8).* Cambridge, England: Cambridge University Press, 1976.

Yen, James (Yan Yangchu, 1890–1990)

Educator and rural reformer, James Yen is considered one of the most important advocates of mass education in modern China.

Yen was born to an intellectual family in Sichuan. At the age of fourteen, while studying at a missionary school, he became a Christian. Shortly after the Revolution of 1911, Yen went to Hong Kong to continue his education there. In 1916, he left for the United States and enrolled at Yale University. Upon receiving a B.A. in political economy in 1918, he volunteered to go to France to help the Chinese laborers who had been sent there to assist the Allied nations' war effort during World War I. This initial experience in mass education apparently had a tremendous impact on Yen, and he developed great interest in the endeavor. In a meeting of young Chinese laborers held in Paris in 1919, Yen for the first time presented his thoughts on the methods and texts suitable for mass education.

That same year Yen returned to the United States and pursued graduate studies at Princeton University, where he received an M.A. in history in 1920. While in America, Yen was already active in campus activities among Christian students. When he returned to China in the summer of 1920, he began a career in the national headquarters of the Chinese Young Men's Christian Association (Y.M.C.A.) in Shanghai, in charge of its newly established section on mass education. With a focus on eastern China, Yen carefully modified the approaches he had used in France and adjusted them to the needs of Chinese society. In 1922, he chose the province of Hunan as the first experimental ground for his mass education program. With the cooperation of the provincial government, then under the militarist Zhao Hengti, the experiment proved to be successful. He then implemented his program in Shandong and Zhejiang, again with the support of the local authorities. In 1923, he helped found the Chinese Association for the Promotion of Mass Education (Mass Education Association, *Pingjiaohui*) in Beijing. This privately funded organization declared as its purpose "eliminating illiteracy and creating new people." Yen's principal colleagues in the association included Tao Xingzhi, Jiang Menglin and Zhang Boling. The latter two headed the prestigious Beijing University and Nankai University, respectively.

Yen soon resigned his position with the Y.M.C.A. and devoted himself entirely to the work of the Mass Education Association (MEA).

He recruited a group of young intellectuals, many of whom had received higher degrees in the United States, as his assistants and dramatically expanded the activities of the MEA. In 1924, they selected the areas of Baoding and Wanping in Hebei province as the MEA's "experiment zones." In 1925, Ding county (Ting hsien) in Hebei also became an "experiment zone." The latter project was especially ambitious. With the help of Qinghua University and the Rockefeller Foundation, the MEA was not only to spread literacy but to improve agriculture in the sixty-two villages in the county.

After the nominal unification of the country by the Guomindang(GMD), Yen's work caught the attention of the new national government in Nanjing. At the invitation of the government, the MEA assisted in several popular education projects in Jiangsu in 1928. In the years that followed, the experiment in Ding county received increasing government support as a showcase of rural reform under Guomindang rule, and Yen himself became closely associated with the government. Naturally he opposed the rural revolution that was being carried out by the Chinese Communist Party (CCP).

When the Sino-Japanese War broke out in 1937, Ding county quickly fell into the hands of the invading Japanese. Soon most of the MEA projects in northern and eastern China were also lost. During the war, Yen served as a member of the People's Political Council and contributed to the war effort mostly by mobilizing popular resistance and training rural workers. In 1943, he went to the United States on a government mission and did not return to China until after the end of the war. His lecture tours in America further enhanced his international reputation as an educator and rural reformer.

From 1946 to 1949, Yen functioned essentially as a bureaucrat in the GMD government. His plans for rural reconstruction were halted by the civil war between the GMD and the CCP, and he spent much effort in securing American aid to the government. In 1948, he played a crucial role in the formation of the Sino-American Rural Reconstruction Commission *(Nongfuhui)*, which later became an important instrument in the GMD's land reform in Taiwan. As the CCP was winning the civil war, Yen moved with the GMD first to the Southwest and then to Taiwan, but he left the country again in 1950. In the 1950s, Yen traveled to various parts of the world, working for the Sino-American Committee on Mass Education as well as for the United Nations' Organization on Culture and Education. In 1952, he accepted the invitation of the government of the Philippines to supervise the rural reconstruction projects in that country. An International Rural Reconstruction College, subsequently founded in Manila, accepted students from Asia, Africa, and Latin America. They were trained to promote rural education and agricultural improvement in their own countries.

Yen once saw his effort as part of a global struggle against Communism. As a result of the change in the international environment and in the situation in China, however, he finally reached a rapprochement with the CCP government on the mainland. In 1985 and 1987 he visited the People's Republic and was warmly welcomed by its leaders, who openly praised his experiments in the 1930s. Yen lived to the age of 100 when he died of illness in New York.

Yen described the key components of his ideas on mass education as the "three Cs," namely, Confucius, Christ, and Collie. His lifetime work was clearly motivated by a strong religious belief, but also by a sense of nationalism. In his lectures during the 1930s he linked rural movement with "national self-salvation" and "national rebuilding." He perceived it as essential to educate the masses to be "knowledgeable, productive, and public-spirited" citizens in order to develop the country and enhance its international status. His personal and intellectual background made it difficult for him to understand the radical and violent approaches to rural reform proposed by the Communists, and in pursuing his goals he often found it necessary to recognize and cooperate with the sociopolitical status quo. This moderate stance led him to side with the establishment in the political struggle of the republican era. In the end, his work failed to stem the rising tide of Chinese revolution.

Wang Ke-wen

References

Hayford, Charles W. *To the People: James Yen and Village China.* New York, NY: Columbia University Press, 1990.

Young China Association

First organized in mid-1918 and formally established in July 1919, the Young China Association *(Shaonian Zhongguo Xuehui)* was probably the most influential study society *(xuehui)* in the May Fourth era. It was initiated by Wang Guangqi, Zeng Qi, Li Dazhao and a few other young intellectuals, many of whom had recently returned from their studies in Japan in protest against Japan's increasing encroachment on China. Its subsequent growth was substantially aided by the nationalist student protest on May 4, 1919.

With headquarters in Beijing, the association established branches in Nanjing, Shanghai, Chengdu, and Paris. A monthly, *Young China (Shaonian Zhongguo),* founded in 1919, served as its organ. During its existence of seven years, the association maintained a total membership of around one hundred. Many of these later became prominent leaders of the Chinese Communist Party, the Chinese Youth Party, and the Guomindang.

These members were motivated by the desire for a strong and unified China and the belief that it was the responsibility of the young intellectuals like themselves to accomplish that goal. In this sense, the association epitomized the major political theme of the May Fourth movement. Yet its declared purpose, "to engage in social services under the guidance of a scientific spirit, so as to create a young China," sounded utterly nonpolitical, and it never produced a formal program or platform.

In fact, the association was divided from its inception on the issue of how political it should be. Wang Guangqi, who was influenced by anarchism, stressed social reform, whereas Li Dazhao was interested in direct political action. After 1920, however, with the radicalization of Chinese politics, the dividing issue became what political direction, whether left or right, the association should pursue. Li and a few others, such as Deng Zhongxia, Yun Daiying, Mao Zedong, and Zhang Guotao, openly supported Marxism and assisted in the formation of the Chinese Communist Party in 1921. In response, Zeng Qi led a group of anti-Communist members, then studying in France, into organizing the Chinese Nationalist Youth (*i.e.,* Chinese Youth Party). Thereafter the association was paralyzed by internal disputes and, following several unsuccessful meetings, it quietly disappeared in 1925.

The experience of the Young China Association reflected that of the entire May Fourth generation. The Chinese youth were united, initially, by an urgent sense of nationalism and vague ideals such as "Young China," but they soon became confused and divided as to what was the most effective approach to national salvation. The association's demise was therefore inevitable, as the *Realpolitik* of the revolution in the 1920s replaced the youthful idealism of the New Culture movement.

Wang Ke-wen

References

Chan, Lau Kit-ching. *The Chinese Youth Party, 1923–1945.* Hong Kong: University of Hong Kong Press, 1972.

Chow, Tse-tsung. *The May Fourth Movement: Intellectual Revolution in Modern China.* Cambridge, MA: Harvard University Press, 1960.

Levine, Marilyn A. *The Found Generation: Chinese Communists in Europe during the Twenties.* Seattle: University of Washington Press, 1993.

Yuan Shikai (1859–1916)

Founder of the Beiyang Army and first president of the Chinese Republic, Yuan Shikai was at one time described by the West as the "George Washington of China." Yuan, however, ended his life and career in the midst of a national upheaval caused by his attempt to make himself an emperor.

Yuan Shikai was born to an official-gentry family in Xiangcheng, Henen province. His grandfather and father had established local fame and influence by organizing militia *(tuanlian).* Yuan initially followed the conventional path and sought a government career through the examination system. After two failures in the examinations, however, he abandoned the path and joined the Huai Army in Shandong as a low-ranking officer. In the 1880s, the Qing government dispatched the Huai Army to Korea to suppress a *coup d'état.* The incident gave Yuan the first opportunity to demonstrate his talents in military and foreign affairs. From 1882 to 1894, he stayed in Korea, winning the respect of the Korean government and assisting it in military training and reform. His performance impressed Li Hongzhang, China's *de facto* premier and foreign minister in the late nineteenth century. He soon appointed Yuan as trade representative of the Qing government in Korea. As the Korean political crisis deepened in the early 1890s, leading to a deterioration of relations between China and Japan, Yuan's work became increasingly difficult. He returned to China on the eve of the first Sino-Japanese War (1894–95) and was immediately ordered to participate in the war effort.

China's defeat in the war persuaded the Qing to consider military modernization. Capitalizing on his experience in Korea, Yuan obtained the trust of Empress Dowager Cixi and the Manchu general Ronglu for the charge of this new project. In 1895 he was given the Dingwu Army, a small but modern-equipped force established during the Sino-Japanese War, to be the foundation of a Newly Created Army *(Xinjian lujun)*. Yuan set up his base at Xiaozhan, near Tianjin, where he began the project with about seven thousand men. During the following four years, he carefully organized and trained a powerful army, with the help of German advisers, Western weapons, and a group of capable officers who eventually became Yuan's chief assistants and followers throughout his career. Among these men were Xu Shichang, Duan Qirui, Feng Guozhang, Cao Kun, and Zhang Xun.

It was also during these years that Yuan showed strong interest in political reform. He befriended such reformers as Kang Youwei and Tan Sitong, and joined the reformist organization Qiangxuehui (Society for the Study of National Strengthening). His enthusiasm, as well as his command of the Newly Created Army, attracted the attention of the reformers. During the final days of the Hundred Days Reform in 1898, they sought his cooperation in eliminating the anti-reform faction, including the empress dowager and Ronglu, by force. Yuan allegedly betrayed the reformers by leaking this information to Ronglu, which led to the empress dowager's *coup d'état* against the reformers and Emperor Guangxu. Shortly after the coup, Yuan was promoted to high office and his army was reorganized into one of the five Wuwei armies commanded by Ronglu.

When the Boxer Uprising began in 1899, Yuan was acting governor of Shandong. A shrewd and realistic politician, he recognized the danger of the Boxers' violent anti-foreignism and adopted stern measures against them. Even after the Qing court had openly supported the uprising in 1900, Yuan reached a tacit agreement with the foreign powers for the maintenance of peace and order in his province. Yuan's handling of the crisis of 1899 to 1900 further enhanced his position in the post-Boxer Qing government.

In 1901, Li Hongzhang died. Yuan, now controlling an army of nearly 20,000 men, succeeded Li as governor of Zhili (Hebei) and commissioner of the northern ports. He established a Military-Political Office of the Northern Ports at Baoding for the purpose of expanding his army into a Beiyang (Northern Ports) Army. By 1905, the Beiyang Army had emerged as the best-equipped and trained force in China. It totaled more than sixty thousand men, with almost all of its senior officers issuing from Yuan's entourage at Xiaozhan. This was the institutional origin of the Beiyang group that was to dominate China for the next two decades.

The growing military and political power of Yuan, a Han official, eventually alarmed the Manchu Qing court. In 1907, Yuan was deprived of the critical post of commissioner of the northern ports, and in 1908, after the death of Empress Dowager Cixi and Emperor Guangxu, he was forced to retire to his home in Henan. In "retirement," he maintained close contact with his followers in the Beiyang Army. When the revolution broke out in 1911, therefore, the Qing court still found Yuan the only person who could control the Beiyang forces and thus the only person to whom to turn for help. Yuan was appointed premier and ordered

Yuan Shikai. (Courtesy of Nationalist Party Archives.)

to command his troops to fight the revolutionaries in Wuhan. Keenly aware of the decisive role which his powerful army played in the conflict, Yuan maneuvered between the Qing and the revolutionaries during the following months, bargaining for the best political terms for himself. By early 1912, he had reached an agreement with the revolutionaries, who promised him the presidency of the new republic in exchange for his assistance in the overthrow of the Qing. In February, Yuan carried out the agreement by forcing the six-year-old Emperor Xuantong to abdicate; days later, the revolutionary government in Nanjing elected him to be its first president. The former premier of the Qing empire thus assumed supreme leadership of the Chinese Republic.

As president, Yuan found his power seriously challenged by the old revolutionaries under Sun Yatsen, now reorganized into the Guomindang. In early 1913, the Guomindang won the majority seats in China's newly established parliament. Its leader Song Jiaoren called for a cabinet system that would make the president a figurehead. Yuan quickly moved to destroy the opposition. In March, he ordered the assassination of Song in Shanghai; the Guomindang retaliated by an open rebellion. In April, Yuan secured financial and political support from the foreign powers through the "Reorganization Loan," then mobilized the Beiyang Army and swiftly suppressed the Guomindang's Second Revolution. Later that year, he dissolved the Guomindang and the parliament.

The domestic and international mood at the time favored Yuan. The Chinese elite desired national unity and peace, whereas the foreign powers generally believed that China needed a "strong man" for post-revolutionary reconstruction and for the protection of their interests in China. Yuan had established rapport with the Western countries, especially Great Britain and the United States, since the Boxer Uprising and through his handling of the issue of Manchuria in the early 1900s. They now saw him as more capable than anyone else for the task of stabilizing the young Republic. The Japanese were somewhat less friendly. In early 1915, taking advantage of the eclipse of Western influence in Asia during World War I, Japan presented the Twenty-One Demands to Yuan's government. Unable to solicit Western intervention, Yuan eventually accepted most of those demands excepting the most damaging ones, which Japan agreed to withdraw.

From 1914 to 1915, Yuan worked to concentrate power in his hands. He also tried to reverse the trend of regional autonomy that had begun in the mid-nineteenth century by centralizing Beijing's administrative and financial control over the provinces. With the backing of his military, his effort met with a degree of success. That initial success, as well as the realization of obstacles ahead, led Yuan to reevaluate the feasibility of the presidency. His allegiance to the Republic was not deeper than his former loyalty to the Qing. Before 1911, he had supported the system of constitutional monarchy; that position apparently remained unchanged. When his American adviser, the political scientist Frank J. Goodnow, also suggested in August 1915 that a constitutional monarchy might be more suitable to China than a republican democracy, Yuan became convinced that a return to monarchy was necessary. Later that year, he orchestrated a national "petition" for a change of polity. He then accepted this "petition" and announced his decision of enthroning himself as an emperor. The new monarchy, with the reign title of "Hongxian," was to commence on January 1, 1916.

To Yuan's surprise and frustration, the monarchical attempt provoked immediate attack from all quarters. Sun Yatsen's revolutionaries launched new waves of revolt; the gentry elite, fearing that a monarchy would further enhance centralization at the expense of their regional power bases, also criticized Yuan's action. Even Yuan's own generals in the Beiyang Army opposed the Hongxian monarchy because it would eliminate their chances of succession to Yuan's position. In late December, Cai E declared the independence of Yunnan province from Yuan's government. His National Protection movement (Huguo yundong) was supported by the provincial military leaders as well as the Jinbudang (Progressive Party), which had cooperated with Yuan during the suppression of the Second Revolution in 1913. Other provinces in south and central China soon followed Yunnan's example. The foreign powers, opportunistic as always, now expressed their disapproval of Yuan. In March, Yuan announced the cancellation of the monarchical plan but retained the presidency. Opposition from the provinces continued to rise, and the Beiyang generals refused to help. Panic and humiliation impaired Yuan's health; he fell ill in May and died on June 6. His government, as well as the best opportunity for a stable and unified Chinese Republic, disappeared with him.

An accidental victim of Yuan's aborted Hongxian monarchy was Confucianism. In advocating a return to monarchy, Yuan sought to revive the ideological foundation of the Chinese imperial system by honoring Confucius and promoting the study of Confucian classics. He also employed Confucianist symbols and rituals in elevating his personal authority. This attempt at associating Confucianism with a reactionary political movement—and a defunct political institution—undermined the autonomy of China's most important intellectual tradition. When the Hongxian monarchy failed, Confucianism and, in fact, traditional Chinese culture in general, became fatally discredited in the eyes of the country's educated elite. Yuan's rule thus paved the way for the iconoclastic May Fourth movement.

Wang Ke-wen

References

Ch'en, Jerome. *Yuan Shih-k'ai, 1859–1916.* Stanford, CA: Stanford University Press, 1961.

Mackinnon, Stephen R. *Power and Politics in Late Imperial China: Yuan Shikai in Beijing and Tianjin, 1901–1908.* Berkeley: University of California Press, 1980.

Young, Ernest P. *The Presidency of Yuan Shih-k'ai: Liberalism and Dictatorship in Early Republican China.* Ann Arbor: University of Michigan Press, 1977.

Yung Wing (Rong Hong, 1828–1912)

One of the earliest foreign-educated reformers in modern China, Yung Wing was born in Xiangshan, Guangdong province, just north of Macao. His family placed him in the first small class for boys in the earliest Protestant missionary school for girls in Macao; this school was subsequently transferred to Hong Kong and became the Morrison School. Yung completed his elementary schooling at this institution as a classmate of Tong King-sing (Tang Tingshu), the preeminent businessman-*comprador* of nineteenth-century China.

Through the assistance of the missionary teachers at the Morrison School, Yung Wing continued his studies in America at the Monson Academy in Monson, Massachusetts. He remained in the United States after his graduation and enrolled in Yale College as a member of the class of 1854. He was the first Chinese to graduate from an American university. His academic performance at Yale was outstanding, and he was twice awarded prizes in English composition. During his time at Yale, he formally converted to Christianity and also became a naturalized American citizen.

Returning to China in 1855, Yung Wing became dedicated to the cause of modernizing and strengthening China in the face of the unwarranted impositions on Chinese national sovereignty under the unequal treaties and the growing threats to Chinese commercial interests and territorial integrity in the late nineteenth century. Yung worked with the Qing government as well as with anti-Qing radicals to achieve his nationalistic goals. His earliest reform activities began in 1863, when Zeng Guofan commissioned him to visit the United States to purchase equipment for a government arsenal; he returned to China with this machinery in 1865 and helped to establish the Jiangnan Arsenal.

In 1870, while serving as adviser to Zeng Guofan and Li Hongzhang in the settlement of the Tianjin Incident, Yung Wing submitted a four-point reform plan that foreshadowed the major self-strengthening undertakings of the 1870s and 1880s. His proposal called for the formation of a steamship company owned and operated by Chinese, the launching of an education mission to the United States to provide a cadre of Chinese with Western technical skills, the development of mines and railways under Chinese ownership and control, and the exclusion of foreign intervention in Chinese judicial administration, beginning with a prohibition on missionaries from exercising jurisdiction over converts. The third of these proposals was of greatest interest to Yung Wing and led to the launching of the Chinese Educational Mission in 1872 under his supervision. At the same time, Yung was appointed vice minister to the United States, Spain, and Peru. He participated in opening the Chinese legation in Washington, and he traveled to Peru to investigate the conditions of coolie labor and negotiate an improvement in their treatment. He was deeply disappointed when the mission, headquartered in Hartford, Connecticut, was cancelled prematurely in 1881 and the students ordered to return to China.

During the Sino-Japanese War of 1894 to 1895, Yung Wing attempted to raise a loan in London on behalf of Zhang Zhidong to help finance the military effort against Japan. Al-

Y

though he was successful, this loan later fell through because of disagreements within China. Yung then attempted to launch a national bank and a coastal railway, but the effort for these projects proved abortive. He finally left China in 1898 because of his close links with the Hundred Days Reform. United States secretary of state John Sherman withdrew his American citizenship at the time on the basis of the racist legislation of the 1880s, so Yung Wing's return to his home and family in the United States in 1902 was technically illegal. Sun Yatsen invited Yung Wing to return to China to serve the newly declared Republic in 1911, but Yung declined because of old age and poor health, and died shortly thereafter in 1912.

Louis T. Sigel

References

Worthy, Edmund H., Jr. "Yung Wing in America." *Pacific Historical Review* no. 34 (1965): 265–87.

Yung, Wing. *My Life in China and America.* New York, NY: Henry Holt & Co., 1909.

Z

Zeng Guofan (1811–72)

A prominent Han official during the late Qing, Zeng Guofan was the founder of the Hunan Army that suppressed the Taiping Rebellion (1851–64) and the leader of the Self-Strengthening movement of the 1870s.

The Qing court in late 1852 decided to commission locally prominent members of the gentry to organize militia forces *(tuanlian)* to reestablish local order in the aftermath of the Taiping rebels' drive north from Guangxi to Nanjing, after the regular armies had proved largely ineffective in fighting the rebellion. While this was not an unprecedented measure, it was a risky one because it raised the prospect of encouraging local power at the central government's expense.

Zeng Guofan, who had returned to his native province of Hunan to mourn the death of his mother in 1852, was one of the prominent officials called out of retirement. Bringing together trusted friends and colleagues from Hunan to be his officers, he formed the Hunan Army *(Xiangjun)*, which succeeded with some difficulty in clearing most of Hunan of rebellion by 1854. Zeng subsequently expanded the scope of his operations beyond the provincial boundaries and his efforts spawned similar armies led by his principal lieutenants.

As he moved beyond the province to fight the Taipings in the broader theater of the Yangtze valley, Zeng mobilized resources to support his expanding campaign, including revenue sources and the construction of arsenals, and created an elaborate personnel and fiscal organization. Although the Manchu government was reluctant to endorse these expanded efforts, it was forced to do so when the government armies invading the Taiping capital at

Nanjing were disastrously defeated in 1860. In that year, Zeng was given plenipotentiary powers as governor-general of LiangJiang, president of the Board of War, and imperial commissioner for military operations in Jiangnan. Subsequently, by 1864, the armies under his overall command led by his brother Zeng Guoquan and his protégé Li Hongzhang, crushed the Taipings in the Lower Yangtze region.

To the extent that the Taipings assaulted the foundations of the Confucian tradition and the alien Manchu rule, while offering a new way of life for the Chinese, they could be considered a proto-nationalist movement. But to Zeng and his fellow Confucian scholar-officials, they were an anathema. In an impassioned proclamation, he appealed to the gentry to come to the defense of the Confucian tradition which he saw imperiled by the radical revolutionary challenge of the Taiping program and its ideology. Patriotism in this context was something quite different from loyalty to a nation; it encompassed an entire culture, which was more than a nation yet was the culture of the dominant class.

Zeng remained loyal to the dynasty and supported the reform programs of the Tongzhi Restoration (1862–74), including the Self-Strengthening movement, as a means to defend and preserve the traditional culture. Zeng was the last great Confucian statesman for whom the link between tradition and nationalism was so clear. After him, that connection was increasingly weakened by the progressive failure of the traditional order to deal with the Western challenge.

Nevertheless, in his later career Zeng became involved with events that were rapidly eroding the tradition he defended. Already in

Zeng Guofan. (Courtesy of Nationalist Party Archives.)

1861 at Anqing, he had established an arsenal that became the precursor of such modern industrial enterprises as the Jiangnan Arsenal at Shanghai. As governor-general of Zhili in 1870 he negotiated a preliminary settlement of the Tianjin Incident, and just before he died, he sponsored the proposal which led to the Chinese Educational Mission to the United States in 1872.

Jonathan Porter

References

Porter, Jonathan. *Tseng Kuo-fan's Private Bureaucracy.* Berkeley: University of California Press, 1972.

Zhan Tianyou (1861–1919)

Zhan Tianyou was the chief engineer of the first Chinese-built railway in modern China. Born in Nanhai, Guangdong, Zhan was among the first group of Chinese children whom the Qing government sent to attend school in the United States in 1872. In 1878, Zhan enrolled at Yale University, where he majored in civil engineering. He returned to China shortly after his graduation in 1882, whereupon the government ordered him to study navigation in the Fuzhou Arsenal and Naval Academy. In 1888, he became an engineer at the Tianjin Railway Company and subsequently supervised the construction of the Luanhe Bridge in the British-financed Tianjin-Yulin Railway. In that project he introduced for the first time the use of pneumatic caissons in constructing the bridge piers. Zhan also helped to build a number of other railways during the twelve years which he spent with that company. His work received the attention of Yuan Shikai, then viceroy at Tianjin in charge of railway enterprises.

In 1905, when the Russians objected to the use of a British engineer in constructing a railway in their "sphere of influence," Yuan appointed Zhan as chief engineer of the Beijing-Kalgan Railway project. Amid general doubts that the task could be managed by a Chinese, Zhan completed the railway, including the section at the Nankou Pass that required four long tunnels, within budget and ahead of schedule. The feat testified not only to Zhan's own extraordinary abilities but to the high morale and courage of his Chinese staff and workers, who worked with little experience and little modern equipment. Upon the opening of the railway in 1909, Zhan was given an honorary *jinshi* degree by the government and made a consulting engineer in the Ministry of Communications. He became a national hero.

When the Revolution of 1911 broke out, Zhan was constructing the Canton-Hankou Railway. He supported the Railway Protection movement that had triggered the Wuchang Uprising. In 1912 the new republican government, headed by Yuan Shikai, appointed Zhan director-general of the Canton-Hankou-Sichuan railroad system, which was financed by a consortium of British, French, German and American loans. The construction was postponed because of the shortage of funds following the outbreak of World War I in 1914. The government soon asked Zhan to serve as the Chinese representative on the Allied Technical Board that assisted the Allied occupation of the Trans-Siberian Railway and the Chinese Eastern Railway. He died of an illness in Hankou in 1919.

Zhan was one of the few eminently successful examples in the late Qing experiment of educating Chinese youth in the West and importing Western knowledge, not just personnel and equipments, onto Chinese soil. While all of his construction projects were financed by foreign loans, his achievements, especially the

Beijing-Kalgan Railway, demonstrated to both Westerners and the Chinese themselves that it was possible for China to master Western science and technology and to realize the goal of self-strengthening. In this sense, his career represented an important chapter in the development of modern Chinese nationalism.

Wang Ke-wen

References

Boorman, Howard L., and Richard C. Howard, eds. *Biographical Dictionary of Republican China*, vol. 1. New York, NY: Columbia University Press, 1967.

Zhang Binglin (1869–1935)

Combining scholarship with political activities, Zhang Binglin (Taiyan) supported efforts to reform the Qing monarchy in the 1890s but turned to anti-Manchu revolution after the turn of the century. Zhang was the foremost proponent of nationalism between 1900 and the Revolution of 1911. He tended to argue that a distinctive Han Chinese race had evolved a particular culture over the millennia. Manchu rule over Han Chinese was therefore a grave injustice, and, in addition, the imperialism of the white race threatened the Chinese nation and culture.

Zhang was born into a scholarly family in Zhejiang province and educated in the Han learning tradition of textual and philological studies. He read such early-Ming loyalists as Wang Fuzhi and Gu Yanwu, and turned away from a government career. He opposed the "new text" scholarship of Kang Youwei and despised Kang's view of Confucius as a religious figure, but he supported the reformers led by Kang in the 1890s in their efforts to modernize China along the lines of Meiji Japan. After the failure of the Hundred Days Reform of 1898, Zhang fled to Taiwan, but refused to support the reformist cause of the emperor against the empress dowager. Instead, he began to press for revolution and, back in Shanghai in 1900, cut off his queue to symbolize his resistance to Manchu rule. Jailed for his anti-Manchu polemics in the *Subao* case, he emerged from prison in 1906 to great acclaim and edited the chief revolutionary organ, *Minbao (The People's Report)* for the next two years.

After the Revolution of 1911, Zhang supported the presidency of Yuan Shikai but soon turned against Yuan and was under house arrest from 1913 to Yuan's death. Thereafter, Zhang played little active role in politics, although much of his scholarship continued to revolve around trying to define a Chinese essence of history, language and literature, and philosophy. He conducted a "National Learning Seminar" to keep Chinese culture alive no matter how dark the political situation might be. He opposed both the conservative attempts to turn Confucianism into a religion and the radical iconoclasm of the May Fourth movement, including the use of vernacular Chinese. He derided Communism in the 1920s as a threat to Chinese culture but urged the Guomindang to reconcile with the Chinese Communists in the 1930s in order to resist Japanese aggression.

At one time or another, Zhang quarreled with nearly all of his revolutionary comrades, including Wu Zhihui and Sun Yatsen, and his skeptical mind prevented him from belonging to any party. Nonetheless, erudite prose as well as scholarly prestige made Zhang an intellectual leader even for those who could barely read his essays. Although Zhang frequently modified his views, he accepted much of the Spencerian notion of social evolution based on racial group competition, which he synthesized with the Chinese intellectual tradition, particularly the "naturalism" of Xunzi. He believed that the white and yellow races were best adapted to social organization, and his goal was to reintegrate the sociopolitical order of China to defend it against Western imperialism. In this sense, anti-Manchuism was but a secondary, instrumentalist aspect of Zhang's anti-imperialism. He was also interested in Pan-Asian resistance to the West.

Zhang became best known for his ethnic nationalism. He linked Chinese culture to blood (descent from the yellow emperor), land, and language. Although at times he condemned the Manchus as inherently inferior, the Chinese revolution was *not* to be directed against the Manchu people but against the incompetent and racist Qing. As soon as it was overthrown, the Manchu people could either join with the Chinese or return to their homeland. Zhang's nationalism was thus explicitly pluralistic. *All* peoples had the right to resist domination and foreign aggression; all peoples had the right to explore their cultural uniqueness. In other words, Zhang's nationalism was neither aggrandizing nor imperialistic. Yet for all that, and even if anti-Manchuism was a propaganda ploy and the real concern was Western imperialism, Zhang's polemics perhaps had the unfortunate effect of poisoning an ethnically conscious patriotism with racial hatred. Anti-Manchuism dominated radical discourse before 1911 to such a degree that other important issues received only a fraction of the attention they deserved.

Modernization, Zhang believed, had to occur in a national context. He generally supported the Republic after 1912, although he remained skeptical about the capacity of parliamentary democracy. Elections, as he saw them in Japan and the West, served largely to ratify the power of the wealthy. A strong streak of egalitarianism and moral concern infused Zhang's nationalism from the beginning of his political career. He favored redistributing land in the countryside, giving workers profit-shares in industry, making taxation progressive, and abolishing inheritance rights.

The relationship between Zhang's political career and his prodigious scholarly product in philosophy and textual studies of all sorts has not been thoroughly explored. Among other subjects, he investigated Buddhist *(Yogacara)* and Daoist philosophy, and Legalism formed part of the basis of his early revolutionary theory. Broadly speaking, a concern with Chinese culture linked his scholarship and his politics. Zhang was an important contributor to the National Essence *(guocui)* movement, which affirmed and expanded various aspects of the Chinese tradition. Zhang's researches into noncanonical schools of thought upset the Confucian worldview of earlier generations. The national essence also served as a bulwark of Chinese nationalism: because the Chinese could take pride in the cultural achievements of the past, and because their very identity as a people was defined by that past. Nonetheless, Zhang's religious beliefs should probably be considered separately from his political activities, although they were not in contradiction. Indeed, Zhang pointed out that his interpretation of Mahayana Buddhism encouraged the moral heroism needed in revolutionary endeavor. It also supplied him with a universalist perspective in counterpoint to his nationalism.

Zhang was a brilliant scholar whose chief historical significance lies in his impact on modern Chinese nationalism. Yet he also foreshadowed, for all of his traditionalism, some of the continuing revolutionism in culture, as well as in society and politics, in twentieth-century China. He hoped to facilitate changes which would bear an organic relationship to the Chinese tradition.

Peter Zarrow

References

Furth, Charlotte. "The Sage as Rebel: The Inner World of Chang Ping-lin," in *The Limits of Change: Essays on Conservative Alternatives in Republican China,* ed. Charlotte Furth, 113–150. Cambridge, MA: Harvard University Press, 1976.

Shimada, Kenji. *Pioneer of the Chinese Revolution: Zhang Binglin and Confucianism.* Trans. Joshua A. Fogel. Stanford, CA: Stanford University Press, 1990.

Wong, Young-tsu. *Search for Modern Nationalism: Zhang Binglin and Revolutionary China, 1869–1936.* Hong Kong: Oxford University Press, 1989.

Zhang Jian (1853–1926)

Leading gentry reformer and industrialist in late Qing and early republican China, Zhang Jian was known as the "last *Zhuangyuan* (top place in the palace examination)" in Chinese history. He received that honor in 1894, eleven years before the abolition of the civil service examinations by the Qing in 1905. It was also the year when the first Sino-Japanese War broke out. China's defeat in that conflict shocked the whole country and stirred up a new wave of reform demands.

Zhang, now a new member of the Hanlin Academy, shared the enthusiasm for reform with his scholar-official friends. His desire to strengthen China, however, prompted him to take an unprecedented route. Zhang soon abandoned a promising career in officialdom and engaged himself in education and industry, because he believed the latter to be the most effective way of modernizing the country. In 1899, he founded, with political assistance from officials and financial contributions from friends, the Dasheng Cotton Mill in his hometown of Nantong, Jiangsu province. The financial success of the mill enabled him to experiment with a variety of other businesses in the following years: a flour mill, an oil mill, shipping lines, and a machine shop, in addition to some pioneering ventures in land reclamation and river conservation projects. He also established normal schools (the first in China, which also educated women) and technical schools, a library, a museum and a gymnastic stadium. Almost all of these enterprises were located in the Nantong area, but Zhang's reputation as China's most prominent private entrepreneur and educator became known throughout the country.

In the meantime, Zhang remained active in politics. Again, he chose to enter politics as a member of the gentry elite instead of a government official. During the Boxer Uprising in 1899 and 1900 Zhang persuaded regional officials such as Liu Kunyi and Zhang Zhidong to form the Southeast Autonomous movement *(dongnan hubao)* and disassociate the Yangtze provinces from the Qing court in Beijing. In the early 1900s, after a brief tour in Japan, Zhang became a strong advocate for constitutional monarchy. He helped to draft a memorandum for those same officials who were then petitioning the Qing court to adopt a constitution, and translated the Meiji Constitution of Japan into Chinese. In 1906, following the announcement by the Qing of its plan to adopt a constitution, Zhang organized the As-sociation for the Preparation of Constitutionalism to press for the speedy formation of a constitutional government. He was then elected chairman of the newly established provincial assembly of Jiangsu. Zhang's leadership in the Constitutional movement was comparable to that of Liang Qichao overseas.

During the Revolution of 1911, Zhang shifted his support to the new Republic and headed the provisional parliament of the revolutionary government in Nanjing. Because of his longtime friendship with Yuan Shikai, he played a critical role in the negotiation between Yuan and the revolutionaries. And it was Zhang who drafted the abdication decree for the Qing, which Yuan subsequently delivered to the court. When Yuan became the first president, Zhang was appointed minister of agriculture and forestry, and later minister of industry and commerce. A supporter of Yuan, Zhang was nevertheless disappointed by Yuan's monarchical attempt in 1915. He resigned from the government in protest and returned to Nantong, continuing his works in education and business. In the late 1910s, he turned his attention to charitable works, establishing facilities for the poor, the disabled, and children. On cultural issues, however, Zhang found himself on the opposite side of reform by criticizing the rising New Culture movement. He died shortly after the Guomindang began its Northern Expedition from Canton.

Zhang's unusual life reflected a transitional period in modern China. A *zhuangyuan*, he was a leading example of the traditional gentry, yet he chose to engage in modern industry and business instead of government office. His decision, motivated by a strong nationalist concern, revealed China's need for social and economic modernizations and the changing character of her Confucian elite. The multiple roles which Zhang played in the early twentieth century positioned him between the scholar-official and the modern entrepreneur, symbolic indeed of the last generation of the Chinese gentry.

Wang Ke-wen

References

Chang, P'eng-yuan. "The Constitutionalists." *China in Revolution: The First Phase, 1900–1913*, ed. Mary C. Wright, 143–183. New Haven, CT: Yale University Press, 1968.

Chu, Samuel C. *Reformer in Modern China: Chang Chien, 1853–1926*. New York, NY: Columbia University Press, 1965.

Zhang Xueliang (b. 1901)

Commander of the Northeast Army and plotter of the Xian Incident in 1936, Zhang Xueliang (Hanqing) was popularly known as the "Young Marshal." He was born in Taishan county, Liaoning, at a time when banditry was widespread in Manchuria in the wake of the Boxer Uprising. His father, Zhang Zuolin, a leader of 300 bandits, received amnesty from the Manchu government and was appointed a battalion commander. His mother was a daughter of a local landlord; she died when the young Zhang was only eleven years old. The elder Zhang had achieved supremacy in Manchuria by the time Xueliang reached adolescence. Xueliang was placed under the care of several erudite Confucian scholars, but he was fond of Western sports and lifestyle and made some Western friends. He entered the first class of the Northeast Military Academy, majoring in artillery, in 1919. He graduated with distinction the following year.

The twenty-year-old Zhang started out by commanding his father's guards brigade. With the help of Guo Songling, he enjoyed remarkable success in training troops and showed much prowess on the battlefield, particularly in the two wars between Zhang Zuolin and Wu Peifu, a northern warlord who then dominated the Beijing government. After the assassination of his father by the Japanese, the young marshal was able to succeed him, but not without some challenge. To consolidate his rule, he was obliged to kill Yang Yuting and Chang Yinhuai, his two rivals, thereby making himself the undisputed leader of Manchuria. He made a dramatic move in 1928 in joining Chiang Kaishek's Nanjing government in order to accomplish the unification of China, regardless of strong objection from Japan. In 1930, during the War of the Central Plains between Chiang Kaishek and the anti-Chiang militarists, Yan Xishan and Feng Yuxiang, the Young Marshal became an arbitrator. He first remained neutral, but later lent support to Chiang, which brought the immediate downfall of Yan and Feng.

When the Young Marshal moved his major forces inside the Great Wall to suppress Shi Youshan's revolt in 1931, the Japanese staged the Manchurian Incident that drove him out of Manchuria. After the loss of Jehol province to Japan, he was forced to resign from all of his political and military positions. Having cured his narcotics habit, Zhang embarked on a European tour. He was so impressed by the revival of Germany and Italy under fascism that, upon returning to China in early 1934, he advocated the adoption of fascism in China with Chiang Kaishek as dictator. But he soon became disillusioned with fighting the Chinese Communists in a civil war, while the true enemy, Japan, devoured China.

By early 1936, Zhang Xueliang and General Yang Hucheng of the Northwest Army had become allies of the Chinese Communists. When Chiang ignored Zhang and Yang's suggestion concerning the suspension of the civil war and the unification of China to fight against Japan, they staged a coup and put Chiang under house arrest at Xian on December 12, 1936, known as the Xian Incident. After Chiang verbally accepted their demands, the most important of which was to stop the civil war, the Young Marshal released Chiang and escorted him back to Nanjing. Once in Nanjing, Chiang took Zhang prisoner. Neither Chiang nor his son Jingguo would set Zhang free during their lifetimes. After fifty-three years under strict surveillance, Zhang was freed on his 90th birthday in Taiwan by President Li Denghui.

Tien-wei Wu

References

Boorman, Howard L., and Richard C. Howard, eds. *Biographical Dictionary of Republican China,* vol. 1. New York, NY: Columbia University Press, 1967.

Wu, Tien-wei. *The Sian Incident: A Pivotal Point in Modern Chinese History.* Ann Arbor: University of Michigan Press, 1976.

Zhang Xun (1854–1923)
See QING RESTORATION ATTEMPT

Zhang Zhidong (1837–1909)

A major reformer in late-nineteenth-century China, Zhang Zhidong participated in all reform movements undertaken by the late Qing government: the Self-Strengthening movement (1862–75), the Hundred Days Reform (1898), and the post-Boxer reform of 1900 to 1911. Like Li Hongzhang, Zhang used his political influence at court and his administrative skills as a scholar-official to bring Western military know-how and industrial technologies into China.

Born to a gentry family in the remote southwestern province of Guizhou, Zhang passed the civil service examination in 1863 at the age of twenty-six. While serving in the capital as a minor official at the Hanlin Academy, Zhang joined the conservative Pure Stream Group *(Qing liu dang)* in criticizing Li Hongzhang's reform. Although it may seem ironic that Zhang criticized Li, whose reform program he would soon adopt, two points need to be borne in mind. The first is that Zhang's criticism of Li focused on his handling of foreign affairs, not on the contents of his reform. Zhang's disagreement with Li was more on tactics than on the necessity of reform. The second is that Zhang's early association with the conservative camp proved to be essential to his later success as a reformer. Not only did he earn the respect of the conservatives but, more importantly, he won the trust of Empress Dowager Cixi, who was the *de facto* ruler of late Qing China. Because of his conservative credentials, Zhang enjoyed a freedom in implementing reforms that other reformers lacked.

In his first assignment as the governor of Shanxi between 1882 and 1884, Zhang was brought face to face with the harsh reality of life in rural China. There he met with Timothy Richard, the Baptist missionary from Wales. Through Richard, Zhang learned firsthand the superiority of Western technology; but it took the Sino-French War (1884–85) to convince Zhang that sweeping reform was necessary to save China. As governor-general of Guangdong and Guangxi during the war, Zhang shouldered the responsibility of defending Chinese territory against the French. The outcome of the war disheartened Zhang; it disclosed not only the inadequacy of Chinese defenses but also the corruption of the Chinese government. Zhang was incredulous that the Chinese government accepted a humiliating treaty with the French even though its soldiers won the war. After the war, Zhang implemented military reforms in Guangdong and Guangxi. He established arsenals, military academies, iron mills, coal mines, and government-sponsored industries.

The Chinese defeat in the Sino-Japanese War (1894–95) gave another impetus to Zhang's reform. In his joint capacities as governor-general of Hubei and Hunan and the temporary governor of Jiangsu and Zhejiang, Zhang was given the task of providing logistical support to the frontline. The swiftness with which China fell to her East Asian neighbor horrified Zhang. The war revealed that China lacked the infrastructure to fight a land and sea war. After the war, therefore, Zhang carried out a much larger-scale reform. Known as the Hubei Reform, it covered communications, finance, heavy industry, and education. Among the different aspects of his reform, Zhang was particularly noted for the improvement of education. He established several modern academies that taught special skills, such as mining, arithmetic, agriculture, and foreign languages. By doing so, Zhang quietly changed the nature of Chinese education. No longer was education simply a guide for future scholar-officials to pass the civil service examinations; it was to train technocrats to build a strong and stable China.

As an exemplary reformer in late Qing China, Zhang Zhidong exhibited the strength and the weakness of a scholar-official engaged in reform. For Zhang, the purpose of reform was to strengthen China against foreign invasions. He was eager to do anything to improve the Chinese defense and its related industry. But political reform was beyond Zhang's vision because too much was at stake. Not only would political reform disrupt the existing political alliances, it would undermine the interests of scholar-officials who were the beneficiaries of the status quo.

Zhang's reformism reached its limits in the Hundred Days Reform. When a new generation of reformers—such as Kang Youwei and Liang Qichao—emerged on the scene demanding a constitutional monarchy, Zhang could not comply. Although he played no part in crushing the short-lived reform, he was clearly on the side of Empress Dowager Cixi in rejecting Emperor Guangxu's reform program. After the Boxer Uprising of 1900, Zhang supervised the eleventh-hour reform by introducing a limited form of constitutional government into China. By then, however, the senior reformer was too old and too sick to be effective. He died one year after Cixi's death and two years before the Qing dynasty fell to the republican revolutionaries.

Tze-ki Hon

References

Ayers, William. *Chang Chih-tung and Educational Reform in China.* Cambridge, MA: Harvard University Press, 1971.

Bays, Daniel H. *China Enters the Twentieth Century: Chang Chih-tung and the Issues of a New Age, 1895–1909.* Ann Arbor: University of Michigan Press, 1978.

Zhang Zuolin (1873–1928)

The warlord who ruled the three northeastern provinces of Manchuria as a virtually autonomous region from 1919 until his death in 1928, Zhang Zuolin was born in Haicheng, Fengtian province (modern Liaoning), to an impoverished peasant family. He never attended school. While still in his teens, he enlisted in a military unit and fought in the Sino-Japanese War of 1894 and 1895. Thereafter he returned to Fengtian and formed his own military force to protect his home area. His troops became allies of the Japanese during the Russo-Japanese War of 1904 to 1905, thereby establishing a pattern for his international relationships in the future. In the final years of the Qing dynasty, Zhang's local power grew under the patronage of Zhao Ersan, who eventually became the governor-general of Manchuria. Zhang became a general in Yuan Shikai's Beiyang Army in the early years of the Republic, and through shrewd political maneuvering, he became military and civil governor of Fengtian after Yuan's death in 1916. Between 1917 and 1919, Zhang emerged victorious in political in-fighting, and extended his power over all of Manchuria. For the next eleven years, his authority there would be seriously challenged only by the Japanese.

Zhang's political ambitions soon extended beyond the borders of Manchuria to encompass all of China. In 1920, his Fengtian Army (named for his original home base) joined with troops of the Zhili Clique, led by Cao Kun and Wu Peifu, to crush the political aspirations of the Anhui Clique led by Duan Qirui. Soon the victorious allies were fighting each other to determine who would dominate the government of the Republic of China in Beijing. Zhang Zuolin lost the first of the Zhili-Fengtian wars, in 1922, and won the second, in 1924, thereby becoming the most powerful leader in north China.

In 1925, Zhang sent troops as far south as the Yangtze River, hoping to extend his power and eventually unify the country under his authority. His ambitions were thwarted when his Fengtian troops were defeated by Sun Chuanfang in the Yangtze provinces and Feng Yuxiang in Henan. Then Sun and Feng united with Zhang's old nemesis, Wu Peifu, in an effort to drive the Fengtian Army out of north China. They were joined by one of Zhang's own generals, Guo Songling, who, purportedly feared the consequences of Zhang's increasingly close relations with the Japanese. Guo urged Zhang to retire in favor of his son Zhang Xueliang. Japanese intervention saved Zhang. Guo Songling was executed.

A greater threat to Zhang's ambitions emerged in 1926, when the Guomindang-led National Revolutionary Army began its Northern Expedition. Zhang joined other warlords, including his old enemies, Sun Chuanfang and Wu Peifu, to form the National Pacification Army *(Anguojun)* to stop the Guomindang (GMD). Zhang was commander-in-chief. The *Anguojun* soon fell apart as the National Revolutionary Army won over major warlords, such as Yen Xishan and Feng Yuxiang, and defeated others. Zhang withdrew his troops to Shandong and Zhili (Hebei) provinces, where he hoped to make a stand with help from his Japanese allies. The Japanese, however, hoped to avoid a premature major confrontation with the GMD. They advised Zhang to pull his troops back to Manchuria and warned him that they would block his retreat if he were defeated in an engagement with the National Revolutionary Army. Zhang had little choice but to accede. On June 3, he left Beijing by train. Early in the morning of June 4, the train was blown up on the orders of a Japanese staff officer. Zhang

Zuolin was killed. The action was locally conceived and executed, but it signaled the ambitions of the Japanese Guandong Army in Manchuria which, in 1931, launched an attack that separated the three Manchurian provinces from the rest of China until the end of World War II in 1945.

Some analysts credited Zhang Zuolin with having unified Manchuria under a single government, an action that contributed to the overall political unification of China during the years of warlord chaos. Some also praised him for maintaining relative peace and stability in Manchuria during those difficult years. Detractors point out, on the other hand, that his concessions to the Japanese, in exchange for nine loans and other help, strengthened Japan's vested interests in Manchuria and encouraged the aggressive military action that resulted in the establishment of the puppet Manchukuo state in 1932. The peace and stability claim is countered by the accusation that Zhang and his cronies impoverished the populace while enriching themselves. Zhang's costly military ventures necessitated the raising of taxes to an unbearable level. He then issued paper currency (which he would not accept for tax payments), causing inflation that wiped out savings, fostered corruption, and ruined many local business ventures. When Zhang was murdered, many Chinese honored him as a patriot, but historians in China today are more inclined to regard his warlord battles as divisive and his concessions to the Japanese as self-serving and, ultimately, counterproductive for nationalism in China.

Peter J. Seybolt

References

Boorman, Howard L., and Richard C. Howard, eds. *Biographical Dictionary of Republican China*, vol. 1. New York, NY: Columbia University Press, 1968.

McCormack, Gavan. *Chang Tso-lin in Northeast China, 1911–1928: China, Japan, and the Manchurian Idea.* Stanford, CA: Stanford University Press, 1977.

Zhao Ziyang (b. 1919)

Premier of the People's Republic from 1980 to 1987 and general secretary of the Chinese Communist Party (CCP) from 1987 to 1989, Zhao Ziyang was the leading Dengist reformer in post-Mao China.

Zhao Ziyang joined the CCP, and worked as a local cadre in his native province of Henan, during the Sino-Japanese War (1937–45). He rose steadily in Party ranks during the civil war of 1945 to 1949, crossing the Yangtze River with the victorious People's Liberation Army on its way to "liberate" the whole country. After the founding of the People's Republic, he was transferred to Guangdong province and eventually became the provincial Party secretary shortly before the eruption of the Cultural Revolution in 1966. A pragmatist and self-made man with innovative ability, Zhao survived the early months of the Cultural Revolution by siding with the Red Guards, but he could not escape purge by the radical Maoists. He was dismissed from office in 1967. After Lin Biao's downfall in 1971, Premier Zhou Enlai reinstated him as a leader in Inner Mongolia and later transferred him back to his old post in Guangdong as the leader of the provincial Party branch. In 1975, when Sichuan province was in agricultural difficulties, Zhao was reassigned as governor and Party leader there with full authority. In Sichuan, Zhao made his reputation as a daring innovator who disbanded Mao's commune system. He personally visited the fields to inspire farmers to work for their own material betterment. His effort resulted in a miraculous increase in agricultural productivity. The prosperity of Sichuan's rural population earned Zhao nationwide reputation.

After Deng Xiaoping's victory over Hua Guofeng in the post-Mao power struggle, Zhao was promoted by Deng to be vice-premier in charge of agriculture. His previous performance in Sichuan apparently impressed the pragmatic Deng. When Hua resigned in early 1980 Zhao succeeded him as premier. Together with Hu Yaobang, the CCP's general secretary at the time, Zhao served as Deng's partner in reform and potential successor. Throughout most of the 1980s, the three men formed a solid troika which led China out of the Maoist stagnation and chaos.

As premier, Zhao was a cautious and smooth leader. His careful planning and administration were critical to the implementation of Deng's market-oriented reforms. He also frequently traveled abroad and was well-versed in public dialogues with foreign governments and press. In 1984, he signed the Sino-British Agreement on Hong Kong with the British prime minister Margaret Thatcher, ensuring the return of that British colony to China in 1997.

In 1987, following the student unrest, Hu Yaobang was dismissed from his post of CCP general secretary, and Zhao was named by Deng Xiaoping as Hu's successor. As head of the Party Zhao devoted much of his attention to theoretical development, as Hu did before him, in order to bring ideology closer to the reality of economic reform. He announced, at the thirteenth Party Congress in October 1987, his famous theory of "primary stage of socialism," which mapped out a long-term reform goal for economic, social, and political development in China within the framework of socialism. The concept of a "primary stage socialism" promised moderate improvements in living standards for the entire population by the fourth decade of the twenty-first century. It promised liberalization of the political system and the diminishing of Party interference in governmental operations. Meanwhile, Zhao worked hard to carry out wage and price reform against the opposition from conservatives in the Party.

When the student demonstration began in Spring 1989, Zhao appeared to be sympathetic with the students. On the eve of the Tiananmen Incident on June 4, he was removed from the post of Party general secretary for his failure to handle the crisis and for "creating a split within the Party." The political crisis of 1989 forced a temporary retreat on Deng's part to appease the conservatives, and Zhao, following the footsteps of Hu, was sacrificed by Deng as a result.

David Wen-wei Chang

References

Ch'i, Hsi-sheng. *Politics of Disillusionment: The Chinese Communist Party under Deng Xiaoping.* Armonk, NY: M. E. Sharpe, 1991.

Shambaugh, David L. *The Making of a Premier: Zhao Ziyang's Provincial Career.* Boulder, CO: Westview Press, 1984.

Zhenbao Island Incident

The Zhenbao Island Incident was a bloody battle in 1969 between the Chinese and Soviet patrols at Zhenbao Island along the Sino-Soviet border. Zhenbao Island, called Damansky by the Russians, is among some six hundred islands on the Ussuri River that are claimed by both China and the Soviet Union. The incident resulted from an intensifying hostility and steady escalation of border conflicts between the two Communist countries in the 1960s.

Chinese troops at Zhenbao Island. (Xinhua News Agency.)

China and the Soviet Union share a common border of four thousand miles along which the two countries have had serious territorial disputes. As the ideological chasm began to widen in the early 1960s, the hitherto controlled territorial issue emerged at the fore. From 1963 to 1965, Moscow and Beijing had reinforced their military positions in the border regions. The Chinese Cultural Revolution that was anti-Soviet as well as anti-West convinced the Soviet leadership that China under Mao Zedong had embarked upon a dangerous nationalist adventure. Consequently, the Soviet deployments of troops along the border increased rapidly.

For the Chinese, the perceived Soviet threat loomed large when Soviet tanks invaded Czechoslovakia in August 1968. Moscow's decision to use military force against another Communist country on the basis of the Brezhnev Doctrine sent a stern warning to the Chinese leaders. Beijing, however, chose to challenge Moscow head-on.

On March 2, 1969, a Chinese ambush force crossed the frozen Ussuri River from the Chinese bank to Zhenbao Island. Wearing white uniforms and taking cover in the snow, the Chinese soldiers caught the Soviet border patrols by surprise. They overwhelmed the Soviet unit and killed seven Russians outright. On March 15, the two sides engaged in a much larger battle. Prepared this time, Soviet troops inflicted a few hundred casualties on the Chinese side with a loss of about sixty of their own men. As the border conflict peaked in Septem-ber, China and the Soviet Union were on the verge of a major war, with the likelihood of nuclear exchanges. A brief meeting between the Chinese premier Zhou Enlai and the Soviet premier Kosygin at Beijing Airport on September 11 averted a military showdown almost at the last minute.

Most scholars agree that China initiated the incident. There is no consensus, however, on why China decided to risk a full-scale war with the Soviet Union by provoking this incident; perhaps it was to force a test of wills with the Soviets. Political factions within the Chinese leadership all seemed to have certain motives for triggering this crisis. Concerned about the possibility of a simultaneous confrontation with two superpowers, Zhou Enlai's faction might have needed this incident to promote a prompt rapprochement with the United States. The military faction of Lin Biao might have used the Soviet danger to elevate the importance of the Chinese military. The radical faction headed by Mao's wife, Jiang Qing, probably wanted to exploit the crisis and launch another propaganda campaign. Ultimately, the decision would have had to come from Mao himself. Unless the armed clash on Zhenbao Island was simply a random incident triggered by restless local commanders, Mao must have concluded that China had to stand firm against the mounting pressure from the Soviet Union.

Shi-ping Zheng

References

Garver, John W. *Foreign Relations of the People's Republic of China*. Englewood Cliffs, NJ: Prentice-Hall, 1993.

Robinson, Thomas. "China Confronts the Soviet Union: Warfare and Diplomacy on China's Inner Asian Frontiers." *The Cambridge History of China*, ed. Roderick MacFarquhar and John K. Fairbank, vol. 15, 218–301. Cambridge, England: Cambridge University Press, 1991.

Zheng Guanying (1842–1923)

Comprador, writer, and one of the leading reformers of nineteenth-century China, Zheng Guanying was a unique figure. Unlike all the other reformers in the late Qing, he did not pursue an academic or official career but entered a profession that was traditionally despised by Confucian literati. He was a *comprador*. Zheng's hometown, Xiangshan, was not far from Canton, the first focal point of Sino-Western contact. As a young man, Zheng studied English with the British missionary John Fryer and may have converted to Christianity. In 1858 he turned away from the civil service examinations and went to Shanghai to work for British companies there. Although quite successful in commerce, Zheng was not an ordinary businessman. His profession led him into close contact with foreigners and the foreign concessions in China. The impressions he obtained from this contact deepened his concern for China's current crisis and her future. In the 1870s and 1880s, Zheng wrote numerous essays on his ideas of reform. He first published them in Hong Kong under the title *Yiyan (Words of Change),* and then expanded the book into the five-volume *Shengshi weiyan (Warnings to a Prosperous Age)* in 1893. The book advocated a combination of Chinese and Western learnings as the means to achieve wealth and power for China.

In 1880, Zheng's knowledge and reputation was recognized by Li Hongzhang, who recruited Zheng to assist the various projects of the Self-Strengthening movement. Among the important positions which Zheng held was head of the China Merchants' Steam Navigation Company. He also participated in the defense and diplomatic work during the Sino-French War (1884–85). After a period of semi-retirement, Zheng returned to the government-supervised merchant-operated enterprises in the 1890s, in charge of the Hanyang Steel Mill and the Canton-Hankou Railway. With the fall of the Qing dynasty in 1911, Zheng's association with the government came to an end. During the early years of the Republic, he voiced opposition to the monarchical attempts by Yuan Shikai and Zhang Xun, and was clearly frustrated by the deterioration of China's political crisis. He wrote a sequel to *Shengshi weiyan.*

The most prominent expression of Zheng's nationalism, as well as his most important contribution to the late Qing reformist thought, may be found in his discussion of commerce and parliament. Much like another reformer with a non-traditional background, Wang Tao, Zheng was keenly aware of the importance of wealth as the basis of power for a modern country. He advocated government support for private business and recommended the elevation of the social status of merchants. His idea of a war of commerce *(shangzhan)* to protect China's rights and interests resembles European mercantilism, and may be described as a form of economic nationalism. More significantly, Zheng proposed the establishment of parliament as the core of a constitutional monarchy. He believed that this Western institution could help bridge the gulf that separated the government and the people (*i.e.,* the propertied class) and enhance national unity. It was apparently based on such a belief that he supported the Constitutional movement on the eve of the Revolution of 1911.

Wang Ke-wen

References

Hao, Yen-p'ing. "Changing Chinese Views of Western Relations, 1840–95." *The Cambridge History of China,* ed. John K. Fairbank and Kwang-ching Liu, vol. 11, 142–201. Cambridge, England: Cambridge University Press, 1980.

———. "Cheng Kuan-ying: The Comprador as Reformer." *Journal of Asian Studies* 29, no. 1 (November 1969): 15–22.

Zhili Clique

See FENG GUOZHANG

Zhili-Anhui War

The Zhili-Anhui War was fought in July 1920 between the Zhili and Anhui military cliques, both of which sought political dominance of the ostensible government of the Chinese Republic in Beijing. The Anhui Clique was a loose coalition of forces backing the political aspirations of Duan Qirui, a native of Anhui province and head of the Anfu Club. Duan, who at various times had served as premier and minister of war in the Beijing government, aspired to unite China by military force and bring an end to the chaotic era of warlord politics that followed the death of President Yuan Shikai in 1916. In pursuit of his ambitions, Duan had contracted a series of loans from Japan and arranged for Japanese help to train and equip his troops. In exchange, through secret agreements, he had granted Japan vast railroad and mining concessions in China and allowed Japanese troops to be stationed in Manchuria and Mongolia. He also secretly arranged to have Japan take over German concessions in Shandong province following Germany's defeat in World War I. News of the latter arrangement touched off the famous May Fourth demonstrations and fueled the political aspirations of Duan's chief military rivals, the Zhili Clique.

The Zhili Clique, headed by Cao Kun and Wu Peifu (and formerly Feng Guozhang) had been members of Yuan Shikai's Beiyang Army before its dissolution following Yuan's death. Like the Anhui Clique, the Zhili Clique sought to dominate the Beijing government, and ultimately to reunite China under its authority. Threatened by the increasing power of Duan, it built support by criticizing his strategy of uniting China by force, and his agreements with Japan for loans and concessions. Its opposition to Duan was supported by warlord Zhang Zuolin, head of the Fengtian Clique that was then predominant in Manchuria. Zhang was especially upset by Duan's sponsorship of General Xu Shuzheng, who was rapidly expanding his power in Inner Mongolia.

In a brief series of battles, the Zhili-Fengtian forces, led by Wu Peifu, defeated Duan's army. This effectively terminated the activities and aspirations of the Anhui Clique and the Anfu Club. Henceforth, the struggle for political dominance in north China would be decided between the Zhili and Fengtian cliques that had allied against their mutual rival.

The significance of the Zhili-Anhui War for nationalism in China is complex. On the one hand, the leaders of all military factions in China aspired to reunite the country and make it strong and independent. On the other hand, the Anhui Clique was criticized by its rivals for seeking foreign aid and granting concessions; but it differed from other factions in that regard only in quantity. Its Fengtian rival Zhang Zuolin was also backed by Japan, and Zhili leaders Cao Kun and Wu Peifu enjoyed support from the United States and Great Britain. Furthermore, the nationalist aspirations of all of these leaders cannot be separated from their personal ambitions, with the latter almost always taking precedence over the former in times of crisis. Ultimately, the warlord period became the antithesis of nationalism. The Chinese nation could not be unified until the warlord factions had been eliminated by superior military force.

Peter J. Seybolt

Zhili-Fengtian Wars

The Zhili-Fengtian wars, fought in 1922 and 1924, involved troops of the Zhili Clique, headed by Cao Kun and Wu Peifu, and those of the Fengtian Clique, headed by Zhang Zuolin. The Zhili Clique derived its name from the capital district—Zhili (modern Hebei province). The Fengtian Clique was named for Zhang Zuolin's home province—Fengtian (modern Liaoning province). Both cliques originated in Yuan Shikai's Beiyang Army, which had broken apart after Yuan's death in 1916. Both cliques aspired to dominate the Beijing government, and ultimately to reunite China under their control. To that end, they had cooperated to defeat the Anhui Clique of Duan Qirui in 1920.

Thereafter, the victors disagreed about the formation of a new government, and Zhang Zuolin withdrew his forces to Manchuria; but by 1921, in cooperation with his defeated rival Duan Qirui, he managed to have a protégé, Liang Shiyi, installed as premier in Beijing. Alarmed at Zhang's growing powers, Wu Peifu forced Liang to resign in early 1922. In response, Zhang moved his troops south of the Great Wall, and after several months of bluffing and threatening telegrams, the Zhili and Fengtian forces clashed in a major battle on May 3. Zhang's forces were defeated and withdrew to their home base in Manchuria. For the next two years, the Zhili faction dominated the Beijing government and large parts of China from the Great Wall to the Yangtze River.

Zhang Zuolin, who still had about 100,000 troops under his command and the backing of the Japanese in Manchuria, awaited his opportunity for revenge. It came in September 1924, when Zhang announced his support of a Zhejiang warlord in his struggle against a Jiangsu warlord supported by the Zhili Clique. Wu Peifu assembled an army of 250,000, considerably larger than Zhang's revitalized force of 170,000, but the victory went to Zhang, when troops in Wu Peifu's coalition, led by warlord Feng Yuxiang, turned traitor. Feng led his troops to Beijing, where he arrested the co-leader of the Zhili Clique, Cao Kun, then president of the Republic. Wu Peifu was cut off and defeated by the Fengtian army and thereafter fled to the Yangtze region with his remnant troops. The Zhili Clique never recovered its power, and Zhang Zuolin's Fengtian forces dominated the political scene in north China for the next several years.

The Zhili and Fengtian cliques were but two of many warlord forces contending for power in China. Virtually all of them aspired to reunite wartorn China and free it of imperialist domination. But all of them were caught in a web of special interests and factional relationships, and few of them could operate effectively beyond the bounds of their regional bases of power. Despite their avowed patriotism, the warlords themselves were a major obstacle to nationalism in China.

Peter J. Seybolt

Zhonghua minzu

The term *Zhonghua minzu* was created by the Chinese Republic to describe the multiethnic "Chinese nation" on which it perceived itself as being founded.

The revolutionary movement that toppled the Qing dynasty had been shaped, to a great extent, by anti-Manchuism. The explicit goal of the Han revolutionaries had been the expulsion of Manchus and the restoration of Han rule in China. As soon as the Revolution of 1911 succeeded, however, the new Republic declared a new position. Concerned about the possible fragmentation of the Chinese state, it abandoned the initial anti-Manchu agenda and proposed instead a commonwealth *(gonghe)* of the five major ethnic groups, *i.e.,* Han, Manchus, Mongols, Muslims, and Tibetans, that it currently governed.

In 1912, President Yuan Shikai first used the term *Zhonghua minzu* (Chinese nation) in his letter to the leader of Outer Mongolia, arguing that the Mongols were in fact part of the greater nation of China. *Zhonghua* had been used in premodern times as one of several forms in reference to China. Both *min* and *zu* had appeared in ancient Chinese texts as well, meaning "commoners" and "tribes," respectively, but the combined term was borrowed from Japan at the turn of the century as a translation of the English word "nation." Yuan's government declared that all the ethnic groups in *Zhonghua minzu* enjoyed equal status, but it also encouraged the non-Han minorities to assimilate themselves with the Han majority.

The introduction of the term and concept of *Zhonghua minzu* represented an important attempt by the Han-dominated Chinese state to forge a unified ethnic foundation for itself. Although in the short run the attempt failed to prevent Outer Mongolia and Tibet from pursuing political independence, since then *Zonghua minzu* has become an ideal of all modern Chinese who try to preserve the existing size and shape of the Chinese state.

Wang Ke-wen

Zhou Enlai (1898–1976)

Leader of the Chinese Communist Party (CCP) and long-time premier of the People's Republic of China (PRC), Zhou Enlai was the preeminent diplomat and administrator in modern China.

Zhou was widely recognized as a patriotic revolutionary and a skilled negotiator. His effective administration, as China's premier from 1949 to 1976, inspired a team of dedicated followers who worked with him to preserve the well-being of the country in the midst of political chaos and economic setbacks. Even more significant than his administration were his achievements in the field of diplomacy. Zhou earned high praise for his performance in negotiating, on behalf of the CCP, with domestic political opponents and foreign countries.

What made Zhou such a successful negotiator? The answer in part comes from his family background and early life. Zhou was born to a large and respectable family in Jiangsu province. His mother died when he was very young. His father, who was well-educated but became disoriented and unmotivated, could not take care of Zhou in person. Young Zhou lived with different uncles and aunts, moving from Shanghai to Manchuria and back to the rural northern Jiangsu. Such an unstable life, shifting from one relative to another as their dependent, taught Zhou the skill of surviving in changing environments. He had to please his relatives, learn to respect and befriend cousins, and work hard to prove his own worthiness. These qualities—loyalty to friends, respect for others, shrewdness, and hard work—remained with him throughout his life and greatly helped his political and diplomatic careers.

Zhou joined the Chinese Communist movement while studying in France in the early 1920s. He became a leader of the European Branch of the Chinese Communist Party and the Chinese Socialist Youth Corps. In 1924, he returned to China and, under the Guomindang–Chinese Communist party (GMD-CCP) United Front, went to Canton and worked for the Political Department of the Whampoa Military Academy. During the Northern Expedition (1926–28) Zhou led the workers' uprisings in Shanghai that helped to secure the city for the National Revolutionary Army in April 1927.

However, Zhou's commandant at Whampoa, Chiang Kaishek, soon turned against the Communists and terminated the United Front. Zhou escaped Chiang's bloody purge in Shanghai and joined the CCP underground.

From the late 1920s to the mid-1930s, Zhou was an important member of the CCP's top leadership. At first he worked closely with the Comintern and its followers in the Party, but when Mao Zedong's "indigenous" force was gaining momentum in the Chinese Communist movement, Zhou quickly readjusted his position. The critical turning point came at the Zunyi Conference in 1935, during the Long March, when Zhou lent his support to Mao in toppling the "Internationalists" as Party leaders. By then, Zhou had established himself as a major CCP representative in dealing with the ruling Guomindang as well as with other non-CCP political forces in China. During the Xian Incident in 1936, for example, Zhou went to Xian as the CCP representative to secure Chiang Kaishek's release from the hands of a Manchurian general. The Communists, at the time, believed that only Chiang could lead a united China to resist Japanese aggression.

During the Sino-Japanese War (1937–45), Zhou served as the main contact person between the CCP and the GMD government, then working under a new United Front. Chiang appointed him to a high position in the GMD government's Military Committee and as a member of the People's Political Council. In Chongqing, the GMD's wartime capital, Zhou's diplomatic talent and mild manners won sympathy and respect for himself and for his Party from all quarters, including many Westerners. In 1945 to 1947, following the end of the war, Zhou worked with George C. Marshall of the United States to seek compromise with the GMD government in order to avert a civil war in China. That effort was not only a public-relations success for the CCP, but bought time for the Party to prepare itself, militarily and politically, for a showdown with the GMD on the battlefield.

After the founding of the People's Republic, Zhou became premier and, for a while, foreign minister. In 1954, Zhou represented the PRC at the Geneva Conference which terminated the French Indochina War. The following year, he attended the Bandung Conference of Afro-Asian leaders. On both occasions, he emerged as the spokesperson for Third World countries and as a reasonable and compassionate participant in international politics. Zhou's most impressive diplomatic success was managing China's negotiations with United States President Richard M. Nixon and his National Security Adviser, Henry A. Kissinger, in 1971 and 1972. The negotiations ended the twenty-year Sino-American hostility without antagonizing the Soviet Union, China's most determined enemy since the early 1960s. The Nixon-Zhou Shanghai Communiqué (1972) will likely be recorded in diplomatic history as one of the most important successes that reduced the Cold War tension.

In domestic politics, Zhou usually emerged on the winning side of intra-party struggles. He organized no faction of his own and championed no particular ideological position, yet his mediating skill and national prestige made him indispensable to every faction and resented almost by none. As Mao Zedong's chief assistant, Zhou seldom challenged Mao's radical endeavors, such as the Great Leap Forward (1958–61) and the Great Proletarian Cultural Revolution (1966–76), although he sometimes worked quietly to moderate their negative impacts. He was never attacked by the radicals during the violent early years of the Cultural Revolution. In the aftermath of the Lin Biao affair in 1971, a helpless Mao turned to Zhou for the restoration of political order. It was through Zhou's effort that Deng Xiaoping was rehabilitated in the early 1970s, and Deng continued Zhou's moderate and practical line after Zhou's death.

The keys to Zhou's political survival lay in flexibility and pragmatism, as well as a lack of personal ambition for supreme leadership. Still, he never betrayed his own integrity, his loyalty to the overall cause of Communism, and his love for China. The contributions he made to the PRC's international prestige and domestic stability made him one of the most respected Communist leaders in the world, and the most admired national leader in twentieth-century China.

David Wen-wei Chang
Wang Ke-wen

References

Han, Suyin. *Eldest Son: Zhou Enlai and the Making of Modern China, 1898–1976.* New York, NY: Hill and Wang, 1994.
Wilson, Dick. *Zhou Enlai: A Biography.* New York, NY: The Viking Press, 1984.

Zhu De (1886–1976)

Founder and principal leader of the Chinese

Communist armed forces, Zhu De was born in Sichuan into a farm worker family. After finishing high school, he briefly worked as a teacher of physical education at an elementary school. In 1909, he started his military career as a student at the Yunnan Military Academy. He joined Sun Yatsen's Tongmenghui (Revolutionary Alliance) in that same year. Zhu achieved moderate fame during the Revolution of 1911, when he participated in the Yunnan Uprising. He later fought for the National Protection movement of 1915, which opposed Yuan Shikai's monarchical attempt.

Zhu De met Zhou Enlai and other Chinese Communists in Berlin during his trip to Germany in 1922. Disillusioned with the warlord politics in China, he soon joined the Chinese Communist Party (CCP). He then went to Moscow and studied military affairs for several months between 1925 and 1926. Returning to China in 1926, he was instructed by the CCP to develop Communist organizations within the Sichuan Army. When the Guomindang (GMD) launched its bloody purge against the CCP in 1927, Zhu was head of the Public Security Bureau in Nanchang, Jiangxi, and controlled the major military forces in the city. He thus played a critical role in the CCP's Nanchang Uprising, which commenced the Party's new strategy of armed uprising and resulted in the creation of the Red Army.

In April 1927, following the failure of the uprising, Zhu De and his troops joined forces with Mao Zedong in the Jinggang Mountains. As commander of the CCP's Fourth Army, Zhu soon became a legendary military leader. The name "Zhu-Mao" came to symbolize the Red Army in the Jiangxi Soviet, which controlled an area between southern Jiangxi and western Fujian. In November 1931, Zhu became chairman of the Soviet's Military Committee and commander of the Chinese Red Army. He was elected into the Politburo of the CCP Central Committee in January 1934, shortly before the collapse of the Jiangxi Soviet under GMD attack. At the Zunyi Conference during the Long March, Zhu supported Mao in his effort to recapture military leadership from the hands of the "Internationalists." He subsequently helped Mao to direct some of the most important battles that saved the Party and the Red Army from extinction.

During the Sino-Japanese War of 1937 to 1945, Zhu De was commander of the GMD government's Eighth Route Army, reorganized from the Red Army under the wartime GMD-CCP United Front. While Mao and the CCP Center were based in Yan'an, Zhu led the Eighth Route Army into battles in north China and created anti-Japanese base areas behind enemy lines. He was largely responsible for the CCP's effective guerrilla warfare against the invading Japanese. Returning to Yan'an in 1940, Zhu proposed to the Party the "Nanniwan model," which encouraged the CCP forces to engage in agriculture production, so that they could support themselves economically rather than further taxing the peasants. This model later developed into the Big Production movement and became one of the main economic policies of the wartime CCP.

Zhu De was also a key supporter of Mao during the Rectification campaign in Yan'an in 1942 to 1944. The campaign was a political victory for Mao in consolidating his power within the Party. In 1945, following the Japanese surrender, Zhu ordered the CCP forces to disarm the Japanese troops in north and northeast China, thus consolidating and expanding the CCP-controlled areas. During the civil war of 1946 to 1949, Zhu was commander-in-chief of the People's Liberation Army and one of the vital military strategists who helped to secure the CCP's final victory over the GMD.

After the establishment of the People's Republic of China (PRC), Zhu De's political influence declined. He still held top positions in the Party and the government, such as vice-chairman of the PRC, chairman of the Standing Committee of the People's Congress, and vice-chairman of the CCP Central Military Committee, vice-chairman of the CCP Central Committee, but he enjoyed little power in policymaking. He was also given the rank of marshal in 1955, an extremely honorable title in the PRC. In reality, however, Mao did not want Zhu to share his leadership. Mao was especially upset by Zhu's approval of Khrushchev's secret report in 1956, whose anti-Stalinism and attack on personal cults offended Mao.

Aware of his own powerless position, Zhu De kept a low profile in the CCP's internal struggle in the 1950s through the 1970s. Unlike other Party leaders, for example, he offered only mild criticism of Peng Dehuai at the 1959 Lushan Conference. During the Cultural Revolution, Zhu was under attack by Lin Biao and Jiang Qing's radical groups, but Mao kept Zhu from total humiliation. The relatively lenient treatment which Zhu received in this violent campaign may reflect the fact that he posed little threat to Mao. Zhu died in July 1976, two months before Mao.

He Gaochao

References

MacFarquhar, Roderick. *The Politics of China, 1949–1989.* Cambridge England: Cambridge University Press, 1993.

Smedley, Agnes. *The Great Road: The Life and Times of Chu Teh.* New York, NY: Monthly Review Press, 1956.

Zilijun Uprising

The only uprising staged by the Baohuanghui (Emperor Protection Society) during the late Qing was the Zilijun Uprising. Following the failure of the Hundred Days Reform in 1898, many of the reformers fled to Japan. Among them was Tang Caichang, a native of Hunan and a close friend of Tan Sitong, a martyr of the Reform movement. In Japan, Tang, like Liang Qichao and some others, came into contact with the revolutionaries under Sun Yatsen and their radical strategies. Although still loyal to the cause of protecting Emperor Guangxu instead of overthrowing the Qing dynasty, Tang now believed that an armed revolt was necessary to accomplish his political goals. In 1900, as the Boxer Uprising raged through north China, Tang returned to the country and organized the Zhengqihui (Uprightness Society), later renamed Zilihui (Independent Society), in Shanghai. With the help of Qin Lishan, he also enlisted the assistance of the secret societies in the Yangtze River valley and formed the Zilijun (Independent Army). In a manifesto, Tang displayed an ideological ambivalence that many of Liang Qichao's group shared during this period. It called for the restoration of a Manchu emperor, yet at the same time expressed anti-Manchu feelings.

In early August, the Zilijun planned to stage an uprising in central China, the goal of which was to topple Empress Dowager Cixi and establish a constitutional monarchy under Emperor Guangxu. The uprising was postponed several times because of delays in the delivery of overseas funds by Kang Youwei. A misunderstanding in communications, however, caused Qin Lishan's men to revolt in Datong prematurely. The revolt was crushed by the government within two days. Tang then decided to launch the uprising on August 23. But before that day, the government of the governor-general of Hunan and Hubei discovered his secret

organization in Hankou. Tang, together with more than twenty of his co-conspirators, was arrested and executed.

Wang Ke-wen

References

Li, Chien-nung. *The Political History of China, 1840–1928.* Trans. Ssu-yu Teng and Jeremy Ingalls. Princeton, NJ: Princeton University Press, 1956.

Smythe, E. Joan. "The Tzu-li Hui: Some Chinese and Their Rebellions." *Harvard Papers on China* no. 12 (1958): 51–68.

Zongli Yamen

Zongli Yamen was the shortened and most commonly used name for the *Zongli geguo shiwu yamen,* or General Office for Managing the Affairs of the Various Countries, usually translated as Office of Foreign Affairs. The Zongli Yamen was created in 1861 as part of the Tongzhi Restoration, and was designed to provide the imperial government in Beijing with a more effective bureaucratic institution for dealing with the threat posed by foreign powers after the shock of China's defeat and the foreign occupation of the capital in the Second Opium War (1857–60).

The establishment of a new office to handle all aspects of relations with the foreign powers became increasingly necessary after the Qing court had been forced to concede the principle of equality in Sino-British correspondence in the 1842 Treaty of Nanjing and the right of permanent diplomatic residence in Beijing in the 1858 Treaty of Tianjin. A new *ad hoc* department to deal with foreign diplomats would insulate the Qing court from direct contact and communication with these "barbarians," but would coordinate the work of gathering information about them and recommending action on how to control them more effectively.

The Zongli Yamen was established in response to a memorial submitted by Prince Gong, Wenxiang, and Guiliang, all of whom were members of the Grand Council. The memorial stipulated that the Zongli Yamen was to operate under the direction of princes and ministers and to be a temporary bureau that would be abolished once the military campaigns had been concluded and foreign relations simplified. The responsibility for conducting foreign relations would then revert to the Grand Council. The Zongli Yamen always retained this peripheral and temporary character and functioned as a subcommittee of the Grand Council. It never achieved significant bureaucratic authority in its own right but depended on the power and influence held by grand councillors who served concurrently on the Zongli Yamen. Essentially, the importance of the Zongli Yamen in Chinese diplomacy depended upon Prince Gong and Wenxiang, and this function was vastly diminished after 1884 with the ouster of Prince Gong.

A major weakness of the Zongli Yamen was that it never succeeded in centralizing the management of foreign relations. The same memorial advocating the establishment of the Zongli Yamen also proposed that the positions of commissioner of the northern ports and commissioner of southern ports be created to handle foreign affairs in those regions. In practice, the governors-general in Tianjin and Canton held these titles and were major players in the formulation and implementation of Chinese foreign policy. Governors in each province similarly dealt with matters associated with foreigners within their jurisdiction.

The abolition of the Zongli Yamen and its replacement by the *Waiwubu* or Ministry of Foreign Affairs, established in that year, was one of the demands imposed upon China in the Boxer Protocols of 1901. The Ministry of Foreign Affairs was a regular ministry within the central bureaucracy, and it enjoyed first rank among all of the central government departments. Its officials were now substantive and significant functionaries rather than being temporary and secondary. This change marked the beginning of a new era in the conduct of Chinese diplomacy.

Louis T. Sigel

References

Banno, Masataka. *China and the West, 1858–1861: The Origins of the Tsungli Yamen.* Cambridge, MA: Harvard University Press, 1964.

Meng, S. M. *The Tsungli Yamen: Its Organization and Functions.* Cambridge, MA: Harvard University Press, 1962.

Wright, Mary C. *The Last Stand of Chinese Conservatism: The T'ung-chih Restoration, 1862–1874.* Stanford, CA: Stanford University Press, 1962.

Zou Rong (1885–1905)

Anti-Manchu revolutionary and propagandist,

Zou Rong. (Courtesy of Nationalist Party Archives.)

Zou Rong was born into a merchant family in Baxian, Sichuan, and received a good classical education at an early age. Inspired by the writings of Tan Sitong, martyr of the Hundred Days Reform (1898), he refused to take the civil service examination but turned to the new learning instead. In 1898, he studied English and Japanese with two Japanese at Chongqing. Under their influence, Zou went to Shanghai in 1901 and enrolled in the Jiangnan Arsenal's language school. The next year he continued his studies in the Tokyo Dobun Shoin.

In Japan, Zou was quickly converted to revolution. He played an active role in the anti-Russian movement organized by the Chinese students, and drafted the anti-Manchu pamphlet, *The Revolutionary Army (Gemingjun)*. In early 1903, he returned to Shanghai after getting into conflict with a Qing official in Tokyo.

In Shanghai, Zou made the acquaintance of Zhang Binglin, who edited and prefaced *The Revolutionary Army* before its publication in May 1903. Afterward, Zhang contributed two essays to *Subao,* a revolutionary newspaper: the first one condemned the reformers and Emperor Guangxu; the second reviewed Zou's work in a favorable light. The seditious articles drew the attention of the Qing government, which pressured the police of the international settlement to arrest Zhang, Zou, and four other radicals. Zhang was arrested on June 29 and Zou gave himself up several days later. The Qing government attempted to have them extradited, but the British consul refused to accede to Chinese demands on the pretext that the prisoners might suffer the same fate as Shen Jin, a reporter and a friend of Tang Caichang (leader of the Zilijun Uprising in 1900), who was beaten to death by the Beijing authorities. The *Subao* case, as it was called, was tried by the Mixed Court in Shanghai. Zhang received a sentence of three years, and Zou two years. Zou died in prison in 1905, at the age of twenty.

Zou Rong's work was regarded as the most popular tract in the anti-Manchu republican. Its popularity lay in Zou's bombastic style of writing and militant radicalism. Consisting of seven chapters, the pamphlet began with a direct call to revolution. Borrowing from Carlyle's *French Revolution,* the ideas of John Stuart Mill, Rousseau, Montesquieu, and Herbert Spencer, he defined the concepts of "nation" and "race," and analyzed China's decline from the Social Darwinist point of view. Zou attributed his country's existing crisis to Manchu racist policies, and urged the Chinese to overthrow the despotic regime before fighting against foreign aggression. In the last few chapters, he outlined a new political order based on Western republicanism and on an educated Chinese citizenry.

Zou Rong's death indirectly helped to publicize his work. In subsequent years, as many as twenty editions and about one million copies were printed in Hong Kong, Singapore, Shanghai, Yokohama, and San Francisco. They appeared under different titles: *Tucunpian (Plan for Survival), Geming xianfeng (Revolutionary Vanguard),* and *Jiushi zhengyen (The Key to Salvation).* For his contribution to the anti-Manchu revolution, the provisional government at Nanjing conferred on Zou Rong the title of "great general" *(dajiangjun)* posthumously in 1912.

Henry Y. S. Chan

References

Rankin, Mary B. *Early Chinese Revolutionaries: Radical Intellectuals in Shanghai and Chekiang, 1902–1911.* Cambridge, MA: Harvard University Press, 1971.

Tsou, Jung. *The Revolutionary Army: A Chinese Nationalist Tract of 1903.* Intro. and trans. John Lust. Paris: Mouton, 1968.

Zuo Zongtang (1812–85)

Zuo Zongtang was the Hunanese commander who significantly aided the defeat of the Taiping forces, the Nian rebels, and the Northwestern Muslim armies from the 1850s through the 1870s. He also supervised the rehabilitation of the war-damaged areas.

Zuo was born into a modest gentry family and studied for the imperial examinations, attaining the *zhuren* degree in 1832. He thrice failed the metropolitan examination and abandoned that route. In his studies, Zuo investigated topics such as geography, history, and agriculture, among others. These three areas of expertise would serve him well in his later career.

Like some of his peers, Zuo met prominent statesmen who became promoters of his abilities. Tao Zhu, He Changling, and Lin Zexu, who attempted to transform provincial governments in the 1820s and 1830s, discerned in the young Hunanese scholar the potential for important service. In fact, Zuo had marriage ties with Tao and He, among a series of kinship and quasi-kin relations linking that generation of reformers with the later generation of Statecraft scholar officials, such as Zeng Guofan and Hu Linyi.

In the 1850s, when the Taiping menace loomed over Hunan, Zuo ably served two governors there. In 1860, he was given command of his own force of volunteers, which fought the Taipings from 1860 to 1866. Apart from helping to defeat the enemy, Zuo, like his peers, energetically began a rehabilitative program of reconstruction and relief.

Following the defeat of the Taipings, Zuo was given the task of restoring the Northwest to central government control, but before that effort could commence, Zuo was summoned to help destroy the Nian rebels. That came in 1868, along with additional imperial honors. Zuo soon returned to his original task and began his northwestern campaign. From 1868 to 1873, he concentrated on defeating the Muslim rebels in Shaanxi and Gansu. Through many successes and setbacks, Zuo succeeded in clearing Shaanxi, Gansu, and Qinghai. The losses were heavy on both sides. As in Zhejiang and Fujian earlier, Zuo began programs to reconstruct the war-devastated areas. He promoted cotton growing, wool production, land reclamation, and the establishment of an arsenal. Some of the economic acts were meant to revitalize the region and to replace the income losses from his ban on opium production.

After the last rebel center fell, Zuo turned his attention to Chinese Turkestan. While laying careful plans, Zuo also had to convince the imperial court that the effort would be worth the expenditure of millions. Li Hongzhang, whose responsibilities included defense of the coastal areas of China, opposed the new campaign. The debate finally concluded in Zuo's favor. The logistic problems of fully equipping and supplying nearly sixty thousand soldiers daunted many, but not Zuo. The attack commenced in 1876 and concluded in late 1877. Again, heavy fighting brought great losses.

In succeeding years, Zuo's health declined, but his abilities and reputation brought him task after task. He subdued one uprising in Shandong and arrived back in Fujian to take charge of the anti-French effort there during the Sino-French War (1884–85), where he soon died.

Zuo earned a reputation as a blunt but patriotic statesman. His talent as a commander and as an administrator brought many high honors. He followed a policy of limited westernization, but continued to believe strongly in Confucian ideals and practices. One of his most notable achievements was the incorporation of Chinese Turkestan into the Qing empire as the province of Xinjiang in 1884.

Lanny B. Fields

References

Fields, Lanny B. *Tso Tsung-t'ang and the Muslims: Statecraft in Northwest China, 1868–1880*. Kingston, Ontario: The Limestone Press, 1978.

Z

Index